GOLF COURSES
in Great Britain & Ireland & Europe

Published by RAC Publishing,
RAC House, PO Box 100, South Croydon CR2 6XW

© RAC Enterprises Limited and Links Publications Limited 1993
© Mapping RAC Enterprises Limited 1993

This book is sold subject to the condition that it shall not, by way of trade, or otherwise, be lent, re-sold, hired out or otherwise circulated without the publisher's prior consent in any form of binding, or cover other than that in which it is published.

All rights reserved. No parts of this work may be reproduced, stored in a retrieval system or transmitted by any means without permission. Whilst every effort has been made to ensure that the information contained in this publication is accurate and up-to-date, the publisher does not accept any responsibility for any error, omission or misrepresentation. All liability for loss, disappointment, negligence or other damage caused by reliance on the information contained in this guide, or in the event of bankruptcy, or liquidation, or cessation of trade of any company, individual or firm mentioned is hereby excluded.

ISBN 0 86211 220 6

Written and compiled for RAC Enterprises Limited by
Links Publications Limited
Additional text: David Brenner
Editorial: John Latimer Smith
Cover photograph: Royal St. George's Golf Club, Sandwich, Kent
Photographs with kind permission from Brian Morgan Golf Photography. Sporting Pictures (UK) Limited
Typeset from disks prepared by SafeSet

Advertising Managers:
Kingslea Press Limited, 137 Newhall Street, Birmingham B3 1SF
Telephone 021-236 8112

Printed in Spain by Grafo SA, Bilbao

Contents

INTRODUCTION	4
HOW TO USE THIS GUIDE	7
HOW TO BOOK A ROUND	8
HANDICAPS	10
GOLF COURSE DESIGN AND ARCHITECTURE	12
GREAT EUROPEAN COURSES	14
ENGLAND	16
SCOTLAND	90
WALES	121
NORTHERN IRELAND	131
REPUBLIC OF IRELAND	138
AUSTRIA	153
BELGIUM	157
DENMARK	160
FINLAND	166
FRANCE	168
GERMANY	189
ITALY	199
NETHERLANDS	206
NORWAY	211
PORTUGAL	213
SPAIN	218
SWEDEN	229
SWITZERLAND	238
MAPS WITH COURSES	241
INDEX	262

Introduction

GOLF is the fastest-growing participant sport in the world today. The design and construction of new courses, particularly in the British Isles, is taking place at a rate almost unprecedented in the game's history and the estimate by the Royal and Ancient in the late 1980s that an additional 700 courses in Britain alone would be needed by the end of the century will certainly be met and probably exceeded.

There are three main reasons for this phenomenon. The first is the growth in golf's popularity as a television spectator sport and this in turn has been entirely due to the resurgence of European golfers at the game's very highest levels. It would be wrong to credit any single player for this, but pride of place must be given to the European golfers who over the past few years have won one of the four 'Major Championships'. (The Open; the US Open; the US masters and the US PGA). Severiano Ballesteros, Nick Faldo, Sandy Lyle, Bernhard Langer and Ian Woosnam, who have all won at least one 'Major', have in turn gone on to form the backbone of the European Ryder Cup team, whose successes against their American counterparts have been avidly followed by both written and electronic media. With blanket coverage of virtually every tournament on both the European and American Tours now available to the European public, it's no wonder there is now such intense and ever-increasing interest in the game.

A natural progression from watching golf is wanting to play and here lies the second reason for the sport's growth. Golf, unlike so many other sporting activities, doesn't demand a particularly high level of fitness from the average player. The ability to walk the four miles or so round a golf course and swing a golf club with reasonable freedom are really the only two basic prerequisites. (And in America, with the reliance on golf buggies, even the walking element has now largely been eliminated!). Additionally, almost uniquely, golf is not exclusively a young person's game. Newcomers in their late forties and fifties who've never held a club in their lives needn't feel in the slightest intimidated, and given average health and mobility, there's absolutely no reason why players can't go on into their sixties, seventies - and beyond.

Harnessed to the desire to play comes whether or not a person has the ability to play. Golf isn't an easy game to learn, but thanks to recent enormous advances in golf equipment technology it is unquestionably easier to learn than ever before. Innovation in golf club design and the increasing use of materials other than the traditional wood and steel to make clubs lighter and stronger - and to hit the ball straighter and further - means that clubs are now far more 'user-friendly' to the novice. This in turn leads to a basic competence being

INTRODUCTION

Royal Birkdale

achieved more quickly, interest being maintained and, consequently, a lower 'drop-out' rate among novices who previously might have found golf simply too difficult to master.

The final reason for golf's ever-increasing popularity is the social factor. It's pleasant to belong to a golf club and to meet new friends and new golf partners of similar ability to your own. Golf club membership, as will be explained elsewhere, is still at a premium in Great Britain, even with the enormous course-building programme currently underway, but once membership has been achieved, not only does it bring the guarantee of regular golf at whatever level - competitive or purely social - you choose, it also, (thanks to the basic courtesies and conventions of the game), ensures a welcome at virtually every other club in the land. Further afield, British golfers now take playing holidays in Spain, Portugal and the United States, while Japanese and American players are drawn to the great links courses of Great Britain and Ireland. Golf tourism, along with every other facet of the game, is a growth industry and it can be only a matter of time before the wonderful courses of the Southern Hemisphere, currently out of the European holidaymaker's reach, become popular and familiar destinations.

The appeal of golf is truly international; its lore, traditions and customs are unique; the variety of courses on which to play is infinite. Some of the finest golf courses in Europe have been included in this Guide: whether you play off scratch or have just taken up the game, you'll find where - and how - to match your golfing tastes and abilities against the challenge of this great sport. Play away!

GOLF COURSES

The Belfry

HOW TO USE THIS GUIDE

ALL the golf courses included in this Guide will admit Golf Societies and individual players on a regular or semi-regular basis, but it's important to remember that the vast majority of clubs, particularly in Great Britain, are private members clubs and that admission to the casual visitor, irrespective of whether or not they may be a member of another club, can be extremely limited. Some clubs insist that you do belong to another club and can produce either a membership card, or a letter of introduction from your Club Secretary before you'll be allowed to play. In other instances, you'll be asked to produce a current handicap certificate; there may even be a minimum handicap stipulation. In most cases, it will be essential to book a tee-off time - see *'How To Book A Round'* - well in advance. With restrictions that you may encounter in your efforts to enjoy a day's golf, a little forward planning is essential. Not only will this Guide tell you which golf clubs are to be found in practically every area of the British Isles and mainland Europe, it will also give you a reasonable indication as to whether or not you'll be able to play at that club without too many problems. Do study the restrictions carefully, for nothing can be more annoying or frustrating - or embarrassing - than to turn up at a course and discover you're unable to play. Each golf club entry in this Guide consists of: The Club's name. Its address and basic directions to reach it.

CONTACT:. The telephone number of either the Secretary or Professional, with whom to book a round.
Course: Its length, par, standard scratch score and type.
SOC RESTR'S: Restrictions, if any, to bookings and course availability for Golf Societies.
SOC GF: The average green fees charged for each round and/or day per player to Golf Societies.
SOC PACK: Special packages and offers available to Golf Societies.
VIS RESTR'S: Restrictions, if any, to bookings and course availability for individual players.
VIS GF: The average green fees charged for each round and/or to individual players. **Wd** = Weekday **We** = Weekend. **N/A** = Not available
FACILITIES: Whether food and drink are readily available to the visitor and details of other golf-related amenities at the club.
HOTELS: RAC-recommended hotels in the area.

Club entries for England, Wales, Northern Ireland and the Republic of Ireland are listed alphabetically by county; for Scotland, listings are alphabetically by region. Club entries for mainland Europe are listed according to Country and, where appropriate, arranged alphabetically within the various districts of each Country. There is a full alphabetical index of every club included, together with location maps, at the end of the Guide.

EXAMPLE

GALASHIELS   MAP 9 B3

Ladhope Recreation Ground, Galashiels TD1 2NJ.
Situated north-east side of town, quarter of a mile from A7.
CONTACT: R Gass, Secretary. Tel: 0896 55307.
Course: 5,311yds, PAR 68, SSS 67. Hillside parkland course.
SOC RESTR'S: Contact in advance.
SOC GF - Round: Wd £8. We £12. **Day:** Wd £12. We £16.
SOC PACK: On application from Secretary.
VIS RESTR'S: No restrictions.
VIS GF - Round: Wd £8, We £12. **Day:** Wd £12. We £16.
FACILITIES: Catering (Weekends only), Bar.

How to Book a Round

A LARGE part of golf's appeal lies in the ability of the average player to go round the same courses used for Championships and important professional and amateur tournaments. The downside to this is that an ever-increasing number of golfers want to play the same, comparatively small, number of courses, with the result that opportunities for the casual visitor will be both limited and expensive. That's not to say it's impossible to get onto such courses, but it will require planning and foresight on your part. Paradoxically, to play the Old Course at St Andrews, the most hallowed golfing tract in the world, can require no more planning and foresight than to be successful in the daily ballot for tee-off times - a longshot, but by no means impossible - whilst the absolute reverse applies if permission is sought to be admitted into the portals of the Honourable Company of Edinburgh Golfers at Muirfield; a privilege granted to so few each year as to make an application little more than an exercise in futility, but how sweet the moment if and when your request is granted!

St Andrews and Muirfield represent the extremes of Championship golf course availability. The other courses on the current Open roster - Royal St George's, Royal Birkdale, Royal Troon, Royal Lytham & St Anne's and Turnberry - will admit Societies and individuals, but pre-booking, probably in writing to the Secretary and with as much notice as possible, is essential and a handicap certificate, together with a minimum handicap of 24 or, more likely

Turnberry

18, may well be required too. The same stipulations will apply to courses used across Europe on the PGA Tour, with the proviso that some courses on mainland Europe may waive minimum handicap requirements, while others may prove more accessible at shorter notice than their British counterparts. Regardless of whichever of these important courses you'd like to play however, the golden rule is always pre-book - and with the maximum notice you can give. The chances of your turning up on spec and getting onto any of these golf courses are virtually non-existent, whilst the security of a guaranteed, pre-booked tee-off time will only add to your anticipation and enjoyment.

Of course not every club in this Guide hosts major tournaments, but a surprisingly large number will at some time have done so, while other clubs will attract a large number of visitors because of their location, tradition, design or place within the game. The best approach to adopt when wanting to play these clubs is that the more famous or prestigious it is, the more difficult and restrictive - and expensive - you're likely to find it. At the very least, you'll always need to pre-book and be prepared to produce a club membership card or handicap certificate.

If all this seems unpleasantly daunting, the good news is that having decided on the spur of the moment on any given day of the week that you'd like a round of golf and aren't too bothered where within reasonable distance you play, you'd be extremely unlucky not to be accommodated. You'll find it a little more difficult, but not impossibly so, at weekends, when demand is greatest and in this particular example, bear in mind that the less prestigious and renowned a course is, the more likely you are to get on. Even so, it's always sensible to telephone first, but at this end of the market, you won't be asked for membership cards or handicap certificates.

There are two other factors to bear in mind: if you've set your heart on playing a major course, your chances will be immeasurably increased if you're prepared to accept a very early or very late tee-off time when demand for course access in all probability might be lessened, or if you're prepared to play in winter when the course might be less attractive, playing less well and with winter rules/winter greens in operation, but at least you'll be on! Remember too when booking that many courses, whether famous or not, are none too keen to admit single players on their own, particularly at times of high demand. Even if you've booked you may be denied your tee-off time and may even find yourself tacked onto a threeball or made to wait until another 'singleton' turns up. If you want to play on your own, make this absolutely clear when you pre-book, but it's surely preferable to play with friends wherever possible.

Handicaps

IT'S no exaggeration to say that the handicapping system is one of golf's fundamental cornerstones, for not only does the level of your handicap provide evidence of your ability as a golfer, but it also enables you to play any other golfer on equal terms. Such is the importance of the handicap, it is perhaps unsurprising that its administration is so closely governed. You'll need a handicap if you want to play anything other than basic, social golf on an irregular basis, or if you want to try your hand over courses where a handicap certificate is a prerequisite for admission, but obtaining that elusive piece of paper provides, so the story has it, a classic example of 'Catch-22' in operation. You can only obtain a handicap if you're a member of a golf club...but you can only become a member of a golf club if you've already got a handicap. Happily for the non-handicapper, this item of perceived golf wisdom isn't entirely accurate...

There are in fact three totally legitimate ways of obtaining a handicap. The first is to join a golf club where possession of a handicap certificate isn't a prerequisite for membership. Many smaller clubs, and not a few of the more recent, large, prestige developments are aware of the 'handicap problem' and will accept as members those who can show a basic proficiency in the game. These individuals then submit three scorecards for rounds played over the course in question which are assessed by the club's handicap committee who will subsequently decide an appropriate handicap for the player concerned. Some clubs are even more accommodating. If a prospective member is not of sufficiently high standard to obtain a handicap, some form of temporary or probationary membership may be granted on the understanding that a player has tuition within the club until sufficient improvement is made for a handicap to be awarded. It's sadly impossible to list clubs that offer these opportunities as some do so as a matter of course, while others will judge each individual case on its merits. The clubs do exist and finding them is a matter of perseverance and word-of-mouth recommendation but it does give lie to the belief that 'no handicap means no club'.

The reverse of that statement is 'no club means no handicap' and that's also not strictly speaking true. It's not easy joining a golf club, irrespective of whether you've got a handicap or not, but it can be extremely simple - and inexpensive too - to join a Golf Society. Perhaps one already exists where you work or at a local pub or club. If so, the procedure's the same as it would be if you were a golf club member: you play three rounds, (which will probably be at three different courses on Society visits), have those rounds assessed and then receive an appropriate handicap.

If you don't know of a Golf Society, you can even form your own. You'll need to gather up a total of twenty like-minded friends and contact the English (or Scottish, or Welsh, or Irish) Golf Union - see 'Useful Numbers' - who'll send you an information pack. As regards the English Golf Union, (and the other Home Unions operate broadly similar schemes), it'll cost you £35 plus VAT, plus £1 per member to register and once your Society's approved you'll be able to issue handicaps.

The last easy and recognised way of obtaining a handicap is to join the Golf Club of Great Britain. This organisation - see 'Useful Numbers' - isn't affiliated to any Home Union, but it does hold regular golf days at courses around the country at which you can play for your handicap. The 1993 subscription was £55, which compares very favourably to standard club subs. One word of warning: some golf clubs may not recognise GCGB or Society handicap certificates as being 'legitimate', but you'd be unlucky to be denied access to a course for this reason alone. And surely any fairly-obtained handicap is better than no handicap at all?

Stoke Poges

GOLF COURSE DESIGN AND ARCHITECTURE

A GREAT part of golf's appeal must surely lie in its sheer diversity; the fact that every hole on every golf course in the world is different, presents golfers with a literally unending challenge to their skills. With the exception of the great Scottish links courses, where the game was created and developed on strips of coastal wasteland too poor for farming and unsuitable for building and where Nature alone largely decided the positions of tee, greens, fairways and bunkers, that challenge to a golfer's skills has been laid down by an individual who can be as reviled as he is revered - the golf course designer.

With all due deference to American designers of the late 19th and early 20th centuries when the first great boom in golf course construction took place, the best in the world at that time were all British: Donald Ross, originally apprenticed to Old Tom Morris at St Andrews, who can list Oak Hill, Inverness, Seminole and the matchless Pinehurst No 2 among his designs. Alister Mackenzie, whose courses span the world from Cypress Point to Royal Melbourne to Fulford and, in collaboration with Bobby Jones, the peerless beauty of Augusta National while Harry Colt was responsible for the great Surrey heathland layouts at Wentworth and Sunningdale New, together with the Eden Course at St Andrews and, ultimately, arguably the best inland course in world golf today, Pine Valley. All these courses share one common factor: a naturalness and harmony with their surroundings and a design philosophy that rewards the good golf shot without harshly penalising the bad one. In short, the majority of older courses can be equally enjoyed and appreciated by low and high handicappers alike.

It can be difficult to be equally appreciative of some modern courses. That's not to say that some superb layouts in the British Isles haven't been opened within the past quarter-of-a-century - the likes of, in no special order, Woburn, St Mellion, East Sussex National, St Pierre and, in Ireland, Mount Juliet are clear evidence to the contrary - but in some, particularly American, new courses, there's an excess of gimmicry and punitive design. Perhaps the view taken by Robert Trent Jones, the one great designer whose career spanned the pre-and post-war periods, has been taken too literally to heart. He said that a golf course was like a battleground, with the players attacking it and the architect building its defences. Those Trent Jones defences can be sampled at, among others, Moor Allerton in Yorkshire and Sotogrande in Spain.

While Robert Trent Jones and, in more recent years, the work of his two sons, is generally respected within golf, the one modern course architect whose work is guaranteed to divide opinions is the American Pete Dye. At its best his early work, as represented by Harbour Town in South Carolina, may fairly said

GOLF COURSE DESIGN AND ARCHITECTURE

St Mellion

to be among the very best in the world. Judgement has not been so generous about some of his more recent creations like the fearsome Ocean Course at Kiawah Island, venue of the 1991 Ryder Cup. The polite view is that modern Pete Dye courses like Kiawah are tough for the pro and impossible for the handicapper; the less diplomatic view is that these courses are punitively unfair. 'Unforgiving' might be a kinder description, such is the absolute premium placed on length and accuracy. As yet, there is no Pete Dye course in Britain, but you can play an allegedly exact replica of his notorious 17th hole at the Tournament Players' Club at Sawgrass in Florida, which has been recreated at Singing Hills in Sussex.

One curious modern phenomenon which may profit designers is the attraction to a great many golfers of the newer, tougher courses. There's a perverse pride in having tried - and failed - to drive the 10th at the Belfry, despite the fact that played conservatively, it's an absurdly easy par-4, while other heroic shots on other modern courses are equally popular. It's true that modern club and golfball technology has drawn the teeth of many older courses, but has their attraction been consequently lessened? The key question is if, in one hundred years time, we will hold today's courses in the same affection and respect with which we currently hold those built a century ago.

GREAT EUROPEAN COURSES

St Andrews

SCOTLAND
THE OLD COURSE, ST ANDREWS

There is no other tract of land in the world that's attracted quite the same amount of attention and adulation as this stretch of sandy scrubland, shaped like a shepherd's crook, lying between what is fondly referred to as 'the old grey toon' and the North Sea.

Despite the central role the Old Course has played in the creation and development of golf and the matchless venue it has proved for great championships and great champions, it nevertheless has its critics as a golf course, who point to its anachronistic double greens, in play on all holes except the 1st, 9th, 17th and 18th; the allegedly 'unfair' placing of many of the fairway bunkers; and the fact that modern advances in golf course management and equipment technology have combined to make the course far easier to play in recent times.

With the American Curtis Strange making a decent stab at breaking 60 over the Old Course in the Dunhill Cup, there is some substance to the last of these observations, even though - especially as regards the 14th and 17th - many of the holes still pose problems that take some solving, but to agree with the others is surely to miss the point about St Andrews. Only its most starry-eyed admirers would claim it to be the perfect golf course. It isn't, but it still is a truly great course. The subtle - and not so subtle - contouring of greens and fairways, which can result in bewildering and frustrating kicks, bounces and borrows, (and thus give lie to the 'unfair' bunker myth), has evolved, without the aid of man or machine, over hundreds of years. To play

GREAT EUROPEAN COURSES

the Old Course is to play golf in its purest, most natural form, to accept 'the rub of the green' and the good and bad fortune that every round played here produces.

Thankfully, the Old Course is not an exclusive preserve. The opportunity to sample its heritage is open to all and only by playing it themselves will golfers begin to understand something of its thrill and mystique.

SPAIN
VALDERRAMA

Originally called Sotogrande New, before - under the direction of Club President Jaime Patino - being remodelled by Robert Trent Jones. The money necessary to make Valderrama one of the world's great golf-courses was never a problem - and it shows. Valderrama hosts the end-of-season Volvo Masters on the European PGA Tour and is reckoned by the pros to be the toughest course they play all year. Does toughest equal best? Some would say it does. There is no doubting that Valderrama is a truly magnificent course, but is is fiendishly difficult. All the Trent Jones trademarks are here: length, dog-legs, small and cunningly-borrowed greens and just a little water - on the 4th and 10th - to add variety. The course provides a fresh challenge on every hole, for nowhere is the golfer allowed to rest and gather resources. The recovery from anything off-line will be hampered by the profusion of cork oaks, while necklaces of bunkers surround most greens, particularly the sharply-tiered landing area of the short 6th; the huge bunker in front of the plateau-greened 8th; and the 9th, where the combined perils of a tree *in* a bunker add to the perils awaiting a wayward approach.

The closing stretch is classic. The 15th is the longest par 3 on the course requiring a hefty carry over trees off the tee; the 16th fairway slopes right to left and consequently second shots tend to get pulled off into bunkers guarding the left-hand side of the green; the 17th is a long par 5, dog-legged right, with trouble all the way up the right-hand side of the fairway; the 18th is as tough a finishing hole as anywhere in the world, with cork oaks awaiting anything pushed off the tee and then a long iron to a sloping green.

Valderrama is being mooted as a possible Ryder Cup venue when the event is played in Spain for the first time in 1997. Whether it has the ancilliary facilities to cope with the event and the pressures the Ryder Cup brings both on and off the course is, at the time of this Guide, open to argument, but what is indisputable is that as a pure test of golf, Valderrama would be a perfect Ryder Cup course.

NETHERLANDS/SWEDEN
KENNEMER/FALSTERBO

It's a golfing fallacy that links course are exclusive to the British Isles: especially so when talk turns to 'great' links courses. The Netherlands and Sweden can boast perhaps two finest examples on mainland Europe, courses which, had they been in Britain, would certainly have been regular and rightful members of the Open Championship roster. Kennemer, in the dunes of Zandvoort, started life in the early years of this centry as a flat, 9-hole meadowland course, but its full potential was only realised by the addition of 18, Harry Colt-designed holes in the late 1920s. These holes are laid out in two loops of 9, each returning to the striking thatched clubhouse from which virtually the entire course can be seen.The 1st hole, which measures over 450 yards provides an inviting drive from an elevated tee to a generous fairway and this hole sets the tone of the course. If the weather is kind, Kennemer can be a driver's delight. As with all the best links courses, placement is crucial and the rough can be penal, but in general the fairways are wide and inviting and the entrances to the greens are not dauntingly narrow. The par 3s are particularly good, especially the 15th, where an underhit shot will be mercilessly gathered by one of three large bunkers.

Falsterbo is on the southernmost tip of Sweden from Denmark, meets the Baltic. It differs from the British style of links course by having a substantial amount of inland water and marsh in play on many holes, particularly the 4th, 5th and 11th, but the closing three holes, all of which hug the coastline, provide links golf in its truest form. On the 17th, views of distant Denmark across the Oresund can provide sufficient distraction for a slice into the Baltic, as can the 18th, a shortish but testing dogleg par 5.

Neither Kennemer nor Falsterbo is punishingly long, but each has that rare ability to please both the average player and the low handicapper. It would be hard to find two better laid out or more visually appealing courses on mainland Europe.

ENGLAND

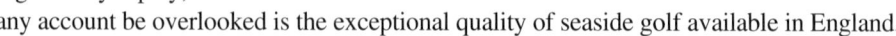

G OLF traditionalists will tell you that golf played over links courses is the truest form of the sport there is and that additionally, the very best links courses in the world are to be found in Scotland. That view point is one to be mulled over with friends at the 19th hole after a good day's play, but what musn't on any account be overlooked is the exceptional quality of seaside golf available in England.

The names of the Open Championship courses in England - Royal Lytham, Royal St George's and Royal Birkdale - will be familiar enough, as will Royal Liverpool, now sadly off the Open roster, but only for logistical reasons. Less familiar might be the names of Royal North Devon, the oldest links course in England, and the truly magnificient links at Saunton a few miles away along the north Devon coast. Combine these with the curiosity of the Church course at St Enodoc for a links trio that would be hard to beat .

At the opposite end of the south coast, clustered around Royal St George's are the twin jewels of Royal Cinque Ports and Prince's; East Anglia can boast Royal West Norfolk and Hunstanton; the north-east has Seaton Carew and, even further north, Berwick-upon -Tweed, all these courses - and more - giving lie to the myth that links golf means Scottish golf.

When it comes to inland courses, England perhaps has the edge. There's even the unique golfing oddity of an inland links course at Royal Worlington and Newmarket, which is acknowledged as the greatest 9-hole course in the world. Nowhere, not even on traditional seaside championship courses, will you find faster, truer greens.

Due to a topographical accident that laid down a belt of sandy, heathery heathland studded with pine, silver birch and gorse, the county of Surrey has perhaps more that its fair share of inland masterpieces: Wentworth, Sunningdale and Walton Heath leading the way, West Hill and Worplesdon not far behind (and infinitely cheaper!) and nearby Hankley Common a regular Open Championship qualifying course.

As for the rest of the country, choices must by necessity be brief and subjective. Of the newer layouts, both Duke and Duchess courses at Woburn are outstanding; the American-style East Sussex National full of promise; Jack Nicklaus's design at St Mellion, after initial unease, has developed into a fine course and Portal in Cheshire has an air of maturity and spaciousness - and extreme length! - unusual in more recent developments. Of the more established courses, the Notts Club at Hollinwell is thought by some to be the best inland course in Britain; devotees of Woodhall Spa and Ganton and Lindrick would doubtless disagree. The list of courses is near-endless, as are opportunities for golfers of any ability. What should by now be apparent is that for sheer diversity, Britain in general and England in particular cannot be equalled by any other country in the world.

൴

Avon

BATH GOLF CLUB   MAP 2 B3

Sham Castle, North Road, Bath, Avon BA2 6JG.
1. 5 miles south-east from City. Turn off A36.

CONTACT: P Edwards, Secretary. Tel: 0225 463834.
COURSE: 6,369yds, PAR 71, SSS 70. Downland course.
SOC RESTR'S: Welcome.
SOC GF - Round: Wd £22. We £26 **Day:** Wd £22. We £26.
SOC PACK: Available on booking.
VIS RESTR'S: Please phone prior to play.
VIS GF - Round: Wd £22. We £26 **Day:** Wd £22. We £26.
FACILITIES: Bar & Restaurant.

BRISTOL & CLIFTON GOLF CLUB   MAP 2 B2

Begger Brush Lane, Failand, Clifton, Avon BS8 3TH.
3 miles south of Junction 19 M5.

CONTACT: P. Wiliams. Secretary. Tel: 0275 393474.
COURSE: 6,290yds, PAR 70, SSS 70. Parkland course.
SOC RESTR'S: Must book with Secretary.
SOC GF - Round: Wd £25. We N/A. **Day:** Wd £40. We N/A.
SOC PACK: Available on booking.
VIS RESTR'S: Times limited at We to 11-12.30 & after 5
VIS GF - Round: Wd £25. We £30. **Day:** Wd £25. We £30.
FACILITIES: Bar & Restaurant.

CHIPPING SODBURY GOLF CLUB   MAP 2 B2

Chipping Sodbury, Bristol, Avon BS16 6PU.
12 miles N of Bristol, 9 miles from J 14 M5, 3 miles from J 18 M4.

CONTACT: KG Starr, Secretary. Tel: 0454 319042.
COURSE: 6,912yds, PAR 71, SSS 73. Downland course.
SOC RESTR'S: Must have Handicap Certificates at We.
SOC GF - Round: Wd £20. We £25. **Day:** Wd £20. We £25.
SOC PACK: Prior arrangement. Coffee, Lunch & Dinner.
VIS RESTR'S: No visitors Saturday or Sunday morning.
VIS GF - Round: Wd £20. We £25. **Day:** Wd £20. We £25.
FACILITIES: 9-hole course, £2. 50 any day. Bar & Restaurant.

BEDFORDSHIRE

KNOWLE GOLF CLUB   MAP 2 B3

Fairway, West Town Lane, Brislington, Bristol BS4 5DF.
M32 - A4 - Bath - Brislington, 3 miles south of Bristol, off A4.

CONTACT: Mrs JD King. Tel: 0272 770660.
COURSE: 6,016yds, PAR 69, SSS 69. Parkland course.
SOC RESTR'S: Welcome Thursdays.
SOC GF-Round: Wd £21. We N/A. **Day:** Wd £26. We N/A.
SOC PACK: None.
VIS RESTR'S: Wd check with Pro (0272 779193). H'cap Cert's.
VIS GF - Round: Wd £21. We £26. **Day:** Wd £26. We £31.
FACILITIES: Bar & Restaurant.

൴

Bedfordshire

JOHN O'GAUNT GOLF CLUB   MAP 3 A2

Sutton Park, Sandy, Bedfordshire SG19 2LY.
B1040 between Biggleswade (3 miles NE) & Potton.

CONTACT: IM Simpson, General Manager. Tel: 0767 260360.
COURSE: 6,513yds, PAR 71, SSS 71. Parkland course.
SOC RESTR'S: Min. 12. Weekdays.
SOC GF - Round: Wd N/A. We N/A. **Day:** Wd £35. We N/A.
SOC PACK: £50 approx.
VIS RESTR'S: H'cap Cert's at We. Advisable to phone before visit.
VIS GF - Round: Wd N/A. We N/A. **Day:** Wd £35. We £50.
FACILITIES: Bar & Restaurant.

JOHN O'GAUNT G C (CARTHAGENA)   MAP 3 A2

Sutton Park, Sandy, Bedfordshire SG19 2LY.
B1040 between Biggleswade (3 miles NE) & Potton.

CONTACT: IM Simpson, General Manager. Tel: 0767 260360.
COURSE: 5,869yds, PAR 69, SSS 68. Undulating parkland course.
SOC RESTR'S: Min. 12. Weekdays.
SOC GF - Round: Wd N/A. We N/A. **Day:** Wd £35. We N/A.
SOC PACK: £50 approx.
VIS RESTR'S: H'cap Cert at We. Advisable to phone before visit.
VIS GF - Round: Wd N/A. We N/A. **Day:** Wd £35. We £50.
FACILITIES: Bar & Restaurant.

ENGLAND

Berkshire

MILL RIDE GOLF CLUB MAP 7 A2

Mill Ride, North Ascot, Berkshire SL5 8LT.
2 miles west of Ascot.
CONTACT: Mrs S Watt, Secretary. Tel: 0344 886777.
COURSE: 6,745yds, PAR 72, SSS 72. Parkland course.
SOC RESTR'S: Welcome Weekdays with prior booking.
SOC GF - Round: Wd N/A. We N/A. Day: Wd £50. We N/A.
SOC PACK: Coffee, Ploughmans Lunch, Dinner, 36 holes, £65.
VIS RESTR'S: Welcome W/days & W/ends after 12. Phone first.
VIS GF - Round: Wd £35. We N/A. Day: Wd £50. We N/A.
FACILITIES: Restaurant, Bar, Pro-shop, Practice area.

CALCOT PARK GOLF CLUB MAP 3 A2

Calcot, Reading, Berkshire RG3 5RN.
3 miles west of Reading on A4.
CONTACT: AL Bray, Secretary. Tel: 0734 427124.
COURSE: 6,283yds, PAR 70, SSS 70. Parkland course.
SOC RESTR'S: No restrictions Wd. Not at We.
SOC GF - Round: Wd £30. We N/A. Day: Wd N/A. We N/A.
SOC PACK: By arrangement.
VIS RESTR'S: Welcome weekdays.
VIS GF - Round: Wd £30. We N/A. Day: Wd N/A. We N/A.
FACILITIES: Bar, Restaurant, Pro shop.

READING GOLF CLUB MAP 3 A2

17 Kidmore End Road, Emmer Green, Reading RG4 8SG.
2 miles N of Reading, 1 mile N of Caversham, off B481.
CONTACT: J Weekes, Secretary. Tel: 0734 472909.
COURSE: 6,212yds, PAR 70, SSS 70. Tree-lined parkland.
SOC RESTR'S: Welcome. Wed 20-25, Tues & Thur 25-75.
SOC GF - Round: Wd N/A. We N/A. Day: Wd £31. We N/A.
SOC PACK: Coffee, Ploughmans Lunch, Dinner, 36 holes, £50.
VIS RESTR'S: Mon /Thur Club or Soc h'cap req Fri/We as Guest.
VIS GF - Round: Wd N/A. We N/A. Day: Wd £27. We N/A.
FACILITIES: Pro-shop, Indoor/Outdoor Practice, Restaurant & Bar.

DOWNSHIRE GOLF COURSE MAP 7 A2

Easthampstead Park, Wokingham, Berkshire RG11 3DH.
2 miles south of Bracknell towards M3.
CONTACT: Professional. Tel: 0344 302030.
COURSE: 6,395yds, PAR 72, SSS 71. Parkland course.
SOC RESTR'S: Welcome Weekdays with advance booking.
SOC GF - Round: Wd £10.20. We N/A. Day: Wd N/A. We N/A.
SOC PACK: Coffee/Breakfast, Lunch, Dinner, 36 holes.
VIS RESTR'S: Seven day booking system. Some walk on times.
VIS GF - Round: Wd £10.20. We N/A. Day: Wd £11.90. We N/A.
FACILITIES: Public golf complex incl.; Range, Par 3 & Lessons.

BERKSHIRE GC (RED) MAP 7 A2

Swinley Road, Ascot, Berkshire SL5 8AY.
3 miles from Ascot on A332.
CONTACT: Mjr PD Clarke, Secretary. Tel: 0344 21496.
COURSE: 6,369yds, PAR 72, SSS 70. Heathland course.
SOC RESTR'S: Letter of Intro & H'cap Cert required. No We.
SOC GF - Round: Wd N/A. We N/A. Day: Wd N/A. We N/A.
SOC PACK: On application.
VIS RESTR'S: Letter of Intro Wd. With Member We. GF on applic.
VIS GF - Round: Wd N/A. We N/A. Day: Wd N/A. We N/A.
FACILITIES: Bar, Restaurant, Pro shop.

GORING & STREATLEY GOLF CLUB MAP 3 A2

Rectory Road, Streatley-on-Thames, Reading RG8 9QA.
10 miles north-west of Reading on A417.
CONTACT: J Menzies, Secretary/Manager. Tel: 0491 873229.
COURSE: 6,286yds, PAR 71, SSS 70. Moorland course.
SOC RESTR'S: Mon (18 players), Tues (60 players), Fri (30 players).
SOC GF - Round: Wd N/A. We N/A. Day: Wd £45. We N/A.
SOC PACK: Coffee/Breakfast, Lunch, Dinner, 36 holes.
VIS RESTR'S: Closed to visitors at We & Bank Hols.
VIS GF - Round: Wd N/A. We N/A. Day: Wd £28. We N/A.
FACILITIES: Excellent Restaurant & Bar facilities.

BERKSHIRE GC (BLUE) MAP 7 A2

Swinley Road, Ascot, Berkshire SL5 8AY.
3 miles from Ascot on A332.
CONTACT: Mjr PD Clarke, Secretary. Tel: 0344 21496.
COURSE: 6,260yds, PAR 71, SSS 70. Heathland course.
SOC RESTR'S: Letter of Intro & H'cap Cert required. No We.
SOC GF - Round: Wd N/A. We N/A. Day: Wd N/A. We N/A.
SOC PACK: On application.
VIS RESTR'S: Letter of Intro Wd. With Member We. GF on applic.
VIS GF - Round: Wd N/A. We N/A. Day: Wd N/A. We N/A.
FACILITIES: Bar, Restaurant, Pro shop.

BUCKINGHAMSHIRE

WEST BERKSHIRE GOLF CLUB   MAP 3 A2

Chaddleworth, Newbury, Berkshire RG16 0HS.
M4 Junctions 13/14. Signpost RAF Welford.

CONTACT: Mrs CM Clayton, Director. Tel: 0488 638574.
COURSE: 7,069yds, PAR 73, SSS 74. Downland course.
SOC RESTR'S: Welcome Weekdays.
SOC GF - Round: Wd N/A. We N/A. **Day:** Wd £22. We N/A.
SOC PACK: Coffee, Lunch, Dinner, 36 holes - £40. total.
VIS RESTR'S: Welcome Weekdays.
VIS GF - Round: Wd N/A. We N/A. **Day:** Wd £22. We N/A.
FACILITIES: Bar & Restaurant.

WINTER HILL GOLF CLUB   MAP 7 A2

Grange Lane, Cookham, Berkshire SL6 9RP.
4 miles north of Maidenhead.

CONTACT: GB Charters-Rowe, Sec. Tel: 0628 527513.
COURSE: 6,408yds, PAR 72, SSS 71. Parkland course.
SOC RESTR'S: Best day Wednesday. Booking required.
SOC GF - Round: Wd £22. We N/A. **Day:** Wd £22. We N/A.
SOC PACK: Available on booking.
VIS RESTR'S: Weekday. Phone call first advisable.
VIS GF - Round: Wd £22. We N/A. **Day:** Wd £22. We N/A.
FACILITIES: Bar & Restaurant.

Buckinghamshire

ELLESBOROUGH GOLF CLUB   MAP 7 A1

Butlers Cross, Aylesbury, Bucks HP17 0TZ.
On B4010, 1. 5 miles west of Wendover.

CONTACT: KM Flint, Secretary. Tel: 0296 622114.
COURSE: 6,271yds, PAR 71, SSS 70. Hilly parkland course.
SOC RESTR'S: Welcome Wed & Thur up to 40.
SOC GF - Round: Wd £20. We N/A. **Day:** Wd N/A. We N/A.
SOC PACK: Coffee, Lunch, Dinner plus 36 holes - £52.
VIS RESTR'S: Welcome except Tues - Competition Day & We.
VIS GF - Round: Wd £20. We N/A. **Day:** Wd £30. We N/A.
FACILITIES: Bar & Restaurant.

STOKE POGES GOLF CLUB   MAP 7 A2

North Drive, Park Road, Stoke Poges, Bucks SL2 4PG.
From London on A40, 2 miles north of Slough.

CONTACT: RC Pickering, Secretary. Tel: 0753 526385.
COURSE: 6,654yds, PAR 71, SSS 72. Parkland course.
SOC RESTR'S: Welcome Mon-Fri (except Tues).
SOC GF - Round: Wd £27. We N/A. **Day:** Wd £37. We N/A.
SOC PACK: Coffee, Lunch & Tea, 36 holes- £62.
VIS RESTR'S: Welcome Wd except Tues am. Hand Cert required.
VIS GF - Round: Wd £27. We N/A. **Day:** Wd £37. We N/A.
FACILITIES: Practice Ground.

WAVENDON GOLF CENTRE   MAP 7 A1

Tower End Road, Wavendon, Milton Keynes MK17 8DA.
1 mile from M1. 10 minutes from centre of Milton Keynes.

CONTACT: N Elmer, Managing Director. Tel: 0908 281811.
COURSE: 5,468yds, PAR 66, SSS 67. Parkland course.
SOC RESTR'S: Welcome with prior booking.
SOC GF - Round: Wd £9. We N/A. **Day:** Wd N/A. We N/A.
SOC PACK: Coffee, Snack Lunch, Dinner, 36 holes £35.
VIS RESTR'S: Welcome.
VIS GF - Round: Wd £9. We £12. **Day:** Wd N/A. We N/A.
FACILITIES: Range, 9-hole Par 3 Course, Pro-shop & Bar Food.

WEXHAM PARK GOLF COURSE   MAP 7 A2

Wexham Street, Slough, Bucks SL3 6NB.
2 miles from Slough towards Gerrards X. Opp Hospital.

CONTACT: P Gale, Secretary. Tel: 0753 663271.
COURSE: 5,390yds, PAR 67, SSS 66. Parkland course.
SOC RESTR'S: Min. 12. Welcome Weekdays.
SOC GF - Round: Wd £8. We N/A. **Day:** Wd £11. We N/A.
SOC PACK: Available on booking.
VIS RESTR'S: Pay & Play. Public course.
VIS GF - Round: Wd £8. We N/A. **Day:** Wd £11. We N/A.
FACILITIES: Range, 9-hole Par 3 Course, Pro-shop, Bar Food.

WOBURN G & CC (DUKE'S)   MAP 7 A1

Bow Brickhill, Milton Keynes, Bucks MK17 9LJ.
Exit J13 M1, half a mile turn left for Woburn & follow signs.

CONTACT: Secretary. Tel: 0908 677987.
COURSE: 6,940yds, PAR 72, SSS 74. Parkland course.
SOC RESTR'S: Ring in advance. Green fees not confirmed.
SOC GF - Round: Wd N/A. We N/A. **Day:** Wd N/A. We N/A.
SOC PACK: Available on booking.
VIS RESTR'S: Wd, booking essential & h'cap cert required.
VIS GF - Round: Wd N/A. We N/A. **Day:** Wd N/A. We N/A.
FACILITIES: Bar & Restaurant.

ENGLAND

WOBURN G & CC (DUCHESS)   MAP 7 A1

Bow Brickhill, Milton Keynes, Bucks MK17 9LJ.
Exit J13 M1, half a mile turn left for Woburn & follow signs.
CONTACT: Secretary. Tel: 0908 677987.
COURSE: 6,641yds, PAR 72, SSS 72. Parkland course.
SOC RESTR'S: Ring in advance. Green fees not confirmed.
SOC GF - Round: Wd N/A. **We** N/A. **Day:** Wd N/A. **We** N/A.
SOC PACK: Available on booking.
VIS RESTR'S: Wd, booking essential & h'cap cert required.
VIS GF - Round: Wd N/A. **We** N/A. **Day:** Wd N/A. **We** N/A.
FACILITIES: Bar & Restaurant.

CAMBRIDGESHIRE MOAT HOUSE   MAP 3 A2

Bar Hill, Cambridge, Cambs CB3 8EU.
On A604 5 miles north-west of Cambridge.
CONTACT: D Vernon, Manager/Pro. Tel: 0954 780555.
COURSE: 6,734yds, PAR 72, SSS 72. Undulating parkland.
SOC RESTR'S: Min 12. Non-res: Mon-Thur. Res: Fri-Sun.
SOC GF - Round: Wd £19. **We** £25. **Day:** Wd N/A. **We** N/A.
SOC PACK: Coffee, Ploughmans Lunch, Dinner, 36 holes £38.
VIS RESTR'S: Prior telephone call required.
VIS GF - Round: Wd £19. **We** £25. **Day:** Wd N/A. **We** N/A.
FACILITIES: Squash, Tennis, Swimming, & Leisure Club.

ELY CITY GOLF CLUB   MAP 3 B2/3

Cambridge Road, Ely, Cambs CB7 4HX.
On A10, southern outskirts of City.
CONTACT: GA Briggs, Secretary. Tel: 0353 662751.
COURSE: 6,602yds, PAR 72, SSS 72. Parkland course.
SOC RESTR'S: Tuesday-Friday.
SOC GF - Round: Wd £19-£22. **We** N/A. **Day:** Wd £19-£22. **We** N/A.
SOC PACK: £30-£34.
VIS RESTR'S: No restrictions. Handicap Certificates required.
VIS GF - Round: Wd N/A. **We** N/A. **Day:** Wd £22. **We** £30.
FACILITIES: Full Bar & Restaurant facilities.

Cambridgeshire

ABBOTSLEY GOLF CLUB   MAP 3 A2

St. Neots, Huntingdon, Cambs PE19 4XN.
A45 follow signs to Abbotsley. 12 miles W of Cambridge.
CONTACT: Andrew Bailey, Manager. Tel: 0480 215153.
COURSE: 6,200yds, PAR 72, SSS 70. Wooded parkland.
SOC RESTR'S: On application from Club Secretary.
SOC GF - Round: Wd £10. **We** £12. **Day:** Wd N/A. **We** N/A.
SOC PACK: From £30 Wd & from £40 We.
VIS RESTR'S: Please phone prior to play.
VIS GF - Round: Wd £10. **We** £12. **Day:** Wd N/A. **We** N/A.
FACILITIES: 2nd 18-hole course. Range, Bar & Restaurant.

PETERBOROUGH MILTON   MAP 3 A1

Milton Ferry, Peterborough, Cambs PE6 7AG.
On A47, 2 miles west of Peterborough.
CONTACT: Mrs Diana Adams, Secretary. Tel: 0733 380489.
COURSE: 6,450yds, PAR 71, SSS 71. Parkland course.
SOC RESTR'S: No limit to numbers. Tues, Wed & Thur.
SOC GF - Round: Wd N/A. **We** N/A. **Day:** Wd £30. **We** N/A.
SOC PACK: Coffee, Breakfast, Lunch & Dinner. £40
VIS RESTR'S: None other than Handicap Certificates required.
VIS GF - Round: Wd £20. **We** £25. **Day:** Wd £25. **We** N/A.
FACILITIES: None.

BRAMPTON PARK GOLF CLUB   MAP 3 A2

Buckden Road, Brampton, Huntingdon, Cambs PE18 6NF.
Half-a-mile east off A1 between Brampton & Huntingdon.
CONTACT: C Burrows, Secretary. Tel: 0480 434700.
COURSE: 6,364yds, PAR 71, SSS 73. Meadowland course.
SOC RESTR'S: Min. 10. Max. 120. Welcome Weekdays.
SOC GF - Round: Wd N/A. **We** N/A. **Day:** Wd £24. **We** N/A.
SOC PACK: Summer Pack: Coffee, Lunch, Dinner 36 holes £45.
VIS RESTR'S: Welcome.
VIS GF - Round: Wd £18. **We** N/A. **Day:** Wd £24. **We** £36.
FACILITIES: Soc Winter Pack Breakfast, Lunch, 18 holes. £30.

GOG MAGOG   MAP 3 A2

Shelford Bottom, Cambridge CB2 4AB.
2 miles south of Cambridge on A1307 (A604).
CONTACT: JE Riches, Secretary. Tel: 0223 247626.
COURSE: 6,386yds, PAR 70, SSS 70. Undulating high ground.
SOC RESTR'S: Tue & Thu only. H'cap Cert required.
SOC GF - Round: Wd N/A. **We** N/A. **Day:** Wd £35. **We** N/A.
SOC PACK: Tailored to requirements.
VIS RESTR'S: Wd with Intro or H'cap Cert. Only with Member We.
VIS GF - Round: Wd £29. **We** N/A. **Day:** Wd £35. **We** N/A.
FACILITIES: 2nd 18-hole (New) Par 68, Bar, Pro shop.

CHESHIRE

Cheshire

MOTTRAM HALL GOLF CLUB   MAP 8 A3

Wilmslow Rd, Mottram St Andrews, Prestbury SK10 4QT.
4 miles south-east of Wilmslow.

CONTACT: Amanda Penney, Secretary. Tel: 0625 828135.
COURSE: 6,905yds, PAR 72, SSS 72. Flat parkland course.
SOC RESTR'S: Handicap Certificate required.
SOC GF - Round: Wd £25. **We** N/A. **Day:** Wd N/A. **We** N/A.
SOC PACK: Special rates vary on party size.
VIS RESTR'S: Handicap Certificate required.
VIS GF - Round: Wd £25. **We** £30. **Day:** Wd N/A. **We** N/A.
FACILITIES: Bar, Pro shop, Leisure centre.

CALDY GOLF CLUB   MAP 2 A1

Links Hey Road, Caldy, Wirral L48 1NB.
1.5 miles south of West Kirby.

CONTACT: TDM Bacon, Secretary. Tel: 051 625 5660.
COURSE: 6,675yds, PAR 72, SSS 73. Parkland course.
SOC RESTR'S: Not before 9.30 & 1-2 Wd. Must book.
SOC GF - Round: Wd N/A. **We** N/A. **Day:** Wd £30. **We** N/A.
SOC PACK: Please discuss at time of booking.
VIS RESTR'S: Not before 9.30 & 1-2 Wd. Must book in advance.
VIS GF - Round: Wd N/A. **We** N/A. **Day:** Wd N/A. **We** N/A.
FACILITIES: Buggies, Bar, Restaurant, Pro shop, Snooker.

PORTAL GOLF COMPLEX   MAP 2 B1

Cobblers Cross Lane, Tarporley, Cheshire CW6 0DJ.
Off the Chester to Nantwich road in Tarporley.

CONTACT: D Wills, General Manager. Tel: 0829 733933.
COURSE: 7,145yds, PAR 73, SSS 74. Undulating parkland.
SOC RESTR'S: Welcome.
SOC GF - Round: Wd £30. **We** £30. **Day:** Wd N/A. **We** N/A.
SOC PACK: Soup/Sandwiches - 18 holes - Dinner: £40.
VIS RESTR'S: Please phone prior to play.
VIS GF - Round: Wd £30. **We** £40. **Day:** Wd £100*. **We** £150*.
FACILITIES: Bar & Restaurant. *For 4 people.

DISLEY GOLF CLUB   MAP 8 A3

Stanley Hall Lane, Disley, Stockport.
6 miles south of Stockport.

CONTACT: JA Lomas, Hon Secretary. Tel: 0663 762071.
COURSE: 6,015yds, PAR 70, SSS 69. Parkland/moorland course.
SOC RESTR'S: Not Wed-Fri or Bank Holidays.
SOC GF - Round: Wd N/A. **We** N/A. **Day:** Wd N/A. **We** N/A.
SOC PACK: On application.
VIS RESTR'S: Not Wed-Fri or BH. GF on application.
VIS GF - Round: Wd N/A. **We** N/A. **Day:** Wd N/A. **We** N/A.
FACILITIES: Bar, Restaurant, Pro shop, Snooker.

STAMFORD GOLF CLUB   MAP 8 A2

Huddersfield Road, Stalybridge, Cheshire SK15 3PY.
B6175 off the A6018.

CONTACT: FE Rowles, Hon. Secretary. Tel: 0457 832126.
COURSE: 5,701yds, PAR 70, SSS 68. Moorland course.
SOC RESTR'S: Welcome except on Mondays.
SOC GF - Round: Wd N/A. **We** N/A. **Day:** Wd £17.50. **We** £22.
SOC PACK: Details on application.
VIS RESTR'S: Not Tues (Ladies day). We GF available after 3.
VIS GF - Round: Wd £17.50. **We** £22. **Day:** Wd N/A. **We** N/A.
FACILITIES: None.

MARPLE GOLF CLUB   MAP 8 A3

Barnsfold Road, Hawk Green, Stockport, Cheshire SK6 7EL.
Off A6 at High Lane - left at Hawk Green.

CONTACT: B Ogden, Secretary. Tel: 061 449 0690.
COURSE: 5,565yds, PAR 68, SSS 67. Parkland/meadowland.
SOC RESTR'S: Not Thursdays or Weekend.
SOC GF - Round: Wd N/A. **We** N/A. **Day:** Wd N/A. **We** N/A.
SOC PACK: Soup/Sandwiches - 27 holes - Dinner - £22.50.
VIS RESTR'S: Not Thursday.
VIS GF - Round: Wd £20. **We** £30. **Day:** Wd N/A. **We** N/A.
FACILITIES: Bar Catering.

TYTHERINGTON   MAP 8 A3

Macclesfield, Cheshire SK10 2JP.
On Manchester road (A523), near Macclesfield.

CONTACT: Mrs R Dawson, Secretary. Tel: 0625 434562.
COURSE: 6,737yds, PAR 72, SSS 72. Parkland course.
SOC RESTR'S: Wd only. Handicap Certificate required.
SOC GF - Round: Wd £20. **We** N/A. **Day:** Wd £30. **We** N/A.
SOC PACK: Please discuss at time of booking.
VIS RESTR'S: Handicap Certificate required.
VIS GF - Round: Wd £25. **We** N/A. **Day:** Wd £35. **We** N/A.
FACILITIES: Driving Range, Bar, Restaurant, Shop, Leisure centre.

ENGLAND

VICARS CROSS GOLF CLUB   MAP 2 B1

Tarvin Road, Littleton, Chester, Cheshire CH3 7HN.
2 miles east of Chester on the A51.

CONTACT: A Rodgers, Secretary. Tel: 0244 335174
COURSE: 6,238yds, PAR 71, SSS 70. Meadowland course.
SOC RESTR'S: Welcome Tuesday & Thursday. Min 20.
SOC GF - Round: Wd N/A. **We** N/A **Day: Wd** £20 **We** N/A
SOC PACK: Available on booking.
VIS RESTR'S: Welcome Monday-Thursday.
VIS GF - Round: Wd N/A. **We** N/A **Day: Wd** £20 **We** N/A
FACILITIES: Bar.

WILMSLOW GOLF CLUB   MAP 8 A3

Great Warford, Mobberley, Knutsford WA16 7AY.
3 miles west of Alderley Edge.

CONTACT: A Laurence, Secretary. Tel: 0565 872148.
COURSE: 6,607yds, PAR 72, SSS 72. Parkland course.
SOC RESTR'S: Handicap Certificate required. Not Weds.
SOC GF - Round: Wd N/A. **We** N/A. **Day: Wd** £40. **We** N/A.
SOC PACK: On application.
VIS RESTR'S: Handicap Certificate required. Not before 3 Weds.
VIS GF - Round: Wd £25. **We** £40. **Day: Wd** N/A. **We** N/A.
FACILITIES: Bar, Restaurant, Pro shop.

Cleveland

SEATON CAREW (OLD)   MAP 5 B2

Tees Road, Hartlepool, Cleveland TS25 1DE.
2 miles from Hartlepool.

CONTACT: PR Wilson, Secretary. Tel: 0429 261473.
COURSE: 6,613yds, PAR 72, SSS 72. Links course.
SOC RESTR'S: Welcome with booking.
SOC GF - Round: Wd N/A. **We** N/A. **Day: Wd** £22. **We** N/A.
SOC PACK: Detailed packages available.
VIS RESTR'S: No restrictions.
VIS GF - Round: Wd N/A. **We** N/A. **Day: Wd** £22. **We** £30.
FACILITIES: Bar, Restaurant, Pro shop.

SEATON CAREW (BRABAZON)   MAP 5 B2

Tees Road, Hartlepool, Cleveland TS25 1DE.
2 miles from Hartlepool.

CONTACT: PR Wilson, Secretary. Tel: 0429 261473.
COURSE: 6,855yds, PAR 72, SSS 73. Links course.
SOC RESTR'S: Welcome with booking.
SOC GF - Round: Wd N/A. **We** N/A. **Day: Wd** £22. **We** N/A.
SOC PACK: Detailed packages available.
VIS RESTR'S: No restrictions.
VIS GF - Round: Wd N/A. **We** N/A. **Day: Wd** £22. **We** £30.
FACILITIES: Bar, Restaurant, Pro shop.

Cornwall

BODMIN GOLF CLUB   MAP 1 A3

Lanhydrock, Bodmin, Cornwall PL30 5AQ.
From Bodmin on Lostwithiel Road, 3 miles out of town on right.

CONTACT: C Willis, Manager. Tel: 0208 73600.
COURSE: 6,142yds, PAR 71, SSS 69. Parkland/moorland course.
SOC RESTR'S: Welcome. Min 12.
SOC GF - Round: Wd £15. **We** N/A. **Day: Wd** £25. **We** N/A.
SOC PACK: Available on booking.
VIS RESTR'S: Welcome. Please phone for tee time.
VIS GF - Round: Wd £19. **We** £19. **Day: Wd** £34. **We** N/A.
FACILITIES: Bar & Restaurant.

CARLYON BAY GOLF CLUB   MAP 1 A3

Carlyon Bay, St. Austell, Cornwall PL25 3RD.
Main Plymouth to Truro road, 1 mile west of St. Blazey.
See advertisement.

CONTACT: N Sears, Professional. Tel: 072 681 4228.
COURSE: 6,501yds, PAR 72, SSS 71. Parkland/hilltop course.
SOC RESTR'S: Please book through professional.
SOC GF - Round: Wd £20. **We** £20. **Day: Wd** £20. **We** £20.
SOC PACK: Available on booking.
VIS RESTR'S: Book in advance through professional.
VIS GF - Round: Wd £20. **We** £20. **Day: Wd** £20. **We** £20.
FACILITIES: Bar, Pro-shop & Club Hire.

CORNWALL

THE CREAM OF GOLF
at Cornwall's Finest...

THE CARLYON BAY & GOLF COURSE is set amidst the finest scenary in Cornwall. Savour the luxuries of the Cornish Riviera's leading hotel and enjoy FREE GOLF on our championship 6500 yard, 18 hole course, lying just a short level walk from our hotel, plus the use of our superb 9 hole approach course, situated within the hotel's own gardens, providing similarly spectacular coastal views of the unique bay.

Also at your disposal will be the full Clubhouse facilities including Bar, Restaurant, Locker rooms and the Resident Professional's shop, offering the complete range of equipment and tuition. Golfers and non-golfers alike can enjoy use of both indoor and outdoor heated pools, tennis courts, sauna, solarium, spa bath and large snooker room. The hotel itself is renowned for its high standards of cuisine, comfort and service, all bedrooms having private bath, colour satellite TV, radio and telephone, most enjoying panoramic views.

For Free Colour Brochure and Breaks Tariff. Please contact: Mr P. Brennan

The Carlyon Bay Hotel
★★★★ RAC

AND GOLF COURSE

Brend Hotels

Nr St. Austell, Cornwall. PL25 3RD. Telephone: (0726) 812304

Coombe Farm
WIDEGATES NR LOOE — CORNWALL PL13 1QN
(Situated on the B3253 from Hessenford to Looe)
Telephone: Widegates (050-34) 223 (Management) or 329 (Guests)
RAC Highly Acclaimed
ETB 2 Crowns Highly Commended

A lovely country house surrounded by lawns, meadows, woods, streams and ponds with superb views to the sea. Log fires. Candlelit dining. Delicious home cooking. Licensed. In the grounds many birds, animals and flowers, a heated outdoor pool, croquet lawn and stone barn for snooker and table tennis. Nearby golf, fishing, tennis, horse riding and glorious walks and beaches. All rooms en-suite

Bed & Breakfast from £16.50. 4-course dinner from £10.50.
A warm welcome assured by Alexander and Sally Low.

MULLION GOLF CLUB — MAP 1 A3

Cury, Helston, Cornwall. TR12 7BP.
Off the A 3083, 6 miles south of Helston.
Recommended Hotel: Housel Bay Hotel, Lingard.

CONTACT: D Watts, Secretary. Tel: 0326 240685.
COURSE: 6,022yds, PAR 69, SSS 69. Undulating course.
SOC RESTR'S: Welcome with prior agreement.
SOC GF - Round: Wd £18. We £18. Wd £18. We £18.
SOC PACK: Seasonal variations to Green Fees.
VIS RESTR'S: Welcome with Handicap Certificate.
VIS GF - Round: Wd £18. We £18. Day: Wd £18. We £18.
FACILITIES: Bar, Snacks, Practice area & Pro-shop.

NEWQUAY GOLF CLUB — MAP 1 A3

Tower Road, Newquay, Cornwall TR7 1LT.
Adjacent to Fistral Beach just outside Newquay town.

CONTACT: P Muscroft, Professional. Tel: 0637 874830.
COURSE: 6,140yds, PAR 69, SSS 69. Sandy seaside course.
SOC RESTR'S: Welcome except Sunday.
SOC GF - Round: Wd £14. We £16. Wd N/A, We N/A.
SOC PACK: By prior arrangement.
VIS RESTR'S: Welcome with Handicap Certificate.
VIS GF - Round: Wd £18, We £20. Day: Wd N/A, We N/A.
FACILITIES: Tennis, Gym, Snooker. Weekly Green Fee £70.

ENGLAND

Western Promise

At the Housel Bay we promise you'll be able to relax in complete seclusion, peace and quiet. We promise comfortable rooms, all en-suite, and many with one of the most stunning views in Britain. We promise friendly service, fine traditional cuisine and a really warm welcome.

We also promise lovely scenery, from spectacular cliffs and sheltered beaches to windswept moorland and hidden wooded valleys. All perfect for walking . . .

. . . and for golf. There are four courses only a short drive from the hotel.

At Housel Bay we don't promise the earth – just a small and beautiful part of it.

The Housel Bay Hotel
Housel Bay, The Lizard, Cornwall, TR12 7PG

CALL FOR BROCHURE
0326 290417

ST MELLION GC (NICKLAUS)   MAP 1 B3

St. Mellion, Saltash, Cornwall PL12 6SD.
10 mls from Plymouth M5/A38 to Saltash - A388 to St. Mellion.
See advertisement.

CONTACT: Mrs Baxter, Co-ordinator. Tel: 0579 50101.
COURSE: 6,626yds, PAR 72, SSS 72. Championship parkland.
SOC RESTR'S: Max. 60. Handicap Certificates required.
SOC GF - Round: Wd £35. **We** N/A. **Day:** Wd N/A. **We** N/A.
SOC PACK: Coffee, Lunch, 18 holes, Drinks midway, Dinner: £52.
VIS RESTR'S: Closed for major events e.g. Benson & Hedges.
VIS GF - Round: Wd £42. **We** N/A. **Day:** Wd N/A. **We** N/A.
FACILITIES: Indoor Pool, Sauna, Jacuzzi, Solarium & Snooker.

ST MELLION GOLF CLUB (OLD)   MAP 1 B3

St. Mellion, Saltash, Cornwall PL12 6SD.
10 miles from Plymouth M5/A38 to Saltash - A388 to St. Mellion.

CONTACT: Mrs Baxter, Co-ordinator. Tel: 0579 50101.
COURSE: 5,927yds, PAR 70, SSS 68. Parkland course.
SOC RESTR'S: Max. 60. No Weekends.
SOC GF - Round: Wd £17. **We** N/A. **Day:** Wd N/A. **We** N/A.
SOC PACK: Coffee, 18 holes, Drinks half way, Dinner: £32.
VIS RESTR'S: Welcome - Prior booking essential.
VIS GF - Round: Wd £22. **We** N/A. **Day:** Wd N/A. **We** N/A.
FACILITIES: Badminton, Squash, Tennis & Table Tennis.

PERRANPORTH GOLF CLUB   MAP 1 A3

Budnick Hill, Perranporth, Cornwall TR6 0AB.
On B3285, half-a-mile north-east of town.

CONTACT: P Barnes, Secretary. Tel: 0872 573701.
COURSE: 6,286yds, PAR 72, SSS 70. Links course.
SOC RESTR'S: Welcome, but prior notice required. Min 10.
SOC GF - Round: Wd N/A. **We** N/A. **Day:** Wd £15. **We** £15.
SOC PACK: Available to suit requirements.
VIS RESTR'S: Welcome, but H'cap Cert required at We.
VIS GF - Round: Wd N/A. **We** N/A. **Day:** Wd £20. **We** £25.
FACILITIES: Bar, Restaurant etc.

ST ENODOC GC (CHURCH)   MAP 1 A3

Rock, Wadebridge, Cornwall PL28 6LG.
3 miles from Port Isaac on the B3314. Turn left onto Rock.

CONTACT: L Guy, Secretary. Tel: 0208 863216.
COURSE: 6,615yds, PAR 72, SSS 70. Seaside links course.
SOC RESTR'S: Book in advance - 3 days a week.
SOC GF - Round: Wd £22. **We** N/A. **Day:** Wd £25. **We** N/A.
SOC PACK: Available on booking. (above GF exclude catering).
VIS RESTR'S: Min handicap 24 Men; 28 Ladies
VIS GF - Round: Wd £22. **We** £27. **Day:** Wd £34. **We** £40.
FACILITIES: 18-hole Holywell Course, Clubhouse & Catering.

YOUR VERY OWN 19th
– WITH FREE GOLF

When you take a luxury lodge at St. Mellion – for a few days, a week or longer – these are just a few of the pleasures that await you.

Golf on either the Nicklaus Championship Course or the Old Course, the heated pool and all the other sports facilities at the Country Club and, not least, your choice of two excellent restaurants.

Add to that the tranquil Cornish countryside, nearby Plymouth and excellent beaches and your holiday will be complete.

Take the first step now. Find out about availability and rates – for parties of two to eight people – from our Reservation Staff on 0579 50101.

ST. MELLION GOLF & COUNTRY CLUB
DEPT RAC · SALTASH · CORNWALL PL12 6SD
TEL 0579 50101   FAX 0579 50116

CUMBRIA

TREVOSE GOLF CLUB   MAP 1 A3

Constantine Bay, Padstow, Cornwall PL28 8JB.
4 miles west of Padstow on B3276.

CONTACT: L Grindley, Secretary. Tel: 0841 520208.
COURSE: 6,608yds, PAR 70, SSS 72. Links course.
SOC RESTR'S: On application from Club Secretary.
SOC GF - Round: Wd N/A. **We** N/A. **Day:** Wd £20/£30. **We** £20/£30.
SOC PACK: Seasonal variation to GF. Weekly rates available.
VIS RESTR'S: Phone first. 3 & 4-ball. H'cap Cert required.
VIS GF - Round: Wd N/A **We** N/A. **Day:** Wd £28. **We** £28.
FACILITIES: 9-hole Course, Restaurant where all meals available.

WEST CORNWALL GOLF CLUB   MAP 1 A3

Church Lane, Lelant, St. Ives Cornwall TR26 3DZ.
Off the A30. 2 miles east of St. Ives.

CONTACT: MC Lack, Secretary. Tel: 0736 753401.
COURSE: 5,879yds, PAR 69, SSS 68. Links course.
SOC RESTR'S: By written application.
SOC GF - Round: Wd N/A. **We** N/A. **Day:** Wd £15.**We** £20.
SOC PACK: 5-day Green Fee £60. 7-day Green Fee £80.
VIS RESTR'S: Welcome. Please book by telephone.
VIS GF - Round: Wd £20. **We** £25. **Day:** Wd £20. **We** £25.
FACILITIES: Restaurant, Bar & Snooker.

Cumbria

APPLEBY GOLF CLUB   MAP 5 A2

Brackenber Moor, Appleby-in-Westmorland, Cumbria CA16 6LP.
2 miles south of Appleby-in-Westmorland on the A66.

CONTACT: BW Rimmer, Secretary. Tel: 0930 07683.
COURSE: 5,755yds, PAR 68, SSS 68. Moorland course.
SOC RESTR'S: With prior agreement from the Secretary.
SOC GF - Round: Wd N/A. **We** N/A. **Day:** Wd £11. **We** £15.
SOC PACK: Catering can be arranged.
VIS RESTR'S: Welcome.
VIS GF - Round: Wd N/A **We** N/A. **Day:** Wd £11. **We** £15.
FACILITIES: Clubhouse.

BRAMPTON GOLF CLUB   MAP 5 A2

Brampton, Cumbria CA8 1HN.
Club is 1.5 miles south-east from Brampton on B6413.

CONTACT: S. Harrison, Professional. Tel: 06977 2000.
COURSE: 6,420yds, PAR 72, SSS 71. Fellside/moorland course.
SOC RESTR'S: Welcome except weekends.
SOC GF - Round: Wd £16. **We** N/A. **Day:** Wd £16. **We** N/A.
SOC PACK: Approx. £22 incl. Lunch & 3-course Meal.
VIS RESTR'S: Welcome but advise telephone for tee bookings.
VIS GF - Round: Wd N/A. **We** N/A. **Day:** Wd £16. **We** £20.
FACILITIES: Snooker.

KESWICK GOLF CLUB   MAP 5 A2

Threlkeld Hall, Threlkeld, Keswick, Cumbria CA12 4SX.
4 miles east of Keswick off A66.

CONTACT: D Bell Secretary. Tel: 07687 79324.
COURSE: 6,175yds, PAR 71, SSS 72. Parkland course.
SOC RESTR'S: Max 24. Welcome Wd. We can play 11.30-12.30.
SOC GF - Round: Wd N/A. **We** N/A. **Day:** Wd £12. **We** £15.
SOC PACK: Approx. £24 We, £21 Wd incl. Lunch & Dinner.
VIS RESTR'S: Welcome except Ladies day Thur 12.-1.30.
VIS GF - Round: Wd N/A. **We** N/A. **Day:** Wd £15. **We** £20.
FACILITIES: Bar & Restaurant.

MARYPORT GOLF CLUB   MAP 4 B3

Bankend, Maryport, Cumbria CA15 6PA.
1 mile north of Maryport on Silloth road (B5300).

CONTACT: A Carlton, Hon. Secretary. Tel: 0900 812605.
COURSE: 6,272yds, PAR 71, SSS 71. Mainly a links course.
SOC RESTR'S: Welcome.
SOC GF - Round: Wd N/A. **We** N/A. **Day:** Wd £10. **We** £15.
SOC PACK: Reductions for parties of 10-19 & 20+.
VIS RESTR'S: Welcome.
VIS GF - Round: Wd N/A. **We** N/A. **Day:** Wd £10. **We** £15.
FACILITIES: Catering by arrangement.

SEASCALE GOLF CLUB   MAP 4 B3

The Banks, Seascale, Cumbria CA20 1QL.
Off A595 and on coast to north of Seascale.

CONTACT: C Taylor, Secretary. Tel: 09467 28202.
COURSE: 6,419yds, PAR 71, SSS 71. Links course.
SOC RESTR'S: No restrictions - arrangement with Secretary.
SOC GF - Round: Wd N/A. **We** N/A. **Day:** Wd £18. **We** £22.
SOC PACK: Catering costs depend on menu.
VIS RESTR'S: No restrictions check availability on the day.
VIS GF - Round: Wd N/A. **We** N/A. **Day:** Wd £18. **We** £22.
FACILITIES: Bar & Restaurant.

ENGLAND

SILLOTH-ON-SOLWAY GOLF CLUB MAP 4 B3

The Clubhouse, Silloth, Cumbria CA5 4BL.
22 miles west of Carlisle off the B5302 Silloth.

CONTACT: JG Proudlock, Secretary. Tel: 06973 31304.
COURSE: 6,357yds, PAR 72, SSS 71. Seaside links course.
SOC RESTR'S: Welcome, Max 40 Wd. We. One round per day.
SOC GF - Round: Wd N/A. We N/A. **Day:** Wd £20. We N/A.
SOC PACK: None.
VIS RESTR'S: Welcome, one round per day at Weekends.
VIS GF - Round: Wd N/A. We £25. **Day:** Wd £20. We N/A.
FACILITIES: Full Catering.

KEDLESTON PARK GOLF CLUB MAP 2 B1

Kedleston, Quarndon, Derby DE6 4JD.
Follow RAC signs from Outer Ring Road (A38) to Kedleston Hall.

CONTACT: K Wilson, Managing Secretary. Tel: 0332 840035.
COURSE: 6,585yds, PAR 72, SSS 71. Natural parkland course.
SOC RESTR'S: Welcome Weekdays.
SOC GF - Round: Wd £25. We N/A. **Day:** Wd N/A, We N/A.
SOC PACK: Lunch, Dinner, 1 Round golf - £40.
VIS RESTR'S: Welcome Weekdays.
VIS GF - Round: Wd £25. We N/A. **Day:** Wd N/A, We N/A.
FACILITIES: Restaurant.

MICKLEOVER GOLF CLUB MAP 2 B1

Uttoxeter Road, Mickleover, Derby DE3 5AD.
A516/B5020, 3 miles west of Derby.

CONTACT: D Rodgers, Secretary. Tel: 0332 518662.
COURSE: 5,631yds, PAR 69, SSS 67. Meadowland course.
SOC RESTR'S: Welcome Tues & Thur, 9 4.
SOC GF - Round: Wd £18. We N/A. **Day:** Wd £18. We N/A.
SOC PACK: Full facilities available.
VIS RESTR'S: Welcome.
VIS GF - Round: Wd N/A. We N/A. **Day:** Wd £18. We £25.
FACILITIES: Snooker.

Derbyshire

EREWASH VALEY GOLF CLUB MAP 3 A1

Stanton-by-Dale, Ilkeston, Derby DE7 4QR.
M1 Junction 25 to Stanton village.

CONTACT: JA Beckett, Secretary. Tel: 0602 322984.
COURSE: 6,444yds, PAR 72, SSS 72. Meadowland/parkland.
SOC RESTR'S: Welcome except Tuesday & Weekends.
SOC GF - Round: Wd £22. We N/A. **Day:** Wd £27. We N/A.
SOC PACK: Available on booking.
VIS RESTR'S: Welcome except before 9.
VIS GF - Round: Wd £22. We £22. **Day:** Wd £27. We £27.
FACILITIES: Snooker, Bowling Green & Full Catering Services.

Devon

HORSLEY LODGE GOLF CLUB MAP 3 A1

Smalley Mill Road, Horsley, Derby DE2 5BL.
Turn for Horsley at Rose & Crown on A608 Derby-Heanor road.

CONTACT: Simon Berry, Professional. Tel: 0332 781400.
COURSE: 6,402yds, PAR 72, SSS 71. Parkland course.
SOC RESTR'S: Not Weekends and Competition days.
SOC GF - Round: Wd £15. We N/A. **Day:** Wd N/A. We N/A.
SOC PACK: Coffee, Lunch, Dinner & 36 holes - £26-£36.
VIS RESTR'S: Any day except during We Competitions.
VIS GF - Round: Wd £17. We £25. **Day:** Wd £17. We £25.
FACILITIES: Floodlit Driving Range & Accommodation.

AXE CLIFF GOLF CLUB MAP 1 B3

Squires Lane, Axmouth, Seaton, Devon EX12 2AZ.
Through Axmouth half-a-mile, turn left before bridge.

CONTACT: D Rogers (Mrs), Secretary. Tel: 0297 24371
COURSE: 4,867yds, PAR 67, SSS 65. Seaside course.
SOC RESTR'S: Welcome except Wed & Sun closed until 11.
SOC GF - Round: Wd £21. We £27. **Day:** Wd £21. We £27.
SOC PACK: Above Green Fees includes catering.
VIS RESTR'S: Closed Wed & Sun until 11.
VIS GF - Round: Wd £12. We £16. **Day:** Wd £14. We £17.
FACILITIES: None.

DEVON

ILFRACOMBE GOLF CLUB   MAP 1 B2

Hele Bay, Ilfracombe, North Devon EX34 9RT.
On main road between Ilfracombe & Combe Martin.

CONTACT: RC Beer, Secretary. Tel: 0271 862176.
COURSE: 5,893yds, PAR 70, SSS 68. Parkland type course.
SOC RESTR'S: Not 12-2 Wd or before 10 on We & Bank Hols.
SOC GF - Round: Wd N/A. We N/A. **Day:** Wd £17. We £20.
SOC PACK: To be negotiated.
VIS RESTR'S: Not 12-2 Wd or before 10 on We & Bank Hols.
VIS GF - Round: Wd N/A. We N/A. **Day:** Wd £17. We £20.
FACILITIES: 5-day Ticket at £70.

MANOR HOUSE GOLF CLUB   MAP 1 B3

Moretonhampstead, Devon TQ13 8RE.
12 miles south-west from Exeter, on the B3212.

CONTACT: R Lewis, Manager/Pro. Tel: 0647 40355.
COURSE: 6,016yds, PAR 69, SSS 69. Parkland course.
SOC RESTR'S: Must be booked well in advance.
SOC GF - Round: Wd £22.50. We £28. **Day:** Wd £30. We £35.
SOC PACK: £44.
VIS RESTR'S: Must be booked in advance.
VIS GF - Round: Wd £22.50. We £28. **Day:** Wd £30. We £35.
FACILITIES: Squash, Tennis & Snooker.

ROYAL NORTH DEVON   MAP 1 B2

Golf Links Road, Westward Ho! EX39 1HD.
2 miles north of Bideford (A39).

CONTACT: JE Linaker, General Manager. Tel: 0237 473817.
COURSE: 6,662yds, PAR 71, SSS 72. Links course with sea views.
SOC RESTR'S: Welcome weekdays. H'cap Cert required.
SOC GF - Round: Wd N/A. We N/A. **Day:** Wd £23. We N/A.
SOC PACK: On application.
VIS RESTR'S: Not Thu am or We before 9.30. H'cap Cert req.
VIS GF - Round: Wd N/A. We N/A. **Day:** Wd N/A. We N/A.
FACILITIES: Bar, Pro shop, Club hire.

SAUNTON GOLF CLUB (EAST)   MAP 1 B2

Saunton, Nr. Braunton, North Devon EX33 1LG.
A361 from Barnstaple 7 miles- B3231 to Croyde Bay.

CONTACT: WE Geddes, Secretary. Tel: 0271 812436.
COURSE: 6,703yds, PAR 71, SSS 73. Championship links course.
SOC RESTR'S: Welcome.
SOC GF - Round: Wd N/A. We N/A. **Day:** Wd £28. We £33.
SOC PACK: £39 incl. GF, Coffee, Lunch & Dinner.
VIS RESTR'S: Must be Members of Golf Club with H'cap Cert.
VIS GF - Round: Wd N/A. We N/A. **Day:** Wd £28. We £33.
FACILITIES: None.

SAUNTON GOLF CLUB (WEST)   MAP 1 B2

Saunton, Nr. Braunton, North Devon EX33 1LG.
A361 from Barnstaple 7 miles- B3231 to Croyde Bay.

CONTACT: WE Geddes, Secretary. Tel: 0271 812436.
COURSE: 6,356yds, PAR 71, SSS 71. New links course.
SOC RESTR'S: Welcome.
SOC GF - Round: Wd N/A. We N/A. **Day:** Wd £28. We £33.
SOC PACK: £39 incl. GF, Coffee, Lunch & Dinner.
VIS RESTR'S: Must be Members of Golf Club with H'cap Cert.
VIS GF - Round: Wd N/A. We N/A. **Day:** Wd £28. We £33.
FACILITIES: None.

GLORIOUS GOLF IN DEVON

Westcliff HOTEL

RAC MERIT AWARDS

SIDMOUTH, DEVON EX10 8RU

SPECIAL FREE GOLF PROMOTION
from this superbly located family run hotel set in two acres of award winning gardens. All public rooms and most of the 32 double and twin bedrooms enjoy outstanding sea views overlooking the Esplanade and Lyme Bay. Outdoor Heated Pool, Lift, Satellite TV, Games Room, Jacuzzi, Sun Bed, Ample Car Parking. For colour brochure

TEL: 0395 513252
Ashley Courtenay and Les Routiers recommended

SIDMOUTH GOLF CLUB   MAP 1 B3

Peak Hill, Cotmaton Road, Sidmouth, Devon EX10 8SX.
Exeter Station Rd to Woodlands Hotel. Turn right Cotmaton Rd.
Recommended Hotel: Westcliff Hotel, Sidmouth.

CONTACT: IM Smith, Secretary. Tel: 0395 513023.
COURSE: 5,178yds, PAR 68, SSS 66. Parkland course.
SOC RESTR'S: By written application.
SOC GF - Round: Wd N/A. We N/A. **Day:** Wd £18. We £18.
SOC PACK: On application.
VIS RESTR'S: Book by telephone.
VIS GF - Round: Wd N/A. We N/A. **Day:** Wd £18. We £18
FACILITIES: Restaurant, Bar & Snooker.

ENGLAND

Dorset

BROADSTONE GOLF CLUB MAP 2 B3

Wentworth Drive, Broadstone, Dorset BH18 8DQ.
Located on the B3074, 3 miles to the north of Poole Harbour.

CONTACT: Secretary's Office. Tel: 0202 692595.
COURSE: 6,183yds, PAR 69, SSS 70. Heathland course.
SOC RESTR'S: Not at We. Please book through secretary.
SOC GF - Round: Wd £27. We N/A. **Day:** Wd £330. We N/A.
SOC PACK: GF + Catering charges £16-£31 dep on menu.
VIS RESTR'S: Wd & not before 9.30. Not Thur mornings.
VIS GF - Round: Wd £27. We N/A. **Day:** Wd £33. We N/A.
FACILITIES: None.

CAME DOWN GOLF CLUB MAP 2 B3

Came Down, Dorchester, Dorset DT2 8NR.
2 miles south of Dorchester.

CONTACT: DE Matthews, Manager. Tel: 0305 813494.
COURSE: 6,224yds, PAR 70, SSS 71. Downland course.
SOC RESTR'S: Welcome Wednesday.
SOC GF - Round: Wd £20. We N/A. **Day:** Wd £20. We N/A.
SOC PACK: Food mandatory. Total cost £30.
VIS RESTR'S: Welcome after 9. Sunday after 11.
VIS GF - Round: Wd £20. We £25. **Day:** Wd £20. We £25.
FACILITIES: Bar & Restaurant.

EAST DORSET GOLF CLUB MAP 2 B3

Hyde, Wareham, Dorset BH20 7NT.
5 miles west of Wareham.

CONTACT: B Lee, General Manager. Tel: 0929 472244.
COURSE: 6,550yds, PAR 71, SSS 71. Parkland course.
SOC RESTR'S: Welcome.
SOC GF - Round: Wd £18. We £25. **Day:** Wd £23. We £30.
SOC PACK: Coffee, Lunch, Dinner, 36 holes on either course - £47.
VIS RESTR'S: Welcome.
VIS GF - Round: Wd £18. We £25. **Day:** Wd £23. We £30.
FACILITIES: 18-hole (Woodland), Range & Computerised Teaching.

FERNDOWN GOLF CLUB MAP 2 B3

119 Golf Links Road, Ferndown, Dorset BH22 0LX.
8 miles north of Bournemouth - A347 to Golf Club.
Recommended Hotel: Coach House Inn, Ferndown.

CONTACT: Secretary/Manager. Tel: 0202 874602.
COURSE: 6,466yds, PAR 71, SSS 71. Parkland course.
SOC RESTR'S: Welcome Tuesday & Friday.
SOC GF - Round: Wd N/A. We N/A. **Day:** Wd £35. We N/A.
SOC PACK: £50.
VIS RESTR'S: Welcome prior arrangement required.
VIS GF - Round: Wd N/A. We N/A. **Day:** Wd £35. We £40.
FACILITIES: 9-hole (New course), Bar & Restaurant.

Coach House Inn
Restaurant & Motel
579 Wimborne Road East
Ferndown, Dorset BH22 9NW
Tel: 0202 861222

Set amidst beautiful pines within two miles of three golf courses. The Coach House Inn has all the comforts of modern facilities, rooms have bathrooms, Sky TV, tea/coffee facilities, telephone and mini bar.

HYDE HOUSE GOLF CLUB (OLD) MAP 2 B3

Hyde, Nr. Wareham, Dorset BH20 7NY.
15 miles south of Poole just outside Wareham.

CONTACT: C Reynard, MD. Tel: Head Office: 081 940 7782
COURSE: 6,450yds, PAR 72, SSS 72. Challenging course.
SOC RESTR'S: Welcome.
SOC GF - Round: Wd N/A. We N/A. **Day:** Wd £20. We £30.
SOC PACK: Various with 10%/20% discounts for larger groups.
VIS RESTR'S: Visits booked through London Head Office.
VIS GF - Round: Wd N/A. We N/A. **Day:** Wd £20. We £30.
FACILITIES: Multi-activities.

HYDE HOUSE GOLF CLUB (NEW) MAP 2 B3

Hyde, Nr. Wareham, Dorset BH20 7NY.
15 miles south of Poole just outside Wareham.

CONTACT: C Reynard, MD. Tel: Head Office: 081 940 7782
COURSE: 6,230yds, PAR 72, SSS 71. Challenging course.
SOC RESTR'S: Welcome.
SOC GF - Round: Wd N/A. We N/A. **Day:** Wd £20. We £30.
SOC PACK: Various with 10%/20% discounts for larger groups.
VIS RESTR'S: Visits booked through London Head Office.
VIS GF - Round: Wd N/A. We N/A. **Day:** Wd £20. We £30.
FACILITIES: Multi-activities.

DORSET

ISLE OF PURBECK GOLF CLUB MAP 2 B3

Studland, Swanage, Dorset BH19 3AB.
Overlooking Poole Harbour on the B3351.

CONTACT: Mrs. J Robinson, Secretary. Tel: 0929 44361.
COURSE: 6,295yds, PAR 70, SSS 71. Undulating heathland.
SOC RESTR'S: On application from Club Secretary.
SOC GF - Round: Wd £23. We £28. Day: Wd £30.50. We £35.50.
SOC PACK: Coffee, Lunch, Dinner & 36 holes £40 Wd, £45 We.
VIS RESTR'S: Please phone prior to play.
VIS GF - Round: Wd £22.50. We £27.50. Day: Wd £30. We £35.
FACILITIES: 9-hole (Dean Course), Bar & Restaurant.

 TEE OFF FROM THE RAC ★★★
GROSVENOR HOTEL
■ BOURNEMOUTH ■
SUPERIOR GOLFING BREAKS ● 7 FIRST-CLASS COURSES
● FREE GOLF BOOKING SERVICE ● MON/FRI & WEEKENDS AVAILABLE ● GREEN FEES PAYABLE AT COURSE ● DISCOUNTS FOR GROUP BOOKINGS ● "HOW TO GET THERE" MAPS AVAILABLE
Send for Hotel Col. Brochure & Golf Leaflet

BATH ROAD · BOURNEMOUTH
TEL: 0202 558858 FAX: 0202 298332

LYME REGIS GOLF CLUB MAP 2 B3

Timber Hill, Lyme Regis, Dorset DT7 3HQ.
Off A3052 Charmouth Road, 1 mile east of Lyme Regis.

CONTACT: RG Fry, Secretary. Tel: 0297 442963.
COURSE: 6,220yds, PAR 71, SSS 70. Undulating Meadowland.
SOC RESTR'S: Min. 12. Mon, Tues, Fri after 9.30.
SOC GF - Round: Wd £20 after 2. We N/A. Day: Wd £24. We £24.
SOC PACK: None.
VIS RESTR'S: Thur after 1.30, Sun after 2. H'Cap Cert req.
VIS GF - Round: Wd £20 after 2. We £24. Day: Wd £24. We £24.
FACILITIES: Bar & Restaurant.

SHERBORNE GOLF CLUB MAP 2 B3

Clatcombe, Sherborne, Dorset DT9 4RN.
1 mile north of Sherborne.

CONTACT: Mrs JMC Guy, Secretary. Tel: 0935 814431.
COURSE: 5,949yds, PAR 70, SSS 68. Parkland course.
SOC RESTR'S: H'cap Cert required. Not Thursday.
SOC GF - Round: Wd N/A. We N/A. Day: Wd £32. We N/A.
SOC PACK: Lunch, Dinner, 36 holes: £47.
VIS RESTR'S: H'cap Cert required. Not Thursday.
VIS GF - Round: Wd £20. We £23. Day: Wd N/A. We N/A.
FACILITIES: Bar, Restaurant, Pro shop.

TEE OFF FROM THE RAC ★★★
EAST CLIFF COURT HOTEL
■ BOURNEMOUTH ■
SUPERIOR GOLFING BREAKS ● 7 FIRST-CLASS COURSES
● FREE GOLF BOOKING SERVICE ● MON/FRI & WEEKENDS AVAILABLE ● GREEN FEES PAYABLE AT COURSE ● DISCOUNTS FOR GROUP BOOKINGS ● "HOW TO GET THERE" MAPS AVAILABLE
Send for Hotel Col. Brochure & Golf Leaflet

EAST OVERCLIFF DRIVE · BOURNEMOUTH
TEL: 0202 554545 FAX: 0202 557456

WEYMOUTH GOLF CLUB MAP 2 B3

Links Road, Weymouth, Dorset DT4 0PF.
A354 from Dorchester, right at Manor R/about, Town Centre.

CONTACT: C Robinson, Secretary. Tel: 0305 773981.
COURSE: 6,009yds, PAR 70, SSS 69. Parkland/seaside course.
SOC RESTR'S: Welcome Tuesday & Thursday.
SOC GF - Round: Wd N/A. We N/A. Day: Wd £20. We N/A.
SOC PACK: £26 incl. Coffee, Lunch, Dinner.
VIS RESTR'S: No restrictions. Handicap Certificate required.
VIS GF - Round: Wd N/A. We N/A. Day: Wd £20. We £26.
FACILITIES: Full Bar & Catering facilities.

PARKSTONE GOLF CLUB MAP 2 B3

Links Road, Poole, Dorset BH14 9JU.
A33 to Poole, 3 miles west of Bournemouth off A35.

CONTACT: AS Kinnear, Secretary. Tel: 0202 707138.
COURSE: 6,250yds, PAR 72, SSS 70. Heathland course.
SOC RESTR'S: Handicap Certificate essential. Please book.
SOC GF - Round: Wd £24. We £30. Day: Wd £32. We £40.
SOC PACK: Catering as required.
VIS RESTR'S: Not Tuesday am. Weekend very limited.
VIS GF - Round: Wd £24. We £30. Day: Wd £32. We £40.
FACILITIES: None.

RAC National Road Maps

Clear, easy-to-read, up-to-date route planning maps at a scale of approximately 8 miles to 1 inch

Price £3.99
Available from bookshops
or direct from the RAC on 0235 834885

ENGLAND

Durham

CROOK GOLF CLUB MAP 5 A2

Low Job's Hill, Crook, Durham DL15 9AA.
6 miles west of Durham City A689.

CONTACT: Mr P Willis, Secretary. Tel: 0388 762429.
COURSE: 6,075yds, PAR 68, SSS 69. Demanding hilly course.
SOC RESTR'S: Welcome except on competition days.
SOC GF - Round: Wd N/A. We N/A. Day: Wd £12. We £15.
SOC PACK: £20-£50 - incl. Coffee, Lunch & High Tea.
VIS RESTR'S: Welcome any time but not on competitions days.
VIS GF - Round: Wd N/A. We N/A. Day: Wd £12. We £20.
FACILITIES: None.

BARNARD CASTLE GOLF CLUB   MAP 5 A2

Harmire Road, Barnard Castle DL12 8QN.
North boundary of Barnard Castle on B6278.

CONTACT: AW Lavender, Secretary. Tel: 0833 38355.
COURSE: 5,838yds, PAR 71, SSS 68. Flat moorland course.
SOC RESTR'S: Not Monday. Limited at weekends.
SOC GF - Round: Wd N/A. We N/A. Day: Wd £18. We N/A.
SOC PACK: Several packages available.
VIS RESTR'S: No restrictions.
VIS GF - Round: Wd £15. We £24. Day: Wd £18. We N/A.
FACILITIES: Food by arrangement, Bar, Pro shop, Snooker.

BISHOP AUCKLAND GOLF CLUB   MAP 5 A2

High Plains, Durham Rd, Bishop Auckland, Durham DL14 8DC.
Leave Market Place on road to Durham. Half-a-mile north-east.

CONTACT: G Thatcher, Secretary. Tel: 0388 663648.
COURSE: 6,420yds, PAR 72, SSS 71. Parkland course.
SOC RESTR'S: Max. 50. Not Wed, Thur & Fri. 1-2 (Members).
SOC GF - Round: Wd £18. We £24. Day: Wd £22. We N/A.
SOC PACK: Parties over 20 have reduction to £18 for day.
VIS RESTR'S: No catering Mon. Ladies Day Tues.
VIS GF - Round: Wd £18. We £24. Day: Wd £22. We N/A.
FACILITIES: 2 Snooker Tables.

BRANCEPETH CASTLE GOLF CLUB MAP 5 A2

Brancepeth, Durham DH7 8EA.
4 miles west of Durham City on A690.

CONTACT: JT Ross, Secretary. Tel: 091 378 0075.
COURSE: 6,415yds, PAR 70, SSS 71. Undulating parkland.
SOC RESTR'S: Welcome Weekdays.
SOC GF - Round: Wd N/A. We N/A. Day: Wd £23. We N/A.
SOC PACK: Around £33.
VIS RESTR'S: Welcome Weekdays. Weekends by arrangement.
VIS GF - Round: Wd N/A. We N/A. Day: Wd £23. We £30.
FACILITIES: Practice Ground.

DARLINGTON GOLF CLUB   MAP 5 B2

Haughton Grange, Darlington, Durham DL1 3JD.
Darlington North A1M to A167 to A1150 Salters Lane North.

CONTACT: N Adair, Hon. Secretary. Tel: 0325 355324.
COURSE: 6,271yds, PAR 71, SSS 71. Level parkland course.
SOC RESTR'S: Max. 40. We & Bank Hols not available.
SOC GF - Round: Wd £20. We N/A. Day: Wd N/A. We N/A.
SOC PACK: Full Dining Room facilities available except Mon.
VIS RESTR'S: Welcome Weekdays.
VIS GF - Round: Wd £22. We N/A. Day: Wd £22. We N/A.
FACILITIES: Practice Area, Good Clubhouse facilities &Snooker.

DURHAM CITY GOLF CLUB   MAP 5 A2

Littleburn, Langley Moor, Durham DH7 8HL.
Turn off A690, 1.5 miles west of Durham.

CONTACT: I Wilson, Hon. Secretary. Tel: 091 378 0806.
COURSE: 6,326yds, PAR 71, SSS 70. Parkland course.
SOC RESTR'S: Welcome Weekdays.
SOC GF - Round: Wd N/A. We N/A. Day: Wd £16. We N/A.
SOC PACK: £2 reduction per person for parties over 20.
VIS RESTR'S: Not before 9 & Club competitions days.
VIS GF - Round: Wd N/A. We N/A. Day: Wd £18. We £24.
FACILITIES: Large Practice Area.

MOUNT OSWALD GOLF CLUB   MAP 5 A2

South Road, Durham City, Durham DH1 3TQ.
West of Durham City on A1050.

CONTACT: SE Reeve, General Manager. Tel: 091 386 7527.
COURSE: 6,101yds, PAR 71, SSS 69. Parkland course.
SOC RESTR'S: Welcome. Min 12.
SOC GF - Round: Wd N/A. We N/A. Day: Wd £21. We £23.
SOC PACK: Coffee, Lunch, Dinner, 27 holes - Price as above.
VIS RESTR'S: Welcome.
VIS GF - Round: Wd £10 after 2. We £12 Day: Wd £17 We £21.
FACILITIES: Full catering available.

ESSEX

SEAHAM GOLF CLUB   MAP 5 B2

Clubhouse, Shrewsbury Street, Seaham, Durham SR7 7RD.
Dawdon, 2 miles north-east of A19.

CONTACT: V Smith, Secretary. Tel: 091 581 2345.
COURSE: 5,972yds, PAR 70, SSS 69. Heathland course.
SOC RESTR'S: Welcome midweek. Afternoon at We.
SOC GF - Round: Wd N/A. We N/A. Day: Wd £15. We £18.
SOC PACK: Coffee, Lunch, Dinner, 36 holes - £25.
VIS RESTR'S: Welcome Weekdays & Sunday.
VIS GF - Round: Wd N/A. We N/A. Day: Wd £15. We £18.
FACILITIES: Snooker, Bar & Bar Meals.

WOODHAM GOLF CLUB   MAP 5 A2

Burnhill Way, Newton Aycliffe, Durham DH5 4PN.
2 miles from A1M. North of Aycliffe.

CONTACT: Leslie Kenna, Business Manager. Tel: 0325 320574.
COURSE: 6,767yds, PAR 73, SSS 72. Parkland course.
SOC RESTR'S: Welcome.
SOC GF - Round: Wd £15. We £20. Day: Wd £20. We £25.
SOC PACK: Discount for golf parties over 20.
VIS RESTR'S: Welcome Weekdays & before 10.30 Weekends.
VIS GF - Round: Wd £15. We £20. Day: Wd £20. We £25.
FACILITIES: Bar, Restaurant, Bar Meals & A la Carte.

Essex

BALLARDS GORE GOLF CLUB   MAP 3 B2

Gore Road, Canewdon, Essex SS4 2DA.
2 miles north-east of Rochford.

CONTACT: NG Patient, Secretary. Tel: 0702 258917.
COURSE: 7,062yds, PAR 73, SSS 74. Parkland course.
SOC RESTR'S: Min. 15 - Max. 36, Welcome Weekdays.
SOC GF - Round: Wd N/A. We N/A. Day: Wd £20. We N/A.
SOC PACK: 2 rounds - Coffee - Lunch - Dinner - £38.
VIS RESTR'S: Welcome Weekdays.
VIS GF - Round: Wd £20. We N/A. Day: Wd £20. We N/A.
FACILITIES: Full Catering facilities.

BASILDON GOLF CLUB   MAP 3 B2

Clayhill Lane, Basildon, Essex SS16 5HL.
Off A176, 1 mile south of Basildon

CONTACT: Professional. Tel: 0268 533532.
COURSE: 6,122yds, PAR 70, SSS 69. Undulating woodland.
SOC RESTR'S: Welcome Weekdays. Book through Council.
SOC GF - Round: Wd N/A. We N/A. Day: Wd N/A. We N/A.
SOC PACK: Contact Basildon Council Leisure Officer or Club Sec.
VIS RESTR'S: Welcome anytime, booking system at Weekends.
VIS GF - Round: Wd £9. We £14.50. Day: Wd N/A. We N/A.
FACILITIES: Club Bar & Catering.

BENTLEY GOLF CLUB   MAP 3 B2

Ongar Road, Brentwood, Essex CM15 9SS.
Midway between Brentwood and Ongar on A128.

CONTACT: J Vivers, Secretary. Tel: 0277 373179.
COURSE: 6,709yds, PAR 72, SSS 72. Parkland course.
SOC RESTR'S: Min. 20 - Max. 80. Not Wed or We.
SOC GF - Round: Wd £19. We N/A. Day: Wd £25. We N/A.
SOC PACK: Coffee, Lunch, Dinner, 36 holes - £40.
VIS RESTR'S: Welcome Weekdays after 8.
VIS GF - Round: Wd £20. We N/A. Day: Wd £26. We N/A.
FACILITIES: Practice Area & Pro-shop.

BRAINTREE GOLF CLUB   MAP 3 B2

Kings Lane, Stisted, Braintree, Essex CM7 8DA.
1st left on A120 after exiting Braintree bypass eastwards.

CONTACT: GJ Bardsley, Secretary/Manager. Tel: 0376 346079.
COURSE: 6,026yds, PAR 70, SSS 69. Parkland course
SOC RESTR'S: Max 80. Welcome Mon, Wed & Thur.
SOC GF - Round: Wd N/A. We N/A. Day: Wd £24. We N/A.
SOC PACK: £42-£45.
VIS RESTR'S: Welcome any day but Sunday.
VIS GF - Round: Wd N/A. We N/A. Day: Wd £24. We £40.
FACILITIES: Bar & Restaurant.

RAC Regional Road Maps

Large scale (3 miles to 1 inch) maps for the motorist. Each sheet contains details of motorway junctions, dual carriageways, town plans, a full index of towns and villages, and tourist information including golf courses.

Price £3.99
Available from bookshops
or direct from the RAC on 0235 834885

ENGLAND

CHIGWELL GOLF CLUB   MAP 7 B2

High Road, Chigwell, Essex IG7 5BH.
A133, 14 miles from London.

CONTACT: M Farnsworth, Secretary. Tel: 081 500 2059.
COURSE: 6,279yds, PAR 71, SSS 70. Undulating testing course.
SOC RESTR'S: Min. 20 - Max. 40 Welcome Mon, Wed & Thur.
SOC GF - Round: Wd £45. We N/A. **Day:** Wd £55. We N/A.
SOC PACK: 1 or 2 rounds plus Full Catering: £55.
VIS RESTR'S: Welcome Weekdays.
VIS GF - Round: Wd £28. We N/A. **Day:** Wd £35. We N/A.
FACILITIES: Bar & Restaurant.

FORRESTER PARK GOLF CLUB   MAP 3 B2

Beckingham Road, Gt. Totham, Nr. Maldon, Essex CM9 8EA.
4 mls north of Maldon & 12 mls south of Colchester on B1022.

CONTACT: T Forrester-Muir, Proprietor. Tel: 0621 891406.
COURSE: 6,073yds, PAR 71, SSS 69. Parkland course.
SOC RESTR'S: Min. 12. Max. 44. Welcome Mon, Thur & Fri from 8.30.
SOC GF - Round: Wd N/A. We N/A. **Day:** Wd £13. We N/A.
SOC PACK: Coffee Lunch, Dinner - 36 holes - £33.
VIS RESTR'S: Welcome except Tues 9-10, Wed 8.30-10, We before 1.
VIS GF - Round: Wd £13. We £18. **Day:** Wd £18. We N/A.
FACILITIES: Bar & Restaurant.

FRINTON GOLF CLUB   MAP 3 B2

The Esplanade, Frinton-on-Sea, Essex CO13 9EP.
18 miles east of Colchester on A133 to B1033.

CONTACT: Lt Col RW Attrill, Secretary. Tel: 0255 674618.
COURSE: 6,260yds, PAR 71, SSS 70. Links course.
SOC RESTR'S: Welcome Wednesday & Thursday.
SOC GF - Round: Wd N/A. We N/A. **Day:** Wd £22. We N/A.
SOC PACK: £42. 50 - 36 holes, Lunch, Dinner.
VIS RESTR'S: Welcome anytime with H'cap Cert but phone first.
VIS GF - Round: Wd N/A. We N/A. **Day:** Wd £22. We £22.
FACILITIES: 9-hole shorter course with no restrictions.

RAC Motoring Atlas Europe

A fully updated edition of this handy-sized atlas which encompasses unified Germany and other newly defined frontiers. Clear and detailed mapping at 1:1 million scale (16 miles to 1 inch) for Western Europe. Comprehensive index of over 52,000 place names. Compact format ideal for car use.

Price £10.99
Available from bookshops
or direct from the RAC on 0235 834885

HAINAULT FOREST GOLF CLUB   MAP 7 B2

Romford Road, Chigwell Row, Essex IG7 4QW.
A12 - signposted to Chigwell.

CONTACT: HG Richards, Secretary/Manager. Tel: 081 500 2470.
COURSE: 6,600yds, PAR 71, SSS 71. Undulating woodland.
SOC RESTR'S: Pease book through Secretary.
SOC GF - Round: Wd N/A. We N/A. **Day:** Wd £17.50. We N/A.
SOC PACK: None.
VIS RESTR'S: Welcome. Public course.
VIS GF - Round: Wd £9.20. We £11.50. **Day:** Wd £17.50. We £17.50. **FACILITIES:** 2nd 18 hole course.

LANGDON HILLS GOLF CLUB   MAP 3 B2

Lower Dunton Road, Bulphan, Essex RM14 3TY.
At A127 Dunton Ford Research Centre turn-off.

CONTACT: Mrs C Hamond, Secretary. Tel: 0268 548444.
COURSE: 6,485yds, PAR 72, SSS 71. Undulating parkland course.
SOC RESTR'S: Min. 12. Welcome Tues, Wed & Thur.
SOC GF - Round: Wd £18.50. We N/A. **Day:** Wd £26.50. We N/A.
SOC PACK: From £27-£52.
VIS RESTR'S: Welcome.
VIS GF - Round: Wd £18.50. We £25. **Day:** Wd £26.50. We N/A.
FACILITIES: Range, 3 Practice Holes & Large Short Game Area.

ORSETT GOLF CLUB   MAP 3 B2

Brentwood Road, Orsett, Essex RM16 3DS.
A13 to Southend-on-Sea — course 400yds on A128.

CONTACT: P Pritchard, Secretary. Tel: 0375 891352.
COURSE: 6,614yds, PAR 72, SSS 72. Heathland course.
SOC RESTR'S: Mon, Tues, Wed. EGU Registered Societies.
SOC GF - Round: Wd N/A. We N/A. **Day:** Wd £30. We N/A.
SOC PACK: £48 incl. Golf, Lunch & Dinner.
VIS RESTR'S: Not Thur & We. H'cap Cert required. Phone first.
VIS GF - Round: Wd N/A. We N/A. **Day:** Wd £30. We N/A.
FACILITIES: Bar & Restaurant.

QUIETWATERS (LINKS)   MAP 3 B2

Colchester Road, Tolleshunt Knights, Maldon, Essex CM9 8HX.
8 miles south of Colchester on B1026.

CONTACT: PD Keeble, Director of Golf. Tel: 0621 868888.
COURSE: 6,194yds, PAR 71, SSS 70. Seaside course.
SOC RESTR'S: Min. 15. Welcome Weekdays.
SOC GF - Round: Wd N/A. We N/A. **Day:** Wd N/A. We N/A.
SOC PACK: On application.
VIS RESTR'S: Welcome any day except Sun mornings.
VIS GF - Round: Wd £18. We £22.50. **Day:** Wd £25. We £30.
FACILITIES: Tennis, Squash, Health Centre, Restaurant & Bars.

ESSEX

QUIETWATERS (LAKES)   MAP 3 B2

Colchester Road, Tolleshunt Knights, Maldon, Essex CM9 8HX.
3 miles south of Colchester on B1026.

CONTACT: PD Keeble, Director of Golf. Tel: 0621 868888.
COURSE: 6,767yds, PAR 72, SSS 72. European Tour Course
SOC RESTR'S: Min. 15. Welcome Weekdays.
SOC GF - Round: Wd N/A. **We** N/A. **Day:** Wd N/A. **We** N/A.
SOC PACK: On application.
VIS RESTR'S: Welcome any day except Sun mornings.
VIS GF - Round: Wd £30. **We** £30. **Day:** Wd £45. **We** £45.
FACILITIES: Health & Fitness Centre, Restaurant & Bars.

STAPLEFORD ABBOTTS (ABBOTTS) MAP 7 B2

Horseman's Side, Stapleford Abbotts, Essex RM41 1JU.
M25, Junction 28 — 2 miles from Romford off B175.

CONTACT: K Fletcher, Secretary. Tel: 0708 381108.
COURSE: 6,648yds, PAR 72, SSS 72. Parkland course.
SOC RESTR'S: Welcome Weekdays.
SOC GF - Round: Wd £20. **We** N/A. **Day:** Wd N/A. **We** N/A.
SOC PACK: Vary, depending on requirements. Brochure available.
VIS RESTR'S: Welcome Weekdays.
VIS GF - Round: Wd £20. **We** N/A. **Day:** Wd £28. **We** N/A.
FACILITIES: 9-hole course ('Friars'), 2 Practice Areas & Spikes Bar.

STAPLEFORD ABBOTTS (PRIORS)   MAP 7 B2

Horsemans Side, Stapleford Abbotts, Essex RM41 1JU.
M25, Junction 28 — 2 miles from Romford off B175.

CONTACT: K Fletcher, Secretary. Tel: 0708 381108.
COURSE: 5,965yds, PAR 70, SSS 70. Challenging parkland course.
SOC RESTR'S: Welcome Weekdays.
SOC GF - Round: Wd £15. **We** N/A. **Day:** Wd N/A. **We** N/A.
SOC PACK: Vary, depending on requirements. Brochure available.
VIS RESTR'S: Welcome Weekdays.
VIS GF - Round: Wd £15. **We** N/A. **Day:** Wd £28. **We** N/A.
FACILITIES: 9 hole ('Friars') £5 per round &Tearoom.

STOKE-BY-NAYLAND (GAINSBOROUGH)   MAP 3 B2

Keepers Lane, Leavenheath, Colchester, Essex CO6 4PZ.
A134 north from Colchester - B1068 to Stoke-by-Nayland.

CONTACT: Alan McLundie, Secretary. Tel: 0206 262836.
COURSE: 6,516yds, PAR 72, SSS 71. Undulating parkland course.
SOC RESTR'S: Welcome Weekdays (By booking form).
SOC GF - Round: Wd £22. **We** £25. **Day:** Wd £30. **We** N/A.
SOC PACK: Lunch, Dinner plus days golf: £32-£44.50.
VIS RESTR'S: Wd None. We after 10.30. Must have H'cap Cert.
VIS GF - Round: Wd £22. **We** £25. **Day:** Wd £30. **We**
FACILITIES: Bar & Restaurant.

STOKE-BY-NAYLAND (CONSTABLE)   MAP 3 B2

Keepers Lane, Leavenheath, Colchester, Essex CO6 4PZ.
A134 north from Colchester - B1068 to Stoke-by-Nayland.

CONTACT: Alan McLundie, Secretary. Tel: 0206 262836.
COURSE: 6,544yds, PAR 72, SSS 71. Undulating parkland.
SOC RESTR'S: Welcome Weekdays (By booking form).
SOC GF - Round: Wd £22. **We** £25. **Day:** Wd £30. **We** N/A.
SOC PACK: Lunch, Dinner plus days golf: £40.
VIS RESTR'S: Wd None. We after 10.30. Must have H'cap Cert.
VIS GF - Round: Wd £22. **We** £25. **Day:** Wd £30. **We** £25.
FACILITIES: Bar & Restaurant.

THREE RIVERS GOLF CLUB   MAP 3 B2

Stow Road, Purleigh, Chelmsford, Essex CM3 6RR.
12 miles from Chelmsford on the B1012.

CONTACT: G Packer, Director of Golf. Tel: 0621 828631.
COURSE: 6,515yds, PAR 70, SSS 72. Parkland course.
SOC RESTR'S: Welcome Weekdays.
SOC GF - Round: Wd N/A. **We** N/A. **Day:** Wd N/A. **We** N/A.
SOC PACK: Coffee, Lunch, Dinner, 36 holes - £30-£60.
VIS RESTR'S: Welcome Weekdays.
VIS GF - Round: Wd £18. **We** £20. **Day:** Wd £25. **We** £30.
FACILITIES: 9-hole Par 3 Course, Squash & 6 Twin-bed rooms.

UPMINSTER GOLF CLUB   MAP 3 B2

114 Hall Lane, Upminster, Essex RM14 1AU.
A127 towards Southend, 1 mile from Upminster Station.

CONTACT: PR Taylor, Secretary/Manager. Tel: 0708 222788.
COURSE: 5,931yds, PAR 69, SSS 68. Parkland course.
SOC RESTR'S: Max. 40. Welcome Wed, Thur & Fri.
SOC GF - Round: Wd £25. **We** N/A. **Day:** Wd £30. **We** N/A.
SOC PACK: Approx £45 for Breakfast, Lunch, Dinner.
VIS RESTR'S: Welcome except Tues morning, We & Bank Hols.
VIS GF - Round: Wd £25. **We** N/A. **Day:** Wd £30. **We** N/A.
FACILITIES: Bar & Restaurant.

WARREN GOLF CLUB   MAP 3 B2

Woodhan Walter, Maldon, Essex CM9 6RW.
8 miles east of Chelmsford on A414.

CONTACT: t Cole, Catering Manager. Tel: 0245 223258.
COURSE: 6,229yds, PAR 70, SSS 70. Parkland course.
SOC RESTR'S: Welcome Mon, Tues, Thur & Fri.
SOC GF - Round: Wd £25. **We** N/A. **Day:** Wd £30. **We** N/A.
SOC PACK: £45 - Breakfast, Lunch, Dinner 36 holes.
VIS RESTR'S: Welcome Weekdays except Wednesday.
VIS GF - Round: Wd £27. **We** N/A. **Day:** Wd £35. **We** N/A.
FACILITIES: Bar & Restaurant.

ENGLAND

Gloucestershire

GLOUCESTER G & CC   MAP 2 B2

Matson Lane, Robinswood Hill, Glos GL4 9EA.
2 miles south of Gloucester Centre on B4073 to Painswick.

CONTACT: P Darnell, Professional. Tel: 0452 411331.
COURSE: 6,137yds, PAR 70, SSS 69. Parkland course.
SOC RESTR'S: On written application to Club Professional.
SOC GF - Round: Wd £14. We £21. **Day:** Wd £21. We N/A.
SOC PACK: Coffee, Ploughmans (£5.50), Dinner (from £9. 75).
VIS RESTR'S: Tee time bookings necessary.
VIS GF - Round: Wd £19. We £25. **Day:** Wd N/A. We N/A.
FACILITIES: Bar, Driving Range & 9-hole Course.

CIRENCESTER GOLF CLUB   MAP 2 B2

Cheltenham Road, Cirencester, Glos GL7 7BH.
On A435 Cirencester- Cheltenham Rd 1.5 mls from Cirencester.

CONTACT: N D Jones, Secretary/Manager. Tel: 0285 652465.
COURSE: 6,002yds, PAR 70, SSS 69. Undulating Cotswold course.
SOC RESTR'S: Max. 60. Welcome Tues, Wed & Fri.
SOC GF - Round: Wd £20. We £25. **Day:** Wd £20. We £25.
SOC PACK: £40.
VIS RESTR'S: Not Competition Days. H'cap Cert required.
VIS GF - Round: Wd £20. We £25. **Day:** Wd £20. We £25.
FACILITIES: Practice Ground & Indoor Training School.

CLEEVE HILL GOLF CLUB   MAP 2 B2

Cleeve Hill, Nr Prestbury, Cheltenham, Glos GL52 3PN.
3 miles north of Cheltenham on A46.

CONTACT: S Gilman, Manager. Tel: 0242 672592.
COURSE: 6,444yds, PAR 72, SSS 71. An inland links course.
SOC RESTR'S: Welcome except Sun mornings.
SOC GF - Round: Wd N/A. We N/A. **Day:** Wd N/A. We N/A.
SOC PACK: On application.
VIS RESTR'S: Welcome except Sat 12-3 & Sun 7-11.
VIS GF - Round: Wd £7. We £8. **Day:** Wd £14. We £16.
FACILITIES: Bar, Restaurant, Snooker & Skittle Alley.

COTSWOLD EDGE GOLF CLUB   MAP 2 B2

Upper Rushmire, Wotton-under-Edge, Glos GL12 7PT.
Approx 7 miles from Junct 14 (M5) B4058 Tetbury Road.

CONTACT: N Newman, Secretary. Tel: 0453 844167.
COURSE: 5,816yds, PAR 71, SSS 68. Meadowland course.
SOC RESTR'S: On application from Club Secretary.
SOC GF - Round: Wd £15. We N/A. **Day:** Wd £15. We N/A.
SOC PACK: Available on booking.
VIS RESTR'S: Weekdays. Please phone first.
VIS GF - Round: Wd £15. We N/A. **Day:** Wd £15. We N/A.
FACILITIES: Bar & Restaurant.

MINCHINHAMPTON (OLD)   MAP 2 B2

New Course, Minchinhampton, Stroud, Glos GL6 9BE.
1 mile west of Minchinhampton (on the Common).

CONTACT: DR Vickers, Secretary/Manager. Tel: 0453 833866.
COURSE: 6,295yds, PAR 71, SSS 70. Meadowland course.
SOC RESTR'S: On written application to Club Secretary.
SOC GF - Round: Wd N/A. We N/A. **Day:** Wd £10. We £13.
SOC PACK: Coffee, Lunch, Dinner: £25-£30.
VIS RESTR'S: Welcome but bookings essential.
VIS GF - Round: Wd N/A. We N/A. **Day:** Wd £10. We £13.
FACILITIES: None.

MINCHINHAMPTON (NEW)   MAP 2 B2

New Course, Minchinhampton, Stroud, Glos GL6 9BE.
1 mile east of Minchinhampton on Avening Road.

CONTACT: DR Vickers, Secretary/Manager. Tel: 0453 833866.
COURSE: 6,675yds, PAR 72, SSS 72. Cotswold plateau, parkland.
SOC RESTR'S: On written application to Club Secretary.
SOC GF - Round: Wd N/A. We N/A. **Day:** Wd £24. We £30.
SOC PACK: Coffee, Lunch, Dinner, 27 holes: £40.
VIS RESTR'S: Welcome with H'cap Cert. Bookings essential.
VIS GF - Round: Wd N/A. We N/A. **Day:** Wd £24. We £30.
FACILITIES: None.

PUCKRUP HALL GOLF CLUB   MAP 2 B2

Puckrup, Tewkesbury, Glos GL20 6EL.
On A38 two miles N of Tewkesbury. J8 of the M5, via J1 M50.
See advertisement.

CONTACT: K Pickett, Professional. Tel: 0684 296200.
COURSE: 6,400yds, PAR 71, SSS 70. Parkland course.
SOC RESTR'S: Contact in advance. Green fees not confirmed.
SOC GF - Round: Wd N/A. We N/A. **Day:** Wd N/A. We N/A.
SOC PACK: Available on booking.
VIS RESTR'S: Contact in advance. Green fees not confirmed.
VIS GF - Round: Wd £17.50. We £22.50. **Day:** Wd £27.50. We £30.
FACILITIES: All fees under review at the time of Publication.

HAMPSHIRE

Hampshire

TEWKESBURY PARK GOLF CLUB MAP 2 B2

Lincoln Green Lane, Tewkesbury, Glos GL20 7DN.
Off Junction 9 of the M5. Half-a-mile south of Tewkesbury.

CONTACT: Emma Durham, Catering Manager. Tel: 0684 295405.
COURSE: 6,533yds, PAR 73, SSS 72. Parkland course.
SOC RESTR'S: Non-res min 12 Mon-Thur. Res no restr's.
SOC GF - Round: Wd N/A. We N/A. **Day:** Wd N/A. We N/A.
SOC PACK: On application.
VIS RESTR'S: Welcome Handicap Certificates required.
VIS GF - Round: Wd £25. We £30. **Day:** Wd £40. We £50.
FACILITIES: 6-hole Par 3 Practice Area, Pro-shop & Range.

BASINGSTOKE GOLF CLUB MAP 3 A3

Kempshott Park, Basingstoke, Hants RG23 7LL.
Exit Junction 7 on the M3. 3 miles west of Basingstoke.

CONTACT: K Maplesden, Secretary. Tel: 0256 465990.
COURSE: 6,259yds, PAR 70, SSS 70. Parkland course.
SOC RESTR'S: Welcome Wednesday & Thursday.
SOC GF - Round: Wd £20. We N/A. **Day:** Wd £30. We N/A.
SOC PACK: Golf & Catering: £44.
VIS RESTR'S: Welcome Weekdays.
VIS GF - Round: Wd £20. We N/A. **Day:** Wd £30. We N/A.
FACILITIES: Bar & Restaurant.

BLACKMOOR GOLF CLUB MAP 7 A3

Whitehill, Bordon, Hants GU35 9EH.
Half-mile west of Whitehill on A325.

CONTACT: Maj HRG Spiller, Secretary. Tel: 0420 472775.
COURSE: 6,213yds, PAR 690, SSS 70. Moorland course.
SOC RESTR'S: No weekends. H'cap Cert required.
SOC GF - Round: Wd N/A. We N/A. **Day:** Wd £35. We N/A.
SOC PACK: Lunch, Dinner, 36 holes: £50.
VIS RESTR'S: No weekends. H'cap Cert required.
VIS GF - Round: Wd £26. We N/A. **Day:** Wd £35. We N/A.
FACILITIES: Bar, Restaurant, Pro shop.

PUCKRUP HALL HOTEL & GOLF CLUB

An elegant Regency Manor set on the edge of the Cotswolds, surrounded by its own 18 hole, par 71, golf course, set in 140 acres of natural wood and parkland.

Take advantage of our inclusive weekend Golf Breaks or improve your game with our resident golf professional.

Societies welcome.

PUCKRUP HALL HOTEL & GOLF CLUB
PUCKRUP · TEWKESBURY
GLOUCESTERSHIRE · GL20 6EL
Telephone: (0684) 296200
Fax: (0684) 850788

BRAMSHAW (MANOR) MAP 2 B3

Brook, Lyndhurst, Hants SO43 7HE.
M27 Junction 1 mile north to Brook.

CONTACT: R Tingey, General Manager. Tel: 0703 813433.
COURSE: 6,233yds, PAR 71, SSS 70. Parkland course.
SOC RESTR'S: Welcome Weekdays by arrangement.
SOC GF - Round: Wd N/A. We N/A. **Day:** Wd N/A. We N/A.
SOC PACK: Coffee, Buffet Lunch, Dinner: £22-£48.
VIS RESTR'S: Welcome Weekdays.
VIS GF - Round: Wd £20. We N/A. **Day:** Wd £30. We N/A.
FACILITIES: Practice Ground, & Full Clubhouse facilities.

35

ENGLAND

BRAMSHAW (FOREST)　　MAP 2 B3

Brook, Lyndhurst, Hants SO43 7HE.
M27 Junction 1. 1 mile north to Brook.

CONTACT: R Tingey, General Manager. Tel: 0703 813433.
COURSE: 5,774yds, PAR 69, SSS 68. Typical New Forest land.
SOC RESTR'S: Welcome Weekdays by arrangement.
SOC GF - Round: Wd N/A. We N/A. **Day:** Wd N/A. We N/A.
SOC PACK: Coffee, Buffet Lunch, Dinner: £22-£48.
VIS RESTR'S: Welcome Weekdays.
VIS GF - Round: Wd £20. We N/A. **Day:** Wd £30. We N/A.
FACILITIES: Practice Ground & Full Clubhouse facilities.

BROCKENHURST MANOR GC　　MAP 2 B3

Sway Road, Brockenhurst, Hants SO41 7SG.
A337 to Brockenhurst - B3055 S to Sway from village centre.

CONTACT: Stuart Craven, Secretary/Manager. Tel: 0590 23332.
COURSE: 6,222yds, PAR 70, SSS 70. Parkland/forest course.
SOC RESTR'S: Welcome Thursdays.
SOC GF - Round: Wd N/A. We N/A. **Day:** Wd N/A. We N/A.
SOC PACK: From £35 for 30. Under 30 from £31.50.
VIS RESTR'S: Please phone prior to play.
VIS GF - Round: Wd £25. We £40. **Day:** Wd £35. We £40.
FACILITIES: Catering 7 days 10-5 -other times seasonal.

CORHAMPTON GOLF CLUB　　MAP 3 A3

Sheeps Pond Lane, Droxford, Southampton, Hants SO3 1QZ.
9 miles south of Winchester. 1 mile from Corhampton village.

CONTACT: P Taylor, Secretary. Tel: 0489 877279.
COURSE: 6,088yds, PAR 69, SSS 69. Downland course.
SOC RESTR'S: Welcome Monday & Thursday.
SOC GF - Round: Wd £20. We N/A. **Day:** Wd £28. We N/A.
SOC PACK: Coffee, Lunch, Dinner, 36 holes: £41.
VIS RESTR'S: Welcome Weekdays.
VIS GF - Round: Wd £20. We N/A. **Day:** Wd £28. We N/A.
FACILITIES: Fully stocked Pro-shop.

DIBDEN GOLF CENTRE　　MAP 3 A3

Main Road, Dibden, Southampton, Hants SO4 5TB.
Leave A326 at Dibden Roundabout, course half-a-mile on right.

CONTACT: A Bridge, Professional. Tel: 0703 845596.
COURSE: 6,206yds, PAR 71, SSS 70. Undulating parkland.
SOC RESTR'S: Max. 32. Welcome Weekdays & Sat pm.
SOC GF - Round: Wd £6.50. We £9.50. **Day:** Wd N/A. We N/A.
SOC PACK: Contact Catering Manager on 0703 845460.
VIS RESTR'S: Welcome. Public course.
VIS GF - Round: Wd £6.50. We £9.50. **Day:** Wd N/A. We N/A.
FACILITIES: Driving Range & 9-hole Course.

HAYLING GOLF CLUB　　MAP 3 A3

Links Lane, Hayling Island, Hants PO11 0BX.
5 miles south of Havant on A3023.

CONTACT: RCW Stokes, Secretary. Tel: 0705 464446
COURSE: 6,489yds, PAR 71, SSS 71. Links course.
SOC RESTR'S: Welcome Tue & Wed. Must have Club H'cap.
SOC GF - Round: Wd £25 We N/A. **Day:** Wd £25 We N/A.
SOC PACK: £40.
VIS RESTR'S: Welcome Handicap Certificate required.
VIS GF - Round: Wd £25. We £31. **Day:** Wd £25. We £31.
FACILITIES: None.

HOCKLEY GOLF CLUB　　MAP 3 A3

Twyford, Winchester, Hants SO21 1PL.
Off Winchester Bypass - Twyford Road - Quarter of a mile.

CONTACT: JR Digby, Secretary. Tel: 0962 713165.
COURSE: 6,279yds, PAR 71, SSS 70. Downland course.
SOC RESTR'S: 20-50, welcome Wednesday only.
SOC GF - Round: Wd £25. We N/A. **Day:** Wd £25. We N/A.
SOC PACK: On application.
VIS RESTR'S: Welcome Weekdays.
VIS GF - Round: Wd £25. We N/A. **Day:** Wd £25. We N/A.
FACILITIES: Bar & Restaurant.

LEE-ON-THE-SOLENT GOLF CLUB　　MAP 3 A3

Brune Lane, Lee-on-the-Solent, Hants PO13 9PB.
M27, Exit Junct 9, 4 miles south of Fareham.

CONTACT: M Topper, Manager. Tel: 0705 551170.
COURSE: 5,959yds, PAR 69, SSS 69. Heathland/parkland.
SOC RESTR'S: Welcome Thursday.
SOC GF - Round: Wd £21. We N/A. **Day:** Wd £26. We N/A.
SOC PACK: £36 including catering.
VIS RESTR'S: Welcome Weekdays with Handicap Certificate.
VIS GF - Round: Wd £21. We N/A. **Day:** Wd £26. We N/A.
FACILITIES: Catering available.

LIPHOOK GOLF CLUB　　MAP 7 A3

Wheatsheaf Enclosure, Liphook, Hants GU30 7EH.
1 mile south of Liphook on A3.

CONTACT: Maj JB Morgan, Secretary. Tel: 0428 723785.
COURSE: 6,247yds, PAR 70, SSS 70. Heatherland course.
SOC RESTR'S: Max. 28. Welcome Wednesday to Friday.
SOC GF - Round: Wd N/A. We N/A. **Day:** Wd N/A. We N/A.
SOC PACK: Available on booking.
VIS RESTR'S: Sun after 1. H'cap Cert required. Phone first.
VIS GF - Round: Wd £24. We N/A. **Day:** Wd £33. We £45.
FACILITIES: Bar & Restaurant.

HAMPSHIRE

MEON VALLEY G & CC   MAP 3 A3

Sandy Lane, Shedfield, Southampton, Hants SO3 2HG.
2 miles north of Wickham.

CONTACT: GF McMenemy, Secretary. Tel: 0329 833455.
COURSE: 6,519yds, PAR 71, SSS 71. Parkland course.
SOC RESTR'S: Welcome Weekdays.
SOC GF - Round: Wd N/A. We N/A. **Day:** Wd N/A. We N/A.
SOC PACK: Various packages on application.
VIS RESTR'S: Welcome Weekdays.
VIS GF - Round: Wd £24. We £30. **Day:** Wd £36. We N/A.
FACILITIES: 9-hole Course, Tennis, Squash, Gym & Swimming.

NEW FOREST GOLF CLUB   MAP 2 B3

Southampton Road, Lyndhurst, Hants SO43 7BU.
A35 Southampton to Lyndhurst road.

CONTACT: Mrs W Swann, Secretary. Tel: 0703 282752.
COURSE: 5,742yds, PAR 69, SSS 68. Heathland course.
SOC RESTR'S: Max. 24. Welcome Tues, Wed & Thur.
SOC GF - Round: Wd £12. We N/A. **Day:** Wd £14. We N/A.
SOC PACK: Coffee, Lunch, Dinner & Golf-: £27.
VIS RESTR'S: Mon-Fri after 9. Sat after 10, Sun after 1.30.
VIS GF - Round: Wd £10. We £12. **Day:** Wd £10. We £12.
FACILITIES: None.

NORTH HANTS GOLF CLUB   MAP 3 A2

Minley Road, Fleet Hampshire GU13 8RE.
5 miles south-east of Camberley off Junction 4a M3.

CONTACT: I Goodliffe, Secretary. Tel: 0252 616443.
COURSE: 6,257yds Par 69, SSS 70. Parkland course.
SOC RESTR'S: Welcome Tuesday & Wednesday.
SOC GF - Round: Wd N/A. We N/A. **Day:** Wd £30. We N/A.
SOC PACK: On application from Secretary.
VIS RESTR'S: Welcome Wd. Must book. H'cap Cert required.
VIS GF - Round: Wd £24. We N/A. **Day:** Wd £30. We N/A.
FACILITIES: Bar & Restaurant.

OLD THORNS GOLF CLUB   MAP 7 A3

Longmoor Road, Liphook, Hants GU30 7PE.
A3 to Liphook - 1 mile down B2131.

CONTACT: Reception. Tel: 0428 724555.
COURSE: 6,447yds, PAR 72, SSS 71. Undulating parkland course.
SOC RESTR'S: Welcome.
SOC GF - Round: Wd £25. We £35. **Day:** Wd £40. We N/A.
SOC PACK: Coffee, Light Lunch, Dinner, 36 holes-: £55.
VIS RESTR'S: Welcome.
VIS GF - Round: Wd £25. We £35. **Day:** Wd £40. We N/A.
FACILITIES: Japanese Restaurant & Hotel Accommodation.

PETERSFIELD GOLF CLUB   MAP 3 A3

Heath Road, Petersfield, Hants GU31 4EJ.
Half-a-mile east of Town Centre.

CONTACT: Neil Garfoot, General Manager. Tel: 0730 262386.
COURSE: 5,649yds, PAR 69, SSS 67. Heath/parkland course.
SOC RESTR'S: 15-40, Welcome Wed, Thur & Fri.
SOC GF - Round: Wd £15. We N/A. **Day:** Wd £21. We N/A.
SOC PACK: Green Fee & Catering £30.
VIS RESTR'S: Welcome Weekdays & Weekend afternoons.
VIS GF - Round: Wd £15. We £21. **Day:** Wd £21. We £30.
FACILITIES: Bar & Restaurant.

ROMSEY GOLF CLUB   MAP 2 B3

Nursling, Southampton, Hants SO1 9XW.
2 miles SE of Romsey on A3057 near M27/M271, Junction 3.

CONTACT: P Hargraves, Manager. Tel: 0703 734637.
COURSE: 5,851yds, PAR 69, SSS 68. Parkland course.
SOC RESTR'S: Min. 15. Max. 50. Welcome Mon, Tues & Thur.
SOC GF - Round: Wd £19.50. We N/A. **Day:** Wd £24. We N/A.
SOC PACK: Coffee, Lunch, Dinner, 36 holes: £38.
VIS RESTR'S: Welcome Weekdays.
VIS GF - Round: Wd £19.50. We N/A. **Day:** Wd £24. We N/A.
FACILITIES: Bar & Restaurant.

ROWLANDS CASTLE GOLF CLUB   MAP 3 A3

31 Links Lane, Rowlands Castle, Hants PO9 6AE.
9 miles S of Petersfield off A3(M) or 4 miles N of Havant.

CONTACT: AW Aird, Secretary. Tel: 0705 412784.
COURSE: 6,381yds, PAR 72, SSS 70. Parkland course.
SOC RESTR'S: Welcome Tuesday & Thursday.
SOC GF - Round: Wd N/A. We N/A. **Day:** Wd N/A. We N/A.
SOC PACK: Green Fees plus Meal: £27
VIS RESTR'S: Welcome except Sat; Restricted numbers on Sun.
VIS GF - Round: Wd £22. We £30. **Day:** Wd £22. We £30.
FACILITIES: Bar & Restaurant.

SANDFORD SPRINGS GOLF CLUB   MAP 3 A3

Wolverton, Basingstoke, Hants RG26 5RT.
8 miles north-west of Basingstoke on A339.

CONTACT: G Tipple, Secretary. Tel: 0635 297881.
COURSE: 6,100yds (27 holes), SSS 70. Woodland course.
SOC RESTR'S: Prior booking. No weekends.
SOC GF - Round: Wd N/A. We N/A. **Day:** Wd £25. We N/A.
SOC PACK: Please discuss at time of booking.
VIS RESTR'S: Wd prior booking. We with Member
VIS GF - Round: Wd £20. We N/A. **Day:** Wd £25. We N/A.
FACILITIES: Bar, Restaurant, Pro shop.

ENGLAND

SOUTHWOOD GOLF CLUB MAP 7 A3

Ively Road, Cove, Farnborough, Hants GU14 0LJ.
1 mile west of Farnborough off A325.

CONTACT: B Hammond, Director of Golf. Tel: 0252 548700.
COURSE: 5,738yds, PAR 69, SSS 68. Parkland course.
SOC RESTR'S: Min. 16. Welcome Weekdays.
SOC GF - Round: Wd N/A. **We** N/A. **Day:** Wd N/A. **We** N/A.
SOC PACK: £40.
VIS RESTR'S: Welcome. All rounds bookable.
VIS GF - Round: Wd £11.50. **We** £14. **Day:** Wd N/A. **We** N/A.
FACILITIES: Bar & Restaurant.

STONEHAM GOLF CLUB MAP 3 A3

Bassett Green Road, Southampton, Hants SO2 3NE.
2 miles north of Southampton on A27.

CONTACT: Mrs AM Wilkinson, Secretary. Tel: 0703 769272.
COURSE: 6,310yds, PAR 72, SSS 70. Hilly parkland course.
SOC RESTR'S: Welcome Mon, Thur & Fri. Time by arrangement.
SOC GF - Round: Wd N/A. **We** N/A. **Day:** Wd N/A. **We** N/A.
SOC PACK: Coffee, Light Lunch, Dinner, 36 holes: £42.
VIS RESTR'S: Welcome Weekdays. Phone for Weekends.
VIS GF - Round: Wd £27. **We** N/A. **Day:** Wd £27. **We** N/A.
FACILITIES: Bar & Restaurant.

Herefordshire

BELMONT-ON-WEY GOLF CLUB MAP 2 B2

Belmont House, Belmont, Hereford, Herefordshire HR2 9SA.
Turn off A465 Hereford-Abergavenny road.

CONTACT: A Wright, Marketing Manager. Tel: 0432 352666.
COURSE: 6,480yds, PAR 71, SSS 71. Meadowland course.
SOC RESTR'S: Welcome except before 12 noon at We.
SOC GF - Round: Wd £14. **We** £18. **Day:** Wd £24. **We** £28.
SOC PACK: Coffee, Lunch, Golf, Dinner, 36 holes: £37.50.
VIS RESTR'S: Welcome.
VIS GF - Round: Wd £14. **We** £18. **Day:** Wd £24. **We** £28.
FACILITIES: Tennis, Fishing, Bowls & Snooker.

BLACKWELL GOLF CLUB MAP 2 B2

Blackwell, Bromsgrove B60 1PY.
3 miles east of Bromsgrove.

CONTACT: RWA Burns, Secretary. Tel: 021 445 1994.
COURSE: 6,202yds, PAR 71, SSS 71. Parkland course.
SOC RESTR'S: H'cap Cert required. No weekends.
SOC GF - Round: Wd N/A. **We** N/A. **Day:** Wd N/A. **We** N/A.
SOC PACK: On application.
VIS RESTR'S: H'cap Cert required. We with Member.
VIS GF - Round: Wd £36. **We** N/A. **Day:** Wd N/A. **We** N/A.
FACILITIES: Catering available but must be booked.

KING'S NORTON GOLF CLUB MAP 2 B2

Brockhill Lane, Weatheroak, Alvechurch B48 7ED.
8 miles south of Birmingham.

CONTACT: LNW Prince, Secretary/Manager. Tel: 0564 826789.
COURSE: 6,754yds, PAR 72, SSS 73. Parkland course.
SOC RESTR'S: Welcome but no weekends.
SOC GF - Round: Wd N/A. **We** N/A. **Day:** Wd £30. **We** N/A.
SOC PACK: Various packages available.
VIS RESTR'S: Weekdays unrestricted but no weekends.
VIS GF - Round: Wd £27. **We** N/A. **Day:** Wd £30. **We** N/A.
FACILITIES: 9-hole Course, Restaurant (not We), Bar, Shop.

KINGTON GOLF CLUB MAP 2 B2

Bradnor Hill, Kington, Herefordshire HR5 3RE.
1 mile north of Kington.

CONTACT: Dean Oliver, Professional. Tel: 0544 231320.
COURSE: 5,840yds, PAR 70, SSS 68. Moorland course.
SOC RESTR'S: Advanced bookings.
SOC GF - Round: Wd £13. **We** £16. **Day:** Wd £16. **We** £20.
SOC PACK: None.
VIS RESTR'S: Contact Club beforehand.
VIS GF - Round: Wd £13. **We** £16. **Day:** Wd £16. **We** £20.
FACILITIES: Bar & Restaurant.

ROSS-ON-WYE GOLF CLUB MAP 2 B2

Two Park, Gorsley, Ross-on-Wye, Herefordshire HR9 7UT.
Off Junction 3 of the M50. Adjoining Junction.

CONTACT: GH Cason, Hon. Secretary. Tel: 0989 82267.
COURSE: 6,500yds, PAR 72, SSS 73. Parkland course.
SOC RESTR'S: Over 16 welcome Monday & Tuesday.
SOC GF - Round: Wd £24. **We** N/A. **Day:** Wd £24. **We** N/A.
SOC PACK: £35-£40.
VIS RESTR'S: Welcome after 9.30 each day. Please book.
VIS GF - Round: Wd £24. **We** £30. **Day:** Wd £24. **We** £30.
FACILITIES: Good Practice Area & Snooker.

HERTFORDSHIRE

Hertfordshire

BISHOP'S STORTFORD GC MAP 7 B1

Dunmow Road, Bishop's Stortford, Herts CM23 5HP.
Junction 8 off M11. Follow signs for Town Centre on A120.

CONTACT: Maj C Rolls, Secretary. Tel: 0279 654715.
COURSE: 6,440yds, PAR 71, SSS 71. Flat parkland course.
SOC RESTR'S: Min. 15. Max. 40. Welcome Wd except Tues.
SOC GF - Round: Wd £25. We N/A. **Day:** Wd £25. We N/A.
SOC PACK: Coffee, Lunch, Dinner, 36 holes: £47.
VIS RESTR'S: Welcome Weekdays.
VIS GF - Round: Wd £21. We N/A. **Day:** Wd £21. We N/A.
FACILITIES: Bar & Restaurant.

ALDENHAM G & CC MAP 7 A2

Church Lane, Aldenham, Nr. Watford, Herts WD2 8AL.
Leave M1 at J5, take A41 London Rd, turn left at 1st roundabout.

CONTACT: J Phillips, Secretary. Tel: 0923 853929.
COURSE: 6,480yds, PAR 70, SSS 71. Parkland course.
SOC RESTR'S: Welcome.
SOC GF - Round: Wd N/A. We N/A. **Day:** Wd N/A. We N/A.
SOC PACK: Coffee, Lunch, Dinner, 36 holes: Price varies.
VIS RESTR'S: Welcome.
VIS GF - Round: Wd £20. We £28. **Day:** Wd £28. We N/A.
FACILITIES: 9-hole course, Snack Bar & Restaurant.

ARKLEY GOLF CLUB MAP 7 B2

Rowley Green Road, Barnet Herts EN5 3HL.
2 miles north-east of Barnet, off A1(M).
Recommended Hotel: Elstree Moat House, Borehamwood.

CONTACT: G Taylor, Secretary. Tel: 081 449 0394.
COURSE: 6,045yds, PAR 72, SSS 69. Parkland course.
SOC RESTR'S: Welcome Wed, Thur & Fri.
SOC GF - Round: Wd £20. We N/A. **Day:** Wd £25. We N/A.
SOC PACK: On application.
VIS RESTR'S: Welcome Weekdays. Please phone first.
VIS GF - Round: Wd £20. We N/A. **Day:** Wd £25. We N/A.
FACILITIES: Bar & Cartering (not Monday).

ASHRIDGE GOLF CLUB MAP 7 A1

Little Gaddesden, Berkhamstead, Herts HP4 1LY.
5 miles north-west of Berkhamstead on the B4506.

CONTACT: Mrs M West, Secretary. Tel: 0442 842244.
COURSE: 6,508yds, PAR 72, SSS 71. Parkland course.
SOC RESTR'S: Max. 45. Not Thur, We or Bank Hols.
SOC GF - Round: Wd N/A. We N/A. **Day:** Wd N/A. We N/A.
SOC PACK: Coffee, Lunch, Tea, 36 holes: £68.
VIS RESTR'S: Welcome except Thursday.
VIS GF - Round: Wd £34. We N/A. **Day:** Wd £50. We N/A.
FACILITIES: Bar & Catering.

BUSHEY HALL GOLF CLUB MAP 7 A2

Bushey Hall Drive, Bushey, Herts WD2 2EP.
1 mile south-east of Watford off the A4008.

CONTACT: CM Brown, Secretary/Manger. Tel: 0923 225802.
COURSE: 6,099yds, PAR 70, SSS 69. Parkland course.
SOC RESTR'S: Welcome Mon, Tues & Thur.
SOC GF - Round: Wd £21. We N/A. **Day:** Wd £29.50. We N/A.
SOC PACK: Coffee, Lunch, Dinner, 36 holes: £39.
VIS RESTR'S: Welcome Weekdays.
VIS GF - Round: Wd £21. We N/A. **Day:** Wd £29.50. We N/A.
FACILITIES: None.

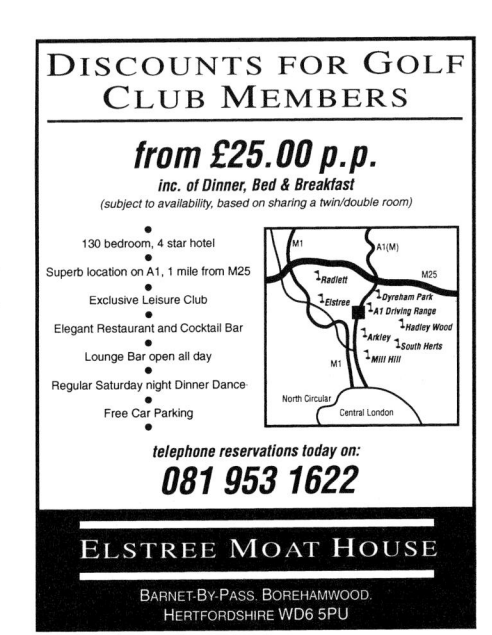

DISCOUNTS FOR GOLF CLUB MEMBERS

from £25.00 p.p.
inc. of Dinner, Bed & Breakfast
(subject to availability, based on sharing a twin/double room)

130 bedroom, 4 star hotel
Superb location on A1, 1 mile from M25
Exclusive Leisure Club
Elegant Restaurant and Cocktail Bar
Lounge Bar open all day
Regular Saturday night Dinner Dance
Free Car Parking

telephone reservations today on:
081 953 1622

ELSTREE MOAT HOUSE

BARNET-BY-PASS, BOREHAMWOOD.
HERTFORDSHIRE WD6 5PU

ENGLAND

CHESHUNT GOLF CLUB   MAP 7 B2/3

The Clubhouse, Park Lane, Cheshunt, Herts EN7 6QD.
M25 Junction 25 - A10 to Hertford, Club signposted.

CONTACT: C. Newton, Professional. Tel: 0992 624009.
COURSE: 6,613yds, PAR 71, SSS 68. Parkland course.
SOC RESTR'S: By arrangement with Professional.
SOC GF - Round: Wd N/A. **We** N/A. **Day:** Wd N/A. **We** N/A.
SOC PACK: On application.
VIS RESTR'S: All times must be booked.
VIS GF - Round: Wd £8. **We** £10.50. **Day:** Wd N/A. **We** N/A.
FACILITIES: Bar.

ELSTREE GOLF CLUB   MAP 7 B2

Watling Street, Elstree, Herts WD6 3AA.
1 mile north of Elstree on A5183.

CONTACT: Kathy Roberts, Administrator. Tel: 081 953 6115.
COURSE: 5,916yds, PAR 69, SSS 68. Parkland course.
SOC RESTR'S: On application from Club Manager.
SOC GF - Round: Wd N/A. **We** N/A. **Day:** Wd N/A. **We** N/A.
SOC PACK: Available on booking.
VIS RESTR'S: Please phone prior to play.
VIS GF - Round: Wd £20. **We** £25. **Day:** Wd £30. **We** N/A.
FACILITIES: Bar/Restaurant open all day. 60-bay Range.

HADLEY WOOD GOLF CLUB   MAP 7 B2

Beech Hill, Barnet, Herts EN4 0JJ.
M25 Junction 24 - A1 - Cockfosters.

CONTACT: Peter Bryan, General Manager. Tel: 081 449 4328.
COURSE: 6,473yds, PAR 72, SSS 71. Parkland course.
SOC RESTR'S: Welcome Weekdays. GF on application.
SOC GF - Round: Wd N/A. **We** N/A. **Day:** Wd N/A. **We** N/A.
SOC PACK: Available on booking.
VIS RESTR'S: Welcome Weekdays. GF on application.
VIS GF - Round: Wd £30. **We** N/A. **Day:** Wd £40. **We** N/A.
FACILITIES: Bar, Restaurant. Fees under review.

HARTSBOURNE G & CC   MAP 7 A2

Bushey Heath, Herts WD2 1JW.
5 miles south-east of Watford, off A411.

CONTACT: DJ Woodman, Secretary. Tel: 081 950 1133.
COURSE: 6,333yds, PAR 72, SSS 70. Parkland course.
SOC RESTR'S: Welcome Mon & Fri by arrangement with Sec.
SOC GF - Round: Wd N/A. **We** N/A. **Day:** Wd N/A. **We** N/A.
SOC PACK: Coffee & Biscuits, Lunch, Dinner, 36 holes -: £55
VIS RESTR'S: Only accompanied by Member.
VIS GF - Round: Wd N/A. **We** N/A. **Day:** Wd N/A. **We** N/A.
FACILITIES: 9-hole course, & Bar.

LETCHWORTH GOLF CLUB   MAP 7 A1

Letchworth Lane, Letchworth, Herts SG6 3NQ.
Quarter-of-a-mile off A505 from Letchworth.

CONTACT: AR Bailey, Secretary. Tel: 0462 683203.
COURSE: 6,181yds, PAR 70, SSS 69. Parkland course.
SOC RESTR'S: Welcome Wed, Thur & Fri.
SOC GF - Round: Wd N/A. **We** N/A. **Day:** Wd N/A. **We** N/A.
SOC PACK: Coffee, Lunch, Dinner, Golf: £48.
VIS RESTR'S: Welcome Weekdays. H'cap Cert required.
VIS GF - Round: Wd £23.50. **We** N/A. **Day:** Wd £32.50. **We** N/A.
FACILITIES: Bar & Restaurant.

MID-HERTS GOLF CLUB   MAP 7 A1

Lamer Lane, Gustard Wood, Wheathampstead, Herts AL4 8RS.
Off B651, 6 miles north of St. Albans.

CONTACT: RJH Jourdan, Secretary. Tel: 0582 832242.
COURSE: 6,094yds, PAR 69, SSS 69. Heathland/parkland course.
SOC RESTR'S: 20-36. Welcome Thur & Fri.
SOC GF - Round: Wd N/A. **We** N/A. **Day:** Wd N/A. **We** N/A.
SOC PACK: Coffee, Lunch, Dinner, 36 holes: £50.
VIS RESTR'S: Welcome Weekdays. H'cap Cert required.
VIS GF - Round: Wd £21. **We** N/A. **Day:** Wd £31. **We** N/A.
FACILITIES: Bar & Restaurant.

MOOR PARK GOLF CLUB (HIGH)   MAP 7 A2

Rickmansworth, Herts WD3 1QN.
1 mile south-east of Rickmansworth off A4145.

CONTACT: JA Davies, Secretary. Tel: 0923 773146.
COURSE: 6,713yds, PAR 72, SSS 72. Parkland course.
SOC RESTR'S: No weekends. H'cap Cert required.
SOC GF - Round: Wd N/A. **We** N/A. **Day:** Wd £50. **We** N/A.
SOC PACK: Tailored packages available.
VIS RESTR'S: H'cap Cert req. We with Member. GF on request.
VIS GF - Round: Wd £30. **We** N/A. **Day:** Wd £50. **We** N/A.
FACILITIES: Bar snacks, Pro shop, Snooker.

MOOR PARK GOLF CLUB (WEST)   MAP 7 A2

Rickmansworth, Herts WD3 1QN.
1 mile south-east of Rickmansworth off A4145.

CONTACT: JA Davies, Secretary. Tel: 0923 773146.
COURSE: 5,823yds, PAR 69, SSS 68. Parkland course.
SOC RESTR'S: No weekends. H'cap Cert required.
SOC GF - Round: Wd N/A. **We** N/A. **Day:** Wd N/A. **We** N/A.
SOC PACK: Tailored packages available.
VIS RESTR'S: H'cap Cert req. Thurs is Ladies Day.
VIS GF - Round: Wd £25. **We** N/A. **Day:** Wd £50. **We** N/A.
FACILITIES: Bar snacks, Pro shop, Snooker.

HERTFORDSHIRE

PORTERS PARK GOLF CLUB   MAP 7 A2

Shenley Hill, Radlett, Herts WD7 7AZ.
M25 Junction 22 to Radlett. Half-a-mile east of Radlett.

CONTACT: JH Roberts, Manager. Tel: 0923 854127.
COURSE: 6,313yds, PAR 70, SSS 70. Undulating parkland.
SOC RESTR'S: Max. 50. Welcome Wed & Thur all day.
SOC GF - Round: Wd N/A. **We** N/A. **Day:** Wd N/A. **We** N/A.
SOC PACK: £65 including catering.
VIS RESTR'S: Welcome Weekdays H'cap Cert req. Please book.
VIS GF - Round: Wd £28. **We** N/A. **Day:** Wd £42. **We** N/A.
FACILITIES: Bar & Restaurant.

POTTERS BAR GOLF CLUB   MAP 7 B1

Darkes Lane, Potters Bar, Herts EN6 1DF.
1 mile north Junction 24 of M25: Half-a-mile Potters Bar Station.

CONTACT: A St. John Williams, Sec/Manager. Tel: 0707 652020.
COURSE: 6,273yds, PAR 71, SSS 70. Parkland course.
SOC RESTR'S: Welcome Mon, Tues, Fri.
SOC GF - Round: Wd N/A. **We** N/A. **Day:** Wd N/A. **We** N/A.
SOC PACK: Coffee, Lunch, Dinner, 36 holes: £50.
VIS RESTR'S: Welcome Weekdays with H'cap Cert.
VIS GF - Round: Wd £18. **We** N/A. **Day:** Wd £27.50. **We** N/A.
FACILITIES: Bar & Restaurant.

REDBOURN GOLF CLUB   MAP 7 A1

Kinsbourne Green Lane, Redbourn, Herts AL3 7QA.
1 miles south of M1 Junction 9. Down Luton Lane.

CONTACT: WM Dunn, Secretary. Tel: 0582 793493.
COURSE: 6,177yds, PAR 70, SSS 69. Parkland course.
SOC RESTR'S: Min. 12. Max. 32. Mon-Thur included.
SOC GF - Round: Wd £14. **We** N/A. **Day:** Wd N/A. **We** N/A.
SOC PACK: On application.
VIS RESTR'S: Welcome Weekdays, Weekends not before 3.
VIS GF - Round: Wd £14. **We** £18. **Day:** Wd N/A. **We** N/A.
FACILITIES: Par 3 Course, Range, Bar & Restaurant.

ROYSTON GOLF CLUB   MAP 7 B1

Baldock Road, Royston, Herts SG8 5BG.
On A505 south-west of Royston.

CONTACT: Mrs S Morris, Secretary/Manager. Tel: 0763 242696.
COURSE: 6,032yds, PAR 70, SSS 69. Undulating heathland.
SOC RESTR'S: Welcome Weekdays.
SOC GF - Round: Wd N/A. **We** N/A. **Day:** Wd £20. **We** N/A.
SOC PACK: Coffee, Lunch, Dinner, Golf: Prices vary.
VIS RESTR'S: Welcome Weekdays.
VIS GF - Round: Wd N/A. **We** N/A. **Day:** Wd £20. **We** N/A.
FACILITIES: Bar, Snooker & TV.

WELWYN GARDEN CITY GC   MAP 7 B1

Mannicotts, High Oaks Road, Welwyn Garden City AL8 7BP.
1 mile north of Hatfield. B197 to Valley Road.

CONTACT: JL Carragher, Secretary. Tel: 0707 325243.
COURSE: 6,100yds, PAR 70, SSS 69. Undulating parkland course.
SOC RESTR'S: No weekends. H'cap Cert required.
SOC GF - Round: Wd N/A. **We** N/A. **Day:** Wd £25. **We** N/A.
SOC PACK: Tailored to requirements.
VIS RESTR'S: H'cap Cert required. Not on Sundays.
VIS GF - Round: Wd £25. **We** £33. **Day:** Wd £25. **We** N/A.
FACILITIES: Bar snacks, Pro shop.

WEST HERTS GOLF CLUB   MAP 7 A2

Cassiobury Park, Watford, Herts WD1 7SL.
Off A412 between Rickmansworth and Watford.

CONTACT: Mrs Verdon. Tel: 0923 236484.
COURSE: 6,488yds, PAR 72, SSS 71. Parkland course.
SOC RESTR'S: Welcome Wed, Thur & Fri.
SOC GF - Round: Wd N/A. **We** N/A. **Day:** Wd N/A. **We** N/A.
SOC PACK: Coffee, Lunch, Dinner, 36 holes: £48.
VIS RESTR'S: Welcome Weekday.
VIS GF - Round: Wd £20. **We** N/A. **Day:** Wd £30. **We** N/A.
FACILITIES: Bar & Restaurant.

WHIPSNADE PARK GOLF CLUB   MAP 7 A1

Studham Lane, Dagnall, Herts HP4 1RH.
M1 J8 at Hemel - A414 to Leighton Buzzard - Dagnall.

CONTACT: Mrs A King, Secretary. Tel: 0442 842330.
COURSE: 6,800yds, PAR 72, SSS 72. Parkland course.
SOC RESTR'S: Max. 60. Welcome Tues - Fri inclusive.
SOC GF - Round: Wd £20. **We** N/A. **Day:** Wd £30. **We** N/A.
SOC PACK: Coffee, Lunch, Dinner 36 holes: £48.
VIS RESTR'S: Welcome Weekday.
VIS GF - Round: Wd £21. **We** N/A. **Day:** Wd £31. **We** N/A.
FACILITIES: Bar & Restaurant.

WHITEHILL GOLF CLUB   MAP 7 B1

Dane End, Ware, Herts SG12 0JS.
2 miles west of A10, turn at Happy Eater.

CONTACT: Miss M Turner. Tel: 0920 438495.
COURSE: 6,636yds, PAR 72, SSS 72. Undulating course.
SOC RESTR'S: Min. 12. Welcome with Handicap Certificate.
SOC GF - Round: Wd N/A. **We** N/A. **Day:** Wd N/A. **We** N/A.
SOC PACK: Coffee, Lunch, Dinner, 36 holes: Prices vary.
VIS RESTR'S: Welcome with Handicap Certificate.
VIS GF - Round: Wd £15. **We** £18. **Day:** Wd £20. **We** N/A.
FACILITIES: Driving Range, Bar & Snooker.

ENGLAND

Humberside

FLAMBROUGH HEAD GOLF CLUB   MAP 5 B3

Lighthouse Road, Bridlington, Humberside YO15 1AR.
Signposted from Flamborough village.

CONTACT: WR Scarle, Secretary. Tel: 0262 850333.
COURSE: 5,438yds, PAR 66, SSS 66. Links course.
SOC RESTR'S: Max. 40. No Sundays or Wednesdays.
SOC GF - Round: Wd N/A. **We** N/A. **Day:** Wd £12. **We** £16.
SOC PACK: Coffee, Lunch, Dinner, 36 holes:Wd £21, We £25.
VIS RESTR'S: Welcome except before 12 on Wed & Sun.
VIS GF - Round: Wd N/A. **We** N/A. **Day:** Wd £12. **We** £16.
FACILITIES: Snooker.

BOOTHFERRY GOLF CLUB   MAP 5 B3

Spaldington Lane, Howden, N Humberside DN14 7NG.
M62 Junction 37 - B1228 Howden to Bubwith road.

CONTACT: S Wilkinson, Pro/Manager. Tel: 0430 430364.
COURSE: 6,700yds, PAR 73, SSS 72. Meadowland course.
SOC RESTR'S: Minimum 12. No other restrictions.
SOC GF - Round: Wd N/A. **We** N/A. **Day:** Wd N/A. **We** N/A.
SOC PACK: Coffee, Lunch, Dinner, 27/36 holes: Prices vary.
VIS RESTR'S: Please phone prior to play.
VIS GF - Round: Wd £7.50. **We** £11 **Day:** Wd £11. **We** £16.
FACILITIES: Practice Area, Chipping & Putting Green & Restaurant.

GANSTEAD PARK GOLF CLUB   MAP 5 B3

Longdales Lane, Coniston, Hull, Humberside HU11 4LB.
A165 Hull to Bridlington (5 miles east of Hull).

CONTACT: M Smee, Professional. Tel: 0482 811121.
COURSE: 6,801yds, PAR 72, SSS 73. Parkland course.
SOC RESTR'S: Welcome by advanced booking.
SOC GF - Round: Wd £15. **We** £24. **Day:** Wd £20. **We** £24.
SOC PACK: Reduction for 20+.
VIS RESTR'S: Not Wednesday or Sunday mornings.
VIS GF - Round: Wd £15. **We** £24. **Day:** Wd £20. **We** £24.
FACILITIES: Bar, Restaurant.

BRIDLINGTON GOLF CLUB   MAP 5 B3

Belvedere Road, Bridlington, Humberside YO15 3NA.
Off A165, 1.5 miles south of Bridlington station.

CONTACT: C Wilson, Hon. Secretary. Tel: 0262 606367.
COURSE: 6,491yds, PAR 71, SSS 71. Seaside course.
SOC RESTR'S: Limited on Wednesday & Sunday.
SOC GF - Round: Wd £10. **We** £15. **Day:** Wd £15. **We** £20.
SOC PACK: Reduction over 25. Full catering.
VIS RESTR'S: Limited on Wednesday & Sunday.
VIS GF - Round: Wd £10. **We** £15. **Day:** Wd £15. **We** £20.
FACILITIES: Bar & Restaurant.

GRIMSBY GOLF CLUB   MAP 5 B3

Littlecoates Road, Grimsby, Humberside DN34 4LU.
1 mile west of Grimsby.

CONTACT: Secretary. Tel: 0472 342630.
COURSE: 6,058yds, PAR 70, SSS 69. Undulating parkland.
SOC RESTR'S: Welcome Mondays & Fridays.
SOC GF - Round: Wd £18. **We** £25. **Day:** Wd £18. **We** £25.
SOC PACK: Available on booking.
VIS RESTR'S: Welcome. Limited play on Weekends.
VIS GF - Round: Wd £18. **We** £25. **Day:** Wd £18. **We** £25.
FACILITIES: Bar & Restaurant.

BROUGH GOLF CLUB   MAP 5 B3

Brough, Humberside HU15 1HB.
10 miles west of Hull on A63.

CONTACT: WG Burleigh, Secretary. Tel: 0482 667291.
COURSE: 6,183yds, PAR 68, SSS 69. Parkland course.
SOC RESTR'S: Welcome except Wednesdays.
SOC GF - Round: Wd N/A. **We** N/A. **Day:** Wd £35. **We** N/A.
SOC PACK: Please discuss at time of booking.
VIS RESTR'S: Welcome except Wednesdays.
VIS GF - Round: Wd £25. **We** N/A. **Day:** Wd N/A. **We** N/A.
FACILITIES: Bar, Restaurant, Pro shop, Snooker.

HOLME HALL GOLF CLUB   MAP 5 B3

Holme Lane, Bottesford, Scunthorpe, Humberside DN16 3RF.
3 miles south of Scunthorpe just off M18.

CONTACT: GD Smith, Secretary. Tel: 0724 862078.
COURSE: 6,475yds, PAR 71, SSS 71. Heathland type course.
SOC RESTR'S: Welcome Weekdays.
SOC GF - Round: Wd N/A. **We** N/A. **Day:** Wd £18. **We** N/A.
SOC PACK: Good catering service available (except Mondays).
VIS RESTR'S: Welcome Weekdays.
VIS GF - Round: Wd N/A. **We** N/A. **Day:** Wd £18. **We** N/A.
FACILITIES: Bar & Restaurant.

KENT

Kent

HORNSEA GOLF CLUB   MAP 5 B3

Rolston Road, Hornsea, Humberside HU18 1XG.
Follow signs for Hornsea Pottery.

CONTACT: BW Kirton, Secretary. Tel: 0964 532020.
COURSE: 6,475yds, PAR 71, SSS 71. Parkland course.
SOC RESTR'S: Welcome Weekdays except Tuesday.
SOC GF - Round: Wd £17.50. **We** N/A. **Day:** Wd £24. **We** N/A.
SOC PACK: Available on booking. to Secretary. Meals available.
VIS RESTR'S: Limited on Tues & We. Phone call advisable.
VIS GF - Round: Wd £17.50. **We** £29. **Day:** Wd £24. **We** £35.
FACILITIES: Bar, Clubhouse & Snooker.

IMMINGHAM GOLF CLUB   MAP 5 B3

Church Lane, Immingham, S Humberside DN40 2EU.
Near St. Andrews Church. 2 miles off A180.

CONTACT: Mrs J Jobling, Secretary. Tel: 0469 575298.
COURSE: 5,809yds, PAR 69, SSS 68. Parkland course.
SOC RESTR'S: Min 12, Max 30. Welcome Weekdays.
SOC GF - Round: Wd N/A. **We** N/A. **Day:** Wd £14. **We** N/A.
SOC PACK: Available on booking through Secretary.
VIS RESTR'S: Welcome except on Thur & Sat am & Sun pm.
VIS GF - Round: Wd £14. **We** £20. **Day:** Wd £20. **We** £20.
FACILITIES: Bar & Restaurant.

NORMANBY HALL GOLF CLUB   MAP 5 B3

Normanby, Nr. Scunthorpe, S Humberside DN15 9HU.
Turn off B1430 5 miles north of Scunthorpe & follow signs.

CONTACT: Civic Centre. Tel: 0724 280444 Ext 852.
COURSE: 6,548yds, PAR 72, SSS 71. Parkland course.
SOC RESTR'S: Max. 40. Welcome except Sun pm or Bank Hols.
SOC GF - Round: Wd £9.50. **We** N/A. **Day:** Wd £15. **We** N/A.
SOC PACK: None.
VIS RESTR'S: Some closure days - ask Professional.
VIS GF - Round: Wd £9.50. **We** £11.50. **Day:** Wd £15. **We** N/A.
FACILITIES: Bar, Restaurant, Clubhouse & Country Park.

RAC National Road Maps

Clear, easy-to-read, up-to-date route planning maps at a scale of approximately 8 miles to 1 inch

Price £3.99
Available from bookshops
or direct from the RAC on 0235 834885

CANTERBURY GOLF CLUB   MAP 3 B3

Scotland Hills, Canterbury, Kent CT1 1TW.
On A257, 1 mile east from City Centre.

CONTACT: EL Ruckert, Secretary. Tel: 0227 453532.
COURSE: 6,249yds, PAR 70, SSS 70. Parkland course.
SOC RESTR'S: Welcome Tues & Thur.
SOC GF - Round: Wd £27. **We** £36. **Day:** Wd £36. **We** N/A.
SOC PACK: Reduction of 5% 30-59. Over 60 - 10% reduction.
VIS RESTR'S: Welcome Weekdays & after 3. at Weekends.
VIS GF - Round: Wd £27. **We** £36. **Day:** Wd £36. **We** N/A.
FACILITIES: Practice Ground (£2).

CHERRY LODGE GOLF CLUB   MAP 7 B3

Jail Lane, Biggin Hill, Kent TN16 3AX.
Off A233 Bromley to Westerham Road.

CONTACT: C Dale, General Manager. Tel: 0959 572250.
COURSE: 6,522yds, PAR 72, SSS 72. Undulating downland.
SOC RESTR'S: Min. 18. Mon-Fri. Full catering with prior booking.
SOC GF - Round: Wd N/A. **We** N/A. **Day:** Wd N/A. **We** N/A.
SOC PACK: Coffee, Lunch, Dinner, 36 holes: £50.
VIS RESTR'S: Welcome Weekdays by prior arrangement.
VIS GF - Round: Wd £18. **We** N/A. **Day:** Wd £28. **We** N/A.
FACILITIES: Restaurant Mon-Sat, Sun Lunches & 2 Bars.

COBTREE MANOR PARK GC   MAP 3 B3

Chatham Road, Boxley, Maidstone, Kent ME14 3AZ.
Take A229 to Chatham, course 3 miles from Maidstone.

CONTACT: Restaurant. Tel: 0662 751881.
COURSE: 5,716yds, PAR 70, SSS 68. Parkland course.
SOC RESTR'S: Welcome Weekdays by prior arrangement.
SOC GF - Round: Wd £12.50. **We** N/A. **Day:** Wd N/A. **We** N/A.
SOC PACK: Standard GF rate applicable. Meals taken extra.
VIS RESTR'S: Welcome Weekdays. Please book for Weekends.
VIS GF - Round: Wd £10.25. **We** £15.35. **Day:** Wd N/A. **We** N/A.
FACILITIES: Bar, Catering, Pro-shop & Practice area.

ENGLAND

CRANBROOK GOLF CLUB   MAP 3 B3

Benenden Road, Cranbrook, Kent TN17 4AL.
M25 - A21 Hastings - A262 Ashford - Sissinghurst Club 2.5 miles.

CONTACT: Alan Gillard Pro/Secretary. Tel: 0580 712833.
COURSE: 6,351yds, PAR 70, SSS 70. Scenic parkland course.
SOC RESTR'S: Not before 10 Tues or Thur. Not Weekends.
SOC GF - Round: Wd £19. We N/A. **Day:** Wd N/A. We N/A.
SOC PACK: Standard GF rate applicable. Meals taken extra.
VIS RESTR'S: Not before 10 Tues or Thur, We not before noon.
VIS GF - Round: Wd £19. We £27.50. **Day:** Wd N/A. We N/A.
FACILITIES: Specialists in Company Golf Days.

CRAY VALLEY GOLF CLUB   MAP 7 B2

Sandy Lane, St. Paul's Cray, Orpington, Kent BR5 3HY.
Ruxley Rondabout A20- turn into Sandy Lane.

CONTACT: Catering Manageress. Tel: 0689 831927.
COURSE: 5,624yds, PAR 70, SSS 67. Parkland course.
SOC RESTR'S: Welcome Weekdays.
SOC GF - Round: Wd £12. We N/A. **Day:** Wd £22. We N/A.
SOC PACK: On application.
VIS RESTR'S: Welcome Weekday anytime, Weekend bookings.
VIS GF - Round: Wd £112. We £16.30. **Day:** Wd N/A. We N/A.
FACILITIES: 9 hole course, Bar & Clubhouse.

DARENTH VALLEY GOLF COURSE   MAP 7 B3

Station Road, Shoreham, Nr. Sevenoaks, Kent TN14 7SA.
A225 Sevenoaks-Dartford - 4 miles north of Sevenoaks.

CONTACT: N Morgan, Clubhouse Manager. Tel: 0959 522944.
COURSE: 6,356yds, PAR 72, SSS 71. Parkland course.
SOC RESTR'S: Min. 20. Not Tues or Weekends.
SOC PACK: Coffee, Lunch, Dinner, 36 holes: £40.
VIS RESTR'S: By arrangement through Professional.
VIS GF - Round: Wd £11. We £15. **Day:** Wd £19. We N/A.
FACILITIES: 100 Cover Restaurant, Bar & Clubhouse.

FAVERSHAM GOLF CLUB   MAP 3 B3

Belmont Park, Faversham, Kent ME13 0HB.
M2 - Faversham exit A251 to Junction A2 - left to Brogdale Road.

CONTACT: DB Christie, Secretary. Tel: 0795 890561.
COURSE: 6,030yds, PAR 70, SSS 69. Parkland course.
SOC RESTR'S: Max. 40. Welcome Wed & Fri. 8.30. & 2.
SOC GF - Round: Wd £25. We N/A. **Day:** Wd £32. We N/A.
SOC PACK: Meals as arranged with Stewardess (0795 89251).
VIS RESTR'S: Welcome Weekdays. H'cap Cert required.
VIS GF - Round: Wd £23. We N/A. **Day:** Wd £30. We N/A.
FACILITIES: Bar & Clubhouse. Teaching by Professional.

GILLINGHAM GOLF CLUB   MAP 3 B3

Woodlands Road, Gillingham, Kent ME7 2AD.
On old A2 from Chatham to Rainham (Watling Street).

CONTACT: LP O'Grady, Secretary. Tel: 0634 853017.
COURSE: 5,863yds, PAR 70, SSS 68. Parkland course.
SOC RESTR'S: Max. 36. Welcome Mon, Tues, Wed 8. to 2.
SOC GF - Round: Wd N/A. We N/A. **Day:** Wd N/A. We N/A.
SOC PACK: Green Fee, Lunch, Dinner: Prices vary.
VIS RESTR'S: Welcome Weekdays. H'cap Cert required.
VIS GF - Round: Wd £22. We N/A. **Day:** Wd £22. We N/A.
FACILITIES: Bar & Restaurant.

KNOLE PARK GOLF CLUB   MAP 7 B3

Seal Hollow Road, Sevenoaks, Kent TN15 0HJ.
Half-a-mile from Town Centre.

CONTACT: DJL Hoppe, Secretary. Tel: 0732 452150.
COURSE: 6,249yds, PAR 70, SSS 70. Parkland course.
SOC RESTR'S: Welcome Weekdays.
SOC GF - Round: Wd £25.50. We N/A. **Day:** Wd £36. We N/A.
SOC PACK: Approx £55 including Dinner.
VIS RESTR'S: By appointment. Not We. H'cap Cert required.
VIS GF - Round: Wd £25.50. We N/A. **Day:** Wd £36. We N/A.
FACILITIES: Full Catering, Bar & Clubhouse.

LANGLEY PARK GOLF CLUB   MAP 7 B2

Barnfield Wood Road, Beckenham, Kent BR3 2SZ.
1 mile from Bromley South Station.

CONTACT: G Ritchie, Professional. Tel: 081 650 1663.
COURSE: 6,488yds, PAR 69, SSS 71. Wooded parkland course.
SOC RESTR'S: No weekends. H'cap Cert required.
SOC GF - Round: Wd N/A. We N/A. **Day:** Wd £35. We N/A.
SOC PACK: On application.
VIS RESTR'S: H'cap Cert required. We with Member.
VIS GF - Round: Wd £35. We N/A. **Day:** Wd £35. We N/A.
FACILITIES: Bar snacks, Pro shop, Club & Trolley hire.

LITTLESTONE GOLF CLUB   MAP 3 B3

St Andrews Road, Littlestone, New Romney, Kent TN28 8RB.
1 mile east of New Romney off the A259.

CONTACT: JD Lewis, Secretary. Tel: 0679 62310.
COURSE: 6,424yds, PAR 71, SSS 72. Links course.
SOC RESTR'S: Welcome Weekdays.
SOC GF - Round: Wd £28. We N/A. **Day:** Wd £36. We N/A.
SOC PACK: Coffee - Light Lunch - Dinner: £50.
VIS RESTR'S: Welcome Weekdays.
VIS GF - Round: Wd £25. We N/A. **Day:** Wd £32. We N/A.
FACILITIES: 9-hole course, Range, Bar & Restaurant.

KENT

NORTH FORELAND GOLF CLUB MAP 3 B3

Kingsgate, Broadstairs, Thanet, Kent CT10 3PU.
B2052, 1.5 miles north of Broadstairs.

CONTACT: BJ Preston, Secretary. Tel: 0843 862140.
COURSE: 6,374yds, PAR 71, SSS 71. Downland seaside course.
SOC RESTR'S: Wed & Fri. H'cap Cert required.
SOC GF - Round: Wd N/A. **We** N/A. **Day:** Wd £30. **We** N/A.
SOC PACK: On application.
VIS RESTR'S: H'cap Cert required. No We mornings.
VIS GF - Round: Wd £20. **We** £30. **Day:** Wd £30. **We** N/A.
FACILITIES: 18-hole Approach & Putt Course, Shop, Bar & Rest.

PRINCE'S GOLF CLUB MAP 3 B3

Sandwich Bay, Sandwich, Kent CT13 9QB.
A2/Canterbury - A257/Sandwich Bypass - A256 (Deal)/Sandwich.

CONTACT: J Adams, Society Bookings. Tel: 0304 611118.
COURSE: 6,506yds, PAR 71, SSS 71. Championship course.
SOC RESTR'S: Welcome as long as course is available. Book.
SOC GF - Round: Wd £29.50. **We** £34. **Day:** Wd £34. **We** £39/£44.
SOC PACK: 18 holes + Lunch: £30 Weekday; £32. 50 Weekend.
VIS RESTR'S: Welcome as long as course is available. Phone.
VIS GF - Round: Wd £29.50. **We** £34. **Day:** Wd £34. **We** £39/£44.
FACILITIES: Three sets of 9 holes, Bar, Restaurant.

ROCHESTER & COBHAM PARK GC MAP 3 B3

Park Pale, by Rochester, Kent ME2 3UL.
3 miles east of Gravesend exit on A2.

CONTACT: JW Irvine, Manager. Tel: 0474 823411.
COURSE: 6,440yds, PAR 72, SSS 71. Undulating parkland course.
SOC RESTR'S: Min. 16. Max. 50. Welcome Tues & Thur.
SOC GF - Round: Wd £28. **We** N/A. **Day:** Wd £39. **We** N/A.
SOC PACK: Coffee, Lunch, Dinner, 36 holes: £55.
VIS RESTR'S: Welcome Weekdays. Handicap Certificate required.
VIS GF - Round: Wd £26. **We** N/A. **Day:** Wd £36. **We** N/A.
FACILITIES: Bar & Restaurant.

ROMNEY WARREN GOLF CLUB MAP 3 B3

St. Andrews Road, Littlestone, New Romney, Kent TN28 8RB.
1 mile east of New Romney off the A259.

CONTACT: JD Lewis, Secretary/Manager. Tel: 0679 62231.
COURSE: 5,100yds, PAR 67, SSS 65. Typical links course.
SOC RESTR'S: Welcome.
SOC GF - Round: Wd N/A. **We** N/A. **Day:** Wd N/A. **We** N/A.
SOC PACK: Coffee - Light Lunch - Dinner: £25.
VIS RESTR'S: Welcome. Please book starting time.
VIS GF - Round: Wd £9.50. **We** £12. **Day:** Wd N/A. **We** N/A.
FACILITIES: Practice area, Putting & Chipping Green.

ROYAL CINQUE PORTS GOLF CLUB MAP 3 B3

Golf Road, Deal, Kent CT14 6RF.
Sandwich - A258 - Upper Deal - Middle Deal Rd- Golf Rd.

CONTACT: Secretary. Tel: 0304 374007.
COURSE: 6,741yds, PAR 72, SSS 72. True links of great renown.
SOC RESTR'S: Max.30. Mon, Tues, Thurs only.
SOC GF - Round: Wd £45. **We** N/A. **Day:** Wd £45. **We** N/A.
SOC PACK: Available on booking. through Secretary.
VIS RESTR'S: As societies. H'cap Cert required. Phone first.
VIS GF - Round: Wd £45. **We** N/A. **Day:** Wd £45. **We** N/A.
FACILITIES: Day GF also applies to play before 1.

ROYAL ST. GEORGE'S GOLF CLUB MAP 3 B3

Sandwich, Kent CT13 9PB.
1 mile from centre of Sandwich.

CONTACT: G Watts, Secretary. Tel: 0304 613090.
COURSE: 6,534yds, PAR 70, SSS 72. Championship links course.
SOC RESTR'S: Welcome Weekdays. H'cap Cert required.
SOC GF - Round: Wd £50. **We** N/A. **Day:** Wd £70. **We** N/A.
SOC PACK: £85 - includes Coffee, Lunch & Tea.
VIS RESTR'S: Welcome Weekdays. H'cap Cert required.
VIS GF - Round: Wd £50. **We** N/A. **Day:** Wd £70. **We** N/A.
FACILITIES: Bar & Restaurant.

RUXLEY PARK GOLF CENTRE MAP 7 B2

Sandy Lane, St. Paul's Cray, Orpington, Kent BR5 3HY.
Off old A20 at Ruxley Roundabout.

CONTACT: P Davies, Secretary. Tel: 0689 871490.
COURSE: 4,466yds, PAR 67, SSS 65. Parkland course.
SOC RESTR'S: Welcome Weekdays.
SOC GF - Round: Wd £10.30. **We** N/A. **Day:** Wd N/A. **We** N/A.
SOC PACK: Coffee, Lunch, Dinner, 36 holes: £34.
VIS RESTR'S: Welcome Weekdays. Weekends after 11.
VIS GF - Round: Wd £10.30. **We** £15.30. **Day:** Wd N/A. **We** N/A.
FACILITIES: Driving Range.

ST. AUGUSTINE'S GOLF CLUB MAP 3 B3

Cottington Road, Cliffsend, Ramsgate, Kent CT12 5JN.
2 miles SW of Ramsgate from A253 or A256 - Follow signs.

CONTACT: RE Freeman, Secretary. Tel: 0843 590333.
COURSE: 5,197yds, PAR 69, SSS 65. Parkland course.
SOC RESTR'S: Min. 12. Max. 40. Welcome Wed & Thur.
SOC GF - Round: Wd £21.50. **We** N/A. **Day:** Wd £21.50. **We** N/A.
SOC PACK: Coffee, Lunch, Dinner, 36 holes: £35. 25.
VIS RESTR'S: H'cap Cert required. Check with Pro for events.
VIS GF - Round: Wd £20. **We** £22. **Day:** Wd £20. **We** £22.
FACILITIES: Bar, Restaurant. £65 weekly GF available.

ENGLAND

SUNDRIDGE PARK GC (EAST)   MAP 7 B2

Garden Road, Bromley, Kent BR1 3NE.
1 mile north of Bromley, by Sundridge Park Station.

CONTACT: D Lowton, Secretary. Tel: 081 460 0278.
COURSE: 6,467yds, PAR 70, SSS 71. Wooded parkland course.
SOC RESTR'S: Weekdays only. H'cap Cert required.
SOC GF - Round: Wd N/A. We N/A. **Day:** Wd £36. We N/A.
SOC PACK: On application.
VIS RESTR'S: Handicap Certificate required.
VIS GF - Round: Wd £36. We N/A. **Day:** Wd £36. We N/A.
FACILITIES: Bar, Restaurant, Pro shop.

Lancashire

SUNDRIDGE PARK GC (WEST)   MAP 7 B2

Garden Road, Bromley, Kent BR1 3NE.
1 mile north of Bromley, by Sundridge Park Station.

CONTACT: D Lowton, Secretary. Tel: 081 460 0278.
COURSE: 6,007yds, PAR 68, SSS 69. Hilly parkland course.
SOC RESTR'S: Weekdays only. H'cap Cert required.
SOC GF - Round: Wd N/A. We N/A. **Day:** Wd £36. We N/A.
SOC PACK: On application.
VIS RESTR'S: Handicap Certificate required.
VIS GF - Round: Wd £36. We N/A. **Day:** Wd £36. We N/A.
FACILITIES: Bar, Restaurant, Pro shop.

ACCRINGTON GOLF CLUB   MAP 8 A2

Devon Avenue, Oswaldtwistle, Accrington, Lancs BB5 4LS.
2 miles east of Blackburn.

CONTACT: JE Pilkington, Secretary. Tel: 0254 232734.
COURSE: 5,954yds, PAR 70, SSS 69. Semi-moorland course.
SOC RESTR'S: Welcome by arrangement.
SOC GF - Round: Wd £16. We £19. **Day:** Wd £16. We £19.
SOC PACK: Coffee, Lunch, Dinner, Golf Fees: £25-£28.
VIS RESTR'S: Welcome by arrangement.
VIS GF - Round: Wd £16. We £19. **Day:** Wd £16. We £19.
FACILITIES: Full Restaurant & Bar facilities.

WILDERNESSE PARK GOLF CLUB   MAP 7 B3

Seal, Sevenoaks, Kent TN15 0JE.
2 miles east of Sevenoaks (A25).

CONTACT: KL Monk, Secretary. Tel: 0732 61199.
COURSE: 6,438yds, PAR 72, SSS 72. Tight, wooded parkland.
SOC RESTR'S: Thur only. H'cap Cert & Letter of Intro required.
SOC GF - Round: Wd N/A. We N/A. **Day:** Wd £37. We N/A.
SOC PACK: On application.
VIS RESTR'S: H'cap Cert & Letter of Intro required.
VIS GF - Round: Wd £26. We N/A. **Day:** Wd £37. We N/A.
FACILITIES: Bar snacks (except Tuesday).

ASHTON & LEA GOLF CLUB   MAP 5 A3

Tudor Avenue, Lea, Preston, Lancs PR4 0XA.
3 miles west of Preston off A583.

CONTACT: MG Gibbs, Secretary. Tel: 0772 726480.
COURSE: 6,289yds, PAR 71, SSS 70. Parkland/heathland course.
SOC RESTR'S: Mon-Wed max. 50. Thur & Fri max. 12.
SOC GF - Round: Wd N/A. We N/A. **Day:** Wd £18 (Fri £20). We N/A.
SOC PACK: Coffee, Lunch, Dinner: £27/£28.
VIS RESTR'S: Reserve tee times with Professional.
VIS GF - Round: Wd N/A. We N/A. **Day:** Wd £18 (Fri £20). We £24.
FACILITIES: Bar, Snooker, Restaurant & Clubhouse.

BLACKBURN GOLF CLUB   MAP 5 A3

Beardwood Brow, Blackburn, Lancs BB2 7AX.
Off Revidge Rd W of town. Easy access from M6, M61, M65/66.

CONTACT: PD Daydock, Secretary. Tel: 0254 51122.
COURSE: 6,147yds, PAR 71, SSS 70. Parkland course.
SOC RESTR'S: Welcome except Tues, We & 12.30-1.30 Wd.
SOC GF - Round: Wd N/A. We N/A. **Day:** Wd £19. We N/A.
SOC PACK: Day's golf & food from £23. Reduced fees for 20+.
VIS RESTR'S: Welcome Weekdays. Please phone for Weekends.
VIS GF - Round: Wd N/A. We N/A. **Day:** Wd £19. We £22.
FACILITIES: Bar & Restaurant.

RAC Regional Road Maps

Large scale (3 miles to 1 inch) maps for the motorist. Each sheet contains details of motorway junctions, dual carriageways, town plans, a full index of towns and villages, and tourist information including golf courses.

Price £3.99
Available from bookshops
or direct from the RAC on 0235 834885

LANCASHIRE

BLACKPOOL NORTH SHORE GC   MAP 5 A3

Devonshire Road, Blackpool, Lancs FY2 0RD.
1.5 miles north of Town Centre.

CONTACT: R Yates, Secretary/Manager. Tel: 0253 52054.
COURSE: 6,420yds, PAR 71, SSS 71. Undulating parkland course.
SOC RESTR'S: Welcome except Thursdays and Weekends.
SOC GF - Round: Wd N/A. We N/A. Day: Wd N/A. We N/A.
SOC PACK: Lunch, Dinner, 27 holes: Prices vary.
VIS RESTR'S: Welcome except Thursdays and Weekends.
VIS GF - Round: Wd N/A. We N/A. Day: Wd £25. We £30.
FACILITIES: Bars & Snooker.

CHORLEY GOLF CLUB   MAP 5 A3

Hall o'th' Hill, Heath Charnock, Chorley, Lancs PR6 9HX.
Just off A673 at junction of A6, 1 mile east of Chorley.

CONTACT: AK Tyrer, Secretary. Tel: 0257 480263.
COURSE: 6,277yds, PAR 71, SSS 70. A challenging course.
SOC RESTR'S: By arrangement. No Mon, We or Bank Hols.
SOC GF - Round: Wd £20. We N/A. Day: Wd £22.50. We N/A.
SOC PACK: No package deals. Catering by prior arrangement.
VIS RESTR'S: By arrangement. No Mon, We or Bank Hols.
VIS GF - Round: Wd £20. We N/A. Day: Wd £22.50. We N/A.
FACILITIES: Bar.

FORMBY GOLF CLUB   MAP 5 A3

Golf Road, Formby, Liverpool L37 1LQ.
By Freshfield Station.

CONTACT: A Thirlwell, Secretary. Tel: 070 48 72164.
COURSE: 6,695yds, PAR 72, SSS 73. Seaside links course.
SOC RESTR'S: No weekends. H'cap Cert required.
SOC GF - Round: Wd £40. We N/A. Day: Wd N/A. We N/A.
SOC PACK: Limited availability.
VIS RESTR'S: H'cap Cert. Not Wed or We.
VIS GF - Round: Wd £40. We N/A. Day: Wd N/A. We N/A.
FACILITIES: Bar snacks (except Monday), Pro shop.

KNOTT END GOLF CLUB   MAP 5 A3

Wyreside, Knott End on Sea, Poulton-le-Fylde, Lancs FY6 0AA.
M55 - A585 (Fleetwood) - B2588 to Knott End.

CONTACT: K Butcher, Secretary. Tel: 0253 810576.
COURSE: 5,900yds, PAR 69, SSS 69. Undulating parkland.
SOC RESTR'S: Welcome Weekdays.
SOC GF - Round: Wd N/A. We N/A. Day: Wd £20. We N/A.
SOC PACK: Golf & Catering: £30.
VIS RESTR'S: Limited on Thur between 10.30 & 1 & We.
VIS GF - Round: Wd N/A. We N/A. Day: Wd £20. We N/A.
FACILITIES: Full Catering & Snooker.

LANCASTER G & CC   MAP 5 A3

Ashton Hall, Ashton with Stodday, Lancaster, Lancs LA2 0AJ.
On A588, 2.5 miles south-west of Lancaster.

CONTACT: Mr D Palmer, Secretary. Tel: 0524 751247.
COURSE: 6,282yds, PAR 71, SSS 71. Undulating parkland.
SOC RESTR'S: Welcome Weekdays.
SOC GF - Round: Wd £26. We N/A. Day: Wd £26. We N/A.
SOC PACK: Available on booking.
VIS RESTR'S: Welcome Weekdays - contact Professional.
VIS GF - Round: Wd £26. We N/A. Day: Wd £26. We N/A.
FACILITIES: Catering, Bar & Hotel facilities.

THE PICKERINGS
Country House Restaurant and Hotel
Catterall, GARSTANG, Lancs

Just a short stroll from Garstang's new Golf Course.
Very comfortable small hotel with delightful food and friendly personal service.
Shooting and coarse fishing can be arranged for guests too.

Reservations and enquiries 0995 602133

LYTHAM GREEN DRIVE GOLF CLUB   MAP 5 A3

Ballam Road, Lytham, Lancs FY8 4LE.
Half-a-mile from centre of Lytham.

CONTACT: R Kershaw, Secretary. Tel: 0253 737390.
COURSE: 6,175yds, PAR 70, SSS 69. Parkland course.
SOC RESTR'S: Welcome Mon, Tues, Thur & Fri.
SOC GF - Round: Wd £19. We N/A. Day: Wd £24. We N/A.
SOC PACK: £33 per day incl. Coffee, Snack Lunch, Dinner.
VIS RESTR'S: Welcome Weekdays limited at Weekends.
VIS GF - Round: Wd £19. We £31. Day: Wd £24. We N/A.
FACILITIES: Bar & Restaurant.

ENGLAND

PENWORTHAM GOLF CLUB   MAP 5 A3

Blundel Lane, Penwortham, Preston, Lancs PR1 0AX.
1.5 miles west of Preston - off the A59.

CONTACT: J Parkinson, Secretary. Tel: 0772 744630.
COURSE: 5,915yds, PAR 69, SSS 68. Parkland course.
SOC RESTR'S: Welcome Wd (except Tues). After 10 & 2.
SOC GF - Round: Wd £22. We N/A. Day: Wd £25. We N/A.
SOC PACK: Prices vary.
VIS RESTR'S: Wd (except Tues) after 10 & 2. Sun after 10.
VIS GF - Round: Wd £22. We £28. Day: Wd £25. We £28.
FACILITIES: Bar & Restaurant.

ROSSENDALE GOLF CLUB   MAP 8 A2

Ewood Lane Head, Haslingden, Rossendale, Lancs BB4 6LH.
Half-a-mile from M66 exit J4, near Haslingden Cricket Ground.

CONTACT: JR Swain, Manager. Tel: 0706 831339.
COURSE: 6,293yds, PAR 72, SSS 71. Parkland course.
SOC RESTR'S: Max. 48. Welcome except Saturdays.
SOC GF - Round: Wd £20. We £25. Day: Wd £20. We £25.
SOC PACK: Coffee, Lunch, Dinner, 36 holes-: £31.66.
VIS RESTR'S: Welcome except Saturdays in season.
VIS GF - Round: Wd £20. We £25. Day: Wd £20. We £25.
FACILITIES: Bar, Snooker & Clubhouse.

ROYAL LYTHAM ST. ANNES   MAP 5 A3

Links Gate, Lytham St. Annes, Lancs FY8 3LQ.
1 mile from centre of St. Annes.

CONTACT: Mrs Harrison, Booking Secretary. Tel: 0253 724206.
COURSE: 6,173yds, PAR 71, SSS 73. Links course.
SOC RESTR'S: Welcome except Tues am and Weekends.
SOC GF - Round: Wd £45. We N/A. Day: Wd £60. We N/A.
SOC PACK: By arrangement when booking.
VIS RESTR'S: Limited on Tues am & Weekends.
VIS GF - Round: Wd £45. We N/A. Day: Wd £60. We N/A.
FACILITIES: Dormy House: £85 per night: Dinner, B&B + 36 holes.

SHAW HILL G & CC   MAP 5 A3

Preston Road, Whittle-le-Woods, Chorley, Lancs PR6 7PP.
Just off M6, Junction 28N - M61, Junction 8N.

CONTACT: Mr Paul Knight. Tel: 0257 269221.
COURSE: 6,405yds, PAR 72, SSS 71. Wooded parkland.
SOC RESTR'S: Welcome Weekdays. H'cap Cert required.
SOC GF - Round: Wd £30. We N/A. Day: Wd N/A. We N/A.
SOC PACK: Coffee, Lunch, Dinner, 27 holes: Prices vary.
VIS RESTR'S: No We or Bank Hols unless by arrangement.
VIS GF - Round: Wd £30. We £40. Day: Wd N/A. We N/A.
FACILITIES: Lovely Georgian Clubhouse, Restaurant & Bar.

SOUTHPORT & AINSDALE GC   MAP 5 A3

Bradshaws Lane, Ainsdale, Southport PR8 3LG.
3 miles south of Southport on A565.

CONTACT: IF Sproule, Secretary. Tel: 0704 78000.
COURSE: 6,612yds, PAR 72, SSS 73. Championshop links course.
SOC RESTR'S: No weekends. H'cap Cert required.
SOC GF - Round: Wd N/A. We N/A. Day: Wd £40. We N/A.
SOC PACK: On application.
VIS RESTR'S: H'cap Cert & Intro required. We occasionally.
VIS GF - Round: Wd £30. We £45. Day: Wd £40. We N/A.
FACILITIES: Restaurant (by arr), Bar, Shop, Snooker.

WILPSHIRE GOLF CLUB   MAP 8 A2

Whalley Road, Wilpshire, Blackburn, Lancs BB1 9LF.
3 miles north of Blackburn on A666.

CONTACT: B Grimshaw, Hon. Secretary. Tel: 0254 248260.
COURSE: 5,911yds, PAR 69, SSS 68. Semi-moorland course.
SOC RESTR'S: Not Competition Days or Ladies Days - Tues.
SOC GF - Round: Wd N/A. We N/A. Day: Wd £22. We £27.
SOC PACK: Available - Contact Hon. Sec or Admin Staff.
VIS RESTR'S: Not Competition Days. Phone call advisable.
VIS GF - Round: Wd N/A. We N/A. Day: Wd £22. We £27.
FACILITIES: Bar & Restaurant.

Leicestershire

BIRSTALL GOLF CLUB   MAP 3 A1

Station Road, Birstall, Leicester LE4 3JQ.
Main A6 to Loughborough (N), turn left as you enter Birstall.

CONTACT: Mrs SE Chilton, Secretary. Tel: 0533 674322.
COURSE: 6,203yds, PAR 70, SSS 70. Parkland course.
SOC RESTR'S: Min. 20. Welcome Wed & Fri.
SOC GF - Round: Wd £20. We N/A. Day: Wd £20. We N/A.
SOC PACK: Available on booking from Secretary.
VIS RESTR'S: Welcome except Tues & Weekends.
VIS GF - Round: Wd £25. We N/A. Day: Wd £25. We N/A.
FACILITIES: Bar, Billiard Room & Dining Area.

LINCOLNSHIRE

COSBY GOLF CLUB   MAP 3 A1

Chapel Lane, off Broughton Road, Cosby, Leicester LE9 5RG.
7 miles south of Leicester. 400yds from Cosby village centre.

CONTACT: MD Riddle, Secretary. Tel: 0533 864759.
COURSE: 6,277yds, PAR 71, SSS 70. Undulating parkland.
SOC RESTR'S: Welcome except Mondays & Weekends.
SOC GF - Round: Wd £20. We N/A. **Day:** Wd £22. We N/A.
SOC PACK: Societies over 20 in number £2 reduction on GF.
VIS RESTR'S: Not Weekends, Bank Hols or after 4. Mon-Fri.
VIS GF - Round: Wd £20. We N/A. **Day:** Wd £22. We N/A.
FACILITIES: All catering requirements must be booked.

HINCKLEY GOLF CLUB   MAP 3 A1

Leicester Road, Hinckley, Leicester LE10 3DR.
A47 - north-east of Hinckley (1 mile).

CONTACT: J Toon, Secretary. Tel: 0455 615124.
COURSE: 6,592yds, PAR 71, SSS 71. Parkland course.
SOC RESTR'S: Over 12. Welcome Mon & Wed.
SOC GF - Round: Wd £20. We N/A. **Day:** Wd £25. We N/A.
SOC PACK: Coffee, Lunch, Dinner, 36 holes: £40.
VIS RESTR'S: Welcome except Tues & Weekends.
VIS GF - Round: Wd £20. We N/A **Day:** Wd £25. We N/A.
FACILITIES: Bar, Snooker, Restaurant & Conference facilities.

KIRBY MUXLOE GOLF CLUB   MAP 3 A1

Station Road, Kirby Muxloe, Leicester LE9 9EP.
3 miles west of Leicester, off Hinckley road.

CONTACT: SF Aldwinckle, Secretary. Tel: 0533 393457.
COURSE: 6,303yds, PAR 71, SSS 70. Parkland course.
SOC RESTR'S: Welcome Wed (limit 50) & Thur (limit 25).
SOC GF - Round: Wd £20. We N/A. **Day:** Wd £25. We N/A.
SOC PACK: Coffee, Lunch, Dinner, £38-£43. according to menu.
VIS RESTR'S: Welcome Weekdays with Handicap Certificate.
VIS GF - Round: Wd £20. We N/A. **Day:** Wd £25. We N/A.
FACILITIES: Range, Snooker, Lounge Bar & Dining facilities.

LONGCLIFFE GOLF CLUB   MAP 3 A1

Snell's Nook Lane, Nanpantan, Loughborough, Leics LE11 3YA.
M1 Junction 23 - A512 to Loughborough - 1st right to course.

CONTACT: G Harle, Secretary. Tel: 0509 239129.
COURSE: 6,551yds, PAR 72, SSS 71. Undulating heathland.
SOC RESTR'S: Welcome Mon, Wed, Thur & Fri.
SOC GF - Round: Wd £22. We N/A. **Day:** Wd £27. We N/A.
SOC PACK: Coffee, Lunch, Dinner, 36 holes: £40.
VIS RESTR'S: No between 12-2 Weekdays or at Weekends.
VIS GF - Round: Wd £22. We N/A. **Day:** Wd £27. We N/A.
FACILITIES: Bar & Restaurant.

ROTHLEY PARK GOLF CLUB   MAP 3 A1

Westfield Lane, Rothley, Leicester LE7 7NH.
West of A6, midway between Leicester & Loughborough.

CONTACT: B Durham, Secretary. Tel: 0533 302809.
COURSE: 6,476yds, PAR 71, SSS 71. Parkland course.
SOC RESTR'S: Welcome Wed &Thur - contact office.
SOC GF - Round: Wd £25. We N/A. **Day:** Wd 37.50. We N/A.
SOC PACK: Available on booking.
VIS RESTR'S: Welcome except Tuesdays & Weekends.
VIS GF - Round: Wd £25. We N/A. **Day:** Wd £37.50. We N/A.
FACILITIES: Bar & Restaurant.

ULLESTHORPE COURT GOLF CLUB   MAP 3 A2

Frolesworth Road, Ullesthorpe, Nr. Lutterworth, Leics LE17 5BZ.
3 miles from A5 between Lutterworth & Hinckley.

CONTACT: Linda Finch, Golf Co-ordinator. Tel: 0455 209023.
COURSE: 6,650yds, PAR 72, SSS 72. Meadowland course.
SOC RESTR'S: Welcome Weekdays.
SOC GF - Round: Wd N/A. We N/A. **Day:** Wd N/A. We N/A.
SOC PACK: Specialist golf day package. Price on request.
VIS RESTR'S: Welcome Weekdays. H'cap Cert required.
VIS GF - Round: Wd £19. We N/A. **Day:** Wd £19. We N/A.
FACILITIES: Hotel & Leisure Centre.

Lincolnshire

BELTON PARK GOLF CLUB   MAP 3 A1

Belton Lane, Grantham, Lincolnshire NG31 9SH.
2 miles north from Grantham on A1.

CONTACT: T Measures, General Manager. Tel: 0476 67399.
COURSE: 6,420yds, PAR 71, SSS 71. Parkland course.
SOC RESTR'S: Welcome except Tuesdays & Weekends.
SOC GF - Round: Wd £16. We N/A. **Day:** Wd N/A We N/A.
SOC PACK: Coffee, Lunch, Dinner, 36 holes: £32.
VIS RESTR'S: Welcome. H'cap Cert required.
VIS GF - Round: Wd £16. We £26. **Day:** Wd N/A We N/A.
FACILITIES: 27 Holes, 7-day Full Catering & Bar facilities.

ENGLAND

BLANKNEY GOLF CLUB   MAP 3 A1

Blankney, Metheringham, Lincolnshire LN4 3AZ.
B1188 - 10 miles south-east of Lincoln.

CONTACT: D Priest, General Manager. Tel: 0526 320263.
COURSE: 6,378yds, PAR 71, SSS 71. Parkland course.
SOC RESTR'S: Welcome Wd with written prior booking.
SOC GF - Round: Wd £15. We N/A. **Day:** Wd £20. We N/A.
SOC PACK: Not possible to quote — separate catering.
VIS RESTR'S: Not Wed am or Weekends. Please phone.
VIS GF - Round: Wd £15. We N/A **Day:** Wd £20. We N/A.
FACILITIES: Bar, All-day Catering & Snooker.

BOSTON GOLF CLUB   MAP 3 A1

Cowbridge, Horncastle Road, Boston, Lincs PE22 7EL.
2 miles north of Boston on B 1183 to Horncastle.

CONTACT: DE Smith, General Manager. Tel: 0205 350589.
COURSE: 5,825yds, PAR 69, SSS 68. Parkland course.
SOC RESTR'S: Max 24. Welcome Weekdays.
SOC GF - Round: Wd £15. We N/A. **Day:** Wd £20. We N/A.
SOC PACK: Coffee, Lunch, Dinner, 36 holes: £33.
VIS RESTR'S: Welcome. H'cap Cert req We and BH.
VIS GF - Round: Wd £15. We £20. **Day:** Wd £20. We £30.
FACILITIES: Bar & Catering.

CANWICK PARK GOLF CLUB   MAP 3 A1

Canwick Park, Washingborough Road, Lincoln LN4 1EF.
1.5 miles east of Lincoln.

CONTACT: AC Hodgkinson, Hon. Secretary. Tel: 0522 522166.
COURSE: 6,257yds, PAR 70, SSS 70. Parkland course.
SOC RESTR'S: Welcome except Thursdays & Weekends.
SOC GF - Round: Wd £13. We N/A. **Day:** Wd £20. We N/A.
SOC PACK: Minimum £50.
VIS RESTR'S: Welcome Weekdays & Weekends after 3.
VIS GF - Round: Wd £13. We £14. **Day:** Wd £20. We £22.
FACILITIES: Bar & Restaurant.

GAINSBOROUGH GOLF CLUB   MAP 3 A1

Thonock, Gainsborough, Lincolnshire DN21 1PZ.
1 mile north-east of Gainsborough.

CONTACT: D Garrison, Manager. Tel: 0427 613088.
COURSE: 6,620yds, PAR 73, SSS 72. Flat parkland course.
SOC RESTR'S: Welcome Weekdays by prior booking.
SOC GF - Round: Wd £20. We N/A. **Day:** Wd £25. We N/A
SOC PACK: From £35.
VIS RESTR'S: Welcome Weekdays. H'cap Cert required.
VIS GF - Round: Wd £20. We N/A. **Day:** Wd £25. We N/A.
FACILITIES: Bar, Restaurant & Range.

HORNCASTLE GOLF CLUB   MAP 3 A1

West Ashby, Nr. Horncastle, Lincolnshire LN9 5PP.
Just off A158, halfway between Lincoln & Skegness.

CONTACT: A Norton, Secretary. Tel: 0507 526800.
COURSE: 5,782yds, PAR 70, SSS 70. Heathland course.
SOC RESTR'S: No restrictions. Phone prior to play.
SOC GF - Round: Wd £10. We £10. **Day:** Wd £15. We £15.
SOC PACK: 2 rounds, Lunch, Dinner: £30 incl. VAT.
VIS RESTR'S: No restrictions.
VIS GF - Round: Wd £10. We £10. **Day:** Wd £15. We £15.
FACILITIES: 25-bay Floodlit Driving Range & Fishing.

LOUTH GOLF CLUB   MAP 3 A1

Crowtree Lane, Louth, Lincolnshire LN11 9LJ.
Half-a-mile west of Louth.

CONTACT: PC Bell, Secretary. Tel: 0507 603681.
COURSE: 6,477yds, PAR 71, SSS 71. Hilly testing course.
SOC RESTR'S: Weekdays only, by appointment.
SOC GF - Round: Wd £15. We N/A. **Day:** Wd £18. We N/A.
SOC PACK: As required.
VIS RESTR'S: Always welcome.
VIS GF - Round: Wd £15. We £18. **Day:** Wd £18. We £20.
FACILITIES: Bar & Restaurant.

MARKET RASEN & DISTRICT GC   MAP 3 A1

Legsby Road, Market Rasen, Lincolnshire LN8 3DZ.
Past racecourse, 1 mile east of town.

CONTACT: E Hill, Hon. Secretary. Tel: 0673 842319.
COURSE: 6,043yds, PAR 70, SSS 69. Wooded heathland.
SOC RESTR'S: Max. 50. Welcome Tuesday & Friday.
SOC GF - Round: Wd £15. We N/A. **Day:** Wd £20. We N/A.
SOC PACK: Available on booking from Sec or Steward.
VIS RESTR'S: Welcome except We & after 10.30 Wednesday.
VIS GF - Round: Wd £15. We N/A. **Day:** Wd £20. We N/A.
FACILITIES: Practice Ground & Good Catering.

SANDILANDS GOLF CLUB   MAP 3 A1

Roman Bank, Sandilands, Sutton-on-Sea, Lincs LN12 2RJ.
1 mile south of Sutton-on-Sea, off A52.

CONTACT: D Mumby, Secretary. Tel: 0507 441617.
COURSE: 5,995yds, PAR 70, SSS 69. Seaside links course.
SOC RESTR'S: Welcome Weekdays.
SOC GF - Round: Wd £12. We £18. **Day:** Wd £18. We £25.
SOC PACK: Coffee, Lunch, Dinner. Approx £12 + Green Fee.
VIS RESTR'S: Welcome.
VIS GF - Round: Wd £12. We £18. **Day:** Wd £18. We N/A.
FACILITIES: Bar & Restaurant.

London

SEACROFT GOLF CLUB MAP 3 B1

Drummond Road, Skegness, Lincolnshire PE25 3AU.
South of Slegness.

CONTACT: HK Brader, Secretary/Manager. Tel: 0754 763020.
COURSE: 6,501yds, PAR 71, SSS 71. Links course.
SOC RESTR'S: Max. 40 Weekdays, 24 at Weekends.
SOC GF - Round: Wd £20. We £25. **Day:** Wd £28. We £35.
SOC PACK: Available on booking from Secretary.
VIS RESTR'S: Not before 9.30 or between 12-2.
VIS GF - Round: Wd £20. We £25. **Day:** Wd £28. We £35.
FACILITIES: Bar & Restaurant.

SLEAFORD GOLF CLUB MAP 3 A1

Willoughby Road, South Rauceby, Sleaford, Lincs NG34 8PL.
1 mile west of Sleaford off A153.

CONTACT: DBR Harris, Hon. Secretary. Tel: 0529 8273.
COURSE: 6,443yds, PAR 72, SSS 71. Inland links course.
SOC RESTR'S: Prior arrangements. Not Weekends.
SOC GF - Round: Wd N/A. We N/A. **Day:** Wd N/A. We N/A.
SOC PACK: Coffee, Lunch, Dinner, 36 holes: £28.50.
VIS RESTR'S: No winter Sundays. No catering on Mondays.
VIS GF - Round: Wd £18. We £26. **Day:** Wd £18. We £26.
FACILITIES: Practice Ground, Putting Green & 6-hole Par 3 Course.

STOKE ROCHFORD GOLF CLUB MAP 3 A1

Stoke Rochford, Nr. Grantham, Lincolnshire NG33 5EW.
A1 northbound, 7 miles south of Grantham.

CONTACT: J Butler, Secretary. Tel: 0476 67035.
COURSE: 6,251yds, PAR 70, SSS 70. Parkland course.
SOC RESTR'S: Handicap Certificates required.
SOC GF - Round: Wd £17. We £26. **Day:** Wd £24. We £35.
SOC PACK: Lunch, Dinner - Cost approx. £35.
VIS RESTR'S: No play before 10.30 We. H'cap Cert required.
VIS GF - Round: Wd £17. We £26. **Day:** Wd £24. We £35.
FACILITIES: Bar, Clubhouse & Snooker.

WOODHALL SPA GOLF CLUB MAP 3 A1

The Broadway, Woodhall Spa, Lincolnshire LN10 6PU.
6 miles south of Horncastle on B1191.

CONTACT: BH Fawcett, Secretary. Tel: 0526 352511.
COURSE: 6,907yds, PAR 73, SSS 73. Championship course.
SOC RESTR'S: Prior booking through Secretary.
SOC GF - Round: Wd £22. We £25. **Day:** Wd £32. We £35.
SOC PACK: None.
VIS RESTR'S: H'cap Cert required (max Gents 20, Ladies 30).
VIS GF - Round: Wd £22. We £25. **Day:** Wd £32. We £35.
FACILITIES: Pitch & Putt Course.

BUSH HILL PARK GOLF CLUB MAP 7 B2

Bush Hill, Winchmore Hill, London N21 2BU.
Half-a-mile south of Enfield town.

CONTACT: H Burnand, Secretary. Tel: 081 360 5738.
COURSE: 5,809yds, PAR 70, SSS 68. Parkland course.
SOC RESTR'S: Min. 30. Welcome Wd except Wed.
SOC GF - Round: Wd £38. We N/A. **Day:** Wd £48. We N/A.
SOC PACK: Coffee, Lunch, Dinner, 36 holes.
VIS RESTR'S: Welcome Weekdays. H'cap Cert required.
VIS GF - Round: Wd £20. We N/A. **Day:** Wd £30. We N/A.
FACILITIES: Bar & Restaurant.

FINCHLEY GOLF CLUB MAP 7 B2

Nether Court, Frith Lane, Mill Hill, London NW7 1PU.
Close to Mill Hill East tube station & A1/M1.

CONTACT: J Pearce, Secretary. Tel: 081 346 2436.
COURSE: 6,411yds, PAR 72, SSS 71. Woodland course.
SOC RESTR'S: Welcome Wednesday & Friday.
SOC GF - Round: Wd £28. We N/A **Day:** Wd £37. We N/A.
SOC PACK: Coffee, Lunch, Dinner, 36 holes: £56.
VIS RESTR'S: Welcome Wd except Thur & afternoon We.
VIS GF - Round: Wd £28. We £37. **Day:** Wd £37. We N/A.
FACILITIES: Bar & Catering Service.

MUSWELL HILL GOLF CLUB MAP 7 B2

Rhodes Avenue, Wood Green, London N22 4UT.
1 mile from Bounds Green Underground.

CONTACT: J Connors, Secretary. Tel: 081 888 1764.
COURSE: 6,474yds, PAR 71, SSS 71. Parkland course.
SOC RESTR'S Mon, Wed & Thur max 40 Fri max 24. 8.30 start.
SOC GF - Round: Wd £23. We N/A. **Day:** Wd £33. We N/A.
SOC PACK: AM round: £30; PM round: £38; All day: £48.
VIS RESTR'S: Wd not before 8.30. We in advance through Pro.
VIS GF - Round: Wd £23. We £35. **Day:** Wd £33. We N/A.
FACILITIES: None.

ENGLAND

NORTH MIDDLESEX GOLF CLUB MAP 7 B2

Friern, Barnet Lane, Whetstone, London N20 0NL.
M25 J23 then A1081 to Barnet & A1000.

CONTACT: MCN Reding, General Manager. Tel: 081 445 1604.
COURSE: 5,625yds, PAR 69, SSS 67. Parkland course.
SOC RESTR'S: Welcome Tuesdays & Thursdays.
SOC GF - Round: Wd £22. We N/A. Day: Wd £27. 50 We N/A.
SOC PACK: £40-£50 depending on menu chosen.
VIS RESTR'S: Advisable to ring Professional. H'cap required.
VIS GF - Round: Wd £22. We £30. Day: Wd £27.50. We N/A.
FACILITIES: Bar & Catering.

WEST ESSEX GOLF CLUB MAP 7 B2

Bury Road, Stewardstonebury, Chingford, London E4 7QL.
1 mile north of Chingford.

CONTACT: PH Galley, Secretary/Manager. Tel: 081 529 7558.
COURSE: 6,289yds, PAR 71, SSS 70. Undulating parkland.
SOC RESTR'S: Min. 20. Max. 60. Welcome Mon, Wed & Fri.
SOC GF - Round: Wd £30. We N/A. Day: Wd £37. We N/A.
SOC PACK: Coffee, Lunch, Dinner, 36 holes: £52.
VIS RESTR'S: Not before 11 on Tues; not after 12 Thur. No We.
VIS GF - Round: Wd £30. We N/A. Day: Wd £37. We N/A.
FACILITIES: Restaurant & Bar facilities.

ROYAL BLACKHEATH GOLF CLUB MAP 7 B2

Court Road, Eltham, London SE9 5AF.
3 miles south-east of Eltham.

CONTACT: R Barriball, Secretary. Tel: 081 850 1795.
COURSE: 6,209yds, PAR 70, SSS 70. Undulating parkland.
SOC RESTR'S: Please apply in writing. Welcome Wd.
SOC GF - Round: Wd N/A. We N/A. Day: £38. We N/A.
SOC PACK: Coffee, Lunch, Dinner, Golf: Prices vary.
VIS RESTR'S: Welcome Wd by booking. GF reduction Nov-Mar.
VIS GF - Round: Wd £28. We N/A. Day: £38. We N/A.
FACILITIES: Bar &Restaurant . 17th century clubhouse.

WIMBLEDON PARK GOLF CLUB MAP 7 B2

Home Park Road, Wimbledon, London SW19 7HR.
Nr Wimbledon Park tube station - 8 miles from Central London.

CONTACT: MK Hale, Secretary. Tel: 081 946 1250.
COURSE: 5,465yds, PAR 66, SSS 66. Parkland course.
SOC RESTR'S: Max. 40. Welcome Tuesday & Thursday.
SOC GF - Round: Wd N/A. We N/A. Day: Wd £34. We N/A.
SOC PACK: Coffee, Lunch, Dinner, 36 holes: £52.
VIS RESTR'S: Welcome Wd, sometimes after 3 We with H'cap Cert.
VIS GF - Round: Wd N/A. We N/A. Day: Wd £25. We £25.
FACILITIES: Bar & Restaurant.

SOUTH HERTS GOLF CLUB MAP 7 B2

Links Drive, Totteridge, London N20 8QU.
4 miles north-west of Finchley.

CONTACT: R Livingston, Professional. Tel: 081 445 2035.
COURSE: 6,470yds, PAR 72, SSS 71. Parkland course.
SOC RESTR'S: By appointment Wed-Fri only.
SOC GF - Round: Wd N/A. We N/A. Day: Wd £22. We £25.
SOC PACK: Please discuss at time of booking.
VIS RESTR'S: Welcome Wd. Must book. H'cap Cert required.
VIS GF - Round: Wd N/A. We N/A. Day: Wd £22. We £25.
FACILITIES: 9-hole course, Bar & Restaurant.

Manchester (Greater)

TRENT PARK GOLF CLUB MAP 7 B2

Bramley Road, Oakwood, London N14 4XS.
3 minutes from Oakwood Station (Piccadilly Line).

CONTACT: G Harris, Professional. Tel: 081 366 7432.
COURSE: 6,008yds, PAR 69, SSS 69. Parkland course.
SOC RESTR'S: Welcome Monday to Thursday.
SOC GF - Round: Wd £8.50. We N/A. Day: Wd N/A. We N/A.
SOC PACK: By arrangement through Secretary.
VIS RESTR'S: Booking advisable & required at Weekend.
VIS GF - Round: Wd £8.50. We £10.50. Day: Wd N/A. We N/A.
FACILITIES: Bar, Snacks & Large Practice Area.

ASHTON-IN-MAKERFIELD G C MAP 5 A3

Garswood Park, Ashton-in-Makerfield, Wigan WN4 0YT.
Close to Junction 24 on M6.

CONTACT: JR Hay, Secretary. Tel: 0942 719330.
COURSE: 6,120yds, PAR 70, SSS 69. Parkland course.
SOC RESTR'S: Welcome Tuesday & Thursday.
SOC GF - Round: Wd £21. We N/A. Day: Wd £21. We N/A.
SOC PACK: Available when booking with Secretary.
VIS RESTR'S: Welcome Wd (not Wed) after 9. 45, by booking.
VIS GF - Round: Wd £21. We N/A. Day: Wd £21. We N/A.
FACILITIES: Bar & Restaurant.

MANCHESTER (GREATER)

BLACKLEY GOLF CLUB   MAP 8 A2

Victoria Avenue East, Blackley, Manchester M9 2HW.
5 miles north from City Centre.

CONTACT: CB Leggott, Secretary. Tel: 061 654 7770.
COURSE: 6,237yds, PAR 70, SSS 70. Parkland course.
SOC RESTR'S: Welcome Mon, Tues, Wed & Fri.
SOC GF - Round: Wd £15. We N/A. **Day:** Wd N/A. We N/A.
SOC PACK: Coffee, Lunch, Dinner, Golf: £25.
VIS RESTR'S: Welcome Weekdays.
VIS GF - Round: Wd £17. We N/A. **Day:** Wd N/A. We N/A.
FACILITIES: Bar, Dinning Room & Billiard Room.

BOLTON OLD LINKS   MAP 8 A2

Chorley Old Road, Montserrat, Bolton BL1 5SU.
3 miles north-west of Bolton off the B6226.

CONTACT: E Monaghan, Hon. Secretary. Tel: 0204 842307.
COURSE: 6,406yds, PAR 72, SSS 72. Parkland course.
SOC RESTR'S: Welcome except Tues or Weekends.
SOC GF - Round: Wd £25. We N/A. **Day:** Wd N/A. We N/A.
SOC PACK: £30.
VIS RESTR'S: Not Wd 12-1.30 & Wed 12-2. Sat before 4.
VIS GF - Round: Wd £25. We £30 **Day:** Wd £25. We N/A.
FACILITIES: Usual Golf Club facilities.

BRAMHALL PARK GOLF CLUB   MAP 8 A3

20 Manor Road, Bramhall, Stockport, Cheshire SK7 3LY.
3 miles south of Stockport off Stockport to Bramhall Road.

CONTACT: JC O'Shea, Hon. Secretary. Tel: 061 485 2205.
COURSE: 6,043yds, PAR 70, SSS 69. Parkland course.
SOC RESTR'S: Max. 60. Welcome Tues & Thur afternoons.
SOC GF - Round: Wd N/A. We N/A. **Day:** Wd £25. We N/A.
SOC PACK: None.
VIS RESTR'S: Welcome except during competitions. Please phone.
VIS GF - Round: Wd N/A. We N/A. **Day:** Wd £25. We £35.
FACILITIES: None.

BRAMHALL GOLF CLUB   MAP 8 A3

Clubhouse, Ladythorn Road, Bramhall, Stockport SK7 2EY.
8 miles south of Manchester on A5102.

CONTACT: JG Lee, Hon. Secretary. Tel: 061 439 6092.
COURSE: 6,280yds, PAR 70, SSS 70. Parkland course.
SOC RESTR'S: Min. 24. Welcome Wednesdays.
SOC GF - Round: Wd N/A. We N/A. **Day:** Wd £25. We N/A.
SOC PACK: Catering arranged through Club Steward.
VIS RESTR'S: Welcome except Thur 8-2; Sat 8-5; Sun 8-12.
VIS GF - Round: Wd N/A. We £35. **Day:** Wd £25. We N/A.
FACILITIES: Snooker, Bar & Dining Room.

BROOKDALE GOLF CLUB   MAP 8 A2/3

Ashbridge, Woodhouse, Failsworth, Manchester M35 9WQ.
5 miles north of Manchester.

CONTACT: G Glass, Hon. Secretary. Tel: 061 681 8996.
COURSE: 6,008yds, PAR 68, SSS 68. Parkland course.
SOC RESTR'S: One months notice required.
SOC GF - Round: Wd £15. We N/A. **Day:** Wd £18. We N/A.
SOC PACK: Coffee, Lunch, Dinner, 27 holes: £25.
VIS RESTR'S: Restricted on Sunday.
VIS GF - Round: Wd £18. We £21. **Day:** Wd N/A. We N/A.
FACILITIES: Usual Golf Club facilities.

DIDSBURY GOLF CLUB   MAP 8 A3

Ford Lane, Northenden, Manchester M22 4NQ.
6 miles south of Manchester.

CONTACT: C Turnbull, Secretary/Manager. Tel: 061 998 9278.
COURSE: 6,273yds, PAR 70, SSS 70. Parkland course.
SOC RESTR'S: Max. 60. Welcome Thur & Fri.
SOC GF - Round: Wd N/A. We N/A. **Day:** Wd £25. We N/A.
SOC PACK: Coffee, Lunch, Dinner, 27 holes: £35-£40.
VIS RESTR'S: Welcome daily 10-12 & 2-4. H'cap Cert required.
VIS GF - Round: Wd N/A. We N/A. **Day:** Wd £22. We £25.
FACILITIES: 2 Practice Grounds, Licensed Dining Room.

DUNHAM FOREST G & CC   MAP 8 A3

Oldfield Lane, Altrincham, Cheshire WA14 4TY.
1.5 miles west off A56.

CONTACT: Mrs S Klaus, Secretary. Tel: 061 928 2605.
COURSE: 6,636yds, PAR 72, SSS 72. Wooded parkland course.
SOC RESTR'S: Min. 20. Welcome Mon, Thur & Fri.
SOC GF - Round: Wd £25. We N/A. **Day:** Wd £30. We N/A.
SOC PACK: £35-£45.
VIS RESTR'S: Welcome except 12.30-1.30 Weekdays. Phone first.
VIS GF - Round: Wd £25. We N/A. **Day:** Wd £30. We N/A.
FACILITIES: Bar & Restaurant.

DUNSCAR GOLF CLUB   MAP 8 A2

Longworth Lane, Bromley Cross, Bolton BL7 9QY.
1.5 miles north of Bolton off A666.

CONTACT: M Yates, Hon. Secretary. Tel: 0204 301090.
COURSE: 6,050yds, PAR 71, SSS 69. Flat moorland course.
SOC RESTR'S: Welcome Weekdays.
SOC GF - Round: Wd N/A. We N/A. **Day:** Wd N/A. We N/A.
SOC PACK: GF for parties: 1-12 ; £20. 13-24; £18. 25+ £17.
VIS RESTR'S: Not before 9.30 nor between 12-1.30.
VIS GF - Round: Wd £20. We £30. **Day:** Wd £20. We £30.
FACILITIES: Bar & Restaurant.

ENGLAND

ELLESMERE GOLF CLUB MAP 8 A2

Old Clough Lane, Worsley, Manchester M28 5HZ.
7 miles west of Manchester, off East Lanes Road.

CONTACT: A Kay, Hon. Assistant Secretary. Tel: 061 790 2122.
COURSE: 5,954yds, PAR 69, SSS 69. Parkland course.
SOC RESTR'S: Welcome Mon, Tues (Wed October to March).
SOC GF - Round: Wd N/A. We N/A. **Day:** Wd £18. We N/A.
SOC PACK: £25.
VIS RESTR'S: Not on Comp days or Bank Hols. Check with Pro.
VIS GF - Round: Wd N/A. We N/A. **Day:** Wd £18. We £22.
FACILITIES: Bar & Meals.

MANCHESTER GOLF CLUB MAP 8 A2

Hopwood Cottage, Middleton, Manchester M24 2QP.
J20 M62 7 miles north of Manchester.

CONTACT: KG Flett, Sec/General Manager. Tel: 061 643 3202.
COURSE: 6,464yds, PAR 72, SSS 72. Parkland/moorland.
SOC RESTR'S: Max 120. Welcome Weekdays.
SOC GF - Round: Wd £25. We N/A. **Day:** Wd £25. We N/A.
SOC PACK: Coffee, Lunch, Dinner, Golf: £35-£38.
VIS RESTR'S: Not on Comp Days, 12-1.30 Weekdays reserved.
VIS GF - Round: Wd £25. We N/A. **Day:** Wd £35. We N/A.
FACILITIES: Bar, Restaurant & Range.

MELLOR & TOWNSCLIFFE GC MAP 8 A3

Gibb Lane, Mellor, Stockport, Cheshire SK6 5NA.
7 miles south-east of Stockport.

CONTACT: DA Ogden, Secretary. Tel: 061 427 2208.
COURSE: 5,925yds, PAR 70, SSS 69. Parkland/hilly course.
SOC RESTR'S: Wed pm. No Sat. No catering Tues
SOC GF - Round: Wd £18. We N/A. **Day:** Wd £18. We £25.
SOC PACK: Weekday approx £28.
VIS RESTR'S: No casual visitors at the Weekend.
VIS GF - Round: Wd £18. We N/A. **Day:** Wd £18. We N/A.
FACILITIES: None.

NEW NORTH MANCHESTER GC MAP 8 A2

Rhodes House, Middleton, Manchester M24 4PE.
5 miles north of Manchester.

CONTACT: A Hodgkinson, Secretary. Tel: 061 643 9033.
COURSE: 6,527yds, PAR 72, SSS 72. Undulating parkland course.
SOC RESTR'S: Welcome Monday to Wednesday.
SOC GF - Round: Wd £18. We N/A **Day:** Wd £22. We N/A.
SOC PACK: Available on booking.
VIS RESTR'S: Welcome except Competition Days or Weekends.
VIS GF - Round: Wd £18. We N/A **Day:** Wd £22. We N/A.
FACILITIES: Catering every day except Tuesday.

REDDISH VALE GOLF CLUB MAP 8 A3

Southcliffe Road, Reddish, Stockport SK5 7EE.
About 1 mile north-east of Stockport.

CONTACT: J Blakey, Hon. Secretary. Tel: 061 480 2359.
COURSE: 6,086yds, PAR 69, SSS 69. Undulating moorland course.
SOC RESTR'S: Welcome Weekdays except between 12.30-1.30.
SOC GF - Round: Wd £20. We N/A. **Day:** Wd £20. We N/A.
SOC PACK: £17 for over 20. Lunch, Dinner, 27 holes: £30.
VIS RESTR'S: Welcome Weekdays except between 12.30-1.30.
VIS GF - Round: Wd £20. We N/A. **Day:** Wd £20. We N/A.
FACILITIES: Bar & Restaurant.

RINGWAY GOLF CLUB MAP 8 A3

Hale Mount, Hale Barns, Altrincham, Cheshire WA15 8SW.
M56 - Junction 6 - 8 miles south of Manchester.

CONTACT: D Wright, Secretary. Tel: 061 980 2630.
COURSE: 6,494yds, PAR 71, SSS 71. Parkland course.
SOC RESTR'S: On application from Club Secretary.
SOC GF - Round: Wd £26. We N/A. **Day:** Wd £26. We N/A.
SOC PACK: Available on booking.
VIS RESTR'S: Not on Tues, Fri or Sat which are Comp Days.
VIS GF - Round: Wd £26. We £32. **Day:** Wd £26. We £32.
FACILITIES: Bar & Restaurant.

ROCHDALE GOLF CLUB MAP 8 A2

Edenfield Road, Bagslate, Rochdale, Lancs OL11 5YR.
M62 Junction 20 then A680 for 3 miles.

CONTACT: S Cockcroft, Hon. Secretary. Tel: 0706 43818.
COURSE: 6,002yds, PAR 71, SSS 69. Parkland course.
SOC RESTR'S: Welcome Wednesday any size - Friday limit 24.
SOC GF - Round: Wd £20. We N/A. **Day:** Wd £20. We N/A.
SOC PACK: None.
VIS RESTR'S: Welcome except Tuesday, Thursday & Saturday.
VIS GF - Round: Wd £20. We £24. **Day:** Wd £40. We £24.
FACILITIES: Bar & Restaurant.

ROMILEY GOLF CLUB MAP 8 A3

Goosehouse Green, Romiley, Stockport SK6 4LJ.
Close to the village centre of Romiley.

CONTACT: F Beard, Hon. Secretary. Tel: 061 430 7257.
COURSE: 6,421yds, PAR 70, SSS 71. Parkland course.
SOC RESTR'S: Welcome Tuesdays & Wednesdays.
SOC GF - Round: Wd £22. We N/A. **Day:** Wd £28. We N/A.
SOC PACK: Over 30 by arrangement, £18 per round, £20 per day.
VIS RESTR'S: Welcome any day.
VIS GF - Round: Wd £22. We £33. **Day:** Wd £28. We N/A.
FACILITIES: Bar & Restaurant.

Merseyside

SADDLEWORTH GOLF CLUB   MAP 8 A2

Mountain Ash, Ladcastle Road, Nr. Oldham, Lancs.
5 miles east of Oldham.

CONTACT: H. A. Morgan, Secretary. Tel: 0457 873653.
COURSE: 5,976yds, PAR 71, SSS 69. Moorland course.
SOC RESTR'S: Welcome Weekdays.
SOC GF - Round: Wd N/A. We N/A. Day: Wd £30. We N/A.
SOC PACK: £30 - Parties of 12 or more.
VIS RESTR'S: Welcome but phone for availability.
VIS GF - Round: Wd £22. We £25. Day: Wd £22. We £25.
FACILITIES: Bar, Snooker & Clubhouse.

SALE GOLF CLUB   MAP 8 A3

Sale Lodge, Golf Road, Sale, Cheshire M33 2LU.
M63, Junction 8 to A6144, north of town.

CONTACT: J Prow, Hon. Secretary. Tel: 061 973 1638.
COURSE: 6,351yds, PAR 71, SSS 70. Parkland course.
SOC RESTR'S: Welcome except Weekends.
SOC GF - Round: Wd N/A. We N/A. Day: Wd £20. We N/A.
SOC PACK: £30.
VIS RESTR'S: Please phone prior to play.
VIS GF - Round: Wd N/A. We N/A. Day: Wd £20. We £30.
FACILITIES: Snooker.

WITHINGTON GOLF CLUB   MAP 8 A3

Palatine Road, West Didsbury, Manchester M20 8UD.
6 miles south of Manchester.

CONTACT: A Larsen, Secretary. Tel: 061 445 9544.
COURSE: 6,411yds, PAR 71, SSS 71. Typical parkland course.
SOC RESTR'S: Welcome Mon, Tues, Wed & Fri.
SOC GF - Round: Wd N/A. We N/A. Day: Wd £22. We N/A.
SOC PACK: Lunch, Dinner, 27 holes: £35
VIS RESTR'S: Welcome Wd except Thur. Phone Pro re times.
VIS GF - Round: Wd £22. We N/A. Day: Wd N/A. We N/A.
FACILITIES: Bar & Restaurant.

BOOTLE GOLF CLUB   MAP 5 A3

Dunnings Bridge Road, Bootle, Merseyside L30 2PP.
5 miles north of Liverpool.

CONTACT: J Morgan, Secretary. Tel: 051 922 4792.
COURSE: 6,362yds, PAR 71, SSS 70. Links course.
SOC RESTR'S: Please book through Secretary.
SOC GF - Round: Wd £4. We £6. Day: Wd N/A. We N/A.
SOC PACK: Available on booking from Secretary.
VIS RESTR'S: Welcome all Weekdays & Weekends pm.
VIS GF - Round: Wd £4. We £6. Day: Wd N/A. We N/A.
FACILITIES: Bar.

GRANGE PARK GOLF CLUB   MAP 2 B1

Prescot Road, St. Helens, Merseyside WA10 3AD.
1.5 miles south-west of St. Helens on A58.

CONTACT: D Wood, Secretary/Manager. Tel: 0744 26318.
COURSE: 6,480yds, PAR 72, SSS 71. Parkland course.
SOC RESTR'S: Welcome Mon, Wed & Fri by arrangement.
SOC GF - Round: Wd £21. We N/A. Day: Wd £28. We N/A.
SOC PACK: Coffee, Lunch, Dinner, 27 holes: £31.50.
VIS RESTR'S: Welcome Mon-Fri & Sun with Letter of Intro.
VIS GF - Round: Wd £21. We £28. Day: Wd £28. We N/A.
FACILITIES: Snooker.

HAYDOCK PARK GOLF CLUB   MAP 5 A3

Rob Lane, Newton-le-Willows, Merseyside WA12 0HX.
Off Junction 23 on M6 - A580.

CONTACT: G Tait, Secretary. Tel: 0925 228525.
COURSE: 6,043yds, PAR 70, SSS 69. Parkland/wooded.
SOC RESTR'S: On application from Club Secretary.
SOC GF - Round: Wd £22. We N/A. Day: Wd £22. We N/A.
SOC PACK: £30 to £35.
VIS RESTR'S: Welcome Weekdays.
VIS GF - Round: Wd £22. We N/A. Day: Wd £22. We N/A.
FACILITIES: Bar & Restaurant.

RAC HOTEL GUIDE
Great Britain & Ireland

Now in its **ninetieth year**,
the authoritative guide to over 6,000 hotels.
Special anniversary competition.
All establishments inspected and approved by the RAC.
Full colour atlas section with all hotel locations shown
Includes discount vouchers worth up to £150
Price £12.99
Available from bookshops
or direct from the RAC on 0235 834885

ENGLAND

HESWELL GOLF CLUB
MAP 2 B1

Cottage Lane, Gayton Heswell, Wirral, Cheshire L60 8PB.
8 miles north-west of Chester, off the A540.

CONTACT: C Peter, R Calvert, Secretaries. Tel: 051 342 1237.
COURSE: 6,472yds, PAR 72, SSS 72. Parkland course.
SOC RESTR'S: Min. 24. Welcome Wednesday & Friday.
SOC GF - Round: Wd N/A. **We** N/A. **Day:** Wd £30. **We** N/A.
SOC PACK: None.
VIS RESTR'S: Not before 9.30. H'cap Cert required.
VIS GF - Round: Wd N/A. **We** N/A. **Day:** Wd £30. **We** £35.
FACILITIES: Bar, Snooker & Large Practice Area.

PRENTON GOLF CLUB
MAP 2 B1

Golf Links Road, Prenton, Birkenhead, Merseyside L42 8LW.
M53 Junction 3 off A552, 2 miles west of Birkenhead.

CONTACT: W Disley, Secretary/Manager. Tel: 051 608 1053.
COURSE: 6,411yds, PAR 71, SSS 71. Level parkland course.
SOC RESTR'S: Welcome usually Wednesdays & Fridays.
SOC GF - Round: Wd £22. **We** N/A. **Day:** Wd £22. **We** N/A.
SOC PACK: By application from Secretary.
VIS RESTR'S: Welcome.
VIS GF - Round: Wd £23. **We** £25. **Day:** Wd £23. **We** £25.
FACILITIES: Full catering available.

ROYAL BIRKDALE GOLF CLUB
MAP 5 A3

Waterloo Road, Birkdale, Southport PR8 2LX.
2 miles south of Southport.

CONTACT: NT Crewe, Secretary. Tel: 0704 67920.
COURSE: 6,703yds, PAR 72, SSS 73. Champ'ship seaside course.
SOC RESTR'S: Welcome Weekdays by arrangement.
SOC GF - Round: Wd N/A. **We** N/A. **Day:** Wd £70. **We** N/A.
SOC PACK: Package for 20+. Details available on booking.
VIS RESTR'S: By arrangement with Sec. H'cap Cert required.
VIS GF - Round: Wd £50. **We** £70. **Day:** Wd £70. **We** N/A.
FACILITIES: Normal Clubhouse facilities.

Balmoral Lodge Hotel
Queens Road, Southport
Tel: (0704) 544298 & 530751
Fax: (0704) 501224

RAC
★★

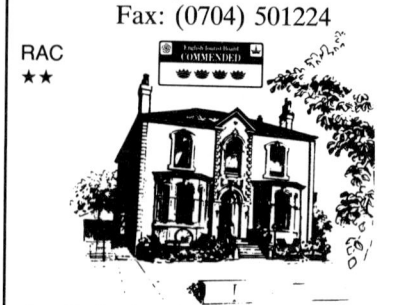

English Tourist Board
COMMENDED

A small select hotel for those requiring a higher than usual standard. All bedrooms have en suite bathrooms, TV, radio, tea/coffee facilities, direct dial telephones, hair dryers and trouser presses. The Tudor style bar has access to picturesque garden for sunbathing or open air lunch. A newly built garden wing offers deluxe twin rooms with garden balconies. A sauna bath is available to all guests free of charge. Comprehensive menu and wine list makes candlelight dining a delight. Short breaks and weekly rates quoted.
Golf packages arranged on request.

HILLSIDE GOLF CLUB
MAP 5 A3

Hastings Road, Hillside, Southport, Merseyside PR8 2LU.
From M6 on to A570 to town centre then A565.

CONTACT: J Graham, Secretary/Manager. Tel: 0704 67169.
COURSE: 6,850yds, PAR 72, SSS 74. Links course.
SOC RESTR'S: Welcome except Tuesday morning & Weekends.
SOC GF - Round: Wd £35. **We** N/A. **Day:** Wd £45. **We** N/A.
SOC PACK: None.
VIS RESTR'S: Wd not Tues am. Occasional Tues pm & Sun.
VIS GF - Round: Wd £35. **We** £45. **Day:** Wd £45. **We** N/A.
FACILITIES: Practice Ground, Snooker, Restaurant & Lounge/Bar.

STUTELEA HOTEL
& Leisure Club

**ALEXANDRA ROAD
SOUTHPORT PR9 0NB
TEL (0704) 544220**

20 De-Luxe Bedrooms (Single to Family Suites) all with Private Bathroom.
8 Apartments (Studio to 2 Bedroomed) all with Private Bathroom and fitted Kitchen.
All Accommodation has Colour TV, Radio, Direct Dial Telephone, Hair Dryers, Trouser Press, and Tea/Coffee Making Facilities.
Heated Indoor Swimming Pool, Jacuzzi, Steam Room, Scandinavian Sauna, Solarium, Gymnasium, Games Room, Gardens and Car Park, 2 Licensed Bars, Restaurant, Lounge with Library. Lift.

FAX: 0704 500232

R.A.C.
★★

MIDDLESEX

THE Bold HOTEL

LORD STREET, SOUTHPORT
Tel: (0704) 532578

Situated on the beautiful Lord St Boulevard convenient for many great golf courses.
23 en-suite bedrooms, recently refurbished Bistro 585. Renowned for fresh fish and gourmet meals at competitive prices. Popular bars and bar food. Raphael's Club at the rear of the hotel with late licence 2am.

★★ RAC   Egon Ronay

WOOLTON GOLF CLUB   MAP 2 B1

Doe Park, Speke Road, Woolton, Liverpool L25 7TZ.
6 miles from City Centre, 1 mile from Woolton village.

CONTACT: KG Jennions, Secretary/Manager. Tel: 051 486 2298.
COURSE: 5,706yds, PAR 69, SSS 68. Parkland course.
SOC RESTR'S: Welcome except Tuesdays & Weekends.
SOC GF - Round: Wd N/A. We N/A. **Day:** Wd £21. We N/A.
SOC PACK: Available on booking.
VIS RESTR'S: Welcome except Tuesdays. Booking required.
VIS GF - Round: Wd £21. We £25. **Day:** Wd £21. We £25.
FACILITIES: Bar & Restaurant.

Middlesex

ROYAL LIVERPOOL GOLF CLUB   MAP 2 A1

Meols Drive, Hoylake, Wirral, Merseyside L47 4AL.
A553 to Hoylake - 10 miles west of Liverpool.

CONTACT: C Moore, Secretary. Tel: 051 632 3101.
COURSE: 6,821yds, PAR 72, SSS 74. Links course.
SOC RESTR'S: Welcome Wednesday & Friday.
SOC GF - Round: Wd £35. We N/A. **Day:** Wd £35. We N/A.
SOC PACK: Light Lunch, Dinner, 36 holes: £60+.
VIS RESTR'S: Not before 9.30 or between 1-2. Some We.
VIS GF - Round: Wd £35. We £50. **Day:** Wd £50. We £75.
FACILITIES: Normal Clubhouse facilities (Snooker).

WALLASEY GOLF CLUB   MAP 5 A3

Bayswater Road, Wallasey, Merseyside L45 8LA.
Junction 1 off M53 take A554 to New Brighton.

CONTACT: Mrs L Dolman, Secretary/Manager. Tel: 051 691 1024.
COURSE: 6,605yds, PAR 72, SSS 73. Seaside links.
SOC RESTR'S: Min. 16. Mon-Fri. 9.30-11.30 & 2.30-4.30 res.
SOC GF - Round: Wd £21. We N/A **Day:** Wd £27. We N/A.
SOC PACK: GF paid to Club. Food as required paid to Caterer.
VIS RESTR'S: Welcome by reservation.
VIS GF - Round: Wd £25. We N/A. **Day:** Wd £30. We N/A.
FACILITIES: Bar, Snooker & Clubhouse.

AIRLINKS GOLF CLUB   MAP 7 A2

Southall Lane, Hounslow, Middlesex TW5 9PE.
Junction 3 on M4, A312 to Hayes.

CONTACT: P Watson, PR Manager. Tel: 081 561 1418.
COURSE: 5,885yds, PAR 71, SSS 69. Flat parkland course.
SOC RESTR'S: Any number considered - 7 days a week.
SOC GF - Round: Wd £10.40 We £13. **Day:** Wd N/A. We N/A.
SOC PACK: Coffee, Lunch, Dinner, 36 holes: £35-£40.
VIS RESTR'S: Booking advised with seven days notice.
VIS GF - Round: Wd £10.40 We £13. **Day:** Wd N/A. We N/A.
FACILITIES: Driving Range, Bar & Restaurant.

EALING GOLF CLUB   MAP 7 A2

Perivale Lane, Greenford, Middlesex UB6 8SS.
Off A40 opposite Hoover Building.

CONTACT: M Scargill, Secretary. Tel: 081 997 0937.
COURSE: 6,216yds, PAR 70, SSS 70. Parkland course.
SOC RESTR'S: Welcome Mon, Wed & Thur. Size by arrangement.
SOC GF - Round: Wd £30. We N/A. **Day:** Wd £30. We N/A.
SOC PACK: Coffee, Lunch, Dinner, 36 holes: £45 + VAT.
VIS RESTR'S: Welcome Weekdays. H'cap Cert required.
VIS GF - Round: Wd £30. We N/A. **Day:** Wd £30. We N/A.
FACILITIES: Bar & Restaurant.

ENGLAND

ENFIELD GOLF CLUB MAP 7 B2

Old Park Road South, Enfield, Middlesex EN2 7DA.
Junction 24 M25 - A1005 to Enfield.

CONTACT: N Challis, Secretary/Manager. Tel: 081 342 0313.
COURSE: 6,154yds, PAR 72, SSS 70. Parkland course.
SOC RESTR'S: Welcome Mon, Wed & Fri.
SOC GF - Round: Wd N/A. **We** N/A. **Day: Wd** £27. **We** N/A.
SOC PACK: Coffee, Lunch, Dinner, 36 holes: £45.
VIS RESTR'S: Welcome Weekdays. Must have H'cap Cert.
VIS GF - Round: Wd £20. **We** N/A. **Day: Wd** £30. **We** N/A.
FACILITIES: Conference facility for up to 150 people.

FULWELL GOLF CLUB MAP 7 A2

Wellington Road, Hampton Hill, Middlesex TW12 1JY.
Opposite Fulwell Station.

CONTACT: CA Brown, Secretary. Tel: 081 977 3188.
COURSE: 6,544yds, PAR 71, SSS 71. Parkland course.
SOC RESTR'S: No weekends. Letter of Intro required.
SOC GF - Round: Wd N/A. **We** N/A. **Day: Wd** £40. **We** N/A.
SOC PACK: On application.
VIS RESTR'S: Letter of Intro required. We occasionally.
VIS GF - Round: Wd £25. **We** £35. **Day: Wd** N/A. **We** N/A.
FACILITIES: Lunch (except Monday), Bar snacks, Pro shop.

HAREFIELD PLACE GOLF CLUB MAP 7 A2

The Drive, Harefield Place, Uxbridge, Middlesex UB10 8PA.
A40 - Harefield turn-off. 2 miles north of Uxbridge.

CONTACT: P Howard, Head Professional. Tel: 0895 237287.
COURSE: 5,753yds, PAR 68, SSS 68. Parkland course.
SOC RESTR'S: Thursdays are Society Days.
SOC GF - Round: Wd N/A. **We** N/A. **Day: Wd** N/A. **We** N/A.
SOC PACK: From £39.50.
VIS RESTR'S: Welcome.
VIS GF - Round: Wd £9.25. **We** £12.50. **Day: Wd** N/A. **We** N/A.
FACILITIES: Function Room, Bar & Restaurant.

PINNER HILL GOLF CLUB MAP 7 A2

Southview Road, Pinner Hill, Middlesex HA5 3YA.
1 mile west from Pinner Green.

CONTACT: J Devitt, Secretary. Tel: 081 866 2109.
COURSE: 6,280yds, PAR 72, SSS 70. Hilly parkland course.
SOC RESTR'S: Welcome Mon & Fri - sometimes Tues.
SOC GF - Round: Wd N/A. **We** N/A. **Day: Wd** N/A. **We** N/A.
SOC PACK: Coffee, Lunch, Dinner, 36 holes: £45.
VIS RESTR'S: Welcome with H'cap Cert by prior arrangement.
VIS GF - Round: Wd £8* **We** £11. **Day: Wd** N/A. **We** N/A.
FACILITIES: *Special Pub Days Wed & Thur, no access to Clubhouse.

SANDY LODGE GOLF CLUB MAP 7 A2

Sandy Lodge Lane, Northwood, Middlesex HA6 2JD.
Adjacent Moor Park Station.

CONTACT: JN Blair, Secretary. Tel: 0923 825429.
COURSE: 6,340yds, PAR 70, SSS 70. Heathland/links-type course.
SOC RESTR'S: H'cap Cert required. Book in advance.
SOC GF - Round: Wd N/A. **We** N/A. **Day: Wd** N/A. **We** N/A.
SOC PACK: On application.
VIS RESTR'S: Must have H'cap Cert or be with Member.
VIS GF - Round: Wd £25. **We** N/A. **Day: Wd** N/A. **We** N/A.
FACILITIES: Bar snacks & Pro-shop.

WEST MIDDLESEX GOLF CLUB MAP 7 A2

Greenford Road, Southall, Middlesex UB1 3EE.
On the A4127 west of Southall.

CONTACT: P Furness, Secretary. Tel: 081 574 3450.
COURSE: 6,242yds, PAR 69, SSS 70. Undulating parkland.
SOC RESTR'S: Applications in writing considered.
SOC GF - Round: Wd £17. **We** N/A. **Day: Wd** £30. **We** N/A.
SOC PACK: On application.
VIS RESTR'S: Welcome Wd. Reduced GF Mon & Wed.
VIS GF - Round: Wd £17. **We** N/A. **Day: Wd** £30. **We** N/A.
FACILITIES: Bar, Restaurant & Pro-shop.

WYKE GREEN GOLF CLUB MAP 7 A2

Syon Lane, Isleworth, Middlesex TW7 5PT.
Half-a-mile north of A4 near Gillette Corner.

CONTACT: D Wentworth-Pollock, Sec/Manager. Tel: 081 560 8777.
COURSE: 6,242yds, PAR 69, SSS 70. Parkland course.
SOC RESTR'S: Min. 20. Welcome Tues, Wed & Thur.
SOC GF - Round: Wd £31. **We** N/A. **Day: Wd** £31. **We** N/A.
SOC PACK: Coffee, Lunch, Dinner + 2 rounds: £49.
VIS RESTR'S: Welcome Wd by appoint. After 3pm We.
VIS GF - Round: Wd £28. **We** N/A. **Day: Wd** £28. **We** N/A.
FACILITIES: Bar, Snacks.

RAC HOTELS IN EUROPE

The ideal 'travel companion' with over 1,500 selected hotels in 20 countries, including Eastern Europe. Hotel entries contain phone and fax numbers, national star rating, restaurant, prices, credit cards and where English is spoken. Full colour atlas section with all hotel locations shown. Parking law - Speed limits - Public holidays - Banks - Shops - Fuel availability
Price £9.99
Available from bookshops
or direct from the RAC on 0235 834885

NORFOLK

Norfolk

HUNSTANTON GOLF CLUB — MAP 3 B1

Golf Links Road, Hunstanton, Norfolk PE36 6JQ.
Half-a-mile north-east of Hunstanton.

CONTACT: RH Cotton, Secretary. Tel: 0485 532811.
COURSE: 6,670yds, PAR 72, SSS 72. Links course.
SOC RESTR'S: Max. 40. Wd after 9.30. H'cap Cert required.
SOC GF - Round: Wd N/A. We N/A. **Day:** Wd £30. We N/A.
SOC PACK: None.
VIS RESTR'S: Wd after 9.30, We restricted. H'cap Cert required.
VIS GF - Round: Wd N/A. We N/A. **Day:** Wd £30. We £36.
FACILITIES: None.

BARNHAM BROOM (HILL) — MAP 3 B1

Barnham Broom, Norwich, Norfolk NR9 4DD.
8 miles south-west of Norwich between A11 & A47.

CONTACT: P Ballingall, Golf Director. Tel: 060 545393.
COURSE: 6,628yds, PAR 72, SSS 72. Meadowland course.
SOC RESTR'S: Welcome on application.
SOC GF - Round: Wd £25. We N/A. **Day:** Wd £30. We N/A.
SOC PACK: Available on application.
VIS RESTR'S: Welcome H'cap Cert required.
VIS GF - Round: Wd £25. We N/A. **Day:** Wd £30. We N/A.
FACILITIES: Full Hotel, Restaurant & Leisure facilities.

BARNHAM BROOM (VALLEY) — MAP 3 B1

Barnham Broom, Norwich, Norfolk NR9 4DD.
8 miles south-west of Norwich between A11 & A47.

CONTACT: P Ballingall, Golf Director. Tel: 060 545393.
COURSE: 6,470yds, PAR 72, SSS 71. Parkland course.
SOC RESTR'S: Welcome on application.
SOC GF - Round: Wd £25. We N/A. **Day:** Wd £30. We N/A.
SOC PACK: Available on application.
VIS RESTR'S: Welcome. H'cap Cert required.
VIS GF - Round: Wd £25. We N/A. **Day:** Wd £30. We N/A.
FACILITIES: Full Hotel, Restaurant & Leisure facilities.

COSTESSEY PARK GOLF CLUB — MAP 3 B1

Costessey Park, Old Costessey, Norwich NR8 5AL.
3 miles west of Norwich.

CONTACT: CL House MD. Tel: 0603 746333.
COURSE: 5,853yds, PAR 72, SSS 68. Parkland course.
SOC RESTR'S: Not usually at Weekends.
SOC GF - Round: Wd N/A. We N/A. **Day:** Wd £14. We N/A.
SOC PACK: Coffee, Lunch, Dinner, 36 holes: £25.
VIS RESTR'S: Welcome all Weekdays & after 11.30 Weekends.
VIS GF - Round: Wd N/A. We N/A. **Day:** Wd £14. We £17.
FACILITIES: Bar & Restaurant.

KING'S LYNN GOLF CLUB — MAP 3 B1

Castle Rising, King's Lynn, Norfolk PE31 6BD.
Take A149 from Kings Lynn. Turn left at Castle Rising sign.

CONTACT: GT Higgins, Secretary. Tel: 0553 631654.
COURSE: 6,646yds, PAR 72, SSS 72. Wooded parkland course.
SOC RESTR'S: Welcome Thursday & Friday.
SOC GF - Round: Wd N/A. We N/A. **Day:** Wd £30. We N/A.
SOC PACK: £40-£50 depending upon catering requirements.
VIS RESTR'S: Welcome except Tues. H'cap Cert required.
VIS GF - Round: Wd £25. We £33. **Day:** Wd £30. We N/A.
FACILITIES: None.

ROYAL CROMER GOLF CLUB — MAP 3 B1

Overstrand Road, Cromer, Norfolk NR27 0JH.
On the B1159, 1 mile east of Cromer.

CONTACT: BA Howson, Secretary. Tel: 0263 512884.
COURSE: 6,508yds, PAR 72, SSS 71. Undulating seaside course.
SOC RESTR'S: On application from Club Secretary for Weekdays.
SOC GF - Round: Wd N/A. We N/A. **Day:** Wd £25. We N/A.
SOC PACK: Available on booking from Secretary.
VIS RESTR'S: Must have H'cap Cert. Seasonal changes to GF.
VIS GF - Round: Wd N/A. We N/A **Day:** Wd £25. We £30.
FACILITIES: Practice Ground & Catering facilities.

ROYAL WEST NORFOLK GC — MAP 3 B1

Brancaster, Nr. King's Lynn, Norfolk PE31 8AX.
7 miles east of Hunstanton on A419.

CONTACT: NA Carrington-Smith, Sec. Tel: 0485 210087.
COURSE: 6,428yds, PAR 71, SSS 71. Links course.
SOC RESTR'S: Not between last week in July - 1st week in Sept.
SOC GF - Round: Wd £30. We £40. **Day:** Wd £30. We £40.
SOC PACK: No packages.
VIS RESTR'S: Not before 10 Sun or Aug-Sept. H'cap Cert req.
VIS GF - Round: Wd £30. We £40. **Day:** Wd £30. We £40.
FACILITIES: Practice Area, Changing Rooms & Dining Room.

ENGLAND

THETFORD GOLF CLUB   MAP 3 B2

Brandon Road, Thetford, Norfolk IP24 3NE.
A11 - B1107 to Brandon - Half-a-mile on left.

CONTACT: RJ Ferguson, Secretary. Tel: 0842 752169.
COURSE: 6,879yds, PAR 72, SSS 73. Long heathland course.
SOC RESTR'S: Welcome Wednesday, Thursday & Friday.
SOC GF - Round: Wd £28. We N/A. **Day:** Wd £28. We N/A.
SOC PACK: With Lunch & Dinner about £42.
VIS RESTR'S: Welcome Weekdays.
VIS GF - Round: Wd £28. We £33. **Day:** Wd £28. We £33.
FACILITIES: None.

WENSUM VALLEY GOLF CLUB   MAP 3 B1

Beech Avenue, Taverham, Norwich NR8 6HP.
4 miles north-west of Norwich on A1067.

CONTACT: Miss B Todd, Secretary. Tel: 0603 261012.
COURSE: 6,000yds, PAR 72, SSS 68. Parkland course.
SOC RESTR'S: No restrictions.
SOC GF - Round: Wd N/A. We N/A. **Day:** Wd £12. We £15.
SOC PACK: Coffee, Lunch, Dinner, 36 holes - £25.
VIS RESTR'S: Welcome all Weekdays & after 12 at Weekends.
VIS GF - Round: Wd N/A. We N/A. **Day:** Wd £12. We £15.
FACILITIES: Bar & Restaurant.

Northamptonshire

COLD ASHBY GOLF CLUB   MAP 3 A2

Cold Ashby, Northampton NN6 7EP.
Between Northampton & Leicester, 5 miles east of J18, M1.

CONTACT: D Croxton, Proprietor. Tel: 0604 740548.
COURSE: 6,007yds, PAR 70, SSS 69. Scenic parkland course.
SOC RESTR'S: Welcome Weekdays.
SOC GF - Round: Wd £14. We N/A. **Day:** Wd £19. We N/A.
SOC PACK: Coffee, Lunch, Dinner + 2 rounds: £33.
VIS RESTR'S: Welcome all Weekdays & after 2. Weekends.
VIS GF - Round: Wd £14. We £15. **Day:** Wd £18. We N/A.
FACILITIES: None.

COLLINGTREE PARK GOLF CLUB   MAP 3 A2

Windingbrook Lane, Northampton NN4 0XM.
Half mile east of M1 junction 15.

CONTACT: Ms Gill Peters, Secretary. Tel: 0604 700000.
COURSE: 6,821yds, PAR 72, SSS 73. Resort course.
SOC RESTR'S: H'cap Cert required. Book in advance.
SOC GF - Round: Wd N/A. We N/A. **Day:** Wd £40. We N/A.
SOC PACK: Seasonal rate available.
VIS RESTR'S: Handicap Certificate required.
VIS GF - Round: Wd £25. We £40. **Day:** Wd N/A. We N/A.
FACILITIES: Driving Range, Bar, Restaurant, Pro shop.

FARTHINGSTONE GOLF CENTRE   MAP 3 A2

Farthingstone, Nr. Towcester, Northamptonshire NN12 8HA.
M1 J16 - A45 to Weedon - Farthingstone - Everdon Rd.

CONTACT: D Donaldson, Proprietor. Tel: 0327 36291.
COURSE: 6,248yds, PAR 71, SSS 71. Parkland course.
SOC RESTR'S: No restrictions.
SOC GF - Round: Wd N/A. We N/A. **Day:** Wd N/A. We N/A.
SOC PACK: £38 Full Day. £29. 50 Half Day.
VIS RESTR'S: Welcome. Please phone prior to play.
VIS GF - Round: Wd £15. We £20. **Day:** Wd £25. We £30.
FACILITIES: 2 Squash Courts, Snooker, Bar & Restaurant.

HELLIDON LAKES G & CC   MAP 3 A2

Hellidon, Nr. Daventry, Northamptonshire NN11 6LN.
M1 Junction 16 - A45 Daventry - A361 Banbury - Hellidon.

CONTACT: P Gill, General Manager. Tel: 0327 62550.
COURSE: 6,700yds, PAR 72, SSS 72. Parkland course.
SOC RESTR'S: Max. 20. Welcome Weekdays.
SOC GF - Round: Wd £19. We N/A. **Day:** Wd N/A. We N/A.
SOC PACK: Coffee, Luncheon, Dinner, 36 holes - £50.
VIS RESTR'S: Welcome. H'cap Cert required at We.
VIS GF - Round: Wd £19. We £26 **Day:** Wd N/A. We N/A.
FACILITIES: Fly Fishing, Tennis, Health Studio & Restaurants.

KETTERING GOLF CLUB   MAP 3 A2

Headlands, Kettering, Northamptonshire NN15 6XA.
South end of Headlands which is continuation of High St.

CONTACT: D Buckby, Secretary. Tel: 0536 511104.
COURSE: 6,087yds, PAR 69, SSS 69. Meadowland course.
SOC RESTR'S: Welcome Wednesday & Friday.
SOC GF - Round: Wd £18. We N/A. **Day:** Wd £18. We N/A.
SOC PACK: Approx £35 per head.
VIS RESTR'S: Welcome Weekdays.
VIS GF - Round: Wd £20. We N/A. **Day:** Wd £20. We N/A.
FACILITIES: Bar & Restaurant.

Northumberland

STAVERTON PARK GOLF COMPLEX MAP 3 A2

Staverton, Daventry, Northamptonshire NN11 6JT.
Situated mins from J16 & 18 of the M1 & J11 & 12 of the M40.

CONTACT: Alexandra Barr, Golf Manager. Tel: 0327 705911.
COURSE: 6,634yds, PAR 71, SSS 72. Parkland course.
SOC RESTR'S: Welcome Weekdays by appointment.
SOC GF - Round: Wd £19.50. We N/A. **Day:** Wd N/A. We N/A.
SOC PACK: From £30-£49.50.
VIS RESTR'S: Welcome. We & Bank Hols available to Residents.
VIS GF - Round: Wd £19.50. We £22.50 **Day:** Wd N/A. We N/A.
FACILITIES: Restaurant, 2 Bars, Sauna & Solarium.

WELLINGBOROUGH GOLF CLUB MAP 3 A2

Harrowden Hall, Wellingborough, Northants NN9 5AD.
2 miles north-east of Wellingborough on A509.

CONTACT: R Tomlin, Secretary/Manager. Tel: 0933 677234.
COURSE: 6,620yds, PAR 72, SSS 72. Undulating parkland.
SOC RESTR'S: Min. 16. Welcome Wed, Thur & Fri after 9 & 2.
SOC GF - Round: Wd £22. We N/A. **Day:** Wd £27. We N/A.
SOC PACK: Coffee, Lunch, Dinner, 36 holes: £40-£45.
VIS RESTR'S: Welcome Weekdays with H'cap Cert.
VIS GF - Round: Wd £22. We N/A. **Day:** Wd £27. We N/A.
FACILITIES: Bar, Snooker & Outdoor Swimming Pool.

WEST PARK G & CC MAP 3 A2

Whittlebury, Towcester, Northants NN12 8XW.
Between Silverstone & Towcester, S of Whittlebury on A413.

CONTACT: P Cane, Director of Golf. Tel: 0327 858092.
COURSE: 6,750yds, PAR 72, SSS 72. Parkland, 3 loops of 9.
SOC RESTR'S: Welcome by advanced booking through Secretary.
SOC GF - Round: Wd £20. We N/A. **Day:** Wd £25. We N/A.
SOC PACK: Details on application.
VIS RESTR'S: Welcome Wd. Some restrictions at We. Please book.
VIS GF - Round: Wd £20. We £25. **Day:** Wd £25. We N/A.
FACILITIES: 9-hole course, Golf Academy, Range & Bar.

BERWICK-UPON-TWEED GC MAP 5 A1

Goswick, Berwick-upon-Tweed, Northumberland TD15 6RW.
Turn off A1 about 3 miles south of Berwick-upon-Tweed.

CONTACT: RC Oliver, Secretary. Tel: 0289 87256.
COURSE: 6,425yds, PAR 72, SSS 71. Links course.
SOC RESTR'S: Welcome except from 10-12, after 2.30 & We.
SOC GF - Round: Wd £18. We N/A. **Day:** Wd £24. We N/A.
SOC PACK: Available on booking from Secretary.
VIS RESTR'S: Welcome any day.
VIS GF - Round: Wd £18. We £24. **Day:** Wd £24. We £32.
FACILITIES: Bar & Restaurant.

DUNSTANBURGH CASTLE G C MAP 5 A1

Embleton, Alnwick, Northumberland NE66 3XQ.
7 miles north-east of Alnwick off A1.

CONTACT: Dr PFC Gilbert, Proprietor. Tel: 0665 576562.
COURSE: 6,298yds, PAR 70, SSS 70. Seaside links course.
SOC RESTR'S: Welcome except before 9.30 at Weekends.
SOC GF - Round: Wd £12. We £14. **Day:** Wd £12. We £18.
SOC PACK: £20 Wd, £22 We (1 round). £26 We (2 rounds).
VIS RESTR'S: Welcome except before 9.30 at Weekends.
VIS GF - Round: Wd £12. We £14. **Day:** Wd £12. We £18.
FACILITIES: Licensed Bar & Catering all day.

HEXHAM GOLF CLUB MAP 5 A2

Spital Park, Hexham, Northumberland NE46 3RZ.
1 mile west of Hexham Town.

CONTACT: JC Oates, Secretary. Tel: 0434 603072.
COURSE: 6,272yds, PAR 70, SSS 70. Scenic parkland.
SOC RESTR'S: Welcome Weekdays.
SOC GF - Round: Wd £18. We N/A. **Day:** Wd £24. We N/A.
SOC PACK: Coffee, Lunch & Dinner.
VIS RESTR'S: Welcome Booking advisable.
VIS GF - Round: Wd £18. We £24. **Day:** Wd £24. We £30.
FACILITIES: Bar, Restaurant & Snooker.

RAC National Road Maps

Clear, easy-to-read, up-to-date route planning maps at a scale of approximately 8 miles to 1 inch

Price £3.99
Available from bookshops
or direct from the RAC on 0235 844885

ENGLAND

MAGDALENE FIELDS GOLF CLUB   MAP 5 A1

Magdalene Fields, Berwick-upon-Tweed TD15 1NE.
1 mile from Berwick-upon-Tweed to the coast.

CONTACT: R Patterson, Secretary. Tel: 0289 305758.
COURSE: 6,551yds, PAR 72, SSS 71. Parkland on clifftop.
SOC RESTR'S: Welcome except Sunday morning.
SOC GF - Round: Wd N/A. **We** N/A. **Day:** Wd £12. **We** £14.
SOC PACK: GF less 10% for 12+. Coffee, Lunch & Dinner - £7.50.
VIS RESTR'S: Welcome except Sunday morning.
VIS GF - Round: Wd N/A. **We** N/A. **Day:** Wd £12. **We** £14.
FACILITIES: Clubhouse & Refreshments.

SLALEY HALL GOLF CLUB   MAP 5 A2

Slaley, Hexham, Northumberland NE47 0BY.
16 mls west of Newcastle, 7 mls south of Corbridge, off A68.

CONTACT: S Brown, Golf Director. Tel: 0434 673350.
COURSE: 7,021yds, PAR 72, SSS 74. Parkland course.
SOC RESTR'S: H'cap Cert required. Contact in advance.
SOC GF - Round: Wd N/A. **We** N/A. **Day:** Wd N/A. **We** N/A.
SOC PACK: On application.
VIS RESTR'S: Handicap Certificate required.
VIS GF - Round: Wd £22.50. **We** £25. **Day:** Wd £35. **We** £40.
FACILITIES: Catering available.

Nottinghamshire

BEESTON FIELDS GOLF CLUB   MAP 3 A1

Old Drive, Beeston Fields, Beeston, Nottinghamshire NG9 3DD.
M1 exit Junction 25 - A52 Derby Road - Wollaton Road.

CONTACT: J Grove, Secretary. Tel: 0602 257062.
COURSE: 6,414yds, PAR 71, SSS 71. Parkland course.
SOC RESTR'S: Welcome Mondays & Wednesdays.
SOC GF - Round: Wd £25. **We** N/A. **Day:** Wd £30. **We** N/A.
SOC PACK: £35-1 round. £45-2 rounds including catering.
VIS RESTR'S: Welcome Wd with res but not Tues before 2.30.
VIS GF - Round: Wd £25. **We** N/A. **Day:** Wd £30. **We** N/A.
FACILITIES: Bar, Restaurant & Snooker.

COXMOOR GOLF CLUB   MAP 3 A1

Coxmoor Road, Sutton-in-Ashfield NG17 5LF.
1.5 miles south of Mansfield, on A611.

CONTACT: JW Tyler, Secretary. Tel: 0623 557359.
COURSE: 6,501yds, PAR 73, SSS 72. Moorland/heathland course.
SOC RESTR'S: Not Tue or We. H'cap Cert required.
SOC GF - Round: Wd N/A. **We** N/A. **Day:** Wd £27. **We** N/A.
SOC PACK: Lunch, Dinner, 36 holes: £48.
VIS RESTR'S: Not Tue or We. H'cap Cert required.
VIS GF - Round: Wd N/A. **We** N/A. **Day:** Wd £27. **We** N/A.
FACILITIES: Bar, Restaurant, Pro shop.

LINDRICK GOLF CLUB   MAP 3 A1

Lindrick Common, Worksop, Notts S81 8BH.
4 miles west of Worksop on A57.

CONTACT: G Bywater, Secretary. Tel: 0909 475282.
COURSE: 6,615yds, PAR 69, SSS 72. Heathland and gorse.
SOC RESTR'S: Wd only. Not Tues. H'cap Cert required.
SOC GF - Round: Wd N/A. **We** N/A. **Day:** Wd £40. **We** N/A.
SOC PACK: Available at time of booking.
VIS RESTR'S: Prior notice. Not Tue am. H'cap Cert required.
VIS GF - Round: Wd £40. **We** £45. **Day:** Wd £40. **We** N/A.
FACILITIES: Bar, Restaurant, Pro shop, Snooker.

NEWARK GOLF CLUB   MAP 3 A1

Coddington, Newark, Nottinghamshire NG24 2QX.
3 miles from Newark on A17 to Sleaford.

CONTACT: AW Morgans, Secretary/Manager. Tel: 0636 626282.
COURSE: 6,421yds, PAR 71, SSS 71. Wooded heathland course.
SOC RESTR'S: Welcome Weekdays except Tuesday.
SOC GF - Round: Wd £18. **We** N/A. **Day:** Wd £24. **We** N/A.
SOC PACK: Green Fees £22 + Catering (approx. £12).
VIS RESTR'S: H'cap Cert required. Limited availability on We.
VIS GF - Round: Wd £18. **We** £24. **Day:** Wd £24. **We** N/A.
FACILITIES: Bar & Restaurant.

NOTTS GOLF CLUB   MAP 3 A1

Hollinwell, Kirby-in-Ashfield NG17 7QR.
4 miles south of Mansfield, on A611.

CONTACT: JR Walker, Secretary. Tel: 0623 753225.
COURSE: 7,030yds, PAR 73, SSS 74. Undulating heathland.
SOC RESTR'S: Not weekends. H'cap Cert required.
SOC GF - Round: Wd N/A. **We** N/A. **Day:** Wd £38. **We** N/A.
SOC PACK: Various packages depending on size.
VIS RESTR'S: We with Member. H'cap Cert required.
VIS GF - Round: Wd £30. **We** N/A. **Day:** Wd £38. **We** N/A.
FACILITIES: Driving Range, Food by arrangement, Pro shop.

Oxfordshire

OAKMERE PARK GOLF CLUB   MAP 3 A1

Oaks Lane, Oxton, Nottinghamshire NG25 0RH.
On A614, 8 miles north-east of Nottingham.

CONTACT: M Gibson, General Manager. Tel: 0602 653545.
COURSE: 6,617yds, PAR 72, SSS 72. Parkland course.
SOC RESTR'S: Min. 12. Welcome any day.
SOC GF - Round: Wd N/A. We N/A. **Day:** Wd £20. We £30.
SOC PACK: Coffee, Lunch, Dinner, 36 holes: £32 (Wd).
VIS RESTR'S: Welcome. Please book Weekends.
VIS GF - Round: Wd £16. We £20. **Day:** Wd £24. We £30.
FACILITIES: 9-hole Course, Range, Bar & Restaurant.

RUDDINGTON GRANGE GOLF CLUB   MAP 3 A1

Wilford Road, Ruddington, Nottinghamshire NG11 6NB.
Junction 24 M1 - A456 to Nottingham - A52 to Ruddington.

CONTACT: D Johnson, Secretary/MD. Tel: 0602 846141.
COURSE: 6,490yds, PAR 71, SSS 72. Parkland course.
SOC RESTR'S: Welcome any weekday.
SOC GF - Round: Wd £20. We N/A. **Day:** Wd £22. We N/A.
SOC PACK: Coffee, Lunch, Dinner, 36 holes: £30.
VIS RESTR'S: Welcome.
VIS GF - Round: Wd £20. We £24. **Day:** Wd £22. We £26.
FACILITIES: Fully Licensed Restaurant & Conference facilities.

SHERWOOD FOREST GOLF CLUB   MAP 3 A1

Eakring Road, Mansfield, Nottinghamshire NE18 3EW.
2 miles east of Mansfield.

CONTACT: DK Hall, Secretary. Tel: 0602 372006.
COURSE: 6,714yds, PAR 71, SSS 73. Heathland course.
SOC RESTR'S: Societies welcome Monday, Thursday & Friday.
SOC GF - Round: Wd £28. We N/A. **Day:** Wd £33. We N/A.
SOC PACK: Available on booking.
VIS RESTR'S: Welcome Weekdays. H'cap Cert required.
VIS GF - Round: Wd £28. We N/A. **Day:** Wd £33. We N/A.
FACILITIES: Bar & Restaurant.

STANTON-ON-THE-WOLDS GC   MAP 3 A1

Stanton-on-the-Wolds, Keyworth, Nottinghamshire NG12 5BH.
A606 S from Nottingham, turn off at Blue Star Garage. 9 miles.

CONTACT: HG Gray, Secretary/Treasurer. Tel: 0602 372006.
COURSE: 6,437yds, PAR 73, SSS 71. Meadowland course.
SOC RESTR'S: By arrangement with Secretary.
SOC GF - Round: Wd £25. We N/A. **Day:** Wd £25. We N/A.
SOC PACK: £25 + Meals to be agreed with caterer (06077 2246).
VIS RESTR'S: Welcome Weekdays but please book through Sec.
VIS GF - Round: Wd £24. We N/A. **Day:** Wd £24. We N/A.
FACILITIES: Bar, Restaurant & Practice Area.

CHESTERTON GOLF CLUB   MAP 3 A2

Chesterton, Nr. Bicester, Oxon, Oxfordshire OX6 8TE.
M40 J9 - A41 to Bicester & 2nd left - left at Red Cow.

CONTACT: JW Wilkshire, Senior Professional. Tel: 0869 242023.
COURSE: 6,224yds, PAR 71, SSS 70. Meadowland course.
SOC RESTR'S: Welcome Weekdays (except Tues). Please book.
SOC GF - Round: Wd N/A. We N/A. **Day:** Wd £15. We N/A.
SOC PACK: 20+. Coffee, Lunch, Dinner: £30.
VIS RESTR'S: Booking required at We & Bank Hols.
VIS GF - Round: Wd £12. We £18. **Day:** Wd £12. We £18.
FACILITIES: Bar, Bar Snacks & Snooker.

WESTWOOD COUNTRY HOTEL

Hinksey Hill, Oxford. Tel: **(0865) 735408**
Comfortable hotel. All en-suite bedrooms. 3½ miles from centre of Oxford. Set in 4 acres of woodland and wildlife gardens (opened by David Bellamy). Excellent restaurant. One of Oxford's Top Ten 1991 *Daily Mail* Hotel Award winner, presented by Judith Chalmers.

RAC ★★   Southern Tourist Board   ETB ●●●

CHIPPING NORTON GOLF CLUB   MAP 3 A2

Southcombe, Chipping Norton, Oxfordshire OX7 5QH.
On A44 Evesham Road, 1 mile east of Chipping Norton.

CONTACT: J Norman, Secretary/Manager. Tel: 0608 642383.
COURSE: 6,280yds, PAR 71, SSS 70. Downland course.
SOC RESTR'S: Max. 40. Welcome except Thursdays & Weekends.
SOC GF - Round: Wd £22. We N/A. **Day:** Wd £22. We N/A.
SOC PACK: Coffee, Lunch, Dinner, 36 holes: £38.
VIS RESTR'S: Welcome Weekdays.
VIS GF - Round: Wd £22. We N/A. **Day:** Wd £22. We N/A.
FACILITIES: Normal Bar & Catering.

ENGLAND

FRILFORD HEATH GC (RED)   MAP 3 A2

Frilford Heath, Abingdon OX13 5NW.
3 miles west of Abingdon on A338.

CONTACT: JW Kleynhans, Secretary. Tel: 0865 390864.
COURSE: 6,768yds, PAR 73, SSS 73. Heathland course.
SOC RESTR'S: Welcome Mon, Wed and Fri.
SOC GF - Round: Wd N/A. We N/A. **Day:** Wd £40. We N/A.
SOC PACK: Full catering and Green Fees.
VIS RESTR'S: Letter of Intro & H'cap required. We with Member.
VIS GF - Round: Wd £40. We N/A. **Day:** Wd £40. We N/A.
FACILITIES: 2nd 18-hole Course, Bar, Restaurant, Pro shop.

LYNEHAM GOLF CLUB   MAP 2 B2

Lyneham, Chipping Norton, Oxfordshire OX7 6QQ.
Off the A361 5 miles west of Chipping Norton.

CONTACT: C Howkins, Secretary. Tel: 0993 831841.
COURSE: 6,669yds, PAR 72, SSS 72. Parkland course.
SOC RESTR'S: Always welcome.
SOC GF - Round: Wd N/A. We N/A. **Day:** Wd £14. We £18.
SOC PACK: Please discuss at time of booking.
VIS RESTR'S: No restrictions.
VIS GF - Round: Wd N/A. We N/A. **Day:** Wd £14. We £18.
FACILITIES: Bar & Restaurant.

TADMARTON HEATH GOLF CLUB   MAP 3 A2

Wigginton, Banbury, Oxon, Oxfordshire OX15 5HL.
5 miles south-west of Banbury - B4035.

CONTACT: RE Wackrill, Secretary. Tel: 0608 737278.
COURSE: 5,917yds, PAR 69, SSS 69. Heathland course.
SOC RESTR'S: Max. 36. Welcome Tues, Wed & Fri.
SOC GF - Round: Wd N/A. We N/A. **Day:** Wd N/A. We N/A.
SOC PACK: Coffee, Lunch, Dinner, 36 holes: £45.
VIS RESTR'S: Welcome Weekdays. H'cap Cert required.
VIS GF - Round: Wd £27. We N/A. **Day:** Wd £27. We N/A.
FACILITIES: Practice Ground.

RAC Regional Road Maps

Large scale (3 miles to 1 inch) maps for the motorist. Each sheet contains details of motorway junctions, dual carriageways, town plans, a full index of towns and villages, and tourist information including golf courses.

Price £3.99
Available from bookshops
or direct from the RAC on 0235 834885

Shropshire

CHURCH STRETTON GOLF CLUB   MAP 2 B1

Trevor Hill, Church Stretton, Shropshire SY6 6JH.
From A49 to Town Centre. Right & 1st left.

CONTACT: R Broughten, Secretary. Tel: 0694 722633.
COURSE: 5,008yds, PAR 66, SSS 65. Hillside course.
SOC RESTR'S: Welcome Weekdays.
SOC GF - Round: Wd N/A. We N/A. **Day:** Wd £12. We N/A.
SOC PACK: Coffee, Lunch, Dinner, 36 holes: £25.
VIS RESTR'S: Not Sat: 9-10.30 & 1.30-3. Sun: pre 10.30 & 12-3.
VIS GF - Round: Wd N/A. We N/A. **Day:** Wd £12. We £18.
FACILITIES: Bar & Restaurant.

HAWSTONE PARK GC (HAWSTONE)   MAP 2 B1

Weston-under-Redcastle, Shrewsbury SY4 5UY.
7 mls south of Whitchurch, 14 mls north of Shrewsbury on A49.

CONTACT: RE Thomas, Secretary. Tel: 093 924 611.
COURSE: 6,465yds, PAR 72, SSS 71. Parkland course.
SOC RESTR'S: After 10.30am. Contact in advance.
SOC GF - Round: Wd N/A. We N/A. **Day:** Wd £50. We N/A.
SOC PACK: On application.
VIS RESTR'S: Welcome after 10.30am.
VIS GF - Round: Wd £25. We £28. **Day:** Wd N/A. We N/A.
FACILITIES: 2nd 18-hole (Weston) Par 65, Buggy Hire, Pro shop.

LLANYMYNECH GOLF CLUB   MAP 2 A1

Pant, Oswestry, Shropshire SY10 8LB.
5 miles south of Oswestry on A483.

CONTACT: NE Clews, Secretary. Tel: 0691 830983.
COURSE: 6,114yds, PAR 70, SSS 69. Upland course.
SOC RESTR'S: Contact in advance.
SOC GF - Round: Wd N/A. We N/A. **Day:** Wd £18. We N/A.
SOC PACK: Lunch, Dinner, 36 holes: £42.
VIS RESTR'S: Unrestricted before 4.30pm with Member after.
VIS GF - Round: Wd £13. We £19. **Day:** Wd £18. We £23.
FACILITIES: Restaurant (except Monday), Bar, Pro shop.

SOMERSET

OSWESTRY GOLF CLUB MAP 2 B1

Aston Park, Oswestry, Shropshire SY11 4JJ.
3 miles east of Oswestry on A5.

CONTACT: Mrs P Lindner, Secretary. Tel: 0691 88535.
COURSE: 6,038yds, PAR 70, SSS 69. Parkland course.
SOC RESTR'S: Max. 60. Welcome Wednesday & Friday.
SOC GF - Round: Wd £17. We N/A. **Day:** Wd £17. We N/A.
SOC PACK: Cost approx. £30 with meals.
VIS RESTR'S: Must be members of recognised Golf Club.
VIS GF - Round: Wd £17. We £25. **Day:** Wd £17. We £25.
FACILITIES: Bar & Restaurant.

PATSHULL PARK GOLF CLUB MAP 2 B1

Pattingham, Nr. Wolverhampton, Shropshire WV6 7HR.
J3, M54 via Albrighton & A454, Burnhill Green to Pattingham.

CONTACT: Mrs Brown-Smith. Tel: 0902 700100.
COURSE: 6,412yds, PAR 72, SSS 72. Parkland course.
SOC RESTR'S: Welcome with prior reservation.
SOC GF - Round: Wd £22. We £27. **Day:** Wd £37. We £42.
SOC PACK: From £28 p. p. incl. 18 holes, Lunch & Coffee.
VIS RESTR'S: Welcome.
VIS GF - Round: Wd £22. We £27. **Day:** Wd £37. We £42.
FACILITIES: Swimming Pool, Fitness Centre, Fishing & Tennis.

SHREWSBURY GOLF CLUB MAP 2 B1

Condover, Shrewsbury, Shropshire SY5 7BL.
4 miles south-west of Shrewsbury.

CONTACT: Mrs. SM Kenny, Secretary. Tel: 0743 872977.
COURSE: 6,212yds, PAR 70, SSS 70. Meadowland course.
SOC RESTR'S: Min. 16. Welcome Mon & Fri (some Sundays).
SOC GF - Round: Wd £15. We N/A. **Day:** Wd £20. We N/A.
SOC PACK: Available on booking from Secretary.
VIS RESTR'S: Welcome everyday.
VIS GF - Round: Wd £15 We £25. **Day:** Wd £20. We £25.
FACILITIES: Bar & Restaurant.

TELFORD G & CC MAP 2 B1

Great Hay, Telford, Shropshire TF7 4DT.
Off A442, 4 miles south of Telford.

CONTACT: J Brigham, Secretary. Tel: 0952 585642.
COURSE: 6,766yds, PAR 72, SSS 72. Wooded parkland.
SOC RESTR'S: Welcome Weekdays.
SOC GF - Round: Wd N/A. We N/A. **Day:** Wd N/A. We N/A.
SOC PACK: Coffee, Lunch, Dinner, 36 holes: £42.50.
VIS RESTR'S: Must reserve tee time. H'cap Cert required.
VIS GF - Round: Wd £25. We £35. **Day:** Wd £25. We £50.
FACILITIES: 9-hole Par 3 course, Full Leisure Centre & Bar.

WORFIELD GOLF CLUB MAP 2 B1

Worfield, Nr. Bridgnorth, Shropshire WV15 5HE.
On A454, 3 miles from Bridgnorth behind Worfield Garage.

CONTACT: W Weaver, Secretary. Tel: 07464 541.
COURSE: 6,801yds, PAR 73, SSS 73. Parkland course.
SOC RESTR'S: Welcome Monday & Thursday.
SOC GF - Round: Wd £15. We £20. **Day:** Wd £20. We £25.
SOC PACK: On application.
VIS RESTR'S: 1st tee reserved for Members till 10.
VIS GF - Round: Wd £15. We £20. **Day:** Wd £20. We £25.
FACILITIES: Excellent Practice facilities, Bar & Restaurant.

Somerset

BREAN GOLF CLUB MAP 2 B3

Coast Road, Brean, Somerset TA8 2RF.
Leave M5 at J22, follow signs to Brean Leisure Park.

CONTACT: A Clarke, Manager. Tel: 0278 751570.
COURSE: 5,714yds, PAR 69, SSS 68. Flat moorland course.
SOC RESTR'S: Welcome Weekdays.
SOC GF - Round: Wd N/A. We N/A. **Day:** Wd N/A. We N/A.
SOC PACK: £20 for 2 rounds & single course meal if 8+.
VIS RESTR'S: Welcome Weekdays, Weekends not before 12 noon.
VIS GF - Round: Wd £15. We £20. **Day:** Wd N/A. We N/A.
FACILITIES: Catering in adjoining leisure Centre.

BURNHAM & BERROW GOLF CLUB MAP 2 B3

St. Christopher's Way, Burnham-on-Sea, Somerset TA8 2PE.
M5 Junction 22, 1 mile north of Burnham-on-Sea.

CONTACT: Mrs EL Sloman, Secretary. Tel: 0278 785760.
COURSE: 6,547yds, PAR 71, SSS 73. Links course.
SOC RESTR'S: Welcome subject to a Handicap of 22 & under.
SOC GF - Round: Wd N/A. We N/A. **Day:** Wd £28. We £40.
SOC PACK: Green Fee - Choice from menu.
VIS RESTR'S: Not before 2.30 on Sat. H'cap Cert required.
VIS GF - Round: Wd N/A. We N/A. **Day:** Wd £28. We £40.
FACILITIES: 9-hole course, Dormy House sleeps 8.

ENGLAND

ENMORE PARK GOLF CLUB MAP 2 A3

Enmore, Bridgwater, Somerset TA5 2AN.
4 miles south-west of Bridgwater.

CONTACT: D Weston, Secretary/Manager. Tel: 0278 671481.
COURSE: 6,406yds, PAR 71, SSS 71. Parkland course.
SOC RESTR'S: Not Fri or Competition Days. Wed is Ladies Day.
SOC GF Round: Wd £18. We £25. **Day:** Wd £25. We £30.
SOC PACK: Available on booking.
VIS RESTR'S: Not Competition Days. Wed is Ladies Day.
VIS GF Round: Wd £18. We £25. **Day:** Wd £25. We £30.
FACILITIES: Bar & Restaurant.

MENDIP GOLF COURSE MAP 2 B3

Gurney Slade, Shepton Mallet, Bath, Somerset BA3 4UT.
3 miles from Shepton Mallet, just off A37.

CONTACT: Mrs. JP Howe Secretary. Tel: 0749 840570.
COURSE: 6,033yds, PAR 71, SSS 70. Undulating downland.
SOC RESTR'S: Welcome Weekdays.
SOC GF - Round: Wd N/A. We N/A. **Day:** Wd £30. We N/A.
SOC PACK: Available on booking from Secretary.
VIS RESTR'S: Please phone before play.
VIS GF - Round: Wd £20. We £30. **Day:** Wd £30. We £30.
FACILITIES: Bar & Restaurant.

MINEHEAD & WEST SOMERSET MAP 2 A3

The Warren, Minehead, Somerset TA24 5SJ.
Just outside town at the east end of seafront.

CONTACT: LS Harper, Secretary. Tel: 0643 702057.
COURSE: 6,228yds, PAR 71, SSS 71. Seaside links course.
SOC RESTR'S: By arrangement with Secretary.
SOC GF - Round: Wd £19.50. We £23. **Day:** Wd £19.50. We £23.
SOC PACK: 10% reduction for parties over 12 in number.
VIS RESTR'S: Res tee time. Not before 10 & between 12-2.
VIS GF - Round: Wd £19.50. We £23. **Day:** Wd £19.50. We £23.
FACILITIES: Catering available except Tuesdays.

SWAN HOTEL
WELLS, SOMERSET
Tel: (0749) 678877

A Best Western Hotel   RAC ***

A 15th-century coaching Inn with 10 original four-poster
beds and log fires.
5 day golfing breaks available. Tee off times arranged and
Golf Societies welcome at special rates.
With a superb view of the West Front of Wells Cathedral
it's just the place if you wish to tour the West Country.
Please write or telephone the Manager for further details.

TAUNTON & PICKERIDGE G C MAP 2 A/B1

Corfe, Taunton, Somerset TA3 7BY.
4 miles south of Taunton on B3170.

CONTACT: GW Sayers, Secretary. Tel: 0823 42537.
COURSE: 5,921yds, PAR 69, SSS 68. Semi-parkland course.
SOC RESTR'S: By arrangement with Secretary.
SOC GF - Round: Wd £19. We N/A. **Day:** Wd £19. We N/A.
SOC PACK: Coffee, Lunch Dinner, GF, average cost £28/£30.
VIS RESTR'S: Reserve tee time with Secretary.
VIS GF - Round: Wd £19. We £24. **Day:** Wd £19. We £24.
FACILITIES: Practice Areas.

WELLS (SOMERSET) GOLF CLUB MAP 2 B3

East Horrington Road, Wells, Somerset BA5 3DS.
From Wells B3139 towards Radstock- Club 1 mile on right.

CONTACT: GE Ellis, Secretary/Manager. Tel: 0749 675005.
COURSE: 5,354yds, PAR 67, SSS 66. Wooded parkland.
SOC RESTR'S: Welcome Weekdays, preferably Tues & Thur.
SOC GF - Round: Wd £16. We N/A. **Day:** Wd £19. We £22.
SOC PACK: Coffee, Lunch, Dinner, Golf: £29-£33.
VIS RESTR'S: Welcome after 9.30 We. H'cap Cert required at We.
VIS GF - Round: Wd £16. We £20. **Day:** Wd £19. We £22.
FACILITIES: Practice Ground, Professional + 2 Assistants.

Staffordshire

BARLASTON GOLF CLUB MAP 2 B1

Meaford Road, Stone, Staffordshire ST15 8UX.
Off A34, 400yds south of Barlaston & 1 mile north of Stone.

CONTACT: MJ Degg, Secretary. Tel: 0781 392867.
COURSE: 5,800yds, PAR 69, SSS 68. Meadowland course.
SOC RESTR'S: Welcome Weekdays.
SOC GF - Round: Wd N/A. We N/A. **Day:** Wd £18. We N/A.
SOC PACK: On application from Secretary.
VIS RESTR'S: Welcome every day except before 10 at We.
VIS GF - Round: Wd N/A. We N/A. **Day:** Wd £18. We £22.50.
FACILITIES: Bar & Restaurant.

STAFFORDSHIRE

BEAU DESERT GOLF CLUB MAP 2 B1

Hazel Slade, Cannock, Staffordshire WS12 5PJ.
4 miles north-east of Cannock.

CONTACT: AJR Fairfield, Admin. Secretary. Tel: 0543 422626.
COURSE: 6,279yds, PAR 70, SSS 71. Heathland course.
SOC RESTR'S: Welcome Monday to Thursday.
SOC GF - Round: Wd £30. We N/A. **Day:** Wd £30. We N/A.
SOC PACK: Coffee, Lunch, Dinner, Golf: £45.
VIS RESTR'S: Welcome Weekdays.
VIS GF - Round: Wd £30. We N/A. **Day:** Wd £30. We N/A.
FACILITIES: Bar & Restaurant.

INGESTRE PARK GOLF CLUB MAP 2 B1

Ingestre, Stafford, Staffordshire ST18 0RE.
6 miles east of Stafford.

CONTACT: DD Humphries, Manager. Tel: 0889 270845.
COURSE: 6,334yds, PAR 70, SSS 70. Undulating Parkland course.
SOC RESTR'S: Wd except Wed & 9.30-10.45 & 1.30-2.45.
SOC GF - Round: Wd £17. We N/A. **Day:** Wd £27. We N/A.
SOC PACK: Coffee, Lunch, Dinner, 27 holes: £30.
VIS RESTR'S: Welcome before 3.30 Weekdays with H'cap Cert.
VIS GF - Round: Wd £17. We N/A. **Day:** Wd £27. We N/A.
FACILITIES: Snooker & Bar.

BURTON-ON-TRENT GOLF CLUB MAP 2 B1

Ashby Road East, Burton-on-Trent, Staffordshire DE15 0PS.
3 miles east of Burton-on-Trent on A50.

CONTACT: D Hartley, Hon. Secretary. Tel: 0283 44551.
COURSE: 6,555yds, PAR 71, SSS 71. Undulating Parkland course.
SOC RESTR'S: Max. 50. Weekdays & not before 9.
SOC GF - Round: Wd £20. We N/A. **Day:** Wd £25. We N/A.
SOC PACK: Minimum 16 to avail package.
VIS RESTR'S: Not before 9. Not between 12.30-2.
VIS GF - Round: Wd £20. We £25. **Day:** Wd £25. We £30.
FACILITIES: Snooker.

LEEK GOLF CLUB MAP 2 B1

Cheddleton Road, Leek, Staffordshire ST13 5RE.
Half-a-mile south of Leek on A520.

CONTACT: F Cutts, Secretary. Tel: 0538 384779.
COURSE: 6,240yds, PAR 70, SSS 70. Moorland course.
SOC RESTR'S: 30-40 players Welcome Wednesday.
SOC GF - Round: Wd £15. We N/A. **Day:** Wd £25. We N/A.
SOC PACK: On application from Secretary.
VIS RESTR'S: Please book tee time. H'cap Cert required.
VIS GF - Round: Wd N/A. We N/A. **Day:** Wd £25. We £35.
FACILITIES: Bar, Restaurant & Snooker.

CRAYTHORNE GOLF CENTRE MAP 2 B1

Craythorne Road, Stretton, Staffordshire DE13 0AZ.
A38/A5121 Junction - Stretton - 1.5 miles north of Burton.

CONTACT: J Bissell, General Manager. Tel: 0283 37992.
COURSE: 5,243yds, PAR 68, SSS 66. Parkland course.
SOC RESTR'S: Max. 40. Welcome Weekdays.
SOC GF - Round: Wd N/A. We N/A. **Day:** Wd N/A. We N/A.
SOC PACK: £24 including Golf & Meals.
VIS RESTR'S: Sunday Green Fees are £2 over Saturdays.
VIS GF - Round: Wd £12. We £14 (Sat). **Day:** Wd £17. We £20 (Sat).
FACILITIES: Driving Range, Par 3 Pitch & Putt & Bar.

TRENTHAM GOLF CLUB MAP 2 B1

Barlaston Old Road, Trentham, Stoke-on-Trent, Staffs ST4 8HB.
Junction 15 M6, A34 to A5035 to Longton, 1st right.

CONTACT: R Irving, Secretary. Tel: 0782 658109.
COURSE: 6,644yds, PAR 72, SSS 72. Parkland course.
SOC RESTR'S: Normally Wednesday or Thursday.
SOC GF - Round: Wd £25. We N/A. **Day:** Wd £30. We N/A.
SOC PACK: £35 per head.
VIS RESTR'S: Welcome except Sat & Sun am. H'cap Cert required.
VIS GF - Round: Wd £25. We £30. **Day:** Wd £30. We N/A.
FACILITIES: Squash & Snooker.

GOLDENHILL GOLF CLUB MAP 2 B1

Mobberley Road, Goldenhill, Stoke-on-Trent, Staffs ST6 5SS.
Between Tunstall and Kidsgrove off main A50.

CONTACT: T Clingan, Professional. Tel: 0782 784715.
COURSE: 5,957yds, PAR 71, SSS 68. Rolling Parkland course.
SOC RESTR'S: Welcome Weekdays after 10.
SOC GF - Round: Wd £6. We N/A. **Day:** Wd N/A. We N/A.
SOC PACK: Variable - Details on application.
VIS RESTR'S: No restrictions. We bookings 7 Days in advance.
VIS GF - Round: Wd £6. We £7. **Day:** Wd N/A. We N/A.
FACILITIES: Clubhouse Restaurant, Bar &Changing Rooms.

TRENTHAM PARK GOLF CLUB MAP 2 B1

Trentham Park, Trentham, Stoke-on-Trent, Staffs ST4 8AE.
4 miles S of Newcastle-under-Lyme on A34. M6 J15 1 mile.

CONTACT: N Portas, Secretary. Tel: 0782 642125.
COURSE: 6,403yds, PAR 70, SSS 71. Woodland course.
SOC RESTR'S: Min. 20. Welcome Wednesday & Friday.
SOC GF - Round: Wd N/A. We N/A. **Day:** Wd £20. We N/A.
SOC PACK: On application from Secretary.
VIS RESTR'S: Welcome Weekdays with booking.
VIS GF - Round: Wd N/A. We N/A. **Day:** Wd £20. We N/A.
FACILITIES: Bar & Restaurant.

ENGLAND

UTTOXETER GOLF CLUB MAP 2 B1

Wood Lane, Uttoxeter, Staffordshire ST14 8JR.
Just under half-a-mile from the town's racecourse.

CONTACT: Mrs G Davies, Secretary. Tel: 0889 564884.
COURSE: 5,468yds, PAR 69, SSS 68. Parkland course.
SOC RESTR'S: Welcome Weekdays - otherwise by appointment.
SOC GF - Round: Wd N/A. We N/A. Day: Wd N/A. We N/A.
SOC PACK: Coffee, Brunch mid-day, Dinner, 36 holes: Min 4 £23.
VIS RESTR'S: Welcome except major Competition Days.
VIS GF - Round: Wd £13. We £17. Day: Wd £20. We £N/A.
FACILITIES: Catering each day but Monday.

FELIXSTOWE FERRY GOLF CLUB MAP 3 B2

Ferry Road, Felixstowe, Suffolk IP11 9RY.
A45 to Felixstowe - follow signs to Yachting Centre.

CONTACT: IH Kimber, Secretary. Tel: 0394 283975.
COURSE: 6,423yds, PAR 72, SSS 69. Links course.
SOC RESTR'S: Welcome Tuesday, Wednesday & Friday.
SOC GF - Round: Wd £22. We N/A. Day: Wd £22. We N/A.
SOC PACK: On application from Secretary.
VIS RESTR'S: Must be member of Golf Club. Please ring first.
VIS GF - Round: Wd £20. We £24. Day: Wd £20. We £24.
FACILITIES: Self-catering flats (golf included). Bar & Restaurant.

FORNHAM PARK G & CC MAP 3 B2

Fornham All Saints, Bury St. Edmunds, Suffolk IP28 6JQ.
2 miles from Bury St. Edmunds on the A1106.

CONTACT: Miss A Num. Tel: 0284 706777.
COURSE: 6,229yds, PAR 71, SSS 70. Parkland course.
SOC RESTR'S: Welcome Monday, Wednesday &Thursday.
SOC GF - Round: Wd N/A. We N/A. Day: Wd £35. We N/A.
SOC PACK: 2 options from £25 to £35.
VIS RESTR'S: Welcome Weekdays but not till 1 at Weekends.
VIS GF - Round: Wd £12.50. We £25. Day: Wd £20. We £20.
FACILITIES: A la Carte Restaurant.

Suffolk

ALDEBURGH GOLF CLUB MAP 3 B2

Saxmundham Road, Aldeburgh, Suffolk IP15 5PE.
6 miles east of A12 between Ipswich and Lowestoft.

CONTACT: RC Van de Velde, Secretary. Tel: 0728 452890.
COURSE: 6,330yds, PAR 68, SSS 71. Heath/seaside course.
SOC RESTR'S: Welcome except We. H'cap Cert required.
SOC GF - Round: Wd N/A. We N/A. Day: Wd £30. We N/A.
SOC PACK: On application from Secretary.
VIS RESTR'S: Welcome by arrangement.
VIS GF - Round: Wd N/A. We N/A. Day: Wd £30. We £36.
FACILITIES: 9-hole Course £12. 50 Day Green Fee.

HINTLESHAM HALL GOLF CLUB MAP 3 B2

Hintlesham, Ipswich, Suffolk IP8 3NS.
4 miles west of Ipswich - 10 mins drive from A12 & A45.

CONTACT: A Spink, Mamager/Pro. Tel: 0473 652761.
COURSE: 6,630yds, PAR 72, SSS 70. Parkland course.
SOC RESTR'S: Welcome with advanced bookings.
SOC GF - Round: Wd £39. We N/A. Day: Wd N/A. We N/A.
SOC PACK: £40 - 18 holes 3-course Lunch & Coffee.
VIS RESTR'S: Please book tee time.
VIS GF - Round: Wd £26. We £45. Day: Wd £45. We £75.
FACILITIES: Clubhouse, 2 Bars, Spa, Sauna & Steam Room.

BURY ST. EDMUNDS GOLF CLUB MAP 3 B2

Tuthill, Bury St. Edmunds, Suffolk IP28 6LG.
Take B1106 off A45 - 400yds on right.

CONTACT: J Sayer, Secretary. Tel: 0284 755979.
COURSE: 6,615yds, PAR 72, SSS 72. Parkland course.
SOC RESTR'S: Welcome Weekdays. 3 per week.
SOC GF - Round: Wd £22. We N/A. Day: Wd £26. We N/A.
SOC PACK: 2 rounds - Coffee - Lunch - Dinner: About £40.
VIS RESTR'S: Welcome Weekdays.
VIS GF - Round: Wd £23. We N/A. Day: Wd £23. We N/A.
FACILITIES: 9-hole Course.

IPSWICH GOLF CLUB MAP 3 B2

Purdis Heath, Bucklesham Road, Ipswich, Suffolk IP3 8UQ.
3 miles east of Ipswich.

CONTACT: Brig AP Wright, Sec/Manager. Tel: 0473 728941.
COURSE: 6,415yds, PAR 71, SSS 71. Heathland course.
SOC RESTR'S: Max. 50. Welcome Mon, Thur & Fri.
SOC GF - Round: Wd £30. We £36. Day: Wd £36. We £36.
SOC PACK: Green Fees £28; Lunch £4; Dinner £11.
VIS RESTR'S: Book with Secretary. H'cap Cert required.
VIS GF - Round: Wd £30. We £36. Day: Wd N/A. We £36.
FACILITIES: 9-hole course open to public.

SURREY

LINKS GOLF CLUB   MAP 3 B2

Cambridge Road, Newmarket, Suffolk CB8 0TG.
Signposted on A1304, 1 mile south of Newmarket.

CONTACT: Mrs. T MacGregor, Secretary. Tel: 0638 663000.
COURSE: 6,424yds, PAR 72, SSS 71. Parkland course.
SOC RESTR'S: Max. 50. Welcome Tues, Wed & Thur.
SOC GF - Round: Wd £24. **We** £28. **Day: Wd** £24. **We** £28.
SOC PACK: On application from Secretary.
VIS RESTR'S: Everyday & Sun after 11.30. H'cap Cert req.
VIS GF - Round: Wd £24. **We** £28. **Day: Wd** £24. **We** £28.
FACILITIES: Bar & Restaurant.

Surrey

ROYAL WORLINGTON & NEWMARKET   MAP 3 B2

Worlington, Bury St Edmunds IP28 8SD.
6 miles north-east of Newmarket, off A11.

CONTACT: CP Simpson, Secretary. Tel: 0638 712216.
COURSE: 6,218yds, PAR 70, SSS 70. 9-hole links course.
SOC RESTR'S: H'cap Cert required. No weekends.
SOC GF - Round: Wd N/A. **We** N/A. **Day: Wd** £30. **We** N/A.
SOC PACK: By arrangement.
VIS RESTR'S: Intro or H'cap required. No We. Phone first.
VIS GF - Round: Wd N/A. **We** N/A. **Day: Wd** £30. **We** N/A.
FACILITIES: Lunch by arrangement, Bar snacks, Pro shop.

THORPENESS GOLF CLUB   MAP 3 B2

Thorpeness, Nr. Leiston, Suffolk IP16 4NH.
A12 at Saxmundham to the B1119, then B1353 to Thorpeness.

CONTACT: Mrs A Davis. Tel: 0728 452176.
COURSE: 6,241yds, PAR 69, SSS 71. Gorse & heather course.
SOC RESTR'S: Welcome by prior appointment.
SOC GF - Round: Wd £20. **We** £25. **Day: Wd** £20. **We** £40.
SOC PACK: On application from Secretary.
VIS RESTR'S: Welcome.
VIS GF - Round: Wd £20. **We** £25. **Day: Wd** £30. **We** £40.
FACILITIES: Bar & Restaurant.

WALDRINGFIELD HEATH   MAP 3 B2

Newbourne Road, Waldringfield, Woodbridge, Suffolk IP12 4PT.
3 miles north of Ipswich off A12/A45 Ring Road.

CONTACT: LJ McWade, Secretary. Tel: 0473 36768.
COURSE: 5,813yds, PAR 71, SSS 68. Heathland course.
SOC RESTR'S: Welcome Weekdays.
SOC GF - Round: Wd £10. **We** N/A. **Day: Wd** £15. **We** N/A.
SOC PACK: Coffee, Lunch, Dinner, 36 holes: £28.
VIS RESTR'S: Welcome Wd & after 12 noon We.
VIS GF - Round: Wd £10. **We** £12. **Day: Wd** £15. **We** N/A.
FACILITIES: Bar & Restaurant.

ADDINGTON COURT (CHAMPIONSHIP)   MAP 7 B2

Featherbed Lane, Croydon, Surrey CR0 9AA.
South Croydon - Selsdon - Addington.

CONTACT: Mrs Philbie, Pro Shop. Tel: 081 657 0281.
COURSE: 5,577yds, PAR 68, SSS 67. Undulating public course.
SOC RESTR'S: Welcome Mon, Tues & Thurs.
SOC GF - Round: Wd N/A. **We** N/A. **Day: Wd** N/A. **We** N/A.
SOC PACK: From £46 per head (36 holes + food).
VIS RESTR'S: Mon, Tues & Thurs. Must be booked.
VIS GF - Round: Wd £12. **We** £12. **Day: Wd** N/A. **We** N/A.
FACILITIES: 18-hole Par 3 Course, 9-hole Course & Bar.

ADDINGTON COURT (FALCONWOOD)   MAP 7 B2

Featherbed Lane, Croydon, Surrey CR0 9AA.
South Croydon - Selsdon - Addington.

CONTACT: J Rees, Secretary. Tel: 081 657 0281.
COURSE: 5,513yds, PAR 68, SSS 67. Undulating public course.
SOC RESTR'S: Welcome Mon, Tues & Thurs.
SOC GF - Round: Wd N/A. **We** N/A. **Day: Wd** N/A. **We** N/A.
SOC PACK: From £46 per head (36 holes + food).
VIS RESTR'S: Welcome but must book.
VIS GF - Round: Wd £11. **We** £11. **Day: Wd** N/A. **We** N/A.
FACILITIES: 18-hole Par 3 Course, 9-hole Course &, Bar.

BANSTEAD DOWNS GOLF CLUB   MAP 7 A3

Burdon Lane, Belmont, Sutton, Surrey SM2 7DD.
1 mile south of Sutton (A217).

CONTACT: AW Schooling, Secretary/Manager. Tel: 081 642 2284.
COURSE: 6,169yds, PAR 69, SSS 69. Downland course.
SOC RESTR'S: Welcome Thursday.
SOC GF - Round: Wd N/A. **We** N/A. **Day: Wd** £25. **We** N/A.
SOC PACK: 36 Holes + Catering: £47.
VIS RESTR'S: Welcome Weekdays H'cap Cert required.
VIS GF - Round: Wd £20. **We** N/A. **Day: Wd** £30. **We** N/A.
FACILITIES: Bar & Restaurant.

ENGLAND

BRAMLEY GOLF CLUB   MAP 7 A3

Bramley, Nr. Guildford, Surrey GU5 0AL.
3 miles south of Guildford on A281.

CONTACT: Mrs Margaret Lambert, Secretary. Tel: 0483 892696.
COURSE: 5,990yds, PAR 69, SSS 69. Parkland course.
SOC RESTR'S: Welcome Weekdays except Tuesday am.
SOC GF - Round: Wd £20.50. We N/A. **Day:** Wd £25.50. We N/A.
SOC PACK: 36 Holes + Catering: £45.
VIS RESTR'S: Welcome Weekdays.
VIS GF - Round: Wd £25. We N/A. **Day:** Wd £30. We N/A.
FACILITIES: Driving Range.

COOMBE HILL GOLF CLUB   MAP 7 B2

Golf Club Drive, Off Coombe Lane West, Kingston KT2 7DG.
1 mile west of New Malden on A238.

CONTACT: DG Seward, General Manager. Tel: 081 942 2284.
COURSE: 6,303yds, PAR 71, SSS 71. Undulating woodland course.
SOC RESTR'S: H'cap Cert required. Contact first.
SOC GF - Round: Wd N/A. We N/A. **Day:** Wd £30. We N/A.
SOC PACK: Limited catering.
VIS RESTR'S: Intro or H'cap required. GF by arrangement.
VIS GF - Round: Wd N/A. We N/A. **Day:** Wd £30. We N/A.
FACILITIES: Bar snacks, Pro shop.

COULSDON COURT GOLF CLUB   MAP 7 B3

Coulsdon Road, Coulsdon, Surrey CR5 2LL.
Junction 7 M25 - A23 Brighton Road, 2 miles south of Croydon.

CONTACT: M Pybus, Manager. Tel: 081 668 0414.
COURSE: 6,037yds, PAR 70, SSS 68. Parkland course.
SOC RESTR'S: Min. 16. Welcome Tues, Thur & Fri.
SOC GF - Round: Wd £38.50. We N/A. **Day:** Wd £47.50. We N/A.
SOC PACK: 36 Holes + Catering: £49.50.
VIS RESTR'S: Welcome everyday. Need to book Weekends.
VIS GF - Round: Wd £11.50. We £14.50. **Day:** Wd N/A. We N/A.
FACILITIES: 4-Star Hotel on-site.

EPSOM GOLF CLUB   MAP 7 A3

Longdown Lane South, Epsom, Surrey KT17 4JR.
Off A240 onto B288, close to Epsom Racecourse.

CONTACT: J Carter, Secretary/Manager. Tel: 0372 721666.
COURSE: 5,607yds, PAR 69, SSS 67. Undulating downland course.
SOC RESTR'S: Min. 12. Max. 40. Welcome Wed 9. Fri 8.30.
SOC GF - Round: Wd £13. We N/A. **Day:** Wd N/A. We N/A.
SOC PACK: From £20 (lunch + afternoon round) to £45 (all day).
VIS RESTR'S: Everyday exc before 12 Tues & We. After 12 We.
VIS GF - Round: Wd £13. We £15. **Day:** Wd £20. We £20.
FACILITIES: Clubhouse, Bar, Large & Small Dining Rooms.

FERNFELL GOLF CLUB   MAP 7 A3

Barhatch Lane, Cranleigh, Surrey GU6 7NG.
Guildford A281 to Horsham take Cranleigh turn-off.

CONTACT: Mr B Templeman, Manager. Tel: 0483 268855.
COURSE: 5,461yds, PAR 68, SSS 67. Woodland/parkland.
SOC RESTR'S: Welcome Weekdays with prior arrangements.
SOC GF - Round: Wd £20. We N/A. **Day:** Wd £30. We N/A.
SOC PACK: £45 a day package.
VIS RESTR'S: Welcome Weekdays. After 12 We.
VIS GF - Round: Wd £20. We £20. **Day:** Wd £30. We N/A.
FACILITIES: Bar & Restaurant.

FOXHILLS (CHERTSEY)   MAP 7 A2/3

Stonehill Road, Ottershaw, Surrey KT16 0EL.
J11 M25 to Woking, right at R/about, left next R/about - next left.

CONTACT: Miss K John, Golf Co-ordinator. Tel: 0932 872050.
COURSE: 6,658yds, PAR 73, SSS 72. Heathland course.
SOC RESTR'S: Min. 20 Max 100 Welcome Weekdays.
SOC GF - Round: Wd £40. We N/A. **Day:** Wd £50. We N/A.
SOC PACK: Coffee, Lunch, Dinner, 36 holes: £97 p.p.
VIS RESTR'S: Welcome Weekdays from 8am. After 12 at We.
VIS GF - Round: Wd £45. We £55. **Day:** Wd £65. We N/A.
FACILITIES: 9-hole Course, 3 Restaurants, Tennis & Squash.

FOXHILLS (LONGCROSS)   MAP 7 A2/3

Stonehill Road, Ottershaw, Surrey KT16 0EL.
J11 M25 to Woking, right at R/about, left next R/about - next left.

CONTACT: Miss K John, Golf Co-ordinator. Tel: 0932 872050.
COURSE: 6,391yds, PAR 72, SSS 70. Heathland course.
SOC RESTR'S: Min. 20 Max 100 Welcome Weekdays.
SOC GF - Round: Wd £40. We N/A **Day:** Wd £50. We N/A.
SOC PACK: Coffee, Lunch, Dinner, 36 holes: £97 p.p.
VIS RESTR'S: Welcome Weekdays from 8am. After 12 at We.
VIS GF - Round: Wd £45. We £55. **Day:** Wd £65. We N/A.
FACILITIES: Swimming, Gymnasium & Conference facilities.

GATTON MANOR GOLF CLUB   MAP 7 A3

Ockley, Nr. Dorking, Surrey RH5 5PQ.
A29, 9 miles south from Dorking.

CONTACT: P Davis, General Manager. Tel: 0306 627555.
COURSE: 6,145yds, PAR 72, SSS 72. Undulating parkland.
SOC RESTR'S: Welcome Weekdays.
SOC GF - Round: Wd N/A. We N/A. **Day:** Wd N/A. We N/A.
SOC PACK: Coffee, Lunch, Dinner, 2 rounds: £52.50 p.p.
VIS RESTR'S: Welcome everyday except Sunday morning.
VIS GF - Round: Wd £15. We £20. **Day:** Wd £26 We £40.
FACILITIES: Club Hire, Bar, Restaurant & Twilight GF.

SURREY

HANKLEY COMMON GOLF CLUB MAP 7 A3

Tilford, Farnham, Surrey GU10 2DD.
3 miles south-east of Farnham on Tilford road.

CONTACT: JKA O'Brien, Secretary. Tel: 025 125 2493.
COURSE: 6,418yds, PAR 71, SSS 71. Heathland course.
SOC RESTR'S: By arrangement with Secretary.
SOC GF - Round: Wd N/A. We N/A. **Day:** Wd N/A. We N/A.
SOC PACK: On application.
VIS RESTR'S: Wd Letter of Intro. We at Sec's discretion.
VIS GF - Round: Wd £27. We £34. **Day:** Wd N/A. We N/A.
FACILITIES: Bar snacks, Pro shop.

HINDHEAD GOLF CLUB MAP 7 A3

Churt Road, Hindhead, Surrey GU26 6HX.
1.5 miles north of Hindhead on A287.

CONTACT: The Office. Tel: 0428 604614.
COURSE: 6,365yds, PAR 70, SSS 70. Heathland course.
SOC RESTR'S: Welcome Wednesday & Thursday.
SOC GF - Round: Wd £25. We N/A. **Day:** Wd £33. We N/A.
SOC PACK: Coffee, Lunch, Dinner, 36 holes: £53.
VIS RESTR'S: H'cap Cert of 20 or below & booking at We.
VIS GF - Round: Wd £27. We £32. **Day:** Wd £35. We £42.
FACILITIES: Bar & Restaurant.

HOME PARK GOLF CLUB MAP 7 A2

Hampton Wick, Kingston-upon-Thames, Surrey KT1 4AD.
Kingston Bridge Gate entrance to Home Park.

CONTACT: Mrs Ness, Asst Manager. Tel: 081 977 2423.
COURSE: 6,600yds, PAR 71, SSS 71. Parkland course.
SOC RESTR'S: Welcome Weekdays.
SOC GF - Round: Wd £18. We N/A. **Day:** Wd £28. We N/A.
SOC PACK: Breakfast, Lunch, Dinner or Carvery, 36 holes: £45.30.
VIS RESTR'S: Welcome.
VIS GF - Round: Wd £15. We £20. **Day:** Wd £24. We N/A.
FACILITIES: Bar & Restaurant.

KINGSWOOD G & CC MAP 7 B3

Sandy Lane, Kingswood, Tadworth, Surrey KT20 6NE.
Just off A217, 5 miles from Sutton. Junction 8 M25.

CONTACT: Miss Lynn Thompson, Administrator. Tel: 0737 832188.
COURSE: 6,855yds, PAR 72, SSS 73. Flat Parkland course.
SOC RESTR'S: Welcome on application.
SOC GF - Round: Wd £28. We N/A. **Day:** Wd £40. We N/A.
SOC PACK: Coffee, Lunch, Carvery Dinner, 36 holes: £70.
VIS RESTR'S: Welcome everyday. Some limitations at the We.
VIS GF - Round: Wd £28. We £40. **Day:** Wd £42. We N/A.
FACILITIES: Snooker &Squash.

LEATHERHEAD GOLF CLUB MAP 7 A3

Kingston Road, Leatherhead, Surrey KT22 0DP.
On A243, just off Junction 9 of M25.

CONTACT: Miss VL Laithwaite, Admin Manager. Tel: 0372 843966.
COURSE: 6,107yds, PAR 71, SSS 69. Parkland course.
SOC RESTR'S: Min 16, Max 100 welcome, not Thur am or We.
SOC GF - Round: Wd £30. We N/A. **Day:** Wd £35. We N/A.
SOC PACK: Coffee, Lunch, Dinner, 36 holes: £67.50.
VIS RESTR'S: Welcome but not Thur or We mornings.
VIS GF - Round: Wd £30. We £42.50. **Day:** Wd £35. We N/A.
FACILITIES: Practice Ground, Putting Green, Restaurant, & Bar.

LONDON SCOTTISH GOLF CLUB MAP 7 B2

Windmill Encl, Wimbledon Common, London SW19 5NQ.
12 miles south-west of London.

CONTACT: J Johnson, Secretary. Tel: 081 789 7517.
COURSE: 5,438yds, PAR 68, SSS 66.
SOC RESTR'S: Welcome Wd - must wear red top.
SOC GF - Round: Wd N/A. We N/A. **Day:** Wd £20. We N/A.
SOC PACK: On application.
VIS RESTR'S: Welcome Wd - must wear red top.
VIS GF - Round: Wd £13.50. We N/A. **Day:** Wd £20. We N/A.
FACILITIES: Use of Wimbledon Common Course.

MALDEN GOLF CLUB MAP 7 B2

Traps Lane, New Malden, Surrey KT3 4RS.
Between Wimbledon & Kingston off A3, Coombe Lane.

CONTACT: Mr Fletcher, Secretary. Tel: 081 942 0654.
COURSE: 6,201yds, PAR 71, SSS 70. Parkland course.
SOC RESTR'S: Welcome Wednesday to Friday.
SOC GF - Round: Wd N/A. We N/A. **Day:** Wd N/A. We N/A.
SOC PACK: Coffee, Lunch, Dinner, 36 holes: £50.
VIS RESTR'S: Welcome Wd. Phone re We restrictions.
VIS GF - Round: Wd £20 We £45. **Day:** Wd £30 We £45.
FACILITIES: Bar & Restaurant.

NORTH DOWNS GOLF CLUB MAP 7 B3

Northdown Road, Woldingham, Caterham, Surrey CR3 7AA.
On A22 roundabout at Caterham take the Woldingham road.

CONTACT: JAL Smith, Manager. Tel: 0883 652057.
COURSE: 5,787yds, PAR 69, SSS 68. Undulating course.
SOC RESTR'S: Welcome Monday, Tuesday & Friday.
SOC GF - Round: Wd N/A. We N/A. **Day:** Wd £40. We N/A.
SOC PACK: Coffee, Lunch, Dinner, 36 holes: £49. (18: £41).
VIS RESTR'S: Welcome Weekdays.
VIS GF - Round: Wd £28. We N/A. **Day:** Wd £28. We N/A.
FACILITIES: Restaurant, Bar, etc.

ENGLAND

OAKS SPORTS CENTRE MAP 7 B3

Woodmansterne Road, Carshalton, Surrey SM5 4AN.
On B2032 past Carshalton, 2 miles from Sutton.

CONTACT: D McNab, General Manager. Tel: 081 643 8363.
COURSE: 5,975yds, PAR 69, SSS 69. Meadowland course.
SOC RESTR'S: By arrangement through Secretary.
SOC GF - Round: Wd £9. **We** £11. **Day:** Wd N/A. **We** N/A.
SOC PACK: On application from Secretary.
VIS RESTR'S: Public course no restrictions.
VIS GF - Round: Wd £9. **We** £11. **Day:** Wd N/A. **We** N/A.
FACILITIES: 9-hole Course, Range, Squash, Restaurant & Bar.

ROYAL MID-SURREY GC (OUTER) MAP 7 B2

Old Deer Park, Richmond, Surrey TW9 2SB.
Near Richmond roundabout, off A316.

CONTACT: MSR Lunt, Secretary. Tel: 081 940 1894.
COURSE: 6,337yds, PAR 69, SSS 70. Parkland course.
SOC RESTR'S: H'cap Cert required. No weekends.
SOC GF - Round: Wd N/A. **We** N/A. **Day:** Wd N/A. **We** N/A.
SOC PACK: On application.
VIS RESTR'S: Wd H'cap or with Member. We with Member.
VIS GF - Round: Wd £43. **We** N/A. **Day:** Wd N/A. **We** N/A.
FACILITIES: Bar snacks, Pro shop.

ROYAL MID-SURREY GC (INNER) MAP 7 B2

Old Deer Park, Richmond, Surrey TW9 2SB.
Near Richmond roundabout, off A316.

CONTACT: MSR Lunt, Secretary. Tel: 081 940 1894.
COURSE: 5,446yds, PAR 68, SSS 67. Parkland course.
SOC RESTR'S: H'cap Cert required. No weekends.
SOC GF - Round: Wd N/A. **We** N/A. **Day:** Wd N/A. **We** N/A.
SOC PACK: On application.
VIS RESTR'S: Wd H'cap or with Member. We with Member.
VIS GF - Round: Wd £43. **We** N/A. **Day:** Wd N/A. **We** N/A.
FACILITIES: Bar snacks, Pro shop.

ST. GEORGE'S HILL GOLF CLUB MAP 7 A2/3

Weybridge, Surrey KT13 0NL.
M25 Junction 10 - A3 - A245 to Woking.

CONTACT: MR Mapsell, Secretary. Tel: 0932 847758.
COURSE: 6,569yds, PAR 70, SSS 71. Heathland course.
SOC RESTR'S: Welcome Wednesday, Thursday & Friday.
SOC GF - Round: Wd N/A. **We** N/A. **Day:** Wd N/A. **We** N/A.
SOC PACK: GF on application. 36 Holes + Food approx £75.
VIS RESTR'S: With H'cap Cert Wd (Wed, Thurs, Fri only).
VIS GF - Round: Wd £30. **We** N/A. **Day:** Wd £40. **We** N/A.
FACILITIES: 9-hole course, Bar & Restaurant.

SELSDON PARK GOLF CLUB MAP 7 B3

Sanderstead, South Croydon, Surrey CR2 8YA.
3 miles south-east of Croydon on the A2022.

CONTACT: Mrs C Streek, Bookings. Tel: 081 657 8811 Ext 604.
COURSE: 6,402yds, PAR 71, SSS 71. Parkland course.
SOC RESTR'S: By arrangement through Secretary.
SOC GF - Round: Wd N/A. **We** N/A. **Day:** Wd N/A. **We** N/A.
SOC PACK: Variety of packages available, £28.50-£62.50.
VIS RESTR'S: Please book. Winter & We Twilight GF reductions.
VIS GF - Round: Wd £20. **We** £30/£35. **Day:** Wd £30. **We** N/A.
FACILITIES: 4-Star Hotel, Bar & Restaurant open to non-residents.

SILVERMERE GOLF CLUB MAP 7 A3

Redhill Road, Cobham, Surrey KT11 1EF.
Half-a-mile on B366 from Junction 10 M25/A3.

CONTACT: Miss C Packer, Admin. Tel: 09328 66007.
COURSE: 6,333yds, PAR 71, SSS 71. Woodland/parkland.
SOC RESTR'S: Welcome Weekdays.
SOC GF - Round: Wd £17.50. **We** N/A **Day:** Wd £35. **We** N/A.
SOC PACK: £47. 50 - Full Day with Meals.
VIS RESTR'S: Welcome everyday except Weekend mornings.
VIS GF - Round: Wd £16.50. **We** £21. **Day:** Wd N/A. **We** N/A.
FACILITIES: Floodlit Driving Range, Sports & Clothing Store.

SUNNINGDALE GOLF CLUB (OLD) MAP 7 A2

Sunningdale, Surrey SL5 9RW.
Off the A30 in Sunningdale, 25 miles south-west of London.

CONTACT: Caddymaster. Tel: 0344 26064.
COURSE: 6,586yds, PAR 72, SSS 71. Heathland course.
SOC RESTR'S: Tue, Wed, Thur. With H'cap Cert.
SOC GF - Round: Wd N/A. **We** N/A. **Day:** Wd £80. **We** N/A.
SOC PACK: Several packages available.
VIS RESTR'S: By arrangement. Letter of intro Weekdays.
VIS GF - Round: Wd N/A. **We** N/A. **Day:** Wd £80. **We** N/A.
FACILITIES: 2nd 18-hole course, Bar & Restaurant.

SUNNINGDALE GOLF CLUB (NEW) MAP 7 A2

Sunningdale, Surrey SL5 9RW.
Off the A30 in Sunningdale, 25 miles south-west of London.

CONTACT: Caddymaster. Tel: 0344 26064.
COURSE: 6,676yds, PAR 72, SSS 71. Championship heathland.
SOC RESTR'S: Tue, Wed, Thur. With H'cap Cert.
SOC GF - Round: Wd N/A. **We** N/A. **Day:** Wd £80. **We** N/A.
SOC PACK: Several packages available.
VIS RESTR'S: By arrangement. Letter of intro Weekdays.
VIS GF - Round: Wd N/A. **We** N/A. **Day:** Wd £80. **We** N/A.
FACILITIES: 2nd 18-hole course, Bar & Restaurant.

SURREY

TANDRIDGE GOLF CLUB MAP 7 B3

Oxted, Surrey RH8 9NQ.
M25 Junction 6 - A25 near Oxted.

CONTACT: AS Furnival, Secretary. Tel: 0883 712274.
COURSE: 6,250yds, PAR 70, SSS 70. Parkland course.
SOC RESTR'S: 40 max. Mon, Wed & Thur H'cap Cert required.
SOC GF - Round: Wd N/A. We N/A. Day: Wd £63. We N/A.
SOC PACK: Coffee, Lunch, Tea/Sandwiches - 2 rounds.
VIS RESTR'S: As societies, by appointment with Secretary.
VIS GF - Round: Wd £40. We N/A. Day: Wd N/A. We N/A.
FACILITIES: Bar & Restaurant.

WALTON HEATH (OLD) MAP 7 B3

Tadworth, Surrey KT20 7TP.
3 miles south of Epsom on A217.

CONTACT: GR James, Secretary. Tel: 0737 812380.
COURSE: 6,801yds, PAR 730, SSS 73. Heathland course.
SOC RESTR'S: H'cap Cert required. No weekends.
SOC GF - Round: Wd N/A. We N/A. Day: Wd N/A. We N/A.
SOC PACK: On application.
VIS RESTR'S: Wd by prior arrangement with H'cap Cert
VIS GF - Round: Wd £57. We N/A. Day: Wd N/A. We N/A.
FACILITIES: Bar snacks, Pro shop.

WALTON HEATH (NEW) MAP 7 B3

Tadworth, Surrey KT20 7TP.
3 miles south of Epsom on A217.

CONTACT: GR James, Secretary. Tel: 0737 812380.
COURSE: 6,609yds, PAR 72, SSS 72. Heathland course.
SOC RESTR'S: H'cap Cert required. No weekends.
SOC GF - Round: Wd N/A. We N/A. Day: Wd N/A. We N/A.
SOC PACK: On application.
VIS RESTR'S: Wd by prior arrangement with H'cap Cert.
VIS GF - Round: Wd £57. We N/A. Day: Wd N/A. We N/A.
FACILITIES: Bar snacks, Pro shop.

WENTWORTH GOLF CLUB (WEST) MAP 7 A2

Wentworth Drive, Virginia Water, Surrey GU25 4LS.
A30 junction A329 Ascot.

CONTACT: Reception. Tel: 0344 842201.
COURSE: 6,945yds, PAR 72, SSS 72. Heathland course.
SOC RESTR'S: Max 100 Welcome Weekdays.
SOC GF - Round: Wd £80. We N/A. Day: Wd N/A. We N/A.
SOC PACK: 1 round East - 1 round West - Coffee, Lunch: £135.
VIS RESTR'S: Welcome Weekdays from 8.30-11 & 2 onwards.
VIS GF - Round: Wd £80. We N/A. Day: Wd N/A. We N/A.
FACILITIES: Restaurant, Private Rooms, Tennis.

WENTWORTH GOLF CLUB (EAST) MAP 7 A2

Wentworth Drive, Virginia Water, Surrey GU25 4LS.
A30 junction A329 Ascot.

CONTACT: Reception. Tel: 0344 842201.
COURSE: 6,176yds, PAR 68, SSS 70. Heathland course.
SOC RESTR'S: Max 100. Welcome Weekdays.
SOC GF - Round: Wd £60. We N/A. Day: Wd N/A. We N/A.
SOC PACK: 1 round East - 1 round West - Coffee, Lunch: £135.
VIS RESTR'S: Welcome Weekdays from 8.30-11 & 2 onwards.
VIS GF - Round: Wd £60. We N/A. Day: Wd N/A. We N/A.
FACILITIES: Restaurant, Private Rooms, Tennis.

WENTWORTH G C (EDINBURGH) MAP 7 A2

Wentworth Drive, Virginia Water, Surrey GU25 4LS.
A30 junction A329 Ascot.

CONTACT: Reception. Tel: 0344 842201.
COURSE: 6,979yds, PAR 72, SSS 73. Heathland course.
SOC RESTR'S: Max 100 Welcome Weekdays.
SOC GF - Round: Wd £65. We N/A. Day: Wd N/A. We N/A.
SOC PACK: 1 r'd E'burgh, 1 r'd East/West, Coffee, Lunch: £135.
VIS RESTR'S: Welcome Weekdays from 8.30-11 & 2 onwards.
VIS GF - Round: Wd £65. We N/A. Day: Wd N/A. We N/A.
FACILITIES: Restaurant, Private Rooms, Tennis.

WEST BYFLEET GOLF CLUB MAP 7 A3

Sheerwater Road, West Byfleet, Surrey KT14 6AA.
M25 Junction 10, on A245 to Woking.

CONTACT: D Lee, General Manager. Tel: 0932 343433.
COURSE: 6,211yds, PAR 70, SSS 70. Heathland course.
SOC RESTR'S: Min. 25 players. Welcome Tues/Wed 8. 45-1.45.
SOC GF - Round: Wd N/A. We N/A. Day: Wd N/A. We N/A.
SOC PACK: Coffee, Lunch, Dinner, 36 holes - £50. (18 - £40)
VIS RESTR'S: Welcome Weekdays. Thur is Ladies Day.
VIS GF - Round: Wd £27. We N/A. Day: Wd £33. We N/A.
FACILITIES: Bar & Restaurant.

WEST HILL GOLF CLUB MAP 7 A3

Bagshot Road, Brookwood, Surrey GU24 0GH.
On the A322 by Brookwood village.

CONTACT: Mrs J Hay, Asst Secretary. Tel: 0483 474365.
COURSE: 6,368yds, PAR 69, SSS 70. Heathland/woodland.
SOC RESTR'S: Welcome Mon, Tues, Thurs & Fri.
SOC GF - Round: Wd N/A. We N/A. Day: Wd N/A. We N/A.
SOC PACK: Lunch, Tea, 36 holes: £58. Lunch, Dinner, 36 holes: £61.
VIS RESTR'S: Welcome Weekdays by arrangement.
VIS GF - Round: Wd £32. We N/A. Day: Wd £42. We N/A.
FACILITIES: Practice Range, Bar & Restaurant.

ENGLAND

WORPLESDON GOLF CLUB   MAP 7 A3

Heath House Road, Woking, Surrey GU22 0RA.
Near Richmond roundabout, off A316.

CONTACT: Maj REE Jones, Secretary. Tel: 0483 472277.
COURSE: 6,440yds, PAR 71, SSS 71. Heathland course.
SOC RESTR'S: H'cap Cert required. No weekends.
SOC GF - Round: Wd N/A. **We** N/A. **Day: Wd** N/A. **We** N/A.
SOC PACK: On application.
VIS RESTR'S: H'cap Cert. We with Member. GF on application.
VIS GF - Round: Wd N/A. **We** N/A. **Day: Wd** N/A. **We** N/A.
FACILITIES: Bar, Pro shop.

East Sussex

ANDERIDA GOLF CLUB   MAP 7 B3

Ashdown Forest Hotel, Forest Row, East Sussex RH18 5BB.
3 miles south of East Grinstead on A22, Forest Row.

CONTACT: Ms K Keen, Reservations. Tel: 0342 824866.
COURSE: 5,549yds, PAR 68, SSS 67. Forest course.
SOC RESTR'S: Min. 12. Welcome by prior arrangement.
SOC GF - Round: Wd £18. **We** £23. **Day: Wd** £23. **We** £28.
SOC PACK: Coffee, Lunch, Dinner, 36 holes: £45-£50.
VIS RESTR'S: Welcome, telephone to check availability.
VIS GF - Round: Wd £15. **We** £20. **Day: Wd** £20. **We** £25.
FACILITIES: A la Carte Restaurant & 15-bedroom Hotel.

DALE HILL GOLF CLUB   MAP 3 B3

Ticehurst, Wadhurst, East Sussex TN5 7DQ.
On B2087, 1 mile off A21.

CONTACT: Mr R Wellyn, Secretary. Tel: 0580 200112.
COURSE: 6,063yds, PAR 69, SSS 69. Wooded parkland.
SOC RESTR'S: By arrangement through Secretary.
SOC GF - Round: Wd £20. **We** £25. **Day: Wd** £35. **We** £50.
SOC PACK: Coffee, Lunch, Dinner, 36 holes: £45.
VIS RESTR'S: Welcome except before 10 Weekends.
VIS GF - Round: Wd £20. **We** £25. **Day: Wd** £35. **We** £50.
FACILITIES: 4-Star/5-Crown luxury hotel attached to Club.

DYKE GOLF CLUB   MAP 3 A3

Dyke Road, Brighton, East Sussex BN1 8YJ.
From A23 take A2038 to Hove follow signs to Devil's Dyke.

CONTACT: KL Butt, Assistant Secretary. Tel: 0273 857296.
COURSE: 6,577yds, PAR 72, SSS 71. Downland course.
SOC RESTR'S: Min. 16. Welcome Weekdays except Tuesday.
SOC GF - Round: Wd £21. **We** N/A. **Day: Wd** £31. **We** N/A.
SOC PACK: Coffee, Lunch, Dinner, 36 holes: £45.
VIS RESTR'S: Welcome everyday with reservation. Not am Sun.
VIS GF - Round: Wd £21. **We** £31. **Day: Wd** £31. **We** N/A.
FACILITIES: Restaurant & Bar.

EAST SUSSEX NATIONAL (EAST)   MAP 3 A3

Little Horsted, Uckfield, East Sussex TN22 5TS.
Off the A22, 2 miles south of Uckfield.
Recommended Hotel: Halland Forge Hotel, Nr Lewes.

CONTACT: G Dukart, Director. Tel: 0825 880088.
COURSE: 7,112yds, PAR 73, SSS 74. Manicured parkland.
SOC RESTR'S: Min 20. Welcome with 6 months prior notice.
SOC GF - Round: Wd £65. **We** £75. **Day: Wd** £85. **We** £95.
SOC PACK: Several available to suit requirements.
VIS RESTR'S: Welcome with 7 days prior booking.
VIS GF - Round: Wd £65. **We** £75. **Day: Wd** £85. **We** £95.
FACILITIES: Restaurant, Bar, Golf Academy, Range & Accomm.

EAST SUSSEX NATIONAL (WEST)   MAP 3 A3

Little Horsted, Uckfield, East Sussex TN22 5TS.
Off the A22, 2 miles south of Uckfield.
Recommended Hotel: Halland Forge Hotel, Nr Lewes.

CONTACT: G Dukart, Professional. Tel: 0825 880088.
COURSE: 7,072yds, PAR 72, SSS 74. Manicured American course.
SOC RESTR'S: Min. 12. Welcome with 6 months prior notice.
SOC GF - Round: Wd £60. **We** £60. **Day: Wd** £80. **We** £80.
SOC PACK: Several, available to suit requirements.
VIS RESTR'S: Welcome with 7 days prior booking, with Member.
VIS GF - Round: Wd £30. **We** £40. **Day: Wd** £30. **We** £40.
FACILITIES: Restaurant, Bar, Golf Academy, Range & Accomm.

HIGHWOODS GOLF CLUB   MAP 3 B3

Ellerslie Lane, Bexhill-on-Sea, East Sussex TN39 4LJ.
A259, 2 miles west of Bexhill-on-Sea.

CONTACT: Mr I Osborough, Secretary. Tel: 0424 212625.
COURSE: 6,218yds, PAR 70, SSS 70. Undulating parkland.
SOC RESTR'S: Min 18. Monday, Wednesday & Thursday.
SOC GF - Round: Wd N/A. **We** N/A. **Day: Wd** N/A. **We** N/A.
SOC PACK: £42 (18 holes: £27) (36 holes: £29) + Food = £42.
VIS RESTR'S: Welcome except Sunday am. H'cap Cert required.
VIS GF - Round: Wd £25. **We** £30. **Day: Wd** £25. **We** £30.
FACILITIES: Restaurant.

WEST SUSSEX

ROYAL ASHDOWN FOREST G C MAP 7 B3

Chapel Lane, Forest Row, Nr. East Grinstead RH18 5LR.
A22 to B2110 - Chapel Lane - Left at top of hill.

CONTACT: D Scrivens, Secretary. Tel: 0342 822018.
COURSE: 6,477yds, PAR 72, SSS 71. Heathland course.
SOC RESTR'S: Welcome Wednesday, Thursday & Friday.
SOC GF - Round: Wd N/A. **We** N/A. **Day:** Wd N/A. **We** N/A.
SOC PACK: Coffee, Lunch, Dinner, 36 Holes: £60.
VIS RESTR'S: Advisable to telephone first.
VIS GF - Round: Wd £27. **We** £32. **Day:** Wd £35. **We** £40.
FACILITIES: Practice Ground.

WEST HOVE GOLF CLUB MAP 3 A3

Church Farm, Hangleton, Hove, East Sussex BN3 8AN.
North of new Link road off A27 to new M/way on to spur road.

CONTACT: N Hill, Secretary. Tel: 0273 419738.
COURSE: 6,266yds, PAR 72, SSS 70. Downland course.
SOC RESTR'S: Welcome Weekdays.
SOC GF - Round: Wd N/A. **We** N/A. **Day:** Wd N/A. **We** N/A.
SOC PACK: £30 to include Ploughmans Lunch & Dinner.
VIS RESTR'S: Welcome after 12 noon, please phone.
VIS GF - Round: Wd £16. **We** £18. **Day:** Wd £16. **We** £18.
FACILITIES: Bar, Restaurant & Twilight Green Fee.

RAC ★★★
Open 7 days a week

The ideal 19th hole

Play golf to your heart's content in Sussex.
Then dine in style and stay a while at the
Halland Forge Hotel and Restaurant.
The Forge Restaurant – *A la Carte and Table d'Hôte*
Luncheon and Dinner. Coffee Shop/Carvery – *Open for
Breakfast, Lunch and Tea from 8.00am to 6.00pm*
Anvil Lounge Bar – *Fully Licensed.*
20 Bedrooms with private facilities.
▲ We are the ideal golf centre for South East England ▲

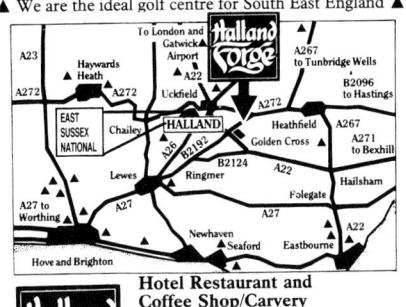

**Hotel Restaurant and
Coffee Shop/Carvery**
Halland, nr Lewes, East Sussex
On A22/B2192 crossroads,
4 miles south of Uckfield just
beyond East Sussex National.

Tel: Halland (0825) 840456 Fax: (0825) 840773

WILLINGDON GOLF CLUB MAP 3 B3

Southdown Road, Eastbourne, East Sussex BN20 9AA.
2 miles north of Eastbourne on A22.

CONTACT: B Kirby, Secretary. Tel: 0323 410981.
COURSE: 6,049yds, PAR 69, SSS 69. Hilly downland course.
SOC RESTR'S: Max. 30. Welcome Wed, Thur, Fri, after 9.
SOC GF - Round: Wd N/A. **We** N/A. **Day:** Wd £26. **We** N/A.
SOC PACK: Coffee, Lunch, Dinner, 36 holes: Under £40.
VIS RESTR'S: Welcome after 9 everyday - not Tues or Sun am.
VIS GF - Round: Wd N/A. **We** N/A. **Day:** Wd £24. **We** £27.
FACILITIES: Clubhouse, Restaurant & Bar.

West Sussex

SEAFORD GOLF CLUB MAP 3 A3

East Blatchington, Seaford, East Sussex BN25 2JD.
1 mile north of Seaford.

CONTACT: Mr P Shenans, Secretary. Tel: 0323 892442.
COURSE: 6,233yds, PAR 69, SSS 69. Downland course.
SOC RESTR'S: Welcome Wednesday, Thursday & Friday.
SOC GF - Round: Wd £24. **We** N/A. **Day:** Wd £30. **We** N/A.
SOC PACK: Ploughmans Lunch, Dinner & 2 rounds: £48.
VIS RESTR'S: Welcome Mon, Wed, Thur, Fri usually after 10.
VIS GF - Round: Wd £24. **We** N/A. **Day:** Wd £30. **We** N/A.
FACILITIES: Dormy House accommodation for 18.

COPTHORNE GOLF CLUB MAP 7 B3

Borers Arms Road, Copthorne, West Sussex RH10 3LL.
1 mile east off Junction 10 off M23.

CONTACT: I Evans, Secretary. Tel: 0342 712508.
COURSE: 6,505yds, PAR 71, SSS 71. Wooded heathland.
SOC RESTR'S: Welcome midweek - all day - any size.
SOC GF - Round: Wd £25. **We** N/A. **Day:** Wd £33. **We** N/A.
SOC PACK: Lunch, Dinner & 2 rounds: £55.
VIS RESTR'S: Welcome Weekdays & after 2pm Weekends.
VIS GF - Round: Wd £25. **We** £30. **Day:** Wd £33. **We** N/A.
FACILITIES: Restaurant.

ENGLAND

COTTESMORE COUNTRY CLUB (OLD)   MAP 7 B3

Buchan Hill, Pease Pottage, Crawley, West Sussex RH11 9AT.
Exit 11 M23(S): Signposted Pease Pottage A23(N).

CONTACT: V Williams, Secretary/Manager. Tel: 0293 528256.
COURSE: 6,113yds, PAR 72, SSS 70. Meadowland course.
SOC RESTR'S: Welcome Monday, Wednesday & Friday.
SOC GF - Round: Wd N/A. **We** N/A. **Day:** Wd N/A. **We** N/A.
SOC PACK: Coffee, Lunch, Dinner, 36 holes: £50.
VIS RESTR'S: Welcome Weekdays & after 11 on Weekends.
VIS GF - Round: Wd £30. **We** £35. **Day:** Wd £30. **We** £38.
FACILITIES: Second 18-hole Course & Hotel.

COTTESMORE COUNTRY CLUB (NEW)   MAP 7 B3

Buchan Hill, Pease Pottage, Crawley, West Sussex RH11 9AT.
Exit 11 M23(S): Signposted Pease Pottage A23(N).

CONTACT: V Williams, Secretary/Manager. Tel: 0293 528256.
COURSE: 5,700yds, PAR 70, SSS 68. Meadowland course.
SOC RESTR'S: Welcome Monday, Wednesday & Friday.
SOC GF - Round: Wd N/A. **We** N/A. **Day:** Wd N/A. **We** N/A.
SOC PACK: Coffee, Lunch, Dinner, 36 holes: £38.
VIS RESTR'S: Welcome Weekdays & after 11 on Weekends.
VIS GF - Round: Wd N/A. **We** N/A. **Day:** Wd £20. **We** £25.
FACILITIES: Second 18-hole Course & Hotel.

COWDRAY PARK GOLF CLUB   MAP 3 A3

Midhurst, West Sussex GU29 0BB.
1 mile east of Midhurst on A272.

CONTACT: K Campbell, Secretary/Manager. Tel: 0730 813599.
COURSE: 6,212yds, PAR 70, SSS 70. Parkland course.
SOC RESTR'S: 20-40, Welcome Mon, Wed, Thur. 9/ 2.
SOC GF - Round: Wd N/A. **We** N/A. **Day:** Wd £20. **We** N/A.
SOC PACK: Coffee, Lunch, Dinner, 36 holes: £45.
VIS RESTR'S: Welcome Weekdays & after 11 on Sat & 3 on Sun.
VIS GF - Round: Wd £20. **We** £25. **Day:** Wd £20. **We** £25.
FACILITIES: Bar & Restaurant.

HAM MANOR GOLF CLUB   MAP 3 A3

West Drive, Angmering, West Sussex BN16 4JE.
Turn off A27 to Angmering village, entrance off Station Rd.

CONTACT: PH Saubergue, Sec/Manager. Tel: 0903 783288.
COURSE: 6,243yds, PAR 70, SSS 70. Parkland course.
SOC RESTR'S: Min. 20. Welcome Weds & Thurs from 8.45.
SOC GF - Round: Wd £25. **We** N/A. **Day:** Wd £25. **We** N/A.
SOC PACK: £40 incl. Full catering & 36 holes.
VIS RESTR'S: Not before 8.45. Handicap Certificate required.
VIS GF - Round: Wd £25. **We** £35. **Day:** Wd £25. **We** £35.
FACILITIES: Snooker.

HAYWARDS HEATH GOLF CLUB   MAP 7 B3

High Beech Lane, Haywards Heath, West Sussex RH16 1SL.
2 miles north of Haywards Heath.

CONTACT: J Duncan, Managing Secretary. Tel: 0444 414457.
COURSE: 6,204yds, PAR 71, SSS 70. Parkland course.
SOC RESTR'S: Min. 20. Welcome Wednesday & Thursday.
SOC GF - Round: Wd N/A. **We** N/A. **Day:** Wd N/A. **We** N/A.
SOC PACK: On booking through Secretary.
VIS RESTR'S: Please book.
VIS GF - Round: Wd £22. **We** £30. **Day:** Wd £27. **We** £35.
FACILITIES: Bar & Restaurant.

HILL BARN GOLF CLUB   MAP 3 A3

Hill Barn Lane, Worthing, West Sussex BN14 9QE.
North-east of Worthing off Upper Brighton Road.

CONTACT: Pro Shop. Tel: 0903 237301.
COURSE: 6,224yds, PAR 70, SSS 70. Downland course.
SOC RESTR'S: Min 11. Please book in advance.
SOC GF - Round: Wd £12. **We** N/A. **Day:** Wd N/A. **We** N/A.
SOC PACK: Available at time of booking.
VIS RESTR'S: Always welcome.
VIS GF - Round: Wd £10.50. **We** £12.50. **Day:** Wd N/A. **We** N/A.
FACILITIES: Bar & Clubhouse.

IFIELD GOLF & COUNTRY CLUB   MAP 7 B3

Rusper Road, Ifield, Crawley, West Sussex RH11 0LW.
Just off the A23 on the outskirts of Crawley.

CONTACT: B Gazzard, Secretary. Tel: 0293 520222.
COURSE: 6,314yds, PAR 71, SSS 70. Parkland course.
SOC RESTR'S: On application from Club Secretary.
SOC GF - Round: Wd £20. **We** N/A. **Day:** Wd £27. **We** N/A.
SOC PACK: Available at time of booking.
VIS RESTR'S: Welcome Mon & Tues. Wed pm. Thur & Fri after 3.
VIS GF - Round: Wd £20. **We** N/A. **Day:** Wd £27. **We** N/A.
FACILITIES: Bar & Catering.

PAXHILL PARK GOLF CLUB   MAP 7 B3

East Mascalls Lane, Lindfield, West Sussex RH16 2QN.
North of Haywards Heath off the B2111 east of Lindfield.

CONTACT: K Moss, Secretary. Tel: 0444 484467.
COURSE: 6,174yds, PAR 71, SSS 69. Parkland course.
SOC RESTR'S: Welcome Weekdays. Weekends pm.
SOC GF - Round: Wd £12.50. **We** £17.50. **Day:** Wd £20. **We** N/A.
SOC PACK: Coffee, Lunch, Dinner, 36 holes: £33.
VIS RESTR'S: Welcome Weekdays. Weekends after 1pm.
VIS GF - Round: Wd £12.50. **We** £17.50. **Day:** Wd £20. **We** N/A.
FACILITIES: Full A la Carte Restaurant facilities.

PYECOMBE GOLF CLUB MAP 3 A3

Clayton Hill, Pyecombe, West Sussex BN45 7FF.
4 miles north of Brighton off A23.

CONTACT: WM Wise, Secretary. Tel: 0273 845372.
COURSE: 6,124yds, PAR 70, SSS 70. Downland course.
SOC RESTR'S: Max 45. Welcome Mon, Weds & Thurs.
SOC GF - Round: Wd N/A. **We** N/A. **Day:** Wd N/A. **We** N/A.
SOC PACK: Coffee, Lunch, Dinner + 2 rounds: £39.
VIS RESTR'S: Welcome after 9. 15 Weekdays - after 2 Weekends.
VIS GF - Round: Wd £15. **We** £25. **Day:** Wd £20. **We** £25.
FACILITIES: Full catering.

SINGING HILLS GOLF CLUB MAP 3 A3

Albourne, West Sussex BN6 9EB.
A23 turn-B2218 to Albourne-B2177 to Henfield-course on right.
See advertisement.
CONTACT: D T Howe, Club Director. Tel: 0273 835353.
COURSE: 6,273yds, PAR 70, SSS 70. 27-Hole Complex.
SOC RESTR'S: No restrictions.
SOC GF - Round: Wd N/A. **We** N/A. **Day:** Wd N/A. **We** N/A.
SOC PACK: Coffee, Lunch, Carvery, 36 holes: £45.
VIS RESTR'S: No restrictions, always welcome.
VIS GF - Round: Wd £20. **We** £25. **Day:** Wd £30. **We** £38.
FACILITIES: Driving Range & Conference Rooms.

Singing Hills Golf Course Ltd

Albourne, Sussex BN6 9EB.
Tel: 0273 835353 Fax: 0273 835444
27 hole complex. Superior Clubhouse facilities include Restaurant & Conference Facilities. Driving Range.

WEST CHILTINGTON GOLF CLUB MAP 3 A3

Broadford Bridge Road, W Chiltington, W Sussex RH20 2YA.
B2133, 2 miles east A29 London/Bognor road - Signposted.

CONTACT: SE Coulson, Secretary. Tel: 0798 813574.
COURSE: 6,000yds, PAR 70, SSS 69. Gently undulating course.
SOC RESTR'S: Welcome Weekdays. Min 10.
SOC GF - Round: Wd £13. **We** N/A. **Day:** Wd N/A. **We** N/A.
SOC PACK: Coffee, Lunch, Dinner, 36 holes: £36.
VIS RESTR'S: Welcome. Public course.
VIS GF - Round: Wd £15. **We** £20. **Day:** Wd £28. **We** £33.
FACILITIES: 9-hole Par 3 Course, Driving Range & Practice Area.

TYNE & WEAR

WEST SUSSEX GOLF CLUB MAP 3 A3

Hurston Lane, Pulborough, West Sussex RH20 2EN.
1.5 miles east of Pulborough on A283.

CONTACT: GR Martindale, Secretary. Tel: 0798 872563.
COURSE: 6,221yds, PAR 68, SSS 70. Heathland course.
SOC RESTR'S: Wednesday & Thursday only.
SOC GF - Round: Wd £28. **We** N/A. **Day:** Wd £38. **We** N/A.
SOC PACK: Lunch, Dinner, 36 holes: £55.
VIS RESTR'S: Wd Intro & H'cap. Fri with Mem. GF on application.
VIS GF - Round: Wd £28. **We** N/A. **Day:** Wd £38. **We** N/A.
FACILITIES: Bar snacks, Pro shop.

Tyne & Wear

CITY OF NEWCASTLE GOLF CLUB MAP 5 A2

Three Mile Bridge, Gosforth, Newcastle-upon-Tyne NE3 2DR.
3 miles north of City Centre.

CONTACT: AJ Matthew, Secretary. Tel: 091 285 1775.
COURSE: 6,508yds, PAR 72, SSS 71. Flat parkland course.
SOC RESTR'S: Welcome Tuesday, Wednesday & Thursday.
SOC GF - Round: Wd N/A. **We** N/A. **Day:** Wd £19. **We** N/A.
SOC PACK: On application from Secretary.
VIS RESTR'S: Welcome everyday. Limited Fri & Men's Comp Days.
VIS GF - Round: Wd N/A. **We** N/A. **Day:** Wd £19. **We** £21.
FACILITIES: Bar, Food, & Snooker.

NEWCASTLE UNITED GOLF CLUB MAP 5 A2

Ponteland Road, Cowgate, Newcastle-upon-Tyne NE5 3JW.
2.5 miles west of City Centre.

CONTACT: G Ritchie, Hon. Secretary. Tel: 091 286 9998.
COURSE: 6,573yds, PAR 72, SSS 71. Moorland links course.
SOC RESTR'S: Welcome Weekdays.
SOC GF - Round: Wd N/A. **We** N/A. **Day:** Wd £12.50. **We** N/A.
SOC PACK: Variable, details on application.
VIS RESTR'S: Welcome Weekdays, limited Weekends.
VIS GF - Round: Wd £12.50. **We** £16.50. **Day:** Wd N/A. **We** N/A.
FACILITIES: Bar Meals.

ENGLAND

SOUTH SHIELDS GOLF CLUB MAP 5 B2

Cleadon Hills, South Shields, Tyne & Wear NE34 8EG.
A1018 north from Sunderland - Quarry Lane.

CONTACT: WH Loades, Secretary. Tel: 091 456 0475.
COURSE: 6,264yds Par 71, SSS 70. Seaside course.
SOC RESTR'S: Please book through Secretary.
SOC GF - Round: Wd £20. We N/A. Day: Wd N/A. We N/A.
SOC PACK: On application from Secretary.
VIS RESTR'S: Always welcome.
VIS GF - Round: Wd £20. We £25. Day: Wd N/A. We N/A.
FACILITIES: Meals available all day. PGA Coaching.

WASHINGTON MOAT HOUSE G C MAP 5 B2

Stonecellar Road, High Usworth, Washington NE37 1PH.
At Washington Moat House Hotel.

CONTACT: B Wardle, Leisure Manager. Tel: 091 417 2626.
COURSE: 6,604yds, PAR 73, SSS 72. Parkland course.
SOC RESTR'S: By arrangement through Leisure Manager.
SOC GF - Round: Wd £15. We N/A. Day: Wd N/A. We N/A.
SOC PACK: Negotiable, depending on size & requirements.
VIS RESTR'S: Please book by phone.
VIS GF - Round: Wd £15. We £22. Day: Wd N/A. We N/A.
FACILITIES: 106-bedroomed hotel on-site.

WHITBURN GOLF CLUB MAP 5 B2

Lizard Lane, South Shields, Tyne& Wear NE34 7AF.
Between Sunderland & South Shields, adj to Coast Rd.

CONTACT: Mrs. V Atkinson, Secretary. Tel: 091 529 4210.
COURSE: 6,046yds, PAR 70, SSS 69. Parkland course.
SOC RESTR'S: Welcome except Tuesday & Weekends.
SOC GF - Round: Wd £15. We N/A. Day: Wd £15. We N/A.
SOC PACK: £2 reduction per person on numbers over 11.
VIS RESTR'S: Welcome with limitations on Tues & Comp We.
VIS GF - Round: Wd £15. We £20. Day: Wd £15. We £20.
FACILITIES: Bar & Catering facilities.

RAC Regional Road Maps

Large scale (3 miles to 1 inch) maps for the motorist. Each sheet contains details of motorway junctions, dual carriageways, town plans, a full index of towns and villages, and tourist information including golf courses.

Price £3.99
Available from bookshops
or direct from the RAC on 0235 834885

Warwickshire

LEAMINGTON & COUNTY G C MAP 2 B2

Golf Lane, Leamington Spa, Warwickshire CV31 2QA.
2 miles south of Leamington Spa off A452.

CONTACT: Mrs SM Cooknell, Secretary. Tel: 0926 425961.
COURSE: 6,424yds, PAR 71, SSS 71. Undulating parkland course.
SOC RESTR'S: Welcome Wednesday & Thursday.
SOC GF - Round: Wd £23. We N/A. Day: Wd £26. We N/A.
SOC PACK: Soup & Sandwich Lunch £3. Eve Meal from £8.
VIS RESTR'S: Welcome.
VIS GF - Round: Wd £25. We £37. Day: Wd £28. We £68.
FACILITIES: Snooker.

NUNEATON GOLF CLUB MAP 2 B1

Golf Drive, Nuneaton, Warwickshire CV11 6QF.
2 miles south of Nuneaton.

CONTACT: G Pinder, Secretary/Manager. Tel: 0203 347810.
COURSE: 6,412yds, PAR 71, SSS 71. Parkland course.
SOC RESTR'S: Min. 12. Welcome Wednesday & Friday.
SOC GF - Round: Wd £22. We N/A. Day: Wd N/A. We N/A.
SOC PACK: Coffee, Lunch, Dinner, 36 Holes: £40.
VIS RESTR'S: Welcome Weekdays.
VIS GF - Round: Wd N/A. We N/A. Day: Wd £22. We N/A.
FACILITIES: Food available except Monday.

PURLEY CHASE G & CC MAP 2 B1

Ridge Lane, Nr. Nuneaton, North Warwickshire CV10 0RB.
M42/A5 junction 6 miles. 4 miles north-west of Nuneaton.

CONTACT: Lesley Newitt. Tel: 0203 393118.
COURSE: 7,000yds, PAR 72, SSS 72. Meadowland course.
SOC RESTR'S: Over 40 by consultation. Weekdays preferred.
SOC GF - Round: Wd £12. We N/A. Day: Wd £17. We N/A.
SOC PACK: £21 min. to £40 for complete day.
VIS RESTR'S: Welcome.
VIS GF - Round: Wd £12. We £18. Day: Wd £17. We N/A.
FACILITIES: Bar, Restaurant & Driving Range.

WEST MIDLANDS

WELCOMBE GOLF CLUB   MAP 2 B2

Warwick Road, Stratford-upon-Avon, Warwickshire CV37 0NR.
Exit M40 at Junction 15, follow signs to Stratford.

CONTACT: Golf Office. Tel: 0789 295252.
COURSE: 6,202yds, PAR 70, SSS 70. Parkland course.
SOC RESTR'S: Upon request. Welcome Weekdays.
SOC GF - Round: Wd £12. We N/A. **Day:** Wd £27.50. We N/A.
SOC PACK: Approx. £55 for a days golf & dinner at hotel.
VIS RESTR'S: Upon request. Hotel Guests £20 Wd & We.
VIS GF - Round: Wd N/A. We N/A. **Day:** Wd £32.50. We £40.
FACILITIES: Practice Area, Putting Green & Tennis.

West Midlands

BELFRY GOLF CLUB (BRABAZON)   MAP 2 B1

Lichfield Road, Wishaw, Sutton Coldfield B76 9PR.
4 miles north of Junction 4 M6.

CONTACT: R Maxfield, Golf Manager. Tel: 0675 470301.
COURSE: 6,975yds, PAR 73, SSS 73. Parkland course.
SOC RESTR'S: On application.
SOC GF - Round: Wd £50. We £50. **Day:** Wd £50. We £50.
SOC PACK: On application from Secretary.
VIS RESTR'S: Bookings 14 days in advance.
VIS GF - Round: Wd £50. We £50. **Day:** Wd £50. We £50.
FACILITIES: Driving Range & Restaurants.

BELFRY GOLF CLUB (DERBY)   MAP 2 B1

Lichfield Road, Wishaw, Sutton Coldfield B76 9PR.
4 miles north of Junction 4 M6.

CONTACT: R Maxfield, Golf Manager. Tel: 0675 470301.
COURSE: 6,077yds, PAR 70, SSS 70. Parkland course.
SOC RESTR'S: On application.
SOC GF - Round: Wd £25. We £25. **Day:** Wd £25. We £25.
SOC PACK: On application from Secretary.
VIS RESTR'S: Bookings 14 days in advance.
VIS GF - Round: Wd £25. We £25. **Day:** Wd £25. We £25.
FACILITIES: Driving Range & Restaurants.

COPT HEATH GOLF CLUB   MAP 2 B2

1220 Warwick Road, Knowle, Solihull B93 9LN.
2 miles south of Solihull on A4141.

CONTACT: W Lenton, Secretary. Tel: 0564 772650.
COURSE: 6,500yds, PAR 71, SSS 71. Parkland course.
SOC RESTR'S: Prior booking. No weekends.
SOC GF - Round: Wd N/A. We N/A. **Day:** Wd N/A. We N/A.
SOC PACK: On application.
VIS RESTR'S: Wd H'cap Cert required. We with Member.
VIS GF - Round: Wd £35. We N/A. **Day:** Wd N/A. We N/A.
FACILITIES: Bar, Restaurant, Pro shop.

FOREST OF ARDEN GC (ARDEN)   MAP 2 B2

Maxstoke Lane, Meriden, Coventry CV7 7HR.
9 miles west of of Coventry, off A45.

CONTACT: R Woolston, Golf Manager. Tel: 0676 23721.
COURSE: 7,100yds, PAR 72, SSS 73. Parkland course.
SOC RESTR'S: Prior booking. No weekends.
SOC GF - Round: Wd N/A. We N/A. **Day:** Wd N/A. We N/A.
SOC PACK: On application.
VIS RESTR'S: Not before 1 at We. GF on application.
VIS GF - Round: Wd N/A. We N/A. **Day:** Wd N/A. We N/A.
FACILITIES: Bar, Restaurant, Pro shop, Leisure centre.

FOREST OF ARDEN (AYLESFORD)   MAP 2 B2

Maxstoke Lane, Meriden, Coventry CV7 7HR.
9 miles west of of Coventry, off A45.

CONTACT: R Woolston, Golf Manager. Tel: 0676 23721.
COURSE: 6,525yds, PAR 72, SSS 71. Parkland course.
SOC RESTR'S: Prior booking. No weekends.
SOC GF - Round: Wd N/A. We N/A. **Day:** Wd N/A. We N/A.
SOC PACK: On application.
VIS RESTR'S: Not before 1 at We. GF on application.
VIS GF - Round: Wd N/A. We N/A. **Day:** Wd N/A. We N/A.
FACILITIES: Bar, Restaurant, Pro shop, Leisure centre.

HANDSWORTH GOLF CLUB   MAP 2 B1

Sunningdale Cl, Handsworth Wood, Birmingham B20 1NP.
5 mins from Junction 1 of M5 or Junction 7 of M6.

CONTACT: JA Whitaker, Asst Secretary. Tel: 021 554 3387.
COURSE: 6,312yds, PAR 70, SSS 70. Parkland course.
SOC RESTR'S: Welcome Monday, Wednesday & Thursday.
SOC GF - Round: Wd £23. We N/A. **Day:** Wd £25. We N/A.
SOC PACK: Coffee, Lunch, Dinner, Golf: £38.
VIS RESTR'S: Welcome except Tues 9.30-2. We H'cap Cert req.
VIS GF - Round: Wd £25. We N/A. **Day:** Wd £25. We N/A.
FACILITIES: Large Practice Area & Squash Courts.

ENGLAND

ROBIN HOOD GOLF CLUB   MAP 2 B2

St. Bernards Road, Solihull, West Midlands B92 7DJ.
7 miles south of Birmingham.

CONTACT: AJ Hanson, Secretary. Tel: 021 706 0061.
COURSE: 6,609yds, PAR 72, SSS 72. Parkland course.
SOC RESTR'S: Min. 16. Welcome Tues afternoon, Thur & Fri.
SOC GF - Round: Wd £28. **We** N/A. **Day:** Wd £33. **We** N/A.
SOC PACK: Range of meals & refreshments available.
VIS RESTR'S: Wd except Bank Hols, Tues am or Wed pm.
VIS GF - Round: Wd £28. **We** N/A. **Day:** Wd £33. **We** N/A.
FACILITIES: Bar & Restaurant.

STOURBRIDGE GOLF CLUB   MAP 2 B2

Worcester Lane, Pedmore, Stourbridge DY8 2RB.
1 mile south of Stourbridge on Worcester Road.

CONTACT: Ms M Cooper, Secretary. Tel: 0384 395566.
COURSE: 6,231yds, PAR 70, SSS 70. Parkland course.
SOC RESTR'S: Welcome Tuesday.
SOC GF - Round: Wd £22. **We** N/A. **Day:** Wd £22. **We** N/A.
SOC PACK: On application from Secretary.
VIS RESTR'S: Welcome Weekdays.
VIS GF - Round: Wd £22. **We** N/A. **Day:** Wd £22. **We** N/A.
FACILITIES: Bar & Restaurant.

SANDWELL PARK GOLF CLUB   MAP 2 B1

Birmingham Road, West Bromwich, West Midlands B71 4JJ.
Adjacent to Junction 1 on M5.

CONTACT: JB Mawby, Secretary. Tel: 021 553 4637.
COURSE: 6,470yds, PAR 71, SSS 72. Parkland course.
SOC RESTR'S: Welcome Tuesday to Friday.
SOC GF - Round: Wd £32.50. **We** N/A. **Day:** Wd £32.50. **We** N/A.
SOC PACK: £27.50 per person if Society exceeds 25.
VIS RESTR'S: Welcome Weekdays.
VIS GF - Round: Wd £32.50. **We** N/A. **Day:** Wd £32.50. **We** N/A.
FACILITIES: Bar & Restaurant.

WALSALL GOLF CLUB   MAP 2 B1

Broadway, Walsall, West Midlands WS1 3EY.
1 mile south of Town Centre.

CONTACT: E Murray, Hon. Secretary. Tel: 0922 613512.
COURSE: 6,300yds, PAR 70, SSS 70. Well wooded parkland.
SOC RESTR'S: Min. 16. Welcome Weekdays.
SOC GF - Round: Wd £25. **We** N/A. **Day:** Wd £35. **We** N/A.
SOC PACK: Variable - £38-£45.
VIS RESTR'S: Welcome Weekdays.
VIS GF - Round: Wd £33. **We** N/A. **Day:** Wd £40. **We** N/A.
FACILITIES: Bar & Restaurant.

SHIRLEY GOLF CLUB   MAP 2 B2

Stratford Road, Monkspath, Shirley, Solihull B90 4EW.
500yds from Junction 4 on M42.

CONTACT: AJ Phillips, Secretary. Tel: 021 744 6001.
COURSE: 6,510yds, PAR 72, SSS 71. Undulating parkland course.
SOC RESTR'S: Main day - Thursday max. 100.
SOC GF - Round: Wd £25. **We** N/A. **Day:** Wd £35. **We** N/A.
SOC PACK: Available at time of booking.
VIS RESTR'S: Welcome Weekdays.
VIS GF - Round: Wd £25. **We** N/A. **Day:** Wd £35. **We** N/A.
FACILITIES: Snooker.

Wiltshire

SOUTH STAFFORDSHIRE G C   MAP 2 B1

Danescourt Road, Tettenhall, Wolverhampton WV6 9BQ.
3 miles west of Wolverhampton off A41.

CONTACT: Mr J Maklin, Secretary/Manager. Tel: 0902 751065.
COURSE: 6,653yds, PAR 72, SSS 72. Parkland course.
SOC RESTR'S: Max. 60. Welcome Weekdays.
SOC GF - Round: Wd £25. **We** N/A. **Day:** Wd £25. **We** N/A.
SOC PACK: Coffee, Lunch, Dinner, 27 holes: £35.
VIS RESTR'S: Welcome except Tuesday am. Please book.
VIS GF - Round: Wd £25. **We** £30. **Day:** Wd N/A. **We** N/A.
FACILITIES: Bar & Restaurant (not Mon).

BROOME MANOR GOLF COMPLEX   MAP 2 B2

Pipers Way, Swindon, Wiltshire SN3 1RG.
2 miles from Junction 15 of M4 towards Swindon.

CONTACT: T Watt, Manager. Tel: 0793 495761.
COURSE: 6,359yds, PAR 71, SSS 70. Modern parkland layout.
SOC RESTR'S: Welcome Monday to Thursday.
SOC GF - Day: Wd N/A. **We** N/A. **Day:** Wd N/A. **We** N/A.
SOC PACK: £12-£36 (incl. meals). Limited 21 to 39 players.
VIS RESTR'S: Welcome. - Booking essential.
VIS GF - Day: Wd £7.50. **We** £9.20. **Day:** Wd N/A. **We** N/A.
FACILITIES: Bar, Restaurant & Driving Range.

WILTSHIRE

CHIPPENHAM GOLF CLUB   MAP 2 B2

Malmesbury Road, Chippenham, Wiltshire SN15 5LT.
Exit M4 at J17, course on right at end of dual carriageway.

CONTACT: D Maddison, Secretary. Tel: 0249 652040.
COURSE: 5,540yds, PAR 69, SSS 67. Meadowland course.
SOC RESTR'S: Welcome Tuesday & Thursday.
SOC GF - Round: Wd £20. **We** N/A. **Day: Wd** £20. **We** N/A.
SOC PACK: Coffee, Lunch, Dinner, 36 holes: £36.
VIS RESTR'S: Please book. H'cap Cert required.
VIS GF - Round: Wd £20. **We** £25. **Day: Wd** £20. **We** £25.
FACILITIES: Bar & Restaurant.

ERLESTOKE SANDS GOLF CLUB   MAP 2 B3

Erlestoke, Devizes, Wiltshire SN10 5UA.
6 miles east of Westbury on the B3098.

CONTACT: T Head, Managing Director. Tel: 0380 830507.
COURSE: 6,649yds, PAR 71, SSS 72. Downland course.
SOC RESTR'S: Welcome Weekdays.
SOC GF - Round: Wd £10. **We** N/A. **Day: Wd** N/A. **We** N/A.
SOC PACK: Coffee, Lunch, Dinner, 36 holes: £32.
VIS RESTR'S: Welcome. - Booking advisable.
VIS GF - Round: Wd £12. **We** £16. **Day: Wd** £20. **We** £25.
FACILITIES: Bar & Restaurant.

MARLBOROUGH GOLF CLUB   MAP 2 B2/3

The Common, Marlborough, Wiltshire SN8 1DU.
Three-quarters-mile from Town Centre on A345 to Swindon.

CONTACT: L Ross, General Manager. Tel: 0672 512147.
COURSE: 6,526yds, PAR 72, SSS 71. Downland course.
SOC RESTR'S: Welcome Weekdays.
SOC GF - Round: Wd £19.50. **We** N/A. **Day: Wd** £29. **We** N/A.
SOC PACK: Coffee, Lunch, Dinner, 36 holes: £42.50-£49.
VIS RESTR'S: Generally welcome but please phone first.
VIS GF - Round: Wd £19.50. **We** £40. **Day: Wd** £29. **We** N/A.
FACILITIES: Bar, Restaurant & Conference Rooms.

NORTH WILTS GOLF CLUB   MAP 2 B3

Bishops' Cannings, Devizes, Wiltshire SN10 2LP.
1 mile east of Calne off A4 - Signposted.

CONTACT: SA Musgrove, Secretary. Tel: 0380 860627.
COURSE: 6,484yds, PAR 72, SSS 71. Downland course.
SOC RESTR'S: Max. 30. Welcome Weekdays by arrangement.
SOC GF - Round: Wd N/A. **We** N/A. **Day: Wd** £25. **We** N/A.
SOC PACK: Coffee, Lunch, Dinner, 36 holes: approx £32.
VIS RESTR'S: Check with Professional on 0380 860830.
VIS GF - Round: Wd £18. **We** £30. **Day: Wd** £25. **We** N/A.
FACILITIES: Full Catering.

SALISBURY & SOUTH WILTS G C   MAP 2 B3

Netherhampton, Salisbury, Wiltshire SP2 8PR.
On A3094, 2 miles Salisbury - 2 miles Wilton.

CONTACT: J Newcomb, Secretary. Tel: 0722 742645.
COURSE: 6,528yds, PAR 71, SSS 71. Parkland course.
SOC RESTR'S: Min. 20. Welcome Weekdays.
SOC GF - Round: Wd N/A. **We** N/A. **Day: Wd** £25. **We** N/A.
SOC PACK: No package. By arrangement.
VIS RESTR'S: Always welcome. Phone call advisable.
VIS GF - Round: Wd N/A. **We** N/A. **Day: Wd** £25. **We** £40.
FACILITIES: Bar & Restaurant.

SHRIVENHAM PARK GOLF CLUB   MAP 2 B2

Penny Hooks, Shrivenham, Nr. Swindon, Wiltshire SN6 8EX.
Exit Junction 15 on M4. Follow signs to Shrivenham.

CONTACT: Mrs. Carole Johnson. Tel: 0793 783853.
COURSE: 5,622yds, PAR 69, SSS 68. Parkland course.
SOC RESTR'S: No restrictions but must have prior booking.
SOC GF - Round: Wd £10. **We** £13. **Day: Wd** £16.50. **We** £20.
SOC PACK: Write for details. Special Winter & Summer offers.
VIS RESTR'S: No restrictions.
VIS GF - Round: Wd £10. **We** £13. **Day: Wd** £16.50. **We** £20.
FACILITIES: Restaurant & Bar.

SWINDON GOLF CLUB   MAP 2 B2

Ogbourne St. George, Nr. Marlborough, Wiltshire SN8 1TB.
Junction 15 M4 - A345 to Marlborough 4 miles.

CONTACT: J Smith, Asstistant Manager. Tel: 0902 897031.
COURSE: 6,226yds, PAR 71, SSS 70. Downland course.
SOC RESTR'S: Max. 45. Welcome Monday, Wednesday & Friday.
SOC GF - Round: Wd £15. **We** N/A. **Day: Wd** £25. **We** N/A.
SOC PACK: Coffee, Lunch, Dinner, Golf: £40.
VIS RESTR'S: Welcome Wd please book. H'cap Cert required.
VIS GF - Round: Wd £15. **We** N/A. **Day: Wd** £25. **We** N/A.
FACILITIES: Practice Ground, Good Clubhouse facilities.

WOOTTON BASSETT GOLF CLUB   MAP 2 B2

Wootton Bassett, Swindon, Wiltshire SN4 7PB.
M4 Junction 16 half a mile south of Wootton Bassett.

CONTACT: M Palmer, Manager. Tel: 0793 849999.
COURSE: 6,627yds, PAR 72, SSS 72. Parkland course.
SOC RESTR'S: Welcome Weekdays by arrangement.
SOC GF - Round: Wd £25. **We** N/A. **Day: Wd** £30. **We** N/A.
SOC PACK: On application.
VIS RESTR'S: Welcome with H'cap Cert.
VIS GF - Round: Wd £25. **We** £30. **Day: Wd** £30. **We** £35.
FACILITIES: Bar & Snooker.

ENGLAND

Worcestershire

KIDDERMINSTER GOLF CLUB MAP 2 B2

Russell Road, Kidderminster, Worcestershire DY10 3HT.
Signposted off the A449 Worcester-Wolverhampton road.

CONTACT: A Biggs, Secretary. Tel: 0562 822303.
COURSE: 6,200yds, PAR 71, SSS 70. Parkland course.
SOC RESTR'S: Max. 60. Welcome Thursdays.
SOC GF - Round: Wd £24. We N/A. **Day:** Wd £24. We N/A.
SOC PACK: Several available to Society's requirements.
VIS RESTR'S: Welcome Weekdays.
VIS GF - Round: Wd £22. We N/A **Day:** Wd £22. We N/A.
FACILITIES: Bar Snacks & Restaurant during normal hours.

ABBEY PARK G & CC MAP 2 B2

Dagnell End Road, Redditch, Worcestershire B98 7BD.
M42 Junction 2 - B435 - A4101 Bedley.

CONTACT: Mrs M Rigby. Tel: 0527 63918.
COURSE: 6,411yds, PAR 71, SSS 71. Parkland course.
SOC RESTR'S: Welcome except Weekends between 11 -12.
SOC GF - Round: Wd £10. We £12.50. **Day:** Wd N/A. We N/A.
SOC PACK: Coffee, Lunch, Dinner, 27 holes: £37.45.
VIS RESTR'S: Welcome, booking advisable at Weekends.
VIS GF - Round: Wd £10. We £12.50. **Day:** Wd N/A. We N/A.
FACILITIES: 32-bedroom Hotel, Restaurant & 2 Bars.

REDDITCH GOLF CLUB MAP 2 B2

Lower Grinsty, Callow Hill, Redditch, Worcestershire B97 5PJ.
Heathfield Road off A441 - 3 miles south-west of Redditch.

CONTACT: Secretary or Professional. Tel: 0527 543309.
COURSE: 6,671yds, PAR 72, SSS 72. Split parkland and forest.
SOC RESTR'S: Welcome Weekdays.
SOC GF - Round: Wd £27.50. We N/A. **Day:** Wd £27.50. We N/A.
SOC PACK: Coffee, Ploughmans Lunch, Dinner, Golf: £40.
VIS RESTR'S: Welcome Weekdays.
VIS GF - Round: Wd £27.50. We N/A. **Day:** Wd £27.50. We N/A.
FACILITIES: Bar & Restaurant.

BROADWAY GOLF CLUB MAP 2 B2

Willersey Hill, Broadway, Worcestershire WR12 7LG.
2.5 miles east of Broadway off A44.

CONTACT: B Carnie, Secretary. Tel: 0386 853683.
COURSE: 6,216yds, PAR 72, SSS 69. Downland course.
SOC RESTR'S: Must contact in advance.
SOC GF - Round: Wd N/A. We N/A. **Day:** Wd N/A. We N/A.
SOC PACK: On application from Secretary.
VIS RESTR'S: Not Sat unless with member. No ladies Sun am.
VIS GF - Round: Wd £23. We £28. **Day:** Wd £28. We £32.
FACILITIES: No catering Monday, Bar & Pro-shop.

WORCESTERSHIRE GOLF CLUB MAP 2 B2

Wood Farm, Malvern Wells, Worcestershire WR14 4PP.
2 miles south of Great Malvern, just off A449.

CONTACT: GR Scott, Secretary. Tel: 0684 575992.
COURSE: 6,449yds, PAR 71, SSS 71. Meadowland/parkland.
SOC RESTR'S: Max. 50. Welcome Thursday & Friday.
SOC GF - Round: Wd £25. We N/A. **Day:** Wd N/A. We N/A.
SOC PACK: Approx. £40 - including Golf & Meals.
VIS RESTR'S: Welcome except We before 10. H'cap Cert req.
VIS GF - Round: Wd £25. We £30. **Day:** Wd N/A. We N/A.
FACILITIES: Bar & Restaurant.

DROITWICH G & CC MAP 2 B2

Ford Lane, Droitwich, Worcestershire WR9 0BQ.
Junction 5 on M5 - Off A38 1 mile north of town.

CONTACT: MJ Taylor, Secretary/Manager. Tel: 0905 774344.
COURSE: 6,040yds, PAR 70, SSS 69. Undulating parkland.
SOC RESTR'S: Max. 36. Welcome Wednesday & Friday.
SOC GF - Round: Wd N/A. We N/A. **Day:** Wd £24. We N/A.
SOC PACK: None.
VIS RESTR'S: Welcome Weekdays.
VIS GF - Round: Wd £24. We N/A. **Day:** Wd £24. We N/A.
FACILITIES: Bar & Restaurant.

RAC HOTEL GUIDE
Great Britain & Ireland
Now in its **ninetieth year**,
the authoritative guide to over 6,000 hotels.
Special anniversary competition.
All establishments inspected and approved by the RAC.
Full colour atlas section with all hotel locations shown
Includes discount vouchers worth up to £150
Price £12.99
Available from bookshops
or direct from the RAC on 0235 834885

North Yorkshire

NORTH YORKSHIRE

FULFORD GOLF CLUB　　MAP 5 B3

Heslington Lane, York YO1 5DY.
2 miles south of York (A64).

CONTACT: Mrs J Hayhurst, Secretary. Tel: 0904 413579.
COURSE: 6,775yds, PAR 72, SSS 72. Parkland/moorland course.
SOC RESTR'S: By prior arrangement with Secretary.
SOC GF - Round: Wd N/A. We N/A. **Day:** Wd £35. We N/A.
SOC PACK: On application.
VIS RESTR'S: By prior arrangement with Secretary.
VIS GF - Round: Wd £20. We N/A. **Day:** Wd £30. We N/A.
FACILITIES: Bar, Restaurant, Pro shop.

CATTERICK GARRISON　　MAP 5 A3

Leyburn Road, Catterick Garrison, N. Yorkshire DL9 3QE.
6 miles SW of Scotch Corner - A1 turn off Catterick Garrison.

CONTACT: JK Mayberry, Secretary. Tel: 0748 833268.
COURSE: 6,331yds, PAR 71, SSS 70. Parkland/moorland.
SOC RESTR'S: By appointment through Secretary.
SOC GF - Round: Wd £16. We £24. **Day:** Wd £16. We £24.
SOC PACK: By arrangement with Caterer.
VIS RESTR'S: Check tee reservations with Professional.
VIS GF - Round: Wd £16. We £24. **Day:** Wd £16. We £24.
FACILITIES: Restaurant, Bar & Pro-Shop.

GANTON GOLF CLUB　　MAP 5 B3

Ganton, Nr. Scarborough, N. Yorkshire YO12 4PA.
A64 York/Malton, 13 miles towards Scarborough.

CONTACT: RG Price, Secretary. Tel: 0944 710329.
COURSE: 6,720yds, PAR 72, SSS 73. Heathland course.
SOC RESTR'S: Welcome Weekdays. After 9.30 & 2.15.
SOC GF - Round: Wd N/A. We N/A. **Day:** Wd £35. We N/A.
SOC PACK: No package. 1994 Green Fees under review.
VIS RESTR'S: Welcome Wd. 1994 Green Fees under review.
VIS GF - Round: Wd N/A. We N/A. **Day:** Wd £35. We £40.
FACILITIES: Bar & Restaurant.

EASINGWOLD GOLF CLUB　　MAP 5 B3

Stillington Road, Easingwold, York YO6 3ET.
1 mile along Stillington Road from A19.

CONTACT: Mr Young, Asst Secretary. Tel: 0904 621301.
COURSE: 6,048yds, PAR 72, SSS 69. Parkland course.
SOC RESTR'S: Max 48. Welcome Wd. Not November to March.
SOC GF - Round: Wd N/A. We N/A. **Day:** Wd £22. We N/A.
SOC PACK: None.
VIS RESTR'S: Welcome everyday but not before 9.30 or 12 to 1.30.
VIS GF - Round: Wd £22. We £27. **Day:** Wd £22. We £27.
FACILITIES: Restaurant & Bar

ALDWARK MANOR GOLF HOTEL
ALDWARK, YORK YO6 2NF
Tel: (0347) 838146 Fax: (0347) 838867
Golf Shop: (0347) 838353
Set in Yorkshire Parkland with its own 18 hole golf course, it has been restored to its Victorian glory. Good friendly service and the finest produce, combine to make this one of Yorkshire's finest and busiest Hotels.

FILEY GOLF CLUB　　MAP 5 B3

West Avenue, Filey, N. Yorkshire YO14 9BQ.
1 mile south of town centre off the end of West Avenue.

CONTACT: TM Thompson, Secretary. Tel: 0723 513293.
COURSE: 5,737yds, PAR 69, SSS 67. Seaside course.
SOC RESTR'S: Please book with Secretary.
SOC GF - Round: Wd N/A. We N/A. **Day:** Wd £18. We N/A.
SOC PACK: On application from Secretary.
VIS RESTR'S: H'cap Cert required. Winter reductions to GF.
VIS GF - Round: Wd N/A We N/A **Day:** Wd £18 We £23.
FACILITIES: Bar & Restaurant.

HARROGATE GOLF CLUB　　MAP 8 B1

Forest Lane Head, Harrogate, N. Yorkshire HG2 7TF.
2 miles on road to Knaresborough - A59 from Harrogate.

CONTACT: J McDougall, Hon. Secretary. Tel: 0423 862999.
COURSE: 6,241yds, PAR 69, SSS 70. Undulating parkland course.
SOC RESTR'S: Welcome Weekdays.
SOC GF - Round: Wd £26. We N/A. **Day:** Wd £30. We N/A.
SOC PACK: None.
VIS RESTR'S: Always welcome. Please book.
VIS GF - Round: Wd £26. We £40. **Day:** Wd £30. We £40.
FACILITIES: Full Catering & Bar.

ENGLAND

KIRKBYMOORSIDE GOLF CLUB   MAP 5 B3

Manor Vale, Kirkbymoorside, York YO6 6EG.
On A170 between Helmsley and Pickering.

CONTACT: Mrs R Rivis, Secretary. Tel: 0751 31525.
COURSE: 5,880yds, PAR 70, SSS 68. Parkland course.
SOC RESTR'S: On application from Steward.
SOC GF - Round: Wd £16. We £20. **Day:** Wd £16. We £20.
SOC PACK: Coffee, Lunch, Dinner, 36 holes: £23.
VIS RESTR'S: Welcome, except Competition Days. Please book.
VIS GF - Round: Wd £16. We £20. **Day:** Wd £16. We £20.
FACILITIES: Bar & Restaurant.

OAKDALE GOLF CLUB   MAP 8 B1

Oakdale, Harrogate, N. Yorkshire HG1 2LN.
Half-a-mile from Town Centre off Ripon Road.

CONTACT: FR Hindmarsh, Secretary/Manager. Tel: 0423 567162.
COURSE: 6,456yds, PAR 71, SSS 71. Undulating parkland course.
SOC RESTR'S: Welcome Weekdays.
SOC GF - Round: Wd £22. We £27.50. **Day:** Wd £29.50. We N/A.
SOC PACK: On application from Secretary.
VIS RESTR'S: Not 8.30-9.30 or 12.30-1.30. Ladies Day Tues.
VIS GF - Round: Wd £22. We £27.50. **Day:** Wd £29.50. We N/A.
FACILITIES: Clubhouse, Bar, Snooker, & TV Rooms.

PANNAL GOLF CLUB   MAP 8 B1

Follifoot Road, Pannal, Harrogate, N. Yorkshire HG3 1ES.
3 miles Leeds side of Harrogate. Just off A61.

CONTACT: TB Davey, Secretary. Tel: 0423 872628.
COURSE: 6,659yds, PAR 72, SSS 72. Moorland/parkland course.
SOC RESTR'S: Welcome Weekdays except Tues am.
SOC GF - Round: Wd £29. We N/A. **Day:** Wd £35. We N/A.
SOC PACK: On application from Secretary.
VIS RESTR'S: Welcome Wd except Tues am. We limited.
VIS GF - Round: Wd £29. We N/A. **Day:** Wd £35. We N/A.
FACILITIES: Bar & Restaurant.

PIKE HILLS GOLF CLUB   MAP 5 B3

Tadcaster Road, Askham Bryan, York YO2 3UW.
3 miles west of York on Leeds Road.

CONTACT: G Rawlings, Hon. Secretary. Tel: 0904 706566.
COURSE: 6,122yds, PAR 71, SSS 69. Parkland course.
SOC RESTR'S: Max. 36. Welcome Tues, Wed & Thur.
SOC GF - Round: Wd £20. We N/A. **Day:** Wd £20. We N/A.
SOC PACK: Coffee, Lunch, Dinner, approx. £30 inclusive.
VIS RESTR'S: Welcome Weekdays.
VIS GF - Round: Wd £20. We N/A. **Day:** Wd £20. We N/A.
FACILITIES: Good Practice Area & Clubhouse.

SCARBOROUGH NORTH CLIFF GC   MAP 5 B3

North Cliff Avenue, Scarborough, N. Yorkshire YO12 6PP.
2 miles north of Scarborough on the coast road.

CONTACT: JR Freeman, Sec/Manager. Tel: 0723 360786.
COURSE: 6,425yds, PAR 71, SSS 71. Parkland course.
SOC RESTR'S: Min. 12. Arranged with Secretary in advance.
SOC GF - Round: Wd N/A. We N/A. **Day:** Wd £21. We £26.
SOC PACK: Several alternatives available on request.
VIS RESTR'S: Competition Days. Not before 10 Sunday.
VIS GF - Round: Wd N/A. We N/A. **Day:** Wd £21. We £26.
FACILITIES: Practice Area, Pro-shop, Bar, Restaurant & TV Room.

SCARBOROUGH SOUTH CLIFF GC   MAP 5 B3

Deepdale Avenue, Scarborough, N. Yorkshire YO11 2UE.
Turn left on Filey Road, 1 mile south of Scarborough.

CONTACT: R Bramley, Secretary. Tel: 0723 374737.
COURSE: 6,085yds, PAR 70, SSS 69. Seaside/parkland.
SOC RESTR'S: Max 12 if Club Competition on.
SOC GF - Round: Wd £20. We £25. **Day:** Wd £25. We £30.
SOC PACK: Liaise directly with private franchise Caterer.
VIS RESTR'S: Book in advance with Secretary.
VIS GF - Round: Wd £20. We £25. **Day:** Wd £25. We £30.
FACILITIES: Bar & Restaurant.

SELBY GOLF CLUB   MAP 5 B3

Mill Lane, Brayton Barff, Selby, N. Yorkshire YO8 9LD.
3 miles south-west of Selby off A19.

CONTACT: B Moore, Secretary/Manager. Tel: 0757 228622.
COURSE: 6,246yds, PAR 70, SSS 70. Inland links type course.
SOC RESTR'S: Welcome Wednesday, Thursday & Friday.
SOC GF - Round: Wd £22. We N/A. **Day:** Wd £24. We N/A.
SOC PACK: 2 rounds plus £2 voucher for Dinner.
VIS RESTR'S: Welcome except 11am-1pm. H'cap Cert required.
VIS GF - Round: Wd £22. We N/A. **Day:** Wd £24. We N/A.
FACILITIES: Bar, Snooker & Restaurant.

SKIPTON GOLF CLUB   MAP 8 A1

Northwest Bypass, Skipton, N. Yorkshire BD23 1LL.
1 mile north-west of Skipton on A65.

CONTACT: D Farnsworth, General Manager. Tel: 0756 793922.
COURSE: 6,010yds, PAR 69, SSS 70. Undulating course.
SOC RESTR'S: Max. 24. Welcome Tues, Weds & Friday.
SOC GF - Round: Wd N/A. We N/A. **Day:** Wd N/A. We N/A.
SOC PACK: £28 midweek. £35 Weekends & Bank Hols.
VIS RESTR'S: Welcome Wd, restricted at We 9.45-10.30 & 2-3.
VIS GF - Round: Wd £22. We £26. **Day:** Wd N/A. We N/A.
FACILITIES: Bar & Restaurant.

South Yorkshire

WHITBY GOLF CLUB   MAP 5 B2

Low Straggleton, Whitby N. Yorkshire YO21 3SR.
2 miles north of Whitby on A174.

CONTACT: A Dyson, Secretary. Tel: 0947 600360.
COURSE: 5,710yds, PAR 69, SSS 67. Clifftop seaside course.
SOC RESTR'S: Must be booked before visiting.
SOC GF - Round: Wd £17.50. We £25. **Day:** Wd £17.50. We £25.
SOC PACK: None.
VIS RESTR'S: Please book.
VIS GF - Round: Wd £17.50. We £25. **Day:** Wd £17.50. We £25.
FACILITIES: Licensed & Full Catering.

YORK GOLF CLUB   MAP 5 B3

Lords Moor Lane, Strensall, York YO3 5XF.
2 miles north of York Ring Road (A1237).

CONTACT: F Appleyard, Secretary. Tel: 0904 490304.
COURSE: 6,285yds, PAR 70, SSS 70. Woodland course.
SOC RESTR'S: Welcome Mon, Wed, Thur & Sun.
SOC GF - Round: Wd £20. We N/A. **Day:** Wd £25. We N/A.
SOC PACK: None.
VIS RESTR'S: Welcome everyday except Tues am & Sat.
VIS GF - Round: Wd £20. We N/A. **Day:** Wd £25. We N/A.
FACILITIES: Practice Ground & Full Catering.

The Town House Hotel

Holgate Road, York YO2 4BB Tel: 0904 636171 Fax: 0904 623044

A fine example of early Victorian town houses, an ideal family run hotel for the tourist, holidaymaker or businessman. First class cuisine and an excellent selection of wines which will complement your stay with us. The Town House is a short walk from the city centre, York's famous Minster and other historical landmarks. The Racecourse is also close by. Private car park.

AUSTERFIELD PARK GOLF CLUB   MAP 5 B3

Cross Lane, Austerfield, Doncaster, S. Yorkshire DN10 6RF.
On A614, 2 miles north-east of Bawtry to Thorne.

CONTACT: A Bradley, Company Secretary. Tel: 0302 710841.
COURSE: 6,854yds, PAR 73, SSS 73. Parkland course.
SOC RESTR'S: Welcome.
SOC GF - Round: Wd £12. We £16. **Day:** Wd £16. We £20.
SOC PACK: On application.
VIS RESTR'S: Welcome.
VIS GF - Round: Wd £12. We £16. **Day:** Wd £16. We £20.
FACILITIES: Driving Range, Bowling Green.

HICKLETON GOLF CLUB   MAP 5 B3

Hickleton, Nr. Doncaster, S. Yorkshire DN5 7BE.
Hickleton village is on A635 between Barnsley & Doncaster.

CONTACT: P Shepherd, Professional. Tel: 0709 895170.
COURSE: 6,231yds, PAR 71, SSS 70. Undulating parkland.
SOC RESTR'S: Welcome except before 2.30 Weekends.
SOC GF - Round: Wd N/A. We N/A. **Day:** Wd N/A. We N/A.
SOC PACK: On application from Secretary.
VIS RESTR'S: By arrangement with Pro. Not before 2.30 We.
VIS GF - Round: Wd N/A. We N/A. **Day:** Wd £17. We £25.
FACILITIES: Bar & Restaurant.

ABBEYDALE GOLF CLUB   MAP 8 B3

Twentywell Lane, Sheffield, S. Yorkshire S17 4QA.
A621 south of Sheffield - 5 miles City Centre.

CONTACT: Mrs KM Johnston, Sec/Manager. Tel: 0742 360763.
COURSE: 6,419yds, PAR 72, SSS 71. Parkland course.
SOC RESTR'S: Welcome Tuesday & Friday by arrangement.
SOC GF - Round: Wd £22.50. We N/A. **Day:** Wd £27.50. We N/A.
SOC PACK: None.
VIS RESTR'S: By arrangement. Some time restrictions Apr-Oct.
VIS GF - Round: Wd £22.50. We N/A. **Day:** Wd £27.50. We N/A.
FACILITIES: Bar & Restaurant.

LEES HALL GOLF CLUB   MAP 8 B3

Hemsworth Road, Norton, Sheffield S8 8LL.
East of A61, 3 miles south of Sheffield off A6102 Ring Road.

CONTACT: J Paulson, Secretary. Tel: 0742 552900.
COURSE: 6,137yds, PAR 71, SSS 69. Undulating parkland.
SOC RESTR'S: By prior booking through Secretary.
SOC GF - Round: Wd £20. We £30. **Day:** Wd £27. We N/A.
SOC PACK: Catering arranged with Steward - Tel: 0742 551526.
VIS RESTR'S: Welcome exc We before 10.30. Ladies priority Wed.
VIS GF - Round: Wd £20. We £30. **Day:** Wd £27. We N/A.
FACILITIES: Bar & Snooker (men).

ENGLAND

RENISHAW PARK GOLF CLUB   MAP 3 A1

Station Road, Renishaw, Sheffield, S. Yorkshire S31 9UZ.
1.5 miles from Junction 30 on M1.

CONTACT: Mr L Hughes, Secretary. Tel: 0246 432044.
COURSE: 6,253yds, PAR 71, SSS 70. Parkland course.
SOC RESTR'S: Welcome Weekdays after 9.30.
SOC GF - Round: Wd £20. We N/A. **Day:** Wd £28. We N/A.
SOC PACK: On application.
VIS RESTR'S: Please phone before play.
VIS GF - Round: Wd £20. We £33. **Day:** Wd £28. We £33.
FACILITIES: Bar & Restaurant.

ROTHERHAM GOLF CLUB   MAP 3 A1

Thrybergh Park, Thrybergh, Rotherham, S. Yorkshire S65 4NU.
On A630 - about 3.5 miles east of Rotherham.

CONTACT: F Green, Secretary. Tel: 0709 850812.
COURSE: 6,324yds, PAR 70, SSS 70. Parkland course.
SOC RESTR'S: Welcome Weekdays except Wednesday.
SOC GF - Round: Wd N/A. We N/A. **Day:** Wd N/A. We N/A.
SOC PACK: Coffee, Lunch, Dinner: Prices vary.
VIS RESTR'S: Arrange through Professional (0709 850480).
VIS GF - Round: Wd £25. We £30. **Day:** Wd £25. We £30.
FACILITIES: Bar & Restaurant.

SITWELL PARK GOLF CLUB   MAP 3 A1

Shrogswood Road, Rotherham, S. Yorkshire S60 4BY.
3 miles east of Rotherham.

CONTACT: J Straffen, Hon. Secretary. Tel: 0709 541046.
COURSE: 6,203yds, PAR 71, SSS 70. Undulating parkland.
SOC RESTR'S: Welcome except Sat & before 11.30 Sun.
SOC GF - Round: Wd £20. We £24. **Day:** Wd £24. We N/A.
SOC PACK: Arrange through Secretary & Stewardess.
VIS RESTR'S: Welcome exc Sat & before 11.30 Sun. Please book.
VIS GF - Round: Wd £20. We £24. **Day:** Wd £24. We £24.
FACILITIES: Bar & Restaurant.

TANKERSLEY PARK GOLF CLUB   MAP 8 B3

High Green, Sheffield, S. Yorkshire S30 4LG.
M1(N) J35a to A616 - M1(S) J36, A61 Sheffield, left on A616.

CONTACT: PA Bagshaw, Secretary. Tel: 0742 468247.
COURSE: 6,212yds, PAR 69, SSS 70. Inland links course.
SOC RESTR'S: 50/60. Welcome Tues & Wed. Times to be agreed.
SOC GF - Round: Wd £17. We N/A. **Day:** Wd £22. We N/A.
SOC PACK: None.
VIS RESTR'S: Welcome except before 3 on Weekends.
VIS GF - Round: Wd £17. We £22. **Day:** Wd £22. We N/A.
FACILITIES: Practice Area, Bar & Food.

THORNE GOLF CLUB   MAP 5 B3

Kirton Lane, Thorne, S. Yorkshire DN8 5RJ.
Thorne turn-off on M18 Junction 5/6.

CONTACT: ED Highfield, Chairman. Tel: 0405 812084.
COURSE: 5,366yds, PAR 68, SSS 66. Parkland course.
SOC RESTR'S: Please book in advance.
SOC GF - Round: Wd £7.60. We £8.60. **Day:** Wd N/A. We N/A.
SOC PACK: Coffee, Lunch, Dinner, 36 holes.: £18-£60.
VIS RESTR'S: No restrictions.
VIS GF - Round: Wd £7.60. We £8.60. **Day:** Wd N/A. We N/A.
FACILITIES: Changing rooms, Full Clubhouse facilities.

WATH GOLF CLUB   MAP 5 B3

Abdy, Rawmarsh, Rotherham, S. Yorkshire S62 7SJ.
A633 from Rotherham - B6090 to Wentworth - B6089 - Signpost.

CONTACT: J Pepper, Stewardess. Tel: 0709 872149.
COURSE: 5,857yds Par 68, SSS 68. Parkland course.
SOC RESTR'S: Welcome Weekends.
SOC GF - Round: Wd £16. We N/A. **Day:** Wd £16. We N/A.
SOC PACK: Lunch, Dinner, 36 holes: £25.
VIS RESTR'S: Welcome Weekdays.
VIS GF - Round: Wd £16. We N/A. **Day:** Wd £16. We N/A.
FACILITIES: Clubhouse, Meals & Bar.

WORTLEY GOLF CLUB   MAP 8 B3

Hermit Hill Lane, Wortley, Sheffield S30 4DF.
M1 Junction 36 or 35a - A629 West - Wortley village.

CONTACT: JL Dalby, Hon. Secretary. Tel: 0742 885294.
COURSE: 5,983yds, PAR 68, SSS 69. Parkland course.
SOC RESTR'S: Welcome Wednesday & Friday.
SOC GF - Round: Wd £21. We N/A. **Day:** Wd £21. We N/A.
SOC PACK: None.
VIS RESTR'S: Please phone to check availability of 1st tee.
VIS GF - Round: Wd £21. We £25. **Day:** Wd £21. We £25.
FACILITIES: Catering - by arrangement.

RAC National Road Maps

Clear, easy-to-read, up-to-date route planning maps at a scale of approximately 8 miles to 1 inch

Price £3.99
Available from bookshops or direct from the RAC on 0235 834885

WEST YORKSHIRE

West Yorkshire

HALIFAX GOLF CLUB   MAP 8 B2

Union Lane, Ogden, Halifax, W. Yorkshire HX2 8XR.
4 miles north of Halifax off the A629.

CONTACT: JP Clark, Secretary/Manager. Tel: 0422 244171.
COURSE: 6,037yds, PAR 70, SSS 70. Moorland course.
SOC RESTR'S: By arrangement with Secretary.
SOC GF - Round: Wd £15. We £25. **Day:** Wd £15. We £25.
SOC PACK: Midweek £32 all in. Weekends £40 all in.
VIS RESTR'S: Please Book. Reductions with H'cap Cert.
VIS GF - Round: Wd £20. We £30. **Day:** Wd £20. We £30.
FACILITIES: Bar & Restaurant.

BINGLEY ST. IVES GOLF CLUB   MAP 8 B1

St. Ives Estate, Bingley, W. Yorkshire BD16 1AT.
Off B6429 north-west of Bradford Centre.

CONTACT: Secretary or Professional. Tel: 0274 562506.
COURSE: 6,488yds, PAR 71, SSS 71. Parkland course.
SOC RESTR'S: Welcome except Saturdays.
SOC GF - Round: Wd £20. We £25. **Day:** Wd £25. We £25.
SOC PACK: To be negotiated.
VIS RESTR'S: Welcome Weekdays limited at Weekends.
VIS GF - Round: Wd £20. We £25. **Day:** Wd £25. We £25.
FACILITIES: Bar, Restaurant (not Mon).

HALIFAX BRADLEY HALL G C   MAP 8 B2

Holywell Green, Halifax. W. Yorkshire HX4 9AN.
South of Halifax on A6112.

CONTACT: PM Pitchforth, Hon. Secretary. Tel: 0422 374108.
COURSE: 6,213yds, PAR 70, SSS 70. Moorland course.
SOC RESTR'S: Max. 25. Welcome Weekdays by arrangement.
SOC GF - Round: Wd £18. We N/A. **Day:** Wd £23. We N/A.
SOC PACK: On application.
VIS RESTR'S: Welcome assuming availability, no restrictions.
VIS GF - Round: Wd £18. We £28. **Day:** Wd £23. We £35.
FACILITIES: Bar & Snooker.

BRADLEY PARK GOLF CLUB   MAP 8 B2

Bradley Road, Bradley, Huddersfield, W. Yorks HD2 1PZ.
Near Junction 25 on M62, 2 miles - Huddersfield.

CONTACT: PE Reilly, Professional. Tel: 0484 539988.
COURSE: 6,220yds, PAR 70, SSS 69. Parkland course.
SOC RESTR'S: Welcome Weekdays.
SOC GF - Round: Wd £8. We N/A. **Day:** Wd N/A. We N/A.
SOC PACK: Ring for details.
VIS RESTR'S: Welcome please book Weekends.
VIS GF - Round: Wd £8. We £10. **Day:** Wd N/A. We N/A.
FACILITIES: Driving Range, Par 3 Course & Clubhouse.

HUDDERSFIELD GOLF CLUB   MAP 8 B2

Fixby Hall, Lightridge Road, Fixby, Huddersfield HD2 2EP.
J24/M62 - Brighouse signs - Right at traffic lights to course.

CONTACT: D Bennett, Secretary. Tel: 0484 426203.
COURSE: 6,402yds, PAR 71, SSS 71. Heathland course.
SOC RESTR'S: Welcome Weekends. Ladies Day Tues.
SOC GF - Round: Wd £30. We N/A. **Day:** Wd £40. We N/A.
SOC PACK: On application.
VIS RESTR'S: Always welcome except Sat. Please Book.
VIS GF - Round: Wd £30. We £40. **Day:** Wd £40. We £50.
FACILITIES: Bar & Snooker.

CALVERLEY GOLF CLUB   MAP 8 B2

Woodhall Lane, Pudsey, Leeds, W. Yorks LS28 5QY.
7 miles from Leeds - 4 miles from Bradford.

CONTACT: D Johnson, Professional. Tel: 0532 569244.
COURSE: 5,527yds, PAR 68, SSS 67. Parkland course.
SOC RESTR'S: On application from Secretary.
SOC GF - Round: Wd N/A. We N/A. **Day:** Wd N/A. We N/A.
SOC PACK: On application.
VIS RESTR'S: Please book.
VIS GF - Round: Wd £10. We £15. **Day:** Wd £15. We N/A.
FACILITIES: 9-hole Course, Bar & Restaurant.

LEEDS GOLF CLUB   MAP 8 B1

Elmete Lane, Leeds, W. Yorkshire LS8 2LJ.
Off A58 Leeds/Wetherby - 4 miles from City Centre.

CONTACT: GW Backhouse, Secretary. Tel: 0532 658775.
COURSE: 6,097yds Par 69, SSS 69. Parkland course.
SOC RESTR'S: Welcome Weekdays. Limited catering Monday.
SOC GF - Round: Wd £19. We N/A. **Day:** Wd £25. We N/A.
SOC PACK: On application from Secretary.
VIS RESTR'S: Welcome Weekdays. Limited catering Monday.
VIS GF - Round: Wd £19. We N/A. **Day:** Wd £25. We N/A.
FACILITIES: Bar & Restaurant.

ENGLAND

LOW LAITHES GOLF CLUB   MAP 8 B2

Parkmill Lane, Flushdyke, Ossett, W. Yorks WF5 9AP.
M1/Exit Junction 40 - Follow signs to Low Laithes.

CONTACT: D Wilson, Hon. Secretary. Tel: 0924 273275.
COURSE: 6,203yds, PAR 72, SSS 70. Parkland course.
SOC RESTR'S: Welcome Weekdays.
SOC GF - Round: Wd £21. We N/A. Day: Wd £21. We N/A.
SOC PACK: Coffee, Lunch, Dinner - £31.
VIS RESTR'S: Welcome Weekday after 10 & Weekend after 2.
VIS GF - Round: Wd £21. We £27. Day: Wd £21. We £27.
FACILITIES: Bar.

MELTHAM GOLF CLUB   MAP 8 B2

Thick Hollins Hall, Meltham, Huddersfield HD7 3DQ.
5 miles west of Huddersfield.

CONTACT: P Davies, Professional. Tel: 0484 850227.
COURSE: 6,145yds, PAR 70, SSS 70. Parkland course.
SOC RESTR'S: By appointment - Not Saturdays.
SOC GF - Round: Wd N/A. We N/A. Day: Wd £22. We £25.
SOC PACK: None.
VIS RESTR'S: Welcome Weekdays & Sunday.
VIS GF - Round: Wd N/A. We N/A. Day: Wd £22. We £25.
FACILITIES: Excellent catering.

MOOR ALLERTON GOLF CLUB   MAP 8 B1

Coal Road, Wike Leeds, W. Yorkshire LS17 9NH.
6 miles north-west of Leeds.

CONTACT: Pam Hobson. Tel: 0532 661154.
COURSE: 6,550yds, PAR 72, SSS 72. Undulating parkland.
SOC RESTR'S: On application from Secretary.
SOC GF - Round: Wd N/A. We N/A. Day: Wd £35. We N/A.
SOC PACK: Coffee, Lunch, Dinner, Golf: Prices vary.
VIS RESTR'S: Welcome Wd by booking. GF reduction Nov-Mar.
VIS GF - Round: Wd N/A. We N/A. Day: Wd £35. We £45
FACILITIES: Bar, Restaurant & Bowling Green.

MOORTOWN GOLF CLUB   MAP 8 B1

Harrogate Road, Leeds, W. Yorkshire LS17 7DB.
On A61 Leeds/Harrogate Road. 5 miles from City Centre.

CONTACT: Mr T Hughes, Secretary. Tel: 0532 686521.
COURSE: 6,544yds, PAR 71, SSS 72. Moorland course.
SOC RESTR'S: On application to Secretary.
SOC GF - Round: Wd £35. We £40. Day: Wd £40. We N/A.
SOC PACK: None.
VIS RESTR'S: Welcome apply to Secretary.
VIS GF - Round: Wd £35. We £40. Day: Wd £40. We £45.
FACILITIES: Bar & Restaurant.

NORTHCLIFFE GOLF CLUB   MAP 8 B1

High Bank Lane, Shipley, Bradford, W. Yorks BD18 4LJ.
3 miles north-west of Bradford off A650 Keighley Road.

CONTACT: H Archer, Secretary. Tel: 0274 596731.
COURSE: 5,839yds, PAR 71, SSS 68. Parkland course.
SOC RESTR'S: Welcome Weekdays.
SOC GF - Round: Wd N/A. We N/A. Day: Wd £20. We N/A.
SOC PACK: None.
VIS RESTR'S: Welcome except Competition days. Please phone.
VIS GF - Round: Wd N/A. We N/A. Day: Wd £20. We £25.
FACILITIES: Snooker.

SAND MOOR GOLF CLUB   MAP 8 B1

Alwoodley Lane, Leeds, W. Yorkshire LS17 7DJ.
5 miles north of Leeds, just off A61 Harrogate Road.

CONTACT: BF Precious, Secretary. Tel: 0532 685180.
COURSE: 6,429yds, PAR 71, SSS 71. Moorland course.
SOC RESTR'S: Welcome Weekdays by arrangement.
SOC GF - Round: Wd £28. We N/A. Day: Wd £35. We N/A.
SOC PACK: Meals by arrangement with Caterer.
VIS RESTR'S: Welcome most Weekdays by arrangement.
VIS GF - Round: Wd £28. We N/A. Day: Wd £35. We N/A.
FACILITIES: Bar & Restaurant.

SCARCROFT GOLF CLUB   MAP 8 B1

Syke Lane, Scarcroft, Leeds, W. Yorkshire LS14 3BQ.
7 miles north-east of Leeds off A58.

CONTACT: D Barwell, Secretary/Manager. Tel: 0532 892311.
COURSE: 6,426yds Par 71, SSS 71. Parkland course.
SOC RESTR'S: Max. 30. Tuesday/Thursday. Max. 50 Wednesday.
SOC GF - Round: Wd £25. We N/A. Day: Wd 30. We N/A.
SOC PACK: No package - Overall Day approx. £40.
VIS RESTR'S: Welcome after 9.30.
VIS GF - Round: Wd £25. We £35. Day: Wd £30. We N/A.
FACILITIES: Bar & Restaurant.

SHIPLEY GOLF CLUB   MAP 8 B1

Beckfoot Lane, Cottingley Brg, Bingley, W. Yorks BD16 1LX.
6 miles north of Bradford on A650 Bradford/Keighley Road.

CONTACT: M Shaw, Hon. Secretary. Tel: 0274 568652.
COURSE: 6,218yds, PAR 72, SSS 70. Undulating course.
SOC RESTR'S: Welcome Weekdays except Tuesday before 2.
SOC GF - Round: Wd £25. We N/A. Day: Wd £25. We N/A.
SOC PACK: No package - meals by negotiation with the Steward.
VIS RESTR'S: Welcome except before 2 Tues, 4 Sat & 9.30 Sun.
VIS GF - Round: Wd £25. We £33. Day: Wd £25. We £33.
FACILITIES: Snooker, Bar & Mixed Lounge.

Isle of Man

WEST BOWLING GOLF CLUB MAP 8 B2

Newall Hall, Rooley Lane, Bradford, W. Yorks BD5 8LB.
Junction of M606 & Bedford Ring Road (East).

CONTACT: ME Lynn, Secretary/Manager. Tel: 0274 724449.
COURSE: 5,657yds, PAR 69, SSS 67. Parkland course.
SOC RESTR'S: 30/40. Welcome Tues, Wed & Thur after 9.30.
SOC GF - Round: Wd N/A. **We** N/A. **Day:** Wd N/A. **We** N/A.
SOC PACK: On application. Catering by arrangement.
VIS RESTR'S: Welcome Wd & limited We. Reduct with H'cap Cert.
VIS GF - Round: Wd N/A. **We** N/A. **Day:** Wd £22. **We** £28.
FACILITIES: Bar, Restaurant & Snooker.

WEST END GOLF CLUB (HALIFAX) MAP 8 B2

Paddock Lane, Highroad Well, Halifax, W. Yorks HX2 0NT.
2 miles west of Halifax.

CONTACT: B Thomas, Secretary/Manager. Tel: 0422 353608.
COURSE: 6,003yds, PAR 69, SSS 69. Moorland course.
SOC RESTR'S: Welcome exc Tue & Sat. Must have H'cap Cert.
SOC GF - Round: Wd £15. **We** £18. **Day:** Wd £20. **We** N/A.
SOC PACK: No package.
VIS RESTR'S: Please phone Professional before play.
VIS GF - Round: Wd £15. **We** £18. **Day:** Wd £20. **We** £25.
FACILITIES: Bar & Restaurant.

CASTLETOWN GOLF CLUB MAP 4 A/B1

Fort Island, Derbyhaven, Isle of Man.
1 mile east of Castletown.

CONTACT: M Crowe, Professional. Tel: 0624 822211.
COURSE: 6,716yds, PAR 72, SSS 72. Seaside links course.
SOC RESTR'S: Prior booking.
SOC GF - Round: Wd N/A. **We** N/A. **Day:** Wd N/A. **We** N/A.
SOC PACK: On application.
VIS RESTR'S: No restrictions. Prior booking essential.
VIS GF - Round: Wd £35. **We** N/A. **Day:** Wd N/A. **We** N/A.
FACILITIES: Bar, Restaurant, Pro Shop, Leisure centre.

Channel Islands

LA MOYE GOLF CLUB

La Moye, St Brelade, Jersey.
6 miles west of St Helier.

CONTACT: P Clash, Secretary. Tel: 0534 43401.
COURSE: 6,741yds, PAR 72, SSS 72. Seaside links course.
SOC RESTR'S: H'cap Cert. 9.30-11am & 2.30-4pm only.
SOC GF - Round: Wd N/A. **We** N/A. **Day:** Wd N/A. **We** N/A.
SOC PACK: On application.
VIS RESTR'S: H'cap Cert & Letter or Intro required.
VIS GF - Round: Wd £35. **We** £35. **Day:** Wd N/A. **We** N/A.
FACILITIES: Driving Range, Bar, Restaurant, Pro shop, Snooker.

SCOTLAND

WHAT is there to be said about golf in Scotland that hasn't been said a thousand times before? Whether the Scots or the Dutch invented the game is really irrelevent; what surely must be of more importance is that it was the Scots who took the game for their own, who nurtured it and who gave it to the world. And not only the game, for it was the Scots who introduced to the vocabulary of golfers everywhere the evocative names of the greatest links courses it is possible to play - St Andrews, Carnoustie, Turnberry, Troon, Prestwick, Dornoch, Muirfield...the list is near-endless.

Away from her coastline, Scotland is blessed with an embarrassment of inland riches. In the Ochil Hills, there is stirring golf to be had at Gleneagles; in Glasgow, Haggs Castle might be accessible only with a member, but a round can be pre-arranged at the Glasgow club, laid out in 1878; both courses at Cawder offer excellent challenges and a little further afield, the development at Loch Lomond looks to have been rescued from possible abandonment to the extent that one of Tom Weiskopf's original two 'dream courses' should be in play.

In Edinburgh, you can sample Dalmahoy, where Europe's women golfers triumphed in the Solheim Cup; Perth has the curiosity of the King James VI club, a shortish parkland layout on an island in the middle of the River Tay, accessible by a footbridge; while Brora, on the coast between Dornoch and Helmsdale, takes full advantage of the long days and short nights of midsummer, by staging a midnight competition in June; in truth, each of Scotland's courses legitimately demand a page of this Guide in its own right.

With its profusion of municipal courses in addition to its grand and prestigious clubs, Scotland still offers the finest golf bargains to be had anywhere in the world. Yes, the very best can become hideously crowded, but with so many to choose from, that shouldn't be any great problem. Golf in Scotland is unique and an experience that all golfers should savour at least once in their lives.

Borders

GALASHIELS   MAP 9 B3

Ladhope Recreation Ground, Galashiels TD1 2NJ.
Situated north-east side of town, quarter of a mile from A7.
CONTACT: R Gass, Secretary. Tel: 0896 55307.
Course: 5,311yds, PAR 68, SSS 67. Hillside parkland course.
SOC RESTR'S: Contact in advance.
SOC GF - Round: Wd £8. We £12. **Day:** Wd £12. We £16.
SOC PACK: On application from Secretary.
VIS RESTR'S: No restrictions.
VIS GF - Round: Wd £8, We £12. **Day:** Wd £12. We £16.
FACILITIES: Catering (Weekends only), Bar.

HAWICK GOLF CLUB   MAP 9 B3

Vertish Hill, Hawick, Roxburghshire.
Situated south of town, on A7.
CONTACT: Mr Riley, Secretary. Tel: 0450 75294.
Course: 5,929yds, PAR 68, SSS 69. Hillside course.
SOC RESTR'S: Welcome on application.
SOC GF - Round: Wd £12. We N/A. **Day:** Wd £18. We N/A.
SOC PACK: On application from Secretary.
VIS RESTR'S: Welcome please book.
VIS GF - Round: Wd £12. We £18. **Day:** Wd £18. We £18.
FACILITIES: Bar, Catering & Pro-shop.

KELSO GOLF CLUB   MAP 9 B3

Berrymoss Racecourse Road, Kelso TD5 7SL.
1 mile north of town centre, within National Hunt Racecourse.
CONTACT: JP Payne. Secretary. Tel: 0573 223009.
Course: 6,061yds, PAR 70, SSS 69. Parkland course.
SOC RESTR'S: Booking required.
SOC GF - Round: Wd £12. We £16. **Day:** Wd £18. We £25.
SOC PACK: On application from Secretary.
VIS RESTR'S: No restrictions.
VIS GF - Round: Wd £12. We £16. **Day:** Wd £18. We £25.
FACILITIES: Catering Wednesday to Sunday, Pro-shop.

CENTRAL

PEEBLES GOLF CLUB   MAP 9 A3

Kirkland Street, Peebles EH45 8EU.
23 miles south of Edinburgh. Signposted in town.
CONTACT: H Gilmore, Secretary. Tel: 0721 720197.
Course: 6,137yds, PAR 70, SSS 69. Parkland course.
SOC RESTR'S: Limited to 24 at Weekends - 8 x 3 ball.
SOC GF - Round: Wd N/A. We N/A. **Day:** Wd N/A. We N/A.
SOC PACK: Coffee, Lunch, High Tea: Prices vary.
VIS RESTR'S: Welcome.
VIS GF - Round: Wd £12. We £18, **Day:** Wd £18. We £25.
FACILITIES: Bar, Lounge, Locker room & Showers.

WEST LINTON GOLF CLUB   MAP 9 A2

West Linton, Peeblesshire EH46 7HN.
On A702, 15 miles south of Edinburgh.
CONTACT: G Scott, Hon. Secretary. Tel 0968 60463.
Course: 6,132yds, PAR 69, SSS 69. Moorland course.
SOC RESTR'S: Max. 35. Welcome except Weekends.
SOC GF - Round: Wd £14. We N/A. **Day:** Wd £18. We N/A.
SOC PACK: On application.
VIS RESTR'S: Welcome except before 1. 15 at Weekends.
VIS GF - Round: Wd £14. We £22. **Day:** Wd £18. We N/A.
FACILITIES: Bar, Restaurant & Practice Area.

Central

ABERFOYLE GOLF CLUB   MAP 4 B1

Braeval, Aberfoyle, Stirlingshire FK8 3UY.
On A81 from Glasgow - Stirling.
CONTACT: R Steele, Secretary. Tel: 08772 493.
Course: 5,205yds, PAR 68, SSS 66. Scenic hillside course.
SOC RESTR'S: Welcome parties limited to 20.
SOC GF - Round: Wd £12. We £16. **Day:** Wd £16. We £24.
SOC PACK: On application from Secretary.
VIS RESTR'S: Welcome. No teeing off before 10. 30 at We.
VIS GF - Round: Wd £12. We £16. **Day:** Wd £16. We £24.
FACILITIES: Light lunches during summer.

SCOTLAND

ALLOA GOLF CLUB
MAP 4 B1

Shawpark, Sauchie, By Alloa, Clackmannanshire FK10 3AX.
1 mile north of Alloa.

CONTACT: AM Frame, Hon. Secretary. Tel: 0259 750100.
Course: 6,240yds, PAR 70, SSS 70. Undulating parkland course.
SOC RESTR'S: Not Wed after 2. 15 & not before 11.30 We.
SOC GF - Round: Wd £12. We £15. Day: Wd £20. We £24.
SOC PACK: Around £30.
VIS RESTR'S: Not Wed after 2.15 & not before 11.30 We.
VIS GF - Round: Wd £12. We £15. Day: Wd £20. We £24.
FACILITIES: Bar & Restaurant.

BRAEHEAD GOLF CLUB
MAP 4 B1

Cambus, By Alloa, Clackmannanshire FK10 2NT.
On A907, 1 mile west of Alloa.

CONTACT: P MacMichael, Secretary. Tel: 0259 722078.
Course: 6,041yds, PAR 71, SSS 69. Parkland course.
SOC RESTR'S: Restricted availability of Weekend times.
SOC GF - Round: Wd £12. We £18. Day: Wd £18. We N/A.
SOC PACK: Fees + £6.
VIS RESTR'S: Few restrictions, advisable to phone in advance.
VIS GF - Round: Wd £12. We £18. Day: Wd £18. We N/A.
FACILITIES: Full catering.

BUCHANAN CASTLE GOLF CLUB
MAP 4 B1

Drymen, Glasgow G63 0HY.
1 mile west of town, 18 miles north-west of Glasgow.

CONTACT: R Kinsella, Secretary. Tel: 0360 60307.
Course: 6,086yds, PAR 70, SSS 69. Parkland course.
SOC RESTR'S: Contact in advance. Max 12.
SOC GF - Round: Wd £25. We N/A. Day: Wd £35. We N/A.
SOC PACK: On application from Sec. Catering by arrangement.
VIS RESTR'S: Contact in advance.
VIS GF - Round: Wd £25. We N/A. Day: Wd £35. We N/A.
FACILITIES: Bar, Catering, Pro-shop & Club Hire.

CALLANDER GOLF CLUB
MAP 4 B1

Aveland Road, Callander, Perthshire FK17 8EN.
A48 from Stirling.

CONTACT: S Galloway, Secretary. Tel: 0877 30090.
Course: 4,450yds, PAR 66, SSS 66. Parkland course.
SOC RESTR'S: 3 months notice required.
SOC GF - Round: Wd £12. We £16. Day: Wd £17. We £21.
SOC PACK: Full catering facilities from Bar Snacks to Dinner.
VIS RESTR'S: Wed not before 9.30. Sun not before 9. 30 & 1-2.
VIS GF - Round:Wd £12. We £16. Day: Wd £17. We £21.
FACILITIES: Bar & Practice Area.

DOLLAR GOLF CLUB
MAP 4 B1

Brewlands House, Dollar FK14 7EA.
Beside Dollar Town.

CONTACT: M Shea, Secretary. Tel: 0259 42400.
COURSE: 5,144yds, PAR 68, SSS 66. Hilly course.
SOC RESTR'S: By arrangement with Secretary.
SOC GF - Round: Wd £7. We £15. Day: Wd £11. We £15.
SOC PACK:Catering available with day ticket
VIS RESTR'S: Always welcome.
VIS GF - Round: Wd £7. We £15. Day: Wd £11. We £15.
FACILITIES: Bar & Restaurant.

DUNBLANE NEW GOLF CLUB
MAP 4 B1

Perth Road, Dunblane, Perthshire.
East side of town on A9, 6 miles north of Stirling.

CONTACT: B Jamieson, Professional. Tel: 0786 823711.
Course: 5,876yds, PAR 69, SSS 68. Parkland course.
SOC RESTR'S: Welcome Monday & Thursday. Contact in advance.
SOC GF - Round: Wd £16. We £23. Day: Wd £23. We £23.
SOC PACK: On application from Secretary.
VIS RESTR'S: Welcome some restrictions at Weekends.
VIS GF - Round: Wd £16. We £23. Day: Wd £23. We £23.
FACILITIES: Bar, Restaurant, Pro-shop & Club Hire.

FALKIRK GOLF CLUB
MAP 4 B1

Stirling Road, Camelon, Falkirk FK2 7YP.
2 miles west of Falkirk on A9.

CONTACT: J Elliot, Secretary. Tel: 0324 611061.
Course: 6,282yds, PAR 71, SSS 69. Parkland course.
SOC RESTR'S: Welcome except Wed, Sat & Sun before 10.30.
SOC GF - Round: Wd £10. We N/A. Day: Wd £15. We N/A.
SOC PACK: Coffee, Lunch, Dinner.
VIS RESTR'S: Welcome except Weekends.
VIS GF - Round: Wd £10. We N/A. Day: Wd £15. We N/A.
FACILITIES: Bar & Restaurant.

FALKIRK TRYST GOLF CLUB
MAP 4 B1

86 Burnhead Road, Larbert.
1 mile north-east of town off A88/B905.

CONTACT: D Wallis, Secretary. Tel: 0324 562415.
Course: 6,053yds, PAR 70, SSS 69. Windy moorland course.
SOC RESTR'S: Welcome except Wednesday & Weekends.
SOC GF - Round: Wd £12. We N/A. Day: Wd £17. We N/A.
SOC PACK: On application from Secretary.
VIS RESTR'S: Welcome except Wednesday & Weekends.
VIS GF - Round: Wd £12. We N/A. Day: Wd £17. We N/A.
FACILITIES: Restaurant (Sat eve only), Bar Snacks & Pro-shop.

DUMFRIES

GLENBERVIE GOLF CLUB MAP 4 B1

Stirling Road, Larbert, Stirlingshire FK5 4SJ.
1 mile north of town on A9 between Larbert & Stirling.

CONTACT: Mrs M Purves, Secretary. Tel: 0324 562605.
Course: 6,469yds, PAR 71, SSS 71. Parkland course.
SOC RESTR'S: Max. 40. Welcome Tuesday & Thursday only.
SOC GF - Round: Wd £20. We N/A. **Day:** Wd £30. We N/A.
SOC PACK: 1 round + High Tea approx. £32.
VIS RESTR'S: Welcome Weekdays.
VIS GF - Round: Wd £20. We N/A. **Day:** Wd £30. We N/A.
FACILITIES: Bar, Catering & Practice Area.

GRANGEMOUTH GOLF CLUB MAP 4 B1

Polmont Hill, Polmont, Falkirk FK2 0YA.
3 miles east of Falkirk.

CONTACT: DG Walls, Secretary. Tel: 0324 711500.
Course: 6,314yds, PAR 71, SSS 71. Parkland course.
SOC RESTR'S: Max 40. Welcome at Weekends.
SOC GF - Round: Wd £6.30. We £8.40. **Day:** Wd £9.45. We £11.55.
SOC PACK: On application from Secretary.
VIS RESTR'S: Please phone in advance.
VIS GF - Round: Wd £6.30. We £8.40. **Day:** Wd £9.45. We £11.55.
FACILITIES: Catering by prior arrangement, Bar & Pro-shop.

MUCKHART GOLF CLUB MAP 4 B1

Drumburn Rd, Muckhart, By Dollar Fk14 7JH.
On side road between A91 & A823 just south of village.

CONTACT: J Muston, Manager. Tel: 0259 781423.
Course: 6,192yds, PAR 70, SSS 70. Moorland course.
SOC RESTR'S: Not every Weekend.
SOC GF - Round: Wd £12.50. We £18. **Day:** Wd £18. We £24.
SOC PACK: £26 Weekdays - £32 Weekends.
VIS RESTR'S: Welcome except before 9. 45 at Weekends.
VIS GF - Round: Wd £12.50. We £18. **Day:** Wd £18. We £24.
FACILITIES: Bar & Catering,

STIRLING GOLF CLUB MAP 4 B1

Queen's Road, Stirling FK8 2QY.
Half-a-mile west of town centre on A811.

CONTACT: W McArthur, Hon. Sec. Tel: 0786 464098.
Course: 6,438yds, PAR 72, SSS 71. Parkland course.
SOC RESTR'S: Welcome by arrangement with Secretary.
SOC GF - Round: Wd £17. We N/A. **Day:** Wd £23. We N/A.
SOC PACK: Coffee, Lunch, High Tea, 36 holes. Approx. £33.
VIS RESTR'S: Welcome Weekdays subject to time. Please phone.
VIS GF - Round: Wd £17. We £17. **Day:** Wd £23. We £23.
FACILITIES: Bar & Restaurant.

TULLIALLAN GOLF CLUB MAP 4 B1

Alloa Road, Kincardine-On-Forth, By Alloa FK10 4QH.
5 miles east of Alloa.

CONTACT: K Weir. Tel: 0259 730396.
Course: 5,970yds, PAR 69, SSS 69. Parkland course.
SOC RESTR'S: Welcome. Max 24 on Sunday.
SOC GF - Day: Wd £14. We £16. **Day:** Wd £18.50. We £23.
SOC PACK: On application from Secretary.
VIS RESTR'S: Welcome except Friday & Saturday.
VIS GF - Day: Wd £14. We £16. **Day:** Wd £18.50. We £23.
FACILITIES: Bar & Restaurant.

Dumfries

DUMFRIES & COUNTY GC MAP 4 B2

Edinburgh Road, Dumfries DG1 1JX.
1 mile north of Dumfries town on A701.

CONTACT: EC Pringle, Secretary. Tel: 0387 53585.
Course: 5,928yds, PAR 69, SSS 68. Parkland course.
SOC RESTR'S: Apply in writing.
SOC GF - Round: Wd N/A. We N/A. **Day:** Wd £21. We £25.
SOC PACK: On application from Secretary.
VIS RESTR'S: Welcome except on Sat Mar-Oct. Please phone.
VIS GF - Round: Wd N/A. We N/A. **Day:** Wd £21. We £25.
FACILITIES: Bar, Restaurant, Pro-shop & Club Hire.

DUMFRIES & GALLOWAY GC MAP 4 B2

2 Laurieston Avenue, Dumfries DG2 7NY.
The course is on the A75 west of Dumfries.

CONTACT: J Donnachie, Secretary. Tel: 0387 63848.
Course: 5,803yds, PAR 68, SSS 68. Parkland course.
SOC RESTR'S: Max 40. Welcome Weekdays except Tuesday.
SOC GF - Round: Wd £16. We N/A. **Day:** Wd £16. We N/A.
SOC PACK: Private Caterers.
VIS RESTR'S: Welcome except Club Competition day.
VIS GF - Round: Wd £16. We £20. **Day:** Wd £16. We £20.
FACILITIES: Full catering.

SCOTLAND

KIRKCUDBRIGHT GOLF CLUB MAP 4 B3

Stirling Crescent, Kirkcudbright DG6 4EZ.
Turn left at sign on B727 on way into town.

CONTACT: Secretary or Stewardess. Tel: 0557 30314.
Course: 5,598yds, PAR 67, SSS 67. Hilly parkland course.
SOC RESTR'S: Welcome. H'cap Cert required.
SOC GF - Round: Wd £15. We £15. **Day:** Wd £20. We £20.
SOC PACK: On application.
VIS RESTR'S: Always welcome except for Club Competitions.
VIS GF - Round: Wd £15. We £15. **Day:** Wd £20. We £20.
FACILITIES: Bar & Catering.

POWFOOT GOLF CLUB MAP 4 B3

Powfoot, Cummertrees, Annan, Dumfries.
Off Annan to Dumfries road approx 3 miles west from Annan.

CONTACT: R Anderson, Secretary. Tel: 0461 202866.
Course: 6,266yds, PAR 71, SSS 70. Semi links course.
SOC RESTR'S: Max. 40 on Weekdays, 24 on Sunday after 2.45.
SOC GF - Round: Wd £15. We N/A. **Day:** Wd £23. We N/A.
SOC PACK: No package - GF £23, catering arrange with Steward.
VIS RESTR'S: Welcome except Sat & before 2. 45 on Sun.
VIS GF - Round: Wd £15. We N/A. **Day:** Wd £23. We N/A.
FACILITIES: Practice ground. Full bar & Catering facilities.

LOCKERBIE GOLF CLUB MAP 4 B2

Corrie Road, Lockerbie, Dumfries DG11 2ND.
East side of town centre off B7068.

CONTACT: J Thomson, Secretary. Tel: 0576 202462/203363.
Course: 5,418yds, PAR 67, SSS 66. Parkland course.
SOC RESTR'S: Apply in writing.
SOC GF - Round: Wd N/A. We N/A. **Day:** Wd £14. We £16/£18.
SOC PACK: On application from Secretary.
VIS RESTR'S: No restrictions.
VIS GF - Round: Wd N/A. We N/A. **Day:** Wd £14. We £16/£18.
FACILITIES: Bar & Restaurant.

SOUTHERNESS GOLF CLUB MAP 4 B3

Southerness, Dumfries DG2 8AZ.
16 miles south-west of Dumfries on A710.

CONTACT: Mr Ramage, Hon. Sec. Tel: 0387 88677.
Course: 6,554yds, PAR 72, SSS 72. Championship links course.
SOC RESTR'S: May play Wd 10-12 & 2-4 We 11-12 & 2-4.30.
SOC GF - Round: Wd N/A. We N/A. **Day:** Wd £23. We £30.
SOC PACK: None. Catering requirements: confirm 14 days prior.
VIS RESTR'S: Restrictions as shown for Societies.
VIS GF - Round: Wd N/A. We N/A. **Day:** Wd £23. We £30.
FACILITIES: Practice area, Bar & Catering. 5 day GF £80.

MOFFAT GOLF CLUB MAP 4 B2

Coatshill, Moffat, Dumfries DG10 9SB.
Leave A74 at Beattock & take A701 for 1 ml; club signposted.

CONTACT: Mrs McGregor. Tel: 0683 20020.
Course: 5,218yds, PAR 69, SSS 66. Scenic moorland.
SOC RESTR'S: No restrictions except Wednesday afternoons.
SOC GF - Round: Wd N/A. We N/A. **Day:** Wd £16. We £24.
SOC PACK: £20 Wd, £30 We, 36 holes, Coffee, Lunch & Eve meal.
VIS RESTR'S: No restrictions, except Wed afternoons.
VIS GF - Round: Wd N/A. We N/A. **Day:** Wd £16. We £24.
FACILITIES: Bar & Catering, Caddy cart hire, 5 day GF £35.

STRANRAER GOLF CLUB MAP 4 A3

Creachmore, Leswalt, Stranraer, Dumfries DG9 0LF.
2.5 miles north-west of Stranraer on A718.

CONTACT: WI Wilson, Secretary. Tel: 0776 87245.
Course: 6,300yds, PAR 70, SSS 71. Parkland course.
SOC RESTR'S: Contact in advance. 1994 GF under review.
SOC GF - Round: Wd N/A. We N/A. **Day:** Wd N/A. We N/A.
SOC PACK: On application from Secretary.
VIS RESTR'S: Restricted We. Contact first.
VIS GF - Round: Wd £15.75. We £21. **Day:** Wd £21. We £26.25.
FACILITIES: Restaurant (by arrangement), Bar Snacks & Shop.

PORTPATRICK (DUNSKEY) GC MAP 4 A3

Golf Course Rd, Portpatrick, Stranraer DG9 8TB.
A77 or A75 to Stranraer - Portpatrick fork right at War Memorial.

CONTACT: JA Horberry, Hon. Secretary. Tel: 0776 81273.
Course: 5,732yds, PAR 70, SSS 68. Links course.
SOC RESTR'S: Welcome Weekdays. H'cap Cert required.
SOC GF - Round: Wd £13. We N/A. **Day:** Wd £20. We N/A.
SOC PACK: Coffee, Lunch, High Tea, 18 holes: £27.
VIS RESTR'S: Prior booking essential. H'cap Cert required.
VIS GF - Round: Wd £13. We £16. **Day:** Wd £20. We £24.
FACILITIES: 9-hole Par 3 course & Bar.

THORNHILL GOLF CLUB MAP 4 B2

Blacknest, Thornhill, Dumfries DG3 5DW.
1 mile east of Thornhill, off the A76.

CONTACT: J Davidson, Club Steward. Tel: 0848 330546.
Course: 6,011yds, PAR 71, SSS 69. Parkland course.
SOC RESTR'S: Contact Club Steward.
SOC GF - Round: Wd N/A. We N/A. **Day:** Wd £16. We £20.
SOC PACK: None.
VIS RESTR'S: Open Competition Days - contact Club Steward.
VIS GF - Round: Wd N/A. We N/A. **Day:** Wd £16. We £20.
FACILITIES: Bar & Restaurant. Weekly GF £75.

FIFE

WIGTOWNSHIRE COUNTY GC MAP 4 A3

Mains of Park, Newton Stewart, Wigtownshire DG8 0NN.
8 miles east of Stranraer on the A75.

CONTACT: R McKnight, Treasurer. Tel: 0581 3420.
Course: 5,716yds, PAR 70, SSS 68. Links course.
SOC RESTR'S: Requires to be booked with R McCubbin.
SOC GF - Round: Wd £12. We £14. **Day:** Wd £16. We £18.
SOC PACK: 10+ players £1 each disc on GF. Meals approx £8.
VIS RESTR'S: Welcome except Wed eve & before 9.30 Sun.
VIS GF - Round: Wd £12. We £14. **Day:** Wd £16. We £18.
FACILITIES: Bar & Restaurant. Weekly GF £45.

BURNTISLAND GOLF HOUSE CLUB MAP 9 A2

Dodhead, Burntisland, Fife.
On B923, 1 mile north-east of the town centre.

CONTACT: I MacLean, Secretary. Tel: 0592 874093.
Course: 5,497yds, PAR 69, SSS 69. Moorland course.
SOC RESTR'S: Max. 24. Welcome exc We. Tee off 9.45 & 2.45.
SOC GF - Round: Wd £15. We N/A. **Day:** Wd £21. We N/A.
SOC PACK: On application.
VIS RESTR'S: Welcome but must book.
VIS GF - Round: Wd £15. We £25. **Day:** Wd £21. We £35.
FACILITIES: Visitors room, Shower room, Food & Bar.

CANMORE GOLF CLUB MAP 9 A2

Venturefair Avenue, Dunfermline, Fife.
1 mile north of Dunfermline on A823.

CONTACT: J Duncan, Secretary. Tel: 0383 724969.
Course: 5,474yds, PAR 67, SSS 66. Undulating parkland.
SOC RESTR'S: Contact in advance. Welcome except Weekends.
SOC GF - Round: Wd N/A. We N/A. **Day:** Wd N/A. We N/A.
SOC PACK: On application from Secretary.
VIS RESTR'S: Welcome except Weekends.
VIS GF - Round: Wd £12. We £18. **Day:** Wd £18. We £25.
FACILITIES: Bar & Pro-shop.

Fife

ABERDOUR GOLF CLUB MAP 9 A2

Seaside Place, Aberdour, Fife KY3 0TX.
South side of village, by the coast.

CONTACT: J Train, Secretary. Tel: 0383 860256.
Course: 5,469yds, PAR 67, SSS 67. Scenic parkland course.
SOC RESTR'S: Welcome except Saturday.
SOC GF - Round: Wd £15. We N/A. **Day:** Wd £22. We N/A.
SOC PACK: On application from Secretary.
VIS RESTR'S: Welcome Weekdays. Contact first.
VIS GF - Round: Wd £15. We £22. **Day:** Wd £22. We £22.
FACILITIES: Bar & Restaurant.

CRAIL GOLFING SOCIETY MAP 9 B1

Balcomie Clubhouse, Fifeness, Crail, Fife KY10 3XN.
1.5 miles from Crail centre.

CONTACT: Mrs CW Penhale, Secretary. Tel: 0333 50278.
Course: 5,202yds, PAR 69, SSS 68. Classic links course.
SOC RESTR'S: Max. 40 on Weekdays, Max. 30 at Weekends.
SOC GF - Round: Wd £16. We £20. **Day:** Wd £24. We £30.
SOC PACK: On application from Secretary.
VIS RESTR'S: No bookings before 10 & 12 to 2.
VIS GF - Round: Wd £16. We £20. **Day:** Wd £24. We £30.
FACILITIES: Bar & Catering. 3-5 day GF £16 a day. 2 weeks £128.

BALBIRNIE PARK GOLF CLUB MAP 9 A2

Balbirnie Park, Markinch, Glenrothes KY7 6NR.
From A92 turn to B4130 to Markinch. 1 ml turn left signposted.

CONTACT: A Gordon, Secretary. Tel: 0592 752006.
Course: 6,210yds, PAR 71, SSS 70. Parkland course.
SOC RESTR'S: Max. 24. Only restriction Comps have priority.
SOC GF - Round: Wd £18. We £26. **Day:** Wd £25. We £32.
SOC PACK: Coffee, Lunch, High Tea or Dinner by arrangement.
VIS RESTR'S: Welcome except before 10 on Sun & Comp times
VIS GF - Round: Wd £18. We £26. **Day:** Wd £25. We £32.
FACILITIES: Bar & Restaurant.

DUNFERMLINE GOLF CLUB MAP 9 A2

Pitfirrane, Crossford, Dunfermline, Fife KY12 8QV.
2 miles west of Dunfermline at Crossford on A994.

CONTACT: H Matheson, Secretary. Tel: 0383 723534.
Course: 6,237yds, PAR 72, SSS 70. Parkland course.
SOC RESTR'S: Max. 36. Welcome Weekdays.
SOC GF - Round: Wd £18. We N/A. **Day:** Wd £25. We N/A.
SOC PACK: Coffee, Snack lunch, High Tea + 36 holes: £32.50.
VIS RESTR'S: Welcome Weekdays, 10-12 & 2-4. H'cap required.
VIS GF - Round: Wd £18. We N/A. **Day:** Wd £25. We N/A.
FACILITIES: 9-hole Par 3 Course, Practice Area & Billiard Table.

95

SCOTLAND

DUNNIKIER PARK GOLF CLUB   MAP 9 A2

Dunnikier Way, Kirkcaldy, Fife KY1 3LP.
North side of town (Kirkcaldy).

CONTACT: R Waddell, Secretary. Tel: 0592 261599.
Course: 6,601yds, PAR 72, SSS 72. Parkland course.
SOC RESTR'S: Min. 12. Max. 30. Welcome by arrangement.
SOC GF - Round: Wd £8. We £10. **Day:** Wd £13.50. We £15.50.
SOC PACK: Coffee, Lunch, High Tea, 36 holes: £20.
VIS RESTR'S: Welcome but please book.
VIS GF - Round: Wd £8. We £10. **Day:** Wd £13.50. We £15.50.
FACILITIES: Practice Ground, Bar & Catering.

KIRKCALDY GOLF CLUB   MAP 9 A2

Balwearie Road, Kirkcaldy, Fife KY2 5LT.
Just outside the town to the west.

CONTACT: J Brodley, Hon. Secretary. Tel: 0592 260370.
Course: 6,004yds, PAR 71, SSS 70. Parkland course.
SOC RESTR'S: No parties Tuesdays or Saturdays.
SOC GF - Round: Wd £15. We £18. **Day:** Wd £20. We £25.
SOC PACK: None.
VIS RESTR'S: Welcome except Saturday & limited on Tuesday.
VIS GF - Round: Wd £15. We £18. **Day:** Wd £20. We £25.
FACILITIES: Bar.

ELIE GOLF CLUB   MAP 9 B2

Elie, Leven, Fife KY9 1AS.
12 miles from St. Andrews on A915.

CONTACT: A Sneddon, Secretary. Tel: 0333 330301.
Course: 6,214yds, PAR 70, SSS 70. Seaside links course.
SOC RESTR'S: Not We May-Sept. or any day June-Aug.
SOC GF - Round: Wd £22. We £33. **Day:** Wd £30. We £42.
SOC PACK: £40 including Lunch & High Tea.
VIS RESTR'S: Not before 10. No visitors on Sun May-Sept.
VIS GF - Round: Wd £22. We £33. **Day:** Wd £30. We £42.
FACILITIES: 9-hole Course, Driving Range, Putting & Tennis.

LADYBANK GOLF CLUB   MAP 9 A1

Annsmuir, Ladybank, Fife KY7 7RA.
6 mls S of Cupar on Edinburgh-Dundee road. N of village.

CONTACT: A Dick, Secretary. Tel: 0337 30814.
Course: 6,641yds, PAR 71, SSS 72. Heathland course.
SOC RESTR'S: Must contact in advance.
SOC GF - Round: Wd £24. We £26. **Day:** Wd £32. We £35.
SOC PACK: On application from Secretary.
VIS RESTR'S: Please phone before play.
VIS GF - Round: Wd £24. We £26. **Day:** Wd £32. We £35.
FACILITIES: Bar, Restaurant, Pro-shop & Club Hire.

GLENROTHES GOLF CLUB   MAP 9 A2

Golf Course Road, Glenrothes, Fife KY6 2LA.
Follow signs to Glenrothes west.

CONTACT: P Landells, Secretary. Tel: 0592 758686.
Course: 6,444yds, PAR 71, SSS 71. Hilly parkland course.
SOC RESTR'S: Min 12. Max 30. Book 1 month in advance.
SOC GF - Round: Wd £8. We £10. **Day:** Wd £13.50. We £15.50.
SOC PACK: Full day plus meals approx. £21.
VIS RESTR'S: Always welcome.
VIS GF - Round: Wd £8. We £10. **Day:** Wd £13.50. We £15.50.
FACILITIES: Clubhouse.

LEVEN LINKS GOLF CLUB   MAP 9 A1

Links Road, Leven, Fife. KY8 4HS.
9 miles east of Kirkcaldy on the A955.

CONTACT: B Jackson, Secretary. Tel: 0333 428859.
Course: 6,435yds, PAR 71, SSS 71. Links course.
SOC RESTR'S: Must apply in writing.
SOC GF - Round: Wd £18. We £24. **Day:** Wd £26. We £36.
SOC PACK: On application from Secretary.
VIS RESTR'S: Welcome except Saturday.
VIS GF - Round: Wd £18. We £24. **Day:** Wd £26. We £36.
FACILITIES: Bar, Restaurant & Pro-shop.

KINGHORN GOLF CLUB   MAP 9 A2

Macduff Crescent, Kinghorn, Fife KY3 9RE.
Off A92, 3 miles west of Kirkcaldy.

CONTACT: J Robertson, Secretary. Tel: 0592 890345.
Course: 5,269yds, PAR 65, SSS 317. Municipal course.
SOC RESTR'S: Contact in writing.
SOC GF - Round: Wd £8. We £10. **Day:** Wd £13. We £15.
SOC PACK: On application from Secretary.
VIS RESTR'S: No restrictions.
VIS GF - Round: Wd £8. We £10. **Day:** Wd £13. We £15.
FACILITIES: Bar.

LOCHGELLY GOLF CLUB   MAP 9 A2

Cartmore Road, Lochgelly, Fife.
West side of town, off the A910.

CONTACT: R Stuart, Secretary. Tel: 0592 780174.
Course: 5,491yds, PAR 68, SSS 67. Parkland course.
SOC RESTR'S: Max. 2 at Weekends. Must apply in writing.
SOC GF - Round: Wd £9.50. We £13. **Day:** Wd £16.50. We £21.
SOC PACK: On application from Secretary.
VIS RESTR'S: No restrictions.
VIS GF - Round: Wd £9.50. We £13. **Day:** Wd £16.50. We £21.
FACILITIES: Catering (prior arrangement) &Bar.

FIFE

LUNDIN GOLF CLUB MAP 9 A1

Golf Road, Lundin Links, Fife KY8 6BA.
3 miles east of Leven on the A915.

CONTACT: A McBride, Secretary. Tel: 0333 320202.
Course: 6,377yds, PAR 71, SSS 71. Links course.
SOC RESTR'S: Welcome except Weekends.
SOC GF - Round: Wd £18. **We** N/A. **Day:** Wd £27. **We** N/A.
SOC PACK: On application from Secretary.
VIS RESTR'S: Welcome Mon-Thur 9-3.30, Fri 9-3, Sat after 2.30.
VIS GF - Round: Wd £18. **We** N/A. **Day:** Wd £27. **We** N/A.
FACILITIES: Bar & Restaurant.

PITREAVIE GOLF CLUB MAP 9 A2

Queensferry Road, Dunfermline, Fife KY11 5PR.
South- east of town on A823, midway to Rosyth.

CONTACT: D Carter, Secretary. Tel: 0383 722591.
Course: 6,086yds, PAR 70, SSS 69. Woodland course.
SOC RESTR'S: Must book in advance.
SOC GF - Round: Wd £13. **We** N/A. **Day:** Wd £18. **We** £24.
SOC PACK: On application from Secretary.
VIS RESTR'S: Please book. H'cap Cert required.
VIS GF - Round: Wd £13. **We** N/A. **Day:** Wd £18. **We** £24.
FACILITIES: Restaurant (except Tue), Bar Snacks & Pro-shop.

SCOONIE GOLF CLUB MAP 9 A1/2

North Links, Leven, Fife KY8 4SP.
5 mins drive from town centre, 10 miles SW of St. Andrews.

CONTACT: S Kuzcepra, Secretary. Tel: 0333 427057.
Course: 4,854yds, PAR 67, SSS 66. Flat parkland course.
SOC RESTR'S: Min. 12, Max. 30. Welcome except Thur &Sat.
SOC GF - Round: Wd £8. **We** £10. **Day:** Wd £13. **We** N/A.
SOC PACK: Wd £18, We £20 incl Coffee, Lunch & High Tea.
VIS RESTR'S: Welcome except Thursday & Saturday.
VIS GF - Round: Wd £8. **We** £10. **Day:** Wd £13. **We** N/A.
FACILITIES: Bar & Restaurant.

SCOTSCRAIG GOLF CLUB MAP 9 B1

Golf Road, Tayport, Fife DD6 9DZ.
10 miles north of St. Andrews.

CONTACT: S Kuzcepra, Secretary. Tel: 0382 552315.
Course: 6,496yds, PAR 71, SSS 71. Seaside links course.
SOC RESTR'S: Limited to 24 at Weekends. GF on application.
SOC GF - Round: Wd N/A. **We** £25. **Day:** Wd N/A. **We** N/A.
SOC PACK: On application from Secretary.
VIS RESTR'S: Welcome Wd, We by booking. GF on application.
VIS GF - Round Wd £20. **We** £25. **Day:** Wd £32. **We** £40.
FACILITIES: Bar & Restaurant.

ST. ANDREWS (OLD COURSE) MAP 9 B1

Links Management Committee, St. Andrews, Fife KY16 9JA.
Signposted from outskirts of St. Andrews on A91..

CONTACT: Mrs Smith, Reservation Manager. Tel: 0334 75757.
Course: 6,566yds, PAR 72, SSS 72. Links course.
SOC RESTR'S: Welcome except Saturday.
SOC GF - Round: Wd £40. **We** £40. **Day:** Wd N/A. **We** N/A.
SOC PACK: None.
VIS RESTR'S: Availability; check by phone. H'cap Cert required.
VIS GF - Round: Wd £40. **We** £40. **Day:** Wd N/A. **We** N/A.
FACILITIES: Practice Area, Shop & Caddies always available.

ST. ANDREWS (EDEN COURSE) MAP 9 B1

Links Management Committee, St. Andrews, Fife KY16 9JA.
Signposted from outskirts of St. Andrews on A91.

CONTACT: Mrs Smith, Reservation Manager. Tel: 0334 75757.
Course: 6,315yds, PAR 70, SSS 70. Links course.
SOC RESTR'S: Welcome except Saturday.
SOC GF - Round: Wd £16. **We** £16. **Day:** Wd N/A. **We** N/A.
SOC PACK: None.
VIS RESTR'S: Availability; check by phone.
VIS GF - Round: Wd £16. **We** £16. **Day:** Wd N/A. **We** N/A.
FACILITIES: 3-Day Ticket £40. Weekly Ticket £80-Under 16's 50% less.

ST. ANDREWS (NEW COURSE) MAP 9 B1

Links Management Committee, St. Andrews, Fife KY16 9JA.
Signposted from outskirts of St. Andrews on A91.

CONTACT: Mrs Smith, Reservation Manager. Tel: 0334 75757.
Course: 6,604yds, PAR 71, SSS 72. Links course.
SOC RESTR'S: Welcome except Saturday.
SOC GF - Round: Wd £18. **We** £18. **Day:** Wd N/A. **We** N/A.
SOC PACK: None.
VIS RESTR'S: Availability; check by phone.
VIS GF - Round: Wd £18. **We** £18. **Day:** Wd N/A. **We** N/A.
FACILITIES: Practice Area. 3-Day & Weekly Ticket.

ST. ANDREWS (JUBILEE COURSE) MAP 9 B1

Links Management Committee, St. Andrews, Fife KY16 9JA.
Signposted from outskirts of St. Andrews on A91.

CONTACT: Mrs Smith, Reservation Manager. Tel: 0334 75757.
Course: 6,805yds, PAR 72, SSS 73. Links course.
SOC RESTR'S: Welcome except Saturday.
SOC GF - Round: Wd £16. **We** £16. **Day:** Wd N/A. **We** N/A.
SOC PACK: None.
VIS RESTR'S: Availability must be ascertained by telephone.
VIS GF - Round: Wd £16. **We** £16. **Day:** Wd N/A. **We** N/A.
FACILITIES: Practice Area, Golf Shop, Tickets.

SCOTLAND

THORNTON GOLF CLUB MAP 9 A2

Station Road, Thornton, Fife KY1 4DW.
Via Station Road in Thornton village.

CONTACT: N Robertson, Secretary. Tel: 0592 771111.
Course: 6,177yds, PAR 70, SSS 69. Undulating parkland.
SOC RESTR'S: Please book through Secretary.
SOC GF - Round: Wd £11. We £16. **Day:** Wd £17. We £25.
SOC PACK: Coffee, Lunch, High Tea, 36 holes.
VIS RESTR'S: Always welcome but please book.
VIS GF - Round: Wd £11. We £16. **Day:** Wd £17. We £25.
FACILITIES: Practice Pitching & Putting Green & Driving Net.

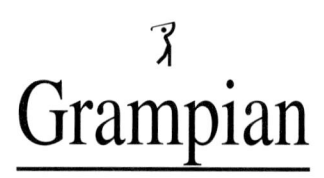

Grampian

ABOYNE GOLF CLUB MAP 6 B2

Formaston Park, Aboyne, Aberdeenshire AB3 5HD.
North of A93 on east side of village.

CONTACT: Mrs McLean, Secretary. Tel: 03398 87078.
Course: 5,910yds, PAR 68, SSS 68. Parkland course.
SOC RESTR'S: Prior booking essential.
SOC GF - Round: Wd £14. We £16. **Day:** Wd £18. We £21.
SOC PACK: On application from Secretary.
VIS RESTR'S: Please phone before play.
VIS GF - Round: Wd £14. We £16. **Day:** Wd £18. We £21.
FACILITIES: Bar, Restaurant, Pro-shop & Club Hire.

BALLATER GOLF CLUB MAP 6 B2

Victoria Road, Ballater, Aberdeenshire AB3 5QX.
42 miles west of Aberdeen, 62 miles north of Perth on the A93.

CONTACT: A Ingram, Manager. Tel: 0339 755567.
Course: 5,638yds, PAR 67, SSS 68. Moorland course.
SOC RESTR'S: Booking by prior notification.
SOC GF - Round: Wd £15. We £18. **Day:** Wd £22.50. We £27.
SOC PACK: On application from Manager.
VIS RESTR'S: Always welcome but please book in advance.
VIS GF - Round: Wd £15. We £18. **Day:** Wd £22.50. We £27.
FACILITIES: Practice Area. Weekly GF £63, Season £150.

BALNAGASK GOLF CLUB MAP 6 B2

St. Fitticks Road, Aberdeen.
2 miles south-east of city centre.

CONTACT: Secretary. Tel: 0224 876407.
Course: 5,986yds, PAR 72, SSS 70. Undulating seaside links.
SOC RESTR'S: Book in advance.
SOC GF - Round: Wd £6. We £6. **Day:** Wd £12. We £12.
SOC PACK: On application from Secretary.
VIS RESTR'S: Welcome.
VIS GF - Round: Wd £6. We £6. **Day:** Wd £12. We £12.
FACILITIES: Bar & Restaurant.

BANCHORY GOLF CLUB MAP 6 B2

Kinneskie Road, Banchory, Kincardine AB31 3TA.
18 miles west of Aberdeen on Deeside.

CONTACT: W Donaldson, Secretary. Tel: 0330 22365.
Course: 5,245yds, PAR 67, SSS 66. Parkland course.
SOC RESTR'S: Welcome except Thursday & Weekends.
SOC GF - Round: Wd £14. We N/A. **Day:** Wd £17.50. We N/A.
SOC PACK: Coffee, Lunch, Evening Meal approx. £10-£12.
VIS RESTR'S: Welcome.
VIS GF - Round: Wd N/A. We N/A. **Day:** Wd £17.50. We £19.50.
FACILITIES: Bar & Restaurant.

BON ACCORD GOLF CLUB MAP 6 B2

19 Golf Road, Aberdeen AB2 1QB.
Beside Pittodrie Stadium, near the beach.

CONTACT: J Miller, Secretary. Tel: 0224 633464.
Course: 6,433yds, PAR 72, SSS 71. Links coastal course.
SOC RESTR'S: Must contact in advance.
SOC GF - Round: Wd £6. We £6. **Day:** Wd £12. We £12.
SOC PACK: On application from Secretary.
VIS RESTR'S: No restrictions.
VIS GF - Round: Wd £6. We £6. **Day:** Wd £12. We £12.
FACILITIES: Lunch (prior arrangement), Bar Snacks & Snooker.

BUCKPOOL GOLF CLUB MAP 6 B2

Barhill Road, Buckie, Banffshire AB56 1DU.
Leave A98 towards Buckpool.

CONTACT: Mrs Geddes, Secretary. Tel: 0542 32236.
Course: 6,257yds, PAR 70, SSS 70. Seaside links.
SOC RESTR'S: By prior arrangement.
SOC GF - Day : Wd £6. We £10. **Day:** Wd £10. We £15.
SOC PACK: £25 approx.
VIS RESTR'S: Not on Competition Days.
VIS GF - Day : Wd £6. We £10. **Day:** Wd £10. We £15.
FACILITIES: Catering (prior arrangement), Squash & Snooker.

GRAMPIAN

CRUDEN BAY GOLF CLUB   MAP 6 B2

Aulton Road, Cruden Bay, Peterhead AB4 7NN.
7 miles S of Peterhead, 23 miles NE of Aberdeen on coast.

CONTACT: G Donald, Secretary. Tel: 0779 812285.
Course: 6,370yds, PAR 70, SSS 71. Seaside links course.
SOC RESTR'S: Apply in writing.
SOC GF - Round: Wd N/A. **We** N/A. **Day:** Wd N/A. **We** N/A.
SOC PACK: On application from Secretary.
VIS RESTR'S: Welcome with H'cap Cert, restrictions at We.
VIS GF - Round: Wd N/A. **We** N/A. **Day:** Wd £20. **We** £28.
FACILITIES: Bar, Restaurant, Pro-shop & Club Hire.

ELGIN GOLF CLUB   MAP 6 B2

Hardhillock, Birnie Road, Elgin, Moray IV30 3SX.
Half-a-mile south of Elgin.

CONTACT: DJ Chambers, Secretary. Tel: 0343 542338.
Course: 6,401yds, PAR 69, SSS 71. Gently undulating parkland.
SOC RESTR'S: Subject to existing course loading.
SOC GF - Round: Wd £14. **We** £20. **Day:** Wd £20. **We** £28.
SOC PACK: £9+ depending on menu. GF discount for 25+.
VIS RESTR'S: Subject to previous bookings.
VIS GF - Round: Wd £14. **We** £20. **Day:** Wd £20. **We** £28.
FACILITIES: Bar & Restaurant.

CULLEN GOLF CLUB   MAP 6 B2

The Links, Cullen, Buckie, Banffshire.
Half-a-mile west of Cullen off trunk road A98.

CONTACT: I Findlay, Secretary. Tel: 0542 40685.
Course: 4,610yds, PAR 63, SSS 62. Links course.
SOC RESTR'S: Parties limited to 40 & We. Written application.
SOC GF - Round: Wd N/A. **We** N/A. **Day:** Wd £8. **We** N/A.
SOC PACK: Coffee, Lunch, High Tea approx £25.
VIS RESTR'S: As Societies but small parties accommodated at We.
VIS GF - Round: Wd N/A. **We** N/A. **Day:** Wd £8. **We** £11.
FACILITIES: 18-hole Putting Green & Net Practice Area.

FORRES GOLF CLUB   MAP 6 A2

Muiryshade, Forres, Moray IV36 0RD.
1 mile south-east side of town centre, off B9010.

CONTACT: DF Black, Secretary. Tel: 0309 672949.
Course: 6,203yds, PAR 70, SSS 70. Undulating parkland.
SOC RESTR'S: Welcome Weekdays.
SOC GF - Round: Wd N/A. **We** N/A. **Day:** Wd £12. **We** £17.
SOC PACK: On application from Secretary.
VIS RESTR'S: Welcome but phone re competitions.
VIS GF - Round: Wd N/A. **We** N/A. **Day:** Wd £12. **We** £17.
FACILITIES: Bar, Restaurant, Pro-shop & Club Hire.

DEESIDE GOLF CLUB   MAP 6 B2

Golf Road, Bieldside, Aberdeen.
3 miles west of city centre, off A93.

CONTACT: A Urquart, Secretary. Tel: 0224 869457.
Course: 6,000yds, PAR 69, SSS 69. Scenic parkland course.
SOC RESTR'S: Welcome Thursday only.
SOC GF - Round: Wd N/A. **We** N/A. **Day:** Wd £17. **We** N/A.
SOC PACK: On application from Secretary.
VIS RESTR'S: Welcome Wd between 9 & 4, We after 4.
VIS GF - Round: Wd N/A. **We** N/A. **Day:** Wd £20. **We** £25.
FACILITIES: Catering (not Mon), Shop. Weekly GF £60.

FRASERBURGH GOLF CLUB   MAP 6 B2

Corbie Hill, Philorth, Fraserburgh AB4 5TL.
1 mile east of Fraserburgh on A92.

CONTACT: J Grant, Secretary. Tel: 0346 518287.
Course: 6,217yds, PAR 70, SSS 70. Seaside course.
SOC RESTR'S: Contact in advance. Green fees not confirmed.
SOC GF - Round: Wd N/A. **We** N/A. **Day:** Wd N/A. **We** N/A.
SOC PACK: On application from Secretary.
VIS RESTR'S: No restrictions. 1994 GF not confirmed.
VIS GF - Round: Wd N/A. **We** N/A. **Day:** Wd £11. **We** £15.
FACILITIES: Bar, Restaurant & Pro-shop.

DUFFTOWN GOLF CLUB   MAP 6 B2

Mether Cluny, Glenrinnes, Dufftown.
1 mile west of town.

CONTACT: DF Duncombe, Treasurer. Tel: 0340 20335.
Course: 5,308yds, PAR 67, SSS 67. Parkland course.
SOC RESTR'S: Welcome.
SOC GF - Round: Wd £7. **We** £8. **Day:** Wd £7. **We** £8.
SOC PACK: Less than £20. Food to be negotiated in advance.
VIS RESTR'S: Always welcome.
VIS GF - Round: Wd £7. **We** £8. **Day:** Wd £7. **We** £8.
FACILITIES: Dufftown is the 'Whisky Capital' of Scotland.

GARMOUTH & KINGSTON GC   MAP 6 B2

Garmouth, Fochabers, Moray IV32 7LU.
In Garmouth village, on B9015.

CONTACT: Secretary. Tel: 0343 87388.
Course: 5,656yds, PAR 67, SSS 67. Seaside/parkland course.
SOC RESTR'S: Must telephone in advance.
SOC GF - Round: Wd £10. **We** £14. **Day:** Wd £12. **We** £18.
SOC PACK: On application from Secretary.
VIS RESTR'S: Restricted on Competition Days. Please phone.
VIS GF - Round: Wd £10. **We** £14. **Day:** Wd £12. **We** £18.
FACILITIES: Catering (May-Sept or prior booking) & Bar.

SCOTLAND

GRANTOWN-ON-SPEY GOLF CLUB MAP 6 A2

Golf Course Road, Grantown-on-Spey, Moray.
Leave A9 at Aviemore, continue on A939 to Grantown.

CONTACT: Secretary. Tel: 0479 2079 (summer).
Course: 5,745yds, PAR 70, SSS 67. Parkland/woodland.
SOC RESTR'S: Telephone in advance, write in winter.
SOC GF - Round: Wd N/A. We N/A. Day: Wd £13. We £18.
SOC PACK: On application from Secretary.
VIS RESTR'S: Welcome except Wd 5. 30-6.30, We 8-10,1-2 & 5-6.
VIS GF - Round: Wd N/A We N/A Day: Wd £13. We £16.
FACILITIES: Catering (prior arrangement) & Pro-shop.

HAZELHEAD CLUB (NO. 1) MAP 6 B2

Hazelhead Park, Aberdeen.
4 miles west of city centre, off A944.

CONTACT: J Murchie, Secretary. Tel: 0224 315417.
Course: 6,595yds, PAR 70, SSS 70. Treelined moorland.
SOC RESTR'S: Contact in advance.
SOC GF - Round: Wd £6. We N/A. Day: Wd N/A. We N/A.
SOC PACK: On application from Secretary.
VIS RESTR'S: No restrictions.
VIS GF - Round: Wd £6. We £6. Day: Wd N/A. We N/A.
FACILITIES: 9-hole Course, Pro-shop & Club Hire.

HAZELHEAD GOLF CLUB (NO. 2) MAP 6 B2

Hazelhead Park, Aberdeen.
4 miles west of city centre, off A944.

CONTACT: J Murchie, Secretary. Tel: 0224 315417.
Course: 5,800yds, PAR 69, SSS 68. Parkland course.
SOC RESTR'S: Contact in advance.
SOC GF - Round: Wd £6. We N/A. Day: Wd N/A. We N/A.
SOC PACK: On application from Secretary.
VIS RESTR'S: No restrictions.
VIS GF - Round: Wd £6. We £6. Day: Wd N/A. We N/A.
FACILITIES: 9-hole Course, Pro-shop & Club Hire.

HOPEMAN GOLF CLUB MAP 6 A2

Hopeman, Moray IV30 2SS.
East side of village, off B9012.

CONTACT: WH Dumbar, Secretary. Tel: 0343 830578.
Course: 5,511yds, PAR 67, SSS 67. Links course.
SOC RESTR'S: Apply by letter 2 weeks in advance.
SOC GF - Round: Wd N/A. We N/A. Day: Wd £10. We £15.
SOC PACK: On application from Secretary.
VIS RESTR'S: Welcome except Tuesday 5-6 & some Weekends.
VIS GF - Round: Wd N/A. We N/A. Day: Wd £10. We £15.
FACILITIES: Bar & Restaurant.

INVERALLOCHY GOLF CLUB MAP 6 B2

24 Shore St., Inverallochy, Nr Fraserburgh.
4 miles south of Fraserburgh off the A92.

CONTACT: G Young, Secretary. Tel: 0346 582000.
Course: 5,137yds, PAR 64, SSS 65. Links course.
SOC RESTR'S: Apply in writing.
SOC GF - Round: Wd N/A. We N/A. Day: Wd N/A. We N/A.
SOC PACK: On application from Secretary.
VIS RESTR'S: No restrictions.
VIS GF - Round: Wd N/A. We N/A. Day: Wd £8. We £10.
FACILITIES: Catering (evenings & weekends). Unlicensed.

KEITH GOLF CLUB MAP 6 B2

Fife Park, Keith, Banffshire.
North-west side of town centre off A96 Keith-Dufftown Road.

CONTACT: J Edwards, Secretary. Tel: 0542 22469.
Course: 5,767yds, PAR 69, SSS 68. Parkland course.
SOC RESTR'S: By arrangement with Secretary
SOC GF - Round: Wd N/A. We N/A. Day: Wd £9. We £12.
SOC PACK: On application from Secretary.
VIS RESTR'S: No restrictions.
VIS GF - Round: Wd N/A. We N/A. Day: Wd £9. We £12.
FACILITIES: Bar.

KINTORE GOLF CLUB MAP 6 B2

Balbithan Road, Kintore, Inverurie, Aberdeenshire.
12 miles north-west of Aberdeen, leave A96 in centre of Kintore.

CONTACT: J Smith, Secretary. Tel: 0467 32631.
Course: 6,208yds, PAR 70, SSS 71. Undulating moorland course.
SOC RESTR'S: Welcome Weekdays.
SOC GF - Round: Wd N/A. We N/A. Day: Wd £12. We N/A.
SOC PACK: On application from Secretary.
VIS RESTR'S: No restrictions. Twilight GF after 6 £6.
VIS GF - Round: Wd N/A. We N/A. Day: Wd £12. We £17.
FACILITIES: Catering (not Mondays). Weekly GF available.

MACDONALD GOLF CLUB MAP 6 B2

Hospital Road, Ellon, Aberdeenshire AB4 9AW.
Quarter of a mile north of Ellon on A948.

CONTACT: K Clouston, Secretary. Tel: 0358 720576.
Course: 5,986yds, PAR 70, SSS 69. Tight parkland course.
SOC RESTR'S: By arrangement with Secretary.
SOC GF - Round: Wd N/A. We N/A. Day: Wd N/A. We N/A.
SOC PACK: On application from Secretary.
VIS RESTR'S: Welcome but at the We book & not before 10.
VIS GF - Round: Wd N/A. We N/A. Day: Wd £14. We £16/£20.
FACILITIES: Bar.

GRAMPIAN

MORAY GOLF CLUB (OLD) — MAP 6 B2

Stotfield Road, Lossiemouth, Moray IV31 6QS.
5 miles north of Elgin.
CONTACT: J Hamilton, Secretary. Tel: 0343 812018.
Course: 6,643yds, PAR 71, SSS 72. Links course.
SOC RESTR'S: Welcome except Sat all day & Sun before 10.30.
SOC GF - Round: Wd N/A. We N/A. **Day:** Wd £21. We £30.
SOC PACK: 10% reduction for parties of over 12.
VIS RESTR'S: Not before 9.30 &1-2 Wd. Sun before 10.30 &1-2.
VIS GF - Round: Wd N/A. We N/A. **Day:** Wd £21. We £30.
FACILITIES: Bar & Restaurant.

OLDMELDRUM GOLF CLUB — MAP 6 B2

Kirk Brae, Oldmeldrum, Inverurie, Aberdeenshire AB51 1OU.
On A947, 17 miles N of Aberdeen, signposted from main road.
CONTACT: D Petrie, Secretary. Tel: 0651 872383.
Course: 5,988yds, PAR 69, SSS 69. Parkland course.
SOC RESTR'S: After 10.30 on Competition Days.
SOC GF - Round: Wd N/A. We N/A. **Day:** Wd £10. We £15.
SOC PACK: Please phone.
VIS RESTR'S: Restrictions only on Club & Open Comp Days.
VIS GF - Round: Wd N/A. We N/A. **Day:** Wd £10. We £15.
FACILITIES: Licensed Bar & Catering.

MORAY GOLF CLUB (NEW) — MAP 6 B2

Stotfield Road, Lossiemouth, Moray IV31 6QS.
5 miles north of Elgin.
CONTACT: J Hamilton, Secretary. Tel: 0343 812018.
Course: 6,005yds, PAR 69, SSS 69. Links - many fine holes.
SOC RESTR'S: Welcome except Sat all day & Sun before 10.30.
SOC GF - Round: Wd N/A. We N/A. **Day:** Wd £15. We £20.
SOC PACK: 10% reduction for parties of over 12.
VIS RESTR'S: Not before 9. 30 &1-2 Wd. Sun before 10. 30 &1-2.
VIS GF - Round: Wd N/A. We N/A. **Day:** Wd £15. We £20.
FACILITIES: Bar & Restaurant.

PETERHEAD GOLF CLUB — MAP 6 B2

Craigewan Links, Peterhead, Aberdeenshire AB42 6LT.
Off Golf Road at north boundary of town.
CONTACT: A Brandie, Secretary. Tel: 0779 72149.
Course: 6,190yds, PAR 70, SSS 70. Links course.
SOC RESTR'S: Welcome any time except Sat. Prior booking only.
SOC GF - Round: Wd N/A. We N/A. **Day:** Wd £12. We £16.
SOC PACK: Coffee, Lunch, High Tea, 36 holes approx. £17-£21.
VIS RESTR'S: Always welcome.
VIS GF - Round: Wd N/A. We N/A. **Day:** Wd £12. We £16.
FACILITIES: Lounge Bar.

MURCAR GOLF CLUB — MAP 6 B2

Bridge of Don, Aberdeen AB2 8BD.
On A92 4 miles north-east from Aberdeen centre.
CONTACT: R Matthews, Sec. A White, Pro. Tel: 0224 704354.
Course: 6,241yds, PAR 71, SSS 70. Typical links course.
SOC RESTR'S: Max. 40. Not after noon on Wed & not on We.
SOC GF - Round: Wd £16. We N/A. **Day:** Wd £20. We N/A.
SOC PACK: £20 + meal (approx. £6).
VIS RESTR'S: Welcome except after noon on Wed & on We.
VIS GF - Round: Wd £16. We £22.50. **Day:** Wd £20. We £22.50.
FACILITIES: Bar & Catering.

ROYAL ABERDEEN GOLF CLUB — MAP 6 B2

Balgownie, Links Rd, Bridge of Don, Aberdeen AB2 8AT.
4 miles north of Aberdeen, off A92 Ellon road.
CONTACT: R MacAskill, Professional. Tel: 0224 702221.
Course: 6,372yds, PAR 70, SSS 71. Championship links course.
SOC RESTR'S: Please book in advance.
SOC GF - Round: Wd N/A. We N/A. **Day:** Wd £35. We N/A.
SOC PACK: By arrangement.
VIS RESTR'S: Letter of Intro and H'cap Cert required.
VIS GF - Round: Wd £28. We £35. **Day:** Wd £35. We N/A.
FACILITIES: 2nd 18-hole (Par 64), Food by arr, Bar, Restaurant.

NEWMACHER GOLF CLUB — MAP 6 B2

Newmacher, Aberdeen AB5 0NU.
2 miles north of Dyce, off A947.
CONTACT: G MacIntosh, Secretary. Tel: 0651 863002.
Course: 6,605yds, PAR 72, SSS 73. Championship parkland.
SOC RESTR'S: Apply in writing.
SOC GF - Round: Wd £16. We £20. **Day:** Wd £24. We N/A.
SOC PACK: On application from Secretary.
VIS RESTR'S: Please book. H'cap Cert required.
VIS GF - Round: Wd £16. We £24. **Day:** Wd £24. We £30.
FACILITIES: Bar, Restaurant, Pro-shop & Club Hire.

ROYAL TARLAIR GOLF CLUB — MAP 6 B2

Buchan Street, Macduff AB4 1TA.
On A98 - 48 miles from Aberdeen city.
CONTACT: Mrs T Watt, Secretary. Tel: 0261 32897.
Course: 5,866yds, PAR 69, SSS 68. Seaside links course.
SOC RESTR'S: Open tournaments from fixture list.
SOC GF - Round: Wd N/A. We N/A. **Day:** Wd £12. We £15.
SOC PACK: Full catering plus 36 holes by arrangement.
VIS RESTR'S: Always welcome.
VIS GF - Round: Wd £8. We £10. **Day:** Wd £12. We £15.
FACILITIES: Bar.

SCOTLAND

SPEY BAY GOLF CLUB　　MAP 6 B2

Spey Bay Hotel, Spey Bay, By Fochabers, Moray IV32 7PN.
Turn off A96 at Fochabers to Spey Bay (3 miles).
CONTACT: Manager. Tel: 0343 820424.
Course: 6,059yds, PAR 71, SSS 69. Links course.
SOC RESTR'S: Welcome.
SOC GF - Round: Wd £8. We £9.50. Day: Wd £11. We £13 (Sun).
SOC PACK: Coffee, Lunch, High Tea, 36 holes: Wd £16. We £18.
VIS RESTR'S: Always welcome. Phone for Sundays.
VIS GF - Round: Wd £8. We £9.50. Day: Wd £11. We £13 (Sun).
FACILITIES: Driving Range, Putting & Tennis.

Highlands

STONEHAVEN GOLF CLUB　　MAP 6 B2

Cowie, Stonehaven AB3 2RH.
Half-a-mile north of town - access from town.
CONTACT: RO Blair, Club Manager. Tel: 0569 62124.
Course: 4,804yds, PAR 66, SSS 65. Cliff-top course.
SOC RESTR'S: Welcome except Sat & from Jul-Aug Sun.
SOC GF - Round: Wd N/A. We N/A. Day: Wd £13. We £18.
SOC PACK: Weekday £21. Weekends £26.
VIS RESTR'S: Always welcome except Saturday.
VIS GF - Round: Wd N/A. We N/A. Day: Wd £13. We £18.
FACILITIES: Full Catering & Pro-shop.

BOAT OF GARTEN GOLF CLUB　　MAP 6 A2

Boat of Garten, Inverness-shire PH24 3BQ.
5 miles north of Aviemore on A9.
CONTACT: JR Ingram, Secretary. Tel: 0479 83282.
Course: 5,762yds, PAR 69, SSS 69. Narrow parkland course.
SOC RESTR'S: By arrangement only.
SOC GF - Round: Wd N/A. We N/A. Day: Wd £15. We £20.
SOC PACK: None.
VIS RESTR'S: Welcome except before 9.15 Wd & 10 We.
VIS GF - Round: Wd N/A. We N/A. Day: Wd £15. We £20.
FACILITIES: Bar & Restaurant.

STRATHLENE GOLF CLUB　　MAP 6 B2

Portessie, Buckie, Banffshire AB5 2DJ.
On the coast between Buckie & Cullen.
CONTACT: G Clark, Club Secretary. Tel: 0542 31798.
Course: 5,957yds, PAR 69, SSS 69. Seaside moorland.
SOC RESTR'S: By prior arrangement.
SOC GF - Round: Wd £10. We £12. Day: Wd £12. We £15.
SOC PACK: On application.
VIS RESTR'S: Always welcome.
VIS GF - Round: Wd £10. We £12. Day: Wd £12. We £15.
FACILITIES: Clubhouse.

BRORA GOLF CLUB　　MAP 6 A1

Golf Road, Brora, Sutherland KW9 6QS.
Signposted in village to beach.
CONTACT: H Baillie, Secretary. Tel: 0408 621417.
Course: 6,100yds, PAR 69, SSS 69. Natural seaside links.
SOC RESTR'S: On Competition Days.
SOC GF - Round: Wd £13. We £13. Day: Wd £15. We £15.
SOC PACK: Please phone for details.
VIS RESTR'S: On Competition Days.
VIS GF - Round: Wd £13. We £13. Day: Wd £15. We £15.
FACILITIES: Catering from Easter-October. Weekly GF £60.

TURRIFF GOLF CLUB　　MAP 6 B2

Rosehall, Turriff, Aberdeenshire AB53 7BB.
From A947, signposted on south side of Turriff.
CONTACT: Secretary. Tel: 0888 62982.
Course: 6,145yds, PAR 69, SSS 69. Parkland course.
SOC RESTR'S: Max. 30. Welcome except Wed &We.
SOC GF - Round: Wd £9. We £13. Day: Wd £13. We £16.
SOC PACK: Coffee, Lunch, High Tea, 36 holes: £21 Wd, £24 We.
VIS RESTR'S: Not before 10 at Weekends.
VIS GF - Round: Wd £12. We £15. Day: Wd £15. We £20.
FACILITIES: Changing Room, Showers, Meals & Bar.

FORT WILLIAM GOLF CLUB　　MAP 6 A2

North Road, Torlundy, Fort William. PH33 6RD.
2 miles north of Fort William, off A82.
CONTACT: J Allen, Secretary. Tel: 0397 704464.
Course: 5,640yds, PAR 70, SSS 68. Moorland course.
SOC RESTR'S: Contact in writing.
SOC GF - Round: Wd £8. We £8. Day: Wd £10. We £10.
SOC PACK: On application from Secretary.
VIS RESTR'S: No restrictions.
VIS GF - Round: Wd £8. We £8. Day: Wd £10. We £10.
FACILITIES: Bar, Restaurant & Club Hire.

HIGHLANDS

FORTROSE & ROSEMARKIE GC MAP 6 A2

Ness Road East, Fortrose IV10 8SE.
A9 north of Inverness to Tore Roundabout, A832 to Fortrose.
CONTACT: Margaret Collier, Secretary. Tel: 0381 620529.
Course: 5,462yds, PAR 71, SSS 69. Seaside links course.
SOC RESTR'S: Welcome by arrangement through Secretary.
SOC GF - Round: Wd £12. **We** £17. **Day:** Wd £17. **We** N/A.
SOC PACK: Depending on size.
VIS RESTR'S: No restrictions. Parties of 8+ book with Secretary.
VIS GF - Round: Wd £12. **We** £17. **Day:** Wd £17. **We** N/A.
FACILITIES: Bar & Catering. 5 day GF £40, 10 day GF £60.

MUIR OF ORD GOLF CLUB MAP 6 A2

Great North Road, Muir of Ord, Ross & Cromarty IV6 7SX.
12 miles north of Inverness on A862.
CONTACT: R Ewart, Secretary. Tel: 0463 870825.
Course: 5,202yds, PAR 67, SSS 65. Heathland course.
SOC RESTR'S: Apply in writing.
SOC GF - Round: Wd N/A. **We** N/A. **Day:** Wd £12. **We** £15.
SOC PACK: On application from Secretary.
VIS RESTR'S: Welcome except some We times. Please phone.
VIS GF - Round: Wd N/A. **We** N/A. **Day:** Wd £12. **We** £15.
FACILITIES: Shop, Club Hire & Snooker. 6-day GF £30, Mthly £100.

GOLSPIE GOLF CLUB MAP 6 A1

Ferry Road, Golspie, Sutherland KW10 6TQ.
Off the A9 half-a-mile from town.
CONTACT: M MacLeod, Assistant Administrator. Tel: 0408 633266.
Course: 5,836yds, PAR 68, SSS 67. Split links/parkland.
SOC RESTR'S: Societies welcome with bookings in advance.
SOC GF - Round: Wd N/A. **We** N/A. **Day:** Wd £15. **We** £15.
SOC PACK: None.
VIS RESTR'S: Always welcome.
VIS GF - Round: Wd N/A. **We** N/A. **Day:** Wd £15. **We** £15.
FACILITIES: Bar facilities & meals served all day during Apr -Sept.

NAIRN GOLF CLUB MAP 6 A2

Seabank Road, Nairn IV12 4HB.
West side of town by seashore.
CONTACT: J Somerville, Secretary. Tel: 0667 53208.
Course: 6,722yds, PAR 72, SSS 71. Seaside links course.
SOC RESTR'S: Prior booking required.
SOC GF - Round: Wd £25. **We** £30. **Day:** Wd £35. **We** £40.
SOC PACK: None.
VIS RESTR'S: Always welcome. H'cap Cert required.
VIS GF - Round: Wd £25. **We** £30. **Day:** Wd £35. **We** £40.
FACILITIES: 9-hole Course & Practice Ground.

INVERNESS GOLF CLUB MAP 6 A2

The Clubhouse, Culcabock, Inverness IV2 3XQ.
1 mile south of Inverness on A9.
CONTACT: G Thomson, Secretary. Tel: 0463 239882.
Course: 6,226yds, PAR 69, SSS 70. Parkland course.
SOC RESTR'S: Welcome to book with Secretary.
SOC GF - Round: Wd £15. **We** £18. **Day:** Wd £20. **We** £22.
SOC PACK: Depending on size.
VIS RESTR'S: Welcome except Saturday from Mar-Oct.
VIS GF - Round: Wd £15. **We** £18. **Day:** Wd £20. **We** £22.
FACILITIES: Catering & Bar.

NAIRN DUNBAR GOLF CLUB MAP 6 A2

Lochloy Road, Nairn IV12 5AE.
East side of town, off A96, on southern shore of Moray Firth.
CONTACT: Mrs S MacLennan, Secretary. Tel: 0667 52741.
Course: 6,431yds, PAR 71, SSS 71. Seaside links course.
SOC RESTR'S: Must contact in advance.
SOC GF - Round: Wd £15. **We** £20. **Day:** Wd £20. **We** £25.
SOC PACK: On application from Secretary.
VIS RESTR'S: Welcome.
VIS GF - Round: Wd £15. **We** £20. **Day:** Wd £20. **We** £25.
FACILITIES: Bar, Restaurant, Pro-shop & Club Hire.

KINGUSSIE GOLF CLUB MAP 6 A2

Gynack Road, Kingussie, Inverness-shire PH21 1LR.
Half-a-mile north of town. Turn off at Duke of Gordon Hotel.
CONTACT: ND McWilliam, Secretary. Tel: 0540 661600.
Course: 5,504yds, PAR 67, SSS 66. Upland course.
SOC RESTR'S: No societies at We except 10-12 & 2-4.
SOC GF - Round: Wd£10.50. **We** £12.50. **Day:** Wd£13.50. **We**£16.50.
SOC PACK: On application from Secretary.
VIS RESTR'S: Not We 8.30-9.30, 12.30-1.30 & 5.30-6.30.
VIS GF - Round: Wd£10.50. **We** £12.50. **Day:** Wd£13.50. **We**£16.50.
FACILITIES: None.

NEWTONMORE GOLF CLUB MAP 6 A2

Golf Course Road, Newtonmore, Inverness-shire PH20 1AP.
East side of village, off A9. 45 miles south of Inverness.
CONTACT: R Cheyne, Secretary. Tel: 0540 673328.
Course: 5,880yds, PAR 70, SSS 68. Moor/parkland course.
SOC RESTR'S: Please apply in writing.
SOC GF - Round: Wd £10. **We** £13. **Day:** Wd £13. **We** £16.
SOC PACK: On application from Secretary.
VIS RESTR'S: Not many. Advised to contact in advance.
VIS GF - Round: Wd £10. **We** £13. **Day:** Wd £13. **We** £16.
FACILITIES: Catering (Mar-Oct except Tues), Bar & Pro-shop.

SCOTLAND

REAY GOLF CLUB MAP 6 A1

Reay, Thurso, Caithness KE14 7RE.
11 miles west of Thurso towards Bettyhill.

CONTACT: Miss P Peebles, Secretary. Tel: 0847 81288.
Course: 5,865yds, PAR 69, SSS 68. Seaside links course.
SOC RESTR'S: Please apply in writing.
SOC GF - Round: Wd N/A. We N/A. Day: Wd £10. We £10.
SOC PACK: On application from Secretary.
VIS RESTR'S: Restricted Competition Days.
VIS GF - Round: Wd N/A. We N/A. Day: Wd £10. We £10.
FACILITIES: Catering (Weekdays in summer). Weekly GF £30.

ROYAL DORNOCH GOLF CLUB MAP 6 A2

Golf Road, Dornoch, Sutherland IV25 3LW.
1 mile from A9 to Wick.

CONTACT: ICR Walker, Secretary. Tel: 0862 810219.
Course: 6,581yds, PAR 70, SSS 72. Championship links.
SOC RESTR'S: Must be arranged through Secretary.
SOC GF - Round: Wd £30. We £35. Day: Wd N/A. We N/A.
SOC PACK: None.
VIS RESTR'S: Always welcome - except major competitions.
VIS GF - Round: Wd £30. We £35. Day: Wd N/A. We N/A.
FACILITIES: Bar & Catering.

STRATHPEFFER SPA GOLF CLUB MAP 6 A2

Strathpeffer, Ross-shire IV14 9AS.
5 miles west of Dingwall, to the north of village.

CONTACT: N Roxburgh, Hon. Sec. Tel: 0997 421219.
Course: 4,792yds, PAR 65, SSS 65. Upland course.
SOC RESTR'S: Min. 10. Restriction competition days. Usually Sat.
SOC GF - Round: Wd £10. We £12. Day: Wd £15. We £18.
SOC PACK: Coffee, Snack, High Tea & 36 holes: £23.
VIS RESTR'S: Welcome except before 10 Sun. Check other times.
VIS GF - Round: Wd £10. We £12. Day: Wd £15. We £18.
FACILITIES: Bar & Catering - not Monday.

TAIN GOLF CLUB MAP 6 A2

Chapel Road, Tain, Ross-shire IV19 1PA.
35 miles north of Inverness on A9.

CONTACT: Mrs Kathleen Ross, Secretary. Tel: 0862 892314.
Course: 6,238yds, PAR 70, SSS 70. Part links/heathland.
SOC RESTR'S: Not before 10am.
SOC GF - Round: Wd £12. We £18. Day: Wd £18. We £24.
SOC PACK: 18 holes - £13 Wd, £17 We. 36 holes- add £6 Incl.
VIS RESTR'S: Welcome but phone first.
VIS GF - Round: Wd £12. We £18. Day: Wd £18. We £24.
FACILITIES: Bar & Restaurant.

THURSO GOLF CLUB MAP 6 A1

Newlands of Geise, Thurso, Caithness.
2 miles south-west of Thurso on B874.

CONTACT: W Meilklejohn, Secretary. Tel: 0847 63807.
Course: 5,818yds, PAR 69, SSS 69. Windy parkland course.
SOC RESTR'S: Please book through Secretary.
SOC GF - Round: Wd N/A. We N/A. Day: Wd £10. We £10.
SOC PACK: On application from Secretary.
VIS RESTR'S: No restrictions.
VIS GF - Round: Wd N/A. We N/A. Day: Wd £10 We £10.
FACILITIES: Lunch/Dinner (sum only), Bar Snacks & Pro-shop.

TORVEAN GOLF CLUB MAP 6 A2

Glenurquhart Road, Inverness.
2 miles south-west on A82 towards Fort William.

CONTACT: Secretary. Tel: 0463 711434.
Course: 5,784yds, PAR 69, SSS 68. Parkland course.
SOC RESTR'S: Advance bookings required.
SOC GF - Round: Wd £8.20. We £9.50. Day: Wd £10.90. We £12.30.
SOC PACK: On application from Secretary.
VIS RESTR'S: Restricted Comp Days. Contact in advance.
VIS GF - Round: Wd £8.20. We £9.50. Day: Wd £10.90. We £12.30.
FACILITIES: Catering (prior arrangement) & Bar (Apr-Oct).

WICK GOLF CLUB MAP 6 B1

Reiss, Wick, Caithness KW1 4RW.
Signposted on A9, 3 miles north of Wick.

CONTACT: Mrs M Abernethy, Secretary. Tel: 0955 2726.
Course: 5,976yds, PAR 69, SSS 69. Typical links course.
SOC RESTR'S: Welcome except Wednesday & Thursday.
SOC GF - Round: Wd N/A. We N/A. Day: Wd £10. We £12.
SOC PACK: Available from Secretary on booking.
VIS RESTR'S: Always welcome.
VIS GF - Round: Wd N/A. We N/A. Day: Wd £10. We £12.
FACILITIES: Bar. Limited catering at Weekends.

RAC Regional Road Maps

Large scale (3 miles to 1 inch) maps for the motorist. Each sheet contains details of motorway junctions, dual carriageways, town plans,
a full index of towns and villages, and tourist information including golf courses.

Price £3.99
Available from bookshops

Lothian

BABERTON GOLF CLUB   MAP 9 A2

Baberton Avenue, Juniper Green, Edinburgh EH14 5DU.
South-west side of Edinburgh on the A70.

CONTACT: E W Horberry, Sec/Treasurer. Tel: 031 453 4911.
Course: 6,098yds, PAR 69, SSS 69. Parkland course.
SOC RESTR'S: Max. 40. Welcome Weekdays 9. 30-3.30.
SOC GF - Round: Wd £17. We N/A. Day: Wd £25. We N/A.
SOC PACK: On application from Secretary.
VIS RESTR'S: Welcome by arrangement. No Weekends.
VIS GF - Round: Wd £17. We N/A. Day: Wd £25. We N/A.
FACILITIES: Bar.

BATHGATE GOLF CLUB   MAP 9 A2

Edinburgh Road, Bathgate, West Lothian EH48 1BA.
Half-a-mile east of Bathgate town centre.

CONTACT: W Gray, Secretary. Tel: 0506 52232.
Course: 6,328yds, PAR 71, SSS 70. Parkland course.
SOC RESTR'S: Welcome Weekends.
SOC GF - Round: Wd £15. We £15. Day: Wd £20. We £25.
SOC PACK: On application.
VIS RESTR'S:. Welcome except competition days.
VIS GF - Round:Wd £15. We £15. Day: Wd £20. We £25.
FACILITIES: Bar & Restaurant.

BRAIDS UNITED GOLF CLUB   MAP 9 A2

22 Braids Hill Approach, Edinburgh EH10 6JY.
South side of Edinburgh.

CONTACT: Secretary. Tel: 031 452 9408.
Course: 5,731yds, PAR 70, SSS 68. Hillside course.
SOC RESTR'S: Welcome. Public course.
SOC GF - Round: Wd £6.60. We £6.60. Day: Wd N/A. We N/A.
SOC PACK: On application from Secretary.
VIS RESTR'S: Saturdays very busy. Public course.
VIS GF - Round: Wd £6.60. We £6.60. Day: Wd N/A. We N/A.
FACILITIES: Course open to all. 2nd 18 hole course, SSS 64.

LOTHIAN

BROOMIEKNOWE GOLF CLUB   MAP 9 A2

Golf Course Road, Bonnyrigg, Midlothian EH19 2HZ.
Half-a-mile north-east off B704.

CONTACT: I Nimmo, Secretary. Tel: 031 663 9317.
Course: 5,754yds, PAR 68, SSS 68. Mature parkland course.
SOC RESTR'S: Must write first. Deposit required.
SOC GF - Round: Wd £15. We £25. Day: Wd £25. We £50.
SOC PACK: On application from Secretary.
VIS RESTR'S: Restricted Wednesday. We H'cap Cert preferred.
VIS GF - Round: Wd £15. We £25. Day: Wd £25. We £50.
FACILITIES: Catering (except Mon). Bar & Pro-shop.

DALMAHOY G & CC (EAST)   MAP 9 A2

Kirknewton, Midlothian EH27 8EB.
7 miles west of Edinburgh on A71.

CONTACT: Country Club Reception. Tel: 031 333 4105.
Course: 6,664yds, PAR 72, SSS 72. Rolling parkland course.
SOC RESTR'S: Weekends limited to Hotel guests & Members.
SOC GF - Round: Wd £33. We £44. Day: Wd N/A. We N/A.
SOC PACK: Ryder Package £60, Masters Package £75 per round.
VIS RESTR'S: Welcome Weekdays. Weekends by arrangement.
VIS GF - Round: Wd £33. We £44. Day: Wd N/A. We N/A.
FACILITIES: Swimming, Snooker, Squash, Tennis & Health Centre.

DALMAHOY G & CC (WEST)   MAP 9 A2

Kirknewton, Midlothian EH27 8EB.
7 miles west of Edinburgh on A71.

CONTACT: Country Club Reception. Tel: 031 333 4105.
Course: 5,317yds, PAR 69, SSS 66. Short parkland course.
SOC RESTR'S: Welcome Weekdays.
SOC GF - Round: Wd £22. We £33. Day: Wd N/A. We N/A.
SOC PACK: Ryder Package £49, Masters Package £75 per round.
VIS RESTR'S: Welcome Weekdays. Weekends by arrangement.
VIS GF - Round: Wd £22. We £33. Day: Wd N/A. We N/A.
FACILITIES: Swimming, Snooker, Squash, Tennis & Health Centre.

DEER PARK GOLF CLUB   MAP 9 A2

Carmondean, Livingston, West Lothian.
North side of town, off the A809.

CONTACT: W Yule, Secretary. Tel: 0506 38843.
Course: 6,636yds, PAR 71, SSS 72. Long testing course.
SOC RESTR'S: Book through Secretary.
SOC GF - Round: Wd £14. We £22. Day: Wd £19. We £31.
SOC PACK: On application from Secretary.
VIS RESTR'S: No restrictions.
VIS GF - Round: Wd £14. We £22. Day: Wd £19. We £31.
FACILITIES: Bar, Pro-shop & Club Hire.

SCOTLAND

DUDDINGSTON GOLF CLUB   MAP 9 A2

Duddingston Road West, Edinburgh EH15 3QD.
3 miles south-east of city centre off A1.

CONTACT: JC Small, Secretary. Tel: 031 661 7688.
Course: 6,647yds, PAR 72, SSS 72. Undulating parkland.
SOC RESTR'S: Welcome Tuesday & Thursday only.
SOC GF - Round: Wd N/A. We N/A. **Day:** Wd N/A. We N/A.
SOC PACK: On request from Secretary.
VIS RESTR'S: Welcome Weekdays only.
VIS GF - Round: Wd £20. We N/A. **Day:** Wd £26. We N/A.
FACILITIES: Bar & Catering.

DUNBAR LINKS GOLF CLUB   MAP 9 B2

East Links, Dunbar EH42 1LT.
East side of Dunbar.

CONTACT: D Thompson, Secretary. Tel: 0368 62317.
Course: 6,441yds, PAR 71 SSS 71. Seaside links course.
SOC RESTR'S: Welcome by prior arrangement.
SOC GF - Round: Wd N/A. We N/A. **Day:** Wd £25. We £40.
SOC PACK: None.
VIS RESTR'S: All Thu. Wd prior 9.30 & 1.30-2. We prior 9.30 & 12-2.
VIS GF - Round: Wd N/A. We N/A. **Day:** Wd £25. We £40.
FACILITIES: Bar & Catering.

GLEN GOLF CLUB   MAP 9 B2

Tantallon Terrace, North Berwick EH39 4LE.
Half-a-mile east of A198.

CONTACT: D Montgomery, Secretary. Tel: 0620 5288.
Course: 6,079yds, PAR 69, SSS 69. Seaside links.
SOC RESTR'S: Advance booking required.
SOC GF- Round: Wd £11. We £14. **Day:** Wd £16. We £20.
SOC PACK: Coffee, Lunch, High Tea/Dinner & 36 holes.
VIS RESTR'S: Always welcome.
VIS GF - Round: Wd £11. We £14. **Day:** Wd £16. We £20.
FACILITIES: Bar & Catering.

GLENCORSE GOLF CLUB   MAP 9 A2

Milton Bridge, Penicuik, Midlothian EH 26 0RD.
9 miles south of Edinburgh on A701.

CONTACT: DA McNiven, Secretary. Tel: 0968 677177.
Course: 5,205yds, PAR 64, SSS 66. Parkland course.
SOC RESTR'S: Max. 24. Welcome most Wd after 9.30.
SOC GF - Round: Wd £15. We N/A. **Day:** Wd £20. We N/A.
SOC PACK: On application from Secretary.
VIS RESTR'S: Individuals - no restrictions. Check for Competitions.
VIS GF - Round: Wd £15. We £20. **Day:** Wd £20. We N/A.
FACILITIES: Bar & Restaurant.

GULLANE GOLF CLUB (NO. 1)   MAP 9 B2

Gullane, East Lothian EH31 2BB.
18 miles east of Edinburgh on A198.

CONTACT: Starter's Office. Tel: 0620 843115.
Course: 6,466yds, PAR 71, SSS 71. Championship downland.
SOC RESTR'S: On application.
SOC GF - Round: Wd N/A. We N/A. **Day:** Wd £50. We N/A.
SOC PACK: On application.
VIS RESTR'S: Welcome at all times.
VIS GF - Round: Wd £35. We £45. **Day:** Wd £50. We N/A.
FACILITIES: Par 66 course, Free childrens' 6-hole, Bar, Restaurant.

GULLANE GOLF CLUB (NO. 2)   MAP 9 B2

Gullane, East Lothian EH31 2BB.
18 miles east of Edinburgh on A198.

CONTACT: Starter's Office. Tel: 0620 843115.
Course: 6,244yds, PAR 70, SSS 70. Downland course.
SOC RESTR'S: On application.
SOC GF - Round: Wd N/A. We N/A. **Day:** Wd N/A. We N/A.
SOC PACK: On application.
VIS RESTR'S: Welcome at all times.
VIS GF - Round: Wd £16. We £20. **Day:** Wd £24. We £30.
FACILITIES: Par 66 course, Free childrens' 6-hole, Bar, Restaurant.

HADDINGTON GOLF CLUB   MAP 9 B2

Amisfield Park, Haddington, East Lothian EH41 4QE.
17 miles east of Edinburgh.

CONTACT: T Shaw, Secretary Tel: 0620 823627.
Course: 6,280yds, PAR 71, SSS 70. Parkland course.
SOC RESTR'S: Welcome all Wd. We between 10-12 & 2-4.
SOC GF - Round: Wd £10. We £13. **Day:** Wd £13.50. We £17.
SOC PACK: Coffee, Lunch, High Tea; Wd £26, We £29.
VIS RESTR'S: Welcome all Wd. We between 10-12 & 2-4.
VIS GF - Round: Wd £10. We £13. **Day:** Wd £13.50. We £17.
FACILITIES: Bar & Catering.

HARBURN GOLF CLUB   MAP 9 A2

West Calder, West Lothian EH55 8RS.
2 miles from west Calder off A71.

CONTACT: F Vinter, Secretary. Tel: 0506 871131.
Course: 5,853yds, PAR 69, SSS 68. Parkland course.
SOC RESTR'S: By advanced arrangement.
SOC GF - Round: Wd £12.50. We £18.50. **Day:** Wd £18.50. We £25.
SOC PACK: None.
VIS RESTR'S: Always welcome.
VIS GF - Round: Wd £12.50. We £18.50. **Day:** Wd £18.50. We £25.
FACILITIES: Catering.

LOTHIAN

LINLITHGOW GOLF CLUB MAP 9 A2

Braehead, Linlithgow, West Lothian EH49 6QF.
18 miles west of Edinburgh off M9.

CONTACT: Mr Thompson, Secretary. Tel: 0506 842585.
Course: 5,729yds, PAR 70, SSS 68. Undulating parkland.
SOC RESTR'S: Welcome except Saturdays.
SOC GF - Round: Wd £10. We £15. **Day:** Wd £15. We £20.
SOC PACK: On application from Secretary.
VIS RESTR'S: Welcome except Saturdays.
VIS GF - Round: Wd £10. We £15. **Day:** Wd £15. We £20.
FACILITIES: Catering.

LONGNIDDRY GOLF CLUB MAP 9 B2

Links Road, Longniddry, East Lothian EH32 0NL.
From Edinburgh A1-A198 north. Berwick 5 miles - Left at Inn.

CONTACT: GC Dempster, Secretary. Tel: 0875 52141.
Course: 6,219yds, PAR 68, SSS 70. Split links/parkland.
SOC RESTR'S: Welcome except Friday to Sunday incl.
SOC GF - Round: Wd £22. We N/A. **Day:** Wd £32. We N/A.
SOC PACK: Lunch, High Tea, 36 holes-: £36.
VIS RESTR'S: Welcome Weekdays with booking.
VIS GF - Round: Wd £22. We N/A. **Day:** Wd £32. We N/A.
FACILITIES: Bar & Restaurant.

LOTHIANBURN GOLF CLUB MAP 9 A2

Biggar Road, Edinburgh EH10 7DU.
Left of Edinburgh bypass going west at Lothianburn Exit.

CONTACT: W Jardine, Secretary. Tel: 031 445 5067.
Course: 5,750yds, PAR 71, SSS 69. Hillside course.
SOC RESTR'S: No restrictions Wd. Some restrictions We.
SOC GF - Round: Wd £11. We £15. **Day:** Wd £16. We N/A.
SOC PACK: Coffee, Lunch, High Tea, 36 holes - approx. £22.
VIS RESTR'S: Wd not after 4.30. Not We am or Comp days.
VIS GF - Round: Wd £11. We £15. **Day:** Wd £16. We £20.
FACILITIES: Bar & Catering.

LUFFNESS NEW GOLF CLUB MAP 9 B2

Aberlady, East Lothian EH32 0QA.
A198 from Edinburgh 1 mile outside Aberlady.

CONTACT: I Tedford, Secretary. Tel: 0620 843336.
Course: 6,122yds, PAR 69, SSS 69. Links course.
SOC RESTR'S: Welcome Weekly except Thursdays/Weekends.
SOC GF - Round: Wd £25. We N/A. **Day:** Wd £35. We N/A.
SOC PACK: No package deals. Lunch £6/£7. Jacket & ties.
VIS RESTR'S: Welcome Weekdays.
VIS GF - Round: Wd £25. We N/A. **Day:** Wd £35. We N/A.
FACILITIES: Caddies call 0620 843111. No Pro-shop.

MUIRFIELD GOLF CLUB MAP 9 B2

Muirfield, Gullane, East Lothian EH31 2EG.
Duncur Road (off A98 on north-east side of village).

CONTACT: JA Prideaux, Secretary. Tel: 0620 842123.
Course: 6,610yds, PAR 70, SSS 73. Championship links course.
SOC RESTR'S: Welcome on acceptance by Secretary.
SOC GF - Round: Wd £48. We N/A. **Day:** Wd £64. We N/A.
SOC PACK: On application from Secretary.
VIS RESTR'S: Welcome Tue & Thu, also Fri am. Contact with intro.
VIS GF - Round: Wd £48. We N/A. **Day:** Wd £64. We N/A.
FACILITIES: Lunch available. Bar.

MUSSELBURGH GOLF CLUB MAP 9 A2

Monktonhall, Musselburgh, Midlothian EH21 6SA.
From the A1 take the B6415 to Musselburgh.

CONTACT: G Finlay, Administrator. Tel: 031 665 2005.
Course: 6,614yds, PAR 71, SSS 72. Championship parkland.
SOC RESTR'S: Subject to negotiation.
SOC GF - Round: Wd £15. We £19. **Day:** Wd £22. We £26.
SOC PACK: Subject to negotiation.
VIS RESTR'S: Weekdays not before 9.30. Weekends 10.00.
VIS GF - Round: Wd £15. We £19. **Day:** Wd £22. We £26.
FACILITIES: Catering - except Tuesdays.

NORTH BERWICK GOLF CLUB MAP 9 B2

West Links, Beach Road, North Berwick EH39 4BB.
West side of town on A198.

CONTACT: D Huish, Professional. Tel: 0620 2135.
Course: 6,315yds, PAR 71, SSS 70. Championship links.
SOC RESTR'S: Contact in advance.
SOC GF - Round: Wd £20. We £30. **Day:** Wd £30. We £40.
SOC PACK: On application from Secretary.
VIS RESTR'S: Welcome except Saturday. Contact first.
VIS GF - Round: Wd £20. We £30. **Day:** Wd £30. We £40.
FACILITIES: Catering (prior arrangement), Bar & Snacks.

PRESTONFIELD GOLF CLUB MAP 9 A2

6 Priestfield Road North, Edinburgh EH16 5HS.
2 miles south-east of Edinburgh.

CONTACT: M Dillon, Secretary. Tel: 031 667 1273.
Course: 6,216yds, PAR 70, SSS 70. Parkland course.
SOC RESTR'S: Welcome Weekdays.
SOC GF - Round: Wd £17. We £25. **Day:** Wd £25. We £35.
SOC PACK: Not pre-packaged.
VIS RESTR'S: Not 8-10.30 on Sat or before 11.30 on Sun.
VIS GF - Round: Wd £17. We £25. **Day:** Wd £25. We £35.
FACILITIES: Bar & Meals.

SCOTLAND

RATHO PARK GOLF CLUB   MAP 9 A2

Ratho, Newbridge, Midlothian EH28 8NX.
8 miles west of Edinburgh adjacent to Airport.

CONTACT: JC McLafferty, Secretary. Tel: 031 333 1752.
Course: 5,900yds, PAR 69, SSS 68. Parkland course.
SOC RESTR'S: Welcome Tuesday, Wednesday & Thursday.
SOC GF - Round: Wd £17.50. We N/A. **Day:** Wd £27. We N/A.
SOC PACK: None.
VIS RESTR'S: No restrictions.
VIS GF - Round: Wd £17.50. We £30. **Day:** Wd £27. We £30.
FACILITIES: Catering, Practice Area, Putting & Snooker.

ROYAL BURGESS GOLFING SOC   MAP 9 A2

181 Whitehouse Road, Edinburgh EH4 6BY.
West of city centre on Queensferry Road.

CONTACT: J Audis, Secretary. Tel: 031 339 2075.
Course: 6,494yds, PAR 71, SSS 71. Parkland course.
SOC RESTR'S: Welcome Tue, Thur & Fri. **(Male only).**
SOC GF - Round: Wd £27. We N/A. **Day:** Wd £37. We N/A.
SOC PACK: None.
VIS RESTR'S: Welcome Weekdays. **(Male only).**
VIS GF - Round: Wd £27. We £40. **Day:** Wd £37. We £40.
FACILITIES: Bar.

ROYAL MUSSELBURGH GC   MAP 9 A2

Prestongrange House, Prestonpans, East Lothian.
West side of town centre, off A59.

CONTACT: TH Hardie, Secretary. Tel: 0875 810276.
Course: 6,237yds, PAR 70, SSS 70. Treelined parkland.
SOC RESTR'S: Contact in writing.
SOC GF - Round: Wd £16.50. We £27.50. **Day:** Wd £27.50. We N/A.
SOC PACK: On application from Secretary.
VIS RESTR'S: Welcome Wd not before 9.30 or after 3 & Fri pm.
VIS GF - Round: Wd £16.50. We £27.50. **Day:** Wd £27.50. We N/A.
FACILITIES: Catering (prior arrangement), Bar & Snacks.

UPHALL GOLF CLUB   MAP 9 A2

Uphall, West Lothian.
On A899, West side of village.

CONTACT: A Dobie, Secretary. Tel: 0506 856404.
Course: 5,567yds, PAR 69, SSS 67. Meadowland course.
SOC RESTR'S: Contact in advance. Green fees not confirmed.
SOC GF - Round: Wd N/A. We N/A. **Day:** Wd N/A. We N/A.
SOC PACK: On application from Secretary.
VIS RESTR'S: We not until 11. Green fees not confirmed.
VIS GF - Round: Wd £13. We £17. **Day:** Wd £17. We £25.
FACILITIES: Bar.

WEST LOTHIAN GOLF CLUB   MAP 9 A2

Airngarth Hill, Linlithgow, West Lothian EH49 7RH.
Off A706, 1 mile south.

CONTACT: TB Fraser, Secretary. Tel: 0506 826030.
Course: 6,578yds, PAR 71, SSS 71. Hilly parkland course.
SOC RESTR'S: Welcome please ring in advance.
SOC GF - Round: Wd £10. We £14. **Day:** Wd £15. We £20.
SOC PACK: On application from Secretary.
VIS RESTR'S: Welcome except Saturday.
VIS GF - Round: Wd £10. We £14. **Day:** Wd £15. We £20.
FACILITIES: Bar.

Strathclyde

ANNANHILL GOLF CLUB   MAP 4 B2

Irvine Road, Kilmarnock KA3 1DW.
1 mile west on main Kilmarnock-Irvine Road (A71).

CONTACT: D McKie, Secretary. Tel: 0563 21644.
Course: 6,269yds, PAR 71, SSS 70. Tree-lined parkland.
SOC RESTR'S: Ring in advance. Welcome except Saturday.
SOC GF - Round: Wd £8. We £12. **Day:** Wd £12. We £15.
SOC PACK: On application from Secretary.
VIS RESTR'S: Welcome except Saturday.
VIS GF - Round: Wd £8. We £12. **Day:** Wd £12. We £15.
FACILITIES: Lunch (excl. Tues & Thurs), Dinner, Bar & Snacks.

ARDEER GOLF CLUB   MAP 4 A2

Greenhead, Stevenston, Ayrshire.
Half-a-mile north off A78.

CONTACT: T Cummins, Secretary. Tel: 0294 64542.
Course: 6,500yds, PAR 72, SSS 72. Parkland course.
SOC RESTR'S: Contact in advance.
SOC GF - Round: Wd £10. We £12. **Day:** Wd £18. We £24.
SOC PACK: On application from Secretary.
VIS RESTR'S: Welcome except Saturday.
VIS GF - Round: Wd £10. We £14. **Day:** Wd £18. We £24.
FACILITIES: Bar, Restaurant, Pro-shop & Snooker.

STRATHCLYDE

BALLOCHMYLE GOLF CLUB   MAP 4 B2

Ballochmyle, Mauchline, Ayrshire KA5 6LE.
One mile south-east on B705.

CONTACT: DG Munro, Secretary. Tel: 0290 550469.
Course: 5,952yds, PAR 70, SSS 69. Wooded parkland.
SOC RESTR'S: Max. 30. Apply in writing.
SOC GF - Round: Wd £18. We N/A. **Day:** Wd £25. We £30.
SOC PACK: On application from Secretary.
VIS RESTR'S: Welcome except Saturday.
VIS GF - Round: Wd £18. We N/A. **Day:** Wd £25, We £30.
FACILITIES: Catering (seasonal), Bar, Squash & Snooker.

BARSHAW GOLF CLUB   MAP 4 B1

Barshaw Park, Glasgow Road, Paisley, Renfrewshire.
1 mile east of Paisley, of A737.

CONTACT: W Collins, Secretary. Tel: 041 889 2908.
Course: 5,703yds, PAR 68, SSS 67. Municipal parkland.
SOC RESTR'S: On application to Superintendent Parks Dept.
SOC GF - Round: Wd £6. We £6. **Day:** Wd N/A. We N/A.
SOC PACK: On application from Secretary.
VIS RESTR'S: No restrictions.
VIS GF - Round: Wd £6. We £6. **Day:** Wd N/A. We N/A.
FACILITIES: Changing Rooms.

BELLEISLE GOLF CLUB   MAP 4 A2

Belleisle Park, Ayr.
Situated in the south of Ayr.

CONTACT: Starter's Office. Tel: 0292 441258.
Course: 6,545yds, PAR 71, SSS 70. Parkland course.
SOC RESTR'S: No more than 40 to a party.
SOC GF - Round: Wd £15. We £15. **Day:** Wd N/A. We N/A.
SOC PACK: On application from Secretary.
VIS RESTR'S: Always welcome but book Weekends
VIS GF - Round: Wd £15. We £15. **Day:** Wd N/A. We N/A.
FACILITIES: Day GF shared with Seafield Golf Club.

BIGGAR GOLF CLUB   MAP 4 B2

The Park, Broughton Road, Biggar, Lanarkshire.
1 mile east of Biggar, on the Broughton Road.

CONTACT: D Baxter. Tel: 0899 20618.
Course: 5,229yds, PAR 67, SSS 69. Municipal parkland.
SOC RESTR'S: Early booking essential.
SOC GF - Round: Wd N/A. We N/A. **Day:** Wd £9. We £11.
SOC PACK: None.
VIS RESTR'S: Always welcome. Phone 0899 20319 for tee time.
VIS GF - Round: Wd N/A. We N/A. **Day:** Wd £9. We £11.
FACILITIES: Catering, Bar & Pro-shop.

BOTHWELL CASTLE GOLF CLUB   MAP 4 B1

Blantyre Road, Bothwell, Glasgow G71 8PJ.
3 miles north of Hamilton.

CONTACT: ADC Watson, Secretary. Tel: 0698 853177.
Course: 6,243yds, PAR 71, SSS 70. Parkland course.
SOC RESTR'S: Max 30. Welcome on Tue, 9.30-3.30,
SOC GF - Round: Wd £18. We N/A. **Day:** Wd £25. We N/A.
SOC PACK: None.
VIS RESTR'S: Welcome Weekdays, 9.30-3.30.
VIS GF - Round: Wd £18. We N/A. **Day:** Wd £25. We N/A.
FACILITIES: Clubhouse, Bar & Professional.

CAMPSIE GOLF CLUB   MAP 4 B1

Crow Road, Lennoxtown, Glasgow G65 7HX.
Half-a-mile north on B822 from Lennoxtown.

CONTACT: J Donaldson, Secretary. Tel: 0360 310244.
Course: 5,515yds, PAR 70, SSS 67. Scenic hillside course.
SOC RESTR'S: Contact 1 month in advance.
SOC GF - Round: Wd £10. We N/A. **Day:** Wd £16.50. We N/A.
SOC PACK: Green fees reduced for parties of 12 or more.
VIS RESTR'S: Welcome Weekdays & Weekends by booking.
VIS GF - Round: Wd £10. We £12.50. **Day:** Wd £16.50. We £18.
FACILITIES: Catering, Bar & Pro-shop.

CARDROSS GOLF CLUB   MAP 4 A1

Cardross, Dumbarton G82 5LB.
4 miles west of Dumbarton.

CONTACT: R Evans, Secretary. Tel: 0389 841754.
Course: 6,466yds, PAR 71, SSS 71, Undulating parkland.
SOC RESTR'S: Weekdays only. Arrange with Secretary.
SOC GF - Round: Wd N/A. We N/A. **Day:** Wd 25. We N/A.
SOC PACK: Full catering and Green Fees.
VIS RESTR'S: Unrestricted Wd. Only with Member at We.
VIS GF - Round: Wd £15. We N/A. **Day:** Wd £25. We N/A.
FACILITIES: Food arrangement, Bar, Pro shop.

CARLUKE GOLF CLUB   MAP 4 B2

Mauldslie Road, Hallcraig, Carluke, Lanarkshire ML8 5HG.
West from Carluke Cross for 2 miles.

CONTACT: J Muir, Hon. Secretary. Tel: 0555 771070.
Course: 5,800yds, PAR 70, SSS 68. Parkland course.
SOC RESTR'S: Max. 40. Welcome Weekdays only till 4.00.
SOC GF - Round: Wd £12. We N/A. **Day:** Wd £18. We N/A.
SOC PACK: Coffee, Light lunch, Dinner, 36 holes: £22.
VIS RESTR'S: Welcome up to 4. 00 Weekdays only.
VIS GF - Round: Wd £12. We N/A. **Day:** Wd £18. We N/A.
FACILITIES: Clubhouse, Bar, Dining Room & Spikes Bar.

SCOTLAND

CARNWATH GOLF CLUB   MAP 4 B2

Main Street, Carnwath ML11 8JX.
On A70 - 10 miles from Carluke towards Peebles.

CONTACT: A Thom, Party Bookings. Tel: 0555 840251.
Course: 5,222yds, PAR 66, SSS 66. Tight undulating course.
SOC RESTR'S: Max 30. Wd except Tue, Thu & Bank Hols. 40 on Sun.
SOC GF - Round: Wd N/A. We N/A. **Day:** Wd £17. We N/A.
SOC PACK: Coffee, Lunch, High Tea, 36 holes: £26 Wd. £29 We.
VIS RESTR'S: Welcome Mon, Wed, Fri & Sun.
VIS GF - Round: Wd N/A. We N/A. **Day:** Wd £17. We N/A.
FACILITIES: Bar & Catering.

CAWDER GOLF CLUB   MAP 4 B1

Cadder Road, Bishopbriggs, Glasgow.
North of Glasgow, off A803 Kirkintilloch road.

CONTACT: GT Stoddart, Secretary. Tel: 041 772 5167.
Course: 6,295yds, PAR 70, SSS 71. Hilly parkland course.
SOC RESTR'S: Weekdays only. Arrange with Secretary.
SOC GF - Round: Wd N/A. We N/A. **Day:** Wd £22. We N/A.
SOC PACK: Lunch, Dinner, 36 holes: £35.
VIS RESTR'S: Welcome weekdays.
VIS GF - Round: Wd £22. We N/A. **Day:** Wd £22. We N/A.
FACILITIES: 2nd 18-hole Par 68, Restaurant, Bar, Pro shop.

CLOBER GOLF CLUB   MAP 4 B1

Carigton Road, Milngavie, Glasgow G26 7HP.
9 miles north of Glasgow.

CONTACT: J Anderson, Secretary. Tel: 041 956 1685.
COURSE: 5,070yds, PAR 65, SSS 65. Parkland course.
SOC RESTR'S: By appointment with Secretary.
SOC GF - Round: Wd £9. We N/A. **Day:** Wd N/A. We N/A.
SOC PACK: None.
VIS ESTR'S: Welcome Wd before 4pm
VIS GF - Round: Wd £9. We N/A. **Day:** Wd N/A. We N/A.
FACILITIES: Full catering, Bar & Shop.

CLYDEBANK & DISTRICT GC   MAP 4 B1

Glasgow Road, Hardgate, Clydebank G81 5QY.
Off Great Western Road, Clydebank.

CONTACT: Professional. Tel: 0389 73289.
Course: 5,825yds, PAR 68, SSS 68. Parkland course.
SOC RESTR'S: Not accepted.
SOC GF - Round: Wd £12. We N/A. **Day:** Wd N/A. We N/A.
SOC PACK: Not accepted.
VIS RESTR'S: Welcome Weekdays.
VIS GF - Round: Wd £12. We N/A. **Day:** Wd N/A. We N/A.
FACILITIES: Bar & Restaurant.

COLVILLE PARK GOLF CLUB   MAP 4 B1

Jerviston Estate, Motherwell, Strathclyde.
2 miles east of Motherwell town centre.

CONTACT: S Connacher, Secretary. Tel: 0698 263017.
Course: 6,250yds, PAR 71, SSS 70. Parkland course.
SOC RESTR'S: Welcome Weekdays only before 3.30.
SOC GF - Round: Wd N/A. We N/A. **Day:** Wd £20. We £20.
SOC PACK: On request.
VIS RESTR'S: Welcome with prior written agreement.
VIS GF - Round: Wd N/A. We N/A. **Day:** Wd N/A. We N/A.
FACILITIES: Bar & Restaurant

COWAL GOLF CLUB   MAP 4 A1

Ardenslate Road, Kirn, Dunoon, Argyll PA23 8LT.
Ardenslate Road is half-a-mile from Western Ferries Terminal.

CONTACT: BR Chatham, Secretary. Tel: 0369 5673.
Course: 6,251yds, PAR 70, SSS 70. Moorland type course.
SOC RESTR'S: Min. 12 Max 24. Wd Tee times 10-11 & 2-3.30.
SOC GF - Round: Wd £13. We £20. **Day:** Wd £20. We £30.
SOC PACK: Coffee, Lunch, High Tea GF- Wd £27. We £31.
VIS RESTR'S: Welcome Weekdays. Some Weekend restrictions.
VIS GF - Round: Wd £13. We £20. **Day:** Wd £20. We £30.
FACILITIES: Bar & Restaurant.

COWGLEN GOLF CLUB   MAP 4 B1

301 Barrhead Road, Glasgow G43 1AA.
4 miles south-west of Glasgow.

CONTACT: RJ Jamieson, Secretary. Tel: 0292 266600.
COURSE: 6,010yds, PAR 69, SSS 69. Undulating parkland.
SOC RESTR'S: On application to Secretary.
SOC GF - Round: Wd N/A. We N/A. **Day:** Wd £35. We N/A.
SOCPACK: None.
VIS RESTR'S: H'cap Cert & Letter of Intro required.
VIS GF - Round: Wd £20. We N/A. **Day:** Wd £35. We N/A.
FACILITIES: Bar & Restaurant.

CROW WOOD GOLF CLUB   MAP 4 B1

Muirhead, Glasgow G69 9JF.
1 mile north of Stepps on A80.

CONTACT: I McInnes, Secretary. Tel: 041 779 4954.
Course: 6,249yds, PAR 71, SSS 70. Wooded parkland course.
SOC RESTR'S: Max 32, midweek before 4.
SOC GF - Round: Wd £16. We N/A. **Day:** Wd £24. We N/A.
SOC PACK: £31 incl. Coffee, Snack lunch, Evening meal.
VIS RESTR'S: Welcome Weekdays when booked.
VIS GF - Round: Wd £16. We N/A. **Day:** Wd £24. We N/A.
FACILITIES: Snooker Table.

STRATHCLYDE

DALMILLING GOLF CLUB MAP 4 A2

Westwood Crescent, Whitletts, Ayr.
Situated in Dalmilling Housing Scheme in North Ayr.

CONTACT: P Cheyney, Starter's Office. Tel 0292 263893.
Course: 5,752yds, PAR 69, SSS 68. Lush parkland course.
SOC RESTR'S: Welcome by prior agreement.
SOC GF - Round: Wd £10. We £10. **Day:** Wd £18. We £18.
SOC PACK: On application from Secretary.
VIS RESTR'S: No restrictions but advisable to phone.
VIS GF - Round: Wd £10. We £10. **Day:** Wd £18. We £18.
FACILITIES: Table licensed restaurant.

DARLEY GOLF CLUB MAP 4 A2

Harling Drive, Troon.
All Troon clubs are located together at Harling Drive.

CONTACT: Starter's Office. Tel: 0292 312464.
Course: 6,501yds, PAR 71, SSS 71. A heather/moorland course.
SOC RESTR'S: Welcome - first come, first served basis.
SOC GF - Round: Wd £15. We £15. **Day:** Wd £22. We £22.
SOC PACK: On application from Secretary.
VIS RESTR'S: Always welcome - first come, first served basis.
VIS GF - Round: Wd £15. We £15. **Day:** Wd £22. We £22.
FACILITIES: Table licensed restaurant.

DOUGALSTON GOLF CLUB MAP 4 B1

Strathblane Road, Milngavie, Glasgow.
North-east side of town, on A81.

CONTACT: G Wilson, Golf Manager. Tel: 041 956 5750.
Course: 6,683yds, PAR 72, SSS 71. Treelined parkland.
SOC RESTR'S: Contact in advance.
SOC GF - Round: Wd £12. We N/A. **Day:** Wd £18. We N/A.
SOC PACK: Welcome.
VIS RESTR'S: Contact in advance.
VIS GF - Round: Wd £12. We N/A. **Day:** Wd £18. We N/A.
FACILITIES: Restaurant & Bar.

DRUMPELLIER GOLF CLUB MAP 4 B1

Drumpellier Avenue, Coatbridge ML5 1RX.
8 miles east of Glasgow.

CONTACT: W Brownlie, Secretary. Tel: 0236 428723.
Course: 6,227yds, PAR 71, SSS 70. Parkland course.
SOC RESTR'S: Welcome except Thursdays & Weekends.
SOC GF - Round: Wd £18. We N/A. **Day:** Wd £25. We N/A.
SOC PACK: None.
VIS RESTR'S: Welcome Weekdays when booked.
VIS GF - Round: Wd £18. We N/A. **Day:** Wd £25. We N/A.
FACILITIES: Bar - 2 lounges.

EAST RENFREWSHIRE GC MAP 4 B2

Pilmuir, Newton Mearns, Glasgow G77 6RT.
Approx 1 mile from Mearns Cross - Kilmarnock Road.

CONTACT: A Gillespie, Secretary. Tel: 041 226 4311.
Course: 6,097yds, PAR 70, SSS 70. Moorland course.
SOC RESTR'S: Welcome with prior agreement from Secretary.
SOC GF - Round: Wd £20. We N/A. **Day:** Wd £30. We N/A.
SOC PACK: On application.
VIS RESTR'S: Welcome except Sat. Must always book with Pro.
VIS GF - Round: Wd £20. We N/A. **Day:** Wd £30. We N/A.
FACILITIES: Bar & Restaurant.

EASTWOOD GOLF CLUB MAP 4 B2

'Muirshield,' Loganswell, Newton Mearns G77 6RX.
South of Newton Mearns - towards Kilmarnock.

CONTACT: CB Scouler, Secretary. Tel: 0355 5261.
Course: 5,864yds, PAR 68, SSS 68. Moorland course.
SOC RESTR'S: By negotiation with Secretary.
SOC GF - Round: Wd £18. We N/A. **Day:** Wd £26. We N/A.
SOC PACK: £35 if meals & drinks taken.
VIS RESTR'S: Welcome Wd with prior agreement form Sec.
VIS GF - Round: Wd £18. We N/A. **Day:** Wd £26. We N/A.
FACILITIES: Bar & Restaurant.

FERENEZE GOLF CLUB MAP 4 B1

Fereneze Avenue, Barrhead G78 1HJ.
9 miles south-west of Glasgow centre.

CONTACT: A Gourley, Sec/Treasurer. Tel: 041 221 6394.
Course: 5,821yds, PAR 70, SSS 68. Delightful parkland course.
SOC RESTR'S: Welcome by arrangement with Secretary.
SOC GF - Round: Wd N/A. We N/A. **Day:** Wd £17.50. We N/A.
SOC PACK: £21. 50 - Coffee, Snack lunch & High Tea.
VIS RESTR'S: Welcome Weekdays. Please book.
VIS GF - Round: Wd N/A. We N/A. **Day:** Wd £17.50. We N/A.
FACILITIES: Fully stocked Pro-shop with Caddy car hire.

GIRVAN GOLF CLUB MAP 4 A2

Golf Course Road, Girvan, Ayrshire.
Golf club is well signposted on the main Ayr-Girvan road (A77).

CONTACT: Starter's Office. Tel: 0465 4346.
Course: 5,095yds, PAR 64, SSS 65. Seaside/meadowland course.
SOC RESTR'S: Welcome by arrangement through Secretary.
SOC GF - Round: Wd £10. We £10. **Day:** Wd £18. We £18.
SOC PACK: On application.
VIS RESTR'S: Welcome, please book through Starter.
VIS GF - Round: Wd £10. We £10. **Day:** Wd £18. We £18.
FACILITIES: Bar & Restaurant.

SCOTLAND

GLASGOW GAILES GOLF CLUB   MAP 4 A2

Gailes, Irvine, Ayrshire KA11 5AE.
1 mile south of Irvine.

CONTACT: DW Deas, Secretary. Tel: 041 942 2011.
Course: 6,493yds, PAR 71, SSS 72. Links/parkland course.
SOC RESTR'S: Arrange with Secretary. Letter of Intro required.
SOC GF - Round: Wd N/A. **We** N/A. **Day:** Wd £30. **We** N/A.
SOC PACK: Full catering and Green Fees.
VIS RESTR'S: Letter of Intro (Wd). Only with Member at We.
VIS GF - Round: Wd £27. **We** £33. **Day:** Wd £30. **We** N/A.
FACILITIES: Lunch daily (except Monday).

GLASGOW GOLF CLUB   MAP 4 A2

Killermont, Bearsden, Glasgow G61 2TW.
5 miles north-west of Glasgow.

CONTACT: D Deas, Secretary. Tel: 041 942 2011.
COURSE: 5,966yds, PAR 69, SSS 69. Undulating parkland.
SOC RESTR'S: On application from Secretary.
SOC GF - Round: Wd N/A. **We** N/A. **Day:** Wd £35. **We** N/A.
SOC PACK: Coffee, Lunch, Dinne, Golf: Prices vary.
VIS RESTR'S: Welcome Wd by booking. GF reduction Nov-Mar.
VIS GF - Round: Wd N/A. **We** N/A. **Day:** Wd £35. **We** £45
FACILITIES: Bar & Restaurant.

GLEDDOCH G & CC   MAP 4 A1

Langbank, Renfrewshire PA14 6YE.
B789 Langbank/Houston exit M8 – follow Gleddoch signs.

CONTACT: P Morrison, Secretary. Tel: 0475 54304.
Course: 5,661yds, PAR 68, SSS 67. Park/heathland course.
SOC RESTR'S: Welcome Wd by arrangement with Secretary.
SOC GF - Round: Wd N/A. **We** N/A. **Day:** Wd £25. **We** N/A.
SOC PACK: On application from Secretary.
VIS RESTR'S: Welcome.
VIS GF - Round: Wd N/A. **We** N/A. **Day:** Wd £25. **We** N/A.
FACILITIES: Restaurant, Bar, 50% reduction on GF to Hotel Guests.

GOUROCK GOLF CLUB   MAP 4 A1

Cowal View, Gourock, Inverclyde PA19 6HD.
2 miles west of Gourock railway station.

CONTACT: CM Campbell, Hon. Secretary. Tel: 0475 631001.
Course: 6,493yds, PAR 73, SSS 71. Moorland course.
SOC RESTR'S: Parties Weekdays only.
SOC GF - Round: Wd £12. **We** N/A. **Day:** Wd £18. **We** N/A.
SOC PACK: On application.
VIS RESTR'S: Welcome but must book in advance.
VIS GF - Round: Wd £12. **We** N/A. **Day:** Wd £18. **We** N/A.
FACILITIES: Bar & Catering.

GREENOCK GOLF CLUB   MAP 4 A1

Forsyth Street, Greenock, Renfrewshire PA16 8RE.
South-west side of town off A770.

CONTACT: E Black, Secretary. Tel: 0475 20793.
Course: 5,838yds, PAR 68, SSS 68. Testing moorland course.
SOC RESTR'S: Advanced booking through Secretary.
SOC GF - Round: Wd £11.50. **We** £15. **Day:** Wd £15. **We** £20.
SOC PACK: On application from Secretary.
VIS RESTR'S: Welcome except Saturday. Please book.
VIS GF - Round: Wd £11.50. **We** £15. **Day:** Wd £15. **We** £20.
FACILITIES: Bar, Restaurant & Pro-shop.

HAGGS CASTLE GOLF CLUB   MAP 4 B1

70 Drumbeck Road, Drumbeck, Glasgow G41 4SN.
South-west Glasgow (B768).

CONTACT: I Harvey, Secretary. Tel: 041 427 1157.
Course: 6,464yds, PAR 72, SSS 71. Wooded parkland course.
SOC RESTR'S: Wednesdays only.
SOC GF - Round: Wd £24. **We** N/A. **Day:** Wd £36. **We** N/A.
SOC PACK: Lunch, Dinner, 36 holes: £50.
VIS RESTR'S: H'cap Cert required Wd. With Member at We.
VIS GF - Round: Wd £24. **We** N/A. **Day:** Wd £36. **We** N/A.
FACILITIES: Bar, Restaurant, Pro shop, Club & Trolley hire.

HAYSTON GOLF CLUB   MAP 4 B1

Campsie Road, Kirkintilloch Road, Glasgow G66 1RN.
11 miles east of Glasgow.

CONTACT: Mr Carmichael, Secretary. Tel: 041 775 0723.
Course: 6,042yds, PAR 70, SSS 69. Undulating parkland course.
SOC RESTR'S: Welcome Tuesday & Thursday.
SOC GF - Round: Wd £15. **We** N/A. **Day:** Wd £25. **We** N/A.
SOC PACK: £28.
VIS RESTR'S: Welcome Wd. We when booked in advance.
VIS GF - Round: Wd £15. **We** N/A. **Day:** Wd £25. **We** N/A.
FACILITIES: Bar.

HELENSBURGH GOLF CLUB   MAP 4 A1

Abercromby Street, Helensburgh G84 9JD.
25 miles west of Glasgow on A82.

CONTACT: Mrs A McEwan, Secretary. Tel: 0436 74173.
Course: 6,058yds, PAR 69, SSS 69. Moorland course.
SOC RESTR'S: Welcome Mondays & Thursdays only.
SOC GF - Round: Wd £15, **We** N/A. **Day:** Wd £23. **We** N/A.
SOC PACK: On application from Secretary.
VIS RESTR'S: Welcome Weekdays only.
VIS GF - Round: Wd £15. **We** N/A. **Day:** Wd £23. **We** N/A.
FACILITIES: Bar & Sacks.

STRATHCLYDE

HOLLANDBUSH GOLF CLUB   MAP 4 B2

Acretophead, Lesmahagow, Lanarkshire.
Off M74 at Lesmahagow.

CONTACT: I Rae, Professional. Tel: 0555 893646.
Course: 6,110yds, PAR 71, SSS 70. Parkland course.
SOC RESTR'S: By arrangement through Professional.
SOC GF - Round: Wd £6. We £8. **Day:** Wd £10. We £12.
SOC PACK: None.
VIS RESTR'S: Always welcome.
VIS GF - Round: Wd £6. We £8. **Day:** Wd £10. We £12.
FACILITIES: Clubhouse & Catering.

KILARNOCK (BARASSIE) GC   MAP 4 A2

Hillhouse Road, Barassie, Troon KA10 6SY.
Opposite Barassie railway station, north of Troon.

CONTACT: R Bryce, Secretary. Tel: 0292 313920.
Course: 6,177yds, PAR 69, SSS 69. Seaside course.
SOC RESTR'S: Welcome by arrangement through Secretary.
SOC GF - Round: Wd N/A. We N/A. **Day:** Wd £35. We N/A.
SOC PACK: None.
VIS RESTR'S: Welcome except Weekends & Friday morning.
VIS GF - Round: Wd £35. We N/A. **Day:** Wd £35. We N/A.
FACILITIES: Bar & Catering.

IRVINE GOLF CLUB   MAP 4 A2

Bogside, Irvine KA12 8SN.
North side of town, off A737.

CONTACT: A Morton, Secretary. Tel: 0294 275979.
Course: 6,400yds, PAR 71, SSS 71. Testing links course.
SOC RESTR'S: Wd only. Book in advance, 0294 75979.
SOC GF - Round: Wd £25. We N/A. **Day:** Wd £35. We N/A.
SOC PACK: On application from Secretary.
VIS RESTR'S: Not before 3 at We. Contact in advance.
VIS GF - Round: Wd £25. We £35. **Day:** Wd £35. We N/A.
FACILITIES: Bar, Restaurant & Pro-shop.

LANARK GOLF CLUB   MAP 4 B2

The Moor, Whitelees Road, Lanark ML11 7RX.
1 mile from Lanark town - well signposted.

CONTACT: G Cuthill, Secretary/Manager. Tel: 0555 663219.
Course: 6,423yds, PAR 70, SSS 71. Moorland course.
SOC RESTR'S: Max. 36. Mon, Tue & Wed. Max. 16. Thur & Fri.
SOC GF - Round: Wd £18. We N/A. **Day:** Wd £28. We N/A.
SOC PACK: Coffee, Lunch, High Tea, 36 holes: £35.
VIS RESTR'S: Welcome before 4 Weekdays only.
VIS GF - Round: Wd £18. We N/A. **Day:** Wd £28. We N/A.
FACILITIES: Bar.

IRVINE RAVENSPARK GOLF CLUB   MAP 4 A2

Kidsneuk Lane, Irvine, Ayrshire KA12 8SR.
North side of town, on A737.

CONTACT: G Robertson, Secretary. Tel: 0294 279550.
Course: 6,702yds, PAR 71, SSS 71. Parkland course.
SOC RESTR'S: Max. 30. Welcome Weekdays & Sunday.
SOC GF - Round: Wd £5. We £8.80. **Day:** Wd £8.80. We £14.
SOC PACK: On application from Secretary.
VIS RESTR'S: Welcome except Sat 7-10 or 12-2.
VIS GF - Round: Wd £5. We £8.80. **Day:** Wd £8.80. We £14.
FACILITIES: Bar, Restaurant (not Tue or Thur) & Pro-shop.

LARGS GOLF CLUB   MAP 4 A2

Irvine Road, Largs, Ayrshire KA30 8EV.
28 miles North of Glasgow on A78.

CONTACT: F Gilmour, Secretary. Tel: 0475 673594.
Course: 6,290yds, PAR 70, SSS 70. Parkland/seaside course.
SOC RESTR'S: Welcome Tue & Thur by prior agreement.
SOC GF - Round: Wd £18. We N/A. **Day:** Wd £24. We N/A.
SOC PACK: £35.
VIS RESTR'S: Welcome. Phone re competition days.
VIS GF - Round: Wd £18. We £18. **Day:** Wd £24. We £24.
FACILITIES: Bar & Restaurant.

KILMACOLM GOLF CLUB   MAP 4 A1

Porterfield Road, Kilmacolm, Renfrewshire PA13 3PD.
10 miles west of Paisley.

CONTACT: RF McDonald, Secretary. Tel 050 587 2139.
Course: 5,890yds, PAR 69, SSS 68. Moorland course.
SOC RESTR'S: Welcome by arrangement through Secretary.
SOC GF - Round: Wd £18. We N/A. **Day:** Wd £24. We N/A.
SOC PACK: On application from Secretary.
VIS RESTR'S: Welcome Weekdays.
VIS GF - Round: Wd £18. We N/A. **Day:** Wd £24. We N/A.
FACILITIES: Bar & Restaurant.

LETHAMHILL GOLF CLUB   MAP 4 B1

Cumbernauld Road, Glasgow G33 1AH.
On A80, 3 miles north-east of city centre.

CONTACT: Secretary. Tel: 041 770 6220.
Course: 5,859yds, PAR 70, SSS 68. Municipal parkland.
SOC RESTR'S: Welcome by arrangement through Secretary.
SOC GF - Round: Wd N/A. We N/A. **Day:** Wd N/A. We N/A.
SOC PACK: On application from Secretary.
VIS RESTR'S: Welcome by arrangement through Secretary.
VIS GF - Round: Wd £4. We £4. **Day:** Wd £8. We £8.
FACILITIES: Changing Rooms.

SCOTLAND

LOCHGREEN GOLF CLUB   MAP 4 B2

Harling Drive, Troon.
All Troon clubs are located together at Harling Drive.
CONTACT: Starter's Office. Tel: 0292 312464.
Course: 6,303yds, PAR 74, SSS 73. Links course.
SOC RESTR'S: Welcome.
SOC GF - Round: Wd £15. We £15. Day: Wd £22. We £22.
SOC PACK: On application from Secretary.
VIS RESTR'S: Always welcome.
VIS GF - Round: Wd £15. We £15. Day: Wd £22. We £22.
FACILITIES: Table licensed restaurant.

LOCHWINNOCH GOLF CLUB   MAP 4 A1

Burnfoot Road, Lochwinnoch, Renfrewshire PA12 4AN.
On Largs-Kilbirnie Road.
CONTACT: Mrs EM McBride, Secretary. Tel: 0505 842153.
Course: 6,202yds, PAR 70, SSS 70. Parkland course.
SOC RESTR'S: Welcome Weekdays only.
SOC GF - Round: Wd N/A. We N/A. Day: Wd N/A. We N/A.
SOC PACK: £25.
VIS RESTR'S: Welcome Weekdays.
VIS GF - Round: Wd N/A. We N/A. Day: Wd £20. We N/A.
FACILITIES: Bar & Restaurant.

LOUDOUN GOLF CLUB   MAP 4 B2

Galston, Ayrshire KA4 8PA.
5 miles east of Kilmarnock on A71.
CONTACT: TR Richmond, Secretary. Tel: 0563 821 993.
Course: 5,607yds, PAR 67, SSS 67. Parkland course.
SOC RESTR'S: Max. 40. Welcome Weekdays only.
SOC GF - Round: Wd £13. We N/A. Day: Wd £20. We N/A.
SOC PACK: Coffee, Lunch, High Tea, 36 holes: £28.
VIS RESTR'S: Welcome Weekdays only. Last tee time 3.
VIS GF - Round: Wd £13. We N/A. Day: Wd £20. We N/A.
FACILITIES: Bar & Restaurant.

MACHRIE GOLF CLUB

Port Ellen, Isle of Islay.
5 miles north of Port Ellen.
CONTACT: M Macpherson, Secretary. Tel: 0496 2310.
Course: 6,477yds, PAR 71, SSS 71. Links course.
SOC RESTR'S: Arrange with Secretary. H'cap Cert required.
SOC GF - Round: Wd N/A. We N/A. Day: Wd £40. We N/A.
SOC PACK: On application.
VIS RESTR'S: Handicap Certificate required.
VIS GF - Round: Wd £25. We N/A. Day: Wd £40. We N/A.
FACILITIES: Driving Range, Bar, Restaurant, Pro shop.

MACHRIHANISH GOLF CLUB   MAP 4 A2

Machrihanish, Campbeltown, Argyl PA28 6PT.
5 minute drive from Campbeltown.
CONTACT: Mrs A Anderson, Secretary. Tel: 0586 81213.
Course: 6,228yds, PAR 70, SSS 70. Links course.
SOC RESTR'S: Welcome by arrangement through Secretary.
SOC GF - Round:Wd £15. We N/A. Day: Wd £20. We £20.
SOC PACK: Discount for 12 or more. Special Fly drive package.
VIS RESTR'S: Welcome, some restrictions on Club Comp days.
VIS GF - Round: Wd £15. We N/A. Day: Wd £20. We £20.
FACILITIES: 9-hole Course & Practice area.

MILLPORT GOLF CLUB   MAP 4 A1/2

Golf Road, Millport, Isle of Cumbrae KA28 0BA.
Cumbrae Slip to Millport Pier to Golf Rd. (7 min. ferry ride)
CONTACT: Starter's Office. Tel: 0475 530305.
Course: 5,314yds, PAR 68, SSS 66. Seaside/moorland course.
SOC RESTR'S: Welcome by arrangement through Secretary.
SOC GF - Round: Wd £11. We N/A. Day: Wd £15. We N/A.
SOC PACK: Approx £25 per head.
VIS RESTR'S: Virtually none.
VIS GF - Round: Wd £11. We £15. Day: Wd £15. We £20.
FACILITIES: Catering, Bar & Showers.

THE *Glynhill* HOTEL
AND LEISURE CLUB

The gateway to Scotland hotel offering businessmen and tourists alike a quality product and service. Facilities range from Diplomat Suites, American-style bedrooms, convention centre, gourmet and carverie restaurants, all complemented by a luxurious leisure centre. Privately owned, excellent value, well located hotel for the West of Scotland. Glasgow International Airport 1 mile.

THE GLYNHILL HOTEL AND LEISURE CLUB
169 Paisley Road, Renfrew PA4 8XB *(300 yds M8 J27)*
Tel: (041) 886 5555 Fax: (041) 885 2838

STRATHCLYDE

PAISLEY GOLF CLUB MAP 4 B1

Braehead, Paisley, Renfrewshire PA2 8TZ.
On Gleniffer Braes south-west of Paisley.
CONTACT: WJ Cunningham, Secretary. Tel: 041 884 3903.
Course: 6,424yds, PAR 71, SSS 71. Moorland course.
SOC RESTR'S: Welcome by arrangement through Secretary.
SOC GF - Round: Wd £19. **We** N/A. **Day:** Wd £24. **We** N/A.
SOC PACK: Coffee, Snack lunch, High Tea - £8.
VIS RESTR'S: Welcome Weekdays by booking.
VIS GF - Round: Wd £19. **We** N/A. **Day:** Wd £24. **We** N/A.
FACILITIES: Bar, Catering & Snooker.

PORT GLASGOW GOLF CLUB MAP 4 A1

Devol Farm Ind Est, Port Glasgow, Renfrewshire PA14 5XE.
1 mile south of town.
CONTACT: Mr Mitchell, Secretary. Tel: 0475 704181.
Course: 5,712yds, PAR 68, SSS 68. Hilltop moorland course.
SOC RESTR'S: Apply in writing.
SOC GF - Round: Wd £12. **We** N/A. **Day:** Wd £18. **We** N/A.
SOC PACK: On application from Secretary.
VIS RESTR'S: Welcome Weekdays until 4.00.
VIS GF - Round: Wd £12. **We** N/A. **Day:** Wd £18. **We** N/A.
FACILITIES: Bar. Catering (on request).

PRESTWICK GOLF CLUB MAP 4 A2

2 Links Road, Prestwick, Ayrshire KA9 1QG.
Prestwick Airport 1 mile, near Railway Station.
CONTACT: DE Donaldson, Secretary. Tel: 0292 77404.
Course: 6,668yds, PAR 71, SSS 72. Seaside links course.
SOC RESTR'S: Arrange with Secretary. Letter of Intro required.
SOC GF - Round: Wd £50. **We** N/A. **Day:** Wd N/A. **We** N/A.
SOC PACK: On application.
VIS RESTR'S: Letter of Intro on Wd and by prior agreement.
VIS GF - Round: Wd £50. **We** N/A. **Day:** Wd N/A. **We** N/A.
FACILITIES: Bar, Restaurant, Pro shop.

PRESTWICK ST. NICHOLAS GC MAP 4 A2

Grangemuir Road, Prestwick, Ayrshire KA9 1SN.
Off A79, from Main Street into Grangemuir Road.
CONTACT: JR Leishman, Secretary. Tel: 0292 77608.
Course: 5,926yds, PAR 67, SSS 68. Links course.
SOC RESTR'S: Max. 30. Welcome Weekdays only.
SOC GF - Round: Wd N/A. **We** N/A. **Day:** Wd £30. **We** N/A.
SOC PACK: Normal catering charges.
VIS RESTR'S: Welcome Weekdays by booking.
VIS GF - Round: Wd £18. **We** N/A. **Day:** Wd £30. **We** N/A.
FACILITIES: Bar & Catering, Games room & Caddy cart hire.

RANFURLY CASTLE GOLF CLUB MAP 4 A1

Golf Road, Bridge of Weir, Renfrewshire PA11 3HN.
Junct 29 on M8 from Glasgow - A240 - A761 to Bridge of Weir.
CONTACT: J Walker, Secretary. Tel: 0505 612609.
Course: 6,284yds, PAR 70, SSS 70. Undulating moorland course.
SOC RESTR'S: Welcome Tuesday only.
SOC GF - Round: Wd £22. **We** N/A. **Day:** Wd £27. **We** N/A.
SOC PACK: No package.
VIS RESTR'S: Welcome Wd by arrangement with Professional.
VIS GF - Round: Wd £22. **We** N/A. **Day:** Wd £27. **We** N/A.
FACILITIES: Full restaurant facilities.

ROYAL TROON (OLD COURSE) MAP 4 A2

Craigend Road, Troon Ayrshire KA10 6EP.
Off A77 to Prestwick Airport.
CONTACT: JD Montgomerie, Sec/Manager. Tel: 0292 311555.
Course: 7,097yds, PAR 72, SSS 74. Championship links.
SOC RESTR'S: Mon to Thur only. H'cap Cert max 20.
SOC GF - Round: Wd N/A. **We** N/A. **Day:** Wd £75. **We** N/A.
SOC PACK: £75 incl coffee & choice of lunch or high tea.
VIS RESTR'S: Welcome Mon, Tue &Thur 9. 30-11 & 2. 30-3.
VIS GF - Round: Wd N/A. **We** N/A. **Day:** Wd £75. **We** N/A.
FACILITIES: Bar & Restaurant. (No Ladies or under 18s on course).

ROYAL TROON (PORTLAND) MAP 4 A2

Craigend Road, Troon Ayrshire KA10 6EP.
Off A77 to Prestwick Airport.
CONTACT: JD Montgomerie, Sec/Manager. Tel: 0292 311555.
Course: 6,274yds, PAR 71, SSS 71. Seaside links.
SOC RESTR'S: Max 24. Welcome by arrangement through Sec.
SOC GF - Round: Wd N/A. **We** N/A. **Day:** Wd £45. **We** N/A.
SOC PACK: £45 incl morning coffee & choice of lunch or high tea.
VIS RESTR'S: As Old Course.
VIS GF - Round: Wd N/A. **We** N/A. **Day:** Wd £45. **We** N/A.
FACILITIES: Bar & Restaurant.

SEAFIELD GOLF CLUB MAP 4 A2

Belleisle Park, Ayr.
Situated on the south side of Ayr.
CONTACT: D Gemmell, Starters Office, Tel: 0292 441258.
Course: 5,449yds, PAR 67, SSS 67. Moorland/parkland course.
SOC RESTR'S: Max 40. Welcome by arrangement.
SOC GF - Round: Wd £10. **We** £10. **Day:** Wd £22. **We** £22.
SOC PACK: On application from Secretary.
VIS RESTR'S: Welcome but book. Under 17s. H'cap of 12 or better.
VIS GF - Round: Wd £10. **We** £10. **Day:** Wd £22. **We** £22.
FACILITIES: Days GF shared with Belleisle Golf Course.

SCOTLAND

SHOTTS GOLF CLUB MAP 4 B1

Blairhead, Shotts ML7 5BJ.
Off M8 at Junction 5 (B7057), travel about 1.5 miles.

CONTACT: J McDermott, Secretary. Tel: 0501 820431.
Course: 6,125yds, PAR 70, SSS 70. Moorland/wooded course.
SOC RESTR'S: Welcome Weekdays.
SOC GF - Round: Wd N/A. **We** N/A. **Day:** Wd £14. **We** N/A.
SOC PACK: £20 includes Lunch & High Tea.
VIS RESTR'S: Welcome except Sat before 3. 30 & all day Sun.
VIS GF - Round: Wd N/A. **We** N/A. **Day:** Wd £14. **We** N/A.
FACILITIES: Practice Area. Off season reduction to Green Fee.

STRATHAVEN GOLF CLUB MAP 4 B2

Glasgow Road, Strathaven ML10 6NL.
Outskirts of town on Strathaven to East Kilbride Road.

CONTACT: AW Wallace, Secretary. Tel: 0357 20421.
Course: 6,206yds, PAR 71, SSS 70. Parkland course.
SOC RESTR'S: Max. 40. Welcome Tuesdays only.
SOC GF - Round: Wd £17.50. **We** N/A. **Day:** Wd £25. **We** N/A.
SOC PACK: £33 - Green fee plus full catering for day.
VIS RESTR'S: Welcome Weekdays. Not Weekends up to 4.
VIS GF - Round: Wd £17.50. **We** N/A. **Day:** Wd £25. **We** N/A.
FACILITIES: None.

TURNBERRY GOLF CLUB (AILSA) MAP 4 A2

Turnberry, Ayrshire KA26 9LT.
Off A77 from Glasgow on A719. 15 mls from Prestwick Airport.

CONTACT: Mr Bowman, Operations Officer. Tel: 0655 31000.
Course: 6,950yds, PAR 70, SSS 72. Championship course.
SOC RESTR'S: Requests for non-residents should be sent in writing.
SOC GF - Round: Wd N/A. **We** N/A. **Day:** Wd £75. **We** £75.
SOC PACK: Hotel Guest Green Fees £45.
VIS RESTR'S: As Societies.
VIS GF - Round: Wd N/A. **We** N/A. **Day:** Wd £75. **We** £75.
FACILITIES: Clubhouse, Bar & Restaurant.

TURNBERRY GOLF CLUB (ARRAN) MAP 4 A2

Turnberry, Ayrshire KA26 9LT.
Off A77 from Glasgow on A719. 15 mls from Prestwick Airport.

CONTACT: Mr Bowman, Operations Officer. Tel: 0655 31000.
Course: 6,249yds, PAR 69, SSS 70. Championship course.
SOC RESTR'S: Requests for non-residents should be sent in writing.
SOC GF - Round: Wd N/A. **We** N/A. **Day:** Wd £75. **We** £75.
SOC PACK: Hotel Guest Green Fees £45.
VIS RESTR'S: Please contact in advance.
VIS GF - Round: Wd N/A. **We** N/A. **Day:** Wd £75. **We** £75.
FACILITIES: Clubhouse, Bar & Restaurant.

WESTERN GAILES GOLF CLUB MAP 4 A2

Gailes, Irvine, Ayrshire KA11 5AE.
3 miles north of Troon.

CONTACT: A McBean, Secretary. Tel: 0294 311649.
Course: 6,664yds, PAR 71, SSS 72. Links course.
SOC RESTR'S: Welcome Weekdays except Thursday.
SOC GF - Round: Wd £35. **We** N/A. **Day:** Wd £43. **We** N/A.
SOC PACK: Full catering available. Details on request.
VIS RESTR'S: Welcome Mon, Tue, Wed & Fri. H'cap Cert required.
VIS GF - Round: Wd £35. **We** N/A. **Day:** Wd £43. **We** N/A.
FACILITIES: Bar & Restaurant.

WESTERWOOD G & CC MAP 4 B1

St. Andrews Drive, Westerwood, Cumbernauld G68 0EW.
Adjacent to A80.

CONTACT: Christine Page, Marketing Manager. Tel: 0236 457171.
Course: 6,721yds, PAR 73, SSS 72. Undulating park/woodland.
SOC RESTR'S: By prior arrangement.
SOC GF - Round: Wd £22.50. **We** £27.50. **Day:** Wd N/A. **We** N/A.
SOC PACK: On application from Secretary.
VIS RESTR'S: No restrictions.
VIS GF - Round: Wd £22.50. **We** £27.50. **Day:** Wd N/A. **We** N/A.
FACILITIES: Bar, Restaurant, Tennis, Snooker, Swimming & Gym.

WEST KILBRIDE GOLF CLUB MAP 4 A2

West Kilbride, Ayrshire KA23 9HT.

CONTACT: ED Jefferies, Secretary. Tel: 0294 823911.
Course: 6,4527yds, PAR 71, SSS 71. Seaside links course.
SOC RESTR'S: No Weekends of Bank Holidays.
SOC GF - Round: Wd £25. **We** N/A. **Day:** Wd N/A. **We** N/A.
SOC PACK: On application.
VIS RESTR'S: Welcome Wd. H'cap req. Special pm GF of £16.
VIS GF - Round: Wd £25. **We** N/A. **Day:** Wd N/A. **We** N/A.
FACILITIES: Food by arrangement, Bar, Pro shop.

WHITECRAIGS GOLF CLUB MAP 4 B1

Ayr Road, Giffnock, Glasgow G46 6SW.
On A77, 7 miles south of Glasgow.

CONTACT: RW Miller, Secretary. Tel: 041 639 4530.
Course: 6,230yds, PAR 70, SSS 70. Parkland course.
SOC RESTR'S: Welcome Wednesday only.
SOC GF - Round: Wd £23. **We** N/A. **Day:** Wd £29. **We** N/A.
SOC PACK: On application from Secretary.
VIS RESTR'S: Welcome with letter of introduction.
VIS GF - Round: Wd £23. **We** £23. **Day:** Wd £29. **We** £29.
FACILITIES: Bar & Restaurant.

TAYSIDE

WISHAW GOLF CLUB — MAP 4 B1

Cleland Road, Wishaw, Lanarkshire ML2 7PH.
M74 - Motherwell - end of Main Street.

CONTACT: DD Gallacher, Secretary. Tel: 0698 372869.
Course: 6,051yds, PAR 69, SSS 69. Parkland course.
SOC RESTR'S: Welcome by arrangement through Secretary.
SOC GF - Round: Wd £12. We N/A. **Day:** Wd £20. We N/A.
SOC PACK: Coffee, Lunch, High Tea, 36 holes - £23 Wd, £28 We.
VIS RESTR'S: Welcome before 4.00 Wd & after 11.30-Sun.
VIS GF - Round: Wd £12. We N/A. **Day:** Wd £20. We N/A.
FACILITIES: Bar & Catering.

Tayside

ARBROATH GOLF CLUB — MAP 9 B1

Elliot, by Arbroath, Angus.
1 mile west of town on A92 Arbroath-Dundee.

CONTACT: L Ewart, Professional. Tel: 0241 75837.
Course: 6,098yds, PAR 70, SSS 69. Seaside links.
SOC RESTR'S: Welcome Weekdays. Weekend first tee-off 10.
SOC GF - Round: Wd £10. We £15. **Day:** Wd £16. We £24.
SOC PACK: On application.
VIS RESTR'S: Welcome except before 10 on Sunday.
VIS GF - Round: Wd £10. We £15. **Day:** Wd £16. We £24.
FACILITIES: Bar & Restaurant.

BLAIRGOWRIE (ROSEMOUNT) — MAP 9 A1

Rosemount, Blairgowrie, Perthshire PH10 6LG
1 mile south of Blairgowrie, off A93.

CONTACT: JN Simpson, Secretary/Manager. Tel: 0250 872622.
Course: 6,588yds, PAR 72, SSS 72. Heathland course.
SOC RESTR'S: Contact in advance.
SOC GF - Round: Wd N/A. We N/A. **Day:** Wd £40. We N/A.
SOC PACK: By arrangement.
VIS RESTR'S: Restricted Wed, Fri, We. H'cap only 8-12 &2-3.30.
VIS GF - Round: Wd £30. We £34. **Day:** Wd £40. We N/A.
FACILITIES: 9-hole Course, Bar, Restaurant, Pro shop.

BLAIRGOWRIE (LANDSDOWNE) — MAP 9 A1

Rosemount, Blairgowrie, Perthshire PH10 6LG
1 mile south of Blairgowrie, off A93.

CONTACT: JN Simpson, Secretary/Manager. Tel: 0250 872622.
Course: 6,895yds, PAR 72, SSS 73. Heathland course.
SOC RESTR'S: Contact in advance.
SOC GF - Round: Wd N/A. We N/A. **Day:** Wd £40. We N/A.
SOC PACK: By arrangement.
VIS RESTR'S: Restricted Wed, Fri, We. H'cap only 8-12 &2-3.30.
VIS GF - Round: Wd £30. We £34. **Day:** Wd £40. We N/A.
FACILITIES: Bar, Restaurant, Pro shop.

BRECHIN GOLF CLUB — MAP 6 B3

Trinity, by Brechin, Angus DD9 7PD.
1 mile north of Brechin on the A94.

CONTACT: AB May, Secretary. Tel: 0356 622383.
Course: 5,287yds, PAR 65, SSS 66. Rolling parkland course.
SOC RESTR'S: All party reservations to be made in advance.
SOC GF - Round: Wd £11. We £16. **Day:** Wd £16. We £25.
SOC PACK: Weekdays £21 for 36 holes incl. Min. 12.
VIS RESTR'S: Welcome, please book.
VIS GF - Round: Wd £11. We £16. **Day:** Wd £16. We £25.
FACILITIES: Bar, Catering & 2 Squash Courts.

CAIRD PARK GOLF CLUB — MAP 9 A1

Mains Loan, Dundee, Tayside DD4 9BX.
2 miles north of city centre, off A972.

CONTACT: G Martin, Secretary. Tel: 0382 453606.
Course: 6,281yds, PAR 72, SSS 70. Municipal parkland.
SOC RESTR'S: Contact in advance. Green fees not confirmed.
SOC GF - Round: Wd N/A. We N/A. **Day:** Wd N/A. We N/A.
SOC PACK: On application from Secretary.
VIS RESTR'S: Must book in advance. Green fees not confirmed.
VIS GF - Round: Wd N/A. We N/A. **Day:** Wd £12. We £12.
FACILITIES: Bar & Pro-shop.

CAMPERDOWN GOLF CLUB — MAP 9 A1

Camperdown House, Camperdown Park, Dundee.
Off Coupar Angus Road approx 2 miles from city centre.

CONTACT: Dundee Council. Tel: 0382 21341 Ext 4704.
Course: 6,561yds, PAR 71, SSS 72. Parkland course.
SOC RESTR'S: Welcome by arrangement through Secretary.
SOC GF - Round: Wd N/A. We N/A. **Day:** Wd £12. We £12.
SOC PACK: On application from Secretary.
VIS RESTR'S: Always welcome.
VIS GF - Round: Wd N/A. We N/A. **Day:** Wd £12. We £12.
FACILITIES: Catering available by appointment.

SCOTLAND

CARNOUSTIE (CHAMPIONSHIP) MAP 9 B1

Links Parade, Carnoustie, Angus DD7 7JE.
12 miles east of Dundee, by A92 or A930.
CONTACT: EJC Smith, Secretary. Tel: 0241 53789.
Course: 6,936yds, PAR 72, SSS 74. Seaside links course.
SOC RESTR'S: Welcome by arrangement through Secretary.
SOC GF - Round: Wd £34. We N/A. Day: Wd £60. We N/A.
SOC PACK: On application from Secretary.
VIS RESTR'S: Must book in advance. H'cap cert required.
VIS GF - Round: Wd £34. We N/A. Day: Wd £60. We N/A.
FACILITIES: Bar & Restaurant available locally.

CARNOUSTIE (BURNSIDE) MAP 9 B1

Links Parade, Carnoustie, Angus DD7 7JE.
12 miles east of Dundee, by A92 or A930.
CONTACT: EJC Smith, Secretary. Tel: 0241 53789.
Course: 6,020yds, PAR 68, SSS 69. Seaside links course.
SOC RESTR'S: Welcome by arrangement through Secretary.
SOC GF - Round: Wd £13. We N/A. Day: Wd £20. We N/A.
SOC PACK: On application from Secretary.
VIS RESTR'S: Welcome Wd, Sat after 2, Sun after 11.
VIS GF - Round: Wd £13. We N/A. Day: Wd £20. We N/A.
FACILITIES: Bar & Restaurant available locally.

CARNOUSTIE (BUDDON) MAP 9 B1

Links Parade, Carnoustie, Angus DD7 7JE.
12 miles east of Dundee, by A92 or A930.
CONTACT: EJC Smith, Secretary. Tel: 0241 53789.
Course: 5,300yds, PAR 68, SSS 66. Seaside links course.
SOC RESTR'S: No restrictions.
SOC GF - Round: Wd £8. We N/A. Day: Wd £12. We N/A.
SOC PACK: On application from Secretary.
VIS RESTR'S: Welcome.
VIS GF - Round: Wd £8. We N/A. Day: Wd £12. We N/A.
FACILITIES: Bar & Restaurant available locally.

CRIEFF GC (FERNTOWER) MAP 4 B1

Perth Road, Crieff, Perthshire PH7 3LR.
On A85 Perth to Crieff Road just as you enter Crieff.
CONTACT: LJ Rundle, Secretary. Tel: 0764 652909.
Course: 6,402yds, PAR 71, SSS 71. Parkland course.
SOC RESTR'S: Please ask when booking.
SOC GF - Round: Wd £16. We £20. Day: Wd £27. We £34.
SOC PACK: On application from Secretary.
VIS RESTR'S: Welcome. Weekly & fortnightly tickets available.
VIS GF - Round: Wd £16. We £20. Day: Wd £27. We £34.
FACILITIES: 9-hole Course, Practice Areas & Putting Greens.

DOWNFIELD GOLF CLUB MAP 9 A1

Turnberry Avenue, Dundee DD2 3QP.
North of city centre, off A923.
CONTACT: BF Mole, Secretary. Tel: 0382 825595.
Course: 6,804yds, PAR 73, SSS 73. Undulating woodland.
SOC RESTR'S: Welcome by arrangement through Secretary.
SOC GF - Round: Wd £26. We N/A. Day: Wd £34. We N/A.
SOC PACK: On application from Secretary.
VIS RESTR'S: Welcome.
VIS GF - Round: Wd £26. We £26. Day: Wd £34. We £34.
FACILITIES: Bar, Restaurant, Pro-shop & Snooker.

EDZELL GOLF CLUB MAP 6 B3

High Street, Edzell, Angus DD9 7TF.
From A94 on to B966 for 3 miles.
CONTACT: JM Hutchison, Secretary. Tel: 0356 647283.
Course: 6,281yds, PAR 71, SSS 70. Heathland Course.
SOC RESTR'S: Max 36 between 10-11.30 & 2.30-4 We.
SOC GF - Round: Wd £15. We £20. Day: Wd £22.50. We £30.
SOC PACK: Coffee, Lunch, High Tea, 36 holes: £32.
VIS RESTR'S: Welcome except Weekdays 5-6.15.
VIS GF - Round: Wd £15. We £20. Day: Wd £22.50. We £30.
FACILITIES: Bar & full meal service in Lounge & Dining room.

FORFAR GOLF CLUB MAP 9 B1

Cunninghill, Arbroath Road, Forfar, Angus DD8 2RL.
Follow signs to Arbroath from centre of Forfar.
CONTACT: W Baird, Managing Secretary. Tel: 0307 463773.
Course: 5,946yds, PAR 72, SSS 71. Undulating moorland course.
SOC RESTR'S: Welcome by arrangement through Secretary.
SOC GF - Round: Wd £15. We £25. Day: Wd £20. We £25.
SOC PACK: On application.
VIS RESTR'S: Welcome except 10-12 noon & 2.30-4.
VIS GF - Round: Wd £15. We £25. Day: Wd £20. We £25.
FACILITIES: None.

GLENEAGLES (KING'S COURSE) MAP 9 A1

Auchterarder, Perthshire PH3 1NF.
16 miles south-west of Perth on A9.
CONTACT: S Mailer, Golf Co-ordinator. Tel: 0764 662231.
Course: 6,471yds, PAR 70, SSS 71. Championship moorland.
SOC RESTR'S: Only as guest of member or hotel residents.
SOC GF - Round: Wd £40. We £40. Day: Wd N/A. We N/A.
SOC PACK: On application from Secretary.
VIS RESTR'S: Only as guest of member or hotel residents.
VIS GF - Round: Wd £40. We £40. Day: Wd N/A. We N/A.
FACILITIES: Clay shooting, Horse riding, Restaurants & Bars.

TAYSIDE

GLENEAGLES (QUEEN'S COURSE) MAP 9 A1

Auchterarder, Perthshire PH3 1NF.
16 miles south-west of Perth on A9.

CONTACT: S Mailer, Golf Co-ordinator. Tel: 0764 662231.
Course: 5,965yds, PAR 68, SSS 69. Undulating moorland course.
SOC RESTR'S: Only as guest of member or hotel residents.
SOC GF - Round: Wd £40. We £40. **Day:** Wd N/A. We N/A.
SOC PACK: On application from Secretary.
VIS RESTR'S: Only as guest of member or hotel residents.
VIS GF - Round: Wd £40. We £40. **Day:** Wd N/A. We N/A.
FACILITIES: The infamous 'Wee Course. "

GLENEAGLES (MONARCH'S) MAP 9 A1

Auchterarder, Perthshire PH3 1NF.
16 miles south-west of Perth on A9.

CONTACT: S Mailer, Golf Co-ordinator. Tel: 0764 662231.
Course: 6,134yds, PAR 71, SSS 69. Undulating moorland course.
SOC RESTR'S: Only as guest of member or hotel residents.
SOC GF - Round: Wd £40. We £40. **Day:** Wd N/A. We N/A.
SOC PACK: On application from Secretary.
VIS RESTR'S: Only as guest of member or hotel residents.
VIS GF - Round: Wd £40. We £40. **Day:** Wd N/A. We N/A.
FACILITIES: The infamous 'Wee Course. "

KING JAMES VI GOLF CLUB MAP 9 A1

Moncrieffe Island, Perth PH2 8NR.
On Moncrieffe Island in the Tay River.

CONTACT: T Coles, Professional. Tel: 0738 32460.
Course: 5,661yds, PAR 68, SSS 68. Parkland course.
SOC RESTR'S: Welcome by arrangement through Secretary.
SOC GF - Round: Wd £13. We N/A. **Day:** Wd £20. We N/A.
SOC PACK: Day ticket (midweek) £17. Lunch, Evening meal. £25.
VIS RESTR'S: Welcome except Saturdays. Please book.
VIS GF - Round: Wd £13. We £15. **Day:** Wd £20. We £27.
FACILITIES: Bar meals all day.

LETHAM GRANGE (OLD COURSE) MAP 9 B1

Colliston, by Arbroath, Angus DD11 4RL.
A933 Brechin/Forfar Road - through Colliston.

CONTACT: Miss P Ogilvie, Secretary. Tel: 0241 89373.
Course: 6,939yds, PAR 73, SSS 73. Parkland course.
SOC RESTR'S: Welcome by arrangement through Secretary.
SOC GF - Round: Wd £20. We £25. **Day:** Wd £30. We N/A.
SOC PACK: On application from Secretary.
VIS RESTR'S: Not We before 10.30 &1-2. Tue before 10.
VIS GF - Round: Wd £20. We £25. **Day:** Wd £30. We N/A.
FACILITIES: Bar & Restaurant.

LETHAM GRANGE (NEW COURSE) MAP 9 B1

Colliston, by Arbroath, Angus DD11 4RL.
A933 Brechin/Forfar Road - through Colliston.

CONTACT: Miss P Ogilvie, Secretary. Tel: 0241 89373.
Course: 5,528yds, PAR 68, SSS 68. Parkland course.
SOC RESTR'S: Welcome by arrangement through Secretary.
SOC GF - Round: Wd £12. We N/A. **Day:** Wd £18. We N/A.
SOC PACK: On application from Secretary.
VIS RESTR'S: Welcome with H'cap Cert & booked.
VIS GF - Round: Wd £12. We £15. **Day:** Wd £18. We N/A.
FACILITIES: Bar & Restaurant.

MONIFIETH GOLF LINKS (MEDAL) MAP 9 B1

Princes Street, Monifieth, Dundee DD5 4AW.
6 miles east of Dundee.

CONTACT: Medal Starter's Box. Tel: 0382 532767.
Course: 6,650yds, PAR 71, SSS 72. Heathland course.
SOC RESTR'S: Contact in advance.
SOC GF - Round: Wd N/A. We N/A. **Day:** Wd £32. We N/A.
SOC PACK: Lunch, Dinner, 36 holes: £46.
VIS RESTR'S: Unrestricted Wd. Not before 2 Sat or before 10 Sun.
VIS GF - Round: Wd £22. We £24. **Day:** Wd £32. We £36.
FACILITIES: 2nd 18-hole (Ashludie) Par 66, Bar, Pro shop.

MONTROSE LINKS (MEDAL COURSE) MAP 6 B3

Trail Drive, Montrose, Angus DD10 8SW.
East off A92 between Dundee & Aberdeen.

CONTACT: Mrs M Stewart, Secretary. Tel: 0674 72932.
Course: 6,443yds, PAR 71, SSS 71. True links course.
SOC RESTR'S: Welcome by arrangement through Secretary.
SOC GF - Round: Wd £13. We £19. **Day:** Wd £22. We £30.
SOC PACK: 36 holes golf + catering from £25. 50 per head.
VIS RESTR'S: Welcome except Sat or before 10. 00 Sun.
VIS GF - Round: Wd £13. We £19. **Day:** Wd £22. We £30.
FACILITIES: 2nd 18-hole Course, SSS 64. Weekly GF £60.

MURRAYSHALL GOLF CLUB MAP 9 A1

Murrayshall, by Scone, Perthshire PH2 7PH.
Turn right before New Scone on A94 from Perth.

CONTACT: Christine Page, Marketing Manager. Tel: 0738 51171.
Course: 6,446yds, PAR 73, SSS 71. Undulating parkland course.
SOC RESTR'S: Welcome by arrangement through Secretary.
SOC GF - Round: Wd £20. We £25. **Day:** Wd £30. We £40.
SOC PACK: From £30.
VIS RESTR'S: No restrictions. But please book.
VIS GF - Round: Wd £20. We £25. **Day:** Wd £30. We £40.
FACILITIES: Clubhouse.

SCOTLAND

NORTH INCH GOLF CLUB   MAP 9 A1

North Inch, Perth.
North of central Perth. First tee close to Bells Sports Centre.
CONTACT: C Fraser, Starter. Tel: 0738 36481
Course: 5,178yds, PAR 65, SSS 65. Parkland course.
SOC RESTR'S: Welcome by arrangement through Secretary.
SOC GF - Round: Wd £4.60. We £6.20. **Day:** Wd N/A. We N/A.
SOC PACK: On application from Secretary.
VIS RESTR'S: Pay & Play most times.
VIS GF - Round: Wd £4.60. We £6.20. **Day:** Wd N/A. We N/A.
FACILITIES: None.

PANMURE GOLF CLUB   MAP 9 B1

Barry, Carnoustie DD7 7RT.
1 mile west of Carnoustie.
CONTACT: DA Chidley, Secretary. Tel: 0241 53120.
Course: 6,317yds, PAR 70, SSS 70. Tight links course.
SOC RESTR'S: Welcome weekdays.
SOC GF - Round: Wd £21. We N/A. **Day:** Wd £32. We N/A.
SOC PACK: By arrangement.
VIS RESTR'S: Welcome except Saturdays.
VIS GF - Round: Wd £21. We £21. **Day:** Wd £32. We £32.
FACILITIES: Bar, Restaurant, Pro shop.

PITLOCHRY GOLF CLUB   MAP 6 A3

Golf Course Road, Pitlochry.
On A9, half-a-mile from Pitlochry centre.
CONTACT: Secretary. Tel: 0796 472114.
Course: 5,811yds, PAR 69, SSS 68. Heathland course.
SOC RESTR'S: Welcome by arrangement through Professional.
SOC GF - Round: Wd N/A. We N/A. **Day:** Wd £14. We £17.
SOC PACK: On application from Secretary.
VIS RESTR'S: Welcome. Winter GF Nov-Mar from £6.
VIS GF - Round: Wd N/A. We N/A. **Day:** Wd £14. We £17.
FACILITIES: Catering (prior arrangement), Bar & Snacks.

TAYMOUTH CASTLE GOLF CLUB   MAP 6 A3

Kenmore, Perthshire.
6 miles west of Aberfeldy.
Recommended Hotel: Kenmore.
CONTACT: M Mulcahey, Secretary. Tel: 0887 830397.
Course: 6,078yds, PAR 70, SSS 69. Parkland course.
SOC RESTR'S: Welcome but please book in advance.
SOC GF - Round: Wd £14. We £18. **Day:** Wd £22. We £26.
SOC PACK: Catering requirements should be made with Hotel.
VIS RESTR'S: Welcome but please book in advance.
VIS GF - Round: Wd £14. We £18. **Day:** Wd £22. We £26.
FACILITIES: Bar & Pro-shop.

Taymouth Castle Golf Course

3 Day Breaks fully inclusive from £116.00
Kenmore Hotel, Kenmore, Perthshire
Tel: 0887 830205
"Well above Par"

Rufflets Country House

Strathkinness Low Road, St Andrews, Fife KY16 9TX
Tel: 0334 72594 Fax: 0334 78703
RAC ★★★

Two storey 1920s house set in
10 acres of secluded grounds.
24 bedrooms all en-suite, annexe
3 bedrooms, all en-suite.

CULLEN BAY HOTEL

Magnificent views of Cullen Bay and golf course and close to 12 different courses. Newly refurbished rooms with full facilities, good food, log fires and a friendly welcome will all add up to an unforgettable holiday!
Cullen Bay Hotel, Cullen, Buckie, Banffshire
AB56 2XA.   Tel: 0542 40432 Fax: 0542 40900

WALES

WHEN talk turns to golf in the British Isles and the glories of Scotland, England and Ireland, Wales tends to be rather forgotten which, in view of the courses on offer in the Principality, amounts to negligence.

The keen golfer, coming from southern England, could enjoy a week's unrivalled golf simply by progressing gently along the M4 motorway: first stop would be St Pierre at Chepstow for Parkland golf at its finest; next, Southerndown, a links and downland course at Bridgend, followed by arguably the best links course in Wales, Royal Porthcawl. Progressing further westwards, Ashburnham, handily placed near the Llanelli exit off the motorway. Then, to end the journey, a little bit of golfing history with a round at Tenby, the oldest club in Wales.

North Wales might serve you almost as well. The prize here would be Royal St David's at Harlech, another majestic links layout, closely followed by Conwy and the neighbours North Wales and Llandudno, the latter designed by a certain Tom Jones...

Anglesey

BULL BAY GOLF CLUB   MAP 2 A1

Bull Bay, Amlwch, Anglesey, Gwynedd LL68 9RY.
Half-a-mile from Amlwch on A5025.

CONTACT: D Lewis, Secretary. Tel: 0407 830960.
Course: 6,132yds, PAR 70, SSS 70. Seaside links.
SOC RESTR'S: We restricted to 20 with Handicap Certificate.
SOC GF - Round: Wd N/A. **We** N/A. **Day:** Wd N/A. **We** N/A.
SOC PACK: Above GF for 12 +. Catering by arrangement.
VIS RESTR'S: Welcome except Saturdays 11-12 noon.
VIS GF - ROUND: Wd £15. **We** £20. **Day:** Wd £20. **We** £25.
FACILITIES: Practice Ground & Putting Green.

ANGLESEY GOLF CLUB   MAP 2 A1

Rhosneigr, Anglesey, Gwynedd LL64 5QX.
8 miles south-east of Holyhead, off A4080.

CONTACT: DM Denyer, Manager. Tel: 0407 811202.
Course: 5,713yds, PAR 68, SSS 68. Links course.
SOC RESTR'S: Welcome by arrangement through Secretary.
SOC GF - ROUND: Wd N/A. **We** N/A. **Day:** Wd £15. **We** £20.
SOC PACK: None.
VIS RESTR'S: None but preferably after 10am.
VIS GF - ROUND: Wd N/A. **We** N/A. **Day:** Wd £15. **We** £20.
FACILITIES: Bar.

HOLYHEAD GOLF CLUB   MAP 2 A1

Trearddur Bay, Anglesey LL65 2YG.
1 mile east from Holyhead on Trearddur Bay Road.

CONTACT: D Entwistle, Secretary/Manager. Tel: 0407 763279.
Course: 6,084yds, PAR 70, SSS 70. Heathland course.
SOC RESTR'S: Max. 30. 10. 00 & 2. 00 start. H'cap Cert required.
SOC GF - ROUND: Wd N/A. **We** N/A. **Day:** Wd £20. **We** £25.
SOC PACK: For 20 + a small reduction on GF by arrangement.
VIS RESTR'S: By prior arrangements. 5 day GF £68.
VIS GF - ROUND: Wd £17. **We** £20. **Day:** Wd £20. **We** £25.
FACILITIES: Dormy House (12 beds) 6 rooms, details on

WALES

Clwyd

DENBIGH GOLF CLUB   MAP 2 A1

Henllan Road, Denbigh, Clwyd LL16 5AA.
1 mile outside Denbigh on B5382.
CONTACT: M McArthy, Secretary. Tel: 0745 814159.
Course: 5,580yds, PAR 68, SSS 67. Undulating parkland.
SOC RESTR'S: No Societies Thursdays to Saturdays incl.
SOC GF - ROUND: Wd N/A. We N/A. **Day:** Wd £18. We £24.
SOC PACK: Additional catering package £8.50.
VIS RESTR'S: Welcome except Thursday & Sunday.
VIS GF - ROUND: Wd N/A. We N/A. **Day:** Wd £18. We £24.
FACILITIES: 7-Day Catering. Snooker.

ABERGELE & PENSARN GC   MAP 2 A1

Tan-Y-Goppa Road, Abergele, Clwyd LL22 8DS.
By Gwrych Castle, Abergele.
CONTACT: HE Richards, Secretary. Tel: 0745 824034.
Course: 6,256yds, PAR 72, SSS 70. Tricky parkland course.
SOC RESTR'S: Min. 12 - Max 50. Wd 10.15. We 10.15.
SOC GF - Round: Wd N/A. We N/A. **Day:** Wd £21. We £26.
SOC PACK: Not available, under discussion.
VIS RESTR'S: Priority to members until 10.15+ 12-2.15 daily.
VIS GF - Round: Wd N/A. We N/A. **Day:** Wd £21. We £26.
FACILITIES: Bar, Restaurant & Snooker Room.

OLD PADESWOOD GOLF CLUB   MAP 2 A1

Station Lane, Padeswood, Nr. Mold, Clwyd CH7 4JL.
3 miles south-east of Mold off the A5118.
CONTACT: Mrs B Jones, Co. Secretary. Tel: 0244 550414.
Course: 6,702yds, PAR 72, SSS 72. Undulating parkland.
SOC RESTR'S: Welcome Weekdays.
SOC GF - Round: Wd £16. We £20. **Day:** Wd £25. We N/A.
SOC PACK: Coffee, Lunch, Evening meal, 27 holes: £26/£28.
VIS RESTR'S: Welcome except Comp day. H'cap Cert preferred.
VIS GF - Round: Wd £16. We £20. **Day:** Wd £25. We N/A.
FACILITIES: 9-Hole Par 3 Course, Bar & Restaurant.

ENJOYING A UNIQUE POSITION COMMANDING PANORAMIC SEA VIEWS FROM ALL ROOMS. EXCELLENT CUISINE, SUPERB SURROUNDINGS

◆ *Ideal Touring Base*
◆ *Close to many Golf Clubs*
◆ *Conference & Function Specialists*

THE COLWYN BAY HOTEL

FOR BUSINESS AND PLEASURE

It's Ideal

TELEPHONE: 0492 516555

PENMAENHEAD, OLD COLWYN, COLWYN BAY, CLWYD LL29 9LD

DYFED

Dyfed

PRESTATYN GOLF COURSE MAP 2 A1

Marine Road East, Prestatyn, Clwyd LL19 7HS.
1 mile east of Prestatyn town off coast road A584.
CONTACT: R. Woodruff, Manager. Tel: 0745 854320.
Course: 6,792yds, PAR 72, SSS 73. Championship links.
SOC RESTR'S: Max 50. Welcome except Tuesday & Saturday.
SOC GF - Round: Wd N/A. **We** N/A. **Day:** Wd £18. **We** £25.
SOC PACK: 27 holes & catering - Wd £25, We £29.
VIS RESTR'S: By arrangement with Professional.
VIS GF - Round: Wd N/A. **We** N/A. **Day:** Wd £18. **We** £25.
FACILITIES: Bar & Catering. Snooker.

RHUDDLAN GOLF CLUB MAP 2 A1

Meliden Road, Rhuddlan, Clwyd LL18 6LB.
3 miles south of Rhyl.
CONTACT: D. Morris, Secretary/Manager. Tel: 0745 590217.
Course: 6,487yds, PAR 71, SSS 71. Undulating parkland.
SOC RESTR'S: Max 50 Weekdays 9.30-12 & 1.30-3.00.
SOC GF - Round: Wd N/A. **We** N/A. **Day:** Wd N/A. **We** N/A.
SOC PACK: Coffee, Lunch. Dinner: £30.
VIS RESTR'S: Welcome except Sunday.
VIS GF - Round: Wd N/A. **We** £25. **Day:** Wd £20. **We** N/A.
FACILITIES: Snooker, Bars & Restaurant. Practice Ground.

ABERYSTWYTH GOLF CLUB MAP 2 A2

Bryn-y-Mor Road, Aberystwyth, Dyfed SY23 2HY.
Half-a-mile outside town.
CONTACT: B Thomas, Secretary. Tel: 0970 615104.
Course: 5,868yds, PAR 68, SSS 68. Undulating meadowland.
SOC RESTR'S: No restrictions. Apply to Secretary.
SOC GF - Round: Wd £12. **We** £15. **Day:** Wd £15. **We** £18.
SOC PACK: 10% discount parties of 10 or more.
VIS RESTR'S: Welcome, please book.
VIS GF - Round: Wd £12. **We** £15. **Day:** Wd £15. **We.** £18.
FACILITIES: Clubhouse, Restaurant, Professional & Shop.

ASHBURNHAM GOLF CLUB MAP 2 A2

Cliffe Terrace, Burry Port SA16 0HN.
5 miles west of Llanelli (A484).
CONTACT: DK Williams, Secretary. Tel: 0554 832269.
Course: 6,916yds, PAR 72, SSS 72. Seaside-type course.
SOC RESTR'S: Handicap Certificates required.
SOC GF - Round: Wd N/A. **We** N/A. **Day:** Wd £30. **We** N/A.
SOC PACK: On application.
VIS RESTR'S: Welcome. Handicap Certificates required.
VIS GF - Round: Wd £22.50. **We** £30. **Day:** Wd £30. **We** £35.
FACILITIES: Bar, Restaurant, Pro shop, Pool table.

St. Margaret's Hotel
RAC MERIT AWARDS
H C

Princes Drive, Colwyn Bay, Clwyd LL29 8RP
Tel: 0492 532718

Tailormade Golf Packages from £42 per person per day, including 5 course Dinner, Bed & Breakfast, Full Day's Golf & VAT. Ensuite bedrooms with CTV, central heating and beverage tray.
Societies welcome (max 23)

VALE OF LLANGOLLEN GOLF CLUB MAP 2 A1

The Clubhouse, Holyhead Road, Llangollen, Clwyd LL20 7RP.
2 miles east of town on A5.
CONTACT: TF Ellis, Secretary/Manager. Tel: 0978 860040.
Course: 6,461yds, PAR 72, SSS 72. Parkland course.
SOC RESTR'S: Welcome by arrangement through Secretary.
SOC GF - Round: Wd N/A. **We** N/A. **Day:** Wd £20. **We** £25.
SOC PACK: By arrangement.
VIS RESTR'S: Welcome.
VIS GF - Round: Wd N/A. **We** N/A. **Day:** Wd £20. **We** £25.
FACILITIES: Bar & Catering.

BORTH & YNYSLAS GOLF CLUB MAP 2 A1

Borth, Aberystwyth, Dyfed SY24 5JS.
8 miles north of Aberystwyth.
CONTACT: Mrs Sparks. Tel: 0970 871325.
Course: 6,118yds, PAR 70, SSS 70. Links course.
SOC RESTR'S: Welcome by arrangement through Secretary.
SOC GF - Round: Wd N/A. **We** N/A. **Day:** Wd £12. **We** £16.
SOC PACK: Coffee, Light Lunch, Dinner: £22.
VIS RESTR'S: Welcome, please phone first.
VIS GF - Round: Wd N/A. **We** N/A. **Day:** Wd £15. **We** £20.
FACILITIES: Bar & Catering. August Green Fee £20 a day.

WALES

GLYNHIR GOLF CLUB MAP 2 A2

Glynhir Road, Llandybie, Ammanford, Dyfed SA18 2TF.
3.5 miles north of Ammanford.
CONTACT: EP Rees, Hon. Secretary. Tel: 0269 850472.
Course: 5,952yds, PAR 69, SSS 69. Undulating parkland.
SOC RESTR'S: Weekdays only, preferably Tuesday & Friday.
SOC GF - Round: Wd N/A. We N/A. **Day:** Wd £13. We N/A.
SOC PACK: £25.
VIS RESTR'S: Welcome except Sundays.
VIS GF - Round: Wd N/A. We N/A. **Day:** Wd £15. We £20.
FACILITIES: Bar & Catering. Winter reduction to Green Fee.

Gwent

HAVERFORDWEST GOLF CLUB MAP 1 A2

Arnolds Down, Haverfordwest, Pembs, Dyfed SA61 2XQ.
1 mile East of Haverfordwest on A40.
CONTACT: MA Harding, Secretary Tel: 0437 764523.
Course: 6,005yds, PAR 70, SSS 69. Fairly flat parkland.
SOC RESTR'S: No large Societies after 12 noon on Weekends.
SOC GF - ROUND: Wd N/A. We N/A. **Day:** Wd £16. We £23.
SOC PACK: Green Fees are on a sliding scale above 10 players.
VIS RESTR'S: Welcome Wd. We depends on competitions.
VIS GF - ROUND: Wd N/A. We N/A. **Day:** Wd £16. We £23.
FACILITIES: Licensed Bar & Small Restaurant.

ALICE SPRINGS GOLF CLUB MAP 2 B2

Bettws Newydd, Usk, Gwent NP5 1JY.
North out of Usk on B4598 2 miles - turn right.
CONTACT: W Byard, Secretary. Tel: 0873 880708.
Course: 6,041yds, PAR 67, SSS 69. Undulating parkland.
SOC RESTR'S: Welcome by arrangement through Secretary.
SOC GF - Round: Wd £12.50. We £12.50. **Day:** Wd £17.50. We £17.50.
SOC PACK: Snack lunch. Evening meal. £22.50.
VIS RESTR'S: Always welcome. Book for weekends.
VIS GF - Round: Wd £12.50. We £12.50. **Day:** Wd £17.50. We £17.50.
FACILITIES: Bar.

MILFORD HAVEN GOLF CLUB MAP 1 A2

Woodbine House, Hubberston, Milford Haven, Dyfed SA72 2HQ.
West Boundary - Milford Haven - Dale Road.
CONTACT: IS Harvey, Club Administrator. Tel: 0646 692368.
Course: 6,071yds, PAR 71, SSS 71. Coastal course.
SOC RESTR'S: Welcome.
SOC GF - ROUND: Wd N/A. We N/A. **Day:** Wd £13. We £18.
SOC PACK: On application from Club Administrator.
VIS RESTR'S: Always welcome.
VIS GF - ROUND: Wd N/A. We N/A. **Day:** Wd £13. We £18.
FACILITIES: Bar.

DEWSTON GOLF CLUB MAP 2 B2

Caerwent, Newport, Gwent NP6 4AH.
1 mile off A48 between Newport & Chepstow.
CONTACT: Mrs Hill. Tel: 0291 430444.
Course: 6,100yds, PAR 72, SSS 70. Parkland course.
SOC RESTR'S: Welcome Weekdays.
SOC GF - Round: Wd N/A. We £15. **Day:** Wd £21. We N/A.
SOC PACK: 18 Holes plus meal £18. 36 Holes plus meal £27.
VIS RESTR'S: Always welcome.
VIS GF - Round: Wd £11. We £15. **Day:** Wd £18. We N/A.
FACILITIES: 26-Bay Floodlit Driving Range.

TENBY GOLF CLUB MAP 1 A2

The Burrows, Tenby, Dyfed SA70 7NP.
In Tenby Town.
CONTACT: TC Peake, Manager. Tel: 0834 842978.
Course: 6,232yds, PAR 69, SSS 71. Links course.
SOC RESTR'S: Welcome by arrangement through Secretary.
SOC GF - ROUND: We N/A. We N/A. **Day:** Wd N/A. We N/A.
SOC PACK: Reduced fee for Societies when booked.
VIS RESTR'S: Welcome subject to Club Comp. H'cap Cert required.
VIS GF - Round: Wd N/A. We N/A. **Day:** Wd £18. We £22.50.
FACILITIES: Catering.

MONMOUTHSHIRE GOLF CLUB MAP 2 A/B1

Llanfoist, Abergavenny.
2 miles south-west of Abergavenny.
CONTACT: GJ Swayne, Secretary. Tel: 0873 852606.
Course: 6,045yds, PAR 72, SSS 69. Parkland course.
SOC RESTR'S: Prior booking only.
SOC GF - ROUND: Wd N/A. We N/A. **Day:** Wd £21. We N/A.
SOC PACK: Tailored to suit requirements.
VIS RESTR'S: Handicap Certificates required.
VIS GF - Round: Wd £21. We £26. **Day:** Wd £21. We N/A.
FACILITIES: Bar, Restaurant, Pro shop, Fishing.

GWYNEDD

NEWPORT GOLF CLUB MAP 2 B2

Great Oak, Rogerstone, Newport, Gwent NP1 9FX.
Newport 3 miles on B4591 - Junction 27 - 1 mile.
CONTACT: Mr G Kay, Secretary. Tel: 0633 892643.
Course: 6,370yds, PAR 72, SSS 71. Parkland course.
SOC RESTR'S: Max 48. Welcome Weekdays except Tuesday.
SOC GF - Round: Wd N/A. We N/A. Day: Wd £30. We £40.
SOC PACK: None.
VIS RESTR'S: Welcome Weekdays.
VIS GF - Round: Wd N/A. We N/A. Day: Wd £30. We £40.
FACILITIES: Bar & Restaurant.

ROLLS OF MONMOUTH MAP 2 B2

The Hendre, Monmouth, Gwent NP5 4HG.
Approx 4 miles from Monmouth on B4233.
CONTACT: Mrs S Orton. Tel: 0600 715353.
Course: 6,723yds, PAR 72, SSS 72. Well wooded parkland.
SOC RESTR'S: Please book.
SOC GF - Round: Wd N/A. We N/A. Day: Wd £28. We £32.
SOC PACK: On application.
VIS RESTR'S: Please book in advance.
VIS GF - Round: Wd N/A. We N/A. Day: Wd £28. We £32.
FACILITIES: Bar & Restaurant.

ST. PIERRE GOLF CLUB (OLD) MAP 2 B2

St. Pierre Park, Chepstow, Gwent NP6 6YA.
Take Exit 22 on the M4 to A48.
CONTACT: T Davidson, Manager. Tel: 0291 625261.
Course: 6,748yds, PAR 71, SSS 71. Mature parkland course.
SOC RESTR'S: Welcome Wd. As Hotel residents We.
SOC GF - Round: Wd £35. We £65. Day: Wd £50. We £65.
SOC PACK: £55-£90.
VIS RESTR'S: Welcome with Handicap Certificate.
VIS GF - Round: Wd £35. We £65. Day: Wd £50. We £65.
FACILITIES: Swimming Pool, Sauna, Jacuzzi & Steam Room.

ST. PIERRE GOLF CLUB (NEW) MAP 2 B2

St. Pierre Park, Chepstow, Gwent NP6 6YA.
Take Exit 22 on the M4 on A48.
CONTACT: T Davidson, Manager. Tel: 0291 625261.
Course: 6,748yds, PAR 71, SSS 71. Mature parkland course.
SOC RESTR'S: Welcome Wd. As Hotel residents We.
SOC GF - Round: Wd £25. We £65. Day: Wd £50. We £65.
SOC PACK: £55-£90.
VIS RESTR'S: Welcome with Handicap Certificate.
VIS GF - Round: Wd £25. We £65. Day: Wd £50. We £65.
FACILITIES: Fitness Studio, Badminton, Squash & Snooker.

WEST MONMOUTHSHIRE GC MAP 2 A2

Pond Road, Nantyglo, Gwent NP3 6XS.
Heads of the Valleys Road - North of Brynmawr.
CONTACT: Colin Lewis, Secretary. Tel: 0495 310233.
Course: 6,118yds, PAR 71, SSS 69. Parkland course.
SOC RESTR'S: Welcome by arrangement through Secretary.
SOC GF-Round: Wd N/A. We N/A. Day: Wd £12. We N/A.
SOC PACK: Light Lunch, Dinner, Golf - Wd £16 - We £20.
VIS RESTR'S: Welcome Weekday. By arrangement at Weekend.
VIS GF-Round: Wd N/A. We N/A. Day: Wd £12. We £12/£15.
FACILITIES: Bar & Catering.

Gwynedd

ABERDOVEY GOLF CLUB MAP 2 A1

Aberdovey, Gwynedd LL35 0RT.
On A493 immediately west of village.
CONTACT: JM Griffiths, Secretary. Tel: 0654 767493.
Course: 6,445yds, PAR 71, SSS 71. Classic Links.
SOC RESTR'S: Max 36. Welcome Weekdays after 9.30.
SOC GF - Round: Wd £19. We N/A. Day: Wd £29. We N/A.
SOC PACK: None.
VIS RESTR'S: Welcome except 8-9.30 & 12.30-2.00.
VIS GF - Round: Wd £19. We £21. Day: Wd £29. We £31.
FACILITIES: Bar.

CAERNARFON GOLF CLUB MAP 2 A1

Llanfaglan, Caernarfon, Gwynedd LL54 5RP.
Approx 1 mile from town on Pwllheli Road.
CONTACT: JO Morgan, General Manager. Tel: 0286 673783.
Course: 5,870yds, PAR 69, SSS 69. Parkland course.
SOC RESTR'S: Welcome by arrangement through Secretary.
SOC GF - Round: Wd N/A. We N/A. Day: Wd £15. We £18.
SOC PACK: Reduced Green Fee for 20+.
VIS RESTR'S: Welcome.
VIS GF - Round: Wd N/A. We N/A. Day: Wd £15. We £18.
FACILITIES: Bar & Catering.

WALES

CONWY GOLF CLUB MAP 2 A1

Morfa, Conwy, Gwynedd LL37 8ER.
1 mile west of Conwy off A55.

CONTACT: EC Roberts, Secretary. Tel: 0492 593400.
Course: 6,901yds, PAR 72, SSS 73. Typical seaside course.
SOC RESTR'S: Welcome by arrangement through Secretary.
SOC GF - ROUND: Wd N/A. We N/A. **Day:** Wd £22. We £27.
SOC PACK: None.
VIS RESTR'S: Welcome Wd 10-11.30 & 2-3. We 10-11 & 2.30-4.
VIS GF - ROUND: Wd N/A. We N/A. **Day:** Wd £22. We £27.
FACILITIES: Bar & Catering. 5 day Green Fee £72.

NORTH WALES GOLF CLUB MAP 2 A1

Brymau Road, West Shore, Llandudno, Gwynedd LL30 2DZ.
1 mile from Llandudno Town Centre.

CONTACT: Mr Harwood, Secretary. Tel: 0492 875325.
Course: 6,132yds, PAR 71, SSS 69. Coastal course.
SOC RESTR'S: Welcome by arrangement through Secretary.
SOC GF - ROUND: Wd N/A. We N/A. **Day:** Wd £20. We £25.
SOC PACK: None.
VIS RESTR'S: Visitors welcome after 9.45. H'cap Cert required.
VIS GF - ROUND: Wd N/A. We N/A. **Day:** Wd £20. We £25.
FACILITIES: Full Catering, Bar, Snooker & Pro-shop.

CRICCIETH GOLF CLUB MAP 2 A1

Ednyfed Hill, Criccieth, Gwynedd LL52 0RR.
Criccieth Town Centre.

CONTACT: MG Hamilton, Secretary. Tel: 0766 522154.
Course: 5,787yds, PAR 69, SSS 68. Inland course.
SOC RESTR'S: Welcome by arrangement through Secretary.
SOC GF - Round: Wd N/A. We N/A. **Day:** Wd £10. We £15.
SOC PACK: 15% discount to groups of over 15.
VIS RESTR'S: Welcome please book.
VIS GF - ROUND: Wd N/A. We N/A. **Day:** Wd £10. We £15.
FACILITIES: Bar, Meals Apr-Sept.

PORTMADOG GOLF CLUB MAP 2 A1

Morfa Bychan, Portmadog, Gwynedd LL49 9UU.
2 miles west of Portmadog.

CONTACT: D Morrow, Secretary. Tel: 0766 512037.
Course: 6,309yds, PAR 70, SSS 70. Links course.
SOC RESTR'S: Members tee times 9-10 & 12 -1.30.
SOC GF - ROUND: Wd N/A. We N/A. **Day:** Wd £15. We £20.
SOC PACK: 20% discount on GF for 20 +. Full day's catering £10.
VIS RESTR'S: Welcome, not Club Competitions & Members' times.
VIS GF - ROUND: Wd N/A. We N/A. **Day:** Wd £15. We £20.
FACILITIES: Bar & Snooker Room. Bank Holiday Green Fee £25.

LLANDUDNO (MAESDU) GC MAP 2 A1

Hospital Road, Llandudno, Gwynedd LL30 1HU.
1 mile south of town. Beside General Hospital.

CONTACT: Mr Dean, Secretary. Tel: 0492 876450.
Course: 6,513yds, PAR 73, SSS 73. Parkland/links course.
SOC RESTR'S: Must be members of recognised Golf Clubs.
SOC GF - ROUND: Wd N/A. We N/A. **Day:** Wd £20. We £25.
SOC PACK: On application at time of booking.
VIS RESTR'S: Write or phone for tee availability.
VIS GF - ROUND: Wd N/A. We N/A. **Day:** Wd £20. We £25.
FACILITIES: Bar.

RHOS-ON-SEA GOLF CLUB MAP 2 A1

Penrhyn Bay, Llandudno, Gwynedd LL30 3PU.
A55 to Old Colwyn, follow coastline round.

CONTACT: J John, Steward. Tel: 0492 549641.
Course: 6,064yds, PAR 69, SSS 69. Parkland course.
SOC RESTR'S: Welcome, but booking essential.
SOC GF - ROUND: Wd N/A. We N/A. **Day:** Wd £15. We £20.
SOC PACK: Contact Steward for details.
VIS RESTR'S: Welcome. Booking required at Weekends.
VIS GF - ROUND: Wd N/A. We N/A. **Day:** Wd £15. We £20.
FACILITIES: 2 Full-size Snooker Tables, Catering & Bar.

NEFYN & DISTRICT GOLF CLUB MAP 2 A1

Morfa Nefyn, Pwllheli, Gwynedd LL53 6DA.
20 miles west of Caernarfon.

CONTACT: RW Parry, Secretary. Tel: 0758 720966.
Course: 6,301yds, PAR 72, SSS 71. Clifftop course.
SOC RESTR'S: Only by prior arrangement with Secretary.
SOC GF - Round: Wd £17.50. We £25. **Day:** Wd £22.50. We £30.
SOC PACK: 10% discount for 12+. Catering separate (ring 720218).
VIS RESTR'S: Welcome except Club Competition, please phone.
VIS GF - Round: Wd £17.50. We £25. **Day:** Wd £22.50. We £30.
FACILITIES: Full Catering, Bars & Snooker.

ROYAL ST. DAVID'S GOLF CLUB MAP 2 A1

Harlech, Gwynedd LL46 2UB.
On main A496.

CONTACT: R Jones, Secretary/Manager. Tel: 0766 780361.
Course: 6,427yds, PAR 69, SSS 71. Championship Links.
SOC RESTR'S: Must book well in advance.
SOC GF - ROUND: Wd N/A. We N/A. **Day:** Wd £23. We £28.
SOC PACK: None.
VIS RESTR'S: By prior arrangement. H'cap Cert required.
VIS GF - ROUND: Wd N/A. We N/A. **Day:** Wd £23. We £28.
FACILITIES: Full Catering & Bar.

MID GLAMORGAN

Mid-Glamorgan

ST. DEINIOL GOLF CLUB MAP 2 A1

Penybryn, Bangor, Gwynedd LL57 1PX.
Off A5/A55 Junction, 1 mile east of Bangor on A5122.

CONTACT: JR Harries, Secretary. Tel: 0248 353098.
Course: 5,068yds, PAR 68, SSS 67. Elevated parkland course.
SOC RESTR'S: Subject to prior arrangement.
SOC GF - Round: Wd £10. We £15. Day: Wd £10. We £15.
SOC PACK: By arrangement with Secretary.
VIS RESTR'S: Welcome except Weekends - subject to availability.
VIS GF - Round: Wd £10. We £15. Day: Wd £10. We £15.
FACILITIES: Bar & Snooker. Meals by arrangement.

ABERDARE GOLF CLUB MAP 2 A2

Abernant, Aberdare, Mid Glamorgan CF44 0RY.
Half-a-mile from Town Centre.

CONTACT: L Adler, Secretary. Tel: 0685 872797.
Course: 5,845yds, PAR 69, SSS 69. Mountain/parkland course.
SOC RESTR'S: Max 30. Welcome by arrangement through Sec.
SOC GF - Round: Wd N/A. We N/A. Day: Wd £14. We £18.
SOC PACK:. Meals arranged with Steward (not Mon) approx £7.
VIS RESTR'S: Welcome Weekdays & Sunday. H'cap required.
VIS GF - Round: Wd N/A. We N/A. Day: Wd £14. We £18.
FACILITIES: Full-Size Snooker Table.

BARGOED GOLF CLUB MAP 2 A2

Moorland Road, Bargoed, Mid Glamorgan CF8 9GF.
A469 from Cardiff. Half-a-mile from Town Centre.

CONTACT: W Coleman, Secretary. Tel: 0443 830143.
Course: 5,836yds, PAR 70, SSS 70. Parkland course.
SOC RESTR'S: Welcome Weekdays by appointment.
SOC GF - Round: Wd N/A. We N/A. Day: Wd £15. We £15.
SOC PACK: Coffee, Lunch, Dinner, 36 holes: £20.
VIS RESTR'S: Welcome Weekdays.
VIS GF - Round: Wd N/A. We N/A. Day: Wd £15. We £15.
FACILITIES: Bar & Catering.

BRYN MEADOWS GOLF CLUB MAP 2 A2

The Bryn, Nr. Hengoed, Mid Glamorgan CF8 7SM.
Junction 28 M4. Follow sign for Brynmawr - A4048 4 miles

CONTACT: Mrs Williams, Secretary. Tel: 0495 225590.
Course: 6,132yds, PAR 71, SSS 69. Parkland course.
SOC RESTR'S: Mon, Wed & Fri up to 20. Tue &Thur over 20.
SOC GF - ROUND: Wd N/A. We N/A. Day: Wd N/A. We N/A.
SOC PACK: Coffee, Lunch, Dinner, 27 holes: £35.
VIS RESTR'S: Welcome except Sunday mornings.
VIS GF - Round: Wd £17.50. We £22.50. Day: Wd N/A. We N/A.
FACILITIES: A la Carte Restaurant, Function Suite & Leisure Area.

MAESTEG GOLF CLUB MAP 2 A2

Mount Pleasant, Neath Rd, Maesteg, Mid Glam CF34 9PR.
1 mile west of Maesteg on B4282. M4 J36 (E), J40, (W).

CONTACT: WH Hanford, Hon. Secretary. Tel: 0656 734106.
Course: 5,900yds, PAR 70, SSS 69. Hilltop course.
SOC RESTR'S: Welcome Weekdays by arrangement.
SOC GF - ROUND: Wd N/A. We N/A. Day: Wd £15. We N/A.
SOC PACK: Golf, Lunch & Dinner approx £20.
VIS RESTR'S: Please phone in advance.
VIS GF - ROUND: Wd N/A. We N/A. Day: Wd £15. We £20.
FACILITIES: Bar, Catering every day except Thursday.

MOUNTAIN ASH GOLF CLUB MAP 2 A2

The Clubhouse, Mountain Ash, Mid Glamorgan CF 45 4DT.
4 miles north of Abercyon, 10 miles from Pontypridd.

CONTACT: G Matthews, Secretary. Tel: 0443 479459.
Course: 5,553yds, PAR 69, SSS 68. Semi-woodland course.
SOC RESTR'S: Welcome Weekdays only.
SOC GF - Round: Wd N/A. We N/A. Day: Wd £18. We N/A.
SOC PACK: No definite package.
VIS RESTR'S: Welcome Weekdays.
VIS GF - Round: Wd N/A. We N/A. Day: Wd £18. We N/A.
FACILITIES: Bar.

MOUNTAIN LAKES GOLF CLUB MAP 2 A2

Blaengwynlais, Nr. Caerphilly, Mid Glamorgan CF8 1NG.
M4, Junct 32, 4th Exit on roundabout. 4 miles N of Cardiff.

CONTACT: P Page, Director. Tel: 0222 861128.
Course: 6,500yds, PAR 72, SSS 73. American style course.
SOC RESTR'S: Welcome when booked in advance except Sun.
SOC GF - Round: Wd N/A. We N/A. Day: Wd £15. We £15.
SOC PACK: Coffee, Lunch, Dinner, 27 holes: £29.50.
VIS RESTR'S: Always welcome with H'cap Cert.
VIS GF - Round: Wd N/A. We N/A. Day: Wd £15. We £15.
FACILITIES: Buffet all day.

WALES

PYLE & KENFIG GOLF CLUB MAP 2 A2

Waun-y-Mer, Kenfig, Mid Glamorgan CF33 4PU.
Follow Porthcawl signs from Junction 37, M4.

CONTACT: R Thomas, Secretary. Tel: 0656 783093.
Course: 6,650yds, PAR 71, SSS 73. Downland course.
SOC RESTR'S: Max 50. Tuesdays & Fridays only.
SOC GF - Round: Wd £25. We N/A. **Day:** Wd £30. We N/A.
SOC PACK: No packages.
VIS RESTR'S: Welcome Weekdays with H'cap Cert.
VIS GF - Round: Wd £25. We N/A **Day:** Wd £30. We N/A.
FACILITIES: Full Catering.

Powys

RHONDDA GOLF CLUB MAP 2 A2

Golf House, Penrhys, Rhondda, Mid Glamorgan CF43 3PN.
6 miles west of Pontypridd.

CONTACT: G Rees, Secretary. Tel: 0443 441384.
Course: 6,428yds, PAR 70, SSS 70. Mountain course.
SOC RESTR'S: Welcome Weekdays.
SOC GF - Round: Wd N/A. We N/A. **Day:** Wd £19. We N/A.
SOC PACK: £16 per day to include Lunch & Dinner.
VIS RESTR'S: Welcome with H'cap Cert.
VIS GF - Round: Wd £15. We £20. **Day:** Wd £15. We £20.
FACILITIES: Restaurant, Snooker Table & Pro-shop.

BUILTH WELLS GOLF CLUB MAP 1 B1

The Clubhouse, Golf Links Road, Builth Wells, Powys LD2 3NF.
A483 Llandovery Road.

CONTACT: A Jones, Secretary. Tel: 0982 553296.
Course: 5,386yds, PAR 66, SSS 67. Undulating parkland.
SOC RESTR'S: Max. 30. Welcome by arrangement.
SOC GF - Round: Wd N/A. We N/A. **Day:** Wd £15. We £20.
SOC PACK: Approx. £12 to include Meal & Golf.
VIS RESTR'S: Always Welcome.
SOC GF - Round: Wd N/A. We N/A. **Day:** Wd £15. We £20.
FACILITIES: Bar & Catering. 5 day Green Fee £50.

ROYAL PORTHCAWL GOLF CLUB MAP 2 A2

Rest Bay, Porthcawl, Mid Glamorgan CF36 3UW.
Leave M4 at Junction 37, follow signs to Porthcawl 3 miles.

CONTACT: AW Woolcott, Secretary. Tel: 0656 782251.
Course: 6,691yds, PAR 72, SSS 74. Links course.
SOC RESTR'S: Welcome by arrangement through Secretary.
SOC GF - ROUND: Wd N/A. We N/A. **Day:** Wd £30. We N/A.
SOC PACK: Coffee, Light Lunch, Dinner, 36 holes-: £45.
VIS RESTR'S: Not on Monday or Wednesday am, or all Weekend.
VIS GF - ROUND: Wd N/A. We N/A. **Day:** Wd £30. We N/A.
FACILITIES: Bar & Catering.

CRADOC GOLF CLUB MAP 1 B1

Penoyre Park, Cradoc, Brecon, Powys.
2 miles north of Brecon, off B4520 (signposted).

CONTACT: GSW Davies, Secretary. Tel: 0874 623658.
Course: 6,301yds, PAR 71, SSS 71. Parkland course.
SOC RESTR'S: Welcome Weekdays.
SOC GF - Round: Wd N/A. We N/A. **Day:** Wd £17. We £20.
SOC PACK: None.
VIS RESTR'S: Welcome except Sunday.
VIS GF - Round: Wd N/A. We N/A. **Day:** Wd £17. We £20.
FACILITIES: Practice Ground. Full Catering & Bar.

SOUTHERNDOWN GOLF CLUB MAP 2 A2

Ewenny, Bridgend, Mid Glamorgan CF35 5BF.
In Ogmore-by-Sea. Opposite Ogmore Castle ruins turn left.

CONTACT: KR Wilcox, Secretary. Tel: 0656 480476.
Course: 6,613yds, PAR 70, SSS 73. Downland course.
SOC RESTR'S: Max. 50. Tue & Thur. Tee off 9-4. We possible.
SOC GF - Round: Wd £24. We £30. **Day:** Wd £24. We £30.
SOC PACK: Light Lunch, Dinner, 36 holes: £32-£35.
VIS RESTR'S: Welcome except Club Comp days. H'cap Cert.
VIS GF - Round: Wd £24. We £30. **Day:** Wd £24. We £30.
FACILITIES: Practice Ground, Pro-shop, Full Catering & Bar.

LLANDRINDOD WELLS GC MAP 1 B1

Llandrindod Wells, Powys LD1 5NY.
Well signposted. A483 - Centre of town.

CONTACT: FT James, Secretary/Manager. Tel: 0597 823873.
Course: 5,687yds, PAR 69, SSS 68. Mountain course.
SOC RESTR'S: Welcome. 3 months notice for We outing.
SOC GF - Round: Wd £12 We £16. **Day:** Wd N/A. We N/A.
SOC PACK: On application.
VIS RESTR'S: Please phone in advance.
VIS GF - Round: Wd £15. We £18. **Day:** Wd N/A. We N/A.
FACILITIES: Catering as required. Bar.

SOUTH GLAMORGAN

WELSHPOOL GOLF CLUB   MAP 1 B1

Golfa Hill, Welshpool, Powys.
On A548 west from Welshpool for 4 miles.

CONTACT: DB Pritchard, Secretary Tel: 0938 552215.
Course: 5,708yds, PAR 70, SSS 69. Hilly course.
SOC RESTR'S: Welcome by arrangement through Secretary.
SOC GF - Round: Wd N/A. We N/A. Day: Wd £10. We £20.
SOC PACK: On application.
VIS RESTR'S: Always welcome but book at Weekends.
VIS GF - Round: Wd N/A. We N/A. Day: Wd £10. We £20.
FACILITIES: Catering as required. Bar.

South Glamorgan

BRYNHILL (BARRY) GOLF CLUB   MAP 1 B2

Port Road, Barry, South Glamorgan CF6 7PN.
From M4 follow signs to Barry & Cardiff (Wales) Airport.

CONTACT: K Atkinson, Secretary. Tel: 0446 720277.
Course: 6,077yds, PAR 71, SSS 69. Undulating meadowland.
SOC RESTR'S: By arrangement with Secretary. No Mon. No We.
SOC GF - Round: Wd N/A. We N/A. Day: Wd N/A. We N/A.
SOC PACK: Coffee, Lunch, Dinner, 36 holes approx £25.
VIS RESTR'S: No visitors on Sundays.
VIS GF - Round: Wd N/A. We N/A. Day: Wd £20. We £25.
FACILITIES: Men's Bar, Lounge Bar, Terrace & Dining Room.

CREIGIAU GOLF CLUB   MAP 1 B2

Creigiau, Cardiff, South Glamorgan.
7 miles north-west of Cardiff off A4119.

CONTACT: D Jones, Secretary. Tel: 0222 890263.
Course: 5,979yds, PAR 70, SSS 69. Parkland course.
SOC RESTR'S: Welcome by arrangement through Secretary.
SOC GF- Round: Wd N/A. We N/A Day: Wd £21. We N/A.
SOC PACK: £33.
VIS RESTR'S: Welcome Weekdays.
VIS GF - Round: Wd N/A. We N/A. Day: Wd £21. We N/A.
FACILITIES: Bar & Catering except Mondays.

DINAS POWIS GOLF CLUB   MAP 1 B2

Golf House, Dinas Powis, South Glamorgan CF6 4AJ.
From Cardiff follow signs to Dinas Powis.

CONTACT: JD Hughes, Secretary. Tel: 0222 512727.
Course: 5,357yds, PAR 67, SSS 65. Parkland course.
SOC RESTR'S: Max 40. Welcome by arrangement through Sec.
SOC GF - ROUND: Wd N/A. We N/A. Day: Wd £16. We N/A.
SOC PACK: 9-hole morning. 18-hole afternoon.
VIS RESTR'S: Welcome Weekends. Weekends by arrangement.
VIS GF - ROUND: Wd N/A. We N/A. Day: Wd £20. We £25.
FACILITIES: Bar.

GLAMORGANSHIRE GOLF CLUB   MAP 1 B2

Lavernock Road, Penarth CF6 2UP.
5 miles south of Cardiff.

CONTACT: WG Davies, Secretary. Tel: 0222 701185.
Course: 6,181yds, PAR 70, SSS 70. Parkland course.
SOC RESTR'S: Welcome but contact in advance.
SOC GF - Round: Wd N/A. We N/A. Day: Wd £24. We N/A.
SOC PACK: Lunch, Dinner, 36 holes: £37.50.
VIS RESTR'S: Welcome. Handicap Certificate required.
VIS GF - Round: Wd N/A. We N/A. Day: Wd £24. We £28.
FACILITIES: Bar, Restaurant, Pro shop, Squash, Snooker.

RADYR GOLF CLUB   MAP 1 B2

Radyr, Cardiff, South Glamorgan CF4 8BS.
Junct 32 M4. Follow A470 to Merthyr Tydfil, Radyr 1st Exit.

CONTACT: S Gough, Manager. Tel: 0222 842408.
Course: 6,031yds, PAR 69, SSS 70. Parkland course.
SOC RESTR'S: Max. 60. Welcome Wednesday, Thursday & Friday.
SOC GF - Round: Wd N/A. We N/A. Day: Wd £25. We N/A.
SOC PACK: GF reduction for large groups. All catering arranged.
VIS RESTR'S: Welcome Weekdays. H'cap Cert required.
VIS GF - Round: Wd N/A. We N/A. Day: Wd £25. We N/A.
FACILITIES: Usual Bar & Catering.

WHITCHURCH GOLF CLUB   MAP 1 B2

Pantmawr Road, Whitchurch, Cardiff, South Glam CF4 6XD.
Half mile M4 Junction 32. A470 to Cardiff.

CONTACT: R Burley, Secretary. Tel: 0222 620985.
Course: 6,319yds, PAR 71, SSS 70. Well manicured course.
SOC RESTR'S: Welcome Thursday only.
SOC GF - Round: Wd N/A. We N/A. Day: Wd £23. We £30.
SOC PACK: Separate catering arrangements with chef.
VIS RESTR'S: Welcome Weekdays. Some restrictions Weekends.
VIS GF - Round: Wd N/A. We N/A. Day: Wd £23. We £30.
FACILITIES: Bar & Snooker.

WALES

West Glamorgan

CLYNE GOLF CLUB MAP 1 B2

Owls Lodge Lane, Mayals, Swansea, West Glamorgan SA3 5DP.
A4067 to Mayals Road.

CONTACT: K Crawford, Secretary. Tel: 0792 401989.
Course: 6,344yds, PAR 70, SSS 71. Moorland course.
SOC RESTR'S: Max 60. Welcome by arrangement through Sec.
SOC GF - ROUND: Wd N/A. We N/A. Day: Wd £20. We N/A.
SOC PACK: Under review.
VIS RESTR'S: Welcome Weekdays, Weekends by booking.
VIS GF - ROUND: Wd N/A. We N/A. Day: Wd £20. We £25.
FACILITIES: Practice Area/Green, Bar, Catering & Snooker Table.

FAIRWOOD PARK GOLF CLUB MAP 1 B2

Blackhills Lane, Upper Killay, Swansea, W Glamorgan SA2 7JN.
Blackhills Lane, turn left opp Swansea Airport entrance.

CONTACT: Steward. 0792 297849.
Course: 6,606yds, PAR 72, SSS 72. Parkland course.
SOC RESTR'S: Max 60 Welcome by arrangement through Sec.
SOC GF - Round: Wd N/A. We N/A. Day: Wd £25. We £30.
SOC PACK: Coffee, Lunch, Dinner, 27 holes - Wd £35, We £38.
VIS RESTR'S: Prior arrangement please.
VIS GF - Round: Wd N/A. We N/A. Day: Wd £25. We £30.
FACILITIES: Bar, Restaurant & Snooker.

MORRISTON GOLF CLUB MAP 1 B2

Clasemont Road, Morriston, Swansea, W Glamorgan SA6 6AJ.
East on A48 - Junction 46 M4, 4 miles north of Swansea.

CONTACT: A Jefford, Secretary. Tel: 0792 796528.
Course: 5,785yds, PAR 68, SSS 68. Parkland course.
SOC RESTR'S: Welcome Weekdays.
SOC GF - Round: Wd £18. We £25. Day: Wd £18. We £25.
SOC PACK: Catering arrangements 0792 700310.
VIS RESTR'S: Welcome weekdays.
VIS GF - Round: Wd £18. We £25. Day: Wd £18. We £25.
FACILITIES: Bar.

NEATH GOLF CLUB MAP 1 B2

Cadoxton, Neath, West Glamorgan SA10 8AH.
Turn opposite Cadoxton Church - well signposted.

CONTACT: DM Hughes, Secretary. Tel: 0639 632759.
Course: 6,492yds, PAR 72, SSS 72. Parkland course.
SOC RESTR'S: Welcome by arrangement through Secretary.
SOC GF - ROUND: Wd N/A. We N/A. Day: Wd N/A. We N/A.
SOC PACK: Coffee, Lunch, Dinner, 27 or 36 holes: £20.
VIS RESTR'S: Welcome except Weekends & Bank Holidays.
VIS GF -Round: Wd N/A. We N/A. Day: Wd £17. We N/A.
FACILITIES: Bar & Snooker Room.

PENNARD GOLF CLUB MAP 1 B2

Southgate Road, Southgate, Swansea, W Glamorgan SA3 2BT.
8 miles south-west of Swansea via A4067 & B4436.

CONTACT: M Howell, Hon Secretary. Tel: 0792 233131.
Course: 6,289yds, PAR 71, SSS 71. Clifftop links course.
SOC RESTR'S: Max 30. Welcome Weekdays except Bank Holidays.
SOC GF - ROUND: Wd N/A. We N/A. Day: Wd £18. We N/A.
SOC PACK: Please phone & discuss requirements.
VIS RESTR'S: Not Weekends or Bank Holidays.
VIS GF - ROUND: Wd N/A. We N/A. Day: Wd £18. We £22.
FACILITIES: Bar & Snooker.

WITTEMBERG HOTEL

2 Rotherslade Road,
Langland Bay, Swansea.
Tel: (0792) 369696

Beach 200 yards, golf 600 yards, tennis 300 yards, 1 mile Mumbles, 6 miles Swansea. Ample parking. Short breaks all year.

Resident owners: Andrew & June Thomas

PONTARDAWE GOLF CLUB MAP 1 B2

Cefn Llan, Pontardawe, Swansea, W Glamorgan SA8 4SH.
5 miles on A4067 off Junction 45 on M4.

CONTACT: L Jones, Secretary. Tel: 0792 863118.
Course: 6,061yds, PAR 70, SSS 70. Moorland course.
SOC RESTR'S: By prior arrangement.
SOC GF - ROUND: Wd N/A. We N/A. Day: Wd N/A. We N/A.
SOC PACK: Please phone & discuss requirements.
VIS RESTR'S: Welcome Weekdays. Handicap Certificates required.
VIS GF - ROUND: Wd N/A. We N/A. Day: Wd £18. We N/A.
FACILITIES: Bar.

NORTHERN IRELAND

THE announcement by the Royal and Ancient in the wake of the 1993 Open Championship that Royal Portrush was still very much in mind as a Championship venue will have provided a timely and welcome boost to golf in Northern Ireland. Only once, in 1951, has the Open left the British mainland and in Max Faulkner, Portrush provided a British winner - the last before Tony Jacklin at Royal Lytham in 1969. Should you play the course, drive out by the Antrim coast road. There, as you turn a corner past the ruins of Dunluce Castle, the entire layout will be spread out below you: a magical prospect.

Every bit as scenic, with the almost theatrical backdrop of the Mountains of Mourne, is Royal County Down which, legend has it, Tom Morris was paid £4 to lay out in 1889. Even allowing for inflation, the sum still represents an astonishing bargain!

Should these two wonderful courses leave you wanting more links golf, Castlerock and Portstewart, both within just a few miles of Royal Portrush, are both excellent. Away from the coast, Belfast can offer a host of fine courses, among them Royal Belfast, the equally royal-sounding Balmoral and Shandon Park, while further afield, perhaps combined with a visit to Royal County Down, if you fancy trying your luck over the course where Ronan Rafferty learned his skills, head for Warrenpoint, south of Newry.

In general, golf in Northern Ireland represents perhaps the best value currently to be had in the United Kingdom. True the two jewels in the crown of Royal Portrush and Royal Country Down will charge you a green fee appropriate to their standing, (but still less than an equivalent course on the British mainland), but elsewhere, there really are bargains galore. As with golf in the Republic of Ireland, golf in the North is an experience to savour.

NORTHERN IRELAND

Antrim

BELVOIR PARK GOLF COURSE MAP 10 B1

73 Church Road, Newtownbreda, Belfast, Antrim BT8 4AN.
Off A24 south of Belfast.
CONTACT: K Graham, Manager. Tel: 0232 491693.
COURSE: 6,276yds, PAR 70, SSS 70. Parkland course.
SOC RESTR'S: Welcome Mon, Tues & Thur 25 or over.
SOC GF - Round: Wd N/A. We N/A. DAY: Wd N/A. We N/A.
SOC PACK: Please phone Manager in advance.
VIS RESTR'S: Welcome except Saturday. Wed GF as We.
VIS GF - Round: Wd N/A. We N/A. DAY: Wd £25. We £30.
FACILITIES: Full Bar, Catering & Snooker.

BALLYCASTLE GOLF CLUB MAP 10 B1

Cushendall Road, Ballycastle, Antrim BT54 6QP.
North Antrim coast, between Portrush and Cushendall.
CONTACT: ME Page, Hon. Secretary. Tel: 02657 62536.
COURSE: 5,662yds, PAR 71, SSS 68. Links course.
SOC RESTR'S: Max.30. Must book in advance.
SOC GF - Round: Wd N/A. We N/A. DAY: Wd £12. We £17.
SOC PACK: On application.
VIS RESTR'S: Welcome every day by prior arrangement.
VIS GF - Round: Wd N/A. We N/A. DAY: Wd £12. We £17.
FACILITIES: Bar & Restaurant.

CAIRNDHU GOLF CLUB MAP 10 B1

Coast Road, Ballygally, Larne, Antrim BT40 2QG.
4 miles north of Larne.
CONTACT: Mrs J Robinson, Secretary/Manager. Tel: 0574 583324.
COURSE: 6,122yds, PAR 70, SSS 69. Parkland course.
SOC RESTR'S: Welcome except Thursday & Saturday.
SOC GF - Round: Wd N/A. We N/A. DAY: Wd £12. We £18.
SOC PACK: None.
VIS RESTR'S: Welcome except Saturday.
VIS GF - Round: Wd N/A. We N/A. DAY: Wd £12. We £18.
FACILITIES: Bar, Restaurant & Snooker.

BALLYMENA GOLF CLUB MAP 10 B1

128 Raceview Road, Ballymena, Antrim BT42 4HY.
2 miles east of Ballymena on the A42.
CONTACT: M Conon, Secretary. Tel: 0266 861487.
COURSE: 5,736yds, PAR 68, SSS 67. Parkland course.
SOC RESTR'S: Welcome any day except Tuesday & Saturday.
SOC GF - Round: Wd N/A. We N/A. DAY: Wd £12. We £15.
SOC PACK: On application prior to booking.
VIS RESTR'S: Welcome any day except Tuesday & Saturday.
VIS GF - Round: Wd N/A. We N/A. DAY: Wd £12. We £15.
FACILITIES: Bar, Restaurant, Snooker & Bowls.

CARRICKFERGUS GOLF CLUB MAP 10 B1

North Road, Carrickfergus, Antrim BT38 8LP.
Half-a-mile along North Road from town centre.
CONTACT: ID Jardine, Hon. Secretary. Tel: 0960 363713
COURSE: 5,752yds, PAR 68, SSS 68. Parkland course.
SOC RESTR'S: Welcome Weekdays but not after 1.15 on Friday.
SOC GF - Round: Wd N/A. We N/A. Day: Wd £11. We N/A.
SOC PACK: No special Society package.
VIS RESTR'S: Welcome except on Saturday.
VIS GF - Round: Wd N/A. We N/A. Day: Wd £13. We £18.
FACILITIES: Bar, Catering Service. Well stocked Pro-shop.

BALMORAL GOLF CLUB MAP 10 B1

518 Lisburn Road, Belfast, Antrim BT9 6GX.
3 miles south of City centre.
CONTACT: R McConkey, General Manager. Tel: 0232 381514.
COURSE: 6,235yds, PAR 69, SSS 70. Parkland Course.
SOC RESTR'S: Welcome Monday & Thursday.
SOC GF - Round: Wd N/A. We N/A. DAY: Wd £15. We £22.50.
SOC PACK: Tailored to suit size.
VIS RESTR'S: Welcome except Saturday.
VIS GF - Round: Wd N/A. We N/A. DAY: Wd £15. We £22.50.
FACILITIES: Bar & Snooker.

DUNMURRY GOLF CLUB MAP 10 B1

91 Dunmurry Lane, Belfast, Antrim BT17 9JS.
5 miles south of Belfast on Malone Road to Dunmurry.
CONTACT: A Taylor, Secretary/Manager. Tel: 0232 610834.
COURSE: 6,235yds, PAR 69, SSS 70. Parkland course.
SOC RESTR'S: Large outings Monday.
SOC GF - Round: Wd N/A. We N/A. Day: Wd £13. We £18.
SOC PACK: Special rates for over 40 in number.
VIS RESTR'S: Welcome except Friday & Saturday.
VIS GF - Round: Wd N/A. We N/A. Day: Wd £14. We £20.
FACILITIES: Restaurant all day Tuesday to Sunday.

ANTRIM

FORTWILLIAM GOLF CLUB MAP 10 B1

Downview Avenue, Belfast, Antrim BT15 4EZ.
2 miles north of Belfast.
CONTACT: RJ Campbell, Hon. Secretary. Tel: 0232 370770.
COURSE: 5,933yds, PAR 69, SSS 68. Parkland course.
SOC RESTR'S: Max 40. Mon-Wed & Thur am. Sun after 3.30.
SOC GF - Round: Wd N/A. We N/A. **Day:** Wd N/A. We N/A.
SOC PACK: On application from Secretary.
VIS RESTR'S: Welcome except Fri after 3.15 & Sat all day.
VIS GF - Round: Wd N/A. We N/A. **Day:** Wd £15. We £20.
FACILITIES: Bar & Catering.

KNOCK GOLF CLUB MAP 10 B1

Summerfield, Dundonald, Belfast, Antrim BT16 0QX.
4 miles east of Belfast on the Upper Newtownards Rd.
CONTACT: SG Managh, Secretary/Manager. Tel: 0232 483251.
COURSE: 6,6407yds, PAR 70, SSS 71. Parkland course.
SOC RESTR'S: Welcome Monday & Thursday.
SOC GF - Round: Wd N/A. We N/A. **Day:** Wd N/A. We N/A.
SOC PACK: Catering phone 0232 480915.
VIS RESTR'S: Welcome except Saturdays.
VIS GF - Round: Wd N/A. We N/A. **Day:** Wd £20. We £25.
FACILITIES: Putting Green, Snooker, Bar & Catering.

KNOCKBRACKEN G & CC MAP 10 B1

Ballymaconaghy Rd, Knockbracken, Belfast, Antrim BT8 4SB.
2 miles south-west of Belfast off Saintfield Road.
CONTACT: Caroline Uylett, Secretary. Tel: 0232 401811.
COURSE: 5,400yds, PAR 69, SSS 68. Undulating course.
SOC RESTR'S: Welcome except Weekends.
SOC GF - Round: Wd £8.50. We N/A. **Day:** Wd N/A. We N/A.
SOC PACK: Day package: Incl. Golf & meal £12.
VIS RESTR'S: Welcome except Weekend mornings.
VIS GF - Round: Wd £9. We £11. **Day:** Wd N/A. We N/A.
FACILITIES: Covered Range, Pro-Shop & Golf School.

LISBURN GOLF CLUB MAP 10 B1

Eglantine Road, Lisburn, Antrim BT27 5RQ.
3 miles south of Lisburn on the A1.
CONTACT: G Graham, Secretary/Manager. Tel: 0846 677216.
COURSE: 6,101yds, PAR 72, SSS 72. Parkland course.
SOC RESTR'S: Welcome Mondays, Thursdays & Fridays.
SOC GF - Round: Wd N/A. We N/A. **Day:** Wd N/A. We N/A.
SOC PACK: On application from Secretary.
VIS RESTR'S: Welcome except Weekends & Ladies day Tuesday.
VIS GF - Round: Wd N/A. We N/A. **Day:** Wd £20. We N/A.
FACILITIES: Snooker.

MALONE GOLF CLUB MAP 10 B1

Upper Malone Road, Dunmurry, Belfast BT17 9LB
South of Belfast for 5 miles on Upper Malone Road.
CONTACT: Hon Secretary. Tel: 0232 612758.
COURSE: 6,433yds, PAR 71, SSS 71. Parkland course.
SOC RESTR'S: Welcome Monday & Thursday.
SOC GF - Round: Wd N/A. We N/A. **Day:** Wd N/A. We N/A.
SOC PACK: On application from Secretary.
VIS RESTR'S: Welcome except Wed & Sat before 5.15.
VIS GF - Round: Wd N/A. We N/A. **Day:** Wd £23. We £26.
FACILITIES: Restaurant, Bar & Professional (PM O'Hagan).

MASSEREENE GOLF CLUB MAP 10 B1

Lough Road, Antrim BT41 4DQ.
3 miles from Aldergrove airport & 1 mile south-west of Antrim.
CONTACT: Mrs M Agnew, Secretary/Manager. Tel: 0849 428096.
COURSE: 6,614yds, PAR 72, SSS 71. Parkland course.
SOC RESTR'S: Welcome Tue & Thur 9-12 & 2-3.30. Wed. 9-11.30.
SOC GF - Round: Wd £15. We N/A. **Day:** Wd N/A. We N/A.
SOC PACK: On application.
VIS RESTR'S: Welcome except Friday & Saturday.
VIS GF - Round: Wd N/A. We N/A. **Day:** Wd £16. We N/A.
FACILITIES: Bar, Dining Facilities & Snooker Room.

ROYAL PORTRUSH (DUNLUCE) MAP 10 B1

Dunluce Road, Portrush, Antrim.
Half-a-mile from Portrush on main Bushmills Road.
CONTACT: Miss Wilma Erskine, Sec/Manager. Tel: 0265 822311.
COURSE: 6,694yds, PAR 72, SSS 73. Championship links course.
SOC RESTR'S: Available Weekdays am & Sunday after 10.30.
SOC GF - Round: Wd N/A. We N/A. **Day:** Wd £35. We £40.
SOC PACK: On application from Secretary.
VIS RESTR'S: Welcome except Wed &Fri pm & We am. Book
VIS GF - Round: Wd N/A. We N/A. **Day:** Wd £35. We £40.
FACILITIES: Practice Ground. Lessons from Professional.

ROYAL PORTRUSH (VALLEY) MAP 10 B1

Dunluce Road, Portrush, Antrim.
Half-a-mile from Portrush on main Bushmills Road.
CONTACT: Miss Wilma Erskine, Sec/Manager. Tel: 0265 822311.
COURSE: 6,273yds, PAR 70, SSS 70. Links course.
SOC RESTR'S: Welcome except Weekends am.
SOC GF - Round: Wd N/A. We N/A. **Day:** Wd £15. We £20.
SOC PACK: On application.
VIS RESTR'S: Please book.
VIS GF - Round: Wd N/A. We N/A. **Day:** Wd £15. We £20.
FACILITIES: Bar & Restaurant.

NORTHERN IRELAND

SHANDON PARK GOLF CLUB MAP 10 B1

Shandon Park, Belfast, Antrim BT5 6NY.
3 miles from City centre in East Belfast.

CONTACT: H Wallace, General Manager. Tel: 0232 793730.
COURSE: 6,261yds, PAR 70, SSS 70. Parkland course.
SOC RESTR'S: Welcome Monday & Friday. 24/60 people.
SOC GF - Round: Wd £18. We £25. **DAY:** Wd N/A. We N/A.
SOC PACK: On application from Secretary.
VIS RESTR'S: Welcome everyday but phone first or book.
VIS GF - Round: Wd £18. We £25. **DAY:** Wd N/A. We N/A.
FACILITIES: Bar & Restaurant

TANDRAGEE GOLF CLUB MAP 10 B2

Markethill Road, Tandragee, Armagh BT62 2ER.
A47 from Portadown towards Newry. Turn right in Tandragee.

CONTACT: R McCready, Secretary/Manager. Tel: 0762 841272.
COURSE: 6,035yds, PAR 69, SSS 69. Parkland course.
SOC RESTR'S: Max 60 Wd & 30 Sunday. Prior written booking.
SOC GF - Round: Wd N/A. We N/A. **DAY:** Wd N/A. We N/A.
SOC PACK: Above Green Fee for 20+.
VIS RESTR'S: Welcome each day till 4.15.
VIS GF - Round: Wd N/A. We N/A. **DAY:** Wd £10. We £15.
FACILITIES: Bar & Restaurant.

Armagh

Down

ARMAGH GOLF CLUB MAP 10 B2

Newry Road, Armagh.
On the A28, under a mile away towards Newry.

CONTACT: June McParland Secretary. Tel: 0861 525861.
COURSE: 6,147yds, PAR 70, SSS 69. Mature parkland course.
SOC RESTR'S: Contact in writing.
SOC GF - Round: Wd N/A. We N/A. **Day:** Wd N/A. We N/A.
SOC PACK: On application.
VIS RESTR'S: Welcome except 12-3 Sat & 12-2 Sun.
VIS GF - Round: Wd N/A. We N/A. **Day:** Wd £10. We £15.
FACILITIES: Restaurant, Bar, Pro-shop & Snooker.

ARDGLASS GOLF CLUB MAP 10 B2

Castle Place, Ardglass, Down BT30 7TP.
From Belfast to Downpatrick to Ardglass on B1.

CONTACT: A Cannon, Secretary. Tel: 0396 841219.
COURSE: 6,031yds, PAR 70, SSS 69. Scenic seaside course.
SOC RESTR'S: Welcome except on Saturdays.
SOC GF - Round: Wd N/A. We N/A. **DAY:** Wd £12. We £18.
SOC PACK: Full Catering available.
VIS RESTR'S: Welcome.
VIS GF - Round: Wd N/A. We N/A. **DAY:** Wd £13. We £18.
FACILITIES: Bar & Catering.

PORTADOWN GOLF CLUB MAP 10 B2

Gilford Road, Portadown, Craigavon, Armagh BT63 5LF.
A59, south-east of Portadown for 2 miles, entrance on right.

CONTACT: Mrs L Holloway, Sec/Manager. Tel: 0762 355356.
COURSE: 6,147yds, PAR 70, SSS 70. Parkland course.
SOC RESTR'S: Welcome except Tuesdays & Saturdays.
SOC GF - Round: Wd N/A. We N/A. **Day:** Wd N/A. We N/A.
SOC PACK: On application.
VIS RESTR'S: Welcome except Tue & Sat. Reduced GF for Ladies.
VIS GF - Round: Wd £15. We £18. **Day:** Wd N/A. We N/A.
FACILITIES: Squash, Snooker & Indoor Bowls.

BRIGHT CASTLE GOLF CLUB MAP 10 B2

Coniamstown Road, Bright, Downpatrick, Down BT30 8LU.
Off the main Downpatrick - Killogh Road. Signposted.

CONTACT: G Ennis, Manager. Tel: 0396 841319.
COURSE: 7,143yds, PAR 74, SSS 74. Parkland course.
SOC RESTR'S: Any time - no restrictions.
SOC GF - Round: Wd N/A. We N/A. **Day:** Wd £10. We £12.
SOC PACK: On application.
VIS RESTR'S: Any time. Summer twilight GF £4 after 6.
VIS GF - Round: Wd N/A. We N/A. **Day:** Wd £10. We £12.
FACILITIES: Bar & Catering.

DOWN

CARNALEA GOLF CLUB MAP 10 B1

Station Road, Bangor, Down BT19 1EZ.
2 miles west of Bangor.

CONTACT: JH Crozier, Secretary/Manager. Tel: 0247 270368.
COURSE: 5,550yds, PAR 68, SSS 67. Parkland by Belfast Lough.
SOC RESTR'S: Min 20. Welcome except Weekends.
SOC GF - Round: Wd £9. We N/A. **Day:** Wd N/A. We N/A.
SOC PACK: No package.
VIS RESTR'S: Welcome.
VIS GF - Round: Wd £10. We £13. **Day:** Wd N/A. We N/A.
FACILITIES: Bar & Full Catering. A la Carte menu.

CLANDEBOYE GOLF CLUB MAP 10 B1

Conlig, Newtownards, Down BT23 3PN.
In Conlig off A21 Bangor - Newtownards Road.

CONTACT: I Marks, Secretary/Manager. Tel: 0247 271767.
COURSE: 6,468yds, PAR 71, SSS 72. Parkland/heathland course.
SOC RESTR'S: Min. 20. Welcome except Thur. Winter Mon & Fri.
SOC GF - Round: Wd £15. We N/A. **Day:** Wd N/A. We N/A.
SOC PACK: Cost varies with type of meal required.
VIS RESTR'S: Must be with a Member Sat & certain times Sun.
VIS GF - Round: Wd £17.50. We N/A. **Day:** Wd £23. We N/A.
FACILITIES: Bar, Catering & Practice Ground.

DOWNPATRICK GOLF CLUB MAP 10 B2

43 Saul Road, Downpatrick, Down BT30 6PA.
2 miles south-east of Downpatrick.

CONTACT: Mrs Vaughan. Tel: 0396 615947.
COURSE: 6,400yds, PAR 70, SSS 69. Parkland course.
SOC RESTR'S: Restricted Sundays (max.30).
SOC GF - Round: Wd N/A. We N/A. **Day:** Wd £13. We £18.
SOC PACK: 20% reduction Weekdays for 20+.
VIS RESTR'S: Welcome.
VIS GF - Round: Wd N/A. We N/A. **Day:** Wd £13. We £18.
FACILITIES: Full Clubhouse Facilities incl. Snooker.

KIRKISTOWN CASTLE GOLF CLUB MAP 10 B2

142 Main Road, Cloughey, Newtownards, Down BT22 1HZ.
A20 to Kircubbin, B173 to Cloughey joining A2.

CONTACT: D Ryan, Secretary/Manager. Tel: 02477 71233.
COURSE: 6,167yds, PAR 69, SSS 70. Links course.
SOC RESTR'S: Welcome except Weekends.
SOC GF - Round: Wd £10. We N/A. **Day:** Wd N/A. We N/A.
SOC PACK: None.
VIS RESTR'S: Welcome.
VIS GF - Round: Wd £12. We £20. **Day:** Wd N/A. We N/A.
FACILITIES: Catering.

ROYAL BELFAST MAP 10 B1

Station Road, Craigavad, Holywood, Down BT19 0BP.
2 miles east of Holywood on A2.

CONTACT: IM Piggot, Secretary/Manager. Tel: 0232 428165.
COURSE: 5,963yds, PAR 70, SSS 69. Parkland course.
SOC RESTR'S: By arrangement.
SOC GF - Round: Wd £20. We N/A. **Day:** Wd N/A. We N/A.
SOC PACK: No package.
VIS RESTR'S: Welcome except Thur all day & Sat before 4.30.
VIS GF - Round: Wd £20. We £25. **Day:** Wd N/A. We N/A.
FACILITIES: Full Bar & Catering.

ROYAL COUNTY DOWN MAP 10 B2

Newcastle, Down BT33 0AN.
30 miles south of Belfast.

CONTACT: PE Rolph, Secretary. Tel: 0396 723314.
COURSE: 6,968yds, PAR 71, SSS 73. Championship links course.
SOC RESTR'S: Welcome except Wednesday & Weekends.
SOC GF- Round: Wd £40. We £40. **Day:** Wd £40. We £50.
SOC PACK: No package.
VIS RESTR'S: Welcome except Saturdays.
VIS GF - Round: Wd £30. We £40. **Day:** Wd £40. We £50.
FACILITIES: 18 hole course, Bar & Catering.

SCRABO GOLF CLUB MAP 10 B1

233 Scrabo Road, Newtownards, Down BT23 4SL.
Follow signs for Scrabo Tower.

CONTACT: J Fraser, Secretary/Manager. Tel: 0247 812355.
COURSE: 6,232yds, PAR 71, SSS 71. Hilly course.
SOC RESTR'S: Min. 20. Welcome except Saturday.
SOC GF - Round: Wd N/A. We N/A. **Day:** Wd £14. We £19.
SOC PACK: Contact Secretary/Manager for details.
VIS RESTR'S: Welcome except Saturday.
VIS GF - Round: Wd N/A. We N/A. **Day:** Wd £15. We £20.
FACILITIES: Snooker.

WARRENPOINT GOLF CLUB MAP 10 B2

Lower Dromore Road, Warrenpoint BT34 3LN.
South from Belfast on A24, then east on A2 coastal road.

CONTACT: J McMahon, Secretary. Tel: 0693 753695.
COURSE: 6,288yds, PAR 71, SSS 70. Parkland course.
SOC RESTR'S: Contact in advance.
SOC GF - Round: Wd £12. We N/A. **Day:** Wd N/A. We N/A.
SOC PACK: On application from Secretary.
VIS RESTR'S: Welcome except Tuesday, Wednesday & Saturday.
VIS GF - Round: Wd £12. We £21. **Day:** Wd N/A. We N/A.
FACILITIES: Full Clubhouse Facilities incl Snooker & Squash.

NORTHERN IRELAND

Londonderry

Tyrone

CASTLEROCK GOLF CLUB MAP 10 B1

Circular Road, Castlerock, Londonderry BT51 4TJ.
6 miles west of Coleraine.

CONTACT: RG McBride, Secretary/Manager. Tel: 0265 848314.
COURSE: 6,687yds, PAR 73, SSS 72. Links course.
SOC RESTR'S: Welcome Monday to Friday.
SOC GF - Round: Wd £13. We N/A. **Day:** Wd £20. We N/A.
SOC PACK: No special society rates.
VIS RESTR'S: Welcome except Weekends before 11.
VIS GF - Round: Wd £13. We £25. **Day:** Wd £20. We £30.
FACILITIES: Restaurant & Snooker.

DUNGANNON GOLF CLUB MAP 10 B1

Springfield Lane, Dungannon, Tyrone BT70 1QX.
Half-a-mile leaving Dungannon on Donaghmore Road.

CONTACT: Mr F McNamee, Secretary. Tel: 0868 27338.
COURSE: 5,941yds, PAR 71, SSS 68. Parkland course.
SOC RESTR'S: Any day except Saturday March to October.
SOC GF - Round: Wd £10. We £13. **Day:** Wd N/A. We N/A.
SOC PACK: Meals by arrangement with Caterer.
VIS RESTR'S: Any day except Saturday.
VIS GF - Round: Wd £10. We £13. **Day:** Wd N/A. We N/A.
FACILITIES: Bar.

CITY OF DERRY GOLF CLUB MAP 10 B1

Victoria Road, Londonderry.
2 miles from east end of Craigavon Bridge.

CONTACT: P Doherty, Hon. Secretary. Tel: 0504 46369.
COURSE: 6,487yds, PAR 71, SSS 71. Parkland course.
SOC RESTR'S: Preferably Weekdays am. (negotiable).
SOC GF - Round: Wd N/A. We N/A. **Day:** Wd £12. We N/A.
SOC PACK: Golf + Evening meal £15-£20 per person.
VIS RESTR'S: Welcome except Wd after 4. Sat before 4.
VIS GF - Round: Wd N/A. We N/A. **Day:** Wd £12. We £14.
FACILITIES: 9-hole Course, Bar, Dining Room & Snooker.

KILLYMOON GOLF CLUB MAP 10 B1

Killymoon Road, Cookstown, Tyrone BT80 8TW.
Signposted from A29, south of Cookstown.

CONTACT: Reception. Tel: 06487 63762.
COURSE: 6,012yds, PAR 70, SSS 69. Parkland course.
SOC RESTR'S: Welcome except Sat. Max 20. Sun. Thur ladies.
SOC GF - Round: Wd N/A. We N/A. **Day:** Wd £13. We £15.
SOC PACK: Not available. Above GF for 20+.
VIS RESTR'S: Welcome except Sunday pm.
VIS GF - Round: Wd N/A. We N/A. **Day:** Wd £13. We £15.
FACILITIES: Full Catering.

PORTSTEWART (STRAND) MAP 10 B1

Strand Head, Portstewart, Londonderry.
Just outside the town.

CONTACT: M Moss, Manager. Tel: 0265 832015.
COURSE: 6,714yds, PAR 72, SSS 73. Links course.
SOC RESTR'S: Max. 20. Welcome Tuesday to Friday.
SOC GF - Round: Wd £20. We £28. **Day:** Wd £28. We £37.
SOC PACK: Weekends on application.
VIS RESTR'S: Welcome except Saturdays.
VIS GF - Round: Wd £20. We £28. **Day:** Wd £28. We £37.
FACILITIES: 2nd 18-hole course, SSS 64. Catering & Bowling.

NEWTOWNSTEWART GOLF CLUB MAP 10 B1

Golf Course Road, Newtownstewart, Tyrone BT78 4HU.
B84 from Newtownstewart - approx 2 miles.

CONTACT: Miss D Magee, Sec/Manageress. Tel: 0662 661466.
COURSE: 5,979yds, PAR 70, SSS 69. Parkland course.
SOC RESTR'S: No limit on size or days. Book with Secretary.
SOC GF - Round: Wd N/A. We N/A. **Day:** Wd £8. We £10.
SOC PACK: 25% reduction on Green Fees over £160.
VIS RESTR'S: Welcome except Club Comp day. Please phone.
VIS GF - Round: Wd N/A. We N/A. **Day:** Wd £8. We £10.
FACILITIES: Bar, Restaurant & Snooker.

TYRONE

OMAGH GOLF CLUB MAP 10 B1

Dublin Road, Omagh, Tyrone BT78 1HQ.
Half-a-mile from town centre on A5.

CONTACT: Mrs Florence Caldwell, Secretary. Tel: 0662 243160.
COURSE: 5,695yds, PAR 70, SSS 68. Parkland course.
SOC RESTR'S: Welcome Weekdays.
SOC GF - Round: Wd N/A. **We** N/A. **Day: Wd** £10. **We** N/A.
SOC PACK: Reduction for 20 & over. Meals available.
VIS RESTR'S: Welcome any day except Tuesday & Saturday.
VIS GF - Round: Wd N/A. **We** N/A. **Day: Wd** £10. **We** £15.
FACILITIES: Bar.

STRABANE GOLF CLUB MAP 10 B1

Ballycolman Road, Strabane, Tyrone.
Just off main Omagh-Strabane Road.

CONTACT: T Doherty, Secretary. Tel: 0504 382271.
COURSE: 5,865yds, PAR 69, SSS 69. Parkland course.
SOC RESTR'S: Welcome Weekdays.
SOC GF - Round: Wd N/A. **We** N/A. **Day: Wd** £10. **We** N/A.
SOC PACK: No package.
VIS RESTR'S: Welcome Weekdays.
VIS GF - Round: Wd N/A. **We** N/A. **Day: Wd** £10. **We** N/A.
FACILITIES: Bar, Snooker & Dining room.

REPUBLIC OF IRELAND

IF Northern Ireland can boast two of Europe's greatest links courses in Royal County Down and Royal Portrush, then the golfing fraternity in the South can point with equal pride and justification to Portmarnock and Ballybunion. The former, just north of Dublin, and the latter, deep in the south-west corner of Ireland, provide the unique opportunities of sampling seaside golf both ancient and modern. Portmarnock's original 18 holes were laid down in 1894 and a further 18 have since been added. Ballybunion's Old Course dates from 1896, with its New Course having the distinction of being designed by Robert Trent Jones.

Royal Dublin provides more testing links golf close to the capital, while on the other side of the country on the Atlantic seaboard stands Lahinch, older than either Portmarnock or Ballybunion and laid out by Old Tom Morris and where, so the locals tell you, the club barometer was once replaced by a notice reading 'See Goats - if they're sheltering in the lee of the clubhouse, rain is on the way!'

Not too far from Ballybunion lies the inland gem of the splendidly-named Killarney Golf and Fishing Club. Catering for those with rod-and-line is the fine expanse of Lough Leane, while the golfer will find 36 holes on offer here, most notably the Killeen Course, which has hosted the Irish Open. Head from Dublin towards Waterford and you'll come across Ireland's newest Championship venue, the Jack Nicklaus-designed Mount Juliet, which includes the welcome and sensible addition of a 3-hole teaching academy. And for a little Irish golfing history, sample the delightful 9-holes at Sutton, just north-east of Dublin, where the legendary amateur Joe Carr learned the game.

Golf in Ireland, on both sides of the border, will provide you with a warmth and a welcome unrivalled in Europe. The courses are uncrowded, the value splendid and if there is such a place as Golfers' Paradise, it might bear more than a passing resemblance to the Emerald Isle.

CLARE

Carlow

Clare

CARLOW GOLF CLUB MAP 10 B3

Deerpark, Carlow.
2 miles north of Carlow town on N9.
CONTACT: Margaret Meaney, Secretary. Tel: +353 503 31695.
COURSE: 6,391yds, PAR 70, SSS 70. Undulating parkland course.
SOC RESTR'S: Welcome except Sunday & Tuesday.
SOC GF - Round: Wd N/A. We N/A. **Day:** Wd IR£17. We IR£20.
SOC PACK: Dinner, IR£23.50. Wd - IR£27.50. We.
VIS RESTR'S: Not before 10.30 or 1-2.30, Tuesday before 11.
VIS GF - Round: Wd N/A. We N/A. **Day:** Wd IR£20. We IR£20.
FACILITIES: Practice Ground, Putting Green & Restaurant.

ENNIS GOLF CLUB MAP 10 A3

Drumbiggle, Ennis, Clare.
West off N18 Limerick to Galway Road.
CONTACT: M Walshe, Hon. Sec. Tel: +353 65 24074.
COURSE: 5,813yds, PAR 69, SSS 68. Parkland course.
SOC RESTR'S: Welcome except Sunday.
SOC GF - Round: Wd N/A. We N/A. **Day:** Wd N/A. We N/A.
SOC PACK: On application.
VIS RESTR'S: Welcome.
VIS GF - Round: Wd N/A. We N/A. **Day:** Wd IR£15. We IR£15.
FACILITIES: Bar & Catering.

LAHINCH (OLD COURSE) MAP 10 A2

Lahinch, Clare.
30 miles north-west from Shannon Airport.
CONTACT: Secretary. Tel: +353 65 81003.
COURSE: 6,702yds, PAR 72, SSS 73. Championship links course.
SOC RESTR'S: Welcome Weekdays. 1994 Soc GF on application.
SOC GF - Round: Wd N/A. We N/A. **Day:** Wd N/A. We N/A.
SOC PACK: Under review.
VIS RESTR'S: No restrictions.
VIS GF - Round: Wd IR£25. We IR£25. **Day:** Wd N/A. We N/A.
FACILITIES: Bar, Full Catering, Club Hire & Pro-shop.

Cavan

COUNTY CAVAN GOLF CLUB MAP 10 B2

Arnmore House, Drumelis, Cavan.
Just outside Cavan Town.
CONTACT: N Cinnamond. Tel: +353 49 31283.
COURSE: 6,035yds, PAR 70, SSS 69. Parkland course.
SOC RESTR'S: Welcome except Wednesday & Sunday.
SOC GF - Round: Wd IR£10. We IR£12. **Day:** Wd N/A. We N/A.
SOC PACK: On application.
VIS RESTR'S: Welcome except Wednesday & Sunday.
VIS GF - Round: Wd £10. We £12. **Day:** Wd N/A. We N/A.
FACILITIES: Bar. Limited Catering all week.

LAHINCH (CASTLE COURSE) MAP 10 A2

Lahinch, Clare.
30 miles north-west from Shannon Airport.
CONTACT: Secretary. Tel: +353 65 81003.
COURSE: 5,265yds, PAR 67, SSS 66. Seaside course.
SOC RESTR'S: Welcome Weekdays. 1994 Soc GF on application.
SOC GF - Round: Wd N/A. We N/A. **Day:** Wd N/A. We N/A.
SOC PACK: Under review.
VIS RESTR'S: No restrictions.
VIS GF - Round: Wd IR£15. We IR£15. **Day:** Wd N/A. We N/A.
FACILITIES: Bar, Catering, Club Hire & Pro-shop.

REPUBLIC OF IRELAND

SHANNON GOLF CLUB MAP 10 A3

Shannon, Clare.
15 miles west of Limerick City.

CONTACT: JJ Quigley, Manager. Tel: +353 61 471849.
COURSE: 6,874yds, PAR 72, SSS 74. Parkland course.
SOC RESTR'S: By prior arrangement.
SOC GF - Round: Wd N/A. We N/A. **Day:** Wd IR£20. We N/A.
SOC PACK: Package tailored to society requests.
VIS RESTR'S: Welcome with Handicap Certificate.
VIS GF - Round: Wd N/A. We N/A. **Day:** Wd IR£20. We IR£25.
FACILITIES: Practice Range, Catering & Bar.

CORK GOLF CLUB MAP 10 A3

Little Island, Cork.
5 miles south-east of Cork City.

CONTACT: M Sands, Secretary/Manager. Tel: +353 21 353451
COURSE: 6,630yds, PAR 72, SSS 70. Championship parkland.
SOC RESTR'S: Welcome by arrangement with Secretary.
SOC GF- Round: Wd N/A. We N/A. **Day:** Wd N/A. We N/A.
SOC PACK: Green Fees & Meal. Rates under review.
VIS RESTR'S: Welcome except Thursday & Weekends. Phone first.
VIS GF - Round: Wd N/A. We N/A. **Day:** Wd IR£23. We IR£26.
FACILITIES: Bar, Catering & Pro-shop.

EAST CORK GOLF CLUB MAP 10 A3

Goatacrue, Midleton, Cork.
10 miles east of Cork City on Waterford Rd.

CONTACT: M. Maloney. Secretary. Tel: +353 21 631687.
COURSE: 5,690 yds, PAR 69, SSS 69. Parkland course.
SOC RESTR'S: Welcome, limited at Weekends.
SOC GF- Round: Wd N/A. We N/A. **Day:** Wd IR£10. We IR£10.
SOC PACK: On application.
VIS RESTR'S: Welcome, limited at Weekends
VIS GF - Round: Wd N/A. We N/A. **Day:** Wd IR£10. We IR£10.
FACILITIES: Bar & Catering.

Cork

BANDON GOLF CLUB MAP 10 A3

Castle Bernard, Bandon, Cork.
2 miles west of Bandon town.

CONTACT: B O'Neill, Hon. Secretary. Tel: +353 23 41998.
COURSE: 6,010yds, PAR 70, SSS 68. Parkland course.
SOC RESTR'S: Restrictions on Sat, Sun & Bank Holidays.
SOC GF - Round: Wd N/A. We N/A. **Day:** Wd N/A. We N/A.
SOC PACK: Green Fees & Meals on application.
VIS RESTR'S: Welcome except We & Bank Holidays.
VIS GF - Round: Wd N/A. We N/A. **Day:** Wd IR£12. We IR£12.
FACILITIES: Bar, Restaurant & Pro-shop.

FERMOY GOLF CLUB MAP 10 A3

Corrin, Fermoy, Cork.
2 miles on Cork side of Fermoy.

CONTACT: N McCarthy, Bar Manager. Tel: +353 25 31472.
COURSE: 6,124yds, PAR 70, SSS 69. Undulating course.
SOC RESTR'S: Welcome, limited at Weekends.
SOC GF- Round: Wd N/A. We N/A. **Day:** Wd N/A. We N/A.
SOC PACK: IR£20 including meal.
VIS RESTR'S: Always welcome. Please phone first.
VIS GF - Round: Wd N/A. We N/A. **Day:** Wd N/A. We N/A.
FACILITIES: Bar, Driving Range & Pro-shop.

CHARLEVILLE GOLF CLUB MAP 10 A3

Ardmore, Charleville, Cork
Turn east from Charleville Main Street.

CONTACT: JA Murphy, Hon. Secretary. Tel: +353 63 81257.
COURSE: 6,430yds, PAR 71, SSS 70. Parkland course.
SOC RESTR'S: Welcome except Weekends.
SOC GF - Round: Wd N/A. We N/A. **Day:** Wd N/A. We N/A.
SOC PACK: No package but meals available in bar.
VIS RESTR'S: Welcome except Weekends.
VIS GF - Round: Wd N/A. We N/A. **Day:** Wd IR£12. We IR£15.
FACILITIES: Bar.

MAHON GOLF CLUB MAP 10 A3

Mahon, Blackrock, Cork City, Cork.
2 miles south of Cork City via Douglas Road.

CONTACT: T O'Connor, Secretary/Manager. Tel: +353 21 362480.
COURSE: 5,269yds, PAR 68, SSS 66. Scenic course.
SOC RESTR'S: Welcome except Fri 8.30-10.30 We 7.30-10.30.
SOC GF - Round: Wd N/A. We N/A. **Day:** Wd IR£7.30. We IR£8.50.
SOC PACK: On request.
VIS RESTR'S: Welcome except Fri 8.30-10.30 & We 7.30-10.30.
VIS GF - Round: Wd N/A. We N/A. **Day:** Wd IR£7.50. We IR£8.50.
FACILITIES: Clubhouse with Full Catering Facilities.

DONEGAL

MALLOW GOLF CLUB MAP 10 A3

Ballyellis, Mallow, Cork.
1 mile from town.
CONTACT: M O'Sullivan Secretary. Tel: +353 22 21963.
COURSE: 6,423yds, PAR 72, SSS 71. Parkland course.
SOC RESTR'S: Welcome except Tuesday (Ladies Day) & Sunday.
SOC GF - Round: Wd N/A. We N/A. **Day:** Wd N/A. We N/A.
SOC PACK: On application.
VIS RESTR'S: Welcome except Tuesday (Ladies Day) & Sunday.
VIS GF - Round: Wd N/A. We N/A. **Day:** Wd IR£13. We IR£16.
FACILITIES: Tennis, Squash & Snooker.

Donegal

MONKSTOWN GOLF CLUB MAP 10 A3

Monkstown, Cork.
7 miles south-east of Cork City.
CONTACT: GA Finn, Manager. Tel: +353 21 841376.
COURSE: 6,199yds, PAR 70, SSS 69. Parkland course.
SOC RESTR'S: Welcome Tuesday & Wednesday & Weekends.
SOC GF - Round: Wd N/A. We N/A. **Day:** Wd N/A. We N/A.
SOC PACK: On application.
VIS RESTR'S: Welcome.
VIS GF - Round: Wd N/A. We N/A. **Day:** Wd IR£20. We IR£23.
FACILITIES: Bar & Dining Room.

BALLYLIFFIN GOLF CLUB MAP 10 B1

Ballyliffin, Carndonagh, Donegal.
6 miles from Carndonagh, 11 miles from Buncrana.
CONTACT: K O'Doherty, Hon. Secretary Tel: + 353 77 74417.
COURSE: 6,102yds, PAR 72, SSS 70. Links course.
SOC RESTR'S: Phone for booking preferably Weekdays.
SOC GF - Round: Wd N/A. **Sunday** N/A. **Day:** Wd N/A. We N/A.
SOC PACK: 1994 package not decided.
VIS RESTR'S: Reserved for members: 9.30-10.30 & 1-3.15.
VIS GF - Round: Wd N/A. We N/A. **Day:** Wd IR£8. We IR£12.
FACILITIES: Putting Green & 3-hole Practice Area,

MUSKERRY GOLF CLUB MAP 10 A3

Carrierdhan, Cork.
7 miles north-west of Cork City.
CONTACT: JJ Moyniman, Sec/Manager. Tel: +353 21 385297.
COURSE: 5,786yds, PAR 70, SSS 70. Wooded parkland course.
SOC RESTR'S: Welcome except Weekends & 1-2 daily.
SOC GF - Round: Wd N/A. We N/A. **Day:** Wd N/A. We N/A.
SOC PACK: On application.
VIS RESTR'S: Not Wed afternoon, Thur until 12.30 or We.
VIS GF - Round: Wd IR£10. We N/A. **Day:** Wd N/A. We N/A.
FACILITIES: Bar & Catering.

BUNDORAN GOLF CLUB MAP 10 A1

Bundoran, Donegal.
N15 Sligo-Donegal Road along coast of Donegal Bay.
CONTACT: Secretary. Tel: +353 72 41302.
COURSE: 6,326yds, PAR 70, SSS 71. Seaside/parkland course.
SOC RESTR'S: Contact in advance.
SOC GF - Round: Wd N/A. We N/A. **Day:** Wd N/A. We N/A.
SOC PACK: On application.
VIS RESTR'S: Must contact in advance.
VIS GF - Round: Wd IR£12. We IR£14. **Day:** Wd IR£20. We IR£20.
FACILITIES: Bar, Restaurant, Club Hire & Pro-shop.

DONEGAL GOLF CLUB MAP 10 A1

Murvagh, Donegal.
7 miles south of Donegal on N18.
CONTACT: J Nixon, Secretary. Tel: +353 73 22166.
COURSE: 7,271yds, PAR 72, SSS 73. Links course.
SOC RESTR'S: H'cap Cert required. Not Sundays.
SOC GF - Round: Wd IR£13. We N/A. **Day:** Wd N/A. We N/A.
SOC PACK: On application.
VIS RESTR'S: Handicap Certificate required.
VIS GF - Round: Wd IR£13. We IR£16. **Day:** Wd N/A. We N/A.
FACILITIES: Bar, Restaurant, Club Hire.

**RAC HOTEL GUIDE
Great Britain & Ireland**
Now in its **ninetieth year**,
the authoritative guide to over 6,000 hotels.
Special anniversary competition.
All establishments inspected and approved by the RAC.
Full colour atlas section with all hotel locations shown
Includes discount vouchers worth up to £150
Price £12.99
Available from bookshops
or direct from the RAC on 0235 834885

REPUBLIC OF IRELAND

DUNFANAGHY GOLF CLUB MAP 10 B1

Dunfanaghy, Letterkenny, Donegal.
Main Letterkenny to Dunfanaghy Road - N56.

CONTACT: Mary Quinn, Secretary. Tel: +353 74 36335.
COURSE: 5,066yds, PAR 68, SSS 66. Seaside links course.
SOC RESTR'S: Welcome most days by booking.
SOC GF - Round: Wd IR£7. We IR£7. Day: Wd N/A. We N/A.
SOC PACK: None.
VIS RESTR'S: Welcome at all times.
VIS GF - Round: Wd IR£10. We IR£12. Day: Wd N/A. We N/A.
FACILITIES: Bar & Restaurant.

NARIN & PORTNOO GOLF CLUB MAP 10 A1

Portnoo, Donegal.
From Donegal town to Ardara - 7 miles to course.

CONTACT: S Murphy, Club Steward. Tel: +353 75 45107.
COURSE: 6,750yds, PAR 69, SSS 67. Links course.
SOC RESTR'S: Welcome. No societies during July & August.
SOC GF - Round: Wd N/A. We N/A. Day: Wd N/A. We N/A.
SOC PACK: On application.
VIS RESTR'S: Welcome.
VIS GF - Round: Wd N/A. We N/A. Day: Wd IR£10. We IR£13.
FACILITIES: Bar & Snacks.

NORTH WEST GOLF CLUB MAP 10 B1

Lisfannon, Fahan, Donegal.
12 miles west from Derry on Buncrana Rd.

CONTACT: S McBriarty, Profesional. Tel: +353 77 61027.
COURSE: 6,203yds, PAR 69, SSS 69. Links course.
SOC RESTR'S: Welcome.
SOC GF - Round: Wd N/A. We N/A. Day: Wd N/A. We N/A.
SOC PACK: Can be negotiated with Professional.
VIS RESTR'S: Welcome.
VIS GF - Round: Wd N/A. We N/A. Day: Wd IR£10. We IR£13.
FACILITIES: Bar & Catering.

PORTSALON GOLF CLUB MAP 10 B1

Portsalon, Letterkenny, Donegal.
20 miles north of Letterkenny.

CONTACT: C Toland, Secretary. Tel: +353 74 59459.
COURSE: 5,878yds, PAR 69, SSS 68. Seaside links course.
SOC RESTR'S: Min.15. Welcome Weekdays.
SOC GF - Round: Wd N/A. We N/A. Day: Wd IR£8. We IR£10.
SOC PACK: 18 holes, Lunch, Dinner.
VIS RESTR'S: Welcome.
VIS GF - Round: Wd N/A. We N/A. Day: Wd IR£10. We IR£108.
FACILITIES: Clubhouse, Bar & Restaurant.

ROSAPENNA GOLF CLUB MAP 10 B1

Rosapenna, Letterkenny, Donegal.
22 miles from Letterkenny via Milford.

CONTACT: Secretary. Tel: +353 74 55301.
COURSE: 6,271yds, PAR 70, SSS 71. Links course.
SOC RESTR'S: Contact in advance.
SOC GF - Round: Wd N/A. We N/A. Day: Wd IR£12. We IR£15.
SOC PACK: On application.
VIS RESTR'S: Welcome.
VIS GF - Round: Wd N/A. We N/A. Day: Wd IR£12. We IR£15.
FACILITIES: Bar, Restaurant, Tennis, Snooker & Pro-shop.

Dublin

BALBRIGGAN GOLF CLUB MAP 10 B2

Blackhall, Balbriggan, Dublin.
On main Dublin/Belfast road. South of Balbriggan.

CONTACT: Secretary/Manager. Tel: +353 1 412173.
COURSE: 6,431yds, PAR 71, SSS 70. Parkland course.
SOC RESTR'S: Welcome except 12-2 daily, all day Tue, & We.
SOC GF - Round: Wd IR£14. We N/A. Day: Wd N/A. We N/A.
SOC PACK: Meal, Caddie Car Hire, 18 holes: IR£22.
VIS RESTR'S: Welcome except Tuesday & Weekends.
VIS GF - Round: Wd IR£14. We N/A. Day: Wd N/A. We N/A.
FACILITIES: Bar & Restaurant.

BEAVERSTOWN GOLF CLUB MAP 10 B2

Beaverstown, Donabate, Dublin.
2 miles north of Swords off Main Dublin Road.

CONTACT: LE Smyth, Secretary/Manager. Tel: +353 1 436439.
COURSE: 5,980yds, PAR 71, SSS 70. Parkland course.
SOC RESTR'S: On application.
SOC GF - Round: Wd IR£12. We IR£20. Day: Wd N/A. We N/A.
SOC PACK: IR£25 including meal.
VIS RESTR'S: Welcome except Wednesday & Sunday.
VIS GF - Round: Wd IR£12. We IR£20. Day: Wd N/A. We N/A.
FACILITIES: Bar & Restaurant.

DUBLIN

CLONTARF GOLF CLUB MAP 10 B2

Donnycarney House, Lower Malahide Road, Dublin 3.
NE of City centre - 3 miles via Fairview to Lr Malahide Road.
CONTACT: J Craddock, Professional. Tel: +353 1 331892.
COURSE: 5,970yds, PAR 69, SSS 68. Parkland course.
SOC RESTR'S: Welcome Tuesday & Friday up to 3.30.
SOC GF - Round: Wd IR£21. **We** N/A. **Day:** Wd N/A. **We** N/A.
SOC PACK: Reduced GF for 50+. Meals: IR£12 approx.
VIS RESTR'S: Welcome Weekdays.
VIS GF - Round: Wd IR£21. **We** N/A. **Day:** Wd N/A. **We** N/A.
FACILITIES: Bowling Green.

HERMITAGE GOLF CLUB MAP 10 B2

Lucan, Dublin.
West of Dublin on Galway Road.
CONTACT: K Russell, General Manager. Tel: +353 1 6268491.
COURSE: 6,598yds, PAR 71, SSS 70. Championship parkland.
SOC RESTR'S: Last tee off 2. 00 (check with office).
SOC GF- Round: Wd N/A. **We** N/A. **Day:** Wd N/A. **We** N/A.
SOC PACK: Ranges from IR£36 to IR£42.70 (5 menu choices).
VIS RESTR'S: On application.
VIS GF - Round: Wd IR£25. **We** IR£35. **Day:** Wd N/A. **We** N/A.
FACILITIES: Bar, Restaurant & Pro-shop.

DUN LAOGHAIRE GOLF CLUB MAP 10 B2

Tivoli Road, Dun Laoghaire, Dublin.
7 miles south of Dublin, half-a-mile from Ferry Port.
CONTACT: T Stewart, Manager. Tel: +353 1 2803916.
COURSE: 5,990yds, PAR 70, SSS 69. Parkland course.
SOC RESTR'S: Welcome Tuesday & Friday.
SOC GF - Round: Wd N/A. **We** N/A. **Day:** Wd IR£25. **We** N/A.
SOC PACK: None.
VIS RESTR'S: Welcome except Thursday & Weekends.
VIS GF - Round: Wd N/A. **We** N/A. **Day:** Wd £25. **We** N/A.
FACILITIES: Bar & Restaurant.

HOWTH GOLF CLUB MAP 10 B2

St. Fintan's, Carrickbrack Road, Sutton, Dublin 13.
9 miles north of Dublin City, 1 mile from Sutton Cross.
CONTACT: Ann MacNeice, Secretary. Tel: +353 1 323055.
COURSE: 6,143yds, PAR 71, SSS 69. Moorland course.
SOC RESTR'S: Welcome Weekdays.
SOC GF - Round: Wd IR£16. **We** N/A. **Day:** Wd N/A. **We** N/A.
SOC PACK: None.
VIS RESTR'S: Welcome Weekdays.
VIS GF - Round: Wd IR£16. **We** N/A. **Day:** Wd N/A. **We** N/A.
FACILITIES: Bar Snacks & Drinks.

EDMONDSTOWN GOLF CLUB MAP 10 B2

Edmondstown Road, Rathfarnham, Dublin 14.
5 miles south of Dublin.
CONTACT: SS Davies, Secretary/Manager. Tel: +353 1 931082.
COURSE: 6,193yds, PAR 70, SSS 69. Testing parkland course.
SOC RESTR'S: Min. 25. Larger by arrangement.
SOC GF - Round: Wd IR£16. **We** IR£20. **Day:** Wd N/A. **We** N/A.
SOC PACK: Wd before 11.30 IR£27. Sat morning IR£30.
VIS RESTR'S: Welcome. Dress code in operation.
VIS GF - Round: Wd IR£18. **We** IR£22. **Day:** Wd N/A. **We** N/A.
FACILITIES: Bar & Restaurant.

PORTMARNOCK GOLF CLUB MAP 10 B2

Portmarnock, Dublin.
8 miles north-east Dublin City.
CONTACT: W Bornemann, Sec/Manager. Tel: +353 1 8462968.
COURSE: 6,632yds, PAR 72, SSS 74. Championship links.
SOC RESTR'S: Max. 60. Welcome Mon, Tues & Fri.
SOC GF-Round: Wd IR£40. **We** IR£50. **Day:** Wd IR£40. **We** IR£50.
SOC PACK: No package.
VIS RESTR'S: Welcome Weekdays. Please book.
VIS GF - Round: Wd IR£40. **We** IR£50. **Day:** Wd IR£40. **We** IR£50.
FACILITIES: Bar & Catering.

ELM PARK GOLF CLUB MAP 10 B2

Nutley Lane, Donnybrook, Dublin 4.
2 miles south of Dublin City.
CONTACT: A McCormack, Secretary. Tel: +353 1 2693438.
COURSE: 5,964yds, PAR 69, SSS 68. Parkland course.
SOC RESTR'S: Welcome Tuesday.
SOC GF - Round: Wd IR£30. **We** N/A. **Day:** Wd N/A. **We** N/A.
SOC PACK: On application.
VIS RESTR'S: Welcome with prior booking.
VIS GF - Round: Wd IR£30. **We** IR£35. **Day:** Wd N/A **We** N/A.
FACILITIES: Bar & Restaurant.

ROYAL DUBLIN GOLF CLUB MAP 10 B2

Bull Island, Dollymount, Dublin 3.
3 miles north-east of Dublin on road to Howth.
CONTACT: JA Lambe, Secretary/Manager. Tel: +353 1 336346.
COURSE: 6,848yds, PAR 71, SSS 71. Championship links.
SOC RESTR'S: Max. 100. Monday, Thursday & Friday.
SOC GF - Round: Wd N/A. **We** N/A. **Day:** Wd N/A. **We** N/A.
SOC PACK: IR£40 to include catering & snacks before golf.
VIS RESTR'S: Welcome except Wed, Sat &1-2. every day.
VIS GF - Round: Wd IR£35. **We** IR£45. **Day:** Wd N/A. **We** N/A.
FACILITIES: Large Practice Ground, Indoor Video Tuition & Sauna.

REPUBLIC OF IRELAND

SKERRIES GOLF CLUB   MAP 10 B2

Hacketstown, Skerries, Dublin.
10 miles north of Dublin.

CONTACT: Manager. Tel: +353 1 8491567.
COURSE: 6,174yds, PAR 73, SSS 72. Undulating parkland course.
SOC RESTR'S: Welcome Mon, Tues & Fri. Not between 1-2.
SOC GF - Round: Wd IR£17. We N/A. Day: Wd N/A. We N/A.
SOC PACK: IR£17 plus choice of Snack, Lunch or Dinner.
VIS RESTR'S: Welcome except between 1 & 2.
VIS GF - Round: Wd IR£17. We IR£17. Day: Wd N/A. We N/A.
FACILITIES: Bar, Restaurant & Snooker.

SLADE VALLEY GOLF CLUB   MAP 10 B2

Lynch Park, Brittas, Dublin.
9 miles west of Dublin City.

CONTACT: P Maguire, Secretary/Manager. Tel: +353 1 582183.
COURSE: 5,837yds, PAR 69, SSS 67. Undulating course.
SOC RESTR'S: Welcome Weekdays.
SOC GF - Round: Wd IR£14. We N/A. Day: Wd IR£14. We N/A.
SOC PACK: Approx. IR£25.
VIS RESTR'S: Welcome Weekdays.
VIS GF - Round: Wd IR£14. We N/A. Day: Wd IR£14. We N/A.
FACILITIES: Bar Snacks & Drinks.

WOODBROOK GOLF CLUB   MAP 10 B2

Woodbrook, Bray, Dublin.
8 miles south of Dublin towards Bray.

CONTACT: Mrs O'Grady, Secretary. Tel: +353 1 2824799.
COURSE: 6,541yds, PAR 72, SSS 71. Parkland course.
SOC RESTR'S: Welcome Weekdays.
SOC GF - Round: Wd IR£25. We N/A. Day: Wd N/A. We N/A.
SOC PACK: On application to Secretary.
VIS RESTR'S: Welcome Weekdays some restrictions.
VIS GF - Round: Wd IR£25. We IR£35. Day: Wd N/A. We N/A.
FACILITIES: Snooker.

RAC HOTELS IN EUROPE
The ideal 'travel companion' with over 1,500 selected hotels in 20 countries, including Eastern Europe. Hotel entries contain phone and fax numbers, national star rating, restaurant, prices, credit cards and where English is spoken. Full colour atlas section with all hotel locations shown. Parking law - Speed limits - Public holidays - Banks - Shops - Fuel availability
Price £9.99
Available from bookshops
or direct from the RAC on 0235 834885

Galway

BALLINASLOE GOLF CLUB   MAP 10 A2

Rossgloss, Ballinasloe, Galway.
Off Ballinasloe/Portumna Road - 2 miles from town centre.

CONTACT: T Glynn. Tel: +353 950 42126.
COURSE: 6,445yds, PAR 72, SSS 70. Parkland course.
SOC RESTR'S: Welcome except most Sun. Tee 2 hours max Sat.
SOC GF - Round: Wd N/A We N/A. Day: Wd N/A. We N/A.
SOC PACK: IR£180 per hour on 1st tee. Gold plus meal IR£12.
VIS RESTR'S: Welcome except Tuesday & Saturday.
VIS GF - Round: Wd N/A. We N/A. Day: Wd IR£10. We IR£12.
FACILITIES: Bar & Restaurant.

CONNEMARA GOLF CLUB   MAP 10 A2

Ballyconneely, Clifden, Galway.
9 miles south-west of Clifden.

CONTACT: J McLaughlin, Secretary/Manager. Tel: +353 95 23502.
COURSE: 6,750yds, PAR 72, SSS 73. Links course.
SOC RESTR'S: Minimum 20. Advanced booking required.
SOC GF - Round: Wd IR£10. We N/A. Day: Wd N/A. We N/A.
SOC PACK: IR£10 rate not available mid-June to mid-September.
VIS RESTR'S: Welcome.
VIS GF - Round: Wd IR£16. We IR£16. Day: Wd N/A. We N/A.
FACILITIES: Bar & Restaurant.

PORTUMNA GOLF CLUB   MAP 10 A2

Portumna, Galway.
2 miles from Portumna on Scariffe Road.

CONTACT: F McClearn, Hon. Secretary +353 91 45044.
COURSE: 5,205yds, PAR 68, SSS 69. Wooded/parkland course.
SOC RESTR'S: Welcome except Sat after mid-day & Sun all day.
SOC GF - Round: Wd IR£10. We N/A. Day: Wd N/A. We N/A.
SOC PACK: IR£8 per round per person in groups of over 20.
VIS RESTR'S: Welcome except Sundays.
VIS GF - Round: Wd IR£10. We IR£10. Day: Wd IR£10. We N/A.
FACILITIES: Bar & Restaurant.

KERRY

TUAM GOLF CLUB   MAP 10 A2

Barnacurragh, Tuam, Galway.
COURSE signposted from Tuam town approx 2 miles.

CONTACT: M Tierney, Secretary/Manager. Tel: +353 93 28993.
COURSE: 6,409yds, PAR 72, SSS 70. Parkland course.
SOC RESTR'S: Play Weekdays.
SOC GF - Round: Wd N/A. We N/A. Day: Wd IR£8. We N/A.
SOC PACK: By arrangement. Professional also available.
VIS RESTR'S: Sun, Competition day, Certain match days.
VIS GF - Round: Wd N/A. We N/A. Day: Wd IR£10. We N/A.
FACILITIES: Practice Area, Pro-shop, Clubhouse & Restaurant.

DOOKS GOLF CLUB   MAP 10 A3

Glenbeigh, Kerry.
Ring of Kerry on N70. 8 miles west of Killorglin.

CONTACT: M Shanahan, Hon Sec. Tel: +353 66 68205.
COURSE: 6,010yds, PAR 70, SSS 68. Seaside course.
SOC RESTR'S: Welcome.
SOC GF - Round: Wd N/A. We N/A. Day: Wd IR£15. We IR£15.
SOC PACK: None.
VIS RESTR'S: Welcome except 9-10, 1-2.30 & after 5.
VIS GF - Round: Wd N/A. We N/A. Day: Wd IR£15. We IR£15.
FACILITIES: Bar & Restaurant.

GOLF CHUMANN CEANN SIBEAL   MAP 10 A3

Ballyferriter, Kerry.
Follow Ballyferriter. Turn right half-a-mile after Ballyferriter.

CONTACT: G Partington, Hon. Sec. Tel: +353 66 56255.
COURSE: 6,440yds, PAR 72, SSS 71. Traditional links course.
SOC RESTR'S: Any time except 1-2.30 on Wed & Sun.
SOC GF-Round: Wd N/A. We N/A. Day: Wd IR£11. We IR£11.
SOC PACK: None.
VIS RESTR'S: Avoid 1-2.30 Wed & Sun.
VIS GF - Round: Wd IR£16. We IR£16. Day: Wd IR£21. We IR£21.
FACILITIES: Bar & Restaurant.

Kerry

BALLYBUNION (OLD COURSE)   MAP 10 A3

Sandhill Road, Ballybunion, Kerry.
1 mile west of Ballybunion.

CONTACT: Secretary. Tel: +353 68 27146.
COURSE: 6,593yds, PAR 71, SSS 72. Championship links course.
SOC RESTR'S: Must book in advance. No weekends.
SOC GF - Round: Wd IR£30. We N/A. Day: Wd IR£40. We N/A.
SOC PACK: On application.
VIS RESTR'S: Must book in advance and have H'cap Cert.
VIS GF - Round: Wd IR£30. We IR£30. Day: Wd IR£40. We IR£40.
FACILITIES: Bar, Restaurant & Club Hire.

BALLYBUNION (NEW COURSE)   MAP 10 A3

Sandhill Road, Ballybunion, Kerry.
1 mile west of Ballybunion.

CONTACT: Secretary. Tel: +353 68 27146.
COURSE: 6,130yds, PAR 71, SSS 72. Links course.
SOC RESTR'S: Must book in advance through Secretary.
SOC GF - Round: Wd IR£20. We IR£20. Day: Wd IR£40. We IR£40.
SOC PACK: On application.
VIS RESTR'S: Must book in advance and have H'cap Cert.
VIS GF - Round: Wd IR£20. We IR£20. Day: Wd IR£40. We IR£40.
FACILITIES: Bar, Restaurant & Club Hire.

KILLARNEY (MAHONY'S POINT)   MAP 10 A3

Mahony's Point, Killarney, Kerry.
Ring of Kerry Road, 3 miles west of Killarney.

CONTACT: Reception. Tel: +353 64 31034.
COURSE: 6,726yds, PAR 72, SSS 72. Parkland course.
SOC RESTR'S: Welcome.
SOC GF - Round: Wd N/A. We N/A. Day: Wd N/A. We N/A.
SOC PACK: Contact Secretary/Manager for terms.
VIS RESTR'S: Welcome.
VIS GF - Round: Wd IR£25. We IR£25. Day: Wd N/A. We N/A.
FACILITIES: Bar, Restaurant, Exercise Room & Sauna.

KILLARNEY (KILLEEN COURSE)   MAP 10 A3

Mahony's Point, Killarney, Co. Kerry.
Ring of Kerry Road, 3 miles west of Killarney.

CONTACT: Reception. Tel: +353 64 31034.
COURSE: 7,081yds, PAR 72, SSS 73. Championship parkland.
SOC RESTR'S: Welcome.
SOC GF - Round: Wd N/A. We N/A. Day: Wd N/A. We N/A.
SOC PACK: Contact Secretary/Manager for terms.
VIS RESTR'S: Welcome.
VIS GF - Round: Wd IR£25. We IR£25. Day: Wd N/A. We N/A.
FACILITIES: Bar, Restaurant, Exercise Room & Sauna.

REPUBLIC OF IRELAND

TRALEE GOLF CLUB MAP 10 A3

West Barrow, Ardfert, Tralee, Kerry.
West just outside Tralee town off the N22.

CONTACT: P Colleran, Secretary/Manager. Tel: +353 66 36379.
COURSE: 6,519yds, PAR 71, SSS 72. Links course.
SOC RESTR'S: Welcome Weekdays.
SOC GF - Round: Wd N/A. We N/A. **Day:** Wd N/A. We N/A.
SOC PACK: Information available on booking.
VIS RESTR'S: Restricted Wednesdays and Weekends.
VIS GF - Round: Wd IR£25. We IR£30. **Day:** Wd IR£35. We N/A.
FACILITIES: Bar & Restaurant. Full Catering by prior arrangement.

WATERVILLE GOLF LINKS MAP 10 AA3

Waterville, Kerry.
N70 south side of 'Ring'. 1 mile outside Waterville.

CONTACT: Reception. Tel: +353 66 7 4102.
COURSE: 7,184yds, PAR 72, SSS 74. Links course.
SOC RESTR'S: Welcome Weekdays Monday to Thursday.
SOC GF - Round: Wd N/A. We N/A. **Day:** Wd N/A. We N/A.
SOC PACK: On request for groups of 20 or more.
VIS RESTR'S: No restrictions except for major tournaments.
VIS GF - Round: Wd IR£35. We IR£35. **Day:** Wd N/A. We N/A.
FACILITIES: Practice Range, Clinics, Bar & Restaurant.

Kildare

BODENSTOWN GOLF CLUB (OLD) MAP 10 B2

Sallins, Kildare.
4 miles outside Naas, near Bodenstown Graveyard.

CONTACT: B Mather, Secretary/Manager. Tel: +353 45 97096.
COURSE: 6,329yds, PAR 72, SSS 70. Parkland course.
SOC RESTR'S: Weekdays. No weekends.
SOC GF - Round: Wd IR£10. We N/A. **Day:** Wd N/A. We N/A.
SOC PACK: No package. GF & Meals individually priced.
VIS RESTR'S: Weekdays. No weekends.
VIS GF - Round: Wd IR£10. We N/A. **Day:** Wd N/A. We N/A.
FACILITIES: Clubhouse & Full Catering.

BODENSTOWN G C (LADYHILL) MAP 10 B2

Sallins, Kildare.
4 miles outside Naas, near Bodenstown Graveyard.

CONTACT: B Mather, Secretary/Manager. Tel: +353 45 97096.
COURSE: 5,772yds, PAR 71, SSS 68. Parkland course.
SOC RESTR'S: Weekdays. Available at Weekends.
SOC GF - Round: Wd IR£10. We IR£8. **Day:** Wd N/A. We N/A.
SOC PACK: No package. GF & Meals individually priced.
VIS RESTR'S: Weekdays. Available at Weekends.
VIS GF - Round: Wd IR£10. We IR£8. **Day:** Wd N/A. We N/A.
FACILITIES: Clubhouse & Full Catering.

KILLEEN GOLF CLUB MAP 10 B2

Kill, Kildare.
Right off N7 at Kill village.

CONTACT: P Carey, Manager. Tel: +353 45 66003.
COURSE: 5,252yds, PAR 69, SSS 67. Parkland course.
SOC RESTR'S: Min 25. Unrestricted Wd. After 11 We.
SOC GF - Round: Wd IR£10. We IR£120. **Day:** Wd N/A. We N/A.
SOC PACK: IR£20 - 18 holes, Tea/Sandwichs, 4-course Meal.
VIS RESTR'S: Unrestricted Weekdays. After 11 Weekends.
VIS GF - Round: Wd IR£10. We IR£12. **Day:** Wd N/A. We N/A.
FACILITIES: Bar & Putting Green.

KNOCKANALLY GOLF CLUB MAP 10 B2

Donadea, Kildare.
3 miles off Dublin/Galway Road - between Kilcock & Enfield.

CONTACT: N Lyons, Secretary. Tel: +353 45 69322.
COURSE: 6,484yds, PAR 72, SSS 72. Parkland course.
SOC RESTR'S: Welcome.
SOC GF - Round: Wd N/A. We N/A. **Day:** Wd IR£15. We IR£18.
SOC PACK: GF + 4-course Meal IR£23 (Wd), IR£26 (We).
VIS RESTR'S: Welcome.
VIS GF - Round: Wd N/A. We N/A. **Day:** Wd IR£15. We IR£18.
FACILITIES: Bar & Restaurant.

BARBERSTOWN CASTLE

Barberstown Castle is one of the first great Irish country houses to open up its splendour to the outside world. The Castle Keep was built in the early 13th century by Nicholas Barby to guard its inhabitants in medieval times. The Elizabethan House, built in the second half of the 16th century, is one of the few houses in this area that has been in continuous occupation for over 400 years. The Victorian House, built in the 1830s by Hugh Barton, completes a heritage that embraces over 750 years of Irish history inviting you to discover the unique attractions of Barberstown Castle.
Straffan, Co. Kildare. (01) 6288157/62788206. Fax: 6277007

146

Kilkenny

Laois

KILKENNY GOLF CLUB — MAP 10 B3

Glendine, Kilkenny.
1 mile north of Kilkenny.

CONTACT: S O'Neill, Secretary/Manager. Tel: +353 56 65400.
COURSE: 6,400yds, PAR 71, SSS 70. Championship parkland.
SOC RESTR'S: By arrangement.
SOC GF - Round: Wd N/A. We N/A. **Day:** Wd IR£17. We IR£18.
SOC PACK: Approx IR£20 including Meal.
VIS RESTR'S: Welcome but Weekends usually busy.
VIS GF - Round: Wd N/A. We N/A. **Day:** Wd IR£17. We IR£18.
FACILITIES: Snooker, TV & Meals.

MOUNT JULIET G & C C — MAP 10 B3

Thomastown, Kilkenny.
Main Dublin/Waterford Road - at Thomastown.

CONTACT: P Behan. Tel: +353 56 24725.
COURSE: 7,100yds, PAR 73, SSS 74. Championship parkland.
SOC RESTR'S: Welcome every day. After 12 on Sat & Sun.
SOC GF - Round: Wd IR£43. We IR£48. **Day:** Wd IR£80. We IR£85.
SOC PACK: Lunch, 36 holes, Dinner (min 20). IR£63 Wd, IR£68 We.
VIS RESTR'S: Welcome.
VIS GF - Round: Wd IR£60. We IR£60. **Day:** Wd IR£92. We IR£92.
FACILITIES: Fishing, Equestrian, Clay Shooting & Tennis.

RAC Motoring Atlas Europe
A fully updated edition of this handy-sized atlas which encompasses unified Germany and other newly defined frontiers. Clear and detailed mapping at 1:1 million scale (16 miles to 1 inch) for Western Europe. Comprehensive index of over 52,000 place names. Compact format ideal for car use.

Price £10.99
Available from bookshops
or direct from the RAC on 0235 834885

HEATH GOLF CLUB — MAP 10 B2

The Heath, Portlaoise, Laois.
4 miles north-east of Portlaoise.

CONTACT: T Tyrell. Tel: +353 502 22244.
COURSE: 6,247yds, PAR 71, SSS 70. Heathland with gorse.
SOC RESTR'S: Welcome except Sundays.
SOC GF - Round: Wd N/A. We N/A. **Day:** Wd N/A. We N/A.
SOC PACK: Meal must be arranged with Steward.
VIS RESTR'S: Welcome.
VIS GF - Round: Wd N/A. We N/A. **Day:** Wd IR£10. We IR£16.
FACILITIES: 10-bay Floodlit Covered Driving Range.

Limerick

CASTLETROY GOLF CLUB — MAP 10 A3

Castletroy, Limerick.
3 miles from Limerick City on N7, turn at signpost.

CONTACT: L Hayes, Secretary/Manager. Tel: +353 61 335753.
COURSE: 6,335yds, PAR 71, SSS 71. Parkland course.
SOC RESTR'S: Welcome Mon, Wed, & Fri. (except 1-2.30).
SOC GF - Round: Wd IR£12. We N/A. **Day:** Wd N/A. We N/A.
SOC PACK: Tailored to requirements.
VIS RESTR'S: Welcome Weekdays.
VIS GF - Round: Wd N/A. We N/A. **Day:** Wd IR£24. We IR£24.
FACILITIES: Bar & Full Catering Service.

REPUBLIC OF IRELAND

LIMERICK GOLF CLUB　　MAP 10 A3

Ballyclough, Limerick.
3 miles south of City.

CONTACT: D McDonogh, Manager. Tel: +353 61 415146.
COURSE: 6,445yds, PAR 72, SSS 71. Championship parkland.
SOC RESTR'S: Welcome except Tuesday & Weekends.
SOC GF - Round: Wd N/A. We N/A. Day: Wd IR£15. We N/A.
SOC PACK: On application.
VIS RESTR'S: Welcome except Tuesday & Weekends.
VIS GF - Round: Wd N/A. We N/A. Day: Wd IR£20. We N/A.
FACILITIES: Full Catering.

DUNDALK GOLF CLUB　　MAP 10 B2

Blackrock, Dundalk, Louth.
2 miles south of Dundalk on Blackrock Road.

CONTACT: Secretary. Tel: +353 42 21731.
COURSE: 6,687yds, PAR 72, SSS 72. Parkland course.
SOC RESTR'S: Max. 50. Welcome except Tuesday & Sunday.
SOC GF - Round: Wd N/A. We N/A. Day: Wd IR£16. We IR£20.
SOC PACK: On application.
VIS RESTR'S: Some restrictions Tuesday & Sunday.
VIS GF - Round: Wd N/A. We N/A. Day: Wd IR£16. We IR£20.
FACILITIES: Bar & Restaurant.

GREENORE GOLF CLUB　　MAP 10 B2

Greenore, Louth.
15 miles south of Newry & 15 miles north of Dundalk.

CONTACT: B Rafferty, Secretary/Manager. Tel: +353 42 73212.
COURSE: 6,506yds, PAR 71, SSS 71. Links course.
SOC RESTR'S: Welcome but must be by arrangement.
SOC GF - Round: Wd N/A. We N/A. Day: Wd N/A. We N/A.
SOC PACK: On application.
VIS RESTR'S: Weekdays none. Weekends by arrangement.
VIS GF - Round: Wd N/A. We N/A. Day: Wd IR£12. We IR£18.
FACILITIES: Bar & Restaurant.

Louth

ARDEE GOLF CLUB　　MAP 10 B2

Townparks, Ardee, Louth.
Just outside Ardee Town to the north.

CONTACT: S Kelly, Secretary/Manager. Tel: +353 41 53227.
COURSE: 6,100yds. PAR 69, SSS 69. Parkland course.
SOC RESTR'S: Welcome Monday to Saturday. 9-1 & 2-3.30.
SOC GF - Round: Wd N/A. We N/A. Day: Wd IR£14. We IR£15.
SOC PACK: 4-course Steak Meal + Golf. Wd IR£25, We IR£26.
VIS RESTR'S: Welcome Weekdays & Saturday afternoon.
VIS GF - Round: Wd N/A. We N/A. Day: Wd IR£15. We IR£15.
FACILITIES: Bar & Restaurant.

Mayo

COUNTY LOUTH GOLF CLUB　　MAP 10 B2

Baltray, Drogheda, Louth.
4 miles north-east of Drogheda.

CONTACT: M Delany, Secretary/Manager. Tel: +353 41 22329.
COURSE: 6,792yds, PAR 73, SSS 72. Championship links.
SOC RESTR'S: Welcome except Tuesday & some Weekends.
SOC GF - Round: Wd N/A. We N/A. Day: Wd IR£25. We IR£30.
SOC PACK: Available from Secretary.
VIS RESTR'S: Welcome except Tuesday & some Weekends.
VIS GF - Round: Wd N/A. We N/A. Day: Wd IR£27. We IR£33.
FACILITIES: Bar & Restaurant.

CASTLEBAR GOLF CLUB　　MAP 10 A2

Rocklands, Castlebar, Mayo.
On the N84, 1 mile south of Castlebar Town.

CONTACT: Secretary. Tel: +353 94 21649.
COURSE: 6,109yds PAR 70, SSS 69. Parkland course.
SOC RESTR'S: Welcome Weekdays.
SOC GF - Round: Wd IR£10. We N/A. Day: Wd N/A. We N/A.
SOC PACK: On application through Secretary.
VIS RESTR'S: Welcome Weekdays.
VIS GF - Round: Wd IR£10. We IR£10. Day: Wd N/A. We N/A.
FACILITIES: Pro-shop & Catering.

MONAGHAN

WESTPORT GOLF CLUB — MAP 10 A2

Caroholly, Westport, Mayo.
2 miles from Westport - off Newport Road.

CONTACT: Reception. Tel: +353 98 25113.
COURSE: 6,959yds PAR 73, SSS 73. Links course.
SOC RESTR'S: Welcome except Wed. 1.45-3. We 8-10 &1-3.
SOC GF - Round: Wd N/A. **We** N/A. **Day:** Wd IR£12. **We** IR£15.
SOC PACK: Over 60 - IR£2 reduction. Over 100 - IR£3 reduction.
VIS RESTR'S: Welcome except Wed. 1.45-3. We 8-10 &1-3.
VIS GF - Round: Wd N/A. **We** N/A. **Day:** Wd IR£15. **We** IR£18.
FACILITIES: Pro-shop & Catering.

Meath

BLACKBUSH GOLF CLUB — MAP 10 B2

Thomastown, Dunshaughlin, Meath.
2 miles east of Dunshaughlin on Ratoath Road.

CONTACT: R Craig, Hon. Secretary. Tel: +353 1 8250021.
COURSE: 6,930yds, PAR 73, SSS 73. Parkland course.
SOC RESTR'S: Welcome Monday to Saturday.
SOC GF - Round: Wd IR£12. **We** IR£14. **Day:** Wd N/A. **We** N/A.
SOC PACK: On application.
VIS RESTR'S: Please book.
VIS GF - Round: Wd IR£12. **We** IR£14. **Day:** Wd N/A. **We** N/A.
FACILITIES: 9-hole COURSE, Bar & Restaurant.

LAYTOWN & BETTYSTOWN G C — MAP 10 B2

Bettystown, Meath.
N1 north of Dublin Airport - Julianstown follow coast to course.

CONTACT: Stella Garvey, Secretary. Tel: +353 41 27170.
COURSE: 6,181yds, PAR 70, SSS 69. Seaside links course.
SOC RESTR'S: Welcome Weekdays - Occasional Sat also.
SOC GF - Round: Wd N/A. **We** N/A. **Day:** Wd IR£17. **We** IR£22.
SOC PACK: Tailored to suit individual societies.
VIS RESTR'S: Welcome Weekdays. Phone for Weekends.
VIS GF - Round: Wd N/A. **We** N/A. **Day:** Wd IR£17. **We** IR£22.
FACILITIES: Snooker, Tennis, Full Bar & Restaurant.

ROYAL TARA GOLF CLUB — MAP 10 B2

Bellinter, Navan, Meath.
25 miles north on Dublin City.

CONTACT: P O'Brien, Hon. Secretary. Tel: +353 46 25244.
COURSE: 5,757yds, PAR 71, SSS 70. Parkland course.
SOC RESTR'S: Welcome except Tues & 2-3 each day.
SOC GF - Round: Wd IR£14. **We** IR£18. **Day:** Wd N/A. **We** N/A.
SOC PACK: Rates as above per round. Menu on request.
VIS RESTR'S: Welcome except Tues & 2-3 each day.
VIS GF - Round: Wd IR£14. **We** IR£18. **Day:** Wd N/A. **We** N/A.
FACILITIES: 9-hole COURSE, Pro-shop, Bar & Restaurant.

TRIM GOLF CLUB — MAP 10 B2

Newtownmoynagh, Trim, Meath.
3 miles from Trim on Trim/Longwood road.

CONTACT: P Darby, Club Secretary. Tel: +353 46 31438.
COURSE: 6,720yds, PAR 73, SSS 72. Parkland course.
SOC RESTR'S: Welcome except Thursday & Sunday.
SOC GF - Round: Wd N/A. **We** N/A. **Day:** Wd N/A. **We** N/A.
SOC PACK: On application.
VIS RESTR'S: Welcome except Thursday & Weekends.
VIS GF - Round: Wd IR£12. **We** IR£15. **Day:** Wd N/A. **We** N/A.
FACILITIES: Bar & Restaurant.

Monaghan

NUREMORE GOLF CLUB — MAP 10 B2

Nuremore Hotel, Carrickmacross, Monaghan.
South of Carrickmacross on N2.

CONTACT: M Cassidy, Professional. Tel: +353 42 61438.
COURSE: 6,830yds, PAR 72, SSS 73. Parkland course.
SOC RESTR'S: Welcome.
SOC GF - Round: Wd N/A. **We** N/A. **Day:** Wd N/A. **We** N/A.
SOC PACK: IR£30-IR£35 incl. GF & Meal. Corp Days available.
VIS RESTR'S: Welcome.
VIS GF - Round: Wd N/A. **We** N/A. **Day:** Wd IR£15. **We** IR£18.
FACILITIES: Bar & Restaurant.

REPUBLIC OF IRELAND

Offaly

Sligo

TULLAMORE GOLF CLUB MAP 10 B2

Brookfield, Tullamore, Offaly.
3 miles south-west of Tullamore on Kinnity Road.

CONTACT: A Marsden, Hon. Sec. Tel: +353 506 51317.
COURSE: 6,257yds. PAR 71, SSS 70. Wooded parkland course.
SOC RESTR'S: Welcome except 9.30 to 12.30 on Saturdays.
SOC GF - Round: Wd N/A. We N/A. Day: Wd IR£12. We N/A.
SOC PACK: On application.
VIS RESTR'S: Welcome except Tuesday & some Weekends.
VIS GF - Round: Wd N/A. We N/A. Day: Wd IR£12. We IR£15.
FACILITIES: Bar, Restaurant & Pro-shop.

COUNTY SLIGO GOLF CLUB MAP 10 A2

Rosses Point, Sligo.
5 miles west of Sligo Town.

CONTACT: R Mullen, Secretary/Manager. Tel: +353 71 77134.
COURSE: 6,003yds, PAR 71, SSS 72. Championship links.
SOC RESTR'S: Welcome except Tuesday & Sunday.
SOC GF - Round: Wd IR£15. We N/A. Day: Wd N/A. We N/A.
SOC PACK: 18 holes + 4-course Meal (meal value IR£10).
VIS RESTR'S: Please phone before play.
VIS GF - Round: Wd IR£15. We IR£20. Day: Wd N/A. We N/A.
FACILITIES: Bar & Snacks. Full Dining Room Facilities.

ENNISCRONE GOLF CLUB MAP 10 A2

Enniscrone, Sligo.
7 miles north of Ballina.

CONTACT: A Freeman. Secretary. Tel: +353 96 36297.
COURSE: 6,570yds, PAR 72, SSS 72. Championship links.
SOC RESTR'S: Weekends - Please book in advance.
SOC GF - Round: Wd N/A. We N/A. Day: Wd IR£10. We N/A.
SOC PACK: On application.
VIS RESTR'S: Sunday before 10 & 1-3.30.
VIS GF - Round: Wd N/A. We N/A. Day: Wd IR£15. We IR£15.
FACILITIES: Bar, please order meals before play.

Roscommon

ATHLONE GOLF CLUB MAP 10 A2

Hodson Bay, Athlone, Roscommon.
4 miles from Athlone Town on Roscommon Road.

CONTACT: D Fagan, Hon. Secretary. Tel: +353 902 92073.
COURSE: 6,046yds, PAR 69, SSS 69. Undulating parkland.
SOC RESTR'S: Welcome any day except Tue & Sun to 1.30.
SOC GF - Round: Wd IR£12. We IR£15. Day: Wd N/A. We N/A.
SOC PACK: Full Catering plus presentation dinners by arrangement.
VIS RESTR'S: Welcome any day. Tue & Sun by arrangement.
VIS GF - Round: Wd IR£12. We IR£15. Day: Wd N/A. We N/A.
FACILITIES: Bar, Restaurant & Snooker.

RAC HOTEL GUIDE
Great Britain & Ireland
Now in its **ninetieth year**,
the authoritative guide to over 6,000 hotels.
Special anniversary competition.
All establishments inspected and approved by the RAC.
Full colour atlas section with all hotel locations shown
Includes discount vouchers worth up to £150
Price £12.99
Available from bookshops
or direct from the RAC on 0235 834885

WEXFORD

WATERFORD GOLF CLUB — MAP 10 B3

Newrath, Waterford.
North of Waterford City.

CONTACT: J Condon, Secretary/Manager. Tel: +353 51 76748.
COURSE: 6,237yds, PAR 71, SSS 70. Undulating parkland.
SOC RESTR'S: Mid-week by arrangement.
SOC GF - Round: Wd IR£15. We N/A. Day: Wd N/A. We N/A.
SOC PACK: None.
VIS RESTR'S: Welcome Mon, Thur & Fri to 4. Tue & Wed to 1.15.
VIS GF - Round: Wd IR£15. We IR£17. Day: Wd N/A. We N/A.
FACILITIES: Bar & Catering.

Tipperary

CLONMEL GOLF CLUB — MAP 10 B3

Mountain Road, Clonmel, Tipperary.
2 miles south-west of Clonmel.

CONTACT: O Miles. Tel: +353 52 24020.
COURSE: 6,349yds, PAR 71, SSS 70. Parkland course.
SOC RESTR'S: Must be pre-arranged.
SOC GF - Round: Wd IR£10. We IR£13. Day: Wd N/A. We N/A.
SOC PACK: Full meal IR£10-IR£12.
VIS RESTR'S: Welcome. Prior arrangement due to time sheets.
VIS GF - Round: Wd IR£12. We IR£15. Day: Wd N/A. We N/A.
FACILITIES: Full Catering, Bar, Snooker, Table Tennis & TV.

DOOLEY'S HOTEL

The Quay, Waterford, Ireland.
Tel: 051 73531 Fax: 051 70262
One of Waterford's oldest and most renowned hotels, Dooley's Hotel offers a delightful combination of comfort and friendliness. Excellent food served in our Award Winning "New Ship" Restaurant and "Flag Ship" Bar. Entertainment nightly in season.

Waterford

Wexford

TRAMORE GOLF CLUB — MAP 10 B3

Newtown Hill, Tramore, Waterford.
South from Waterford on R675 to Tramore.

CONTACT: J Cox, Secretary/Manager. Tel: +353 51 86170.
COURSE: 6,660yds, PAR 72, SSS 71. Tree-lined parkland.
SOC RESTR'S: On application.
SOC GF - Round: Wd N/A. We N/A. Day: Wd N/A. We N/A.
SOC PACK: On application.
VIS RESTR'S: Preferred on Weekdays.
VIS GF - Round: Wd N/A. We N/A. Day: Wd IR£17. We IR£21.
FACILITIES: Bar & Catering (summer & weekends).

COURTOWN GOLF CLUB — MAP 10 B3

Kiltennel, Gorey, Wexford.
2 miles off Dublin - Rosslare Road at Gorey.

CONTACT: J Sheehan, Secretary/Manager. Tel: +353 55 25166.
COURSE: 6,398yds, PAR 71, SSS 70. Parkland course.
SOC RESTR'S: Welcome except Tuesday & most Weekends.
SOC GF - Day: Wd N/A. We N/A. Day: Wd N/A. We N/A.
SOC PACK: 1 round + meal from IR£21-IR£30.
VIS RESTR'S: Welcome except Comp Days. Please phone.
VIS GF - Day: Wd IR£15. We IR£20. Day: Wd N/A. We N/A.
FACILITIES: Pro-shop, Restaurant & Bar.

REPUBLIC OF IRELAND

ENNISCORTHY GOLF CLUB   MAP 10 B3

Knockmarshal, Enniscorthy, Wexford.
Off Enniscorthy/New Ross Road. 2 miles from Enniscorthy.

CONTACT: Ann Byrne, Secretary. Tel: +353 54 33191.
COURSE: 5,885yds, PAR 70, SSS 68. Inland course.
SOC RESTR'S: Welcome except Tuesday & Sunday.
SOC GF - Day: Wd IR£10. **We** IR£12. **Day:** Wd N/A. **We** N/A.
SOC PACK: On application.
VIS RESTR'S: Contact in advance. Preferred Weekdays.
VIS GF - Round: Wd IR£10. **We** IR£12. **Day:** Wd N/A. **We** N/A.
FACILITIES: Bar, Restaurant & Club Hire.

Wicklow

ROSSLARE GOLF CLUB   MAP 10 B3

Rosslare, Wexford.
Out of Wexford on coast at Rosslare Point.

CONTACT: J Hall, Secretary. Tel: +353 53 32203.
COURSE: 6,502yds, PAR 74, SSS 71. Links course.
SOC RESTR'S: Preferred Weekdays except Tuesday.
SOC GF - Day: Wd N/A. **We** N/A. **Day:** Wd IR£18. **We** IR£23.
SOC PACK: On application.
VIS RESTR'S: Preferred Weekdays except Tuesday.
VIS GF - Round: Wd N/A. **We** N/A. **Day:** Wd IR£18. **We** IR£23.
FACILITIES: Bar, Restaurant & Club Hire.

BLAINROE GOLF CLUB   MAP 10 B2

Blainroe, Wicklow.
4 miles south of Wicklow on coast road to Brittas Bay.

CONTACT: D O'Donovan, Sec/Manager. Tel: +353 404 68168.
COURSE: 6,735yds, PAR 72, SSS 72. Testing seaside parkland.
SOC RESTR'S: Normally 10-12 noon daily.
SOC GF - Round: Wd N/A. **We** N/A. **Day:** Wd N/A. **We** N/A.
SOC PACK: Full Catering available - Midweek IR£27 incl.
VIS RESTR'S: Welcome but Weekends phone for time sheet.
VIS GF - Round: Wd IR£18. **We** IR£25. **Day:** Wd N/A. **We** N/A.
FACILITIES: Bar & Restaurant.

WEXFORD GOLF CLUB   MAP 10 B3

Mulgannon, Wexford.
Within Wexford Town.

CONTACT: P Roche, Chief Steward. Tel: +353 53 42238.
COURSE: 6,100yds, PAR 71, SSS 69. Parkland course.
SOC RESTR'S: Welcome except Sundays.
SOC GF - Round: Wd N/A. **We** N/A. **Day:** Wd N/A. **We** N/A.
SOC PACK: On application.
VIS RESTR'S: Welcome except Thursday & Sunday.
VIS GF - Round: Wd IR£14. **We** IR£15. **Day:** Wd N/A. **We** N/A.
FACILITIES: Bar & Restaurant.

DELGANY GOLF CLUB   MAP 10 B2

Delgany, Wicklow.
Out of Dublin on N11 coast road - Bray, turn onto R762.

CONTACT: J Deally, Secretary. Tel: +353 1 2874536.
COURSE: 5,920yds, PAR 69, SSS 67. Undulating parkland course.
SOC RESTR'S: Preferred Monday, Thursday & Friday.
SOC GF - Round: Wd N/A. **We** N/A. **Day:** Wd N/A. **We** N/A.
SOC PACK: On application.
VIS RESTR'S: Preferred Monday, Thursday & Friday.
VIS GF - Round: Wd IR£17. **We** IR£20. **Day:** Wd N/A. **We** N/A.
FACILITIES: Bar, Restaurant, Club Hire & Pro-shop.

RAC Motoring Atlas Europe

A fully updated edition of this handy-sized atlas which encompasses unified Germany and other newly defined frontiers. Clear and detailed mapping at 1:1 million scale (16 miles to 1 inch) for Western Europe. Comprehensive index of over 52,000 place names. Compact format ideal for car use.

Price £10.99
Available from bookshops
or direct from the RAC on 0235 834885

GREYSTONES GOLF CLUB   MAP 10 B2

Greystones, Wicklow.
Coast road R761 out of Bray to Greystones.

CONTACT: Mr Walsh. Tel: +353 1 2874136.
COURSE: 5,906yds, PAR 72, SSS 68. Parkland course.
SOC RESTR'S: Must contact in advance.
SOC GF - Round: Wd IR£20. **We** N/A. **Day:** Wd N/A. **We** N/A.
SOC PACK: On application.
VIS RESTR'S: Please book by phone before play.
VIS GF - Round: Wd IR£20. **We** IR£25. **Day:** Wd N/A. **We** N/A.
FACILITIES: Bar & Restaurant.

AUSTRIA

Given the fact that Austria can boast only some three dozen golf clubs, many of them only 9-hole layouts, and is neither geographically nor climatically best-suited to golf, it's unsurprising that the country has scant golfing tradition. What is surprising, bearing in mind that many courses are only open for a few months each year, is that interest in golf is strong and growing and that clubs there provide some excellent golf.

Until well after World War II when the majority of Austria's courses were built, the best the country had to offer was Wien, founded in 1901 and curiously situated inside a racetrack in the very heart of Vienna. Now though, the golfer in Austria has a wider choice. The Jack Nicklaus-designed course at Gut Altentann in Henndorf, a few miles north of Salzburg was opened for play in 1989 and in 1990 hosted the inaugural Austrian Open. Gut Altentann is visually stunning: a park/meadow layout with a backdrop of rolling hills and dark forests, it measures some 6800 yards, but is only playable between April and October each year. Another track worthy of note is Murhof in Frohnleiten just north of Graz, which boasts a conveniently-located hotel alongside the course. If, on the other hand, your achievements on the golf course don't match your aspirations, help is at hand in the shape of the first David Leadbetter Academy of mainland Europe. This is at Bad Tatzmannsdorf and was opened in the summer of 1993. On offer are individual lessons in the famed Leadbetter technique and residential golf schools.

With so many courses closed for much of the year, there can be intense demand for tee-times during the summer months, so booking, especially on the better courses, which may also demand valid handicap certificates, is absolutely essential. The limited playability of courses also has a knock-on effect on green fees, which can be on the high side on 18-hole courses, although they can also be a real bargain on the 9-hole layouts.

AUSTRIA-WÖRTHER SEE GOLF CLUB MAP 11 B2

A-9062 Moosburg, Golfstr 2.
5km north of Wörther See.

CONTACT: M Sullivan, Professional. Tel: +43 4272 83486.
COURSE: 6,216m, PAR 72, SSS 72. Parkland course.
SOC RESTR'S: Welcome with advance bookings.
SOC GF - Round: Wd As500. **We** As600. **Day:** Wd N/A. **We** N/A.
SOC PACK: Please discuss at time of booking from Secretary.
VIS RESTR'S: Welcome.
VIS GF - Round: Wd As500. **We** As600. **Day:** Wd N/A. **We** N/A.
FACILITIES: Range, Restaurant & Bar.

COLONY CLUB GUTENHOF (EAST) MAP 11 B2

Gutenhof, Himberg, A-2325.
25km south-east of Vienna.

CONTACT: S Frazer, Secretary. Tel: +43 2235 88055.
COURSE: 6,335m, PAR 73, SSS 73. Parkland course.
SOC RESTR'S: Welcome with advance bookings.
SOC GF - Round: Wd As550. **We** As700. **Day:** Wd N/A. **We** N/A.
SOC PACK: Please discuss at time of booking with Secretary.
VIS RESTR'S: Phone in advance.
VIS GF - Round: Wd As550. **We** As700. **Day:** Wd N/A. **We** N/A.
FACILITIES: Range, Putting Green, Tennis, Pro-shop & Bar.

AUSTRIA

COLONY CLUB GUTENHOF (WEST) MAP 11 B1

Gutenhof, Himberg, A-2325.
25km sSouth-east of Vienna.

CONTACT: S Frazer, Secretary. Tel: +43 2235 88055.
COURSE: 6,397m, PAR 73, SSS 73. Parkland course.
SOC RESTR'S: Welcome with advance bookings.
SOC GF - Round: Wd As550. We As700. **Day:** Wd N/A. We N/A.
SOC PACK: Please discuss at time of booking with Secretary.
VIS RESTR'S: Phone in advance. Handicap Certificate required.
VIS GF - Round: Wd As550. We As700. **Day:** Wd N/A. We N/A.
FACILITIES: Range, Swimming, Sauna, Tennis, Restaurant & Bar.

GOLF & COUNTRY CLUB BRUNN MAP 11 B1

Brunn, Rennweg 50, A-2345.
10km south of Vienna.

CONTACT: Claudia Dechel, Manager. Tel: +43 2236 33711.
COURSE: 6,088m, PAR 72, SSS 72. Parkland course.
SOC RESTR'S: Welcome by arrangement Weekdays only.
SOC GF - Round: Wd As700. We N/A. **Day:** Wd N/A. We N/A.
SOC PACK: Tailored to suite requirements.
VIS RESTR'S: Welcome except Club Competition days.
VIS GF - Round: Wd As700. We As700. **Day:** Wd N/A. We N/A.
FACILITIES: Range, Bar & Restaurant.

GOLF CLUB DONNERSKIRCHEN MAP 11 B1

Donnerskirchen, A-7082.
45km south-east of Vienna.

CONTACT: S Brunner / P Posseth, Secretaries. Tel : +43 2683 8171.
COURSE: 6,261m, PAR 72, SSS 73. A typical links course.
SOC RESTR'S: Any size on non tournament days. Phone prior.
SOC GF - Round: Wd N/A. We N/A. **Day:** Wd As420. We As520.
SOC PACK: Contact Manager Christa Dernec.
VIS RESTR'S: Any time on non tournament days. Phone prior.
VIS GF - Round: Wd N/A. We N/A. **Day:** Wd As420. We As520.
FACILITIES: Driving Range, Pitch & Putt, Bar & Restaurant.

GOLF CLUB ENZESFELD MAP 11 B1

Enzesfeld, A-2551.
40km south of Vienna.

CONTACT: R Morris, Professional. Tel +43 2256 81272.
COURSE: 6,176m, PAR 72, SSS 72. Mountain course.
SOC RESTR'S: Welcome except Thursday & Weekends.
SOC GF - Round: Wd As500. We N/A. **Day:** Wd N/A. We N/A.
SOC PACK: None.
VIS RESTR'S: Open Apr-Oct. Handicap Certificate required.
VIS GF - Round: Wd As500. We As700. **Day:** Wd N/A. We N/A.
FACILITIES: Range, Putting Green, Pitching Area & Golf Car Hire.

GOLF CLUB FRAUENTHAL MAP 11 B2

Deutschlandsberg, Ulrichsberg 3, A-8530.
45km south-west of Graz.

CONTACT: A Pirker, Organiser. Tel: +43 3462 5717.
COURSE: 5,856m, PAR 72, SSS 71. Quiet parkland course.
SOC RESTR'S: Welcome by prior arrangement.
SOC GF - Round: Wd N/A. We N/A. **Day:** Wd As350. We As450.
SOC PACK: On application from Organiser.
VIS RESTR'S: Please phone before play.
VIS GF - Round: Wd N/A. We N/A. **Day:** Wd As350. We As450.
FACILITIES: Special 1 weeks Green Fee As1,900.

GOLF CLUB FÜRSTENFELD MAP 11 B2

Loipersdorf, Gillersdorf 50, A-8282.
50km east of Graz.

CONTACT: P Kospach, Manager. Tel: +43 3382 8533.
COURSE: 6192m, PAR 72, SSS 72. Parkland/forest course.
SOC RESTR'S: Welcome with prior booking.
SOC GF - Round: Wd N/A. We N/A. **Day:** Wd As450. We As550.
SOC PACK: 5 day Green Fee As1,150. 1 week Green Fee As1,750.
VIS RESTR'S: Welcome phone for availability.
VIS GF - Round: Wd N/A. We N/A. **Day:** Wd As450. We As550.
FACILITIES: Bar & Restaurant.

GUT ALTENTANN GOLF CLUB MAP 11 A1

5302 Henndorf am Wallersee, Salzburg.
Henndorf, 16km north of Salzburg.

CONTACT: J Mannie, Professional. Tel: +43 6214 6026.
COURSE: 6,223m, PAR 72, SSS 72. Parkland with water.
SOC RESTR'S: Open Apr-Oct. Weekdays only.
SOC GF - Round: Wd As800. We N/A. **Day:** Wd N/A. We N/A.
SOC PACK: On application.
VIS RESTR'S: Open Apr-Oct. Weekdays only.
VIS GF - Round: Wd As800. We N/A. **Day:** Wd N/A. We N/A.
FACILITIES: Practice Area, Bar & Restaurant.

GUT BRANDLHOF GOLF CLUB MAP 11 A2

A-5760 Saalfelden, Sporthotel Gut Brandlhof.
65km south-west of Salzburg.

CONTACT: H Lumpi, Professional. Tel: +43 6582 2176.
COURSE: 6,312m, PAR 72, SSS 73. Parkland course.
SOC RESTR'S: Welcome with prior booking.
SOC GF - Round: Wd As520. We As660. **Day:** Wd N/A. We N/A.
SOC PACK: On application.
VIS RESTR'S: Welcome phone for availability. HC required.
VIS GF - Round: Wd As520. We As660. **Day:** Wd N/A. We N/A.
FACILITIES: Bar & Restaurant.

AUSTRIA

GUT MURSTÄTTEN GOLF CLUB   MAP 11 B2

A-8403 Lebring, Oedt 4.
25km south of Graz.

CONTACT: C Prasthofer, Professional. Tel: +43 3182 3555.
COURSE: 6,398m, PAR 72, SSS 74. Parkland course.
SOC RESTR'S: Welcome with prior booking.
SOC GF - Round: Wd As480. We As580. **Day:** Wd N/A. We N/A.
SOC PACK: On application.
VIS RESTR'S: Welcome phone for availability. H'cap Cert required.
VIS GF - Round: Wd As480. We As580. **Day:** Wd N/A. We N/A.
FACILITIES: 9-hole Course, Range, Pitch & Putt, Bar & Restaurant.

KÄRNTNER GOLF CLUB   MAP 11 B2

A-9082 Dellach 16, Maria Wörth.
15km west of Klagenfurt.

CONTACT: M Inglis, Professional. Tel: +43 4273 2515.
COURSE: 5,709m, PAR 70, SSS 70. Undulating forest course.
SOC RESTR'S: Welcome Weekdays with prior booking.
SOC GF - Round: Wd N/A. We N/A. **Day:** Wd As600. We As600.
SOC PACK: On application.
VIS RESTR'S: Welcome phone for availability on Weekends.
VIS GF - Round: Wd N/A. We N/A. **Day:** Wd As600. We As600.
FACILITIES: Range, Bar, & Restaurant.

KITZBÜHEL SCHWARZSEE   MAP 11 A2

A-6370, Hinterstadt 18, Kitzbühel.
5km west of Kitzbühel.

CONTACT: F Porstendorfer-Rothbacher, Director. Tel: +43 5356 71645.
COURSE: 6,247m, PAR 72, SSS 72. Parkland course.
SOC RESTR'S: Welcome with prior agreement.
SOC GF - Round: Wd As600. We As700. **Day:** Wd N/A. We N/A.
SOC PACK: Kitzbühler guests with guestcard-30% reduction.
VIS RESTR'S: Welcome Weekdays. Some Weekend restrictions.
VIS GF - Round: Wd As600. We As700. **Day:** Wd N/A. We N/A.
FACILITIES: Range, Putting Green, Pro-shop & Restaurant.

LINZ-SAINT FLORIAN GOLF CLUB   MAP 11 B1

A-4490 Saint Florian, Tillysburg 28.
15km south-east of Linz.

CONTACT: J Crisp, Professional. Tel: +43 7223 2873.
COURSE: 6098m, PAR 72, SSS 72. Forest course.
SOC RESTR'S: Welcome with prior booking.
SOC GF - Round: Wd As500. We As600. **Day:** Wd N/A. We N/A.
SOC PACK: On application.
VIS RESTR'S: Welcome phone for availability. HC required.
VIS GF - Round: Wd As500. We As600. **Day:** Wd N/A. We N/A.
FACILITIES: Bar & Restaurant.

MURHOF GOLF CLUB   MAP 11 B2

8130 Frohnleiten, Adriach 53.
Frohnleiten, 25km north of Graz, 150km south of Vienna.

CONTACT: P Banks/R Austin, Professionals. Tel: +43 3126 3010.
COURSE: 6,381m, PAR 72, SSS 73. Parkland course.
SOC RESTR'S: Handicap Certificate required.
SOC GF - Round: Wd As600. We N/A. **Day:** Wd N/A. We N/A.
SOC PACK: On application.
VIS RESTR'S: H'cap Cert required. Open Mar-Dec only.
VIS GF - Round: Wd As600. We As750. **Day:** Wd N/A. We N/A.
FACILITIES: Practice Area, Tennis, Bar & Restaurant.

SALZKAMMERGUT GOLF CLUB   MAP 11 B1

A-4820 Bad Ischl, Postfach 506.
50km east of Salzburg. On the outskirts of Strobl town.

CONTACT: P Kospach, Manager. Tel: +43 3382 8533.
COURSE: 5,986m, PAR 70, SSS 71. Parkland course.
SOC RESTR'S: Welcome Weekdays with prior booking.
SOC GF - Round: Wd As500. We N/A. **Day:** Wd N/A. We N/A.
SOC PACK: On application.
VIS RESTR'S: Welcome Weekdays only.
VIS GF - Round: Wd As500. We N/A. **Day:** Wd N/A. We N/A.
FACILITIES: Bar & Restaurant.

SCHLOSS ERNEGG GOLF CLUB   MAP 11 B1

A-3216 Steinakirchen, Schlosshotel Ernegg.
60km south-east of Linz.

CONTACT: P Kreier, Manager. Tel: +43 7488 214.
COURSE: 5,699m, PAR 71, SSS 70. Parkland course.
SOC RESTR'S: Welcome with appointment.
SOC GF - Round: Wd As450. We As550. **Day:** Wd N/A. We N/A.
SOC PACK: On application.
VIS RESTR'S: Welcome.
VIS GF - Round: Wd As450. We As550. **Day:** Wd N/A. We N/A.
FACILITIES: 9-hole Course, Pitch & Putt, Range, Bar & Restaurant.

SCHLOSS PICHLARN GOLF CLUB   MAP 11 B2

A-8952 Irdning, Ennstal Steiermark.
2km east of Irdning.

CONTACT: A Mitchell, Professional. Tel: +43 3682 24393.
COURSE: 6,123m, PAR 72, SSS 72. Parkland course.
SOC RESTR'S: Welcome with appointment.
SOC GF - Round: Wd As500. We As650. **Day:** Wd N/A. We N/A.
SOC PACK: On application.
VIS RESTR'S: Welcome. Open May-Nov.
VIS GF - Round: Wd As500. We As600. **Day:** Wd N/A. We N/A.
FACILITIES: Bar & Restaurant.

AUSTRIA

WALDVIERTEL GOLF CLUB MAP 11 B1

Haugschlag 160, Litschau, A-3874.
130km north-east of Linz, 140km North-West of Vienna.

CONTACT: H Holbach, Hon. Sec. Tel: +43 2865 8441.
COURSE: 6, 319m, PAR 72, SSS 73. Parkland course.
SOC RESTR'S: Welcome with advanced booking.
SOC GF - Round: Wd N/A. **We** N/A. **Day: Wd** As480. **We** As620.
SOC PACK: Please discuss at time of booking.
VIS RESTR'S: Always welcome. H'cap Cert required.
VIS GF - Round: Wd N/A. **We** N/A. **Day: Wd** As480. **We** As620.
FACILITIES: 18-hole Par 3 Course, Range, Golf Clinic & Restaurant.

WIEN GOLF CLUB MAP 11 B1

A-1020 Wien, Freudenau 65a.
4km south-east of Vienna.

CONTACT: Caddymaster Tel: +43 2222 18964.
COURSE: 5, 861m, PAR 71, SSS 71. Parkland course.
SOC RESTR'S: Welcome Weekdays with prior arrangement.
SOC GF - Round: Wd N/A. **We** N/A. **Day: Wd** As720. **We** As720.
SOC PACK: Please discuss at time of booking.
VIS RESTR'S: Welcome Weekdays but please book.
VIS GF - Round: Wd N/A. **We** N/A. **Day: Wd** As720. **We** As720.
FACILITIES: Bar & Restaurant.

BELGIUM

COMPARED to some of the over-priced and over-played courses of the Iberian peninsula, Belgium offers some of the best golfing bargains in Europe with excellent courses and very reasonable prices. The most evocative club, for a variety of reasons, is Royal Waterloo. Strictly speaking, it should be referred to as 'New' Royal Waterloo, for it was designed by Fred Hawtree in 1960 and laid out over the terrain where Napoleon and the Duke of Wellington played out an altogether more serious drama in 1815. The course is now a regular venue for the Belgian Open. The 'Old' Royal Waterloo, a Harry Colt design, holds a different place in British affections, for Henry Cotton was the professional here when he won the first of his three Opens in 1934.

Belgium's oldest club, Royal Antwerp, dates back to 1888. Designed by Willie Park and modified by Tom Simpson, it's reminiscent in many ways of the best of the Surrey heathland courses, with the holes wending their way between stands of pine and silver birch. In sharp contrast, Bercuit, opened for play nearly a hundred years later in 1982, is a typical Robert Trent Jones design - and all that that implies! - while on the North Sea coast, near the resort of Knokke-le-Zoute, is the more traditional links layout of Royal Zoute, another Belgian Open venue.

That so many clubs in Belgium can boast the 'Royal' prefix is down to popularity - and golfing prowess - of the late King Baudouin, a keen and accomplished player who was President of the Royal Belgique Club at Tervuren. Given its royal connections, it's perhaps surprising that golf in Belgium isn't more popular.

That it will become so is inevitable, but at present, with more quality courses being designed and built yearly and with access from Britain so easy, Belgium really is an undiscovered golfing jewel.

BERCUIT GOLF CLUB   MAP 11 B3

Les Gottes 3, 1390 Grez-Doiceau.
30km south-east of Brussels.

CONTACT: P Toussaint, Professional. Tel: + 32 10 841 501.
COURSE: 5,980m, PAR 72, SSS 71. Parkland course.
SOC RESTR'S: Welcome Weekdays with prior agreement.
SOC GF - Round: Wd N/A. **We** N/A. **Day:** Wd Bf1,800. **We** N/A.
SOC PACK: Please discuss at time of booking.
VIS RESTR'S: Welcome phone call prior to play advisable.
VIS GF - Round: Wd N/A. **We** Bf1,800. **Day:** Wd Bf2,700. **We** N/A.
FACILITIES: Bar.

BOSSENSTEIN GOLF CLUB   MAP 11 A3

Bossenstein Kasteel, 2250 Broechem.
15km east of Antwerp.

CONTACT: Secretary. Tel: + 32 3 485 6446.
COURSE: 6,203m, PAR 72, SSS 71. Parkland course.
SOC RESTR'S: Welcome with prior booking.
SOC GF - Round: Wd Bf1,200. **We** N/A. **Day:** Wd Bf1,700. **We** N/A.
SOC PACK: Please discuss at time of booking.
VIS RESTR'S: Welcome please phone to check Weekends.
VIS GF - Round: Wd Bf1,200. **We** Bf1,700. **Day:** Wd N/A. **We** N/A.
FACILITIES: 9-hole Course, Range & Bar.

BELGIUM

CLEYDAEL GOLF CLUB MAP 11 A3

Kasteel Cleydael, 2630 Aartselaar.
10km south of Antwerp.

CONTACT: J Wilkinson, Professional. Tel: + 32 3 887 0079.
COURSE: 6,060m, PAR 72, SSS 72. Parkland course.
SOC RESTR'S: Advanced Reservations only.
SOC GF - Round: Wd Bf1,700. We N/A. **Day:** Wd N/A. We N/A.
SOC PACK: Please discuss at time of booking.
VIS RESTR'S: Welcome Weekdays & Weekends after 2.
VIS GF - Round: Wd Bf1,700. We Bf2,300. **Day:** Wd N/A. We N/A.
FACILITIES: Range Practice Area, Pro-shop & Bar.

KEERBERGEN GOLF CLUB MAP 11 A3

50 Vlieghavenlaan, 3140 Keerbergen.
30km north-east of Brussels.

CONTACT: Secretary. Tel: + 32 15 234 961.
COURSE: 5,530m, PAR 70, SSS 69. Forest course.
SOC RESTR'S: Welcome with prior booking.
SOC GF - Round: Wd Bf1,400. We N/A. **Day:** Wd N/A. We N/A.
SOC PACK: Please discuss at time of booking.
VIS RESTR'S: Welcome please phone to check Weekends.
VIS GF - Round: Wd Bf1,400. We Bf2,000. **Day:** Wd N/A. We N/A.
FACILITIES: Bar, Pro-shop & Practice Area.

DAMME GOLF CLUB MAP 11 A3

Doornstraat 16, 8340 Damme-Sijsele.
9km east of Bruges.

CONTACT: G Pearce, Professional. Tel: + 32 50 353 572.
COURSE: 6,046m, PAR 72, SSS 72. Forest course.
SOC RESTR'S: Welcome with prior booking.
SOC GF - Round: Wd Bf1,500. We N/A. **Day:** Wd N/A. We N/A.
SOC PACK: Please discuss at time of booking.
VIS RESTR'S: Welcome please phone to check Weekends.
VIS GF - Round: Wd Bf1,500. We Bf2,000. **Day:** Wd N/A. We N/A.
FACILITIES: 9-hole Course, Bar, Pro-shop & Practice Area.

LIMBURG GOLF CLUB MAP 11 B3

Golfstraat 1, 3530 Houthalen.
15km north of Hasslet.

CONTACT: J Renders, Professional. Tel: + 32 11 383 543.
COURSE: 6,100m, PAR 72, SSS 72. Undulating course.
SOC RESTR'S: Advanced reservations only.
SOC GF - Round: Wd Bf1,200. We N/A. **Day:** Wd N/A. We N/A.
SOC PACK: Tailored for each outing.
VIS RESTR'S: Phone to check availability. H'cap Cert required.
VIS GF - Round: Wd Bf1,200. We Bf1,700. **Day:** Wd N/A. We N/A.
FACILITIES: Bar, Pro-shop & Practice Area.

FALNUÉE GOLF CLUB MAP 11 A4

Rue E Pirson 55, 5830 Mazy.
20km north of Namur.

CONTACT: Secretary. Tel: + 32 81 633 090.
COURSE: 5,721m, PAR 70, SSS 69. Undulating course.
SOC RESTR'S: Welcome please phone to check availability.
SOC GF - Round: Wd Bf950. We N/A. **Day:** Wd N/A. We N/A.
SOC PACK: Please discuss at time of booking.
VIS RESTR'S: Welcome please phone to check Weekends.
VIS GF - Round: Wd Bf950. We Bf1,400. **Day:** Wd N/A. We N/A.
FACILITIES: Bar, Pro-shop & Practice Area.

MONT GARNI GOLF CLUB MAP 11 A4

Rue du Mont Garni 3, 7331 Saint Ghislain.
65km south-west of Brussels.

CONTACT: L Lafon, Professional. Tel: + 32 50 353 572.
COURSE: 6,353m, PAR 72, SSS 73. Undulating parkland course.
SOC RESTR'S: Welcome with prior booking.
SOC GF - Round: Wd Bf1,100. We N/A. **Day:** Wd N/A. We N/A.
SOC PACK: Please discuss at time of booking.
VIS RESTR'S: Phone to check Weekends. H'cap Cert required.
VIS GF - Round: Wd Bf1,100. We Bf1,500. **Day:** Wd N/A. We N/A.
FACILITIES: Bar, Pro-shop & Practice Area.

INTERNATIONAL GOMZE GOLF CLUB MAP 11 B3

4140 Gomze-Andoumont.
20km south of Liège.

CONTACT: Secretary. Tel: + 32 41 609 207.
COURSE: 6,034m, PAR 72, SSS 72. Forest course.
SOC RESTR'S: Please book through Secretary.
SOC GF - Round: Wd Bf1,200. We N/A. **Day:** Wd N/A. We N/A.
SOC PACK: No set package.
VIS RESTR'S: Welcome please phone to check Weekends.
VIS GF - Round: Wd Bf1,200. We Bf1,350. **Day:** Wd N/A. We N/A.
FACILITIES: Bar, Pro-shop & Practice Area.

RIGENÉE GOLF CLUB MAP 11 A3

Rue de Châtelet 62, 1495 Villers-la-Ville.
35km south of Brussels.

CONTACT: P Belton, Professional. Tel: + 32 71 877 765.
COURSE: 6,155m, PAR 72, SSS 72. Forest course.
SOC RESTR'S: Advanced reservations only.
SOC GF - Round: Wd Bf1,050. We N/A. **Day:** Wd N/A. We N/A.
SOC PACK: Please discuss at time of booking.
VIS RESTR'S: Welcome please phone to check Weekends.
VIS GF - Round: Wd Bf1,050. We Bf1,600. **Day:** Wd N/A. We N/A.
FACILITIES: Bar, Pro-shop & Practice Area.

BELGIUM

ROYAL ANTWERP GOLF CLUB MAP 11 A3

Georges Capiaulei 2, 2950 Kapellen.
20km north of Antwerp.

CONTACT: Secretary. Tel: + 32 3 666 8456.
COURSE: 6,140m, PAR 72, SSS 72. Undulating course.
SOC RESTR'S: Please book through Secretary.
SOC GF - Round: Wd Bf1,900. We N/A. **Day:** Wd N/A. We N/A.
SOC PACK: Tailored for each outing.
VIS RESTR'S: Welcome please phone to check Weekends.
VIS GF - Round: Wd Bf1,900. We Bf2,600. **Day:** Wd N/A. We N/A.
FACILITIES: Bar, Pro-shop & Practice Area.

ROYAL LATEM GOLF CLUB MAP 11 A3

9830 Saint Martens-Latem.
10km south-west of Ghent.

CONTACT: J Verplancke, Professional. Tel: + 32 91 825 411.
COURSE: 5,767m, PAR 72, SSS 70. Parkland course.
SOC RESTR'S: Welcome with prior booking.
SOC GF - Round: Wd Bf1, 500. We N/A. **Day:** Wd N/A. We N/A.
SOC PACK: No set package.
VIS RESTR'S: Welcome please phone to check availability.
VIS GF - Round: Wd Bf1,500. We Bf2,000. **Day:** Wd N/A. We N/A.
FACILITIES: Bar, Pro-shop & Practice Area.

ROYAL OSTEND GOLF CLUB MAP 11 A3

Koninklijke Baan 2, 8420 De Haan.
10km north of Ostend.

CONTACT: D Petrie, Professional. Tel: + 32 59 233 283.
COURSE: 5.265m, PAR 68, SSS 68. Undulating course.
SOC RESTR'S: Welcome with written agreement.
SOC GF - Round: Wd Bf1,600. We N/A. **Day:** Wd N/A. We N/A.
SOC PACK: On application.
VIS RESTR'S: Welcome please phone to check availability.
VIS GF - Round: Wd Bf1,600. We Bf2,300. **Day:** Wd N/A. We N/A.
FACILITIES: Bar, Pro-shop & Practice Area.

ROYAL WATERLOO GOLF CLUB (ONE) MAP 11 A3

Vieux Chemin de Wavre, 1380 Ohain.
20km east of Brussels.

CONTACT: Secretary. Tel: + 32 2 633 1850.
COURSE: 6,275m, PAR 72, SSS 73. Parkland course.
SOC RESTR'S: Please book through Secretary.
SOC GF - Round: Wd N/A. We N/A. **Day:** Wd Bf1,900. We N/A.
SOC PACK: Tailored for each outing.
VIS RESTR'S: Welcome with Handicap Certificates.
VIS GF - Round: Wd N/A. We N/A. **Day:** Wd Bf1,900. We Bf3,200.
FACILITIES: 9-hole Course, Bar, Pro-shop & Practice Area.

ROYAL WATERLOO GOLF CLUB (TWO) MAP 11 A3

Vieux Chemin de Wavre, 1380 Ohain.
20km east of Brussels.

CONTACT: Secretary. Tel: + 32 2 633 1850.
COURSE: 6,270m, PAR 72, SSS 72. Parkland course.
SOC RESTR'S: Please book through Secretary.
SOC GF - Round: Wd N/A. We N/A. **Day:** Wd Bf1,900. We N/A.
SOC PACK: Tailored for each outing.
VIS RESTR'S: Welcome with Handicap Certificates.
VIS GF - Round: Wd N/A. We N/A. **Day:** Wd Bf1,900. We Bf3,200.
FACILITIES: 9-hole Course, Bar, Pro-shop & Practice Area.

ROYAL ZOUTE GOLF CLUB MAP 11 A3

Caddiespad 14, 8300 Knokke.
45km north of Bruges.

CONTACT: Starter. Tel: +32 50 60 37 81.
COURSE: 6,172m, PAR 72, SSS 73. Undulating Forest.
SOC RESTR'S: Max 20. H'cap Cert required. No weekends.
SOC GF - Round: Wd N/A. We N/A. **Day:** Wd Bf1,900. We N/A.
SOC PACK: On application.
VIS RESTR'S: H'cap Cert required. We restricted.
VIS GF-Round: Wd Bf1,500. We Bf1,900. **Day:** Wd Bf1,700. We N/A.
FACILITIES: Second 18-hole Course Par 64, Bar & Restaurant.

SPIEGELVEN GOLF CLUB MAP 11 B3

Wiemesmeerstraat, 3600 Genk.
20 east of Hasselt.

CONTACT: Secretary. Tel: + 32 11 353 516.
COURSE: 6,200m, PAR 72, SSS 72. Parkland course.
SOC RESTR'S: Welcome Weekdays with prior agreement.
SOC GF - Round: Wd Bf1,100. We N/A. **Day:** Wd N/A. We N/A.
SOC PACK: Please discuss at time of booking.
VIS RESTR'S: Welcome phone call prior to play advisable.
VIS GF - Round: Wd N/A. We Bf1,650. **Day:** Wd Bf1,100. We N/A.
FACILITIES: Bar, Pro-shop & Practice Area.

WINGE GOLF CLUB MAP 11 B3

Wingerstraat 6, 3390 Saint Joris Winge.
35km east of Brussels.

CONTACT: P Townsend, Professional. Tel: + 32 16 634 053.
COURSE: 6,149m, PAR 72, SSS 72. Parkland course.
SOC RESTR'S: Welcome Weekdays with prior agreement.
SOC GF - Round: Wd Bf1,900. We N/A. **Day:** Wd N/A. We N/A.
SOC PACK: Seasonal alterations to Green Fee.
VIS RESTR'S: Welcome phone call prior to play advisable.
VIS GF - Round: Wd Bf1,900. We N/A. **Day:** Wd N/A. We N/A.
FACILITIES: Bar & Practice Area.

DENMARK

UNTIL very recently, golf would have figured in the low reaches of any 'favourite sports' poll in Denmark. Badminton? Certainly. Denmark is assuredly Europe's top nation. Soccer? Astonishingly, the Danes are again Europe's number one, as witnessed by the national side's extraordinary success in the 1992 European Championships, but golf? Yes, there are some pleasant, if unspectacular courses, but sustained professional success, which invariably sparks a grass-roots interest in the game, has been sadly lacking.

That's not to say the Danes haven't had their moments. Steen Tinning and Anders Sorenson - both former Danish Amateur Champions - currently represent their country on the European Tour and have at times come tantalisingly close to picking up a winner's cheque, most notably Sorenson, who lost in a play-off for the Atlantic Open in 1990 and in both 1989 and 1990 was second in the World Cup individual standings. Despite those achievements, victories have been elusive. The signs are encouraging however that, spurred by the obvious and rapid successes achieved by Sweden in the professional sphere, Denmark, along with Norway and Finland, could provide the next real growth area in the European game.

For the visitor, Denmark currently represents good value. The oldest course, dating back to 1898, is Copenhagen, some 8 miles north of the capital and delightfully located in a deer park. Other old-established courses are at Fano Island (1900) and Ålborg (1908), while of the more recent developments, Nordbornholms, opened in 1987, has attracted some excellent reviews. The nearby Bornholms is much shorter, (5267 yards as opposed to 6026 yards), but represents a reasonable alternative. Most courses, with the usual reconnaissance telephone call, should be readily accessible and one added bonus for visitors from the British Isles is that many clubs employ young British professionals, so language shouldn't be a problem.

Bornholm Island

BORNHOLMS GOLF CLUB MAP 12 B2

Plantagevej 3B, DK 3700 Rønne.
3km east of Rønne.
CONTACT: Secretary. Tel: +45 56 956854.
COURSE: 4,789m, PAR 68, SSS 68. Hillside course.
SOC RESTR'S: Welcome with prior agreement.
SOC GF - Round: Wd N/A. We N/A. **Day:** Wd dkr165. We dkr165.
SOC PACK: Please discuss at time of booking.
VIS RESTR'S: Fri, Sat & Sun max handicap 50. All other days 54.
VIS GF - Round: Wd N/A. We N/A. **Day:** Wd dkr175. We dkr175.
FACILITIES: Pro-shop, Restaurant & Bar.

NORDBORNHOLMS GOLF CLUB MAP 12 B2

Spellingevej 3, Rø 3760 Gudhjem.
12km north-east of Rønne.
CONTACT: Secretary. Tel: +45 56 484050.
COURSE: 5,512m, PAR 72, SSS 71. Undulating course.
SOC RESTR'S: Welcome with prior agreement.
SOC GF - Round: Wd N/A. We N/A. **Day:** Wd dkr155. We dkr155.
SOC PACK: Please discuss at time of booking.
VIS RESTR'S: Welcome check Weekend availability.
VIS GF - Round: Wd N/A. We N/A. **Day:** Wd dkr170. We dkr170.
FACILITIES: Pro-shop, Restaurant & Bar.

Fyn

ODENSE GOLF CLUB MAP 12 A2

Hestehaven 210, 5220 Odense SØ.
Just outside of Odense to the south-east.
CONTACT: P Seebach Nielsen, Sec. Tel: +45 65 959000.
COURSE: 5,990m, PAR 72, SSS 71. Parkland course.
SOC RESTR'S: Welcome with prior agreement.
SOC GF - Round: Wd dkr190. We dkr190. **Day:** Wd N/A. We N/A.
SOC PACK: Please discuss at time of booking.
VIS RESTR'S: Welcome phone call prior to play advisable.
VIS GF - Round: Wd dkr190. We dkr190. **Day:** Wd N/A. We N/A.
FACILITIES: 9-hole Course & Bar.

SCT KNUDS GOLF CLUB MAP 12 A2

Slipshavnsvej 16, DK 5800 Nyborg.
3km south-east of Nyborg.
CONTACT: Secretary. Tel: +45 65 311212.
COURSE: 6,027m, PAR 72, SSS 71. Undulating course.
SOC RESTR'S: Welcome with prior agreement.
SOC GF - Round: Wd N/A. We N/A. **Day:** Wd dkr230. We dkr390.
SOC PACK: Please discuss at time of booking.
VIS RESTR'S: Welcome phone call prior to play advisable.
VIS GF - Round: Wd dkr180. We N/A. **Day:** Wd dkr230. We dkr390.
FACILITIES: Bar & Restaurant.

VESTFYNS GOLF CLUB MAP 12 A2

Rønnemosegård, Krengerupvej 27, DK 5620 Glamsbjerg.
45km south-west of Odense.
CONTACT: Secretary. Tel: +45 64 721577.
COURSE: 5,751m, PAR 71, SSS 72. Parkland course.
SOC RESTR'S: Welcome with prior agreement.
SOC GF - Round: Wd N/A. We N/A. **Day:** Wd dkr165. We dkr165.
SOC PACK: Please discuss at time of booking.
VIS RESTR'S: Welcome phone call prior to play advisable.
VIS GF - Round: Wd N/A. We N/A. **Day:** Wd dkr165. We dkr165.
FACILITIES: Bar, Restaurant & Practice Area.

DENMARK

Jalland

ÅLBORG GOLF CLUB MAP 12 A1

Jægersprisvej 35, 9000 Ålborg.
6km west of Ålborg.

CONTACT: Anne-Lise Pedersen, Manager. Tel: +45 98 341476.
COURSE: 5,711m, PAR 70, SSS 70. Undulating course.
SOC RESTR'S: Welcome with prior agreement.
SOC GF - Round: Wd N/A. We dkr220. **Day:** Wd N/A. We N/A.
SOC PACK: Under review.
VIS RESTR'S: Please phone prior to play.
VIS GF - Round: Wd dkr180. We dkr220. **Day:** Wd N/A. We N/A.
FACILITIES: Bar & Restaurant.

ÅRHUS GOLF CLUB MAP 12 A2

NY Moesgaardvej 50, 8270 Hojbjerg.
6km south of Århus.

CONTACT: Secretary. Tel: +45 86 276322.
COURSE: 5,796m, PAR 71, SSS 70. Parkland course.
SOC RESTR'S: Welcome with prior agreement.
SOC GF - Round: Wd dkr190. We dkr230. **Day:** Wd N/A. We N/A.
SOC PACK: None.
VIS RESTR'S: Welcome.
VIS GF - Round: Wd dkr190. We dkr230. **Day:** Wd N/A. We N/A.
FACILITIES: Bar & Putting Green.

ESBJERG GOLF CLUB MAP 12 A2

Sønderhedevej 11, 6710 Esbjerg V.
15km north of Esbjerg.

CONTACT: M Wester, Administrator. Tel: +45 75 269219.
COURSE: 6,434m, PAR 71, SSS 74. Parkland course.
SOC RESTR'S: Welcome with prior agreement Weekdays only.
SOC GF - Round: Wd N/A. We N/A. **Day:** Wd dkr190. We N/A.
SOC PACK: dkr190 per person. Less 20% if more than 20.
VIS RESTR'S: Best days Monday, Wednesday & Friday.
VIS GF - Round: Wd N/A. We N/A. **Day:** Wd dkr190. We dkr190.
FACILITIES: Putting Green, Bar & Restaurant.

GOLFKLUBBEN HVIDE KLIT MAP 12 A

Hvideklitvej 28, 9982 Aalbaek.
22km north of Frederikshavn.

CONTACT: Secretary. Tel: +45 98 489021.
COURSE: 5,875m, PAR 72, SS 72. Seaside course with heather.
SOC RESTR'S: Welcome with prior agreement.
SOC GF - Round: Wd N/A. We N/A. **Day:** Wd dkr180. We dkr180.
SOC PACK: Please discuss at time of booking.
VIS RESTR'S: Weekdays 8.00 to 1.00.
VIS GF - Round: Wd N/A. We N/A. **Day:** Wd dkr180. We dkr180.
FACILITIES: On application.

HADERSLEV GOLF CLUB MAP 12 A

Egevej 151, 6100 Haderslev.
Outside Haderslev 1km to the north-east.

CONTACT: C Sahl, Secretary. Tel: +45 74 528301.
COURSE: 5,137m, PAR 69, SSS 67. Meadowland course.
SOC RESTR'S: Welcome with prior agreement.
SOC GF - Round: Wd N/A. We N/A. **Day:** Wd dkr165. We dkr195.
SOC PACK: Please discuss at time of booking.
VIS RESTR'S: Welcome phone call prior to play advisable.
VIS GF - Round: Wd N/A. We N/A. **Day:** Wd dkr165. We dkr195.
FACILITIES: New Clubhouse now open.

HENNE GOLF CLUB MAP 12 A

Hennebysvej 30, 6854 Henne.
4km east of Henne Strand, follow sign Golfbane.

CONTACT: S Mathiasson, Chairman. Tel: +45 75 255610.
COURSE: 6,215m, PAR 73, SSS 73. Parkland course.
SOC RESTR'S: Phone for reservation.
SOC GF- Round: Wd dkr135. We dkr135. **Day:** Wd dkr160. We dkr160.
SOC PACK: Please discuss at time of booking.
VIS RESTR'S: Welcome.
VIS GF - Round: Wd dkr135. We dkr135. **Day:** Wd dkr160. We dkr160.
FACILITIES: 9-hole Par 3 Course, Driving Range & Putting Green.

HERNING GOLF CLUB MAP 12 A

Golfvej 2, 7400 Herning.
2km east of Herning.

CONTACT: Secretary. Tel: +45 97 210033.
COURSE: 5,669m, PAR 70, SSS 70. Links type course.
SOC RESTR'S: Welcome with prior agreement.
SOC GF - Round: Wd N/A. We N/A. **Day:** Wd dkr170. We dkr210.
SOC PACK: None.
VIS RESTR'S: Please phone in advance.
VIS GF - Round: Wd N/A. We N/A. **Day:** Wd dkr170. We dkr210.
FACILITIES: 2nd 18-hole Course, 9-hole Course, Bar, Restaurant.

JALLAND

HJØRRING GOLF CLUB   MAP 12 A1

Vinstrupvej 30, Box 215, 9800 Hjorring.
3km north of Hjorring.
CONTACT: A Routledge, Professional. Tel: + 45 98 900399.
COURSE: 5,886m, PAR 71, SSS 71. An open countryside course.
SOC RESTR'S: Phone for details.
SOC GF - Round: Wd N/A. We N/A. Day: Wd dkr160. We dkr160.
SOC PACK: These prices only applies to 10 + golfers in party.
VIS RESTR'S: Welcome Wd. Some We - phone first.
VIS GF - Round: Wd N/A. We N/A. Day: Wd dkr175. We dkr175.
FACILITIES: Driving Range, Pitch & Putt Course & Putting Green.

RANDERS GOLF CLUB   MAP 12 A1

Himmelbovej 22, 8900 Randers.
5km west of Randers.
CONTACT: Secretary. Tel: +45 86 428869.
COURSE: 5,453m, PAR 72, SSS 71. Very picturesque course.
SOC RESTR'S: Welcome.
SOC GF - Round: Wd dkr160. We dkr190. Day: Wd N/A. We N/A.
SOC PACK: Please discuss at time of booking.
VIS RESTR'S: Welcome.
VIS GF - Round: Wd dkr160. We dkr190. Day: Wd N/A. We N/A.
FACILITIES: 9-hole Course, Bar.

HOLSTEBRO GOLF CLUB   MAP 12 A1

Bransbjergvej 4, 7570 Vemb.
15km west of Holstebro, ringroad Holstebro - Ringkobing.
CONTACT: Secretary. Tel: +45 97 485155.
COURSE: 6,002m, PAR 72, SSS 71. Parkland course.
SOC RESTR'S: Must book through Secretary.
SOC GF - Round: Wd N/A. We N/A. Day: Wd dkr190. We dkr210.
SOC PACK: Discuss when booking.
VIS RESTR'S: Club competition days.
VIS GF - Round: Wd N/A. We N/A. Day: Wd dkr190. We dkr210.
FACILITIES: 9-hole Course, Range, Putting Green, Restaurant.

SILKEBORG GOLF CLUB   MAP 12 A1

Sensommervej 15C, 8600 Silkeborg.
5km east of Silkeborg.
CONTACT: E Lillelund, Director. Tel: + 45 86 853399.
COURSE: 6,950m, PAR 71, SSS 72. Parkland course.
SOC RESTR'S: Welcome with prior agreement.
SOC GF - Round: Wd N/A. We N/A. Day: Wd dkr220. We dkr270.
SOC PACK: Please discuss at time of booking.
VIS RESTR'S: Must have a handicap of 36 or less.
VIS GF - Round: Wd N/A. We N/A. Day: Wd dkr220. We dkr270.
FACILITIES: Driving Range, Pro-shop & Restaurant.

KAJ LYKKE GOLF CLUB   MAP 12 A2

Porsholtsvej 13, DK 6740 Bramming.
18km east of Esbjerg.
CONTACT: L Alsted, Chairman. Tel: +45 75 102246.
COURSE: 6,050m, PAR 72, SSS 72. Flat parkland course.
SOC RESTR'S: Welcome.
SOC GF - Round: Wd N/A. We N/A. Day: Wd dkr150. We dkr170.
SOC PACK: None.
VIS RESTR'S: Welcome.
VIS GF - Round: Wd N/A. We N/A. Day: Wd dkr150. We dkr170.
FACILITIES: Par 3 Course.

VEJLE GOLF CLUB   MAP 12 A2

Fællessletgård, Ibækvej 46, 7100 Vejle.
5km south-east of Vejle.
CONTACT: J Skanderup, Hon. Sec. Tel: +45 75 858185.
COURSE: 6,277m, PAR 73, SSS 73. Parkland course.
SOC RESTR'S: Welcome with prior agreement.
SOC GF - Round: Wd N/A. We N/A. Day: Wd dkr210. We dkr210.
SOC PACK: 25% GF discount to guests at Munkebjerj & Kronprinds.
VIS RESTR'S: Welcome. Handicap Certificate required.
VIS GF - Round: Wd N/A. We N/A. Day: Wd dkr210. We dkr210.
FACILITIES: 9-hole Par 3 Course, Pro-shop & Restaurant.

KOLDING GOLF CLUB   MAP 12 A2

Emerholtsvej 15, 6000 Kolding.
3km north of Kolding.
CONTACT: P Thastum, President. Tel: +45 75 523793.
COURSE: 5,405m, PAR 69, SSS 69. A well kept course.
SOC RESTR'S: Phone for details.
SOC GF - Round: Wd dkr150. We dkr220. Day: Wd N/A. We N/A.
SOC PACK: Please discuss at time of booking.
VIS RESTR'S: Welcome.
VIS GF - Round: Wd dkr150. We dkr220. Day: Wd N/A. We N/A.
FACILITIES: Putting Green, Bar & Restaurant.

VIBORG GOLF CLUB   MAP 12 A1

Møllevej 26, 8800 Viborg.
3km east of Viborg.
CONTACT: HC Hansen, Hon. Sec. Tel: + 45 86 673010.
COURSE: 5, 902m, PAR 72, SSS 71. Gently undulating course.
SOC RESTR'S: Limitations Sundays & daily after 4.
SOC GF - Round: Wd dkr175. We dkr210. Day: Wd N/A. We N/A.
SOC PACK: Please discuss at time of booking.
VIS RESTR'S: Limitations Sundays & daily after 4.
VIS GF - Round: Wd dkr175. We dkr210. Day: Wd N/A. We N/A.
FACILITIES: Bar & Clubhouse.

DENMARK

Zealand

DRAGØR GOLF CLUB   MAP 12 B2

Kalvebodvej 100, 2791 Dragør.
5km south-west of Copenhagen airport.

CONTACT: Edith Johansen, Secretary. Tel: +45 32 538975.
COURSE: 6,404m, PAR 71, SSS 71. Parkland course.
SOC RESTR'S: Weekdays only.
SOC GF - Round: Wd dkr180. We N/A. **Day:** Wd dkr180. We N/A.
SOC PACK: Available on request.
VIS RESTR'S: Weekdays none. Handicap of 36 or better.
VIS GF - Round: Wd dkr180. We N/A. **Day:** Wd dkr180. We N/A.
FACILITIES: 6-hole Par 3 Course.

FURESØ GOLF CLUB   MAP 12 B2

Hestkøbænge 4, 3460 Birkerød.
25km north of Copenhagen.

CONTACT: F Engel, Hon. Sec. Tel: +45 42 817444.
COURSE: 5,692m, PAR 71, SSS 71. Parkland course.
SOC RESTR'S: Welcome with prior agreement.
SOC GF - Round: Wd N/A. We N/A. **Day:** Wd dkr180. We dkr240.
SOC PACK: Please discuss at time of booking.
VIS RESTR'S: Wd after 9, Sat & Sun after 11, Max H'cap 36.
VIS GF - Round: Wd N/A. We N/A. **Day:** Wd dkr180. We dkr240.
FACILITIES: Bar, Clubhouse & Practice Area.

GILLELEJE GOLF CLUB   MAP 12 B2

Ferlevej 52, 3250 Gilleleje.
60km north of Copenhagen.

CONTACT: Secretary. Tel: + 45 49 718056.
COURSE: 6,044m, PAR 72, SSS 72. Links course.
SOC RESTR'S: On We in June & Aug not before 1.15. GF dkr270.
SOC GF - Round: Wd N/A. We N/A. **Day:** Wd dkr210. We dkr250.
SOC PACK: Please discuss at time of booking.
VIS RESTR'S: On We in June & Aug not before 1.15. GF dkr270.
VIS GF - Round: Wd N/A. We N/A. **Day:** Wd dkr210. We dkr250.
FACILITIES: Bar.

GOLF CLUB HEDELAND   MAP 12 B2

Stærkendevej 232A, DK 2640 Hedehusene.
3km south of Hedehusene.
CONTACT: Secretary. Tel + 45 42 136188.
COURSE: 5,735m, PAR 70, SSS 70. Placed in a former gravel pit.
SOC RESTR'S: Welcome.
SOC GF - Round: Wd dkr160. We dkr200. **Day:** Wd N/A. We N/A.
SOC PACK: Please discuss at time of booking.
VIS RESTR'S: Welcome.
VIS GF - Round: Wd dkr160. We dkr200. **Day:** Wd N/A. We N/A.
FACILITIES: Par 3 Course. Driving Range & Putting Green.

GOLF CLUB STORSTRØMMEN   MAP 12 B2

Virketvej 44, 4863 Eskilstrup.
15km north of Copenhagen.

CONTACT: Secretary. Tel: +45 53 838080.
COURSE: 5,945m, PAR 72, SSS 72. Parkland course.
SOC RESTR'S: Always welcome.
SOC GF - Round: Wd N/A. We N/A. **Day:** Wd dkr170. We dkr220.
SOC PACK: Please discuss at time of booking.
VIS RESTR'S: Always welcome with Handicap Certificate.
VIS GF - Round: Wd N/A. We N/A. **Day:** Wd dkr170. We dkr220.
FACILITIES: Par 3 Course, Range, Putting Green & Pro-shop.

HELSINGØR GOLF CLUB   MAP 12 B2

G1 Hellebaekvej, 3000 Helsingør.
2km north of Helsingør town.

CONTACT: Secretary. Tel: +45 49 212970.
COURSE: 5,705m, PAR 71, SSS 71. Undulating course.
SOC RESTR'S: Welcome with prior agreement.
SOC GF - Round: Wd N/A. We dkr260. **Day:** Wd dkr180. We N/A.
SOC PACK: Please discuss at time of booking.
VIS RESTR'S: Wd H'cap: all 36. We Ladies 36, Gentlemen 24.
VIS GF - Round: Wd N/A. We dkr260. **Day:** Wd dkr180. We N/A.
FACILITIES: Bar, Restaurant & Pro-shop.

HILLERØD GOLF CLUB   MAP 12 B2

Nysogårdsvej, Ny Hammersholt, DK 3400 Hillerød.
3km south of Hillerød.

CONTACT: Else Olsen, Secretary. Tel: +45 42 265046.
COURSE: 5,453m, PAR 70, SSS 70. Parkland course.
SOC RESTR'S: Best days are Monday & Thursday.
SOC GF - Round: Wd N/A. We N/A. **Day:** Wd dkr180. We dkr240.
SOC PACK: Please discuss at time of booking.
VIS RESTR'S: Tue Ladies day. Wed Gents day. Not before 12 We.
VIS GF - Round: Wd N/A. We N/A. **Day:** Wd dkr180. We dkr240.
FACILITIES: 6-hole Par 3 Course, Driving Range & Restaurant.

ZEALAND

KØBENHAVNS GOLF CLUB MAP 12 B2

Dyrehaven 2, 2800 Lyngby.
13km north of Copenhagen.

CONTACT: Kate Mogensen, Secretary. Tel: +45 31 630483.
COURSE: 5,696m, PAR 71, SSS 70. Undulating course.
SOC RESTR'S: Welcome with prior agreement.
SOC GF - Round: Wd dkr150. **We** dkr200. **Day:** Wd N/A. **We** N/A.
SOC PACK: Please discuss at time of booking.
VIS RESTR'S: Welcome every day not Tues & after 12 Sat & Sun.
VIS GF - Round: Wd dkr150. **We** dkr200. **Day:** Wd N/A. **We** N/A.
FACILITIES: 6-hole Par 3 Course, Bar, Restaurant & Pro-shop.

KORSØR GOLF CLUB MAP 12 A2

Tårnborgparken, 4220 Korsør.
500m off Motorway, 1km east of Korsør.

CONTACT: M Irving, Professional. Tel: +45 53 571836.
COURSE: 5,998m, PAR 73, SSS 72. Parkland/seaside course.
SOC RESTR'S: Welcome with prior agreement.
SOC GF - Round: Wd N/A. **We** N/A. **Day:** Wd dkr160. **We** dkr200.
SOC PACK: Ring for details.
VIS RESTR'S: All times must be booked in advance.
VIS GF - Round: Wd N/A. **We** N/A. **Day:** Wd dkr160. **We** dkr200.
FACILITIES: 6-hole Par 3 Course, Range, Pro-shop, Restaurant.

RUNGSTED GOLF CLUB MAP 12 B2

Vestre Stationsvej 16, 2960 Rungsted Kyst.
25km north of Copenhagen.

CONTACT: H Stenderup, Secretary. Tel: +45 42 863444.
COURSE: 6,058m, PAR 72, SSS 73. Championship course.
SOC RESTR'S: Welcome with prior booking.
SOC GF - Round: Wd N/A. **We** dkr320. **Day:** Wd N/A. **We** N/A.
SOC PACK: Please contact club for details.
VIS RESTR'S: No visitors before 1 on Sat & Sun.
VIS GF - Round: Wd dkr320. **We** dkr320. **Day:** Wd N/A. **We** N/A.
FACILITIES: Driving Range, Pro-shop & Restaurant.

SØLLERØD GOLF CLUB MAP 12 B2

Øveroduej 239, 2840 Holte.
15km north of Copenhagen.

CONTACT: GK Hansen, Secretary. Tel: +45 42 801884.
COURSE: 5,872m, PAR 72, SSS 72. Parkland hilly course.
SOC RESTR'S: No play before 12 noon on Saturday & Sunday.
SOC GF - Round: Wd dkr180. **We** dkr250. **Day:** Wd N/A. **We** dkr350.
SOC PACK: Please discuss at time of booking.
VIS RESTR'S: Wednesday is Ladies Day, Thursday is Gents Day.
VIS GF - Round: Wd dkr180. **We** dkr250. **Day:** Wd N/A. **We** dkr350.
FACILITIES: Par 3 Course, Range, Putting Green & Restaurant.

SYDSJÆLLANDS GOLF CLUB MAP 12 B2

Præstø Landevej 39, Mogenstrup, 4700 Næstved.
10km south-east of Næstved.

CONTACT: Secretary. Tel: + 45 53 761555.
COURSE: 5,965m, PAR 72, SSS 71. Parkland course.
SOC RESTR'S: Tuesday is Gents Day, Wednesday is Ladies day.
SOC GF - Round: Wd dkr180. **We** dkr210. **Day:** Wd N/A. **We** N/A.
SOC PACK: Please discuss at time of booking.
VIS RESTR'S: Not before 2. match days. Please phone prior.
VIS GF - Round: Wd dkr180. **We** dkr210. **Day:** Wd N/A. **We** N/A.
FACILITIES: Bar, Restaurant & Putting Green.

VALLENSBÆK GOLF CLUB MAP 12 B2

Golfsvinget 16-20, DK 2625 Vallensbæk.
15km west of Copenhagen.

CONTACT: Nina Buchwald, Secretary. Tel: + 45 43 621899.
COURSE: 5,860m, PAR 71, SSS 70. Parkland course.
SOC RESTR'S: Welcome with prior agreement.
SOC GF - Round: Wd dkr190. **We** dkr250. **Day:** Wd N/A. **We** N/A.
SOC PACK: Please discuss at time of booking.
VIS RESTR'S: Welcome phone call prior to play advisable.
VIS GF - Round: Wd dkr190. **We** dkr250. **Day:** Wd N/A. **We** N/A.
FACILITIES: Pro-shop & Restaurant.

FINLAND

WHEN it comes to recommending - or not - golf in Finland, the time-honoured phrase used by other guides comes to mind: more reports are needed. Yes, there is rapid expansion taking place and over a dozen new courses have been opened in the last decade, but given the nature of Finland's climate, it must be extraordinarily difficult to keep courses in reasonable condition during the few short months each year in which they're available for play. Not even the most ardent Finnish nationalist would encourage the casual golfer to visit his country for the specific reason of playing golf, but holidaymakers enjoying Finland's matchless lakes and forests and treating the chance to play golf as a welcome ancilliary could be amply rewarded. A word of warning: choose your venue carefully. the Aura, Espoon, Kymen and Helsingen clubs all have over one thousand members and tee-times are likely to be at a premium. Tawast, in contrast, has a membership of only around 400. Shopping around could pay more dividends here than elsewhere in Europe.

AURA GOLF CLUB MAP 13 B2

Ruissalo 85, 20100 Turku.
9km south-west of Turku on Ruissalo Island.

CONTACT: A Maki, Professional. Tel: +35 921 589201.
COURSE: 5,883m, PAR 72, SSS 71. Links course.
SOC RESTR'S: Welcome with prior agreement.
SOC GF - Round: Wd Fk190. We Fk190. **Day:** Wd N/A. We N/A.
SOC PACK: Please discuss at time of booking.
VIS RESTR'S: Welcome except Competition days.
VIS GF - Round: Wd Fk190. We Fk190. **Day:** Wd N/A. We N/A.
FACILITIES: Pro-shop, Clubhouse, Sauna & Restaurant.

ESPOON GOLF CLUB MAP 13 B1

Box 26, 02781 Espoo.
25km west of Helsinki in Espoo.

CONTACT: R Dance, Professional. Tel: +35 90 811212.
COURSE: 6,183m, PAR 72, SSS 74. Parkland course.
SOC RESTR'S: Welcome by agreement.
SOC GF - Round: Wd Fk140. We Fk150. **Day:** Wd N/A. We N/A.
SOC PACK: Please discuss at time of booking.
VIS RESTR'S: Welcome please check Weekend availability.
VIS GF - Round: Wd Fk140. We Fk150. **Day:** Wd N/A. We N/A.
FACILITIES: Pro-shop, Clubhouse, Sauna & Restaurant.

GREEN ZONE GOLF CLUB MAP 13 B2

Näräntie 95400.
25km north-west of Kemi-Totnio on the Finnish/Swedish border.

CONTACT: E Palsi, Director. Tel: +35 869 843171.
COURSE: 6,853m, PAR 72, SSS 73. Parkland course.
SOC RESTR'S: Welcome Weekdays.
SOC GF - Round: Wd Fk160. We Fk210. **Day:** Wd N/A. We N/A.
SOC PACK: Please discuss at time of booking.
VIS RESTR'S: Welcome Weekdays. Phone for Weekends.
VIS GF - Round: Wd Fk160. We Fk210. **Day:** Wd N/A. We N/A.
FACILITIES: Pro-shop, Clubhouse, Sauna & Restaurant.

HELSINGIN GOLF CLUB MAP 13 B1

Talin Kartano, 00350 Helsinki 35.
10km west of Helsinki.

CONTACT: S Nystrom, Professional. Tel: +35 90 550235.
COURSE: 5,953m, PAR 71, SSS 71. Parkland course.
SOC RESTR'S: Welcome Weekdays.
SOC GF - Round: Wd Fk190. We N/A. **Day:** Wd N/A. We N/A.
SOC PACK: Please discuss at time of booking.
VIS RESTR'S: Welcome please check Weekend availability.
VIS GF - Round: Wd Fk190. We Fk200. **Day:** Wd N/A. We N/A.
FACILITIES: Pro-shop, Clubhouse & Restaurant.

FINLAND

KARELIA GOLF CLUB MAP 13 B2

Porkkatie 1A3 80230 Jœnsuu.
18km from Jœnsuu.
CONTACT: A Vaalas, Professional. Tel: +35 973 732411.
COURSE: 6,220m, PAR 72, SSS 73. Parkland course.
SOC RESTR'S: Welcome with prior booking.
SOC GF - Round: Wd Fk150. We Fk200. **Day:** Wd N/A. We N/A.
SOC PACK: Please discuss at time of booking.
VIS RESTR'S: Welcome.
VIS GF - Round: Wd Fk150. We Fk200. **Day:** Wd N/A. We N/A.
FACILITIES: Pro-shop, Clubhouse, Sauna & Restaurant.

KEIMOLA GOLF CLUB MAP 13 B1

Kirkantie 32, 01750 Vantaa.
15km north of Helsinki.
CONTACT: J Utter, Professional. Tel: +35 90 896991.
COURSE: 5,920m, PAR 72, SSS 74. Parkland course.
SOC RESTR'S: Welcome by agreement.
SOC GF - Round: Wd Fk150. We Fk150. **Day:** Wd N/A. We N/A.
SOC PACK: Please discuss at time of booking.
VIS RESTR'S: Welcome please check Weekend availability.
VIS GF - Round: Wd Fk150. We Fk150. **Day:** Wd N/A. We N/A.
FACILITIES: Pro-shop, Clubhouse, Restaurant.

KYMEN GOLF CLUB MAP 13 B2

Mussalo Golfcourse, 48310 Kotka.
130km east of Helsinki on Mussalo Island.
CONTACT: Secretary. Tel: +35 952 604555.
COURSE: 6,004m, PAR 72, SSS 74. Links course.
SOC RESTR'S: Welcome by agreement.
SOC GF - Round: Wd Fk130. We Fk150. **Day:** Wd N/A. We N/A.
SOC PACK: Please discuss at time of booking.
VIS RESTR'S: Welcome please check Weekend availability.
VIS GF - Round: Wd Fk130. We Fk150. **Day:** Wd N/A. We N/A.
FACILITIES: Pro-shop & Clubhouse.

MASTER GOLF CLUB MAP 13 B1

Puotistentie 4, 02940 Espoo.
25km west of Helsinki in Espoo.
CONTACT: K Tellqvist, Professional. Tel: +35 90 8537002.
COURSE: 6,220m, PAR 72, SSS 74. Parkland course.
SOC RESTR'S: Welcome by agreement.
SOC GF - Round: Wd Fk170. We Fk210. **Day:** Wd N/A. We N/A.
SOC PACK: Please discuss at time of booking.
VIS RESTR'S: Welcome please phone prior to play.
VIS GF - Round: Wd Fk170. We Fk210. **Day:** Wd N/A. We N/A.
FACILITIES: 9-hole Course, Pro-shop & Clubhouse.

MESSILÄ GOLF CLUB MAP 13 B1

Messilä, 15980.
One hour north of Helsinki.
CONTACT: J Mustjoki. Tel: + 35 918 860371.
COURSE: 5,725m, PAR 71, SSS 71. Parkland course.
SOC RESTR'S: Mon to Fri 8 to 3 possible to play.
SOC GF - Round: Wd N/A. We N/A. **Day:** Wd Fk210. We N/A.
SOC PACK: Bed & breakfast & day GF costs about Fk300.
VIS RESTR'S: Mon to Fri 8 to 3 possible to play.
VIS GF - Round: Wd N/A. We N/A. **Day:** Wd Fk210. We N/A.
FACILITIES: On application.

ST LAURENCE GOLF CLUB MAP 13 B1

Kaivurinkatu, 08200 Lohja.
55km west of Helsinki.
CONTACT: Secretary. Tel: +35 912 86603.
COURSE: 6,333m, PAR 73, SSS 74. Parkland course.
SOC RESTR'S: Welcome by agreement.
SOC GF - Round: Wd Fk160. We Fk180. **Day:** Wd N/A. We N/A.
SOC PACK: Please discuss at time of booking.
VIS RESTR'S: Welcome please check Weekend availability.
VIS GF - Round: Wd Fk160. We Fk180. **Day:** Wd N/A. We N/A.
FACILITIES: Par 3 Course, Pro-shop, Clubhouse & Range.

TAWAST GOLF & COUNTRY CLUB MAP 13 B2

Paavola, 13270 Hämeenlinna.
5km from Hämeenlinna to Lahti.
CONTACT: J Kovasiipi, MD. Tel: + 35 917 6197502.
COURSE: 5,741m, PAR 72, SSS 72. Parkland course.
SOC RESTR'S: Welcome with prior agreement.
SOC GF - Round: Wd N/A. We N/A. **Day:** Wd Fk200. We Fk200.
SOC PACK: Call Hotel or Club.
VIS RESTR'S: Welcome.
VIS GF - Round: Wd N/A. We N/A. **Day:** Wd Fk200. We Fk200.
FACILITIES: Tennis Courts, Saunas & Restaurant.

YYTERI GOLF CLUB MAP 13 B2

Pl 36, 28101 Pori.
20km from Pori.
CONTACT: T Nousiainen, Professional. Tel: + 358 17 197502.
COURSE: 5,735m, PAR 72, SSS 72. Parkland course.
SOC RESTR'S: Welcome Weekdays with prior agreement.
SOC GF - Round: Wd Fk170. We N/A. **Day:** Wd N/A. We N/A.
SOC PACK: Available with accommodation arranged.
VIS RESTR'S: Welcome Weekdays only.
VIS GF - Round: Wd Fk170. We N/A. **Day:** Wd N/A. We N/A.
FACILITIES: Bar & Clubhouse.

FRANCE

NOWHERE in Europe has the current boom in golf and golf course construction been more enthusiastically embraced than in France. Perhaps this isn't too surprising, for there has always been a strong golf tradition in France: the national championship dates back to 1906 and is one of Europe's oldest; examples of the work of early course designers can be found throughout the country and for British visitors, especially with the advent of the Channel Tunnel, it's a happy accident that in the 'Sea' and 'Forest' courses at Le Touquet; and at Wimereux and Hardelot, there are four of the best courses to be found anywhere in France, all within easy reach of the coast.

With the exception of links courses, the choice available to the golfer in France is the near-equal of that available in Britain. Parkland layouts in particular are excellent, especially around Paris. The 36 holes on offer at La Boulie; 27 holes at Chantilly; and another 36 holes each at La Prieure and Saint-Cloud all offer a welcome counter-attraction to the regular tourist spots. There's even more: St Nom-la-Breteche, home of the Lancome Trophy, provides a further 36 holes and, potentially the best of them all, no less than 45 holes are in play at the brand-new Paris National Golf club south-west of the city, at Guyancourt near Versailles The latter is a truly fabulous development on a decidedly unprepossessing former landfill site. Credit for it must lie jointly with the French Golf Federation and its Chief Executive and Principal Course Designer Hubert Chesneau. Every standard of golf is catered to here. There is the 9-hole 'Oiselet' course for beginners; the more testing 'Eagle' 18-hole layout for general play; and the 'Albatross' Championship course, the new venue for the French Open. This is stadium golf design at its best and as the courses mature, they can only get better and better. For keen golfers, note that the Albatross course is playable, but minimum handicap requirements are strictly enforced.

It's true to say that wherever you are in France, you'll be near a golf course. Those in the south might soon rival their equivalents in Spain and Portugal as holiday venues, but be warned, golf in France is not cheap, especially in the High Season. However your green fee will allow you access to what are generally extremely well-appointed club-houses offering facilities, (especially in the catering department!) far in excess of what is the norm in Britain. Be warned too that at all the better and more famous clubs, you'll almost certainly need a handicap certificate. Golf in France can be a treat, albeit an expensive one; with a little judicious planning and course selection, it can also be memorable.

Aquitaine

GOLF CLUB DE BIARRITZ   MAP 14 A3

2, Avenue Edith Cavell, 64200 Biarritz.
Centre of Biarritz town.

CONTACT: D Dubos, Manager. Tel: +33 59 03 71 80.
COURSE: 5,373m, PAR 69, SSS 69. Flat parkland course.
SOC RESTR'S: Welcome with prior reservation.
SOC GF – Round: Wd N/A. We 250F. **Day:** Wd 250F. We 300F.
SOC PACK: Seasonal alterations & reserved discount on GF.
VIS RESTR'S: Always welcome. Bookings 24 hours in advance.
VIS GF – Round: Wd N/A. We 250F. **Day:** Wd 250F. We 300F.
FACILITIES: Bar, Restaurant & Clubhouse.

GOLF CLUB DE PERIGUEUX   MAP 14 B3

Domaine de Saltgourde, 24430 Marsac.
120km north-east of Bordeaux on the N89.

CONTACT: E Smith, Professional. Tel: +33 53 53 02 35.
COURSE: 5,860m, PAR 72, SSS 72. A testing course.
SOC RESTR'S: Please book in advance.
SOC GF – Round: Wd N/A. We N/A. **Day:** Wd 195F. We 195F.
SOC PACK: Available on booking.
VIS RESTR'S: Welcome. Public Course.
VIS GF – Round: Wd N/A. We N/A. **Day:** Wd 195F. We 195F.
FACILITIES: Restaurant & Clubhouse.

GOLF D'ARCACHON   MAP 14 A3

35 Boulevard d'Arcachon, 33260, La Teste de Buch.
60km south of Bordeaux off the N250.

CONTACT: Reservations. Tel: +33 56 54 44 00.
COURSE: 5,865m, PAR 71, SSS 70. Testing parkland course.
SOC RESTR'S: Please book in advance.
SOC GF – Round: We N/A. We N/A. **Day** Wd 260F. We 260F.
SOC PACK: Seasonal alterations & reserved discount on GF.
VIS RESTR'S: Advisable to phone prior. H'cap Cert required.
VIS GF – Round: We N/A. We N/A. **Day:** Wd 260F. We 260F.
FACILITIES: Restaurant & Bar.

AQUITAINE

GOLF D'ARCANGUES   MAP 14 A3

Argelous, 64200 Arcangues.
5km south of Biarritz off the D932.

CONTACT: Secretary. Tel: +33 59 43 10 56.
COURSE: 6,037m, PAR 72, SSS 70. Parkland course.
SOC RESTR'S: Out of season – closed on Tuesday.
SOC GF – Round: Wd 280F. We 280F. **Day** Wd N/A We N/A.
SOC PACK: Off season reduction on above GF Wd 140F. We 200F.
VIS RESTR'S: Off season – closed on Tuesday. GF reduction as Soc.
VIS GF – Round: Wd 280F. We 280F. **Day:** We N/A. We N/A.
FACILITIES: Restaurant, Bar & Lounge.

GOLF D'HOSSEGOR   MAP 14 A3

Avenue du Golf, 40150 Hossegor.
20km north-west of Biarritz off the D79.

CONTACT: C Raillard. Tel: +33 58 43 56 99.
COURSE: 5,968m PAR 71, SSS 71. Heathland course.
SOC RESTR'S: Welcome.
SOC GF – Round: Wd N/A. We N/A. **Day:** Wd 200F. We 280F.
SOC PACK: Available on booking.
VIS RESTR'S: Welcome.
VIS GF – Round: Wd N/A. We N/A. **Day:** Wd 200F. We 280F.
FACILITIES: Range, Golf Buggy Hire, Bar & Clubhouse.

GOLF DE CASTELJALOUX   MAP 14 B3

Route de Mont-de-Marsan, 47700 Casteljaloux.
80km south-east of Bordeaux off the D933.

CONTACT: Reservations. Tel: +33 53 93 51 60.
COURSE: 5,916m, PAR 72, SSS 71. Parkland course.
SOC RESTR'S: Always welcome.
SOC GF – Day: Wd 160F. We 200F. **Day:** Wd 190F. We 230F.
SOC PACK: Available on booking.
VIS RESTR'S: Always welcome.
VIS GF – Round: Wd 160F. We 200F. **Day:** Wd 190F. We 230F.
FACILITIES: Bar, Restaurant & Range.

GOLF DE CHIBERTA   MAP 14 A3

104, Boulevard des Plages, 64600, Anglet.
Just 2km north from Biarritz town, in Anglet.

CONTACT: Reservations. Tel: +33 59 63 83 20.
COURSE: 5,606m PAR 71, SSS 70. Forest & Links course.
SOC RESTR'S: Welcome.
SOC GF – Round: Wd N/A. We N/A. **Day:** Wd 200F. We 240F.
SOC PACK: Available on booking.
VIS RESTR'S: From Apr-May & July-Sept daily GF 300F.
VIS GF – Round: Wd N/A. We N/A. **Day:** Wd 200F. We 240F.
FACILITIES: Clubhouse, Bar & Restaurant.

FRANCE

GOLF DE L'ARDILOUSE
MAP 14 A3

33680 Lacanau-Océan.
40km north-west of Bordeaux on D6 to Lacanau.

CONTACT: Reservations. Tel: +33 56 03 25 60.
COURSE: 5,906m PAR 71, SSS 71. Undulating forest course.
SOC RESTR'S: By prior arrangement only.
SOC GF – Round: Wd 160F. **We** 190F. **Day: Wd** 180F. **We** 230F.
SOC PACK: Seasonal alterations & reserved discount on GF.
VIS RESTR'S: Always welcome.
VIS GF – Round: Wd 160F. **We** 190F. **Day: Wd** 180F. **We** 230F.
FACILITIES: Clubhouse, Bar & Restaurant.

GOLF DE LA COTE D'ARGENT
MAP 14 A3

40660 Moliets.
45km north of Biarritz on the D652.

CONTACT: D Breton, Director. Tel: +33 58 48 54 65.
COURSE: 6,172m, PAR 72, SSS 72. Seaside/links course.
SOC RESTR'S: Welcome Weekdays only.
SOC GF – Round: Wd 270F. **We** N/A. **Day: Wd** N/A. **We** N/A.
SOC PACK: Discount for 20 +.
VIS RESTR'S: Weekdays only. Discount for preserved GF bookings.
VIS GF – Round: Wd 270F. **We** N/A. **Day: Wd** N/A. **We** N/A.
FACILITIES 9-hole Par 31 Course, Clubhouse & Bar.

GOLF DE PESSAC
MAP 14 B3

Rue de la Princesse, 33600, Pessac.
7km south-west of Bordeaux off the N250.

CONTACT: Reservations. Tel: +33 56 36 24 47.
COURSE: 6,198m, PAR 72, SSS 72. Forest/links course.
SOC RESTR'S: Always welcome.
SOC GF – Round: Wd N/A. **We** N/A. **Day: Wd** 210F. **We** 270F.
SOC PACK: Available on booking.
VIS RESTR'S: Always welcome. Discount on reserved GF.
VIS GF – Round: Wd N/A. **We** N/A. **Day: Wd** 210F. **We** 270F.
FACILITIES: 3 sets of 9 holes make up this course.

GOLF DE SEIGNOSSE
MAP 14 A3

Carrefour Boucau, 40510, Seignosse.
25km north of Biarritz off the D79.

CONTACT: Reservations. Tel: +33 58 43 17 32.
COURSE: 6,130m, PAR 72, SSS 72. Championship parkland course.
SOC RESTR'S: Please book in advance.
SOC GF – Round: Wd N/A. **We** N/A. **Day: Wd** 210F. **We** 310F.
SOC PACK: Seasonal alterations & reserved discount on GF.
VIS RESTR'S: Always welcome.
VIS GF – Round: Wd N/A. **We** N/A. **Day: Wd** 210F. **We** 310F.
FACILITIES Bar, Restaurant & Clubhouse.

GOLF DU PIAN MEDOC (OLD)
MAP 14 B3

Chemin de Courmateau, Louens le Pian Médoc, 33290.
20km north-west of Bordeaux off the D1.

CONTACT: Reservations. Tel: +33 56 72 01 10.
COURSE: 6,245m, PAR 71, SSS 71. Inland links course.
SOC RESTR'S: Please book in advance.
SOC GF – Round: Wd N/A. **We** N/A. **Day: Wd** 200F. **We** 270F.
SOC PACK: Seasonal alterations & reserved discount on GF.
VIS RESTR'S: Always welcome. Handicap Certificate required.
VIS GF – Round: Wd N/A. **We** N/A. **Day: Wd** 200F. **We** 270F.
FACILITIES Château Clubhouse & Restaurant.

GOLF DU PIAN MEDOC (NEW)
MAP 14 B3

Chemin de Courmateau, Louens le Pian Médoc, 33290.
20km north-west of Bordeaux off the D1.

CONTACT: Reservations. Tel: +33 56 72 01 10.
COURSE: 5,723m, PAR 71, SSS 71. Parkland course.
SOC RESTR'S: Please book in advance.
SOC GF – Round: Wd N/A. **We** N/A. **Day: Wd** 200F. **We** 270F.
SOC PACK: Seasonal alterations & reserved discount on GF.
VIS RESTR'S: Always welcome. Handicap Certificate required.
VIS GF – Round: Wd N/A. **We** N/A. **Day: Wd** 200F. **We** 270F.
FACILITIES Château Clubhouse & Restaurant.

GOLF GUJAN MESTRAS
MAP 14 A3

Route de Souguinet, 33470 Gujan Mestras.
45km south-west of Bordeaux off the RN 250.

CONTACT: Reservations. Tel: +33 56 66 86 36.
COURSE: 6,230m, PAR 72, SSS 72. Moorland course.
SOC RESTR'S: Always welcome.
SOC GF – Round: Wd N/A. **We** N/A. **Day: Wd** 210F. **We** 270F.
SOC PACK: Seasonal alterations & reserved discount on GF.
VIS RESTR'S: Alteration to Green Fee, July-Aug daily 270F.
VIS GF – Round: Wd N/A. **We** N/A. **Day: Wd** 210F. **We** 270F.
FACILITIES 9-hole Par 36 Course, Clubhouse & Bar.

GOLF HOTEL CASTELNAUD
MAP 14 B3

"La Menuisière', 47290 Castelnaud de Gratecambe.
10km north of Villeneuve on N21. 40km north of Agen.

CONTACT: Christian Sill, Manager. Tel: +33 53 01 74 64.
COURSE: 6,317m, PAR 72, SSS 73. Beautiful parkland course.
SOC RESTR'S: Always welcome.
SOC GF – Round: Wd 150F. **We** 170F. **Day: Wd** 170F. **We** 210F.
SOC PACK: Seasonal alterations & reserved discount on GF.
VIS RESTR'S: Always welcome.
VIS GF – Round: Wd 140F. **We** 210F. **Day: Wd** N/A **We** N/A.
FACILITIES: 9-hole Course, Range, Putting Greens, Pro-shop.

Ardenne & Alsace

GOLF DE LA VITARDERIE MAP 15 A1

BP 41 Chemin de la Bourdonnerie, Dormans, 51700.
40km south-west of Reims off the D20.

CONTACT: J Pimenta, Manager. Tel: +33 26 58 25 09.
COURSE: 5,969m, PAR 72, SSS 71. Windy course with water.
SOC RESTR'S: Monday morning.
SOC GF – Round: Wd 130F. We 160F. **Day:** Wd N/A. We N/A.
SOC PACK: Available on booking.
VIS RESTR'S: Welcome but booking is advisable.
VIS GF – Round: Wd 130F. We 160F. **Day:** Wd N/A. We N/A.
FACILITIES: Bar & Restaurant.

METZ TECHNOPOLE MAP 15 B1

3 Rue Félix Savart, Metz, 57070.
10 minutes from Metz. Follow the 'Technopole' signs.

CONTACT: B Lebreton, Director. Tel: +33 87 20 33 11.
COURSE: 5,774m, PAR 71, SSS 70. Parkland course.
SOC RESTR'S: Welcome.
SOC GF – Round: Wd N/A. We N/A. **Day:** Wd 180F. We 210F.
SOC PACK: 'FORMULE Golf' available on 15 courses.
VIS RESTR'S: Welcome. Handicap Certificate required.
VIS GF – Round: Wd N/A. We N/A. **Day:** Wd 180F. We 210F.
FACILITIES: 6-hole Course, Clubhouse & Restaurant.

ROUGEMONT-LE-CHATEAU MAP 15 B2

Route de Masevaux, Rougemont-le-Château, 90110.
150km east of Dijon- exit Belfort to the D12.

CONTACT: J-M Bouilon, Director. Tel: +33 84 23 74 74.
COURSE: 6,002m, PAR 72, SSS 72. Parkland course.
SOC RESTR'S: Welcome.
SOC GF – Round: Wd N/A. We N/A. **Day:** Wd 185F. We 260F.
SOC PACK: On request.
VIS RESTR'S: Welcome.
VIS GF – Round: Wd N/A. We N/A. **Day:** Wd 195F. We 300F.
FACILITIES: Range, Pitch & Putt.

BRITTANY

VITTEL GOLF CLUB (PEUPLIN) MAP 15 B1/2

BP 122, 88804 Vittel- Cedex.
Vittel, 70km south of Nancy.

CONTACT: D Mory, Professional. Tel: +33 29 08 18 80.
COURSE: 6,100m, PAR 72, SSS 72. Parkland course.
SOC RESTR'S: Book in advance.
SOC GF – Round: Wd 200F. We N/A. **Day:** Wd N/A. We N/A.
SOC PACK: On application.
VIS RESTR'S: Book in advance.
VIS GF – Round: Wd 200F. We 250F **Day:** Wd N/A. We N/A.
FACILITIES: 9-hole Course, Range, Bar & Restaurant.

VITTEL GOLF CLUB (ST JEAN) MAP 15 B1/2

BP 122, 88804 Vittel- Cedex.
Vittel, 70km south of Nancy.

CONTACT: D Mory, Professional. Tel: +33 29 08 18 80.
COURSE: 6,326m, PAR 72, SSS 72. Parkland course.
SOC RESTR'S: Book in advance.
SOC GF – Round: Wd 200F. We N/A. **Day:** Wd N/A. We N/A.
SOC PACK: On application.
VIS RESTR'S: Book in advance.
VIS GF – Round: Wd 200F. We 250F. **Day:** Wd N/A. We N/A.
FACILITIES: 9-hole Course, Range, Bar & Restaurant.

Brittany

AJONCS D'OR GOLF CLUB MAP 14 A1

22240 St-Quay Portrieux.
25km north-west of St-Brieuc, just outside on Portrieux.

CONTACT: Secretary. Tel: +33 96 71 90 74.
COURSE: 6,125m, PAR 72, SSS 72. Public parkland course.
SOC RESTR'S: Welcome with prior bookings.
SOC GF – Round: Wd 180F. We 200F. **Day:** Wd N/A. We N/A.
SOC PACK: Discount on reserved Green Fee bookings.
VIS RESTR'S: Welcome.
VIS GF – Round: Wd 180F. We 200F. **Day:** Wd N/A. We N/A
FACILITIES: Pro-shop, Bar & Clubhouse.

FRANCE

GOLF DE BADEN MAP 14 A2

Kernic, 56870 Baden.
50km south-west of Lorient off the N165 on the coast.
CONTACT: Reservations. Tel: +33 97 57 18 96.
COURSE: 6,145m, PAR 72, SSS 73. Pine forest course.
SOC RESTR'S: Always welcome.
SOC GF – Round: Wd N/A. We N/A. **Day:** Wd 160F. We 240F.
SOC PACK: Seasonal alterations & reserved discount on GF.
VIS RESTR'S: Always welcome.
VIS GF – Round: Wd N/A. We N/A. **Day:** Wd 160F. We 240F.
FACILITIES: Practice Green, Pro-shop, Bar & Restaurant.

GOLF DE L'ODET MAP 14 A2

Clohars-Fouesnant, 29950 Benodet.
50km north-west of Lorient on the N165- in Fouesnant.
CONTACT: Reservations. Tel : +33 98 54 87 88.
COURSE: 6,235m, PAR 72, SSS 73. Parkland course.
SOC RESTR'S: Welcome with prior reservation.
SOC GF – Round: Wd 200F. We 250F. **Day:** Wd N/A. We N/A.
SOC PACK: Available on booking.
VIS RESTR'S: Always welcome. Seasonal variations.
VIS GF – Round: Wd 200F. We 250F. **Day:** Wd N/A. We N/A.
FACILITIES: 9-hole Course, Pro-shop, Bar & Restaurant.

GOLF DE BREST-IROISE MAP 14 A1

Parc des Loisirs de Lann-Rohou, St Urbain, Landerneau 29800.
24km east of Brest on the D712.
CONTACT: Director. Tel : +33 98 85 16 17.
COURSE: 5,672m, PAR 72, SSS 72. Hilly/heathland course.
SOC RESTR'S: Welcome with prior reservation.
SOC GF – Round: Wd 220F. We 250F. **Day:** Wd N/A. We N/A.
SOC PACK: Seasonal alterations & reserved discount on GF.
VIS RESTR'S: Welcome with prior reservation.
VIS GF – Round: Wd 220F. We 250F. **Day:** Wd N/A. We N/A.
FACILITIES: 9-hole Course, Bar & Restaurant.

GOLF DE LA FRESLONNIERE MAP 14 A2

Le Bois Briand, 35650, Le Rheu.
3km west of Rennes.
CONTACT: Reservations. Tel : +33 99 60 84 09.
COURSE: 5,694m, PAR 71, SSS 71. Parkland course.
SOC RESTR'S: Welcome with prior reservation.
SOC GF – Round: Wd N/A. We N/A. **Day:** Wd 200F. We N/A.
SOC PACK: Reduction on reserved Green Fee bookings.
VIS RESTR'S: Always welcome.
VIS GF – Round: Wd N/A. We N/A. **Day:** Wd 200F. We 240F.
FACILITIES: Bar & Restaurant.

GOLF DE DINARD MAP 14 A1

35800 St-Briac-Sue-Mer.
8km west of St-Malo.
CONTACT: Reservations. Tel : +33 99 88 32 07.
COURSE: 5,020m, PAR 69, SSS 73. Links course.
SOC RESTR'S: Welcome with reservations Weekdays only.
SOC GF – Round: Wd N/A. We N/A. **Day:** Wd 210F. We N/A.
SOC PACK: Seasonal alterations to daily Green Fee.
VIS RESTR'S: Welcome with Reservation.
VIS GF – Round: Wd 210F. We 240F. **Day:** Wd N/A. We N/A.
FACILITIES: Bar & Restaurant.

GOLF DES ORMES MAP 14 A1

Epiniac, 35120, Dol-de-Bretagne.
35km north of Rennes off the D780.
CONTACT: R Rault, Director. Tel : +33 99 73 49 60.
COURSE: 6,125m, PAR 72, SSS 72. Parkland course.
SOC RESTR'S: Discount on reserved GF bookings.
SOC GF – Round: Wd N/A. We N/A. **Day:** Wd 225F. We N/A.
SOC PACK: Tour operator 20% normal Green Fees.
VIS RESTR'S: GF alter seasonally from Low160F. to High 225F.
VIS GF – Round: Wd N/A. We N/A. **Day:** Wd 225F. We N/A.
FACILITIES: Par 3 Course, Clubhouse & Restaurant.

GOLF DE KERVER MAP 14 A2

Domaine de Kerver, St-Gildas-de-Rhuys, 56730.
70km south-east of Lorient on the N165- off the D780.
CONTACT: J Leroux, Director. Tel: +33 97 45 30 09.
COURSE: 6,147m, PAR 73, SSS 73. Links course.
SOC RESTR'S: Always welcome.
SOC GF – Round: Wd 210F. We 230F. **Day:** Wd N/A. We N/A.
SOC PACK: Green pass for days.
VIS RESTR'S: Seasonal alterations & reserved discount on GF.
VIS GF – Round: Wd 210F. We 230F. **Day:** Wd N/A. We N/A.]
FACILITIES: New Clubhouse.

GOLF DE PLOEMEUR OCEAN MAP 14 A2

St-Jude, Kerham, 56270 Ploemeur.
5km west of Lorient in Ploemeur.
CONTACT: M Bernard, Manager. Tel: +33 97 32 81 82.
COURSE: 5,957m, PAR 72, SSS 72. Links/parkland course.
SOC RESTR'S: Welcome.
SOC GF – Round: Wd N/A. We N/A. **Day:** Wd 240F. We 240F.
SOC PACK: 20% to tour operators. Booking at least one week.
VIS RESTR'S: Seasonal alterations & reserved discount on GF.
VIS GF – Round: Wd N/A. We N/A. **Day:** Wd 240F. We 240F.
FACILITIES: Covered Driving Range, Bar & Restaurant.

BRITTANY

GOLF DE RENNES MAP 14 A2

35136 St-Jacques-de-la-Landes.
4km south-west of Rennes off the N24.

CONTACT: Reservations Tel: +33 99 64 24 18.
COURSE: 6,090m, PAR 72, SSS 71. Parkland course.
SOC RESTR'S: Welcome with prior reservation.
SOC GF – Round: Wd N/A. We N/A. **Day:** Wd 230F. We N/A.
SOC PACK: Available on booking.
VIS RESTR'S: Welcome but booking is advisable.
VIS GF – Round: Wd N/A. We N/A. **Day:** Wd 230F. We N/A.
FACILITIES: 2 extra short 9-hole Courses, Bar & Restaurant.

GOLF DES SABLES-D'OR-LES-PINS MAP 14 A1

22240 Fréhel.
40km west of St-Malo off the D786 along the coast.

CONTACT: Secretary. Tel: +33 96 41 42 57.
COURSE: 5,585m, PAR 71, SSS 70. Open links course.
SOC RESTR'S: Welcome.
SOC GF – Round: Wd N/A. We N/A. **Day:** Wd 170F. We 260F.
SOC PACK: Seasonal alterations & reserved discount on GF.
VIS RESTR'S: Welcome.
VIS GF – Round: Wd N/A. We N/A. **Day:** Wd 170F. We 260F.
FACILITIES: Pro-shop, Bar & Clubhouse.

GOLF DE ST MALO LE TRONCHET MAP 14 A1

35540 Miniac-Morvan.
25km south of St Malo off the N137.

CONTACT: P Dinard, Director. Tel: +33 99 58 96 69.
COURSE: 6,049m, PAR 72, SSS 72. Championship heathland.
SOC RESTR'S: Welcome.
SOC GF – Round: Wd N/A. We N/A. **Day:** Wd 230F. We N/A.
SOC PACK: Discount on reserved GF bookings.
VIS RESTR'S: Welcome.
VIS GF – Round: Wd N/A. We N/A. **Day:** Wd 230F. We N/A.
FACILITIES: 9-hole Par 36 Course, Bar & Clubhouse.

GOLF DE SAINT SAMSON MAP 14 A1

Route de Kérénoc, Pleumeur-Bodou 22560.
50km east of Roscoff on the D788.

CONTACT: L Guillemot, Secretary. Tel: +33 96 23 87 34.
COURSE: 5,688m, PAR 71, SSS 70. Links course.
SOC RESTR'S: Minimum ten people.
SOC GF – Round: Wd N/A. We N/A. **Day:** Wd 200F. We N/A.
SOC PACK: Double room, Breakfast & Meal – 270F.
VIS RESTR'S: Seasonal alterations & reserved discount on GF.
VIS GF – Round: Wd N/A. We N/A. **Day:** Wd 200F. We N/A.
FACILITIES: Heated Pool, Tennis Court, Hostel on site.

GOLF DU VAL QUEVEN MAP 14 A2

Kerruisseau, 56530 Queven.
10km west of Lorient.

CONTACT: Reservations. Tel: +33 97 05 17 96.
COURSE: 6,127m, PAR 72, SSS 72. Parkland course.
SOC RESTR'S: Welcome with prior reservation.
SOC GF – Round: Wd N/A. We N/A. **Day:** Wd 180F. We 230F.
SOC PACK: Seasonal alterations & reserved discount on GF.
VIS RESTR'S: Welcome with prior reservation.
VIS GF – Round: Wd N/A. We N/A. **Day:** Wd 180F. We 230F.
FACILITIES: Practice Green, Pro-shop, Bar & Restaurant.

ROCHERS GOLF CLUB MAP 14 A2

Château des Rochers Sevigne, 35500 Vitré.
30km east of Rennes off the N157.

CONTACT: Secretary. Tel: +33 99 96 52 52.
COURSE: 5,529m, PAR 71, SSS 72. Undulating parkland course.
SOC RESTR'S: Welcome.
SOC GF – Round: Wd N/A. We N/A .**Day:** Wd 170F. We 230F.
SOC PACK: Seasonal alterations & reserved discount on GF.
VIS RESTR'S: Welcome.
VIS GF – Round: Wd N/A. We N/A. **Day:** Wd 170F. We 230F.
FACILITIES: Pro-shop, Bar, Restaurant & Clubhouse.

SAINT LAURENT MAP 14 A2

Ploemel – 56400 Auray.
20km south of Lorient on the D781.

CONTACT: A Piron, Manager. Tel: +33 97 56 85 18.
COURSE: 6,112m, PAR 72, SSS 72. Parkland course.
SOC RESTR'S: Welcome with prior reservation.
SOC GF – Round: Wd N/A. We N/A. **Day:** Wd 150F. We 230F.
SOC PACK: 10 Green Fees = 10% discount.
VIS RESTR'S: Seasonal alterations & reserved discount on GF.
VIS GF – Round: Wd N/A. We N/A. **Day:** Wd 150F. We 230F.
FACILITIES: 9-hole Par 35 Course, Bar & Clubhouse.

RAC HOTELS IN FRANCE

Over 1,300 carefully selected hotels, many illustrated in colour and all cross-referenced to the map section.
For holidaymaker or business traveller alike.
An information source for
regional foods - beaches - châteaux - resorts - theme parks - wine regions - ...and much more
Price £9.99
Available from bookshops
or direct from the RAC on 0235 834885

FRANCE

Burgundy & Rhône

ALBON GOLF CLUB MAP 15 B2

Domaine du Château de Senaud, Albon, 26140.
55km south of Lyon off the A7.

CONTACT: R Gurgui, Secretary. Tel: +33 75 03 03 90.
COURSE: 6,108m, PAR 72, SSS 73. Parkland course.
SOC RESTR'S: Welcome.
SOC GF – Round: Wd 190F. We 260F. Day: Wd N/A. We N/A.
SOC PACK: Available on booking.
VIS RESTR'S: Welcome.
VIS GF – Round: Wd 190F. We 260F. Day: Wd N/A. We N/A.
FACILITIES: Pro-shop, Swimming Pool, Restaurant & Bar.

GOLF DE BOSSEY MAP 15 B2

Château de Crevin, 74160 St-Julien-en-Genevois.
On the French Switzerland border 5km south of Geneva (Swit).

CONTACT: Secretary. Tel: +33 50 43 75 25.
COURSE: 6,022m, PAR 71, SSS 70. Forest course.
SOC RESTR'S: Welcome with booking.
SOC GF – Round: Wd 300F. We N/A. Day: Wd N/A. We N/A.
SOC PACK: Available on booking.
VIS RESTR'S: Welcome but contact in advance.
VIS GF – Round: Wd 300F. We N/A. Day: Wd N/A. We N/A.
FACILITIES: Restaurant, Bar, Pro-shop & Club Hire.

GOLF D'AIX-LES-BAINS MAP 15 B2

Avenue du Golf, 73100 Aix-les-Bains.
On Lake Bourget, 3km south of Aix-les-Bains.

CONTACT: Secretary. Tel: +33 79 61 23 35.
COURSE: 5,599m, PAR 71, SSS 69. Parkland course.
SOC RESTR'S: Open for applications through Secretary.
SOC GF – Round: Wd 210F. We 300F. Day: Wd N/A. We N/A.
SOC PACK: Available on booking.
VIS RESTR'S: Welcome with some seasonal restrictions.
VIS GF – Round: Wd 210F. We 300F. Day: Wd N/A. We N/A.
FACILITIES: Range, Pro-shop, Restaurant & Bar.

GOLF DE BEAUNE MAP 15 B2

Levernois, 21200 Beaune.
40km south of Dijon on the E17 to Beaune – follow signs.

CONTACT: C Piot, Director. Tel: +33 80 24 10 29.
COURSE: 6,400m, PAR 72, SSS 72. Parkland course.
SOC RESTR'S: Welcome with written application.
SOC GF – Round: Wd 150F. We 230F. Day: Wd N/A. We N/A.
SOC PACK: Available on booking.
VIS RESTR'S: Welcome.
VIS GF – Round: Wd 150F. We 230F. Day: Wd N/A. We N/A.
FACILITIES: 9-hole Course, Clubhouse, Restaurant & Bar.

GOLF DE CHAMONIX MAP 15 B2

Route des Praz, 74400 les Pras de Chamonix.
5km north of Chamonix on the N506.

CONTACT: Secretary. Tel: +33 50 53 06 28.
COURSE: 6,076m, PAR 72, SSS 72. Parkland course.
SOC RESTR'S: Advance bookings only.
SOC GF – Round: Wd 200F. We 300F. Day: Wd N/A. We N/A.
SOC PACK: Information provided when booking.
VIS RESTR'S: Welcome. Some restrictions on Weekends.
VIS GF – Round: Wd 200F. We 300F. Day: Wd N/A. We N/A.
FACILITIES: Restaurant, Bar, Pro-shop & Club Hire.

GOLF DE DIJON-BOURGOGNE MAP 15 B2

Bois des Norges, 21200 Ruffey-les-Echirey.
10km north of Dijon towards Langres.

CONTACT: J Lamaison, Professional. Tel: +33 80 35 71 10.
COURSE: 6,179m, PAR 72, SSS 72. Parkland course.
SOC RESTR'S: Book in advance.
SOC GF – Round: Wd N/A. We N/A. Day: Wd 190F. We N/A.
SOC PACK: On application.
VIS RESTR'S: No restrictions.
VIS GF – Round: Wd 190F. We 250F. Day: Wd 190F. We N/A.
FACILITIES: Second 18-hole Course, Range, Bar & Restaurant.

GOLF DE DIVONNE MAP 15 B2

01220 Divonne-les-Bains.
20km north of Geneva (Switz) off the N5.

CONTACT: F Seguin or P Paoletti. Tel: +33 50 40 34 11.
COURSE: 6,035m, PAR 72, SSS 72. A very technical course.
SOC RESTR'S: Please book in advance.
SOC GF – Round: Wd N/A. We N/A. Day: Wd 270F. We 550F.
SOC PACK: Available on booking.
VIS RESTR'S: Guests at The Grand or Hotel du Golf – 50% reduction.
VIS GF – Round: Wd N/A. We N/A. Day: Wd 270F. We 550F.
FACILITIES: Bar & Restaurant.

CENTRE

GOLF DE GIEZ LAC D'ANNECY MAP 15 B2

Giez 74210, Faverges.
Between Annecy & Albertville N508 (50km south of Geneva).

CONTACT: J Marie or J Gavard. Tel: +33 50 44 48 41.
COURSE: 5,850m, PAR 72, SSS 71. Parkland course.
SOC RESTR'S: Welcome. Closed from December to March.
SOC GF-Round: Wd 240F. **We** 240FF **Day: Wd** N/A. **We** N/A.
SOC PACK: Ten or more players only – 20% discount.
VIS RESTR'S: Welcome.
VIS GF – Round: Wd 240F. **We** 240F. **Day: Wd** N/A. **We** N/A.
FACILITIES: Pro-shop, Caddymaster, Restaurant & Bar.

GOLF DE LA SALLE MACON MAP 15 B2

Lugny, 71260 La Salle.
70km north of Lyon off the A6.

CONTACT: Reservations. Tel: +33 85 36 09 71.
COURSE: 6,024m, PAR 71, SSS 71. Hilly parkland course.
SOC RESTR'S: Welcome with prior reservation.
SOC GF – Round: Wd 180F. **We** 250F. **Day: Wd** N/A. **We** N/A.
SOC PACK: For 10 people at least, Wd GF 140F. We GF 200F.
VIS RESTR'S: Always welcome. Green Fees 100F. on Tuesday.
VIS GF – Round: Wd 180F. **We** 250F. **Day: Wd** N/A. **We** N/A.
FACILITIES: Bar, Restaurant, Putting Green & Range.

GOLF DE LYON VILLETTE-D'ANTHON MAP 15 B2

38280 Villette-d'Anthon.
20km east of Lyon.

CONTACT: Reservations. Tel: +33 78 31 11 33.
COURSE: 6,415m, PAR 73, SSS 72. Flat forest course.
SOC RESTR'S: Written applications only.
SOC GF – Round: Wd 210F. **We** 310F. **Day: Wd** N/A. **We** N/A.
SOC PACK: Tailored for each outing.
VIS RESTR'S: Welcome. Some Weekend restrictions.
VIS GF – Round: Wd 210F. **We** 310F. **Day: Wd** N/A. **We** N/A.
FACILITIES: 2nd 18-hole Course, Bar, Restaurant & Pro-shop.

GOLF SAINT-BENIN D'AZY MAP 15 A2

Parc du Château, Saint-Benin, d'Azy, 58290.
15km east of Nevers on the D978.

CONTACT: V Hoefler. Tel: +33 86 58 50 00.
COURSE: 6,157m, PAR 72, SSS 73. Parkland course.
SOC RESTR'S: Please book through Secretary.
SOC GF – Round: Wd 130F. **We** 180F. **Day: Wd** 130F. **We** 180F.
SOC PACK: Available on booking.
VIS RESTR'S: Welcome. Some restrictions in winter.
VIS GF – Round: Wd 150F. **We** 200F. **Day: Wd** 150F. **We** 200F.
FACILITIES: Clubhouse, Bar & Restaurant.

LA BRESSE GOLF CLUB MAP 15 B2

Domaine de Mary, Condessiat, 01400 Chatillon-sur-Chalaronne.
15km west of Boourg-en-Bresse (D936).

CONTACT: JJ Demange, Professional. Tel: +33 74 51 42 09.
COURSE: 6,217m, PAR 72, SSS 72. Parkland course.
SOC RESTR'S: Handicap Certificate at Weekend.
SOC GF – Round: Wd 200F. **We** N/A. **Day: Wd** N/A. **We** N/A.
SOC PACK: On application.
VIS RESTR'S: Handicap Certificate at Weekend.
VIS GF – Round: Wd 200F. **We** 250F. **Day: Wd** N/A. **We** N/A.
FACILITIES: Range, Bar & Restaurant.

ROYAL GOLF CLUB MAP 15 B2

Rive Sud du lac de Genève, Évian 74500.
35 north-east of Geneve on Lake Lausanne.

CONTACT: R Mercier, Director. Tel: + 33 50 26 85 00.
COURSE: 6,074m, PAR 72, SSS 72. Parkland course.
SOC RESTR'S: Welcome with prior reservation.
SOC GF-Round: Wd N/A. **We** N/A. **Day:** 350F. **We** 380F.
SOC PACK: Free to Hotel Guests.
VIS RESTR'S: Welcome but booking is advisable.
VIS GF- Round: Wd N/A. **We** N/A. **Day:** 350F. **We** 380F.
FACILITIES: Range, Putting Green, Pitching Green, Pitch & Putt.

Centre

CHATEAU DE CHEVERNY MAP 15 A2

Domaine de la Rousselière Cheverny, 41700 Contres.
70km south-west of Orléans on A10-D725.

CONTACT: T Noellec, Director. Tel: +33 54 79 24 70.
COURSE: 5,161m, PAR 71, SSS 71. Set along beautiful ponds.
SOC RESTR'S: Welcome every day except We & Bank Hols.
SOC GF – Round: Wd 200F. **We** 280F. **Day: Wd** N/A. **We** N/A.
SOC PACK: Available on booking.
VIS RESTR'S: Always welcome.
VIS GF – Round: Wd 200F. **We** 280F. **Day: Wd** N/A. **We** N/A.
FACILITIES: Bar & Restaurant.

FRANCE

GOLF CLUB VIERZON LA PICARDIERE MAP 15 A2

Chemin de la Picardiere, 18100 Vierzon.
75km south of Orléans on the A71.

CONTACT: D Baert, Secretary. Tel: +33 48 75 21 43.
COURSE: 6,077m, PAR 72, SSS 72. Parkland course.
SOC RESTR'S: Welcome with prior reservation.
SOC GF – Round: Wd 140F. We 200F. Day: Wd N/A. We N/A.
SOC PACK: Available on booking.
VIS RESTR'S: Reduction on reserved Green Fee bookings.
VIS GF – Round: Wd 140F. We 200F. Day: Wd N/A. We N/A.
FACILITIES: Restaurant & Bar.

GOLF D'ARDRÉE MAP 15 A2

Saint Antoine-du-Rocher, 37360.
10km north of Tours off the N138.

CONTACT: C Bied, Director. Tel +33 47 56 77 38.
COURSE: 5,804m, PAR 71, SSS 71. Lakeside course.
SOC RESTR'S: Welcome.
SOC GF – Round: Wd N/A We N/A Day: Wd 210F. We 260F.
SOC PACK: Available on booking.
VIS RESTR'S: Reduction on reserved Green Fee bookings.
VIS GF – Round: Wd N/A. We N/A. Day: Wd 210F. We 260F.
FACILITIES: Pro-shop, Bar & Restaurant.

GOLF DE MARCILLY MAP 15 A2

Domaine de la Plaine, 45240 Marcilly-en-Villette.
20km south of Orléans off the D921.

CONTACT: P Pascal, President. Tel: +33 38 76 11 73.
COURSE: 6,324m, PAR 72, SSS 70. Parkland course.
SOC RESTR'S: Welcome.
SOC GF – Round: Wd N/A. We N/A. Day: Wd 120F. We 180F.
SOC PACK: Available on booking.
VIS RESTR'S: Closed on Tuesday.
VIS GF – Round: Wd N/A. We N/A. Day: Wd 120F. We 180F.
FACILITIES: 9-hole Course, Pro-shop, Snack Bar.

GOLF DE VAUGOUARD MAP 15 A2

Chemin des Bois, Fontenay-sur-Loing, 45210 Ferrières.
70km north-east of Orléans on the N60 – N7.

CONTACT: Director of Golf. Tel: +33 38 95 81 52.
COURSE: 5,914m, PAR 72, SSS 72. Parkland course.
SOC RESTR'S: Welcome with prior reservation.
SOC GF – Round: Wd N/A. We N/A. Day: Wd 200F. We 330F.
SOC PACK: Available on booking.
VIS RESTR'S: Always welcome.
VIS GF – Round: Wd N/A. We N/A. Day: Wd 200F. We 330F.
FACILITIES: Bar & Restaurant.

GOLF DES AISSES MAP 15 A2

La Ferte Saint Aubin, 45240.
20km south of Orléans on the N 20.

CONTACT: M Ducret, Director. Tel: +33 38 64 80 87.
COURSE: 6,542m, PAR 72, SSS 72. Parkland course.
SOC RESTR'S: Welcome.
SOC GF – Round: Wd 150F. We 200F. Day: Wd N/A. We N/A.
SOC PACK: Not yet agreed.
VIS RESTR'S: Welcome.
VIS GF – Round: Wd 150F. We 200F. Day: Wd N/A. We N/A.
FACILITIES: Clubhouse will open mid 93. Also extra 9 holes.

GOLF DU CHATEAU DES SEPT TOURS MAP 15 B2

Courcelles-de-Touraine, 37330.
30km north-west of Tours off the D43.

CONTACT: Secretary. Tel: +33 47 24 69 75.
COURSE: 6,300m, PAR 72, SSS 72. Parkland/forest course.
SOC RESTR'S: Welcome.
SOC GF – Round: Wd 190F. We 220F. Day: Wd N/A. We N/A.
SOC PACK: Seasonal alterations & reserved discount on GF.
VIS RESTR'S: Always welcome.
VIS GF – Round: Wd 190F. We 220F. Day: Wd N/A. We N/A.
FACILITIES: Bar, Restaurant, Pro-shop, Club Hire & Practice Area.

GOLF DU VAL DE L'INDRE MAP 15 A2

Tregonce, 36320 Villedieu-sur-Indre.
80km south-east of Tours on the N143.

CONTACT: Reservations. Tel: +33 54 26 59 44.
COURSE: 6,225m, PAR 72, SSS 71. Parkland course.
SOC RESTR'S: Please book in advance.
SOC GF – Round: Wd 170F. We 200F. Day: Wd N/A. We N/A.
SOC PACK: Available on booking.
VIS RESTR'S: Welcome.
VIS GF – Round: Wd 170F. We 200F. Day: Wd N/A. We N/A.
FACILITIES: Range, Putting Green, Pro-shop, Bar & Restaurant.

LES BORDES GOLF INTERNATIONAL MAP 15 A2

St Laurent-Nouvan 41220.
25km south-west of Orléans on the D951.

CONTACT: Reservations. Tel: +33 54 87 72 13.
COURSE: 6,438m, PAR 72, SSS 73. Championship parkland course.
SOC RESTR'S: Welcome with prior reservation.
SOC GF – Round: Wd 400F. We 700F. Day: Wd N/A. We N/A.
SOC PACK: Available on booking.
VIS RESTR'S: Welcome
VIS GF – Round: Wd 400F. We 700F. Day: Wd N/A. We N/A.
FACILITIES: 3 star hotel on 18th fairway.

Côte d'Azur

VAL DE LOIRE ORLEANS MAP 15 A2

Château de la Touche Donnery, 45450.
10km east of Orléans off the A 60.

CONTACT: Reservations. Tel: +33 38 59 25 15.
COURSE: 5,750m, PAR 71, SSS 71. Parkland & links course.
SOC RESTR'S: Reductions for reserved Green Fee bookings.
SOC GF – Round: Wd 200F. **We** 260F. **Day:** Wd N/A. **We** N/A.
SOC PACK: Available on booking.
VIS RESTR'S: Reductions for reserved Green Fee bookings.
VIS GF – Round: Wd 200F. **We** 260F. **Day:** Wd N/A. **We** N/A.
FACILITIES: Free Range Balls, Bar, Restaurant & Practice Area.

DE CANNES MANDELIEU MAP 15 B3

Route du Golf, 06210 Mandelieu.
1km inland from Cannes Town.

CONTACT: Reservations. Tel: +33 93 49 55 39.
COURSE: 5,892m, PAR 71, SSS 71. Pine parkland course.
SOC RESTR'S: Advance bookings only.
SOC GF – Round: Wd 270F. **We** 310F. **Day:** Wd N/A. **We** N/A.
SOC PACK: Available on booking. Seasonal alteration to GF.
VIS RESTR'S: Always welcome.
VIS GF – Round: Wd 270F. **We** 310F. **Day:** Wd N/A. **We** N/A.
FACILITIES: 9-hole Par 34 course, Bar, Restaurant, Clubhouse.

DE CANNES MOUGINS MAP 15 B3

175 Route d'Antibes, 06250 Mougins.
6km north of Cannes Town.

CONTACT: Reservations. Tel: +33 93 75 79 13.
COURSE: 6,188m, PAR 72, SSS 72. Links/parkland course.
SOC RESTR'S: Advance bookings only.
SOC GF – Round: Wd 340F. **We** 380F. **Day:** Wd N/A. **We** N/A.
SOC PACK: Available on booking.
VIS RESTR'S: Handicap Cert required (Men 24/Ladies 28).
VIS GF – Round: Wd 340F. **We** 380F. **Day:** Wd N/A. **We** N/A.
FACILITIES: Bar, Restaurant, & Clubhouse.

GAP-BAYARD GOLF CLUB MAP 15 B3

Centre d'Oxygénation, 05000 Gap.
7km north of Town.

CONTACT: Reservations. Tel: +33 92 50 16 83.
COURSE: 6,023m, PAR 72, SSS 71. Hilly parkland course.
SOC RESTR'S: Welcome with prior reservation.
SOC GF – Round: Wd N/A. **We** 185F. **Day:** Wd 170F. **We** N/A.
SOC PACK: Special Green Fee 150F. for parties of 20+.
VIS RESTR'S: Special weekly & monthly Green Fees available.
VIS GF – Round: Wd N/A. **We** 185F. **Day:** Wd 170F. **We** N/A.
FACILITIES: Range, Putting Green, Tennis, Bar & Restaurant.

GOLF CLUB DE BARBAROUX MAP 15 B3

Route de Cabasse, 83170 Brignoles.
60km west of Cannes off the A80.

CONTACT: T Huguenin, Director. Tel: +33 94 59 07 43.
COURSE: 6,341m, PAR 72, SSS 73. Parkland with water.
SOC RESTR'S: Welcome.
SOC GF – Round: Wd 300F. **We** 400F. **Day:** Wd N/A. **We** N/A.
SOC PACK: Available on booking.
VIS RESTR'S: Welcome.
VIS GF – Round: Wd 300F. **We** 400F. **Day:** Wd N/A. **We** N/A.
FACILITIES: Golf Car, Trolleys, Swimming Pool & Tennis.

GOLF CLUB DE SERVANES MAP 15 B3

BP 6, 13890 Mouriès.
25km south of Avignon on the D17.

CONTACT: J Reynaud. Tel: +33 90 47 59 95.
COURSE: 6,100m, PAR 72, SSS 71. Parkland course.
SOC RESTR'S: Welcome with prior reservation.
SOC GF – Round: Wd N/A. **We** N/A. **Day:** Wd 180F. **We** 250F.
SOC PACK: Call for brochure.
VIS RESTR'S: Always welcome.
VIS GF – Round: Wd N/A. **We** N/A. **Day:** Wd 180F. **We** 250F.
FACILITIES: Clubhouse, Bar & Restaurant.

GOLF DE DIGNE-LES-BAINES MAP 15 B3

St-Pierre de Gaubert, 04000 Digne-les-Bains.
80km north-west of Cannes on the N85.

CONTACT: Reservations. Tel: +33 92 32 38 38.
COURSE: 5,920m, PAR 71, SSS 73. Parkland course.
SOC RESTR'S: Please book in advance.
SOC GF – Round: Wd 190F. **We** 240F. **Day:** Wd N/A. **We** N/A.
SOC PACK: Seasonal alterations & reserved discount on GF.
VIS RESTR'S: Always welcome.
VIS GF – Round: Wd 190F. **We** 240F. **Day:** Wd N/A. **We** N/A.
FACILITIES: 6 Practice Holes, Range, Pro-shop, Bar & Restaurant.

FRANCE

GOLF DE LA SAINTE-BAUME MAP 15 B3

Domaine de Châteauneuf, 83860 Nans-les-Pins.
35km north-east of Marseilles on the D80.

CONTACT: G Grattepanche, Director. Tel: +33 94 78 60 12.
COURSE: 6,167m, PAR 72, SSS 73. Tight parkland course.
SOC RESTR'S: Always welcome.
SOC GF – Round: Wd 190F. We 270F. Day: Wd N/A. We N/A.
SOC PACK: Available on booking.
VIS RESTR'S: Always welcome.
VIS GF – Round: Wd 190F. We 270F. Day: Wd N/A. We N/A.
FACILITIES: Fitness Centre, Riding, Bar & Clubhouse.

GOLF DE ROQUEBRUNE MAP 15 B3

CD7, 83520 Roquebrune St Angens.
8km west of Frejus on the RN 7.

CONTACT: D Bier Benort, Director. Tel: +33 94 82 92 91.
COURSE: 6,030m, PAR 71, SSS 71. Narrow parkland course.
SOC RESTR'S: Always welcome. Max handicap 35.
SOC GF – Round: Wd N/A. We N/A. Day: Wd 230F. We 250F.
SOC PACK: Reductions for groups & reserved GF bookings.
VIS RESTR'S: Always welcome. Max handicap 35.
VIS GF – Round: Wd N/A. We N/A. Day: Wd 230F. We 250F.
FACILITIES: Bar & Restaurant.

GOLF DE SAINTE-MAXIME MAP 15 B3

Route de Débarquement, 83120 Sainte-Maxime.
30km southof Cannes.

CONTACT: M Wallace, Professional. Tel: +33 94 492660.
COURSE: 6,123m, PAR 71, SSS 73. Hilly course.
SOC RESTR'S: Written bookings only.
SOC GF – Round: Wd 230F. We N/A. Day: Wd N/A. We N/A.
SOC PACK: On application.
VIS RESTR'S: No restrictions. Closed Tue in winter.
VIS GF – Round: Wd 230F We 260F. Day: Wd N/A. We N/A.
FACILITIES: Range, Bar & Restaurant.

GOLF DE VALBONNE MAP 15 B3

Route de Roqufort-la-Paoute, 06560 Valbonne.
10km north-west of Cannes off the N85.

CONTACT: Reservation. Tel: +33 93 40 27 00.
COURSE: 5,897m, PAR 72, SSS 71. Hilly parkland course.
SOC RESTR'S: Reservations as soon as possible.
SOC GF – Round: Wd N/A. We N/A. Day: Wd 300F. We 350F.
SOC PACK: Available on request.
VIS RESTR'S: Seasonal alterations & reserved discount on GF.
VIS GF – Round: Wd N/A. We N/A. Day: Wd 300F. We 350F.
FACILITIES: Bar & Restaurant.

GOLF ESTEREL MAP 15 B3

Avenue du Golf, 83700 St Raphaël.
20km south of Cannes on the N98 along the coast.

CONTACT: M Vichera, Organiser. Tel: +33 94 82 47 88.
COURSE: 5,921m, PAR 71, SSS 71. Undulating course.
SOC RESTR'S: Reservations as soon as possible.
SOC GF – Round: Wd N/A. We N/A. Day: Wd 250F. We 280F.
SOC PACK: 30% less to clients of Latitudes & Residence Hotels.
VIS RESTR'S: Reservations 48 hours before. Seasonal alterations.
VIS GF – Round: Wd N/A. We N/A. Day: Wd 250F. We 280F.
FACILITIES: 9-hole Academy, Swimming Pool & Tennis.

SAINT ENDREOL MAP 15 B3

Route de Bagnols-en-Fôret, 83920 La Motte.
30km north of Saint Tropez. 30km west of Cannes.

CONTACT: B Lombard, Professional. Tel: +33 94 81 80 81.
COURSE: 6,219m, PAR 72, SSS 73. Parkland course.
SOC RESTR'S: Book in advance.
SOC GF – Round: Wd N/A. We N/A. Day: Wd 200F. We N/A.
SOC PACK: Available upon booking.
VIS RESTR'S: No restrictions.
VIS GF – Round: Wd 200F. We 250F. Day: Wd 200F. We 250F.
FACILITIES: Range, Bar & Restaurant.

SPERONE GOLF CLUB MAP 14 A3

Domaine de Sperone, 20169 Bonifacio.
5km from Bonifacio, South Corsica.

CONTACT: J Casabianca, MD. Tel: +33 95 73 13 69.
COURSE: 6,130m, PAR 72, SSS 73. Clifftop links course.
SOC RESTR'S: Closed Thursday afternoons.
SOC GF – Round: Wd N/A. We N/A. Day: Wd 270F. We 270F.
SOC PACK: Special agreements with local hotels for inclusive deals.
VIS RESTR'S: Welcome every day except Thursday afternoons.
VIS GF – Round: Wd N/A. We N/A. Day: Wd 330F. We 330F.
FACILITIES: Restaurant, Bar, Tennis and Clubhouse.

RAC HOTELS IN FRANCE

Over 1,300 carefully selected hotels, many illustrated in colour and all cross-referenced to the map section.
For holidaymaker or business traveller alike.
An information source for
regional foods - beaches - châteaux - resorts - theme parks - wine regions - ...and much more
Price £9.99
Available from bookshops
or direct from the RAC on 0235 834885

Ile de France & Paris

ILE DE FRANCE & PARIS

GOLF DE FORGES-LES-BAINS   MAP 15 A1

Rue du Général Leclerc, 91470 Forges-les-Bains.
35km south-west of Paris off the D97.

CONTACT: S. Floresco, Secretary. Tel: +33 64 91 48 18.
COURSE: 6,142m, PAR 72, SSS 71. Parkland course.
SOC RESTR'S: Always welcome.
SOC GF – Round: Wd 200F. We 300F. **Day:** Wd N/A. We N/A.
SOC PACK: 20% Green Fee Reduction for 16+.
VIS RESTR'S: Always welcome.
VIS GF – Round: Wd 200F. We 300F. **Day:** Wd N/A. We N/A.
FACILITIES: 3-hole compact Practice Course.

COURSON MONTELOUP   MAP 15 A1

91680 Bruyères-le-Châtel.
35km south-west of Paris, off Route D3.

CONTACT: M Wolseley, Professional. Tel: +33 64 58 80 80.
COURSE: 6,171-6,520m, PAR 00, SSS 72-75. 4 x 9-Holes.
SOC RESTR'S: Welcome Weekdays.
SOC GF – Round: Wd N/A. We N/A. **Day:** Wd 350F. We N/A.
SOC PACK: On application.
VIS RESTR'S: Welcome Wd. Seasonal alterations to GF.
VIS GF – Round: Wd 200F. We N/A. **Day:** Wd 200F. We N/A.
FACILITIES: Range, Bar & Restaurant.

GOLF DES VOLCANS   MAP 15 A2

La Bruyère des Moines, 63870 Orcines.
12km west of Clermont-Ferrand on RN141.

CONTACT: L Roux, G Roux, Professionals. Tel: +33 73 62 15 51.
COURSE: 6,286m, PAR 72, SSS 73. Forest/Heather.
SOC RESTR'S: Book in advance. H'cap Cert required.
SOC GF – Round: Wd N/A. We N/A. **Day:** Wd 200F. We N/A.
SOC PACK: Tailored to each party.
VIS RESTR'S: H'cap Cert required. Closed Tue in winter.
VIS GF – Round: Wd 180F. We 250F. **Day:** Wd N/A. We N/A.
FACILITIES: 9-hole Course, Range, Bar & Restaurant.

GOLF CLEMENT ADER   MAP 15 A1

Domaine de Chateau Pereire, Gretz, 77220 Armainvilliers.
35km south of Paris off the N19.

CONTACT: M Kusaba. Tel: +33 64 07 34 10.
COURSE: 6,323m, PAR 72, SSS 72. Parkland course.
SOC RESTR'S: Welcome with advanced booking.
SOC GF – Round: Wd 250F. We 450F. **Day:** Wd N/A. We N/A.
SOC PACK: Available on booking.
VIS RESTR'S: Welcome.
VIS GF – Round: Wd 250F. We 450F. **Day:** Wd N/A. We N/A.
FACILITIES: Restaurant, Bar & Seminar Rooms.

GOLF DES YVELINES   MAP 15 A1

Château de la Couharde, 78940 La Queue les Yvelines.
45km west of Paris off the N12.

CONTACT: Reservations. Tel: +33 86 86 48 89.
COURSE: 6,321m, PAR 72, SSS 72. Forest parkland course.
SOC RESTR'S: Always welcome. But must book in advance.
SOC GF – Round: Wd N/A. We N/A. **Day:** Wd 190F. We 330F.
SOC PACK: Discount on reserved Green Fee bookings.
VIS RESTR'S: Always welcome.
VIS GF – Round: Wd N/A. We N/A. **Day:** Wd 190F. We 330F.
FACILITIES: 9-hole Par 31 Course, Bar & Restaurant.

GOLF DE FONTENAILLES   MAP 15 A1

Domaine de Bois Boudran, 77370 Nangis.
55km south-ast of Paris on N19.

CONTACT: Secretary. Tel: +33 64 60 51 00.
COURSE: 6,263m, PAR 72, SSS 73. Parkland course.
SOC RESTR'S: Always welcome.
SOC GF – Round: Wd 250F. We 450F. **Day:** Wd N/A. We N/A.
SOC PACK: Available on booking.
VIS RESTR'S: Always welcome.
VIS GF – Round: Wd 250F. We 450F. **Day:** Wd N/A. We N/A.
FACILITIES: 9-hole Course, Hotel on site, Restaurants & Bars.

GOLF NATIONAL (L'ALBATROS)   MAP 15 A1

2 Avenue du Golf, 78280 Guyancourt.
Off the D91 20km south-west of Paris.

CONTACT: Reservations Tel: +33 30 43 36 00.
COURSE: 6,506m, PAR 72, SSS 73. Long American style course.
SOC RESTR'S: Pay & Play course. Must book.
SOC GF – Round: Wd 200F. We 300F. **Day:** Wd N/A. We N/A.
SOC PACK: Discount on reserved Green Fee bookings.
VIS RESTR'S: Welcome. Seasonal alterations to GF.
VIS GF – Round: Wd 200F. We 300F. **Day:** Wd N/A. We N/A.
FACILITIES: 9-hole Par 31, Range, Practice Area & Restaurant.

FRANCE

GOLF NATIONAL (L'AIGLE) MAP 15 A1

2 Avenue du Golf, 78280 Guyancourt.
Off the D91 20km south-west of Paris.

CONTACT: Reservations. Tel: +33 30 43 36 00.
COURSE: 5,951m, PAR 71, SSS 70. Parkland course.
SOC RESTR'S: Pay & Play course. Must book.
SOC GF – Round: Wd 140F. We 220F. Day: Wd N/A. We N/A.
SOC PACK: Discount on reserved Green Fee bookings.
VIS RESTR'S: Welcome. Seasonal alterations to GF.
VIS GF – Round: Wd 140F. We 220F. Day: Wd N/A. We N/A.
FACILITIES: 9-hole Par 31 Course, Range & Practice Area.

LA VAUCOULEURS (RIVER) MAP 15 A1

78910 Civry-la-Forêt.
50km west of Paris off the N12.

CONTACT: Reservations. Tel: +33 34 87 62 29.
COURSE: 6,300m, PAR 73, SSS 74. American style parkland.
SOC RESTR'S: Advance bookings only.
SOC GF – Round: Wd N/A. We N/A. Day: Wd 200F. We 400F.
SOC PACK: Discount on reserved Green Fee bookings.
VIS RESTR'S: Welcome. But advisable to phone.
VIS GF – Round: Wd N/A. We N/A. Day: Wd 200F. We 400F.
FACILITIES: Practice Area & Restaurant.

LA VAUCOULEURS (LINKS) MAP 15 A1

78910 Civry-la-Forêt.
50km west of Paris off the N12.

CONTACT: Reservations. Tel: +33 34 87 62 29.
COURSE: 5,694m, PAR 70, SSS 70. Traditional links course.
SOC RESTR'S: Advance bookings only.
SOC GF – Round: Wd N/A. We N/A. Day: Wd 200F. We 400F.
SOC PACK: Discount on reserved Green Fee bookings.
VIS RESTR'S: Welcome. But advisable to phone.
VIS GF – Round: Wd N/A. We N/A. Day: Wd 200F. We 400F.
FACILITIES: Practice Area & Restaurant.

LE PRIEURE GOLF CLUB (EST) MAP 15 A1

78440 Sailly.
Sailly, 10km NW of Meulan (D130). 45km NW of Paris.

CONTACT: J Alsuguren, Professional. Tel: +33 34 76 70 12.
COURSE: 6,157m, PAR 72, SSS 72. Parkland course.
SOC RESTR'S: Handicap Certificate required.
SOC GF – Round: Wd N/A. We N/A. Day: Wd 225F. We N/A.
SOC PACK: On application.
VIS RESTR'S: Handicap Certificate required.
VIS GF – Round: Wd 260F. We 400F. Day: Wd 260F. We 400F.
FACILITIES: Range, Swimming Pool, Bar & Restaurant.

LE PRIEURE GOLF CLUB (OUEST) MAP 15 A1

78440 Sailly.
Sailly, 10km NW of Meulan (D130). 45km NW of Paris.

CONTACT: J Alsuguren, Professional. Tel: +33 34 76 70 12.
COURSE: 6,274m, PAR 72, SSS 72. Parkland course.
SOC RESTR'S: Handicap Certificate required.
SOC GF – Round: Wd N/A. We N/A. Day: Wd 225F. We N/A.
SOC PACK: On application.
VIS RESTR'S: Handicap Certificate required.
VIS GF – Round: Wd 260F. We 400F. Day: Wd 260F. We 400F.
FACILITIES: Range, Swimming Pool, Bar & Restaurant.

SAINT NOM-LA-BRETECHE (ONE) MAP 15 A1

Hameau Tuilerie-Bignon, 78860 St Nom-La-Bretêche.
24km west of Paris on A-13.

CONTACT: A Cadet, R Golias, Professionals. Tel: +33 30 80 04 40.
COURSE: 6,165m, PAR 72, SSS 72. Undulating with water.
SOC RESTR'S: Not at We. Handicap Certificate required.
SOC GF – Round: Wd N/A. We N/A. Day: Wd N/A. We N/A.
SOC PACK: On application.
VIS RESTR'S: Not at We. Handicap Certificate required.
VIS GF – Round: Wd 450F. We N/A. Day: Wd N/A. We N/A.
ACILITIES: Range, Swimming Pool, Bar & Restaurant.

SAINT NOM-LA-BRETECHE (TWO) MAP 15 A1

Hameau Tuilerie-Bignon, 78860 St Nom-La-Bretêche.
24km west of Paris on A-13.

CONTACT: A Cadet, R Golias, Professionals. Tel: +33 30 80 04 40.
COURSE: 6,127m, PAR 72, SSS 72. Undulating course.
SOC RESTR'S: Not at We. Handicap Certificate required.
SOC GF – Round: Wd N/A. We N/A. Day: Wd N/A. We N/A.
SOC PACK: On application.
VIS RESTR'S: Not at We. Handicap Certificate required.
VIS GF – Round: Wd 450F. We N/A. Day: Wd N/A. We N/A.
FACILITIES: Range, Swimming Pool, Bar & Restaurant.

RAC HOTELS IN FRANCE

Over 1,300 carefully selected hotels, many illustrated in colour and all cross-referenced to the map section.
For holidaymaker or business traveller alike.
An information source for
regional foods - beaches - châteaux - resorts - theme parks - wine regions - ...and much more
Price £9.99
Available from bookshops
or direct from the RAC on 0235 834885

LOIRE

Loire

GOLF DE L'ILE D'OR   MAP 14 A2

Le Cellier, 44850 Ligne.
23km north-east of Nantes off the N23.

CONTACT: Secretary. Tel: +33 40 98 58 00.
COURSE: 6,272m, PAR 72, SSS 72. Forest parkland course.
SOC RESTR'S: Phone for reservations.
SOC GF – Round: Wd 190F. We 260F. Day: Wd N/A. We N/A.
SOC PACK: Discount on reserved Green Fee bookings.
VIS RESTR'S: Welcome.
VIS GF – Round: Wd 190F. We 260F. Day: Wd N/A. We N/A.
FACILITIES: 9-hole compact course, Bar & Restaurant.

ANJOU GOLF & COUNTRY CLUB   MAP 14 B2

Route de Cheffe, 49330 Champigné.
20km north on Angers, off the D768.

CONTACT: Reservations. Tel: +33 41 42 01 01.
COURSE: 6,156m, PAR 72, SSS 72. Parkland course.
SOC RESTR'S: Booking required.
SOC GF – Round: Wd 190F. We 240F. Day: Wd N/A. We N/A.
SOC PACK: Discount on reserved Green Fee bookings.
VIS RESTR'S: Welcome. But advisable to phone.
VIS GF – Round: Wd 190F. We 240F. Day: Wd N/A. We N/A.
FACILITIES: Pitch & Putt, Restaurant & Bar.

GOLF DE LA BRETESCHE   MAP 14 A2

Domaine de la Bretesche, 44780 Missillac.
50km north-west of Nantes on the N165.

CONTACT: Isabelle Moreau, Secretary. Tel: +33 40 88 30 03.
COURSE: 6,080m, PAR 72, SSS 72. Forest course.
SOC RESTR'S: Always welcome but please book in advance.
SOC GF – Round: Wd 140F. We 280F. Day: Wd N/A. We N/A.
SOC PACK: Seasonal alterations & reserved discount on GF.
VIS RESTR'S: Welcome with 24 hours prior notice.
VIS GF – Round: Wd 140F. We 280F. Day: Wd N/A. We N/A.
FACILITIES: Bar & Restaurant.

GOLF D'AVRILLE   MAP 14 B2

Château de la Perrière, 49240 Avrillé.
10km north-west of Angers on the R963.

CONTACT: M. Morin, Director. Tel: +33 41 69 22 50.
COURSE: 6,115m, PAR 71, SSS 71. Parkland course with water.
SOC RESTR'S: Always welcome but no catering on Monday.
SOC GF – Round: Wd 195F. We 230F. Day: Wd N/A. We N/A.
SOC PACK: Special reductions for groups. Please ask for details.
VIS RESTR'S: Always welcome except Sun & Competition Days.
VIS GF – Round: Wd 195F. We 230F. Day: Wd N/A. We N/A.
FACILITIES: 9-hole Course, Chateau Clubhouse, Restaurant.

GOLF DE NANTES   MAP 14 A2

44360 Vigneux de Bretagne.
8km north-west from Nantes city.

CONTACT: Secretary. Tel: +33 40 63 25 82.
COURSE: 5,855m, PAR 72, SSS 71. Parkland course.
SOC RESTR'S: Welcome.
SOC GF – Round: Wd 160F. We 280F. Day: Wd N/A. We N/A.
SOC PACK: Discount on reserved Green Fee bookings.
VIS RESTR'S: Welcome.
VIS GF – Round: Wd 160F. We 280F. Day: Wd N/A. We N/A.
FACILITIES: Pro-shop, Bar & Clubhouse.

GOLF DE CHOLET   MAP 14 B2

Allée du Chêne Landry, 49300 Cholet.
42km south-west of Angers on the N160 in Cholet.

CONTACT: Secretary. Tel: +33 41 71 05 01.
COURSE: 6,080m, PAR 72, SSS 72. Forest parkland course.
SOC RESTR'S: Always welcome but please book in advance.
SOC GF – Round: Wd 160F. We 190F. Day: Wd N/A. We N/A.
SOC PACK: Discount on reserved Green Fee bookings.
VIS RESTR'S: Always welcome.
VIS GF – Round: Wd 160F. We 190F. Day: Wd N/A. We N/A.
FACILITIES: Bar & Restaurant.

GOLF DE NANTES ERDRE   MAP 14 A2

Chemin du Bout des Landes, 44300.
5km north on Nantes City.

CONTACT: Secretary. Tel: +33 40 59 21 21.
COURSE: 6,009m, PAR 71, SSS 71. Parkland course.
SOC RESTR'S: Welcome.
SOC GF – Round: Wd N/A. We N/A. Day: Wd 180F. We 220F.
SOC PACK: Discount on reserved Green Fee bookings.
VIS RESTR'S: Welcome.
VIS GF – Round: Wd N/A. We N/A. Day: Wd 180F. We 220F.
FACILITIES: Pro-shop, Bar & Clubhouse.

FRANCE

GOLF DE PORT BOURGENAY MAP 14 A2

Avenue de la Mine, 85440 Talmont-St-Hilaire.
30km south-west of La-Roche-sur-Yon off the D949.

CONTACT: R Le Bar, Manager. Tel: +33 51 22 29 87.
COURSE: 5,865m, PAR 72, SSS 72. Parkland/links course.
SOC RESTR'S: Welcome with prior reservation.
SOC GF – Round: Wd 140F. We 220F. Day: Wd N/A. We N/A.
SOC PACK: Seasonal alterations & reserved discount on GF.
VIS RESTR'S: Always welcome. Seasonal alterations to GF.
VIS GF – Round: Wd 140F. We 220F. Day: Wd N/A. We N/A.
FACILITIES: Bar, Restaurant & Clubhouse.

GOLF DE SAVENAY MAP 14 A2

44260 Savenay.
30km north-west of Nantes on the N165.

CONTACT: Reservations. Tel: +33 40 56 88 05.
COURSE: 6,335m, PAR 73, SSS 72. Parkland course.
SOC RESTR'S: Please book through Club Reservations.
SOC GF – Round: Wd N/A. We N/A. Day: Wd 240F. We 240F.
SOC PACK: Seasonal alterations & reserved discount on GF.
VIS RESTR'S: Welcome.
VIS GF – Round: Wd N/A. We N/A. Day: Wd 240F. We 240F.
FACILITIES: 9-hole Course, Practice Area, Bar & Restaurant.

GOLF DES FONTENELLES MAP 14 A2

l'Aiguillon-sur-Vie, 85220 Coex.
30km north-west of La Roche-sur-Yon on the D38.

CONTACT: Reservations. Tel: +33 51 54 13 94.
COURSE: 6,185m, PAR 72, SSS 71. Parkland course.
SOC RESTR'S: Welcome with prior reservation.
SOC GF – Round: Wd 160F. We 230F. Day: Wd N/A. We N/A.
SOC PACK: Discount on reserved Green Fee bookings.
VIS RESTR'S: Always welcome. Seasonal alterations to GF.
VIS GF – Round: Wd 160F. We 230F. Day: Wd N/A. We N/A.
FACILITIES: Range, Putting Green, Pro-shop, Bar & Restaurant.

GOLF SABLE SOLESMES MAP 14 B2

Domaine de l'Outiniére, 72300 Sablé-sur-Sarthe.
55km north-east of Angers off the D24.

CONTACT: M Moraly. Tel: +33 43 95 28 78.
COURSE: 6,207m, PAR 72, SSS 73. Parkland course.
SOC RESTR'S: Welcome with prior reservation.
SOC GF – Round: Wd 230F. We 330F. Day: Wd N/A. We N/A.
SOC PACK: Discount on reserved Green Fee bookings.
VIS RESTR'S: Welcome. Seasonal alterations to GF.
VIS GF – Round: Wd 230F. We 330F. Day: Wd N/A. We N/A.
FACILITIES: 27-hole Complex, Bar & Restaurant.

LA BAULE GOLF CLUB MAP 14 A2

Domaine de St Denac, 44117 St-André-des-Eaux.
North of La Baule end of RN171. 70km west of Nantes.

CONTACT: Reservations. Tel: +33 40 60 46 18.
COURSE: 6,146m, PAR 72, SSS 72, Championship parkland course.
SOC RESTR'S: Welcome with prior reservation.
SOC GF – Round: Wd 270F. We 270F. Day: Wd N/A. We N/A.
SOC PACK: Seasonal alterations to Green Fee.
VIS RESTR'S: Welcome. Seasonal alterations to GF.
VIS GF – Round: Wd 270F. We 270F. Day: Wd N/A. We N/A.
FACILITIES: Bar & Restaurant.

LA DOMANGERE GOLF CLUB MAP 14 A2

La Roche-sur-Yon, 85310 Nesmy.
6km south of La Roche-sur-Yon on the D747.

CONTACT: Reservations. Tel: +33 51 07 60 15.
COURSE: 6,388m, PAR 72, SSS 72, Inland links course.
SOC RESTR'S: Welcome with prior reservation.
SOC GF – Round: Wd 230F. We 230F. Day: Wd N/A. We N/A.
SOC PACK: Seasonal alterations & reserved discount on GF.
VIS RESTR'S: Always welcome.
VIS GF – Round: Wd 230F. We 230F. Day: Wd N/A. We N/A.
FACILITIES: Bar & Restaurant.

LAVAL GOLF CLUB MAP 14 B1

Le Jariel, 53000 Changé-les-Laval.
70km east of Rennes off the A81.

CONTACT: Secretary. Tel: +33 43 53 16 03.
COURSE: 6,112m, PAR 72, SSS 72. Undulating parkland course.
SOC RESTR'S: Welcome with prior reservation.
SOC GF – Round: Wd N/A. We N/A. Day: Wd 190F. We 230F.
SOC PACK: Seasonal alterations & reserved discount on GF.
VIS RESTR'S: Welcome.
VIS GF – Round: Wd N/A. We N/A. Day: Wd 190F. We 230F.
FACILITIES: 9-hole Par 31, Pro-shop, Bar & Clubhouse.

LE MANS GOLF CLUB MAP 14 B2

Route de Tours, Mulsanne, 72230 Arnage.
10km south from the centre of Le Mans.

CONTACT: Secretary. Tel: +33 43 42 00 36.
COURSE: 5,858m, PAR 71, SSS 71. Undulating forest course.
SOC RESTR'S: Welcome with prior reservation.
SOC GF – Round: Wd N/A. We N/A. Day: Wd 225F. We 330F.
SOC PACK: Seasonal alterations & reserved discount on GF.
VIS RESTR'S: Welcome.
VIS GF – Round: Wd N/A. We N/A. Day: Wd 225F. We 330F.
FACILITIES: Pro-shop, Bar & Clubhouse.

NORD

SAINT JEAN-DE-MONTS MAP 14 A2

Sporting Golf, 85160 Saint Jean-de-Monts.
50km south-west of Nantes.

CONTACT: Reservations. Tel: +33 51 58 82 73.
COURSE: 5,967m, PAR 72, SSS 72, Links/forest course.
SOC RESTR'S: Welcome with prior reservation.
SOC GF – Round: Wd 240F. **We** 240F. **Day: Wd** 240F. **We** 240F.
SOC PACK: Seasonal alterations & reserved discount on GF.
VIS RESTR'S: Always welcome.
VIS GF – Round: Wd 240F. **We** 240F. **Day: Wd** 240F. **We** 240F.
FACILITIES: Club Hire, Bar & Restaurant.

Nord

AA SAINT-OMER GOLF CLUB MAP 14 B1

Chemin des Bois, Acquin-Westbécourt 62380 Lumbres.
40km south-east of Calais off the A26.

CONTACT: Secretary. Tel: +33 21 38 59 90.
COURSE: 6,420m, PAR 72, SSS 73. Undulating parkland course.
SOC RESTR'S: All applications considered.
SOC GF – Round: Wd 240F. **We** 280F. **Day: Wd** N/A. **We** N/A.
SOC PACK: Seasonal alterations & reserved discount to GF.
VIS RESTR'S: Welcome. Handicap Certificate required.
VIS GF – Round: Wd 240F. **We** 280F. **Day: Wd** N/A. **We** N/A.
FACILITIES: 9-hole Course, Bar, Restaurant & Pro-shop.

CHANTILLY (LONGERES) MAP 14 B1

Vineuil Saint Firmin, 60500 Chantilly.
45km north of Paris.

CONTACT: A Chardonnet, Professional. Tel: +33 44 57 04 43.
COURSE: 6,430m, PAR 71, SSS 71. Forest course.
SOC RESTR'S: Not at weekends.
SOC GF – Round: Wd 350F. **We** N/A. **Day: Wd** N/A. **We** N/A.
SOC PACK: On application.
VIS RESTR'S: Welcome weekdays. Closed Tue.
VIS GF – Round: Wd 350F. **We** N/A. **Day: Wd** N/A. **We** N/A.
ACILITIES: Range, Bar & Restaurant.

CHANTILLY (VINEUIL) MAP 14 B1

Vineuil Saint Firmin, 60500 Chantilly.
45km north of Paris.

CONTACT: , G Lamy, Professional. Tel: +33 44 57 04 43.
COURSE: 6,400m, PAR 71, SSS 71. Championship Forest.
SOC RESTR'S: Not at weekends.
SOC GF – Round: Wd 350F. **We** N/A. **Day: Wd** N/A. **We** N/A.
SOC PACK: On application.
VIS RESTR'S: Welcome weekdays. Closed Tue.
VIS GF – Round: Wd 350F. **We** N/A. **Day: Wd** N/A. **We** N/A.
FACILITIES: Range, Bar & Restaurant.

GOLF D'ABBEVILLE MAP 14 B1

Rue du Val, 80132 Grand Laviers.
80km south from Boulogne on the N1 to Abbeville.

CONTACT: Sylvie Lheureux, Secretary. Tel: +33 22 24 94 58.
COURSE: 6,150m, PAR 72, SSS 71. Technical parkland course.
SOC RESTR'S: No societies at Weekends.
SOC GF – Round: Wd 120F. **We** N/A. **Day: Wd** 120F. **We** N/A.
SOC PACK: Available on booking.
VIS RESTR'S: Welcome.
VIS GF – Round: Wd N/A. **We** N/A. **Day: Wd** 130F. **We** 180F.
FACILITIES: Pitch & Putt, Pro-shop, Rest Rooms & Bar.

GOLF D'ARRAS MAP 14 B1

Rue Briquet Taillandier, 62223 Anzin-Saint-Aubin.
105km south-east of Calais off the D34.

CONTACT: Secretary. Tel: +33 21 50 24 24.
COURSE: 6,151m, PAR 72, SSS 72. Hillside course.
SOC RESTR'S: Welcome.
SOC GF – Round: Wd N/A. **We** N/A. **Day: Wd** 160F. **We** 200F.
SOC PACK: Available on booking.
VIS RESTR'S: No visitors on competition days.
VIS GF – Round: Wd N/A. **We** N/A. **Day: Wd** 160F. **We** 200F.
FACILITIES: Range, Equipment & Golf Car Hire, Bar & Restaurant.

GOLF D'HARDELOT 'LES DUNES' MAP 14 B1

3 Avenue du Golf, 62152 Neufchâtel-Hardelot.
15km south of Boulogne off the D940.

CONTACT: J Riou, Director. Tel: +33 21 91 90 90.
COURSE: 6,014m, PAR 72, SSS 73. Hilly/parkland course.
SOC RESTR'S: Always welcome.
SOC GF – Round: Wd 220F. **We** 260F. **Day: Wd** 360F. **We** 400F.
SOC PACK: GF discount for reserved bookings.
VIS RESTR'S: Always welcome.
VIS GF – Round: Wd 260F. **We** 300F. **Day: Wd** 400F. **We** 440F.
FACILITIES: Restaurant, Swimming Pool & Fitness Centre.

183

FRANCE

GOLF D'HARDELOT 'LES PINS' MAP 14 B1

3 Avenue du Golf, 62152 Neufchâtel-Hardelot.
15km south of Boulogne off the D940.

CONTACT: J Riou, Director. Tel: +33 21 83 73 10.
COURSE: 5,870m, PAR 72, SSS 72. Forest course.
SOC RESTR'S: Always welcome.
SOC GF – Round: Wd 220F. **We** 260F. **Day:** Wd 360F. **We** 400F.
SOC PACK: Available on booking.
VIS RESTR'S: Always welcome.
VIS GF – Round: Wd 260F. **We** 300F. **Day:** Wd 400F. **We** 440F.
FACILITIES: Tennis, Swimming Pool & Fitness Centre.

GOLF DE DUNKERQUE MAP 14 B1

Coudekerque-Village, 59380 Bergues.
5km south-east of Dunkerque on D916.

CONTACT: Secretary. Tel: +33 28 61 07 43.
COURSE: 6,250m, PAR 71, SSS 70. Undulating parkland course.
SOC RESTR'S: All applications considered.
SOC GF – Round: Wd 160F. **We** 180F. **Day:** Wd 200F. **We** 200F.
SOC PACK: According to tariff approx. 250F. – 300F.
VIS RESTR'S: Welcome with advance bookings.
VIS GF – Round: Wd 160F. **We** 180F. **Day:** Wd 200F. **We** 200F.
FACILITIES: 30 Bay Driving Range & Excellent Restaurant.

GOLF DE L'AILETTE MAP 15 A1

02000 Laon.
10km south of Laon on the D967.

CONTACT: Reservations. Tel: +33 23 24 83 99.
COURSE: 6,127m, PAR 72, SSS 71. Forest course.
SOC RESTR'S: Please book in advance.
SOC GF – Round: Wd 200F. **We** 250F. **Day:** Wd N/A. **We** N/A.
SOC PACK: Call club for information.
VIS RESTR'S: Welcome.
VIS GF – Round: Wd 200F. **We** 250F. **Day:** Wd N/A. **We** N/A.
FACILITIES: 9-hole Course, Restaurant Service.

GOLF DE MORMAL MAP 15 A1

Bois St-Pierre, 59144 Preux-au-Sart.
45km south-east of Douai on the D16.

CONTACT: M. Cory, Director. Tel: +33 27 63 15 20.
COURSE: 6,022m, PAR 72, SSS 71. Parkland course.
SOC RESTR'S: Welcome except Competition days.
SOC GF – Round: Wd N/A. **We** N/A. **Day:** Wd 170F. **We** 220F.
SOC PACK: Call club for details.
VIS RESTR'S: Welcome except Competition days.
VIS GF – Round: Wd N/A. **We** N/A. **Day:** Wd 170F. **We** 220F.
FACILITIES: Bar & Restaurant.

GOLF DE NAMPONT-ST-MARTIN MAP 14 B1

Maison Forte, 80120 Nampont-Saint-Martin.
70km south of Calais off the N1.

CONTACT: Secretary. Tel: +33 22 29 92 90.
COURSE: 5,505m, PAR 71, SSS 71. Woodland/marshland course.
SOC RESTR'S: No restrictions except Weekends.
SOC GF – Round: Wd N/A. **We** 160F. **Day:** Wd 190F. **We** N/A.
SOC PACK: Will consider applications for special arrangements.
VIS RESTR'S: Recommend visitors to play Weekdays.
VIS GF – Round: Wd N/A. **We** 160F. **Day:** Wd 190F. **We** N/A.
FACILITIES: Practice Facilities, Restaurant & Parking.

GOLF DE WIMEREUX MAP 14 B1

Route d'Ambleteuse, 62930 Wimereux.
25km south-west of Callais off the N1.

CONTACT: Secretary. Tel: +33 21 32 43 20.
COURSE: 6,089m, PAR 72, SSS 72. Flat links course.
SOC RESTR'S: No restrictions except Weekends.
SOC GF – Round: Wd 200F. **We** 250F. **Day:** Wd N/A. **We** N/A.
SOC PACK: Will consider applications for special arrangements.
VIS RESTR'S: GF discount on reserved bookings.
VIS GF – Round: Wd 200F. **We** 250F. **Day:** Wd N/A. **We** N/A.
FACILITIES: Practice Facilities, Bar & Restaurant.

LE TOUQUET 'LE FORTE' MAP 14 B1

Avenue du Golf, 62520 Le Touquet.
25km south of Boulogne off the D940.

CONTACT: Secretary. Tel: +33 21 05 68 47.
COURSE: 5,637m, PAR 72, SSS 71. Parkland course.
SOC RESTR'S: No restrictions except Weekends.
SOC GF – Round: Wd 250F. **We** 320F. **Day:** Wd N/A. **We** N/A.
SOC PACK: Seasonal alterations & discount on reserved GF.
VIS RESTR'S: GF discount on reserved bookings.
VIS GF – Round: Wd 250F. **We** 320F. **Day:** Wd 370F. **We** 440F.
FACILITIES: 9-hole Course, Practice Area, Bar & Restaurant.

LE TOUQUET 'LE MER' MAP 14 B1

Avenue du Golf, 62520 Le Touquet.
25km south of Boulogne off the D940.

CONTACT: Secretary. Tel: +33 21 05 68 47.
COURSE: 6,146m, PAR 72, SSS 72. Championship links course.
SOC RESTR'S: No restrictions except Weekends.
SOC GF – Round: Wd 250F. **We** 320F. **Day:** Wd N/A. **We** N/A.
SOC PACK: Seasonal alterations & discount on reserved GF.
VIS RESTR'S: GF discount on reserved bookings.
VIS GF – Round: Wd 250F. **We** 320F. **Day:** Wd N/A. **We** N/A.
FACILITIES: 9-hole Course, Practice Area, Bar & Restaurant.

Normande

NORMANDE

GOLF DE CAEN MAP 14 B1

Le Vallon, 14112 Bieville – Beuville.
5km north of Cane off the D7.

CONTACT: R Paulette, Director. Tel: +33 31 94 72 09.
COURSE: 6,155m, PAR 72, SSS 72. Parkland course.
SOC RESTR'S: Welcome.
SOC GF – Round: Wd 150F. We 190F. Day: Wd 190F. We 240F.
SOC PACK: Available on booking.
VIS RESTR'S: Welcome.
VIS GF – Round: Wd 150F. We 190F. Day: Wd 190F. We 240F.
FACILITIES: Catering & Bar.

CABOURG GOLF CLUB MAP 14 B1

Le Home Varaville, 14390 Cabourg.
20km north-east of Caen on the D514.

CONTACT: Secretary. Tel: +33 31 91 25 56.
COURSE: 5,259m, PAR 68, SSS 68. Links course.
SOC RESTR'S: Welcome.
SOC GF – Round: Wd 160F. We 180F. Day: Wd 230F. We 260F.
SOC PACK: Discount on reserved Green Fee bookings.
VIS RESTR'S: Welcome.
VIS GF – Round: Wd 160F. We 180F. Day: Wd 230F. We 260F.
FACILITIES: Pro-shop, Bar & Restaurant.

GOLF DE CLECY CANTELOU MAP 14 B1

Manoir de Cantelou, 14570 Clécy.
36km south of Caen off the D562.

CONTACT: M. Racloz Guy, Director. Tel: +33 31 69 72 72.
COURSE: 5,967m, PAR 72 SSS 72. Parkland course.
SOC RESTR'S: Always welcome.
SOC GF – Round: Wd N/A. We N/A. Day: Wd 150F. We 200F.
SOC PACK: Call Club for details.
VIS RESTR'S: Always welcome.
VIS GF – Round: Wd N/A. We N/A. Day: Wd 150F. We 200F.
FACILITIES: Clubhouse, Billiards & Restaurant.

GOLF CLUB DU CHAMP DE BATAILLE MAP 14 B1

Château du Champ de Bataille, 27110 Le Neubourg.
35km south-west of Rouen.

CONTACT: H Prieux. Tel: +33 32 35 03 72.
COURSE: 5,983m, PAR 72, SSS 72. Woodland course.
SOC RESTR'S: Can cater for 50 – 140 people.
SOC GF – Round: Wd 220F. We 330F. Day: Wd N/A. We N/A.
SOC PACK: GF reductions for reserved bookings.
VIS RESTR'S: Welcome but booking is advisable.
VIS GF – Round: Wd 220F. We 330F. Day: Wd N/A. We N/A.
FACILITIES: Range, Putting Green, Golf School & Restaurant.

GOLF DE ST GATIEN-DEAUVILLE MAP 14 B1

Le Mont St-Jean, 14130 St-Gatien-des-Bois.
10km south-east of Deauville off the N17.

CONTACT: P Bardou, Director. Tel: +33 31 65 19 99.
COURSE: 6,174m, PAR 72, SSS 72. Split parkland/forest course.
SOC RESTR'S: Welcome.
SOC GF – Round: Wd N/A. We N/A. Day: Wd 220F. We 300F.
SOC PACK: Seasonal alterations & reserved discount on GF.
VIS RESTR'S: Welcome. Possible to play 1st nine at half price.
VIS GF – Round: Wd 180F. We 240F. Day: Wd 220F. We 300F.
FACILITIES: 9-hole Course, Practice Area, Clubhouse & Restaurant.

GOLF DE BELLEME-ST-MARTIN MAP 14 B1

Les Sablons, 61110 Bellême.
40km north-east of Le Mans on the D301.

CONTACT: V Lanthony. Tel: +33 33 73 00 77.
COURSE: 5,972m, PAR 72, SSS 72. Parkland course.
SOC RESTR'S: Welcome.
SOC GF – Round: Wd 170F. We 230F. Day: Wd N/A. We N/A.
SOC PACK: Special prices for groups or seminars.
VIS RESTR'S: Welcome.
VIS GF – Round: Wd 170F. We 230F. Day: Wd N/A. We N/A.
FACILITIES: Swimming Pool, Tennis Court & Pony Club.

GRANVILLE GOLF CLUB MAP 14 A1

Bréville, 50290 Bréhal.
5km north of Grandville (80km south of Cherbourg) along coast.

CONTACT: Secretary. Tel: +33 33 50 23 06.
COURSE: 5,854m, PAR 72, SSS 72. Links course.
SOC RESTR'S: Welcome.
SOC GF – Round: Wd N/A. We N/A. Day: Wd 190F. We 300F.
SOC PACK: Seasonal alterations & reserved discount on GF.
VIS RESTR'S: Welcome.
VIS GF – Round: Wd N/A. We N/A. Day: Wd 190F. We 300F.
FACILITIES: 9-hole Par 33 Course, Pro-shop, Bar & Restaurant.

FRANCE

LERY-POSES GOLF CLUB MAP 14 B1

Base de Loisirs et de Plein Air, BP 7, 27740 Poses.
15km south-east of Rouen off the N15.

CONTACT: Secretary. Tel: +33 32 59 47 42.
COURSE: 6,242m, PAR 72, SSS 73. Public parkland course.
SOC RESTR'S: Welcome.
SOC GF – Round: Wd N/A. We N/A. Day: Wd 160F. We 220F.
SOC PACK: Available on booking.
VIS RESTR'S: Welcome.
VIS GF – Round: Wd N/A. We N/A. Day: Wd 160F. We 220F.
FACILITIES: 9-hole Course, Bar & Restaurant.

Poitou Charentes

NEW GOLF DEAUVILLE MAP 14 B1

Saint Arnoult, 14800 Deauville.
2km south-west of Deauville.

CONTACT: F. Barba, Manager. Tel: +33 31 88 20 53.
COURSE: 5,934m, PAR 71, SSS 71. Clifftop/links course.
SOC RESTR'S: No restrictions provided availability.
SOC GF – Round: Wd N/A. We N/A. Day: Wd 240F. We 330F.
SOC PACK: Available on booking.
VIS RESTR'S: Welcome but booking is advisable.
VIS GF – Round: Wd N/A. We N/A. Day: Wd 240F. We 330F.
FACILITIES: Hotel, 9-hole Course, Practice Range & Tennis.

GOLF CLUB DU HAUT-POITOU MAP 14 B2

86130 Saint-Cyr.
25km north-west of Poitiers off the N10.

CONTACT: Catherine Marchais, Secretary. Tel: +33 49 62 53 62.
COURSE: 6,590m, PAR 73, SSS 75. Undulating woodland course.
SOC RESTR'S: Welcome with prior reservation.
SOC GF – Round: Wd N/A. We N/A. Day: Wd 170F. We 200F.
SOC PACK: Available on booking.
VIS RESTR'S: Competitions on Sundays.
VIS GF – Round: Wd N/A. We N/A. Day: Wd 170F. We 200F.
FACILITIES: Leisure Park, Sailing, Windsurfing & Fishing.

OMAHA BEACH GOLF CLUB MAP 14 B1

Ferme St-Sauveur, 14520 Port-en-Bessin.
15km north-west of Bayeux on the D154.

CONTACT: Reservations. Tel: +33 31 21 72 94.
COURSE: 6,229m, PAR 72, SSS 72. A Scottish style links course.
SOC RESTR'S: Always welcome.
SOC GF – Round: Wd 180F. We 260F. Day: Wd 260F. We N/A.
SOC PACK: Seasonal alterations in GF from 180-260F.
VIS RESTR'S: Always welcome. Handicap Certificate required.
VIS GF – Round: Wd 180F. We 260F. Day: Wd 260F. We N/A.
FACILITIES: 9-hole Course, Practice Area, Pitch & Putt.

GOLF DU COGNAC MAP 14 B2

Saint Brice, 16100 Cognac.
5km east of Cognac.

CONTACT: Secretary. Tel: +33 45 32 18 17.
COURSE: 6,122m, PAR 72, SSS 72. Undulating parkland course.
SOC RESTR'S: Welcome with reservation.
SOC GF – Round: Wd 180F. We 220F. Day: Wd N/A. We N/A.
SOC PACK: Available on reservation.
VIS RESTR'S: Always welcome.
VIS GF – Round: Wd 180F. We 220F. Day: Wd N/A. We N/A.
FACILITIES: Tennis, Fishing & Swimming Pool.

SAINT-JULIEN PONT-L'EVEQUE MAP 14 B1

Pont-l'Evêque 14130 St-Julien-sur-Calonne.
15km south of Deauville.

CONTACT: Reservations. Tel: +33 31 64 30 30.
COURSE: 6,290m, PAR 72, SSS 73. Parkland course with water.
SOC RESTR'S: Welcome. Seasonal alterations to GF.
SOC GF – Round: Wd 250F. We 290F. Day: Wd N/A. We N/A.
SOC PACK: GF discounts on reserved bookings.
VIS RESTR'S: Welcome. Seasonal alterations to GF.
VIS GF – Round: Wd 250F. We 290F. Day: Wd N/A. We N/A.
FACILITIES: 9-hole Par 33 Course, Clubhouse & Bar.

LOUDUN GOLF CLUB MAP 14 B2

Domaine St Hilaire, 86120 Roiffe.
20km north of Loudun.

CONTACT: Secretary. Tel: +33 49 98 78 06.
COURSE: 6,280m, PAR 72, SSS 73. A wide but really long course.
SOC RESTR'S: Welcome except Tues from 1st Oct to 31 Mar.
SOC GF – Round: Wd N/A. We N/A. Day: Wd 190F. We 230F.
SOC PACK: On application.
VIS RESTR'S: Welcome except Tues from 1st Oct to 31 Mar.
VIS GF – Round: Wd 170F. We 210F. Day: Wd 190F. We 230F.
FACILITIES: Pitch & Putt, Tennis, Fishing & Swimming Pool.

Pyrenees

ROYAN GOLF CLUB MAP 14 A2

Maine – Gaudin, 17420 St Palais.
6km north-west on Royan on the D145.

CONTACT: Secretary. Tel: +33 46 23 16 24.
COURSE: 6,033m, PAR 71, SSS 71. Tight forest course.
SOC RESTR'S: Welcome with advance reservation.
SOC GF – Round: Wd N/A. We N/A. **Day:** Wd 150F. We 230F.
SOC PACK: Discount on reserved Green Fee bookings.
VIS RESTR'S: Always welcome.
VIS GF – Round: Wd 150F. We 230F. **Day:** Wd 150F. We 230F.
FACILITIES: Bar, Restaurant Pro-shop, Range, Pitch & Putt.

CHATEAU DE TERRIDES MAP 14 B3

Domaine de Terrides, 82100 Labourgade.
50km north-westToulouse on the D14.

CONTACT: R Delille, President. Tel: +33 63 95 65 20.
COURSE: 6,420m, PAR 74, SSS 71. Meadowland course.
SOC RESTR'S: Welcome with prior reservation.
SOC GF – Round: Wd 150F. We 200F. **Day:** Wd N/A. We N/A.
SOC PACK: Call club for details.
VIS RESTR'S: Welcome.
VIS GF – Round: Wd 200F. We 250F. **Day:** Wd N/A. We N/A.
FACILITIES: Swimming Pool, Restaurant & Hotel.

GOLF D'ALBI LASBORDES MAP 14 B3

Château de Lasbordes, 81000 Albi.
80km north-east of Toulouse in Albi town.

CONTACT: AT Louis, Director. Tel: +33 63 54 98 07.
COURSE: 6,199m, PAR 72, SSS 72. Hilly parkland course.
SOC RESTR'S: Welcome.
SOC GF – Round: Wd 150F. We 200F. **Day:** Wd N/A. We N/A.
SOC PACK: Discount on reserved Green Fee bookings.
VIS RESTR'S: Welcome.
VIS GF – Round: Wd 150F. We 200F. **Day:** Wd N/A. We N/A.
FACILITIES: Bar & Restaurant.

PYRENEES

GOLF DE TEOULA MAP 14 B3

71 Avenue des Landes, 31830 Plaisance du Touch.
15km west of Toulouse on the D632.

CONTACT: C Rondelé, Director. Tel: +33 61 91 98 80.
COURSE: 5,500m, PAR 69, SSS 69. Natural parkland course.
SOC RESTR'S: Closed Thursday.
SOC GF – Round: Wd N/A. We N/A. **Day:** Wd 150F. We 200F.
SOC PACK: Seasonal alterations & reserved discount on GF.
VIS RESTR'S: Welcome.
VIS GF – Round: Wd N/A. We N/A. **Day:** Wd 150F. We 200F.
FACILITIES: Restaurant.

GOLF DES TUMULUS MAP 14 B3

1 Rue du Bois, 65310 Laloubère.
35km south-east of Pau, 5km south of Tarbes off the A64.

CONTACT: Charles de Ginestet, President. Tel: +33 62 45 14 50.
COURSE: 5,050m, PAR 70, SSS 68. Numerous water hazards.
SOC RESTR'S: Welcome.
SOC GF – Round: Wd N/A. We N/A. **Day:** Wd 120F. We 230F.
SOC PACK: Available on booking.
VIS RESTR'S: Welcome.
VIS GF – Round: Wd N/A. We N/A. **Day:** Wd 120F. We 230F.
FACILITIES: Bar at Weekends.

GOLF INTERNATIONAL TOULOUSE-SEILH MAP 14 B3

Route de Grenade, 31840 Seilh.
12km north-west on Toulouse on the N20.

CONTACT: Marie Simone Jaudin, Manager. Tel: +33 62 13 14 15.
COURSE: 6,122m, PAR 72, SSS 72. American style – water hazards.
SOC RESTR'S: Always welcome.
SOC GF – Round: Wd 200F. We 250F. **Day:** Wd N/A. We N/A.
SOC PACK: 30% reduction for Hotel Clients.
VIS RESTR'S: Always welcome.
VIS GF – Round: Wd 200F. We 250F. **Day:** Wd N/A. We N/A.
FACILITIES: 2nd 18-hole Course, Swimming Pool & Restaurants.

RAC HOTELS IN FRANCE

Over 1,300 carefully selected hotels, many illustrated in colour and all cross-referenced to the map section. For holidaymaker or business traveller alike.
An information source for regional foods - beaches - châteaux - resorts - theme parks - wine regions - ...and much more
Price £9.99
Available from bookshops
or direct from the RAC on 0235 834885

FRANCE

Roussillon

GOLF DES HAUTS DE NIMES MAP 15 A/B3

Vacquerolles, Route de Sauve, 30900 Nîmes.
6km north-west of Nîmes off the D907.

CONTACT: Reservations. Tel: +33 66 23 33 33.
COURSE: 6,280m, PAR 72, SSS 73. Hilly woodland course.
SOC RESTR'S: Prior booking through Reservations.
SOC GF – Round: Wd 190F. **We** 220F. **Day: Wd** N/A. **We** N/A.
SOC PACK: Discount on reserved Green Fee bookings.
VIS RESTR'S: Welcome but please phone first.
VIS GF – Round: Wd 190F. **We** 220F. **Day: Wd** N/A. **We** N/A.
FACILITIES: Bar, Restaurant, Pro-shop & Club Hire.

GOLF DE LA GRANDE-MOTTE MAP 15 A3

34740 La Grand-Motte.
20km east of Montpellier off the D62.

CONTACT: Jay Achacz. Tel: +33 67 56 05 00.
COURSE: 6,210m, PAR 72, SSS 72. Coastal course.
SOC RESTR'S: Always welcome.
SOC GF – Round: Wd 200F. **We** 220F. **Day: Wd** N/A. **We** N/A.
SOC PACK: Reduction of 20% for 12+. Discount for hotel guests.
VIS RESTR'S: Always welcome.
VIS GF – Round: Wd 200F. **We** 220F. **Day: Wd** N/A. **We** N/A.
FACILITIES: 2nd 18-hole Course, Swimming Pool & Sauna.

NIMES CAMPAGNE GOLF CLUB MAP 15 B3

Route de Saint Gilles, 30000 Nîmes.
10km south of Nîmes on the D42.

CONTACT: Reservations. Tel: +33 66 70 17 37.
COURSE: 6.135m, PAR 72, SSS 72. Parkland course.
SOC RESTR'S: Prior booking through Reservations.
SOC GF – Round: Wd 200F. **We** 250F. **Day: Wd** N/A. **We** N/A.
SOC PACK: Available on application.
VIS RESTR'S: Welcome but please phone first.
VIS GF – Round: Wd 210F. **We** 260F. **Day: Wd** N/A. **We** N/A.
FACILITIES: Bar, Restaurant, Pro-shop & Club Hire.

GOLF DE MASSANE MAP 15 A3

Domaine de Massane, 34670 Baillargues.
10km north-east of Montpellier off the N113.

CONTACT: J. Beauvillain. Tel: +33 67 87 87 87.
COURSE: 6,375m, PAR 72, SSS 74. Championship parkland.
SOC RESTR'S: Welcome.
SOC GF – Round: Wd 175F. **We** 230F. **Day: Wd** N/A. **We** N/A.
SOC PACK: The club will organise any Society event.
VIS RESTR'S: Always welcome.
VIS GF – Round: Wd 205F. **We** 280F. **Day: Wd** N/A. **We** N/A.
FACILITIES: Swimming Pool, Tennis, Golf & Training School.

SAINT MARTIN CAP D'AGDE MAP 15 A3

Avenue des Alizés, 34300 Cap d'Agde.
25km south-east of Béziers on the N312.

CONTACT: Reservations. Tel: +33 67 26 54 40.
COURSE: 6.160m, PAR 72, SSS 71. Heathland course.
SOC RESTR'S: Prior booking through Reservations.
SOC GF – Round: Wd 200F. **We** 250F. **Day: Wd** N/A. **We** N/A.
SOC PACK: Tailored to suit requirements.
VIS RESTR'S: Welcome but please phone first.
VIS GF – Round: Wd 210F. **We** 260F. **Day: Wd** N/A. **We** N/A.
FACILITIES: Pitch & Putt, Restaurant, Pro-shop, Club & Cart Hire.

GOLF DE SAINT CYPRIEN MAP 15 A3

66750 Saint Cyprien Plage.
10km south-east of Perpignan on the D11.

CONTACT: P Socquet, Director General. Tel: +33 68 21 01 71.
COURSE: 6,480m, PAR 73, SSS 74. Long, with water hazards.
SOC RESTR'S: Always welcome.
SOC GF – Round: Wd N/A. **We** N/A. **Day: Wd** 195F. **We** 240F.
SOC PACK: Available on booking.
VIS RESTR'S: Always welcome.
VIS GF – Round: Wd N/A. **We** N/A. **Day: Wd** 195F. **We** 240F.
FACILITIES: 9-hole Course, Special rates for Residents.

GERMANY

WOULD golf in Germany have taken off quite as rapidly as it has done in the past decade if Bernhard Langer hadn't been as wonderfully successfully as he has been? Possibly not, but then again, there had to be another outlet for those who couldn't play either football or tennis! It goes without saying that Langer's successes at Augusta; his tournament wins around the world - including winning the World Cup for Germany with Torsten Gideon in 1990; and the steely courage that's seen him overcome the dreaded 'yips' have given him a special place in German affections, but although he has of course given the game a timely boost in his homeland, there was a reasonable golfing tradition in Germany stretching back to the turn of the century.

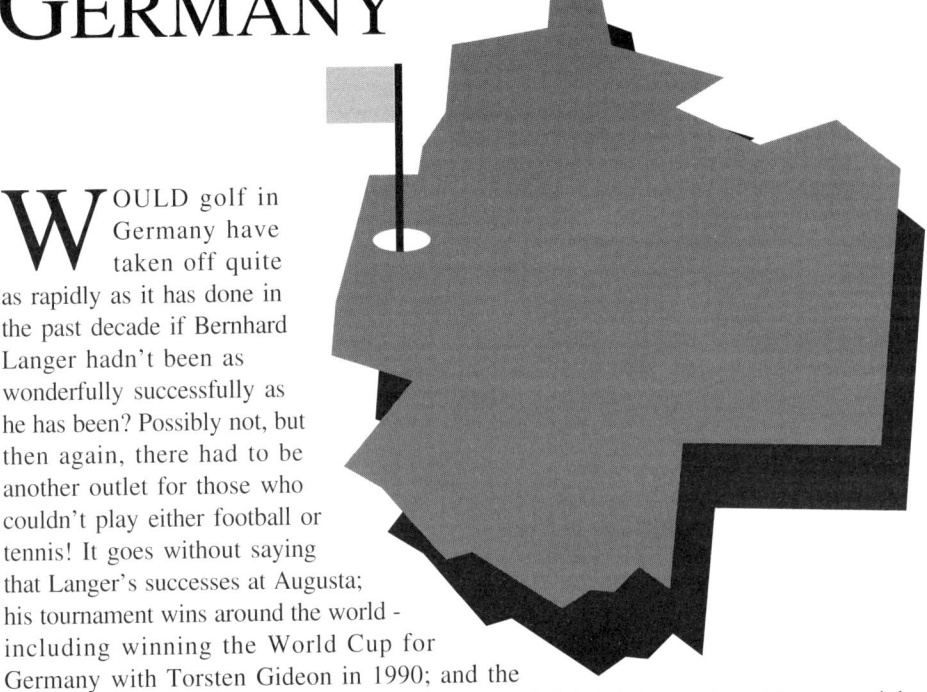

The best example of this German golf tradition can be found at the formidable Club zur Vahr, founded in 1905 and situated about 10 miles north of Bremen. Constructed amidst dark, brooding pines, this is a course of truly Wagnerian proportions and definitely not for the faint-hearted or the short hitter. Off the back tees, it plays in excess of 7200 yards, with a par of 74. The layout includes no fewer than six par-5's, all well over 500 yards. There's a par-3 - the 17th - of 230 yards, while five of the eight par-4's are more than 400 yards. With such prodigious distances to negotiate, it's perhaps just as well - not to mention welcome relief - that there are only 24 bunkers to avoid!

Not all German courses are built on such an heroic scale. The more modern, and gentler parkland courses at Hubbelrath, Gut Kaden and Frankfurt have all hosted European Tour events and many other exciting developments throughout Germany are either in play or under construction. Despite that, in relation to its size, Germany still has substantial pockets of 'golf wilderness' though not, happily, in the major business and tourist areas. There, with the usual provisos about a pre-visit telephone call, few obstacles to a round will be met. That's currently anything but the case in the former East Germany, except in and around Berlin, but it's a situation that looks scheduled for rapid change.

GERMANY

Baden-Würtemberg

HEILBRONN-HOHENLOHE   MAP 16 A3

Postfach 1341, 7100 Neckarsulm.
45km north of Stuttgart by Heilbronn.

CONTACT: B Amara, Professional. Tel: +49 7941 7886.
COURSE: 6,082m, PAR 72, SSS 72. Parkland course.
SOC RESTR'S: Welcome with prior agreement.
SOC GF - Round: Wd DM60 We DM90. **Day:** Wd N/A. **We** N/A.
SOC PACK: Available when booking.
VIS RESTR'S: Welcome.
VIS GF - Round: Wd DM60. We DM90. **Day:** Wd N/A. **We** N/A.
FACILITIES: Bar & Restaurant.

OBERSCHWABEN-BAD WALDSEE   MAP 16 A3

Hofgut Hopfenweiler, 7967 Bad Waldsee.
Off A8 Munich-Stuttgart, take B30 65km south to Bad Waldsee.

CONTACT: Secretary. Tel: +49 7524 5900.
COURSE: 6,148m, PAR 72, SSS 72. Undulating course.
SOC RESTR'S: Welcome with prior booking.
SOC GF - Round: Wd DM55. We DM75. **Day:** Wd N/A. **We** N/A.
SOC PACK: No set package.
VIS RESTR'S: Welcome.
VIS GF - Round: Wd DM55. We DM75. **Day:** Wd N/A. **We** N/A.
FACILITIES: Bar & Restaurant.

SAARBRÜCKEN GOLF CLUB   MAP 16 A3

Oberlimbergerweg, 6634 Wallerfangen-Gisingen.
10km north-west of Saarbrücken towards Saarlouis.

CONTACT: F Le Chevallier, Pro Manager. Tel: +49 6837 401.
COURSE: 6,231m, PAR 72, SSS 73. Parkland course.
SOC RESTR'S: Welcome with written agreement.
SOC GF - Round: Wd DM70. We DM95. **Day:** Wd N/A. **We** N/A.
SOC PACK: On application.
VIS RESTR'S: Welcome with a Handicap of 36 minimum.
VIS GF - Round: Wd DM75. We DM100. **Day:** Wd N/A. **We** N/A.
FACILITIES: Students DM40.

SCHLOSS LIEBENSTEIN   MAP 16 A3

Postfach 27, D-7129 Neckarwestheim.
35km north of Stuttgart.

CONTACT: S Rudiger, Manager. Tel: +49 7133 16019.
COURSE: 5,847m, PAR 72, SSS 71. A very tricky course.
SOC RESTR'S: Welcome with advanced booking.
SOC GF - Round: Wd DM60. We DM80. **Day:** Wd N/A. **We** N/A.
SOC PACK: For special offers call Hotel or Club.
VIS RESTR'S: Welcome phone call advisable to check availability.
VIS GF - Round: Wd DM60. We DM80. **Day:** Wd N/A. **We** N/A.
FACILITIES: Students 50% Green Fee. Max. H'cap 28.

SCHLOSS WEITENBURG   MAP 16 A3

Sommerhalde 11, 7245 Starzach-Sulzau.
50km south-west of Stuttgart

CONTACT: M Straub. Tel: +49 7472 8061.
COURSE: 6,182m, PAR 72, SSS 72. Long parkland course.
SOC RESTR'S: Welcome.
SOC GF - Round: Wd N/A. We N/A. **Day:** Wd DM70. **We** DM90.
SOC PACK: On application.
VIS RESTR'S: Welcome but H'cap Cert is required at Weekends.
VIS GF - Round: Wd N/A. We N/A. **Day:** Wd DM70. **We** DM90.
FACILITIES: 9-hole Course, Bar & Restaurant.

STUTTGART SOLITUDE CLUB   MAP 16 A3

7256 Mönsheim.
15km west of Stuttgart.

CONTACT: Secretary. Tel: +49 7044 5852.
COURSE: 6,045m, PAR 72, SSS 72. Undulating course.
SOC RESTR'S: Welcome with prior booking.
SOC GF - Round: Wd N/A. We N/A. **Day:** Wd DM80. **We** N/A.
SOC PACK: Available when booking.
VIS RESTR'S: Welcome please phone to check availability.
VIS GF - Round: Wd N/A. We N/A. **Day:** Wd DM80. **We** DM110.
FACILITIES: Bar & Restaurant.

ULM GOLF CLUB   MAP 16 A3

Wochenauer Hof 2, 7901 Illerrieden.
15km south of Ulm.

CONTACT: M Emery, Professional. Tel: +49 7306 2102.
COURSE: 6,170m, PAR 72, SSS 72. Undulating course.
SOC RESTR'S: Welcome with prior booking.
SOC GF - Round: Wd DM55. We DM70. **Day:** Wd N/A. **We** N/A.
SOC PACK: Available when booking.
VIS RESTR'S: Welcome please phone to check availability.
VIS GF - Round: Wd DM55. We DM70. **Day:** Wd N/A. **We** N/A.
FACILITIES: Bar & Restaurant.

Bayern

BAD KISSINGEN MAP 16 A2

Euesdorferstr 11, 8730 Bad Kissingen.
95km east of Frankfurt, 2km from Bad Kissingen.

CONTACT: Secretary. Tel: +49 971 3608.
COURSE: 5,680m, PAR 70, SSS 70. Parkland course.
SOC RESTR'S: Welcome with prior booking.
SOC GF - Round: Wd N/A. We N/A. Day: Wd DM55. We DM65.
SOC PACK: On application.
VIS RESTR'S: Welcome any time but must be a member of a club.
VIS GF - Round: Wd N/A. We N/A. Day: Wd DM55. We DM65.
FACILITIES: Bar & Restaurant.

BAD WÖRISHOFEN GOLF CLUB MAP 16 B3

Schlingenstr 27, 8951 Rieden.
10km south of Bad Wörishofen.

CONTACT: Secretary. Tel: +49 8346 777.
COURSE: 6,318m, PAR 72, SSS 71. Parkland course.
SOC RESTR'S: Advanced reservations only.
SOC GF - Round: Wd DM70. We DM90. Day: Wd N/A. We N/A.
SOC PACK: Available when booking.
VIS RESTR'S: Welcome please phone to check times for We.
VIS GF - Round: Wd DM70. We DM90. Day: Wd N/A. We N/A.
FACILITIES: Bar & Restaurant.

BEUERBERG GOLF CLUB MAP 16 B3

Gut Sterz, 8196 Beuerberg.
45km south-west on Munich.

CONTACT: A Hahn, Secretary. Tel: +49 8179 671.
COURSE: 6,518m, PAR 73, SSS 74. Parkland course.
SOC RESTR'S: Welcome with prior agreement.
SOC GF - Round: Wd DM70. We DM95. Day: Wd N/A. We N/A.
SOC PACK: Available when booking. Handicap Cert (max. 28).
VIS RESTR'S: Welcome.
VIS GF - Round: Wd DM70. We DM95. Day: Wd N/A. We N/A.
FACILITIES: Bar & Restaurant.

FELDAFING GOLF CLUB MAP 16 B3

Tutzinger Strasse 15, 8133 Feldafing.
30km south of Munich.

CONTACT: T Flossman, Professional Tel: +49 8175 7005.
COURSE: 5,708m, PAR 71, SSS 70. Undulating course.
SOC RESTR'S: Welcome with prior agreement.
SOC GF - Round: Wd DM70. We DM95. Day: Wd N/A. We N/A.
SOC PACK: Available when booking.
VIS RESTR'S: Welcome please phone to check availability.
VIS GF - Round: Wd DM70. We DM95. Day: Wd N/A. We N/A.
FACILITIES: Pitch & Putt, Bar & Restaurant.

IM CHIEMGAU GOLF CLUB MAP 16 B3

Kötzing 1, 8224 Chieming.
60km west of Salzburg (Austria).

CONTACT: Secretary. Tel: +49 8669 7557.
COURSE: 6,234m, PAR 72, SSS 73. Mountain course.
SOC RESTR'S: Available when booking.
SOC GF - Round: Wd DM55. We DM80. Day: Wd N/A. We N/A.
SOC PACK: On application.
VIS RESTR'S: Welcome please phone to check availability.
VIS GF - Round: Wd DM55. We DM80. Day: Wd N/A. We N/A.
FACILITIES: 9-hole Par 3 Course, Bar & Clubhouse.

MARGARETHENHOF AM CLUB MAP 16 B3

8184 Gmund am Tegernsee.
45km south of Munich in Tegernsee.

CONTACT: Secretary. Tel: +49 8022 7366.
COURSE: 6,056m, PAR 72, SSS 72. Undulating course.
SOC RESTR'S: Welcome with prior agreement.
SOC GF - Round: Wd DM50. We DM70. Day: Wd N/A. We N/A.
SOC PACK: Available when booking.
VIS RESTR'S: Welcome please phone to check availability.
VIS GF - Round: Wd DM50. We DM70. Day: Wd N/A. We N/A.
FACILITIES: Bar & Restaurant. Open Apr-Oct.

RAC HOTELS IN EUROPE

The ideal 'travel companion' with over 1,500 selected hotels in 20 countries, including Eastern Europe. Hotel entries contain phone and fax numbers, national star rating, restaurant, prices, credit cards and where English is spoken.. Full colour atlas section with all hotel locations shown. Parking law - Speed limits - Public holidays - Banks - Shops - Fuel availability

Price £9.99

Available from bookshops
or direct from the RAC on 0235 834885

GERMANY

MÜNCHENER CLUB MAP 16 B3

Tölzerstr, 8021 Strasslach.
10km from Munich in Strasslach.
CONTACT: H Fluss, Professional. Tel: +49 8170 450.
COURSE: 6,177m, PAR 72, SSS 72. Parkland course.
SOC RESTR'S: Welcome Weekdays with booking.
SOC GF - Round: Wd DM80. We N/A. **Day:** Wd N/A. We N/A.
SOC PACK: None.
VIS RESTR'S: Welcome Weekdays.
VIS GF - Round: Wd DM80. We N/A. **Day:** Wd N/A. We N/A.
FACILITIES: 9-hole Par 35 Course, Bar & Restaurant.

MÜNCHEN-NORD EICHENRIED MAP 16 B3

Münchenstr 57, 8059 Eichenried.
19km north-east of Munich.
CONTACT: G Stewart, Professional. Tel: +49 8123 1004.
COURSE: 6,318m, PAR 73, SSS 72. Undulating course.
SOC RESTR'S: Written applications only.
SOC GF - Round: Wd DM70. We N/A. **Day:** Wd N/A. We N/A.
SOC PACK: Limited package.
VIS RESTR'S: Welcome Weekdays. Closed Dec & Jan.
VIS GF - Round: Wd DM70. We N/A. **Day:** Wd N/A. We N/A.
FACILITIES: Pitch & Putt, Indoor Practice Area & Bar.

MÜNCHEN-WEST ODELZHAUSEN MAP 16 B3

Gut Todtenreid, 8063 Odelzhausen.
35km north-west of Munich.
CONTACT: C Burnam, Professionals. Tel: +49 8134 1618.
COURSE: 6,169m, PAR 72, SSS 72. Parkland course.
SOC RESTR'S: Book in advance. Open Apr-Nov.
SOC GF - Round: WdDM60. We N/A. **Day:** Wd N/A. We N/A.
SOC PACK: On application.
VIS RESTR'S: Letter of Intro before 10.45am Wd. Open Apr-Nov.
VIS GF - Round: Wd DM60. We DM80. **Day:** Wd N/A. We N/A.
FACILITIES: Practice Area, Bar & Restaurant.

ST EURACH LAND & GOLF CLUB MAP 16 B3

D-8127 Iffeldorf, Eurach 8.
40km south of Munich.
CONTACT: Secretary. Tel: +49 8801 1332.
COURSE: 6,500m, PAR 72, SSS 74. Forest course.
SOC RESTR'S: Course open 16 Apr-15 Oct. Welcome Weekdays.
SOC GF - Round: Wd DM100. We N/A. **Day:** Wd N/A. We N/A.
SOC PACK: On application.
VIS RESTR'S: Welcome Weekdays only (except pm Wed & Fri).
VIS GF - Round: Wd DM100. We N/A. **Day:** Wd N/A. We N/A.
FACILITIES: On application.

SCHLOß KLINGENBURG GÜNZBURG MAP 16 B3

8876 Jettingen - Scheppach.
40km west of Augsburg. Exit Burgau, Stuttgart-Munich (E 5km).
CONTACT: K Port, Secretary. Tel: +49 8225 3030.
COURSE: 6,218m, PAR 72, SSS 72. Hilly parkland course.
SOC RESTR'S: Welcome with advanced booking.
SOC GF - Round: Wd N/A. We N/A. **Day:** Wd DM60. We DM90.
SOC PACK: On application.
VIS RESTR'S: Open 1st April - 31st October.
VIS GF - Round: Wd N/A. We N/A. **Day:** Wd DM60. We DM90.
FACILITIES: Bar, Restaurant & Clubhouse.

SPORT & KURHOTEL SONNENALP MAP 16 A3

8972 Sonthofen - Ofterschwang.
28km south of Kempten between Sonthofen & Fischen.
CONTACT: Secretary. Tel: +49 8321 7276.
COURSE: 5,938m, PAR 71, SSS 71. Parkland course.
SOC RESTR'S: Welcome. Booking essential.
SOC GF - Round: Wd N/A. We N/A. **Day:** Wd DM95. We DM95.
SOC PACK: On application.
VIS RESTR'S: Welcome. Booking essential.
VIS GF - Round: Wd N/A. We N/A. **Day:** Wd DM95. We DM95.
FACILITIES: Clubhouse, Bar & Restaurant.

TEGERNSEER BAD WIESSEE MAP 16 B3

Robognerhof, 8182 Bad Wiessee.
50km south of Munich on the B318.
CONTACT: Monika Pfletscher, Secretary. Tel: +49 8022 8769.
COURSE: 5,501m, PAR 70, SSS 69. Hilly forest course.
SOC RESTR'S: Welcome with prior booking.
SOC GF - Round: Wd DM75. We DM95. **Day:** Wd N/A. We N/A.
SOC PACK: On application.
VIS RESTR'S: Welcome Mon-Thur. Fri before 1, Sat/Sun before 10.
VIS GF - Round: Wd DM75. We DM95. **Day:** Wd N/A. We N/A.
FACILITIES: Bar & Restaurant.

WALDEGG-WIGGENSBACH MAP 16 A3

Hof Waldegg, D-8961 Wiggensbach, Oberallgau.
From Ulm take A7 south to Kempten. 10km west of Kempten.
CONTACT: Lissie Blumm, Secretary. Tel: +49 8370 733.
COURSE: 5,442m, PAR 69, SSS 69. Mountain course.
SOC RESTR'S: Welcome.
SOC GF - Round: Wd N/A. We N/A. **Day:** Wd DM40. We DM50.
SOC PACK: On application.
VIS RESTR'S: Guests with a Handicap of 36 or better are welcome.
VIS GF - Round: Wd N/A. We N/A. **Day:** Wd DM40. We DM50.
FACILITIES: Bavarian Style Clubhouse.

HAMBURG

Hamburg

GUT WALDHOF GOLF CLUB   MAP 16 A1

Am Waldhof, 2359 Kisdorferwohld.
35km north of Hamburg off the A7.

CONTACT: E Kruger, Caddymaster. Tel: +49 4194 383.
COURSE: 6,073M, PAR 72, SSS 72. Parkland course.
SOC RESTR'S: Only by appointment.
SOC GF - Round: Wd N/A. **We** N/A. **Day: Wd** DM50. **We** DM60.
SOC PACK: None.
VIS RESTR'S: Welcome.
VIS GF - Round: Wd N/A. **We** N/A. **Day: Wd** DM50. **We** DM60.
FACILITIES: Bar, Restaurant & Clubhouse.

AUF DER WENDLOHE GOLF CLUB   MAP 16 A1

Oldesloerstr 251, 2000 Hamburg.
15km north of Hamburg.

CONTACT: G Jones, Professional. Tel: +49 4055 05041.
COURSE: 6,060m, PAR 72, SSS 72. Parkland course.
SOC RESTR'S: Welcome with prior agreement.
SOC GF - Round: Wd DM65. **We** N/A. **Day: Wd** N/A. **We** N/A.
SOC PACK: None.
VIS RESTR'S: Welcome Weekdays.
VIS GF - Round: Wd DM65. **We** N/A. **Day: Wd** N/A. **We** N/A.
FACILITIES: 9 Extra Holes, Bar & Restaurant.

HAMBURG-AHRENSBURG   MAP 16 A/B1

Am Haidschlag 39-45, 2070 Ahrensburg.
20km east of Hamburg.

CONTACT: H Heiser, Professional. Tel: +49 4102 51309.
COURSE: 5,782m, PAR 71, SSS 70. Undulating course.
SOC RESTR'S: Welcome with prior booking.
SOC GF - Round: Wd DM60. **We** N/A. **Day: Wd** N/A. **We** N/A.
SOC PACK: Available when booking.
VIS RESTR'S: Welcome Weekdays.
VIS GF - Round: Wd DM60. **We** N/A. **Day: Wd** N/A. **We** N/A.
FACILITIES: Bar & Restaurant.

CLUB ZUR VAHR   MAP 16 A1

Bgm-Spitta-Allee 34, 2800 Bremen.
15km north of Bremen.

CONTACT: Secretary. Tel: +49 4212 30041.
COURSE: 6,430m, PAR 73, SSS 75. Undulating course.
SOC RESTR'S: Advanced reservations only.
SOC GF - Round: Wd DM70. **We** DM95. **Day: Wd** N/A. **We** N/A.
SOC PACK: Tailored to suit each outing.
VIS RESTR'S: Welcome please phone to check availability.
VIS GF - Round: Wd DM70. **We** DM95. **Day: Wd** N/A. **We** N/A.
FACILITIES: 9-hole Course, Bar & Restaurant.

HAMBURGER GOLF CLUB   MAP 16 A1

In de Bargen, 2000 Hamburg 55.
15km west of Hamburg.

CONTACT: Reservations. Tel: +49 408 12177.
COURSE: 5,925m, PAR 71, SSS 71. Undulating courses.
SOC RESTR'S: Not Weekends, Holidays & Tournament Days.
SOC GF - Round: Wd DM60. **We** DM75. **Day: Wd** N/A. **We** N/A.
SOC PACK: None.
VIS RESTR'S: Not Weekends, Holidays & Tournament Days.
VIS GF - Round: Wd DM60. **We** DM75. **Day: Wd** N/A. **We** N/A.
FACILITIES: On application.

GUT KADEN GOLF CLUB   MAP 16 A1

Kadenerstrasse 9, 2081 Alveslohe.
Alveslohe, 30km north of Hamburg.

CONTACT: W Mych, Professional. Tel: +49 4193 92021.
COURSE: 6,076m, PAR 72, SSS 72. Parkland course.
SOC RESTR'S: Book in advance. Not weekends.
SOC GF - Round: Wd DM50. **We** N/A. **Day: Wd** N/A. **We** N/A.
SOC PACK: On application.
VIS RESTR'S: Welcome weekdays.
VIS GF - Round: Wd DM50. **We** N/A. **Day: Wd** N/A. **We** N/A.
FACILITIES: Bar & Restaurant.

HAMBURGER LAND & GOLF CLUB   MAP 16 A1

Am Golfplatz 24, 2105 Seevetal 1.
25km south of Hamburg.

CONTACT: V Bose, Secretary. Tel: +49 4105 2331.
COURSE: 5,685m, PAR 70, SSS 70. Rolling parkland course.
SOC RESTR'S: Welcome with advanced booking.
SOC GF - Round: Wd DM75. **We** N/A. **Day: Wd** N/A. **We** N/A.
SOC PACK: On application.
VIS RESTR'S: Welcome Weekdays only.
VIS GF - Round: Wd DM75. **We** N/A. **Day: Wd** N/A. **We** N/A.
FACILITIES: Bar & Restaurant.

GERMANY

KÜSTEN GOLF CLUB   MAP 16 A1

Rosenhof 25, 2190 Cuxhaven. z
10km south-west of Cuxhaven on A6.

CONTACT: Reservations. Tel: +49 4721 48057.
COURSE: 6,150m, PAR 72, SSS 72. Undulating course.
SOC RESTR'S: Welcome with prior agreement.
SOC GF - Round: Wd DM50. **We** DM60. **Day: Wd** N/A. **We** N/A.
SOC PACK: Available when booking.
VIS RESTR'S: Welcome please phone to check availability.
VIS GF - Round: Wd DM50. **We** DM60. **Day: Wd** N/A. **We** N/A.
FACILITIES: Bar & Restaurant.

SCHLOSS LÜDERSBURG   MAP 16 B1

D-2127 Lüdersburg, near Lüneburg.
20km east of Lüneburg.

CONTACT: Nicole David, Club Secretary. Tel: +49 4153 6112.
COURSE: 6,180m, PAR 73, SSS 73. Tight parkland course.
SOC RESTR'S: Welcome with advanced booking.
SOC GF - Round: Wd DM50. **We** DM70. **Day: Wd** N/A. **We** N/A.
SOC PACK: On application.
VIS RESTR'S: Maximum Handicap 36.
VIS GF - Round: Wd DM50. **We** DM70. **Day: Wd** N/A. **We** N/A.
FACILITIES: 6 practice holes & Golf apartments to let.

Hessen

FRANKFURTER GOLF CLUB   MAP 16 A2

Golfstr 41, 6000 Frankfurt 71.
5km south-west of Frankfurt beside Airport.

CONTACT: Reservations Tel: +49 6966 62318.
COURSE: 5,870m, PAR 72, SSS 71. Parkland course.
SOC RESTR'S: Welcome with prior agreement.
SOC GF - Round: Wd DM75. **We** DM95. **Day: Wd** N/A. **We** N/A.
SOC PACK: Available when booking.
VIS RESTR'S: Welcome please phone to check availability.
VIS GF - Round: Wd DM75. **We** DM90. **Day: Wd** N/A. **We** N/A.
FACILITIES: Bar & Restaurant.

HANAU GOLF CLUB   MAP 16 A2

Wilhelmsbader Allee, D-6450 Hanau 1.
3km north-west of Hanau which is 15km west of Frankfurt.

CONTACT: Margarete Weipert, Secretary. Tel: +49 6181 82071.
COURSE: 6,192m, PAR 72, SSS 72. Parkland course.
SOC RESTR'S: Welcome with advanced booking.
SOC GF - Round: Wd DM70. **We** DM90. **Day: Wd** N/A. **We** N/A.
SOC PACK: On application.
VIS RESTR'S: Maximum Handicap 28.
VIS GF - Round: Wd DM70. **We** DM90. **Day: Wd** N/A. **We** N/A.
FACILITIES: On application.

KRONBERG GOLF CLUB   MAP 16 A2

Schloss Friedrichshof, Hainstr 25, 6242 Kronberg.
15km north-west on Frankfurt.

CONTACT: J Harder, Professional. Tel: +49 6173 1426.
COURSE: 5,365m, PAR 68, SSS 68. Undulating course.
SOC RESTR'S: Welcome with prior booking.
SOC GF - Round: Wd DM60. **We** DM80. **Day: Wd** N/A. **We** N/A.
SOC PACK: Available when booking.
VIS RESTR'S: Welcome please phone to check times for We.
VIS GF - Round: Wd DM60. **We** DM80. **Day: Wd** N/A. **We** N/A.
FACILITIES: Bar & Restaurant.

RHÖN-FULDA GOLF CLUB   MAP 16 A2

Am Golfplatz, 6417 Hofbieber 1.
10km east of Fulda.

CONTACT: Secretary. Tel: +49 6657 7077.
COURSE: 5,775m, PAR 71, SSS 70. Parkland course.
SOC RESTR'S: Welcome with prior booking.
SOC GF - Round: Wd DM50. **We** DM70. **Day: Wd** N/A. **We** N/A.
SOC PACK: None.
VIS RESTR'S: Welcome please phone to check times for We.
VIS GF - Round: Wd DM50. **We** DM70. **Day: Wd** N/A. **We** N/A.
FACILITIES: Bar & Restaurant.

SCHLOSS BRAUNFELS   MAP 16 A2

Homburger Hof, 6333 Braunfels.
70km north of Frankfurt.

CONTACT: D Erdmann, Director. Tel: +49 6442 4530.
COURSE: 6,288m, PAR 73, SSS 73. Championship parkland course.
SOC RESTR'S: Welcome Weekdays only.
SOC GF - Round: Wd DM80. **We** N/A. **Day: Wd** N/A. **We** N/A.
SOC PACK: None.
VIS RESTR'S: Welcome Weekdays only.
VIS GF - Round: Wd DM80. **We** N/A. **Day: Wd** N/A. **We** N/A.
FACILITIES: 3 Hole Pitch & Putt, Range & Bar.

Niedersachen

NIEDERSACHEN

GÖTTINGEN GOLF CLUB MAP 16 A2

Levershausen, 3410 Northeim 1.
15km north of Göttingen.

CONTACT: W Kreuzer, Professional. Tel: +49 5551 61915.
COURSE: 6,008m, PAR 72, SSS 72. Forest course.
SOC RESTR'S: Advanced reservations only.
SOC GF - Round: Wd DM50. We DM60. **Day:** Wd N/A. We N/A.
SOC PACK: Available when booking.
VIS RESTR'S: Welcome please phone to check availability.
VIS GF - Round: Wd DM50. We DM60. **Day:** Wd N/A. We N/A.
FACILITIES: Bar & Restaurant.

BURGDORF ERGOLF CLUB MAP 16 A1

Waldstr 27, 3167 Burgdorf - Ehlershausen.
20km north-east of Hanover.

CONTACT: Reservations. Tel: +49 5085 7628.
COURSE: 6,426m, PAR 74, SSS 74. Parkland course.
SOC RESTR'S: Must be a member of a golf club.
SOC GF - Round: Wd N/A. We N/A. **Day:** Wd DM45. We DM65.
SOC PACK: On application.
VIS RESTR'S: Must be a member of a golf club.
VIS GF - Round: Wd N/A. We N/A. **Day:** Wd DM45. We DM65.
FACILITIES: Closed Monday & No Dogs.

HANNOVER GOLF CLUB MAP 16 A1

Am Blauen See, 3008 Garbsen 1.
15km north-west of Hanover.

CONTACT: H Koch, Professional. Tel: +49 5137 73235.
COURSE: 5,855m, PAR 72, SSS 71. Forest course.
SOC RESTR'S: Advanced reservations only.
SOC GF - Round: Wd DM50. We DM70. **Day:** Wd N/A. We N/A.
SOC PACK: Tailored to suit each outing.
VIS RESTR'S: Welcome please phone to check times for We.
VIS GF - Round: Wd DM50. We DM70. **Day:** Wd N/A. We N/A.
FACILITIES: Bar & Restaurant.

BUCHHOLZ-NORDHEIDE MAP 16 A1

An der Rehm 25, 2110 Buchholz.
30km south of Hamburg.

CONTACT: P Holley, Club Manager. Tel: +49 4181 36200.
COURSE: 6,130m, PAR 71, SSS 72. Long flat parkland course.
SOC RESTR'S: Welcome Weekdays only.
SOC GF - Round: Wd DM55. We N/A. **Day:** Wd N/A. We N/A.
SOC PACK: None.
VIS RESTR'S: Welcome Weekdays only.
VIS GF - Round: Wd DM55. We N/A. **Day:** Wd N/A. We N/A.
FACILITIES: Driving Range & Practice Hole.

ST DIONYS GOLF CLUB MAP 16 B1

Widukindweg, 2123 St. Dionys.
10km north of Lüneburg.

CONTACT: K Mähl, Professional. Tel: +49 4133 6287.
COURSE: 6,225m, PAR 72, SSS 73. Forest course.
SOC RESTR'S: Welcome with prior booking.
SOC GF - Round: Wd DM70. We DM90. **Day:** Wd N/A. We N/A.
SOC PACK: Tailored to suit each outing.
VIS RESTR'S: Welcome please phone to check times for We.
VIS GF - Round: Wd DM70. We DM90. **Day:** Wd N/A. We N/A.
FACILITIES: Bar & Restaurant.

BUXTEHUDE GOLF CLUB MAP 16 A1

Zum Lehmfeld 1, 2150 Buxtehude.
30km south-west of Hamburg on the A73.

CONTACT: V Niem, Club Manager. Tel: +49 4161 81333.
COURSE: 6,505m, PAR 74, SSS 74. Light hilly parkland course.
SOC RESTR'S: Welcome except Sunday.
SOC GF - Round: Wd DM55. We DM65. **Day:** Wd DM65. We DM85.
SOC PACK: On application.
VIS RESTR'S: Welcome except Sunday before 09.30.
VIS GF - Round: Wd DM55. We DM65. **Day:** Wd DM65. We DM85.
FACILITIES: Clubhouse, Bar & Restaurant.

SCHLOSS SCHWÖBBER (ONE) MAP 16 A2

Schloss Schwöbber, D-3258 Aerzen.
7km on the B1 out of Hameln.

CONTACT: Ursula Cohrs, President. Tel: +49 5154 2004.
COURSE: 6,200m, PAR 74, SSS 72. Hillside forest course.
SOC RESTR'S: Welcome.
SOC GF - Round: Wd DM60. We N/A. **Day:** Wd DM70. We DM80.
SOC PACK: B&B: 2 nights + 3 days DM300
VIS RESTR'S: Welcome.
VIS GF - Round: Wd DM60. We N/A. **Day:** Wd DM70. We DM80.
FACILITIES: Restaurants, Rooms, Bar & Four 9-hole Courses.

GERMANY

SCHLOSS SCHWÖBBER (TWO)   MAP 16 A2

Schloss Schwöbber, D-3258 Aerzen.
7km on B1 out of Hameln.

CONTACT: Ursula Cohrs, President. Tel: +49 5154 2004.
COURSE: 6,032m, PAR 72, SSS 72. Meadowland course.
SOC RESTR'S: Welcome.
SOC GF - Round: Wd DM60 We N/A. Day: Wd DM70 We DM80.
SOC PACK: B&B: 2 nights + 3 days DM300
VIS RESTR'S: Welcome.
VIS GF - Round: Wd DM60. We N/A. Day: Wd DM70. We DM80.
FACILITIES: Short course. - can be played as Par 60 or 56.

Nordrhein-Westfalen

AACHEN GOLF CLUB   MAP 16 A2

Schürzelter Str 300, 5100 Aachen.
5km north-west of Aachen.

CONTACT: W Van Mook, Professional. Tel: +49 2411 2501.
COURSE: 6,105m, PAR 72, SSS 71. Undulating course.
SOC RESTR'S: Welcome with prior booking.
SOC GF - Round: Wd N/A. We N/A. Day: Wd DM60. We DM80.
SOC PACK: None.
VIS RESTR'S: Welcome please phone to check availability.
VIS GF - Round: Wd N/A. We N/A. Day: Wd DM60. We DM80.
FACILITIES: Bar & Restaurant.

BAD GODESBERG   MAP 16 A2

Landgrabenweg, D-5307 Wachtberg-Niederbachen.
5km west of Bad Godesberg.

CONTACT: Mrs Eva Goebels, Secretary. Tel: +49 2283 44003.
COURSE: 5,857m, PAR 71, SSS 72. Hilly forest course.
SOC RESTR'S: Welcome with advanced booking.
SOC GF - Round: Wd N/A. We DM60. Day: Wd DM80. We N/A.
SOC PACK: On application.
VIS RESTR'S: Handicap Certificate required.
VIS GF - Round: Wd N/A. We DM60. Day: Wd DM80. We N/A.
FACILITIES: Clubhouse & Pro-Shop.

DÜSSELDORF HÖSEL CLUB   MAP 16 A2

Grunerstr 13, 4000 Düsseldorf 1.
15km north-east of Düsseldorf in Höstel.

CONTACT: Secretary. Tel: +49 2116 31171.
COURSE: 6,160m, PAR 72, SSS 72. Parkland course.
SOC RESTR'S: Welcome with advanced booking.
SOC GF - Round: Wd DM55. We DM70. Day: Wd N/A. We N/A.
SOC PACK: On application.
VIS RESTR'S: Welcome please phone to check times for We.
VIS GF - Round: Wd DM55. We DM70. Day: Wd N/A. We N/A.
FACILITIES: Bar, Clubhouse & Practice Area.

DÜSSELDORFER GOLF CLUB   MAP 16 A2

Rommerljansweg, D-4030 Ratingen 1.
10km north of Düsseldorf.

CONTACT: M Swan, Secretary. Tel: +49 2102 81092.
COURSE: 5,886m, PAR 71, SSS 71. Parkland course.
SOC RESTR'S: Welcome with advanced booking.
SOC GF - Round: Wd DM80 We N/A. Day: Wd N/A. We N/A.
SOC PACK: On application.
VIS RESTR'S: Welcome Weekdays.
VIS GF - Round: Wd DM80. We N/A. Day: Wd N/A. We N/A.
FACILITIES: Students under 18 half price.

ESSENER HAUS OEFTE GOLF CLUB   MAP 16 A2

Laupendahler Landstr, 4300 Essen.
15km south-west of Essen.

CONTACT: Reservations. Tel: +49 2054 83911.
COURSE: 6,100m, PAR 72, SSS 72. Parkland course.
SOC RESTR'S: Welcome with advanced booking.
SOC GF - Round: Wd DM80. We DM100. Day: Wd N/A. We N/A.
SOC PACK: On application.
VIS RESTR'S: Welcome please phone to check availability.
VIS GF - Round: Wd DM80. We DM100. Day: Wd N/A. We N/A.
FACILITIES: Clubhouse & Practice Area.

HUBBELRATH GOLF CLUB (EAST)   MAP 16 A2

Bergische Landstr 700, 4000 Düsseldorf 12.
Hubbelrath, 13km east of Düsseldorf, on Route B7.

CONTACT: G Danz, HP Ranft, Professionals. Tel: +49 2104 72178.
COURSE: 6,040m, PAR 72, SSS 72. Rolling Parkland.
SOC RESTR'S: Book in advance.
SOC GF - Round: Wd N/A. We N/A. Day: Wd N/A. We N/A.
SOC PACK: On application.
VIS RESTR'S: Book in advance.
VIS GF - Round: Wd DM85. We DM100. Day: Wd N/A. We N/A.
FACILITIES: 2nd18-hole Course (West),Range, Bar & Restaurant.

Schleswig-Holstein

ISSUM-NIEDERRHEIN GOLF CLUB MAP 16 A2

Pauenweg 68, 4174 Issum 1.
10km east of Geldern.

CONTACT: S Tomkinson, Professional. Tel: +49 2835 3626.
COURSE: 5,860m, PAR 71, SSS 71. Undulating course.
SOC RESTR'S: Welcome with prior booking.
SOC GF - Round: Wd DM60. We DM70. Day: Wd N/A. We N/A.
SOC PACK: None.
VIS RESTR'S: Welcome please phone to check availability.
VIS GF - Round: Wd DM60. We DM70. Day: Wd N/A. We N/A.
FACILITIES: Bar & Restaurant.

KÖLN GOLF CLUB MAP 16 A2

Golfplatz 2, 5060 Bergisch Gladbach 1.
15km east of Cologne.

CONTACT: Secretary. Tel: +49 2204 63114.
COURSE: 6,045m, PAR 71, SSS 72. Parkland course.
SOC RESTR'S: Welcome with prior agreement.
SOC GF - Round: Wd DM50. We DM60. Day: Wd N/A. We N/A.
SOC PACK: Available when booking.
VIS RESTR'S: Welcome please phone to check availability.
VIS GF - Round: Wd DM50. We DM60. Day: Wd N/A. We N/A.
FACILITIES: Bar & Restaurant.

KREFELDER GOLF CLUB MAP 16 A2

Eltweg 2, 4150 Krefeld 12.
15km north-west of Düsseldrof, 5km south-east of Krefeld.

CONTACT: KH Tuchel. Tel: +49 2151 570071.
COURSE: 6,060m, PAR 72, SSS 72. Parkland Course.
SOC RESTR'S: Seasonal increase to GF - Wd + DM30. We + DM40.
SOC GF - Round: Wd DM50. We N/A. Day: Wd DM60. We N/A.
SOC PACK: On application.
VIS RESTR'S: Seasonal increase to GF - Wd + DM30. We + DM40.
VIS GF - Round: Wd DM50. We N/A. Day: Wd DM60. We N/A.
FACILITIES: Clubhouse, Pro-shop, Bar & Restaurant.

SCHLOSS GEORGHAUSEN MAP 16 A2

Georghausen 8, 5253 Lindlar-Hommerich.
30km east of Cologne.

CONTACT: G Kessler, Professional. Tel: +49 2207 4938.
COURSE: 6,045m, PAR 72, SSS 72. Parkland course.
SOC RESTR'S: Welcome with prior agreement.
SOC GF - Round: Wd DM60. We DM80. Day: Wd N/A. We N/A.
SOC PACK: Available when booking.
VIS RESTR'S: Welcome please phone to check times for We.
VIS GF - Round: Wd DM60. We DM80. Day: Wd N/A. We N/A.
FACILITIES: Bar & Restaurant.

WESTFÄLISCHER MAP 16 A2

Güterslohstr 127, 4835 Reltberg 2.
8km south-east of Gütersloh.

CONTACT: R Heyse, Secretary. Tel: +49 5244 2340.
COURSE: 6,135m, PAR 72, SSS 71. Parkland course.
SOC RESTR'S: Welcome with prior agreement.
SOC GF - Round: Wd DM70. We N/A. Day: Wd N/A. We N/A.
SOC PACK: None.
VIS RESTR'S: Welcome.
VIS GF - Round: Wd DM70. We DM90. Day: Wd N/A. We N/A.
FACILITIES: Pro-Shop & Clubhouse.

ALTENHOF GOLF CLUB MAP 16 A1

Eckernförde, 2330 Altenhof.
20km north-west of Kiel.

CONTACT: Secretary. Tel: +49 4351 41227.
COURSE: 6,070m, PAR 72, SSS 72. Undulating course.
SOC RESTR'S: Welcome with prior agreement. Not Monday.
SOC GF - Round: Wd DM55. We DM70. Day: Wd N/A. We N/A.
SOC PACK: Available when booking.
VIS RESTR'S: Welcome. Not Mon. H'cap Cert at Weekend.
VIS GF - Round: Wd DM55. We DM70. Day: Wd N/A. We N/A.
FACILITIES: Bar & Restaurant.

AN DER PINNAU GOLF CLUB MAP 16 A1

Pinnerbergerstr, 2085 Rellingen-Quickborn.
22km north-west of Hamburg.

CONTACT: Secretary. Tel: +49 4106 81800.
COURSE: 6,430m, PAR 72, SSS 74. Undulating course.
SOC RESTR'S: Welcome with prior agreement.
SOC GF - Round: Wd DM45. We DM60. Day: Wd N/A. We N/A.
SOC PACK: Available when booking.
VIS RESTR'S: Welcome please phone to check availability.
VIS GF - Round: Wd DM45. We DM60. Day: Wd N/A. We N/A.
FACILITIES: Bar & Restaurant.

GERMANY

GUT GRAMBEK GOLF CLUB   MAP 16 B1

Schlosstr 21, 2411 Grambek.
50km east of Hamburg.

CONTACT: Reservations. Tel: +49 4542 4627.
COURSE: 6,030m, PAR 72, SSS 71. Parkland course.
SOC RESTR'S: Advanced reservations only.
SOC GF - Round: Wd DM50. **We** DM70. **Day: Wd** N/A. **We** N/A.
SOC PACK: Available when booking.
VIS RESTR'S: Welcome please phone to check availability.
VIS GF - Round: Wd DM50. **We** DM70. **Day: Wd** N/A. **We** N/A.
FACILITIES: Bar & Restaurant.

MARITIM GOLF CLUB (NORTH)   MAP 16 B1

Am Golfplatz 3, 2408 Timmendorfer Strand.
15km north of Lübeck.

CONTACT: H Rieckmann, Manager. Tel: +49 4503 5152.
COURSE: 6,095m, PAR 72, SSS 72. Undulating course.
SOC RESTR'S: Welcome Weekdays only.
SOC GF - Round: Wd DM65. **We** N/A. **Day: Wd** N/A. **We** N/A.
SOC PACK: On application.
VIS RESTR'S: Welcome phone call advisable to check availability.
VIS GF - Round: Wd DM65. **We** DM85. **Day: Wd** N/A. **We** N/A.
FACILITIES: Bar, Restaurant & Short Par 61 Course.

ITALY

GOLF in Italy has a long and noble tradition, albeit an eccentric one. More stories, both true and apocryphal, seem to be generated from Italian venues on the European Tour than all the others combined, while in keeping with the Italian philosophy of life, style is everything. It brings to mind the words of the old song 'It ain't what you do, it's the way that you do it' - even, or especially, on the golf course!

That said, golf in Italy is invariably an absolute delight. It can also, if you play the Robert Trent Jones course at Pevero on Sardinia's Costa Smeralda, turn into a surrealistic nightmare. The course was quite literally hacked out of the mountains backing onto Porto Cervo to provide breathtaking views over the Mediterranean and golf which, in another sense, is also breathtaking. Just once, in 1978, did the Italian Open come to Pevero: the South African Dale Hayes won with 293 - 5 over par - the highest score in the event's entire history. 300 was considered a fine effort. The professionals haven't returned.

Gentler, more forgiving and immeasurably more relaxing is Ugolino, just south of Florence. Golf's been played here since 1889 and at Ugolino itself, home of the Florence Open on the European Tour, since 1933. Unusually for a Championship course, it starts with a par-3, albeit a testing one of over 220 yards where a pulled shot will find an impenetrable hedge and a pushed one will roll down a slope into one of two large bunkers. From there, the course meanders pleasantly through the Chianti hills; testing, but not too testing. Tough pin positions provide challenge enough for the pros; for the handicapper, those challenges will be eased.

From the traditional to the super-modern and Le Querce, just north of Rome and built to stage the 1991 World Cup. Le Querce is to Italy what Paris National is to France: a purpose-built Championship course with all the ancilliary features of teaching academies and abundant practice facilities. Unlike the French, who built their showcase course 'in-house', the Italian Golf Federation commissioned the American Tom Faxio, whose reputation, in contrast to other modern designers, is for 'natural-looking' courses. Certainly there's a lack of gimmicry and artificiality at Le Querce, but is the end product just a little bland?

With its golfing tradition, the entire country, perhaps more-so north of Rome, has some excellent courses to offer. Some are extremely expensive for a casual day's golf, but the scenery will usually be timeless and bewitching and the various clubhouses and bars as well-appointed as the best anywhere. But remember to pack that designer golf gear!

ITALY

Emilia Romagna

Lazio

ADRIATIC CERVIA GOLF CLUB MAP 17 A1

Via Jelenia Gora, 48016 Milano.
20km south-east of Ravenna.

CONTACT: Secretary. Tel: +39 544 992 786.
COURSE: 6,275m, PAR 72, SSS 72. Parkland course.
SOC RESTR'S: Please book through Secretary.
SOC GF - Round: Wd N/A. We N/A. **Day:** Wd L65,000. We N/A.
SOC PACK: Available at time of booking.
VIS RESTR'S: Welcome please phone to check Weekends.
VIS GF - Round: Wd N/A. We N/A. **Day:** Wd L65,000. We L80,000.
FACILITIES: Practice Area & Clubhouse.

CASTELGANDOLFO GOLF CLUB MAP 17 A2

Via Santo Spirito 13, 00040 Pavona.
17km south-east of Rome via Appia Nuova towards Albano.

CONTACT: PL Fuga, Director. Tel: 39 69 312 301.
COURSE: 5,855m, PAR 72, SSS 71. Parkland course.
SOC RESTR'S: Welcome Weekdays with prior agreement.
SOC GF - Round: Wd N/A. We N/A. **Day:** Wd L85,000. We N/A.
SOC PACK: On application.
VIS RESTR'S: Welcome Weekdays. Handicap Certificate required.
VIS GF - Round: Wd N/A. We N/A. **Day:** Wd L85,000. We N/A.
FACILITIES: Range, Golf Cars, Swimming Pool, Bar & Restaurant.

BOLOGNA GOLF CLUB MAP 17 A1

Via Sabattini 69, Chiesa Nuova di Monte San Pietro.
20km west of Bologna.

CONTACT: Secretary. Tel: +34 51 969 100.
COURSE: 6,171m, PAR 72, SSS 72. Parkland course.
SOC RESTR'S: Welcome other than Monday as course is closed.
SOC GF - Round: Wd N/A. We N/A. **Day:** Wd L45,000. We L75,000.
SOC PACK: On application.
VIS RESTR'S: Welcome other than Monday as course is closed.
VIS GF - Round: Wd N/A. We N/A. **Day:** Wd L45,000. We L75,000.
FACILITIES: On application.

EUCALYPTUS GOLF CLUB MAP 17 A2

Via Cogna 5, 04011 Aprilia.
20km south of Rome in Aprilia on the A148.

CONTACT: Marina Lanza, Reservations. Tel: +39 6 926 252
COURSE: 6,375m, PAR 72, SSS 72. Parkland course.
SOC RESTR'S: Welcome with advanced booking.
SOC GF - Round: Wd L45,000. We N/A. **Day:** Wd N/A. We N/A.
SOC PACK: No information available.
VIS RESTR'S: Welcome phone call advisable to check availability.
VIS GF - Round: Wd L45,000. We L55,000. **Day:** Wd N/A. We N/A.
FACILITIES: On application.

CROARA GOLF CLUB MAP 17 A1

29010 Croara di Gazzola.
85km south-east of Milan.

CONTACT: Reception. Tel: +39 523 977 105.
COURSE: 6,053m, PAR 72, SSS 72. Undulating course.
SOC RESTR'S: Welcome with prior booking.
SOC GF - Round: Wd L50,000. We N/A. **Day:** Wd N/A. We N/A.
SOC PACK: Tailored for each outing.
VIS RESTR'S: Welcome please phone to check availability.
VIS GF - Round: Wd L50,000. We L60,000. **Day:** Wd N/A. We N/A.
FACILITIES: Clubhouse.

GOLF CLUB PARCO DE'MEDICI MAP 17 A2

Viale Parco de'Medici 20, 00148 Rome.
5km outside Rome.

CONTACT: G Rebeccruni, President. Tel: +39 66 553 477.
COURSE: 6,164m, PAR 72, SSS 72. Parkland course.
SOC RESTR'S: Thursday course closed.
SOC GF - Round: Wd L80,000. We N/A. **Day:** Wd N/A. We N/A.
SOC PACK: On application.
VIS RESTR'S: Thursday course closed.
VIS GF - Round: Wd L80,000. We N/A. **Day:** Wd N/A. We N/A.
FACILITIES: Summer Swimming Pool.

LIGURIA

Liguria

LA QUERCE GOLF CLUB   MAP 17 A2

San Martino, 01015 Sutri (VT).
43km north of Rome.

CONTACT: Professional. Tel: +39 761 68374.
COURSE: 6,433m, PAR 72, SSS 72. Forest course.
SOC RESTR'S: Book in advance.
SOC GF - Round: Wd L70,000. We N/A. Day: Wd N/A. We N/A.
SOC PACK: Available at time of booking.
VIS RESTR'S: No restrictions. Closed Wednesday.
VIS GF - Round: Wd L70,000. We N/A. Day: Wd N/A. We N/A.
FACILITIES: Range, Bar & Restaurant.

OLGIATA GOLF CLUB   MAP 17 A2

Largo Olgiata 15, 00123 Roma.
19km north-west of Rome, near La Storta.

CONTACT: U Grappasonni, Professional. Tel: +39 6 378 9141.
COURSE: 6,396m, PAR 72, SSS 72. Parkland course.
SOC RESTR'S: Book in advance.
SOC GF - Round: Wd L50,000 We N/A. Day: Wd N/A. We N/A.
SOC PACK: On application.
VIS RESTR'S: Book in advance. Difficult.
VIS GF - Round: Wd L50,000. We L100,000. Day: Wd N/A. We N/A.
FACILITIES: 9-hole Course, Range, Bar & Restaurant.

RIVA DEI TESSALI GOLF CLUB   MAP 17 B2

74011 Castellaneta.
35km south-west of Taranto.

CONTACT: Professional. Tel: +39 99 643 9251.
COURSE: 5,960m, PAR 71, SSS 71. Undulating course.
SOC RESTR'S: Prior booking required.
SOC GF - Round: Wd L50,000. We N/A. Day: Wd N/A. We N/A.
SOC PACK: Several available.
VIS RESTR'S: No restrictions.
VIS GF - Round: Wd L50,000. We N/A. Day: Wd N/A. We N/A.
FACILITIES: Range, Tennis, Bar & Restaurant.

ROMA GOLF CLUB   MAP 17 A2

Via Appia Nuova 716, 00178 Rome.
6km south-east of Rome.

CONTACT: Reception. Tel: +39 6 783 407.
COURSE: 5,825m, PAR 72, SSS 72. Parkland course.
SOC RESTR'S: Advanced reservations only.
SOC GF - Round: Wd L70,000. We N/A. Day: Wd N/A. We N/A.
SOC PACK: On application.
VIS RESTR'S: Welcome Weekdays.
VIS GF - Round: Wd L70,000. We N/A. Day: Wd N/A. We N/A.
FACILITIES: On application.

DEGLI ULIVI GOLF CLUB   MAP 17 A1

Via Campo Golf 59, 18038 San Remo.
5km north of San Remo.

CONTACT: Secretary. Tel: +34 184 557 093.
COURSE: 5,230m, PAR 68, SSS 67. Rolling parkland course.
SOC RESTR'S: Welcome other than closed on Tuesday.
SOC GF - Round: Wd N/A. We N/A. Day: Wd L60,000. We N/A.
SOC PACK: On application.
VIS RESTR'S: Welcome other than Tuesday as course is closed.
VIS GF - Round: Wd N/A. We N/A. Day: Wd L60,000. We L80,000.
FACILITIES: On application.

GARLENDA GOLF CLUB   MAP 17 A1

Via Golf 7, 17030 Garlenda.
15km north of Alassio.

CONTACT: G Costa, Manager. Tel: +39 182 580 012.
COURSE: 5,964m, PAR 71, SSS 71. Undulating course.
SOC RESTR'S: Welcome with advanced booking.
SOC GF- Round: Wd N/A. We N/A. Day: Wd L80,000. We L100,000.
SOC PACK: On application.
VIS RESTR'S: Welcome except Weekend in winter time.
VIS GF - Round: Wd N/A. We N/A. Day: Wd L80,000. We L100,000.
FACILITIES: Dormy House, Swimming Pool, Practice Area & Bar.

RAPALLO GOLF CLUB   MAP 17 A1

Via Mameli 377, 16035 Rapallo.
25km south-east of Genoa off the A12.

CONTACT: Secretary. Tel: +34 185 261 777.
COURSE: 5,694m, PAR 70, SSS 70. Parkland course.
SOC RESTR'S: Welcome with booking except Tuesday.
SOC GF- Round: Wd N/A. We N/A. Day: Wd L85,000. We L130,000.
SOC PACK: On application.
VIS RESTR'S: Welcome other than Tuesday as course is closed.
VIS GF - Round: Wd N/A. We N/A. Day: Wd L85,000. We L130,000.
FACILITIES: Equipment Hire, Range, Restaurant & Bar.

ITALY

Lombardia

CIRCOLO GOLF VILLA D'ESTE   MAP 17 A1

Via Cantù 13, 22030 Montorfano.
7km east of Como Town, in the Lecco direction. (40km N Milan)
CONTACT: Secretary. Tel: +39 31 200 200.
COURSE: 5,787m, PAR 69, SSS 71. Hilly parkland course.
SOC RESTR'S: Welcome Weekdays with prior agreement.
SOC GF - Round: Wd N/A. We N/A. Day: Wd L80,000. We N/A.
SOC PACK: None.
VIS RESTR'S: H'cap Cert required plus Letter of Intro.
VIS GF- Round: Wd N/A. We N/A. Day: Wd L80,000. We L120,000.
FACILITIES: Driving Range, Pro-Shop, Bar & Restaurant.

BARLASSINA COUNTRY CLUB   MAP 17 A1

20030 Birago di Camnago Fraz. Lentate.
25km north of Milan on the road to Como.

CONTACT: Susanna Pizzi, Reception. Tel: +39 362 560 621.
COURSE: 6,053m, PAR 72, SSS 72. Slightly undulating course.
SOC RESTR'S: Welcome with prior booking.
SOC GF - Round: Wd L80,000. We N/A. Day: Wd N/A. We N/A.
SOC PACK: No set package.
VIS RESTR'S: Welcome please phone to check availability.
VIS GF- Round: Wd L80,000. We L120,000. Day: Wd N/A. We N/A.
FACILITIES: On application.

LA PINETINA GOLF CLUB   MAP 17 A1

Via al Golf 4, 22070 Appiano Gentile.
15km south of Como.

CONTACT: M Sabbatino, Professional. Tel: +39 31 933 202.
COURSE: 6,000m, PAR 72, SSS 71. Undulating course.
SOC RESTR'S: Welcome with prior booking.
SOC GF - Round: Wd L70,000. We L100,000. Day: Wd N/A. We N/A.
SOC PACK: Available at time of booking.
VIS RESTR'S: Welcome please phone to check Weekends.
VIS GF- Round: Wd L70,000. We L100,000. Day: Wd N/A. We N/A.
FACILITIES: On application.

BERGAMO 'L'ALBENZA'   MAP 17 A1

Via Longoni 12, 24030 Almenno San Bartolomeo.
40km NW of Milan on the A4 to Begamo then NW to Almenno.

CONTACT: A Ripamonti, Secretary. Tel: +39 35 640 028.
COURSE: 6,128m, PAR 72, SSS 72. Parkland course.
SOC RESTR'S: Welcome with prior arrangement.
SOC GF - Round: Wd N/A. We N/A. Day: Wd L60,000. We N/A.
SOC PACK: On application.
VIS RESTR'S: Welcome Weekdays.
VIS GF - Round: Wd N/A. We N/A. Day: Wd L60,000. We N/A.
FACILITIES: 9-hole Course, Caddies, Locker Room & Restaurant.

MENAGGIO & CADENABBIA   MAP 17 A1

Via Golf 12, 22010 Grandola E Uniti.
60km north of Milan on A340 by the west shore of Lake Como.

CONTACT: E Piciotti, Secretary. Tel: +39 34 432 103.
COURSE: 5,277m, PAR 69, SSS 69. Parkland course.
SOC RESTR'S: Welcome with advanced booking.
SOC GF - Round: Wd L60,000. We L100,000. Day: Wd N/A. We N/A.
SOC PACK: On application.
VIS RESTR'S: Welcome phone call advisable to check availability.
VIS GF - Round: Wd L60,000. We L100,000. Day: Wd N/A. We N/A.
FACILITIES: Bar & Restaurant.

CARIMATE GOLF CLUB   MAP 17 A1

Via Airoldi, 22060 Carimate.
30km north of Milan.

CONTACT: E Songia, Professional. Tel: +39 31 790 226.
COURSE: 5,982m, PAR 72, SSS 71. Forest course.
SOC RESTR'S: Please book through Professional.
SOC GF - Round: Wd L65,000. We N/A. Day: Wd N/A. We N/A.
SOC PACK: On application.
VIS RESTR'S: Available at time of booking. H'cap Cert required.
VIS GF - Round: Wd L65,000. We L95,000. Day: Wd N/A. We N/A.
FACILITIES: On application.

RAC HOTELS IN EUROPE

The ideal 'travel companion' with over 1,500 selected hotels in 20 countries, including Eastern Europe. Hotel entries contain phone and fax numbers, national star rating, restaurant, prices, credit cards and where English is spoken.. Full colour atlas section with all hotel locations shown. Parking law - Speed limits - Public holidays - Banks - Shops - Fuel availability
Price £9.99
Available from bookshops
or direct from the RAC on 0235 834885

Piemonte

MILANO GOLF CLUB MAP 17 A1

Monza Park, 20052 Monza.
6km from Monza, 18km north-east from Milan.
CONTACT: R Livraghi, Secretary. Tel: +39 2 303 081.
COURSE: 6,210m, PAR 72, SSS 73. Undulating parkland course.
SOC RESTR'S: Welcome Weekdays with prior booking.
SOC GF - Round: Wd L90,000. **We** N/A. **Day:** Wd N/A. **We** N/A.
SOC PACK: On application.
VIS RESTR'S: Welcome Weekdays with reservation.
VIS GF - Round: Wd L90,000. **We** N/A. **Day:** Wd N/A. **We** N/A.
FACILITIES: 9-hole Par 36, Range, Equipment Hire & Restaurant.

MONTICELLO GOLF CLUB (ONE) MAP 17 A1

Via Volta 4, 22070 Cassina Rizzardi.
10km south-east of Como.

CONTACT: V Damonte, Professional. Tel: +39 31 928055.
COURSE: 6,413m, PAR 72, SSS 72. Forest with lakes.
SOC RESTR'S: Book in advance.
SOC GF - Round: Wd L80,000. **We** N/A. **Day:** Wd N/A. **We** N/A.
SOC PACK: On application.
VIS RESTR'S: Book in advance.
VIS GF - Round: Wd L80,000. **We** L100,000. **Day:** Wd N/A. **We** N/A.
FACILITIES: Swimming Pool, Tennis, Bar & Restaurant.

MONTOCELLO GOLF CLUB (TWO) MAP 17 A1

Via Volta 4, 22070 Cassina Rizzardi.
10km south-east of Como.

CONTACT: A Croce, Professional. Tel: +39 31 928055.
COURSE: 6,122m, PAR 72, SSS 72. Forest course.
SOC RESTR'S: Book in advance.
SOC GF - Round: Wd L80,000. **We** N/A. **Day:** Wd N/A. **We** N/A.
SOC PACK: On application.
VIS RESTR'S: Book in advance.
VIS GF - Round: Wd L80,000. **We** L100,000. **Day:** Wd N/A. **We** N/A.
FACILITIES: Swimming Pool, Tennis, Bar & Restaurant.

ZOATE GOLF CLUB MAP 17 A1

20067 Zoate di Tribiano (M1).
Zoate, 17km south-east of Milan.

CONTACT: A Ferraloni, Professional. Tel: +39 2 9063 2183.
COURSE: 6,122m, PAR 72, SSS 72. Parkland course.
SOC RESTR'S: Handicap Certificate required.
SOC GF - Round: Wd L70,000. **We** N/A. **Day:** Wd N/A. **We** N/A.
SOC PACK: On application.
VIS RESTR'S: No restrictions. H'cap Cert required. Closed Mon.
VIS GF - Round: Wd L70,000. **We** L100,000. **Day:** Wd N/A. **We** N/A.
FACILITIES: Swimming Pool, Tennis, Bar & Restaurant.

ALPINO DI STRESA GOLF CLUB MAP 17 A1

Via Golf Panorama 49, 28040 Vezzo.
8km west of Stresa, 80km from Milan.

CONTACT: Della Francesco, Director. Tel: +39 32 320 642.
COURSE: 5,359m, PAR 69, SSS 67. Hilly parkland courses.
SOC RESTR'S: Welcome with advanced booking.
SOC GF - Round: Wd N/A. **We** N/A. **Day:** Wd L40,000. **We** L60,000.
SOC PACK: No set package.
VIS RESTR'S: Welcome.
VIS GF - Round: Wd N/A. **We** N/A. **Day:** Wd L40,000. **We** L60,000.
FACILITIES: Golf Cars, Club Hire, Bar & Restaurant.

BIELLA 'LE BETULLE' MAP 17 A1

Reg. Valcarozza, 13050 Magnano.
20km south-west of Biella, north-east of Turin.

CONTACT: Reservations. Tel: +39 15 679 151.
COURSE: 6,427m, PAR 73, SSS 72. Parkland course.
SOC RESTR'S: Closed Mon. Open April - November.
SOC GF - Round: Wd L85,000. **We** N/A. **Day:** Wd N/A. **We** N/A.
SOC PACK: On application.
VIS RESTR'S: Welcome phone call advisable to check availability.
VIS GF - Round: Wd L85,000. **We** L100,000. **Day:** Wd N/A. **We** N/A.
FACILITIES: On application.

CASTELCONTURBIA GOLF CLUB MAP 17 A1

Via Suno, 28010 Agrate Conturbia.
25km north of Novara, north-west of Milan.

CONTACT: Secretary. Tel: +39 322 832 093.
COURSE: 6,400m, PAR 72, SSS 72. Forest/parkland course.
SOC RESTR'S: Welcome other than Monday as course is closed.
SOC GF- Round: Wd L80,000. **We** L115,000. **Day:** Wd N/A. **We** N/A.
SOC PACK: On application.
VIS RESTR'S: Welcome other than Monday as course is closed.
VIS GF - Round: Wd L80,000. **We** L115,000. **Day:** Wd N/A. **We** N/A.
FACILITIES: 27-hole complex with comfortable Clubhouse.

ITALY

GOLF CLUB LE FRONDE   MAP 17 A1

Via Sant-Agostino, 68 Avigliana 10051.
20km west of Turin off the E70.

CONTACT: A Rosso, Secretary. Tel: +39 11 938 053.
COURSE: 6,077m, PAR 72, SSS 72. Parkland/woodland course.
SOC RESTR'S: Welcome Weekdays only with prior agreement.
SOC GF - Round: Wd L60,000. **We** N/A. **Day:** Wd N/A. **We** N/A.
SOC PACK: On application.
VIS RESTR'S: Welcome. Restricted to Weekdays from Nov to Feb.
VIS GF - Round: Wd L60,000. **We** L80,000. **Day:** Wd N/A. **We** N/A.
FACILITIES: Bar, Restaurant, Range, Pro-shop & Equipment Hire.

MONTECATINI GOLF CLUB   MAP 17 A1

Via Dei Brogi 5, Loc Pievaccia, 51015 Monsummano Terme.
50km north-west of Florence off the A11.

CONTACT: N Ravinetto, Professional. Tel: +39 57 262 218.
COURSE: 6,145m, PAR 72, SSS 71. Tree lined links course.
SOC RESTR'S: Welcome with prior agreement.
SOC GF - Round: Wd L55,000. **We** N/A. **Day:** Wd N/A. **We** N/A.
SOC PACK: Available at time of booking.
VIS RESTR'S: Welcome please phone to check availability.
VIS GF - Round: Wd L55,000. **We** L70,000. **Day:** Wd N/A. **We** N/A.
FACILITIES: Range, Bar & Restaurant.

I ROVERI GOLF CLUB   MAP 17 A1

Rotta Cerbiatta 24, 10070 Fiano.
15km west of Turin.

CONTACT: M Vinzi, Professional. Tel: +39 11 923 571.
COURSE: 6,218m, PAR 72, SSS 72. Parkland/woodland course.
SOC RESTR'S: Welcome Wd (not Mon) only with prior agreement.
SOC GF - Round: Wd L80,000. **We** N/A. **Day:** Wd N/A. **We** N/A.
SOC PACK: On application.
VIS RESTR'S: Welcome except Monday.
VIS GF- Round: Wd L80,000. **We** L100,000. **Day:** Wd N/A. **We** N/A.
FACILITIES: 9-hole Course, Bar, Restaurant, Range, Pro-shop.

PUNTA ALA GOLF CLUB   MAP 17 A1

Vai del Golf 1, 58040 Punta Ala.
90km south-west of Siena.

CONTACT: G Cavalsani, Secretary. Tel: +39 546 922 121.
COURSE: 6,213m, PAR 72, SSS 72. Coastal parkland course.
SOC RESTR'S: Welcome with advanced reservations.
SOC GF - Round: Wd L50,000. **We** N/A. **Day:** Wd L70,000. **We** N/A.
SOC PACK: Individual arrangement for each Society.
VIS RESTR'S: Welcome Wd only. Seasonal alterations to GF.
VIS GF - Round: Wd L50,000. **We** N/A. **Day:** Wd L70,000. **We** N/A.
FACILITIES: Bar, Restaurant & Clubhouse.

Tuscana

Veneto

FIRENZE UGOLINO GOLF CLUB   MAP 17 A1

Via Chiantigiana 3, 50015 Grassina.
12km south of the Florence Road, leading to Siena.

CONTACT: E Brandi, Secretary. Tel: +39 55 230 1009.
COURSE: 5,728m, PAR 72, SSS 70. Hilly (Italian Open) course.
SOC RESTR'S: Welcome except Competition Days.
SOC GF - Round: Wd L50,000. **We** L70,000. **Day:** Wd N/A. **We** N/A.
SOC PACK: None.
VIS RESTR'S: Welcome except Competition Days.
VIS GF - Round: Wd L50,000. **We** L70,000. **Day:** Wd N/A. **We** N/A.
FACILITIES: Swimming Pool & Tennis Court.

ALBARELLA GOLF CLUB   MAP 17 A1

Isola de Albarella, 45010 Rosolino.
65km south of Venice on the island of Albarella.

CONTACT: Secretary. Tel: +39 42 330 124.
COURSE: 6,065m, PAR 72, SSS 72. Seaside links course.
SOC RESTR'S: Welcome Weekdays with prior booking.
SOC GF - Round: Wd L60,000. **We** N/A. **Day:** Wd N/A. **We** N/A.
SOC PACK: On application.
VIS RESTR'S: Welcome with Handicap Certificate.
VIS GF - Round: Wd L60,000. **We** L90,000. **Day:** Wd N/A. **We** N/A.
FACILITIES: Equipment Hire, Range, Bar & Restaurant.

Sardegna

FRASSANELLE GOLF CLUB MAP 17 A1

35030 Loc Frassanelle di Rovolon (PD).
20km south of Padova, by Via dei Colli.

CONTACT: F Girardi, V Mori, Professionals. Tel: +39 49 991 0722.
COURSE: 6,120m, PAR 72, SSS 72. Parkland course.
SOC RESTR'S: Telephone booking necessary.
SOC GF - Round: Wd L110,000. We N/A. Day: Wd N/A. We N/A.
SOC PACK: On application.
VIS RESTR'S: Prior booking necessary.
VIS GF - Round: Wd L700,000. We N/A. Day: Wd N/A. We N/A.
FACILITIES: Bar & Restaurant.

MODENA GOLF CLUB MAP 17 A1

Via Vandelli 22a, 41050 Colombaro di Formgine.
20km west of Bologna. South of Modena.

CONTACT: N Carrera, Professional. Tel: + 59 553482.
COURSE: 5,785m, PAR 72, SSS 72. Parkland course.
SOC RESTR'S: Written booking necessary.
SOC GF - Round: Wd L100,000. We N/A. Day: Wd N/A. We N/A.
SOC PACK: On application.
VIS RESTR'S: Welcome.
VIS GF - Round: Wd L100,000. We N/A. Day: Wd N/A. We N/A.
FACILITIES: Practice Area, Swimming Pool, Bar & Restaurant.

PADOVA GOLF CLUB MAP 17 A1

35050 Valsanzibio di Galzigano.
20km south of Padua.

CONTACT: A Lionello, Professional. Tel: +39 499 130 078.
COURSE: 6,050m, PAR 72, SSS 72. Forest course.
SOC RESTR'S: Advanced reservations only.
SOC GF - Round: Wd L70,000. We N/A. Day: Wd N/A. We N/A.
SOC PACK: On application.
VIS RESTR'S: Welcome please phone to check Weekends.
VIS GF - Round: Wd L70,000. We L95,000. Day: Wd N/A. We N/A.
FACILITIES: Range, Pro-shop, Bar & Restaurant.

VENEZIA GOLF CLUB MAP 17 A1

Via del Forte, 30011 Alberoni.
In Alberoni at Western end of Lido, 10km south-east of Venice.

CONTACT: Ester Trentin, Secretary. Tel: +39 41 731 015.
COURSE: 6,199m, PAR 72, SSS 73. Tree lined links course.
SOC RESTR'S: Welcome Weekdays but closed on Monday.
SOC GF - Round: Wd L80,000. We N/A. Day: Wd N/A. We N/A.
SOC PACK: On application.
VIS RESTR'S: Welcome with Handicap Certificate.
VIS GF - Round: Wd L80,000. We L95,000. Day: Wd N/A. We N/A.
FACILITIES: Driving Range, Bar & Restaurant.

CIRCOLO GOLF IS MOLAS MAP 17 A3

Santa Margherita di Pula, 00010 (Cagliari) Sardegna.
30km south of Cagliari on the coast road.

CONTACT: M Fulghesu. Tel: +39 709 241 013.
COURSE: 6,131m, PAR 72, SSS 72. Flat parkland course.
SOC RESTR'S: Welcome with advanced booking.
SOC GF - Round: Wd L80,000. We N/A. Day: Wd N/A. We N/A.
SOC PACK: On application.
VIS RESTR'S: Welcome.
VIS GF - Round: Wd L80,000. We L80,000. Day: Wd N/A. We N/A.
FACILITIES: Equipment Hire, Range Swimming Pool & Restaurant.

PEVERO GOLF CLUB MAP 17 A2

07020 Porto Cervo Sardegna.
30km north of Olbia on the coast road.

CONTACT: Secretary. Tel: +39 78 996 072.
COURSE: 6,186m, PAR 72, SSS 72. Undulating parkland/links.
SOC RESTR'S: Welcome with advanced booking.
SOC GF - Round: Wd L80,000. We N/A. Day: Wd N/A. We N/A.
SOC PACK: Seasonal alterations to Green Fee.
VIS RESTR'S: Welcome please phone to check Weekends.
VIS GF - Round: Wd L75,000. We N/A. Day: Wd N/A. We N/A.
FACILITIES: Equipment Hire, Range, Swimming Pool & Restaurant.

NETHERLANDS

WELL, did the Dutch really invent golf before the Scots? Maybe, maybe not: evidence from either side of the North Sea can be seductively conclusive and the argument is a good one that has run - and will run- for many, many years. Irrespective of whether or not colf, or kolf, or kolve, (depending on which scholarly interpretation you prefer), really was the forerunner of the royal and ancient game of gowf, the fact remains that Holland is blessed with some terrific golf courses, especially on the North Sea coast which, as it does in Scotland, lends itself perfectly to the links game.

The best examples of this are at Kennemer, which is dealt with in more detail elsewhere in this Guide, and at Noordwijkse. Both are excellent, both are well worth a special visit and, happily, both are readily accessible for the casual visitor provided he/she has a valid handicap certificate.

Founded in 1910, Kennemer shares with Hilversum the distinction of being Holland's oldest golf course. In appearance, the latter is in many ways reminiscent of the heathland courses of Surrey and in terms of difficulty, further parallels can be drawn. At around 6700 yards, the course is long, but not punishingly so: the real premium here is on accuracy. Some indication of what lies ahead can be tasted on the par-5 opening hole, where a pushed drive will be swallowed up by trees and more trees continue to feature on virtually every hole until the18th - another par-5 - where the timber that might have accounted for your drive on the first will be similarly in play if you try to cut off too much of the dogleg on the last!

Perhaps the Netherlands doesn't yet have quite the number of quality courses to sustain, say, a full week of varied golf; but combined with Belgium, anyone would enjoy some of the very finest that Europe has to offer.

Noord-Oost

DE VERWAEYDE SANDBERGEN MAP 18

Plesmanlaan 30, 8072 PT Nuspeet.
58km north-east of Utrecht off the A28.

CONTACT: Secretary. Tel: +31 3412 58034.
COURSE: 6,283m, PAR 72, SSS 72. Moorland course.
SOC RESTR'S: Please book through Secretary.
SOC GF - Round: Wd fl50. We N/A. Day: Wd N/A. We N/A.
SOC PACK: Catering arrangements on request
VIS RESTR'S: Weekdays only.
VIS GF - Round: Wd fl50. We N/A. Day: Wd N/A. We N/A.
FACILITIES: 9-hole Course, Clubhouse & Restaurant.

NOORD NEDERLANDSE MAP 18

Landgoed De Poll, Pollselaan 5, 9756 GJ Glimmen.
12km south of Groningen.

CONTACT: Reservations. Tel: +31 5906 2004.
COURSE: 5,866m, PAR 71, SSS 71. Parkland course.
SOC RESTR'S: Welcome with advanced booking.
SOC GF - Round: Wd fl65. We fl95. Day: Wd N/A. We N/A.
SOC PACK: On application.
VIS RESTR'S: Welcome phone call advisable to check availability.
VIS GF - Round: Wd fl65. We fl95. Day: Wd N/A. We N/A.
FACILITIES: Clubhouse & Restaurant.

ROSENDAELSCHE GOLF CLUB MAP 18

Apeldoornseweg 450, 6816 SN Arnhem.
On the A12 40km east of Utrrecht in Arnhem.

CONTACT: Secretary. Tel: +31 8542 1438.
COURSE: 6,065m, PAR 72, SSS 72. Meadowland course.
SOC RESTR'S: Welcome by prior arrangement
SOC GF - Round: Wd fl60. We fl85. Day: Wd N/A. We N/A.
SOC PACK: On application.
VIS RESTR'S: Welcome.
VIS GF - Round: Wd fl60. We fl85. Day: Wd N/A. We N/A.
FACILITIES: Clubhouse & Restaurant.

NOORD-WEST

SALLANDSCHE DE HOEK MAP 18

Golfweg 2, 7341 PR Diepenveen.
20km north-east of Arnhem.

CONTACT: Secretary. Tel: +31 5709 1214.
COURSE: 5,995m, PAR 72, SSS 71. Parkland course.
SOC RESTR'S: Prior bookings only.
SOC GF - Round: Wd fl60. We N/A. Day: Wd fl75. We N/A.
SOC PACK: On application.
VIS RESTR'S: Welcome. Weekend handicap max 24.
VIS GF - Round: Wd fl60. We N/A. Day: Wd fl75. We fl90.
FACILITIES: Clubhouse & Restaurant.

Noord-West

ALMEERDERHOUT MAP 18

Watersnipweg 21, 1341 AA Almere.
20km east of Amsterdam in Almere off the A6.

CONTACT: Manager. Tel: +31 3240 21818.
COURSE: 5,969m, PAR 72, SSS 72. Undulating course.
SOC RESTR'S: Please book in advance through the Manager.
SOC GF - Round: Wd fl80. We N/A. Day: Wd N/A. We N/A.
SOC PACK: On application from the Manager.
VIS RESTR'S: Welcome weekdays only.
VIS GF - Round: Wd fl80. We N/A. Day: Wd N/A. We N/A.
FACILITIES: Range, Pitch & Putt, Restaurant & 2 x 9-hole Courses.

ANDERSTEIN GOLF CLUB MAP 18

Woudenbergse Weg 13 A, 3953 ME, Maarsbergen.
20km east of Uthetch off the A12/E30.

CONTACT: Club Secretary. Tel: +31 3433 1330.
COURSE: 6,043m, PAR 72, SSS 72. Meadow/parkland course.
SOC RESTR'S: Welcome with prior booking.
SOC GF - Round: Wd fl75. We N/A. Day: Wd N/A. We N/A.
SOC PACK: On application at the time of booking.
VIS RESTR'S: Welcome Weekdays only. Mon open after 12.
VIS GF - Round: Wd fl75. We N/A. Day: Wd N/A. We N/A.
FACILITIES: Clubhouse, Putting Green & Bar.

NETHERLANDS

DE PURMER GOLF CLUB   MAP 18

Westerweg 60, 1445 AD Purmerend.
18km north of Amsterdam in Purmerend off the A7.
CONTACT: AB Koopman, Secretary. Tel: +31 2990 21392.
COURSE: 6,080m, PAR 72, SSS 70. Moorland course.
SOC RESTR'S: Welcome subject to advanced booking.
SOC GF - Round: Wd fl60. We fl65. **Day:** Wd fl70. We fl80.
SOC PACK: Please discuss with Secretary.
VIS RESTR'S: Welcome but please check for time sheet.
VIS GF - Round: Wd fl60. We fl65. **Day:** Wd fl70. We fl80.
FACILITIES: 9-hole Course, Clubhouse & Restaurant.

HET RIJK VAV NIJMEGEN   MAP 18

Postweg 17, 6561 KJ Groesbeek.
5km south-east of Nijmegen.
CONTACT: Mrs M Steggerda, Manager. Tel: +31 8891 76644.
COURSE: 5,987m, PAR 72, SSS 72. Undulating course.
SOC RESTR'S: Welcome with advanced booking.
SOC GF - Round: Wd fl55. We fl80. **Day:** Wd fl55. We fl80.
SOC PACK: Special price for GF Incl.- Lunch or Dinner on request.
VIS RESTR'S: Always welcome.
VIS GF - Round: Wd fl55. We fl80. **Day:** Wd fl55. We fl80.
FACILITIES: Range, Pitch & Putt, Restaurant & 2 x 9-hole Courses.

HILVERSUMSCHE GOLF CLUB   MAP 18

Soestdijkerstraatweg 172, 1213 XJ Hilversum.
3km east of Hilversum, near Baarn.
CONTACT: M Morbey, R Cattell, Professionals. Tel: +31 35 857060.
COURSE: 5,856m, PAR 71, SSS 71. Flat Forest course.
SOC RESTR'S: Telephone booking necessary.
SOC GF - Round: Wd N/A. We N/A. **Day:** Wd N/A. We N/A.
SOC PACK: On application.
VIS RESTR'S: Welcome weekdays.
VIS GF - Round: Wd fl75. We N/A. **Day:** Wd N/A. We N/A.
FACILITIES: Practice Area, Bar & Restaurant.

KENNEMER GOLF & CC   MAP 18

Kennernweg 78-80, 2042 XT Zandvoor.
5km south-west of Harrlem off the N208.
CONTACT: Secretary. Tel: +31 2507 12836.
COURSE: 6,165m, PAR 72, SSS 72. Championship links course.
SOC RESTR'S: Please book prior through Secretary.
SOC GF - Round: Wd fl85. We fl110. **Day:** Wd N/A. We N/A.
SOC PACK: On application.
VIS RESTR'S: Welcome. Handicap Certificate required.
VIS GF - Round: Wd fl85. We fl110. **Day:** Wd N/A. We N/A.
FACILITIES: 9-hole Course, Clubhouse, Putting Green & Bar.

NOORDWIJKSE GOLF CLUB   MAP 18

Randweg 25, 2004 AL Noordwijk.
20km north of The Hague on the coast off the N208.
CONTACT: Secretary. Tel: +31 2523 73761.
COURSE: 6,282m, PAR 74, SSS 74. Championship links course.
SOC RESTR'S: Welcome but book in advance.
SOC GF - Round: Wd fl100. We fl100. **Day:** Wd N/A. We N/A.
SOC PACK: On application.
VIS RESTR'S: Welcome with Handicap Certificate.
VIS GF - Round: Wd fl100. We fl100. **Day:** Wd N/A. We N/A.
FACILITIES: 9-hole Course, Clubhouse, Putting Green & Bar.

SPAARNWOUDE GOLF CLUB   MAP 18

Het Hoge Land 3, 1981 LT Velsen.
10km north-west of Amsterdam on the A9.
CONTACT: Club Secretary. Tel: +31 2338 2708.
COURSE: 5,965m, PAR 72, SSS 70. Meadow/parkland course.
SOC RESTR'S: Please book prior through Secretary.
SOC GF - Round: Wd fl45. We fl50. **Day:** Wd N/A. We N/A.
SOC PACK: On application.
VIS RESTR'S: Always welcome.
VIS GF - Round: Wd fl45. We fl50. **Day:** Wd N/A. We N/A.
FACILITIES: 9-hole Course, 18-hole Par 3 Course, Clubhouse, Bar.

UTRECHTSE DE PAN   MAP 18

Amersfoortseweg 1, 3735 LJ Bosch en Duin.
10km north-east of Utrecht on the A28 to Amersfoot.
CONTACT: Reservations. Tel: +31 3404 55223.
COURSE: 6,080m, PAR 70, SSS 72. Parkland course.
SOC RESTR'S: Welcome when booked & with H'cap Cert.
SOC GF - Round: Wd fl85. We fl110. **Day:** Wd N/A. We N/A.
SOC PACK: On application.
VIS RESTR'S: Welcome with Handicap Certificates.
VIS GF - Round: Wd fl85. We fl110. **Day:** Wd N/A. We N/A.
FACILITIES: Clubhouse, Putting Green & Bar.

RAC Motoring Atlas Europe

A fully updated edition of this handy-sized atlas which encompasses unified Germany and other newly defined frontiers. Clear and detailed mapping at 1:1 million scale (16 miles to 1 inch) for Western Europe. Comprehensive index of over 52,000 place names. Compact format ideal for car use.

Price £10.99
Available from bookshops
or direct from the RAC on 0235 834885

Zuid-Oost

ZUID-OOST

DE ZUID LIMBURGSE GOLF & CC MAP 18

Dalbissenweg 22, 6281 NC Mechelen.
From Maastricht east to Gulpen approx 25km & follow signs.

CONTACT: GJ Swaen, Secretary. Tel: +31 4455 1397.
COURSE: 5,924m, PAR 71, SSS 71. Parkland course.
SOC RESTR'S: Members of golf clubs only, H'cap 30 at We
SOC GF - Round: Wd fl50. We fl70. **Day:** Wd N/A. We N/A.
SOC PACK: On application.
VIS RESTR'S: As society restrictions.
VIS GF - Round: Wd fl50. We fl70. **Day:** Wd N/A. We N/A.
FACILITIES: Clubhouse & Pro-shop.

BEST GOLF & COUNTRY CLUB MAP 18

Golflaan 1, 5683 RZ Best.
12km north-west of Eindhoven off the N2.

CONTACT: Ingrid M. Westendorp, Manager. Tel: +31 4990 91443.
COURSE: 5,935m, PAR 72, SSS 71. Meadow/parkland course.
SOC RESTR'S: Welcome, always call before play.
SOC GF - Round: Wd fl60. We fl80. **Day:** Wd N/A. We N/A.
SOC PACK: Available on request.
VIS RESTR'S: Welcome phone call advisable to check availability.
VIS GF - Round: Wd fl60. We fl80. **Day:** Wd N/A. We N/A.
FACILITIES: 9 Hole Pitch & Putt, Range & Restaurant.

EINDHOVENSCHE GOLF CLUB MAP 18

Eindhovenscheweg 300, 5553 VB Valkenswaard.
10km south of Eindhoven on the N15.

CONTACT: Secretary. Tel: +31 4902 12713.
COURSE: 5,948m, PAR 71, SSS 71. Parkland course.
SOC RESTR'S: Welcome when booked through Secretary.
SOC GF - Round: Wd fl80. We fl100. **Day:** Wd N/A. We N/A.
SOC PACK: On application.
VIS RESTR'S: Welcome. Handicap Certificate required.
VIS GF - Round: Wd fl80. We fl100. **Day:** Wd N/A. We N/A.
FACILITIES: Clubhouse & Pro-shop.

BRUNSSUM MERHEIDE MAP 18

Rimburger Weg 50, 6445 PA Brunssum.
10km south-east of Geleen.

CONTACT: H Gerrits. Tel: +31 4527 0968.
COURSE: 5,755m, PAR 71, SSS 70. Parkland course.
SOC RESTR'S: Weekdays only. Please book 7 days in advance.
SOC GF - Round: Wd fl50. We N/A. **Day:** Wd N/A. We N/A.
SOC PACK: On application.
VIS RESTR'S: Welcome phone call advisable to check availability.
VIS GF - Round: Wd fl50. We N/A. **Day:** Wd N/A. We N/A.
FACILITIES: 9-hole Course, Bar & Restaurant.

HOENSHUIS G & C CLUB MAP 18

Hoensweg 17, 6367 Gm Voerendaal.
15km south-east of Geleer.

CONTACT: V. D. Elzen, Caddymaster. Tel: +31 457 5330.
COURSE: 6,066m, PAR 72, SSS 72. Parkland course.
SOC RESTR'S: Maximum of 15 players, Weekdays only.
SOC GF - Round: Wd fl60. We N/A. **Day:** Wd N/A. We N/A.
SOC PACK: Call for information.
VIS RESTR'S: Not Sunday between 10 - 2.
VIS GF - Round: Wd fl60. We fl90. **Day:** Wd N/A. We N/A.
FACILITIES: Restaurant.

CROSSMOOR GOLF CLUB MAP 18

Laurabosweg 8, 6006 VR Weert.
25km south-east of Eindhoven off the A2.

CONTACT: Secretary. Tel: +31 4950 18287.
COURSE: 6,021m, PAR 72, SSS 72. Moorland course.
SOC RESTR'S: Golf club or federation members only. Must book.
SOC GF - Round: Wd N/A. We N/A. **Day:** Wd fl65. We fl80.
SOC PACK: On application.
VIS RESTR'S: Golf club or federation members only. Must book.
VIS GF - Round: Wd N/A. We N/A. **Day:** Wd fl65. We fl80.
FACILITIES: Par 3 Course & Chipping / Putting Green.

NOORD BRABANTSE GOLF CLUB MAP 18

Veenstraat 89, 5124 NC Molenschot.
On the outskirts of Breda. 40km south of Rotterdam.

CONTACT: Gemma Jorna, Secretary. Tel: +31 1611 2347.
COURSE: 5,759m, PAR 72, SSS 71. Flat meadowland course.
SOC RESTR'S: Welcome except Competition days & some We.
SOC GF - Round: Wd fl60. We fl90. **Day:** Wd N/A. We N/A.
SOC PACK: On application.
VIS RESTR'S: Always welcome.
VIS GF - Round: Wd fl60. We fl90. **Day:** Wd N/A. We N/A.
FACILITIES: Clubhouse, Putting Green & Bar.

NETHERLANDS

Zuid-West

BROEKPOLDER GOLF CLUB   MAP 18

Watersportweg 100, 3138 HD Vlaardingen.
East on the A20. On the outskirts of Rotterdam.

CONTACT: Mrs EB Knoester, Secretary . Tel: +31 1047 50011.
COURSE: 6,029m, PAR 72, SSS 72. Coastal course.
SOC RESTR'S: Welcome except Weekends.
SOC GF - Round: Wd fl70. We N/A. Day: Wd N/A. We N/A.
SOC PACK: Available at the time of booking.
VIS RESTR'S: Welcome except We. H'cap Cert required.
VIS GF - Round: Wd fl70. We N/A. Day: Wd N/A. We N/A.
FACILITIES: Bar & Restaurant. Three Courses to choose from.

CROMSTRIJEN GOLF CLUB   MAP 18

Veerweg 26, 3281 LX Numansdorp.
20km South of Rotterdam off the A29.

CONTACT: Secretary. Tel: +31 1865 4455.
COURSE: 6,029m, PAR 72, SSS 72. Meadowland course.
SOC RESTR'S: Welcome except Weekends.
SOC GF - Round: Wd fl55. We N/A. Day: Wd N/A. We N/A.
SOC PACK: On application.
VIS RESTR'S: Please phone for availability.
VIS GF - Round: Wd fl55. We N/A. Day: Wd N/A. We N/A.
FACILITIES: 9-hole Course, Clubhouse, Pro-shop & Bar.

GREVELINGENHOUT GOLF CLUB   MAP 18

Oudendijk 2, 4311 NA Bruinisse.
40km south-west of Rotterdam off N59.

CONTACT: Secretary. Tel: +31 1113 2650.
COURSE: 6,429m, PAR 73, SSS 74. Coastal course.
SOC RESTR'S: Welcome except Weekends.
SOC GF - Round: Wd fl60. We N/A. Day: Wd N/A. We N/A.
SOC PACK: On application.
VIS RESTR'S: Welcome except Weekends.
VIS GF - Round: Wd fl60. We N/A. Day: Wd N/A. We N/A.
FACILITIES: Clubhouse, Pro-shop & Restaurant.

KLEIBURG GOLF CLUB   MAP 18

Krabbeweg 9, 3231 NB Brielle.
20km west of Rotterdam on the coast south of the A15.

CONTACT: Manager. Tel: +31 1810 17809.
COURSE: 5,658m, PAR 70, SSS 69. Meadow/parkland course.
SOC RESTR'S: Welcome with reservation.
SOC GF - Round: Wd fl40. We fl50. Day: Wd fl50. We N/A.
SOC PACK: Available on request.
VIS RESTR'S: Advisable to book
VIS GF - Round: Wd fl40. We fl50. Day: Wd fl50. We N/A.
FACILITIES: Clubhouse, Pro-shop & Restaurant.

RIJSWIJKSE GOLF CLUB   MAP 18

Delftweg 59, 2289 AL Rijswijk.
5km south of The Hague on the coast road.

CONTACT: Secretary. Tel: +31 7039 95040.
COURSE: 5,900m, PAR 72, SSS 71. Meadow/parkland course.
SOC RESTR'S: Please book in advance with Secretary.
SOC GF - Round: Wd fl45. We fl60. Day: Wd N/A. We N/A.
SOC PACK: Available on request.
VIS RESTR'S: Advisable to book.
VIS GF - Round: Wd fl45. We fl60. Day: Wd N/A. We N/A.
FACILITIES: Clubhouse, Pro-shop & Restaurant.

ZEEGERSLOOT GOLF CLUB   MAP 18

Kromme Aarweg 5, 2403 NB Alphen an der Rijn.
30km north of Rotterdam.

CONTACT: CP Bos, Manager. Tel: +31 1720 74567.
COURSE: 5,489m, PAR 70, SSS 69. With many water hazards.
SOC RESTR'S: Welcome.
SOC GF - Round: Wd fl40. We fl50. Day: Wd fl50. We fl65.
SOC PACK: Call for information.
VIS RESTR'S: Call Caddymaster +31 1720 41839.
VIS GF - Round: Wd fl40. We fl50. Day: Wd fl50. We fl65.
FACILITIES: Par 3 Course, Clubhouse & Restaurant.

ND# NORWAY

TAKING a golfing holiday in Norway is a bit like going on a skiing trip to Ireland. You might find a hint of what you're looking for but in all probability it might not be all that you expect. The weather and the terrain, plus the lack of any particular golf tradition in Norway, results in a severe shortage of 18-hole courses. The country's oldest club, Oslo, is only 5 miles out of the city to the north-west, but an indication of where golf lies in Norwegian priorities is that you'll only track down the golfcourse by following road signs to an adjacent campsite!

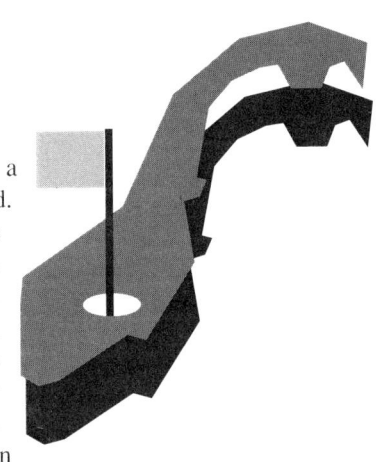

For the greater part of each year, golf in Norway can at best be recommended only as a pleasant alternative, if the weather allows, to the ski slopes. While in summer, it must be said that infinitely more variety is on offer in neighbouring Sweden.

BAERUM GOLF CLUB   MAP 13 A2

Box 31, 1355 Baerum Postterminal.
From Oslo, west to Sandvika, 10km to Lommedalen.

CONTACT: G. Kjolseth, Director. Tel: +47 2 513085.
COURSE: 5,400m, PAR 71, SSS 70. Hilly parkland course.
SOC RESTR'S: Very limited, must book.
SOC GF - Round: Wd N/A. We N/A. **Day:** Wd Kr200. We Kr250.
SOC PACK: On application.
VIS RESTR'S: Welcome with Handicap Certificate.
VIS GF - Round: Wd N/A. We N/A. **Day:** Wd Kr200. We Kr250.
FACILITIES: 9-hole Course, Cafeteria with Snacks & Meals.

KJEKSTAD GOLF CLUB   MAP 13 A2

Boks 201, 3440 Royken.
40km south-west Oslo. 12km south-east of Drammen on R282.

CONTACT: J Yngvar Ohrn, Manager. Tel: +47 3 285350.
COURSE: 5,120m, PAR 67, SSS 67. Surrounded by lakes & forests.
SOC RESTR'S: Handicap of 36 welcome after 3.
SOC GF - Round: Wd Kr150. We Kr150. **Day:** Wd Kr150. We Kr150.
SOC PACK: Available on application.
VIS RESTR'S: Handicap 36 welcome after 3.
VIS GF - Round: Wd Kr150. We Kr150. **Day:** Wd Kr150. We Kr150.
FACILITIES: Bar & Restaurant.

ONSOY GOLF CLUB   MAP 13 A3

Postboks 458, 1601 Fredrikstad.
10km west of Fredrikstad.

CONTACT: S. Meistedt, Professional. Tel: +47 9 333590.
COURSE: 5,634m, PAR 72, SSS 72. Parkland course.
SOC RESTR'S: Welcome with written application.
SOC GF - Round: Wd N/A. We N/A. **Day:** Wd Kr170. We N/A.
SOC PACK: On application.
VIS RESTR'S: Wd before 2 & We after 2. H'cap Cert required.
VIS GF - Round: Wd N/A. We N/A. **Day:** Wd Kr170. We Kr200.
FACILITIES: Pro-shop, Range & Winter Training Room.

OSLO GOLF HOTEL   MAP 13 A2

Bogstad, 0757 Norway 7.
8km north-west Oslo follow road signs to "Bogstad camping".

CONTACT: P Teigen, Secretary. Tel: +47 2 504402.
COURSE: 6,756m, PAR 72, SSS 72. Championship parkland.
SOC RESTR'S: By special appointment.
SOC GF - Round: Wd Kr250. We Kr300. **Day:** Wd N/A. We N/A.
SOC PACK: On application.
VIS RESTR'S: Wd before 2 & We after 2. H'cap Cert required.
VIS GF - Round: Wd Kr250. We Kr300. **Day:** Wd N/A. We N/A.
FACILITIES: Pro-shop, Range & Winter Training Room.

NORWAY

SKJEBERG GOLF CLUB MAP 13 A3

PO Box 149, 1742 Klavestadhaugen.
2km north of Sarpsborg in Hevingen.

CONTACT: G. Midtvoge. Tel: +47 9 166310.
COURSE: 5,550m, PAR 72, SSS 73. Undulating course.
SOC RESTR'S: Welcome with prior booking.
SOC GF - Round: Wd Kr120. **We** Kr140. **Day:** Wd Kr150. **We** N/A.
SOC PACK: On application.
VIS RESTR'S: Welcome.
VIS GF - Round: Wd Kr120. **We** Kr140. **Day:** Wd Kr150. **We** N/A.
FACILITIES: Bar & Practice Area.

STAVANGER GOLF CLUB MAP 13 A3

Longebakke 45, 4042 Hafrsfjord.
5km south-west of Stavanger.

CONTACT: R Lees, Professional. Tel: +47 9 166310.
COURSE: 5,090m, PAR 69, SSS 70. Undulating course.
SOC RESTR'S: Welcome with prior booking.
SOC GF - Round: Wd Kr180. **We** Kr240. **Day:** Wd N/A. **We** N/A.
SOC PACK: On application.
VIS RESTR'S: Welcome.
VIS GF - Round: Wd Kr180. **We** Kr240. **Day:** Wd N/A. **We** N/A.
FACILITIES: Bar & Practice Area.

VESTFOLD GOLF CLUB MAP 13 A3

PO Box 64, 3101 Tønsberg.
8km from Tønsberg.

CONTACT: Secretary. Tel: +47 3 365655.
COURSE: 5,866m, PAR 71, SSS 72. Undulating course.
SOC RESTR'S: Welcome with prior booking.
SOC GF - Round: Wd Kr140. **We** Kr200. **Day:** Wd N/A. **We** N/A.
SOC PACK: On application.
VIS RESTR'S: Welcome please check seasonal closures.
VIS GF - Round: Wd Kr140. **We** Kr200. **Day:** Wd N/A. **We** N/A.
FACILITIES: Bar & Practice Area.

PORTUGAL

GOLF in Portugal - and its neighbour Spain - can represent the very best and the very worst that European golf has to offer. At its best, the climate and the sheer variety and quality of the golf courses available is peerless; at its worst, overplayed, overfull and poorly-maintained courses and exhorbitant green fees charged for the dubious privilege of playing them are nothing short of a national disgrace. Hard on the heels of this indictment however, it must be emphasised that those responsible for golf tourism in Portugal are making strenuous efforts to ensure that the worst excesses are a thing of the past. Whatever measures are imposed however, it has to be accepted that at the very height of the tourist season, some courses can become unpleasantly full. But golf in Portugal can still be a delight, especially so in the less-crowded and cooler months of spring and autumn.

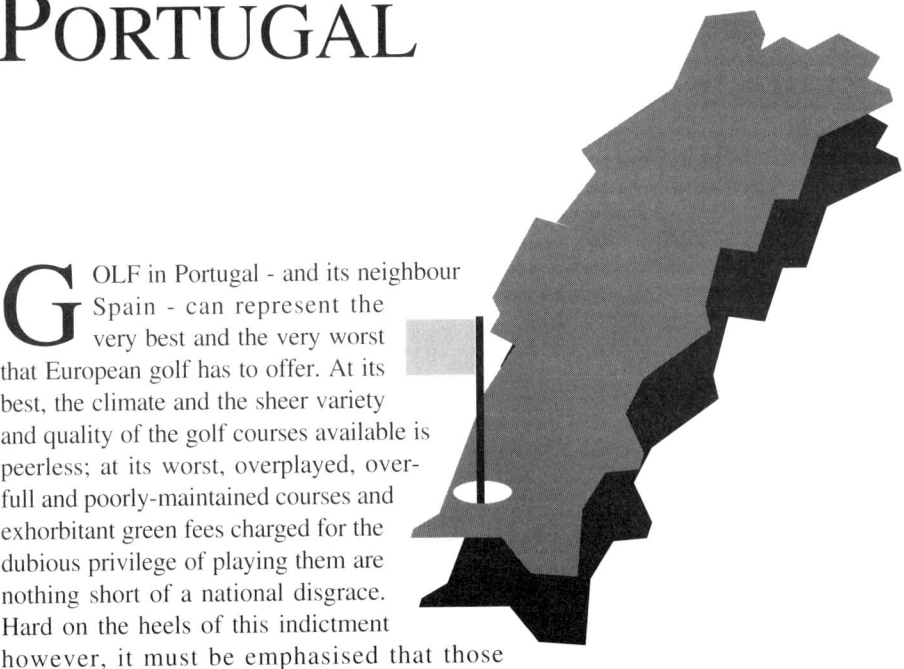

Fittingly, for England's oldest ally, there's a strong expatriate feel about the Estoril club just outside Lisbon, while devotees of links golf will be surprised to find themselves as well catered to as they are at Portugal's oldest club, Oporto, which dates back to 1890, and one of the very newest, Estela.

For the vast majority however, golf in Portugal means the Algarve and in particular, the late Sir Henry Cotton. His designs at Penina and Vale do Lobo are both manificient and fitting monuments to him. Elsewhere on the Algarve, the three 9-hole loops at Quinta do Lago are testing and superbly maintained, (and at least one loop is floodlit now for 24-hour golf!); the new layout at Vila Sol is a worthy Portuguese Open venue; and the Vilamoura complex also offers fine opportunities: Vilamoura 1, the championship course, can get a bit busy, but the newer Vilamoura 2, a little wider and a little easier, (but not by too much!), is nevertheless a super course and much less crowded.

One point to note is that green fees can be very substantially discounted depending on which hotel you stay at, offering the chance to play at some of the prestige courses at bargain prices; and of course, with the profusion of golf package tours available from the UK, it really does pay, more than any other golfing destination (along with Spain) to shop around.

PORTUGAL

Algarve

🏌

GOLF VILA SOL MAP 18

Vila Sol, Alto do Semino, 8125 Quarteira.
Just north of Quarteira off the Faro-Albufeira N125 Road.
CONTACT: Reservations. Tel: +351 89 302144.
COURSE: 6,218m, PAR 72, SSS 71. Undulating forest course.
SOC RESTR'S: Bookings only in advance, details on request.
SOC GF - Round: Wd E10,000. We N/A. **Day:** Wd N/A. We N/A.
SOC PACK: Available on application.
VIS RESTR'S: Welcome, phone call advisable to check availability.
VIS GF - Round: Wd E10,000. We N/A. **Day:** Wd N/A. We N/A.
FACILITIES: Caddy, Club, Trolley & Cart Hire, Range, Bar & Restaurant.

ALTO GOLF MAP 18

Quinta do Alto do Poco, Apartedo 1 Alvor, 8500 Portimão.
Take road to Alvor off main N125, 5km west of Portimão.
CONTACT: A Paixao, Golf Manager. Tel: +351 82 401045.
COURSE: 6,126m, PAR 72, SSS 73. Links/parkland course.
SOC RESTR'S: Welcome with prior arrangement.
SOC GF - Round: Wd E7,800. We N/A. **Day:** Wd N/A. We N/A.
SOC PACK: As required will arrange package.
VIS RESTR'S: Welcome, subject to availability.
VIS GF - Round: Wd E7,800. We N/A. **Day:** Wd N/A. We N/A.
FACILITIES: Range, Teaching Pro, Trolley & Buggy Rental.

PARQUE DA FLORESTA MAP 18

Vale de Poço, 8650 Vila do Bispo.
16km west of Lagos.
CONTACT: T Dodd, Golf Manager. Tel: +351 82 65333.
COURSE: 5,830m, PAR 72, SSS 72. Requires extreme accuracy.
SOC RESTR'S: Always welcome.
SOC GF - Round: Wd N/A. We N/A. **Day:** Wd E6,000. We N/A.
SOC PACK: On application.
VIS RESTR'S: Always welcome.
VIS GF - Round: Wd N/A. We E6,500. **Day:** Wd E6,000. We N/A.
FACILITIES: Pro-shop, Trolley & Buggy Hire, Bar & Restaurant.

CLUB DE GOLF PALMARES MAP 18

Meia Praia, 8600 Lagos, Algarve.
3km east from Lagos Via Meia Praia.
CONTACT: WJ Garvey. Secretary. Tel: +351 82 62961.
COURSE: 5,961m, PAR 71, SSS 72. Links/parkland course.
SOC RESTR'S: No restrictions, subject to availability.
SOC GF - Round: Wd E7,500. We N/A. **Day:** Wd N/A. We N/A.
SOC PACK: Details on application.
VIS RESTR'S: Always welcome. Seasonal alterations on GF.
VIS GF - Round: Wd E7,500. We N/A. **Day:** Wd N/A. We N/A.
FACILITIES: Range, Buggy & Club Hire, Pitch & Putt, Bar & Restaurant.

PENINA GOLF CLUB MAP 18

P.O. Box 146, Penina, 8502 Portimão Codex.
5km west from Portimão, 12km east from Lagos.
CONTACT: L Rio, Golf Secretary. Tel: +351 82 415415.
COURSE: 6,439m, PAR 73, SSS 73. Flat parkland course.
SOC RESTR'S: Priority to all Hotel residence.
SOC GF - Round: Wd E9,500. We N/A. **Day:** Wd N/A. We N/A.
SOC PACK: Free Green Fees to Hotel Residence.
VIS RESTR'S: Phone for daily availability.
VIS GF - Round: Wd E9,500. We N/A. **Day:** Wd N/A. We N/A.
FACILITIES: 2 x 9-holes Monchique GF E6,000 & Quinta E5,000.

DE GOLF DA QUINTA DO LAGO MAP 18

Quinta do Lago, 8135 Almancil.
15km from Faro International Airport.
CONTACT: M Barrauncho, Golf Manager. Tel: +351 89 394782.
COURSE: 6,750m (Champ) PAR 72, SSS 73. 4 x 9-hole courses.
SOC RESTR'S: Bookings only in advance, details on request.
SOC GF - Round: Wd E10,000. We N/A. **Day:** Wd N/A. We N/A.
SOC PACK: Discounts for Guests of Villa do Golf or Quinta do Lago.
VIS RESTR'S: Please phone to check availability.
VIS GF - Round: Wd E10,000. We N/A. **Day:** Wd N/A. We N/A.
FACILITIES: Caddy, Club, Trolley & Cart Hire, Range & Lessons.

QUINTA DO GRAMACHO MAP 18

Carvoeiro Golf, Apartado 24, 8400 Lagoa.
Off the N125 from Albufeira-Lagos, between Carvoeiro & Lagoa.
CONTACT: Reservations. Tel: +351 89 394782.
COURSE: 5,920m, PAR 72, SSS 71. Compact layout.
SOC RESTR'S: Welcome with prior bookings.
SOC GF - Round: Wd E6,000. We N/A. **Day:** Wd N/A. We N/A.
SOC PACK: Limited package.
VIS RESTR'S: Welcome.
VIS GF - Round: Wd E6,000. We E6,000. **Day:** Wd N/A. We N/A.
FACILITIES: Club, Trolley & Cart Hire, Range & Putting Green.

CENTRE

SAN LORENZO GOLF CLUB MAP 18

Quinta do Lago, 8135 Almancil.
15km from Faro International Airport.

CONTACT: A Santos, Golf Manager. Tel: +351 89 396552.
COURSE: 6,238m, PAR 72, SSS 73. Testing parkland course.
SOC RESTR'S: Welcome with prior agreement.
SOC GF - Round: Wd E12,500. **We** N/A. **Day:** Wd N/A. **We** N/A.
SOC PACK: Clients of Hotel Dona Filipa have free access to course.
VIS RESTR'S: Subject to availability, must book 24 hours in advance.
VIS GF - Round: Wd E12,500. **We** E12,500. **Day:** Wd N/A. **We** N/A.
FACILITIES: Driving Range, Golf Tuition, Carts, Shop & Restaurant.

VALE DO LOBO GOLF CLUB MAP 18

Vale do Lobo, Almancil, Algarve.
20km from Faro Airport going West.

CONTACT: Janet Walker. Tel: +351 89 393938.
COURSE: 5,658m, PAR 72, SSS 72. Undulating coastal/parkland.
SOC RESTR'S: None for residents. Otherwise Thur only available.
SOC GF - Round: Wd E10,000. **We** N/A. **Day:** Wd N/A. **We** N/A.
SOC PACK: 50% discount for Villa guests.
VIS RESTR'S: None for residents. Otherwise Thur only available.
VIS GF - Round: Wd E10,000. **We** N/A. **Day:** Wd N/A. **We** N/A.
FACILITIES: 3 sets make up this famous Complex & Clubhouse.

VILAMOURA ONE MAP 18

Vilamoura, Quarteira 8125.
25km west of Faro off the N125.

CONTACT: J Marcelo, Secretary. Tel: +351 89313652.
COURSE: 6,330m, PAR 72, SSS 72. Championship parkland.
SOC RESTR'S: Must book in advance.
SOC GF - Round: Wd E8,500. **We** N/A. **Day:** Wd N/A. **We** N/A.
SOC PACK: On application.
VIS RESTR'S: On application.
VIS GF - Round: Wd E8,500. **We** N/A. **Day:** Wd N/A. **We** N/A.
FACILITIES: Pro-shop, Bar & Restaurants.

VILAMOURA TWO MAP 18

Vilamoura, Quarteira 8125.
25km west of Faro.

CONTACT: E Sousa, Secretary. Tel: +351 89314470.
COURSE: 6,256m, PAR 72, SSS 71. Parkland/forest course.
SOC RESTR'S: Must book in advance.
SOC GF - Round: Wd E7,500. **We** N/A. **Day:** Wd N/A. **We** N/A.
SOC PACK: On application.
VIS RESTR'S: On application.
VIS GF - Round: Wd E7,500. **We** N/A. **Day:** Wd N/A. **We** N/A.
FACILITIES: Pro-shop, Bar & Restaurant.

VILAMOURA THREE MAP 18

Vilamoura, Quarteira 8125.
25km west of Faro.

CONTACT: Susete Calado, Secretary. Tel: +351 89310724.
COURSE: 5,887m, PAR 72, SSS 71. American layout.
SOC RESTR'S: Must book in advance.
SOC GF - Round: Wd E7,500. **We** N/A. **Day:** Wd N/A. **We** N/A.
SOC PACK: On application.
VIS RESTR'S: On application.
VIS GF - Round: Wd E7,500. **We** N/A. **Day:** Wd N/A. **We** N/A.
FACILITIES: Vilamoura Four - 9-hole American style layout.

Centre

CLUB DE CAMPO DE AROEIRA MAP 18

Herdade da Aroeira - Fonte da Telha, 2825 Monte da Caparica.
25km south of Lisbon.

CONTACT: D Leal, Director of Golf. Tel: +351 1 226 3244.
COURSE: 6,040m, PAR 72, SSS 71. Pine forest parkland course.
SOC RESTR'S: Reservations recommended especially We.
SOC GF - Round: Wd E6,500. **We** E6,500. **Day:** Wd N/A. **We** N/A.
SOC PACK: Standard fee 18-holes E6,500 plus catering.
VIS RESTR'S: Welcome.
VIS GF - Round: Wd E6,500. **We** E6,600. **Day:** Wd N/A. **We** N/A.
FACILITIES: Pro-shop, Range, Restaurant & Bar.

GOLF ESTORIL MAP 18

Avenida República, 2765 Estoril.
30km west of Lisbon on the Sintra road.

CONTACT: J Cruz, Secretary. Tel: +351 1 4683248.
COURSE: 5,667m, PAR 69, SSS 69. Links course (with Pines).
SOC RESTR'S: No groups at Weekends.
SOC GF - Round: Wd E6,000. **We** N/A. **Day:** Wd N/A. **We** N/A.
SOC PACK: On application.
VIS RESTR'S: Welcome Weekdays. Some Weekends possible.
VIS GF - Round: Wd E6,000. **We** E8,000. **Day:** Wd N/A. **We** N/A.
FACILITIES: 9-hole Course, Caddies, Range, Bar & Restaurant.

PORTUGAL

LISBON SPORTS CLUB MAP 18

Casal da Carragueira - Belas - Queluz.
Just over 20km north-west from Lisbon.

CONTACT: M Sousa, Secretary. Tel: +351 1 4312482.
COURSE: 5,216m, PAR 68, SSS 69. Parkland course.
SOC RESTR'S: Welcome.
SOC GF -Round: Wd N/A. We N/A. **Day:** Wd E5,500. We E6,500.
SOC PACK: On application.
VIS RESTR'S: Welcome Wd. Please phone regarding We.
VIS GF - Round: Wd N/A. We N/A. **Day:** Wd E5,500. We E6,500.
FACILITIES: Bar & Restaurant.

North

PENHA LONGA GOLF CLUB MAP 18

Longa Azul, Linhó, 2710 Sintra.
30km west of Lisbon and 2km north of Estoril.

CONTACT: Secretary. Tel: +351 1 9240320.
COURSE: 6,176m, PAR 72, SSS 73. Undulating forest course.
SOC RESTR'S: Welcome with advanced booking.
SOC GF -Round: Wd N/A. We N/A. **Day:** Wd E8,000. We E12,000.
SOC PACK: On application.
VIS RESTR'S: Welcome.
VIS GF - Round: Wd N/A. We N/A. **Day:** Wd E8,000. We E12,000.
FACILITIES: Clubhouse. Course surrounds the old Royal Palace.

ESTELA GOLF CLUB MAP 18

Rio Alto - Estela, 4490 Povoa de Varzim.
35km north of Oporto.

CONTACT: F. Pinherio, Director. Tel: +351 52 685567.
COURSE: 6,129m, PAR 72, SSS 73. Genuine links Course.
SOC RESTR'S: Not Tournament Days.
SOC GF - Round: Wd N/A. We N/A. **Day:** Wd E8,000. We E8,000.
SOC PACK: Discount to guests of Sopete Hotels. GF vary seasonally.
VIS RESTR'S: Not Tournament Days.
VIS GF - Round: Wd N/A. We N/A. **Day:** Wd E8,000. We E8,000.
FACILITIES: Clubs, Carts, Buggies, Lockers, Bar & Restaurant.

QUINTA DA MARINHA GOLF MAP 18

Guia, Quinta da Marinha, Cascais 2750.
30km west of Lisbon just beside Estoril.

CONTACT: Secretary. Tel: +351 1 4869881.
COURSE: 6,055m, PAR 71, SSS 71. American style course.
SOC RESTR'S: Welcome with advanced booking.
SOC GF - Round: Wd E6,500. We N/A. **Day:** Wd N/A. We N/A.
SOC PACK: On application.
VIS RESTR'S: Welcome Weekdays.
VIS GF - Round: Wd E6,500. We E7,500. **Day:** Wd N/A. We N/A.
FACILITIES: Accommodation, Bar & Restaurant.

OPORTO GOLF CLUB MAP 18

Lugar do Sisto, Paramos, Espinho 4500.
20km south of Oporto.

CONTACT: Margarida Moreira, Sec. Tel: +351 2 722008.
COURSE: 5,945m, PAR 71, SSS 70. Seaside links Course.
SOC RESTR'S: Closed Mon. We & Bank Hols before 10.
SOC GF - Round: Wd E8,000. We E8,000. **Day:** Wd N/A. We N/A.
SOC PACK: 50% Discount to guests of Solverde & Praia-Golf Hotels.
VIS RESTR'S: As above.
VIS GF - Round: Wd E8,000. We E8,000. **Day:** Wd N/A. We N/A.
FACILITIES: Clubs, Carts, Buggies, Bar & Snacks.

TROIA GOLF MAP 18

Tróia 2,900 Setúbal.
Take the Lisbon to Setubal Motorway South (42km).

CONTACT: J de Carvalho Marques. Tel: +351 6544112.
COURSE: 6,337m, PAR 72, SSS 74. Links (American style) course.
SOC RESTR'S: Welcome.
SOC GF - Round: Wd N/A. We N/A. **Day:** Wd E5,000. We E5,000.
SOC PACK: 10% discount on Hotel & Clubhouse.
VIS RESTR'S: Welcome.
VIS GF - Round: Wd N/A. We N/A. **Day:** Wd E6,000. We E6,000.
FACILITIES: Golf Carts, Trolleys, Restaurant & Bar.

Azores Islands

TERCEIRA ISLAND GOLF CLUB — MAP 18

9760 Praia de Vitoria, Azores.

CONTACT: RJ Pyeatt. Tel: +351 95 25847.
COURSE: 5,760m, PAR 72, SSS 70. Wooded parkland course.
SOC RESTR'S: Welcome.
SOC GF - Round: Wd N/A. **We** N/A. **Day: Wd** E3,000. **We** E3,000.
SOC PACK: For extended periods a 3 day pass is available - E6,000.
VIS RESTR'S: Always welcome.
VIS GF - Round: Wd E3,000. **We** E3,000. **Day: Wd** E3,000. **We** E3,000.
FACILITIES: Bar & Grill for golfers only & Clubhouse.

VERDE GOLF & COUNTRY CLUB — MAP 18

Avendia D. Joao III, Lote 4, 9500 Ponta Delgada.

CONTACT: L Octavia dos Reis Indio. Tel: +351 96 31925.
COURSE: 6,177m, PAR 73, SSS 72. Watch out for the 19th hole.
SOC RESTR'S: On application.
SOC GF - Round: Wd N/A. **We** N/A. **Day: Wd** E3,000. **We** E3,000.
SOC PACK: On application.
VIS RESTR'S: Welcome any day.
VIS GF - Round: Wd N/A. **We** N/A. **Day: Wd** E3,000. **We** E3,000.
FACILITIES: Trolleys, Club Hire & Practice Ground.

SPAIN

WITH the awarding of the 1997 Ryder Cup to Spain, official recognition has been given to the special role that this country has played in the development of golf at all levels in Europe over the past twenty or thirty years. More great courses have been built in Spain over that period than anywhere in the world: special attention is given in this Guide to Valderrama, but the names of others will be familiar to golfers everywhere - La Manga; La Moraleja, where the 10th is named 'El Terror'; Sotogrande; Las Brisas; El Saler; Mas Nou; Torrequebrada, perched above the Mediterranean; Santa Ponsa on Majorca; all have their own special character and all can offer glorious golf.

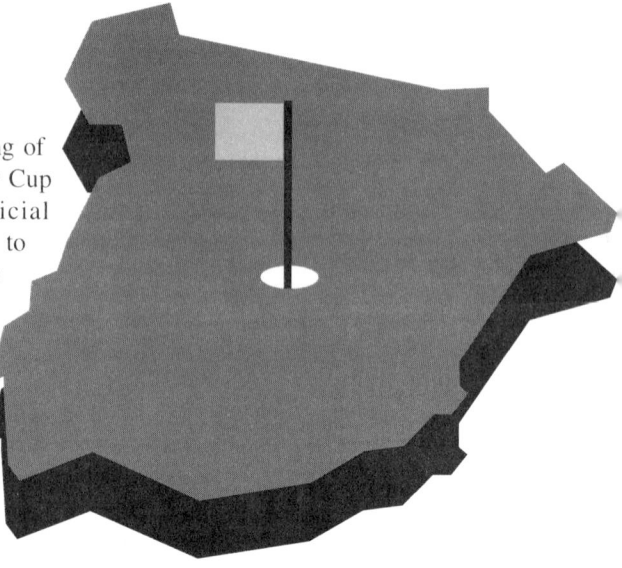

As with Portugal, areas of Spain, particularly in the south, have become 'golfed out' and, again like Portugal, efforts are being made to woo back the golfers who have deserted these courses for the same climate, but better value of America's eastern seaboard. Green fees in southern Spain are dropping and standards are rising. The shoddier developments, which tried to cash in on the boom of the mid-seventies and eighties, will fail and the better courses will again come into their own.

The great advantage Spain has is that golf is not concentrated into just one area. You can follow in the footsteps of a young Seve Ballesteros at Pedrena near Santander in the north, while at the other end of the country at Novo Sancti Petri on the Atlantic coast near Cadiz, you can pit your skills against Ballesteros the designer and judge how - or if - his playing philosophy has coloured his course construction. Madrid offers, appropriately for this Guide, the Real Automovil Club de Espana (Royal Autombile Club of Spain) course that regularly hosts the Spanish Open; each of Spain's major cities - and most of the others too - can boast at least one good course.

The best and most famous clubs charge green fees in line with their reputation, which can lead to temptations to go 'down-market'. That's fine as there can be good value to be had at smaller courses off the beaten track, but do watch out for the cowboys and conmen, especially in the south; it's still all too possible to pay through the nose for indifferent quality golf. As with Portugal, choose to stay in hotels connected to what you know from this Guide to be the better golf courses and scan your local travel agents for good - particularly off-season - bargains.

Basque-Pyrenees

Central

CLUB DE CAMPO LAUKARIZ MAP 19 A2

Laukariz-Munguía Vizcaya.
15km north of Bilbao.

CONTACT: Secretary. Tel: +34 94 6740858.
COURSE: 6,481m, PAR 72, SSS 74. Parkland course.
SOC RESTR'S: Please book in advance.
SOC GF - Round: Wd Pt5,000. We Pt7,000. Day: Wd N/A. We N/A.
SOC PACK: Available on discussion with Secretary.
VIS RESTR'S: Welcome with Handicap Certificate.
VIS GF - Round: Wd Pt5,000. We Pt7,000. Day: Wd N/A. We N/A.
FACILITIES: Bar, Restaurant, Club & Buggy Hire.

CAMPO DE GOLF DE SALAMANCA MAP 19 A2

Monte de Zarapicos, Salamanca.
Sited on the outskirts of Salamanca off the CN 620.

CONTACT: R Lopez Carrillo. Tel: +34 23 329102.
COURSE: 6,480m, PAR 72, SSS 72. Parkland course.
SOC RESTR'S: Welcome by prior arrangement.
SOC GF - Round: Wd N/A. We N/A. Day: Wd Pt5,000. We N/A.
SOC PACK: On application.
VIS RESTR'S: Welcome except competitions days.
VIS GF - Round: Wd N/A. We Pt5,000. Day: Wd Pt5,000. We N/A.
FACILITIES: Bar & Restaurant.

DE NEGURI GOLF CLUB MAP 19 A2

Appo Correos 9, Algorta Vizcaya.
On the La Galea to Guecho road. 20km north of Bilbao.

CONTACT: Secretary. Tel: +34 94 4690200.
COURSE: 6,319m, PAR 72, SSS 73. Parkland course.
SOC RESTR'S: Booking essential.
SOC GF - Round: Wd Pt6,250. We N/A. Day: Wd N/A. We N/A.
SOC PACK: On application.
VIS RESTR'S: Welcome.
VIS GF - Round: Wd Pt6,250. We Pt7,500. Day: Wd N/A. We N/A.
FACILITIES: 6 Practice Holes, Bar, Restaurant, Club & Buggy Hire.

ENTREPINOS GOLF CLUB MAP 19 A2

Carretera de PesqueruelaKM 1. 5, Simancas, Valledolid.
10km south-west of Valledolid in Simancas off the CN 620.

CONTACT: C Pardo, Manager. Tel: +34 83 590511.
COURSE: 5,099m, PAR 69, SSS 69. Tight parkland course.
SOC RESTR'S: Welcome.
SOC GF - Round: Wd Pt2,500. We N/A. Day: Wd N/A. We N/A.
SOC PACK: On application.
VIS RESTR'S: Welcome.
VIS GF - Round: Wd N/A. We N/A. Day: Wd Pt4,300. We Pt4,300.
FACILITIES: Pro-shop, Tennis & Paddle Tennis.

LA PENAZA GOLF CLUB MAP 19 A2

Apartado 3039, Zaragoza.
15km south-west of Zaragoza on Madrid/Barcelona road.

CONTACT: Secretary. Tel: +34 976 342800.
COURSE: 6,160m, PAR 72, SSS 72. Parkland course.
SOC RESTR'S: Welcome but must book in advance.
SOC GF - Round: Wd N/A. We N/A. Day: Wd Pt6,000. We N/A.
SOC PACK: Available at time of booking.
VIS RESTR'S: Welcome.
VIS GF - Round: Wd N/A. We N/A. Day: Wd Pt6,000. We Pt7,500.
FACILITIES: Bar, Restaurant, Club & Buggy Hire.

LA HERRERIA GOLF CLUB MAP 19 A2

San Lorenzo del Escorial, Madrid.
45km north-west of Madrid off A6 to San Lorenzo del Escorial.

CONTACT: L Crespo, Manager. Tel: +34 91 8905111.
COURSE: 6,053m, PAR 72, SSS 72. Parkland/forest course.
SOC RESTR'S: No reservations on Weekends.
SOC GF - Round: Wd Pt5,500. We N/A. Day: Wd N/A. We N/A.
SOC PACK: 18-holes, Lunch & visit to Royal Monastery.
VIS RESTR'S: Not available at Weekends.
VIS GF - Round: Wd Pt5,500. We N/A. Day: Wd N/A. We N/A.
FACILITIES: Restaurant & Tennis.

SPAIN

LA MORALEJA GOLF CLUB   MAP 19 A2

La Moraleja, Alcobendas (Madrid).
9km north of Madrid on Burgos road.
CONTACT: V Barrios, Professional. Tel: +34 91 650 07 00.
COURSE: 6,016m, PAR 72, SSS 72. Parkland with water.
SOC RESTR'S: Written booking necessary.
SOC GF - Round: Wd Pt7,000. We N/A. Day: Wd N/A. We N/A.
SOC PACK: On application.
VIS RESTR'S: Welcome weekdays.
VIS GF - Round: Wd Pt7,000. We N/A. Day: Wd N/A. We N/A.
FACILITIES: Practice Area, Bar & Restaurant.

LOMAS-BOSQUE GOLF CLUB   MAP 19 A2

Urb el Basque, 28670 Villaviciosa de Odón Madrid.
20km from Madrid.
CONTACT: Professional. Tel: +34 91 6167500.
COURSE: 6,141m, PAR 72, SSS 72. Parkland course.
SOC RESTR'S: Welcome Weekdays H'cap Cert's required.
SOC GF - Round: Wd Pt6,000. We N/A. Day: Wd N/A. We N/A.
SOC PACK: Please discuss on application.
VIS RESTR'S: Welcome with Handicap Certificate.
VIS GF - Round: Wd Pt6,000. We Pt10,000. Day: Wd N/A. We N/A.
FACILITIES: 9-hole Course, Bar, Restaurant, Club & Buggy Hire.

NEW MADRID GOLF CLUB   MAP 19 A2

Las Matas, Madrid.
On the La Coruña road, 26km north-west from Madrid.
CONTACT: Secretary. Tel: +3491 6300820.
COURSE: 5,647m, PAR 70, SSS 70. Parkland course.
SOC RESTR'S: Reserved tee times only.
SOC GF - Round: Wd Pt5,000. We N/A. Day: Wd N/A. We N/A.
SOC PACK: On application.
VIS RESTR'S: Reserved tee times only.
VIS GF - Round: Wd N/A. We N/A. Day: Wd Pt5,800. We Pt7,500.
FACILITIES: Bar, Restaurant, Club & Buggy Hire.

PUERTA DE HIERRO GOLF CLUB   MAP 19 A2

Avenida de Miraflores. 28035 Madrid.
4km north of Madrid on the Puera de Hierro road.
CONTACT: Secretary. Tel: +3491 3161745.
COURSE: 6,347m, PAR 72, SSS 73. Parkland course.
SOC RESTR'S: Please book in advance.
SOC GF - Round: Wd Pt6,900. We N/A. Day: Wd N/A. We N/A.
SOC PACK: None.
VIS RESTR'S: Welcome. 1993 Green Fees under review.
VIS GF - Round: Wd Pt6,900. We Pt15,000. Day: Wd N/A. We N/A.
FACILITIES: 2nd 18-hole Course, Bar & Restaurant.

REAL AUTOMOVIL CLUB DE ESPANA   MAP 19 A2

José Abascal 10, 28003 Madrid.
San Sebastián de los Reyes, 28km north of Madrid.
CONTACT: F Alverez, Professional. Tel: +34 91 657 00 01.
COURSE: 6,505m, PAR 72, SSS 72. Parkland course.
SOC RESTR'S: Welcome weekdays.
SOC GF - Round: Wd Pt7,000. We N/A. Day: Wd N/A. We N/A.
SOC PACK: On application.
VIS RESTR'S: Welcome.
VIS GF - Round: Wd Pt7,000. We Pt7,000. Day: Wd N/A. We N/A.
FACILITIES: 9-hole Par 3 Course, Bar & Restaurant.

VILLA DE MADRID   MAP 19 A2

Crta Castilla - 28040 Madrid.
5km north-west from Madrid on the Castilla road.
CONTACT: Secretary. Tel: +34 91 3572132.
COURSE: 6,370m, PAR 72, SSS 74. Parkland course.
SOC RESTR'S: Welcome with advance bookings.
SOC GF - Round: Wd Pt2,000. We N/A. Day: Wd N/A. We N/A.
SOC PACK: Can be arranged at time of booking.
VIS RESTR'S: Welcome but advisable to check time sheet.
VIS GF - Round: Wd Pt2,000. We Pt3,100. Day: Wd N/A. We N/A.
FACILITIES: 9-hole Course, Bar, Restaurant, Club & Buggy Hire.

Costa Blanca

CASTIELLO GOLF CLUB   MAP 19 A2

Apartado de Correos, 161 Gigón.
5km south of Gigon.
CONTACT: Secretary. Tel: +34 985 366313.
COURSE: 4,814m, PAR 68, SSS 67. Parkland course.
SOC RESTR'S: Welcome but group booking essential.
SOC GF - Round: Wd Pt5,300. We Pt5,300. Day: Wd N/A. We N/A.
SOC PACK: On application.
VIS RESTR'S: Welcome, tee times for Guests available everyday.
VIS GF - Round: Wd Pt5,300. We Pt5,300. Day: Wd N/A. We N/A.
FACILITIES: Bar, Restaurant, Club & Buggy Hire.

COSTA BLANCA

CLUB DE CAMPO DEL MEDITERRANEO MAP 19 A1

Urbanizacion La Coma, Borriol, Castellón.
8km north-west of Castellón on the A238.

CONTACT: Reservations. Tel: + 34 964 321227.
COURSE: 6,239m, PAR 72, SSS 68. Undulating course.
SOC RESTR'S: Welcome with prior arrangement.
SOC GF - Round: Wd Pt4,600. **We** N/A. **Day:** Wd N/A. **We** N/A.
SOC PACK: Seasonal alterations to GF.
VIS RESTR'S: Welcome with prior arrangement.
VIS GF - Round: Wd Pt4,600. **We** Pt6,400. **Day:** Wd N/A. **We** N/A.
FACILITIES: Bar & Restaurant.

ESCORPION GOLF CLUB MAP 19 B1

PO 1, 46117 Betera Valencia.
Off road between Valencia & Liria. 20km north of Valencia.

CONTACT: Secretary. Tel: +34 96 1601211.
COURSE: 6,239m, PAR 72, SSS 73. Parkland/forest course.
SOC RESTR'S: Please book in advance.
SOC GF - Round: Wd Pt4,200. **We** N/A. **Day:** Wd N/A. **We** N/A.
SOC PACK: Various packages available.
VIS RESTR'S: Welcome but check availability.
VIS GF - Round: Wd Pt4,200. **We** Pt4,200. **Day:** Wd N/A. **We** N/A.
FACILITIES: Bar, Restaurant, Club & Buggy Hire.

CLUB DE GOLF VILLAMARTIN MAP 19 B2

Apartado 35, Torrevieja Alicante.
10km south of Torrevieja.

CONTACT: J Buendia, Secretary. Tel: +34 6 6765160.
COURSE: 6,132m, PAR 72, SSS 72. Challenging parkland course.
SOC RESTR'S: No restrictions but booking is advisable.
SOC GF - Round: Wd N/A. **We** N/A. **Day:** Wd Pt4,300. **We** Pt8,400.
SOC PACK: To be negotiated with the Club Secretary.
VIS RESTR'S: No restrictions but booking is advisable.
VIS GF - Round: Wd N/A. **We** N/A. **Day:** Wd Pt4,300. **We** Pt8,400.
FACILITIES: Swimming Pool, Tennis, Clubhouse & Restaurant.

LA MANGA CLUB (NORTH) MAP 19 B2

Los Belones, Cartagena.
30km from Cartagena, 75km from Murcia.

CONTACT: Secretary. Tel: +34 968 564511.
COURSE: 5,884m, PAR 70, SSS 71. Parkland/plainland course.
SOC RESTR'S: Please book in advance.
SOC GF - Round: Wd N/A. **We** N/A. **Day:** Wd Pt5,500. **We** N/A.
SOC PACK: Total package including accommodation.
VIS RESTR'S: Welcome but residents have priority.
VIS GF - Round: Wd N/A. **We** N/A. **Day:** Wd Pt5,500. **We** Pt5,500.
FACILITIES: Bar, Restaurant, Club & Buggy Hire.

EL BOSQUE GOLF CLUB MAP 19 B2

Crta Godelleta, 46370 Chiva-Valencia.
Near Chiva, 24km west of Valencia, off Madrid road.

CONTACT: A Pinto, Professional. Tel: +34 96 180 41 42.
COURSE: 6,384m, PAR 72, SSS 74. Parkland with water.
SOC RESTR'S: Prior booking necessary.
SOC GF - Round: Wd Pt5,000. **We** N/A. **Day:** Wd N/A. **We** N/A.
SOC PACK: On application.
VIS RESTR'S: Welcome.
VIS GF - Round: Wd Pt5,000. **We** Pt5,000. **Day:** Wd N/A. **We** N/A.
FACILITIES: Swimming Pool, Tennis, Bar & Restaurant.

LA MANGA CLUB (SOUTH) MAP 19 B2

Los Belones, Cartagena.
30km from Cartagena, 75km from Murcia.

CONTACT: Secretary. Tel: +34 968 564511.
COURSE: 6,268m, PAR 71, SSS 71. Parkland/plainland course.
SOC RESTR'S: Please book in advance.
SOC GF - Round: Wd N/A. **We** N/A. **Day:** Wd Pt5,500. **We** Pt5,500.
SOC PACK: Total package including accommodation.
VIS RESTR'S: Welcome but residents have priority.
VIS GF - Round: Wd N/A. **We** N/A. **Day:** Wd Pt5,500. **We** Pt5,500.
FACILITIES: Bar, Restaurant, Club & Buggy Hire.

EL SALER GOLF CLUB MAP 19 B1

Parador Nacional Luis Vives, 46012 El Saler Valencia.
18km south of Valencia.

CONTACT: Secretary. Tel: +34 96 1611186.
COURSE: 6,485m, PAR 72, SSS 75. Links. (Ex Spanish Open).
SOC RESTR'S: Advanced booking required.
SOC GF - Round: Wd Pt4,700. **We** N/A. **Day:** Wd N/A. **We** N/A.
SOC PACK: On application.
VIS RESTR'S: Welcome Weekdays.
VIS GF - Round: Wd Pt4,700. **We** N/A. **Day:** Wd N/A. **We** N/A.
FACILITIES: Bar, Restaurant, Club & Buggy Hire.

LAS RAMBLAS GOLF CLUB MAP 19 B2

Apartado 35, Alicante.
On the Alicante/Cartagena road, 50 minutes.

CONTACT: J-M Buendia, Secretary. Tel: +34 6 6765160.
COURSE: 5,900m, PAR 72, SSS 72. Forest course.
SOC RESTR'S: No restrictions but booking is advisable.
SOC GF - Round: Wd N/A. **We** N/A. **Day:** Wd Pt4,300. **We** Pt8,400.
SOC PACK: To be negotiated with club secretary.
VIS RESTR'S: No restrictions but booking is advisable.
VIS GF - Round: Wd N/A. **We** N/A. **Day:** Wd Pt4,300. **We** Pt8,400.
FACILITIES: Tennis, Clubhouse Restaurant & Horse Riding.

SPAIN

OLIVA NOVA GOLF CLUB   MAP 19 B1

Marques de Campo 50. 03700 Denia (Alicante).
Junction 61 of A-7, 85km north-east of Alicante along coast.

CONTACT: Secretary. Tel: +34 96 5780650.
COURSE: 6,445m, PAR 72, SSS 71. Parkland course.
SOC RESTR'S: Welcome.
SOC GF - Round: Wd Pt4,300. We Pt5,800. Day: Wd N/A. We N/A.
SOC PACK: No set package.
VIS RESTR'S: Welcome.
VIS GF - Round: Wd Pt4,300. We Pt5,800. Day: Wd N/A. We N/A.
FACILITIES: Bar, Restaurant, Club & Buggy Hire.

QUESADA GOLF CLUB   MAP 19 B2

Avda de las Naciones 168. 03170 Rojales Alicante.
36km south of Alicante near Guardamar.

CONTACT: Secretary. Tel: +34 96 5722179.
COURSE: 6,050m, PAR 72, SSS 72. Parkland course.
SOC RESTR'S: Please book in advance.
SOC GF - Round: Wd Pt4,700. We Pt4,700. Day: Wd N/A. We N/A.
SOC PACK: On application.
VIS RESTR'S: Always welcome.
VIS GF - Round: Wd Pt4,700. We Pt4,700. Day: Wd N/A. We N/A.
FACILITIES: Bar, Restaurant, Club & Buggy Hire.

Costa Brava

CLUB DE GOLF COSTA BRAVA   MAP 19 A1

La Masia, Santa Cristina d'Aro, Girona.
35km south-east of Girona, 6km inland from Plala d'Aro.

CONTACT: A Morros, Manager. Tel: +34 972 837150.
COURSE: 5,445m, PAR 70, SSS 70. Parkland forest course.
SOC RESTR'S: Welcome but July - Aug - Weekends on request.
SOC GF - Round: Wd Pt6,000. We Pt7,000. Day: Wd N/A. We N/A.
SOC PACK: Seasonal Variation to Green Fees.
VIS RESTR'S: Welcome.
VIS GF - Round: Wd Pt6,000. We Pt7,000. Day: Wd N/A. We N/A.
FACILITIES: Special prices with Hotel Members in Association.

CLUB DE GOLF GIRONA   MAP 19 A1

Travessia del Carril 2, Girona.
Gerona is 90km north-east of Barcelona on the A7/E15.

CONTACT: M Ramio, Director. Tel: +34 72 222262.
COURSE: 6,230m, PAR 72, SSS 72. Parkland course.
SOC RESTR'S: Please book through Mr. Ramio.
SOC GF - Round: Wd N/A. We N/A. Day: Wd Pt6,000. We Pt8,000.
SOC PACK: Weekly Green Fee Pt21,000.
VIS RESTR'S: Welcome except Competition days. Please phone.
VIS GF - Round: Wd N/A. We N/A. Wd Pt6,000. We Pt8,000.
FACILITIES: Juniors & children have a 50% reduction.

CLUB GOLF DE PALS   MAP 19 A1

Urb Arenales de Mar, Ctra de la Platja de Pals (Girona).
35km east of Girona.

CONTACT: J. Gispert, Director. Tel: +34 972 636006.
COURSE: 6,222m, PAR 73, SSS 72. Parkland course.
SOC RESTR'S: Limited to 18-holes per day.
SOC GF - Round: Wd Pt5,500. We Pt8,500. Day: Wd N/A. We N/A.
SOC PACK: Limited to 18-holes per day. Seasonal Variation to GF.
VIS RESTR'S: Welcome except Competition Days.
VIS GF - Round: Wd N/A. We N/A. Day: Wd Pt5,500. We Pt8,500.
FACILITIES: Driving Range, Trolleys & Professional available.

GOLF OSONA MONTANYAVA   MAP 19 A1

Masia l'Estanyol, 08553 El Brull.
34km north-east of Barcelona.

CONTACT: J Roqueñi, Professional. Tel: +34 93 8840170.
COURSE: 6,505m, PAR 72, SSS 72. Parkland course.
SOC RESTR'S: Please book in advnce.
SOC GF - Round: Wd Pt4,000. We N/A. Day: Wd N/A. We N/A.
SOC PACK: Group packages available.
VIS RESTR'S: Welcome. Seasonal alteration to GF.
VIS GF - Round: Wd Pt 4,000. We N/A. Day: Wd N/A. We N/A.
FACILITIES: Practice Area, Tennis, Bar & Restaurant.

MAS NOU GOLF CLUB   MAP 19 A1

Urbanizacion Mas Nou, 17250 Playa d'Aro, Costa Brava, Girona.
35km south-east of Girona.

CONTACT: W Tops, President. Tel: +34 972 826118.
COURSE: 6,218m, PAR 72, SSS 72. American course with water.
SOC RESTR'S: Max. H'cap 27 Men, 35 Ladies. Min. 12 players.
SOC GF: Wd Pt4,000. We Pt6,000. Day: Wd N/A. We N/A.
SOC PACK: Special package arrangement with all local hotels.
VIS RESTR'S: Only with advance booking.
VIS GF - Round: Wd Pt4,400. We Pt6,500. Day: Wd N/A. We N/A.
FACILITIES: 9-hole Course, Bar, Restaurant, Club & Buggy Hire.

Costa del Sol - Andalusia

COSTA DEL SOL - ANDALUSIA

REAL CLUB DE GOLF EL PRAT   MAP 19 A1

Aptdo 10, 08080 El Prat.
8km south of Barcelona.

CONTACT: P Marin, Professional. Tel: +34 93 3790278.
COURSE: 6,046m, PAR 72, SSS 72. Pine Forest.
SOC RESTR'S: Please book in advnce.
SOC GF - Round: Wd Pt7,000. We N/A. Day: Wd N/A. We N/A.
SOC PACK: Various packages available.
VIS RESTR'S: Welcome. Seasonal alteration to GF.
VIS GF - Round: Wd Pt 7,000. We N/A. Day: Wd N/A. We N/A.
FACILITIES: 9-hole course, Practoce Area, Bar & Restaurant.

ATALAYA PARK   MAP 19 B3

Crta Benahavis Km 7, Estepona- Málaga.
Between Marbella & Estepona on N340.

CONTACT: D Pascual. Tel: + 34 952 781894.
COURSE: 6,212m, PAR 72, SSS 73. Parkland course.
SOC RESTR'S: Please book in advance.
SOC GF - Round: Wd Pt5,300. We N/A. Day: Wd N/A. We N/A.
SOC PACK: Hotel guests 30% discount.
VIS RESTR'S: Please call to check availability.
VIS GF - Round: Wd Pt5,300. We Pt7,000. Day: Wd N/A. We N/A.
FACILITIES: Bar, Restaurant, Club & Buggy Hire.

CLUB PINEDA DE SEVILLA   MAP 19 B3

P.O. 1. 049, 41080 Sevilla.
3km west of Sevilla.

CONTACT: Secretary. Tel: +34 96 5780650.
COURSE: 6,445m, PAR 72, SSS 72. 9-hole parkland course.
SOC RESTR'S: Welcome with prior agreement.
SOC GF - Round: Wd Pt5,000. We Pt6,900. Day: Wd N/A. We N/A.
SOC PACK: Weekly Green Fee available.
VIS RESTR'S: Some time restrictions. Phone call advisable.
VIS GF - Round: Wd Pt5,000. We Pt6,900. Day: Wd N/A. We N/A.
FACILITIES: Bar, Restaurant, Club & Buggy Hire.

ALOHA GOLF   MAP 19 B3

29660 Nueva Andalucia Marbella (Málaga).
8km south of Marbella.

CONTACT: D Garcia. Tel: +34 952 813750.
COURSE: 8,266m, PAR 72, SSS 74. Parkland course.
SOC RESTR'S: Advance booking is essential.
SOC GF - Round: Wd Pt6,400. We N/A. Day: Wd N/A. We N/A.
SOC PACK: No particular package.
VIS RESTR'S: Welcome weekdays only. Please book.
VIS GF - Round: Wd Pt6,400. We N/A. Day: Wd N/A. We N/A.
FACILITIES: 9-hole Course, Bar, Restaurant, Club & Buggy Hire.

CORTIJO GRANDE   MAP 19 B2

PO box 2, Cortijo Grande, 04630 Turre.
20km west of Turre.

CONTACT: Secretary Tel: +34 951 479164.
COURSE: 6,024m, PAR 72, SSS 71. 9-hole parkland course.
SOC RESTR'S: Societies/groups by prior bookings only.
SOC GF - Round: Wd Pt4,650. We N/A. Day: Wd N/A. We N/A.
SOC PACK: Details available on various packages.
VIS RESTR'S: Fully welcome.
VIS GF - Round: Wd Pt4,650. We Pt4,650. Day: Wd N/A. We N/A.
FACILITIES: Bar, Restaurant, Club & Buggy Hire.

AÑORETA GOLF CLUB   MAP 19 A2

29730 Rincón de la Victoria, Málaga.
11km east of Málaga off the CN340.

CONTACT: Rosa Altamirano, Manager. Tel: +34 952 404000.
COURSE: 5,976m, PAR 72, SSS 71. Parkland with water hazards.
SOC RESTR'S: Welcome with prior arrangement.
SOC GF - Round: Wd Pt4,400. We N/A. Day: Wd N/A. We N/A.
SOC PACK: Please discuss when booking.
VIS RESTR'S: Welcome except Weekends and Comp days.
VIS GF - Round: Wd Pt4,400. We N/A. Day: Wd N/A. We N/A.
FACILITIES: Swimming Pool, Tennis, Bar & Restaurant.

GOLF ALMERIMAR   MAP 19 B2

Urb Almerimar, 04700 El Ejido, Almería.
35km west of Almería.

CONTACT: S Kawaguchi. Tel: +34 951 480234.
COURSE: 6,111m, PAR 72, SSS 72. Undulating course.
SOC RESTR'S: Welcome but booking is mandatory.
SOC GF - Round: Wd N/A. We N/A. Day: Wd Pt6,000. We Pt6,000.
SOC PACK: Weekly Green Fee Pt30,000.
VIS RESTR'S: Welcome. Weekly Green Fee Pt30,400.
VIS GF - Round: Wd N/A. We N/A. Day: Wd Pt6,000. We Pt6,000.
FACILITIES: Discounts for clients of the hotel.

SPAIN

CLUB TORREQUEBRADA MAP 19 B3

Apdo 67, 29630 Benalmadena-Costa.
20km south-west of Málaga on the main coast road.

CONTACT: F Luengo, Secretary. Tel: +34 52 442742.
COURSE: 5,860m, PAR 72, SSS 72. Clifftop parkland course.
SOC RESTR'S: H'cap Cert required, 28 Men, 36 Ladies.
SOC GF - Round: Wd N/A. **We** N/A. **Day:** Wd Pt7,200. **Week** N/A.
SOC PACK: Tailored to requirements. Weekly GF Pt34,000.
VIS RESTR'S: H'cap Cert required. Seasonal variations to GF.
VIS GF - Round: Wd N/A. **We** N/A. **Day:** Wd Pt7,200. **Week** Pt31,500.
FACILITIES: Elec Car, Trolley & Club Hire, Tennis, Squash, & Sauna.

GUADALHORCE CLUB DE GOLF MAP 19 A3

Crtra de Cártama, Km7, Apartado 48, 29590 Campanillas, Málaga.
8km east of Málaga off the CN344.

CONTACT: Caddymaster Tel: +34 952 243682.
COURSE: 6,178m, PAR 72, SSS 72. Championship course.
SOC RESTR'S: Welcome Weekdays between 9 & 12.
SOC GF - Round: Wd Pt6,000. **We** N/A. **Day:** Wd N/A. **We** N/A.
SOC PACK: Call club for details.
VIS RESTR'S: Welcome Weekdays.
VIS GF - Round: Wd Pt6,000. **We** N/A. **Day:** Wd N/A. **We** N/A.
FACILITIES: 9-hole Course, Bar & Restaurant, Changing Rooms.

GUADALMINA CLUB DE GOLF MAP 19 B3

Alta San Pedro de Alcántara, 29678 Málaga.
60km south-west of Málaga off the CN 340.

CONTACT: L Toran Juquera, Manager. Tel: +34 952 883375.
COURSE: 6,065m, PAR 72 SSS 71. Undulating course.
SOC RESTR'S: Welcome with prior reservation.
SOC GF - Round: Wd Pt4,500. **We** N/A. **Day:** Wd N/A. **We** N/A.
SOC PACK: On application.
VIS RESTR'S: Welcome.
VIS GF - Round: Wd Pt4,500. **We** N/A. **Day:** Wd N/A. **We** N/A.
FACILITIES: 2nd 18 Holes, 9-hole Par 3, Sauna & Pool, Restaurant.

LAS BRISAS GOLF CLUB MAP 19 B3

Apdo 147, 29660 Nueva Andalucía, (Málaga).
8km south of Marbella, near Puerto Banus.

CONTACT: S de Miguel, Professional. Tel: +34 952 81 08 75.
COURSE: 6,094m, PAR 73, SSS 72. Undulating Forest.
SOC RESTR'S: Handicap Certificate required.
SOC GF - Round: Wd Pt9,000. **We** N/A. **Day:** Wd N/A. **We** N/A.
SOC PACK: On application.
VIS RESTR'S: Handicap Certificate and booking required.
VIS GF - Round: Wd Pt9,000. **We** N/A. **Day:** Wd N/A. **We** N/A.
FACILITIES: Swimming Pool, Tennis, Bar & Restaurant.

LA QUINTA GOLF & CC MAP 19 B3

Crta de Ronda, Benahavis, Marbella, (Málaga).
5km north of San Pedro de Alcántara.

CONTACT: V Garcia de la Cruz, Director. Tel: +34 952 783462.
COURSE: 5,830m, PAR 71, SSS 71. Parkland course.
SOC RESTR'S: Welcome.
SOC GF - Round: Wd Pt6,200. **We** N/A. **Day:** Wd N/A. **We** N/A.
SOC PACK: Available on request.
VIS RESTR'S: Welcome. Handicap Certificate required.
VIS GF - Round: Wd Pt6,200. **We** N/A. **Day:** Wd N/A. **We** N/A.
FACILITIES: 9-hole Course, Pool, Pro-shop, Bar & Restaurant.

LOS NARANJOS GOLF CLUB MAP 19 B3

Apdo 64, 29660 Nueva Andalucía, Marbella.
7km west of Marbella follow signs in Puerto Banus.

CONTACT: J Bosch, Secretary. Tel: +34 952 815206.
COURSE: 6,438m, PAR 72, SSS 72. Undulating parkland/forest.
SOC RESTR'S: By arrangement only.
SOC GF - Round: Wd N/A. **We** N/A. **Day:** Wd Pt7,500. **We** Pt7,500.
SOC PACK: By agreement.
VIS RESTR'S: Members hour 11 to 12.
VIS GF - Round: Wd N/A. **We** N/A. **Day:** Wd Pt7,500. **We** Pt7,500.
FACILITIES: Pro-shop, Pool, Equipment Rental & Restaurant.

MIJAS GOLF CLUB (LOS LAGOS) MAP 19 A3

Ctra Vieja de Coin 3, Apartado 145, Fuengirola, Málaga.
26km west of Malaga in Coin on the CN 344.

CONTACT: J Guisado Sanches, Secretary. Tel: +34 952 476843.
COURSE: 6,445m, PAR 71, SSS 73. Open meadowland course.
SOC RESTR'S: 12 or more players.
SOC GF-Round: Wd Pt5,000. **We** Pt5,000. **Day:** Wd Pt6,000. **We** Pt6,000.
SOC PACK: Call club for details.
VIS RESTR'S: None.
VIS GF-Round: Wd Pt6,000. **We** Pt6,000. **Day:** Wd Pt7,400. **We** Pt7,400.
FACILITIES: Shop, Driving Range, Putting Green, Bar & Restaurant.

MIRAFLORES GOLF CLUB MAP 19 A3

Urb Riviera del Sol, 29647 Mijas-Costa, Málaga.
3km north of Fuengirola.

CONTACT: K Hewitt, Golf Director. Tel: +34 952 837353.
COURSE: 5,775m, PAR 72, SSS 71. Parkland course.
SOC RESTR'S: Welcome, Reduction for groups.
SOC GF - Round: Wd Pt4,800. **We** N/A. **Day:** Wd N/A. **We** N/A.
SOC PACK: Reduction for groups.
VIS RESTR'S: Welcome weekdays.
VIS GF - Round: Wd Pt4,800. **We** N/A. **Day:** Wd N/A. **We** N/A.
FACILITIES: Bar & Restaurant.

Costa Dorada

NOVO SANCTI PETRI MAP 19 B3

Playa de la Barrosa, 11130 Chiclana de la Frontera, Cádiz.
20km south of Cádiz Town on the CN 340.

CONTACT: M Lafuente, Manager. Tel: +34 956 494005
COURSE: 5,466m, PAR 72, SSS 74. Undulating course.
SOC RESTR'S: Welcome.
SOC GF - Round: Wd Pt6,000. **We** Pt7,300. **Day:** Wd N/A. **We** N/A.
SOC PACK: On application.
VIS RESTR'S: Welcome.
VIS GF - Round: Wd Pt6,000. **We** Pt7,300. **Day:** Wd N/A. **We** N/A.
FACILITIES: 27-hole Complex, Hire of Carts, Electric Cars & Clubs.

SAN ROQUE GOLF CLUB MAP 19 B3

PO 127. 11360 San Roque (Cádiz).
On the Cádiz-Málaga road 3km west of Sotogrande.

CONTACT: Secretary. Tel: +34 956 610649.
COURSE: 6,440m, PAR 72, SSS 74. Parkland course.
SOC RESTR'S: Welcome Weekdays with prior arrangement.
SOC GF - Round: Wd Pt7,000. **We** N/A. **Day:** Wd N/A. **We** N/A.
SOC PACK: Packages available on booking.
VIS RESTR'S: Welcome. Seasonal alterations to GF.
VIS GF - Round: Wd Pt7,000. **We** Pt7,000. **Day:** Wd N/A. **We** N/A.
FACILITIES: Bar, Restaurant, Club & Buggy Hire.

SOTOGRANDE GOLF CLUB MAP 19 B3

Paseo del Parque, PO 14, Sotogrande (Cádiz).
Near Guadiaro on the Cádiz-Málaga road.

CONTACT: Secretary. Tel: +34 956 792050.
COURSE: 6,298m, PAR 72, SSS 74. Parkland course.
SOC RESTR'S: Welcome please book in advance.
SOC GF - Round: Wd Pt8,000. **We** Pt8,000. **Day:** Wd N/A. **We** N/A.
SOC PACK: Many packages to suit most requirements.
VIS RESTR'S: Welcome but walk-on times are difficult.
VIS GF - Round: Wd Pt8,400. **We** Pt8,400. **Day:** Wd N/A. **We** N/A.
FACILITIES: 9-hole Course, Bar, Restaurant, Club & Buggy Hire.

VALDERRAMA GOLF CLUB MAP 19 B3

Avenida Los Cortijos, 11310 Sotogrande, Cádiz.
35km south-west of Málaga turn off CN 340 into Sotogrande.

CONTACT: D Aitken, Manager. Tel: +34 56 795775.
COURSE: 6,419m, PAR 72, SSS 71. Parkland course.
SOC RESTR'S: Maximum 36 players.
SOC GF - Round: Wd N/A. **We** N/A. **Day:** Wd Pt8,750. **We** Pt8,750.
SOC PACK: On application.
VIS RESTR'S: Tee off times available between 11. 30 / 13. 30.
VIS GF - Round: Wd N/A. **We** N/A. **Day:** Wd Pt10,000. **We** Pt10,000.
FACILITIES: 9-hole Course, Bar & Restaurant.

CLUB DE GOLF SANT CUGAT MAP 19 A1

Villa Sin, 08190 Sant Cugat del Valles.
20km north-west of Barcelona in Sant Cugat del Valle.

CONTACT: Secretary. Tel: +34 93 6743908.
COURSE: 5,290m, PAR 70, SSS 68. Parkland course.
SOC RESTR'S: Welcome with prior agreement.
SOC GF - Round: Wd N/A. **We** N/A. **Day:** Wd Pt5,800. **We** Pt8,000.
SOC PACK: None.
VIS RESTR'S: Welcome with reservation.
VIS GF - Round: Wd N/A. **We** N/A. **Day:** Wd Pt5,800. **We** Pt8,000.
FACILITIES: Bar, Restaurant & Clubhouse.

CLUB DE GOLF TERRAMAR MAP 19 A1

Sector Miraplex, 08870 Sitges.
35km south-west of Barcelona along the coast on the N246.

CONTACT: J Morando Grav. Tel: +34 93 8940580.
COURSE: 5,840m, PAR 72, SSS 70. Undulating course.
SOC RESTR'S: Please book through Mr. Morando.
SOC GF - Round: Wd N/A. **We** N/A. **Day:** Wd Pt4,500. **We** Pt7,000.
SOC PACK: On application.
VIS RESTR'S: Phone prior to play.
VIS GF - Round: Wd N/A. **We** N/A. **Day:** Wd Pt4,500. **We** Pt7,000.
FACILITIES: Bar & Restaurant.

COSTA DORADA GOLF CLUB MAP 19 A1

Apartado 600, Tarragona.
90km south-west of Barcelona off the CN 340 Tarragona road.

CONTACT: Secretary. Tel: +34 977 653361.
COURSE: 5,944m, PAR 72, SSS 73. 9-hole parkland course.
SOC RESTR'S: Welcome with advance booking.
SOC GF - Round: Wd Pt4,800. **We** N/A. **Day:** Wd N/A. **We** N/A.
SOC PACK: On application.
VIS RESTR'S: Welcome. Some restrictions please check.
VIS GF - Round: Wd Pt4,800. **We** Pt6,300. **Day:** Wd N/A. **We** N/A.
FACILITIES: Bar, Restaurant, Club & Buggy Hire.

SPAIN

REUS AIGUESVERDS CLUB   MAP 19 A1

Carretera de Cambrils, Mas Guardià 8, 43206 Reus.
85km south-west of Barcelona off the A7/E15.

CONTACT: L Barrionuevo, Director. Tel: +34 977 752725.
COURSE: 6,314m, PAR 72, SSS 72. American style with water.
SOC RESTR'S: Please book in advance.
SOC GF - Round: Wd Pt5,000. **We** N/A. **Day:** Wd N/A. **We** N/A.
SOC PACK: On application.
VIS RESTR'S: Phone prior to play.
VIS GF - Round: Wd Pt5,000. **We** Pt6,000. **Day:** Wd N/A. **We** N/A.
FACILITIES: Pro-shop, Golf School, Club Rental, Bar & Restaurant.

PEDREÑA GOLF CLUB   MAP 19 A2

PO 233, Santander.
24km from Santander, Ferry service to island.

CONTACT: Secretary. Tel: +34 942 500001.
COURSE: 5,721m, PAR 70, SSS 70. Parkland course.
SOC RESTR'S: Welcome with advanced booking.
SOC GF - Round: Wd Pt5,000. **We** N/A. **Day:** Wd N/A. **We** N/A.
SOC PACK: On application.
VIS RESTR'S: Welcome.
VIS GF - Round: Wd Pt5,000. **We** Pt9,000. **Day:** Wd N/A. **We** N/A.
FACILITIES: 9-hole Course, Bar, Restaurant, Club & Buggy Hire.

North-West

Balearic Islands

DE LA CORUÑA GOLF CLUB   MAP 19 A3

PO 737 La Coruna.
In Arteijo, 7km from La Coruna.

CONTACT: Secretary. Tel: +34 981 2852 00.
COURSE: 6,037m, PAR 72, SSS 72. Parkland course.
SOC RESTR'S: Welcome with one months notice minimum.
SOC GF - Round: Wd Pt4,850. **We** N/A. **Day:** Wd N/A. **We** N/A.
SOC PACK: Golf, Lunch & Presentation Dinner available.
VIS RESTR'S: Welcome except Club Competitions days.
VIS GF - Round: Wd Pt4,850. **We** Pt6,500. **Day:** Wd N/A. **We** N/A.
FACILITIES: Bar, Restaurant, Club & Buggy Hire.

CANYAMEL GOLF CLUB   MAP 19 A1

Canyamel, 07580 Capdepera (Mallorca).
60km from Palma on the Cuevas de Artá road.

CONTACT: D Moll, Secretary. Tel: +34 971 56 44 57.
COURSE: 5,982 m, PAR 73, SSS 71. Parkland course.
SOC RESTR'S: Welcome with advanced agreement.
SOC GF - Round: Wd Pt5,900. **We** Pt5,900. **Day:** Wd N/A. **We** N/A.
SOC PACK: Available at time of booking.
VIS RESTR'S: Welcome.
VIS GF - Round: Wd Pt5,900. **We** Pt5,900. **Day:** Wd N/A. **We** N/A.
FACILITIES: Bar, Restaurant, Club & Buggy Hire.

DEPORTIVO LA BARGANIZA   MAP 19 A2

Apartado 227, 33080 Oviedo Asturias.
12km north of Oviedo, 14km from Gijon.

CONTACT: D Faes Hernandez. Tel: + 34 985 742468.
COURSE: 5,598m, PAR 70, SSS 70. Parkland course.
SOC RESTR'S: Please book in advance.
SOC GF - Round: Wd Pt4,800. **We** Pt6,400. **Day:** Wd N/A. **We** N/A.
SOC PACK: Package available but not detailed.
VIS RESTR'S: Welcome except Comp days & some Weekends.
VIS GF - Round: Wd Pt4,800. **We** Pt6,400. **Day:** Wd N/A. **We** N/A.
FACILITIES: Bar, Restaurant, Club & Buggy Hire.

CAPDEPERA GOLF CLUB   MAP 19 A1

Apto 6, 07580 Capdepera, Mallorca.
71km east from Palma, between Artá & Capdepera.

CONTACT: Ingrid Lebrero, Secretary. Tel: +34 971 565875.
COURSE: 6,284m, PAR 72, SSS 73. American style with water.
SOC RESTR'S: Welcome. Large Societies by prior arrangement.
SOC GF - Round: Wd Pt5,500. **We** Pt5,500. **Day:** Wd N/A. **We** N/A.
SOC PACK: Weekly Green Fees available.
VIS RESTR'S: Welcome.
VIS GF - Round: Wd Pt5,500. **We** Pt5,500. **Day:** Wd N/A. **We** N/A.
FACILITIES: Driving Range, Trolleys, Electrocarts & Pro-shop.

Canaries

PONIENTE GOLF CLUB   MAP 19 B1

Cala Figuera 07182 Magalluf.
16km west from Palma on the Andraitx road near Figuera.

CONTACT: Secretary. Tel: +34 971 130148.
COURSE: 6,430m, PAR 72, SSS 72. Parkland course.
SOC RESTR'S: Please book in advance.
SOC GF - Round: Wd Pt6,500. **We** N/A. **Day:** Wd N/A. **We** N/A.
SOC PACK: On application.
VIS RESTR'S: Welcome.
VIS GF - Round: Wd Pt6,500. **We** Pt6,500. **Day:** Wd N/A. **We** N/A.
FACILITIES: Bar & Restaurant.

SANTA PONSA GOLF CLUB   MAP 19 B1

Santa Ponsa Calvia 07180 (Mallorca).
18km from Palma on the Andraitx road.

CONTACT: JM Comez, Secretary. Tel: +34 971 690211.
COURSE: 6,520m, PAR 72, SSS 74. Parkland course.
SOC RESTR'S: Booking is essential for groups.
SOC GF - Round: Wd Pt6,500. **We** Pt6,500. **Day:** Wd N/A. **We** N/A.
SOC PACK: Golf & presentation dinner.
VIS RESTR'S: Always welcome. Some walk-on tee times.
VIS GF - Round: Wd Pt6,500. **We** Pt6,500. **Day:** Wd N/A. **We** N/A.
FACILITIES: Bar, Restaurant, Club & Buggy Hire.

SON VIDA GOLF CLUB   MAP 19 A1

Son Vida 07013 Palma de Mallorca.
5km north-west from Palma. Bus service available.

CONTACT: P Haider, Manager. Tel: +34 971 791210.
COURSE: 5,705m, PAR 72, SSS 71. Parkland course.
SOC RESTR'S: Please book in advance.
SOC GF - Round: Wd Pt6,400. **We** Pt6,400. **Day:** Wd N/A. **We** N/A.
SOC PACK: 20% reduction to Guests of Local hotels.
VIS RESTR'S: Welcome. Seasonal variations to Green Fee.
VIS GF - Round: Wd Pt6,400. **We** Pt6,400. **Day:** Wd N/A. **We** N/A.
FACILITIES: Bar, Restaurant, Club & Buggy Hire.

VALL D'OR GOLF CLUB   MAP 19 B1

Apartado 23, 07660 Cala d'Or, Mallorca.
East from Palma for about 60km.

CONTACT: C Padial. Secretary. Tel: +34 971 837001.
COURSE: 5,880 m, PAR 72, SSS 71. Undulating, tree lined course.
SOC RESTR'S: Welcome with written application.
SOC GF - Round: Wd Pt7,000. **We** Pt7,000. **Day:** Wd N/A. **We** N/A.
SOC PACK: On application.
VIS RESTR'S: Welcome but handicap certificate required.
VIS GF - Round: Wd Pt7,000. **We** Pt7,000. **Day:** Wd N/A. **We** N/A.
FACILITIES: Driving Range, Club Hire, Bar & Restaurant.

AMARILLA GOLF & CC   MAP 19 B1

San Miguel de Abona.
4km from the airport.

CONTACT: E O'Connor, Professional. Tel: +34 922 785777.
COURSE: 5,840m, PAR 72, SSS 72. Undulating course.
SOC RESTR'S: Please book in advnce.
SOC GF - Round: Wd P5,000. **We** N/A. **Day:** Wd N/A. **We** N/A.
SOC PACK: Please discuss at time of booking.
VIS RESTR'S: Welcome.
VIS GF - Round: Wd Pt 5,000. **We** N/A. **Day:** Wd N/A. **We** N/A.
FACILITIES: Practoce area, Tennis, Bar & Restaurant.

CAMPO DE GOLF MASPALOMAS   MAP 19 B1

Av de Africa, Maspalomas, 35100 Las Palmas, Gran Canaria.
50km south of Palma on the main coast road.

CONTACT: J Bosch, Manager. Tel: +34 928 762581.
COURSE: 6,037m, PAR 73, SSS 73. Undulating course.
SOC RESTR'S: Welcome.
SOC GF - Round: Wd N/A. **We** N/A. **Day:** Wd Pt6,000. **We** Pt6,000.
SOC PACK: On application.
VIS RESTR'S: Welcome.
VIS GF - Round: Wd N/A. **We** N/A. **Wd** Pt6,000. **We** Pt6,000.
FACILITIES: Driving Range, Pitching Area, Pro-shop & Restaurant.

DEL SUR GOLF CLUB   MAP 19 B1

San Miguel de Abona, 38312 Tenerife.
2.5km from the airport.

CONTACT: Secretary. Tel: +34 922 704512.
COURSE: 5,111m, PAR 71, SSS 71. Parkland course.
SOC RESTR'S: Welcome but no Groups at the Weekend.
SOC GF - Round: Wd N/A. **We** N/A. **Day:** Wd Pt7,000. **We** N/A.
SOC PACK: Several packages available.
VIS RESTR'S: Welcome. Check Weekend availability.
VIS GF - Round: Wd N/A. **We** N/A. **Day:** Wd Pt7,000. **We** Pt7,000.
FACILITIES: 27-hole Complex, Bar & Restaurant.

SPAIN

LAS PALMAS GOLF CLUB MAP 19 B1

PO 183 Las Palmas, 35310 Gran Canaria.
At Bandama, 14km from Las Palmas.

CONTACT: Secretary. Tel: +34 928 351050.
COURSE: 5,683m, PAR 69, SSS 70. Parkland course.
SOC RESTR'S: Please book in advance.
SOC GF - Round: Wd Pt5,300. **We** Pt5,300. **Day: Wd** N/A. **We** N/A.
SOC PACK: No set package.
VIS RESTR'S: Welcome weekdays only.
VIS GF - Round: Wd Pt5,300. **We** Pt5,300. **Day: Wd** N/A. **We** N/A.
FACILITIES: Pitch & Putt, Bar, Restaurant, Club & Buggy Hire.

TENERIFE GOLF CLUB MAP 19 B1

El Peñón, Taloronte, Tenerife
16km from Santa Cruz, 24km from Puerto de la Cruz.

CONTACT: Secretary. Tel: +34 922 636607.
COURSE: 5922m, PAR 71, SSS 71. Parkland course.
SOC RESTR'S: Welcome with advanced booking.
SOC GF - Round: Wd Pt5,900. **We** Pt5,900. **Day: Wd** N/A. **We** N/A.
SOC PACK: On application when booking.
VIS RESTR'S: Welcome weekdays before 1pm.
VIS GF - Round: Wd Pt5,900. **We** Pt5,900. **Day: Wd** N/A. **We** N/A.
FACILITIES: Bar, Restaurant, Club & Buggy Hire.

SWEDEN

IN Falsterbo, opened in 1909, Sweden had one of Europe's classic courses, but for most people both inside and outside the country, Swedish sport meant Bjorn Borg. Of course golfers of the quality of Anders Forsbrand, Jesper Parnevik, Mats Lanner, Per-Ulrik Johansson and Robert Karlsson, as well as Lotte Neumann and Helen Alfredsson), on both the full European Tour and the satellite Challenge Tour, don't simply drop from the sky and if the credit for their emergence is to be taken by anyone, it must be the Swedish Golf Federation.

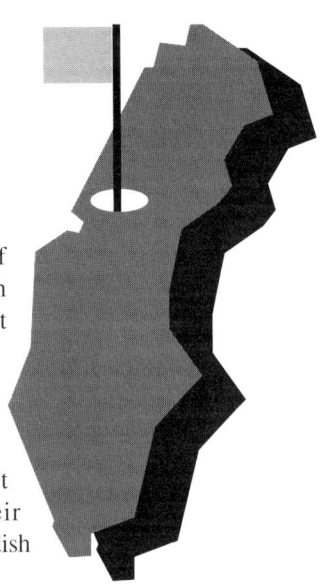

The question why, after years of happy indifference, should so many young Swedes suddenly want to start playing golf, is outside the scope of this Guide, but that desire, once apparent, was nurtured by the Swedish Federation who helped the young hopefuls with money, coaching, travel grants and encouragment and fostered the team spirit that saw Sweden win the Dunhill cup and the World Cup in 1991.

It was an enormous help to the growth of golf in Sweden that much of the infrastructure, in the form of some excellent courses, was already in place. Falsterbo has already been mentioned, alongside it are Flommen and Ljunghusen, while not too far away are Bokskogens and Barseback. All have hosted European Tour events. Drottningholm, just ten miles west of Stockholm, suffers by comparison as a course, but in its own right is good enough; better perhaps is Sven Tumba's Country Club at Ullna; further inland, in the eastern part of the country, Orebro has a fine course - and a little pitch-and-putt track too.

In common with Scandinavia in general, winter can make savage inroads into the game, but that's almost a minor consideration as Sweden's long summer days provide endless golfing opportunities.

Eastern Region

EKERUM GOLF CLUB MAP 13 A3

387 92 Brogholm, Öland.
12km south of Borgholm.

CONTACT: Secretary. Tel: +46 485 80875.
COURSE: 6,658m, PAR 72, SSS 74. Seaside course.
SOC RESTR'S: Best time Mon - Fri. H'cap Cert required.
SOC GF - Round: Wd sk150. **We** sk200. **Day:** Wd N/A. **We** N/A.
SOC PACK: On application.
VIS RESTR'S: Best time Mon - Fri. H'cap Cert required.
VIS GF - Round: Wd sk150. **We** sk200. **Day:** Wd N/A. **We** N/A.
FACILITIES: 9-hole Par 36, Restaurant, Pro-shop & Range.

229

SWEDEN

LAGANS GOLF CLUB   MAP 13 A3

Box 63, 340 14 Lagan.
8km north of Ljungby on the E4 from Motellet Laganalnd.
CONTACT: Secretary. Tel: +46 372 30450.
COURSE: 5,450m, PAR 71, SSS 71. Parkland course.
SOC RESTR'S: Open from the 15th Apr - Sept only.
SOC GF - Round: Wd sk120. We sk150. Day: Wd N/A. We N/A.
SOC PACK: On application.
VIS RESTR'S: Best time Mon - Fri. H'cap Cert required.
VIS GF - Round: Wd sk120. We sk150. Day: Wd N/A. We N/A.
FACILITIES: Restaurant, Pro-shop & Range.

VETLANDA GOLF CLUB   MAP 13 A

Box 249, 574 01 Vetlanda.
2km west of the centre of Vetlanda.
CONTACT: Secretary. Tel: +46 383 18310.
COURSE: 5,764m, PAR 72, SSS 72. Forest/parkland course.
SOC RESTR'S: Open from Apr - Oct only. Best days - Weekday.
SOC GF - Round: Wd sk120. We sk140. Day: Wd N/A. We N/A.
SOC PACK: On application.
VIS RESTR'S: Open from Apr - Oct only.
VIS GF - Round: Wd sk120. We sk140. Day: Wd N/A. We N/A.
FACILITIES: Restaurant, Pro-shop & Range.

NÄSSJÖ GOLF CLUB   MAP 13 A3

Box 5, 571 21 Nässjö.
3km south of Jonkoping.
CONTACT: Secretary. Tel: +46 380 10022.
COURSE: 5,861m, PAR 72, SSS 72. Undulating forest course.
SOC RESTR'S: Open from Apr - Oct only.
SOC GF - Round: Wd sk100. We sk100. Day: Wd N/A. We N/A.
SOC PACK: On application.
VIS RESTR'S: Open from Apr - Oct only.
VIS GF - Round: Wd sk100. We sk100. Day: Wd N/A. We N/A.
FACILITIES: Pro-shop & Range.

Middle Region

TRANÅS GOLF CLUB   MAP 13 A3

N Storgatan 130, 573 00 Tranås.
2km north of Tranås.
CONTACT: S Reese, Professional. Tel: +46 140 11661.
COURSE: 5,830m, PAR 72, SSS 72. Links course.
SOC RESTR'S: Booking necessary.
SOC GF - Round: Wd sk120. We N/A. Day: Wd N/A. We N/A.
SOC PACK: On application.
VIS RESTR'S: Prior booking necessary. Closed Nov-Mar.
VIS GF - Round: Wd sk120. We sk150. Day: Wd N/A. We N/A.
FACILITIES: Practice Area, Bar & Restaurant.

ARVIKA GOLF CLUB   MAP 13 A

Box 197, 671 25 Arvika 1.
10km east of Arvika.
CONTACT: Secretary. Tel: +46 570 54133.
COURSE: 5,764m, PAR 72, SSS 72. 9-hole parkland course.
SOC RESTR'S: Open from Mar - Oct only. Best days - Weekday.
SOC GF - Round: Wd sk130. We sk130. Day: Wd N/A. We N/A.
SOC PACK: On application.
VIS RESTR'S: Open from Mar - Oct only. H'cap Cert required.
VIS GF - Round: Wd sk130. We sk130. Day: Wd N/A. We N/A.
FACILITIES: Restaurant, Pro-shop & Range.

VÄXJÖ GOLF CLUB   MAP 13 A3

Box 227, 351 05 Växjö.
2km north of Växjö.
CONTACT: Secretary. Tel: +46 470 21359.
COURSE: 5,764m, PAR 72, SSS 72. Flat Meadowland course.
SOC RESTR'S: Open from Mar - Oct only. Best days - Weekday.
SOC GF - Round: Wd sk150. We sk180. Day: Wd N/A. We N/A.
SOC PACK: On application.
VIS RESTR'S: Open from Mar - Oct only. Best days - Weekday.
VIS GF - Round: Wd sk150. We sk180. Day: Wd N/A. We N/A.
FACILITIES: Pro-shop & Range.

BILLERUDS GOLF CLUB   MAP 13 A

Box 192, 661 00 Säffle.
15km north of Säffle.
CONTACT: Secretary. Tel: +46 555 91313.
COURSE: 5,764m, PAR 72, SSS 72. Undulating forest course.
SOC RESTR'S: Open from Mar - Oct only. Best days - Weekday.
SOC GF - Round: Wd sk150. We sk150. Day: Wd N/A. We N/A.
SOC PACK: On application.
VIS RESTR'S: Open from Mar - Oct only. H'cap Cert required.
VIS GF - Round: Wd sk150. We sk150. Day: Wd N/A. We N/A.
FACILITIES: Restaurant, Pro-shop & Range.

MIDDLE REGION

HAGGE GOLF CLUB MAP 13 A2

Hagge, 771 00 Ludvika.
6km south of Ludvika.
CONTACT: Secretary. Tel: +46 240 28087.
COURSE: 5,764m, PAR 71, SSS 71. Undulating forest course.
SOC RESTR'S: Open from Mar - Oct only. Best days - Weekday.
SOC GF - Round: Wd sk145. **We** sk145. **Day: Wd** N/A. **We** N/A.
SOC PACK: Weekly Green Fee sk630.
VIS RESTR'S: Open from Mar - Oct only.
VIS GF - Round: Wd sk145. **We** sk145. **Day: Wd** N/A. **We** N/A.
FACILITIES: Restaurant, Pro-shop & Range.

KARLSTAD GOLF CLUB MAP 13 A2

Box 294, 651 07 Karlstad.
10km north-east of Karlstad.
CONTACT: Secretary. Tel: +46 54 36353.
COURSE: 5,764m, PAR 72, SSS 72. Split forest & parkland course.
SOC RESTR'S: Open from Mar - Oct only. Best days - Weekday.
SOC GF - Round: Wd sk170. **We** sk170. **Day: Wd** N/A. **We** N/A.
SOC PACK: On application.
VIS RESTR'S: Open from Mar - Oct only. Max H'cap 36.
VIS GF - Round: Wd sk170. **We** sk170. **Day: Wd** N/A. **We** N/A.
FACILITIES: 9-hole Par 36 Course, Restaurant, Pro-shop & Range.

KILS GOLF CLUB MAP 13 A3

Box 173, 665 00 Kil.
30km north of Säffle.
CONTACT: Secretary. Tel: +46 554 12701.
COURSE: 5,764m, PAR 72, SSS 72. Forest course.
SOC RESTR'S: Open from Mar-Oct only. Best days -Wd before 4.
SOC GF - Round: Wd sk110. **We** sk110. **Day: Wd** N/A. **We** N/A.
SOC PACK: On application.
VIS RESTR'S: Open from Mar - Oct only. Before 4
VIS GF - Round: Wd sk110. **We** sk110. **Day: Wd** N/A. **We** N/A.
FACILITIES: Restaurant, Pro-shop & Range.

LINDE GOLF CLUB MAP 13 A3

Dalkarlshyttan, 711 31 Lindesberg.
5km from Lindesberg.
CONTACT: Secretary. Tel: +46 581 13960.
COURSE: 5,764m, PAR 71, SSS 71. Forest course with water.
SOC RESTR'S: Open from Mar-Oct only. Please book.
SOC GF - Round: Wd sk130. **We** sk160. **Day: Wd** N/A. **We** N/A.
SOC PACK: On application.
VIS RESTR'S: Open from Mar - Oct only. Phone prior to play.
VIS GF - Round: Wd sk130. **We** sk160. **Day: Wd** N/A. **We** N/A.
FACILITIES: Restaurant, Pro-shop & Range.

NORA GOLF CLUB MAP 13 A3

Box 108, 713 23 Nora.
20km north of Karlskoga.
CONTACT: Secretary. Tel: +46 587 11660.
COURSE: 5,832m, PAR 72, SSS 72. Undulating parkland course.
SOC RESTR'S: Open from Mar-Oct only. Best time - Weekday.
SOC GF - Round: Wd sk110. **We** sk130. **Day: Wd** N/A. **We** N/A.
SOC PACK: On application.
VIS RESTR'S: Open from Mar - Oct only. Best time - Weekday.
VIS GF - Round: Wd sk110. **We** sk130. **Day: Wd** N/A. **We** N/A.
FACILITIES: Restaurant, Pro-shop & Range.

ÖREBRO GOLF CLUB MAP 13 A3

Lanna, 710 15 Vintrosa.
18km west of Örebro on Route E18.
CONTACT: M Karlsson, Professional. Tel: +46 19 91065.
COURSE: 5,870m, PAR 71, SSS 72. Undulating course.
SOC RESTR'S: Handicap Certificate required.
SOC GF - Round: Wd sk220. **We** N/A. **Day: Wd** N/A. **We** N/A.
SOC PACK: On application.
VIS RESTR'S: Handicap Certificate required. Closed Nov-Apr.
VIS GF - Round: Wd sk220. **We** N/A. **Day: Wd** N/A. **We** N/A.
FACILITIES: 6-hole Pitch & Putt, Practice Area, Bar & Restaurant.

ROSLAGENS GOLF CLUB MAP 13 A1

Box 110, 761 22 Norrtälje.
10km north of Norrtälje.
CONTACT: Secretary. Tel: +46 176 37194.
COURSE: 5,667m, PAR 71, SSS 71. Forest course.
SOC RESTR'S: Open from Mar-Oct only.
SOC GF - Round: Wd sk160. **We** sk210. **Day: Wd** N/A. **We** N/A.
SOC PACK: On application.
VIS RESTR'S: Open from Mar - Oct only. Max H'cap 36.
VIS GF - Round: Wd sk160. **We** sk210. **Day: Wd** N/A. **We** N/A.
FACILITIES: 9-hole Par 36 Course, Restaurant, Pro-shop & Range.

SUNNE GOLF CLUB MAP 13 A2

Box 108, 686 00 Sunne.
5km south-west of Sunne.
CONTACT: Secretary. Tel: +46 565 14100.
COURSE: 6,234m, PAR 72, SSS 72. Meadowland course.
SOC RESTR'S: Open from Mar-Oct only. Weekdays only.
SOC GF - Round: Wd sk130. **We** sk130. **Day: Wd** N/A. **We** N/A.
SOC PACK: On application.
VIS RESTR'S: Open from Mar - Oct only.
VIS GF - Round: Wd sk130. **We** sk130. **Day: Wd** N/A. **We** N/A.
FACILITIES: Pro-shop & Range.

SWEDEN

UPPSALA GOLF CLUB   MAP 13 A1

Box 12015, 750 12 Uppsala.
10km west of Uppsala.

CONTACT: M Söderberg, Professional. Tel: +46 18 461241.
COURSE: 6,176m, PAR 71, SSS 74. Forest course.
SOC RESTR'S: Please book in advance.
SOC GF - Round: Wd N/A. **We** N/A. **Day:** Wd sk225. **We** N/A.
SOC PACK: On application.
VIS RESTR'S: Welcome.
VIS GF - Round: Wd sk180. **We** sk250. **Day:** Wd N/A. **We** N/A.
FACILITIES: 9-hole Course, Practice Area, Bar & Restaurant.

VÄSTERÅS GOLF CLUB   MAP 13 A3

Bjärby 724 81 Västerås.
2km north of Västerås.

CONTACT: Secretary. Tel: +46 21 357543.
COURSE: 5,588m, PAR 70, SSS 71. Parkland course.
SOC RESTR'S: Open from Mar - Sept only.
SOC GF - Round: Wd sk160. **We** sk160. **Day:** Wd N/A. **We** N/A.
SOC PACK: On application.
VIS RESTR'S: Open from Mar - Sept only.
VIS GF - Round: Wd sk160. **We** sk160. **Day:** Wd N/A. **We** N/A.
FACILITIES: Restaurant, Pro-shop & Range.

Northern Region

HÄRNÖSANDS GOLF CLUB   MAP 13 A2

Box 52, 871 22 Härnösand.
14km north-west of Härnösand.

CONTACT: Secretary. Tel: +46 611 66169.
COURSE: 5,370m, PAR 69, SSS 69. Undulation forest course.
SOC RESTR'S: Open from Mar - Oct only. Best time - Weekday.
SOC GF - Round: Wd N/A. **We** N/A. **Day:** Wd sk170. **We** sk170.
SOC PACK: Weekly Green Fee sk750.
VIS RESTR'S: Open from Mar - Oct only.
VIS GF - Round: Wd N/A. **We** N/A. **Day:** Wd sk170. **We** sk170.
FACILITIES: Restaurant, Pro-shop & Range.

HUDIKSVALLS GOLF CLUB   MAP 13 A2

Tjuvskär Idenor, 824 00 Hudiksvall.
6km south of Hudiksvall.

CONTACT: Secretary. Tel: +46 650 15930.
COURSE: 5,980m, PAR 72, SSS 72. Forest & meadowland course.
SOC RESTR'S: Open from Mar - Oct only. Best time - Weekday.
SOC GF - Round: Wd sk130. **We** sk130. **Day:** Wd N/A. **We** N/A.
SOC PACK: On application.
VIS RESTR'S: Open from Mar - Oct only.
VIS GF - Round: Wd sk130. **We** sk130. **Day:** Wd N/A. **We** N/A.
FACILITIES: Restaurant, Pro-shop & Range.

ÖVIKS GOLF CLUB   MAP 13 B2

Idrottens Hus, 891 32 Örnsköldsvik.
12km north of Örnsköldsvik.

CONTACT: Secretary. Tel: +46 660 62488.
COURSE: 5,842m, PAR 72, SSS 72. Undulating parkland course.
SOC RESTR'S: Open Mar-Oct only. Best time -Tue, Thur & Fri.
SOC GF - Round: Wd sk150. **We** sk150. **Day:** Wd N/A. **We** N/A.
SOC PACK: On application.
VIS RESTR'S: Open from Mar - Oct only.
VIS GF - Round: Wd sk150. **We** sk150. **Day:** Wd N/A. **We** N/A.
FACILITIES: Restaurant, Pro-shop & Range.

SÖDERHAMNS GOLF CLUB   MAP 13 A2

Oxtorget 1C, 826 00 Söderhamn.
8km north-east of Söderhamn.

CONTACT: Secretary. Tel: +46 270 51300.
COURSE: 6,235m, PAR 72, SSS 72. Coastal forest course.
SOC RESTR'S: Open from Mar - Oct only.
SOC GF - Round: Wd sk130. **We** sk130. **Day:** Wd N/A. **We** N/A.
SOC PACK: Weekly Green Fee sk630.
VIS RESTR'S: Open from Mar - Oct only.
VIS GF - Round: Wd sk130. **We** sk150. **Day:** Wd N/A. **We** N/A.
FACILITIES: Restaurant, Pro-shop & Range.

SUNDSVALLS GOLF CLUB   MAP 13 A2

c/o T Bryneholt. Baldersvägen 16, 852 33 Sundsvall.
12km south of Sundsvall.

CONTACT: Secretary. Tel: +46 60 561056.
COURSE: 6,045m, PAR 72, SSS 72. Undulating Parkland course.
SOC RESTR'S: Open from Mar - Sept only. Best time Weekday.
SOC GF - Round: Wd sk170. **We** sk190. **Day:** Wd N/A. **We** N/A.
SOC PACK: Weekly Green Fee available on request.
VIS RESTR'S: Open from Mar - Sept only.
VIS GF - Round: Wd sk170. **We** sk190. **Day:** Wd N/A. **We** N/A.
FACILITIES: Restaurant, Pro-shop & Range.

Southern Region

SOUTHERN REGION

TIMRÅ GOLF CLUB   MAP 13 A2

Box 17, 860 32 Fagervik.
4km from the centre of Sundsvall.

CONTACT: Secretary. Tel: +46 60 570153.
COURSE: 5,686m, PAR 72, SSS 72. Links course.
SOC RESTR'S: Open from Mar - Sept only. Best time Weekday.
SOC GF - Round: Wd sk170. We sk190. Day: Wd N/A. We N/A.
SOC PACK: On application.
VIS RESTR'S: Open from Mar - Sept only.
VIS GF - Round: Wd sk170. We sk190. Day: Wd N/A. We N/A.
FACILITIES: Restaurant, Pro-shop & Range.

ABBEKAS GOLF CLUB   MAP 13 B3

Box 38, 270 11 Abbekas.
1km south of Abbekas.

CONTACT: Secretary. Tel: +46 441 33290.
COURSE: 6,257m, PAR 72, SSS 72. Links course.
SOC RESTR'S: Best time Wd. H'cap Cert required We in Jul-Aug.
SOC GF - Round: Wd sk110. We sk160. Day: Wd N/A. We N/A.
SOC PACK: On application.
VIS RESTR'S: H'cap Cert required at We in Jul -Aug.
VIS GF - Round: Wd sk110. We sk160. Day: Wd N/A. We N/A.
FACILITIES: Restaurant, Pro-shop & Range.

ÄNGELHOLMS GOLF CLUB   MAP 13 A3

Box 1117, 262 22 Ängelholm.
12km east of Ängelholm.

CONTACT: Secretary. Tel: +46 431 30260.
COURSE: 6,257m, PAR 72, SSS 72. Forest/parkland course.
SOC RESTR'S: Best time Wd. H'cap Cert required.
SOC GF - Round: Wd sk110. We sk180. Day: Wd N/A. We N/A.
SOC PACK: On application.
VIS RESTR'S: H'cap Cert required.
VIS GF - Round: Wd sk110. We sk180. Day: Wd N/A. We N/A.
FACILITIES: Restaurant, Pro-shop & Range.

BARSEBÄCK GOLF & CC   MAP 13 B3

Box 274, 240 22 Löddeköpinge.
30km north of Malmö.

CONTACT: Secretary. Tel: +46 46 776230.
COURSE: 6,390m, PAR 72, SSS 72. Seaside/parkland course.
SOC RESTR'S: Best time Wd. Max handicap 36.
SOC GF - Round: Wd N/A. We N/A. Day: Wd sk260. We N/A.
SOC PACK: On application.
VIS RESTR'S: Max handicap 36. Weekdays only.
VIS GF - Round: Wd N/A. We N/A. Day: Wd sk260. We N/A.
FACILITIES: 2nd 18-hole Par 72, Restaurant, Pro-shop & Range.

BOKSKOGEN GOLF CLUB (OLD)   MAP 13 B3

Torups Nygård, 230 40 Bara.
15km south-east of Malmö, off E65.

CONTACT: J Larsson, Professional. Tel: +46 40 481004.
COURSE: 5,992m, PAR 72, SSS 73. Parkland course.
SOC RESTR'S: H'cap Cert required. After 1pm at We.
SOC GF - Round: Wd sk180. We N/A. Day: Wd N/A. We N/A.
SOC PACK: On application.
VIS RESTR'S: H'cap Cert required. After 1pm at We.
VIS GF - Round: Wd sk180. We sk220. Day: Wd N/A. We N/A.
FACILITIES: Bar & Restaurant.

BOKSKOGEN GOLF CLUB (NEW)   MAP 13 B3

Torups Nygård, 230 40 Bara.
15km south-east of Malmö, off E65.

CONTACT: J Larsson, Professional. Tel: 040 481004.
COURSE: 5,499m, PAR 70, SSS 71. Parkland course.
SOC RESTR'S: Handicap Certificate required.
SOC GF - Round: Wd sk150. We N/A. Day: Wd N/A. We N/A.
SOC PACK: On application.
VIS RESTR'S: Handicap Certificate required.
VIS GF - Round: Wd sk150. We sk180. Day: Wd N/A. We N/A.
FACILITIES: Bar & Restaurant.

FALSTERBO GOLF CLUB   MAP 13 B3

Box 71, 230 11 Flasterbo.
30km south of Malmö.

CONTACT: Secretary. Tel: +46 40 475078.
COURSE: 6,197m, PAR 71, SSS 72. Links course.
SOC RESTR'S: Best time Wd. We before 1. Max handicap 36.
SOC GF - Round: Wd sk230. We sk260. Day: Wd N/A. We N/A.
SOC PACK: Seasonal variations to Green Fee.
VIS RESTR'S: We before 1. Max handicap 36.
VIS GF - Round: Wd sk230. We sk260. Day: Wd N/A. We N/A.
FACILITIES: Restaurant, Pro-shop & Range.

SWEDEN

FLOMMENS GOLF CLUB MAP 13 B3

Box 49, 230 11 Flasterbo.
35km south-west of Malmö.

CONTACT: Secretary. Tel: +46 40 475017.
COURSE: 6,266m, PAR 72, SSS 72. Links course.
SOC RESTR'S: Best time Wd. H'cap Cert required from Jun-Aug.
SOC GF - Round: Wd sk180. We sk210. Day: Wd N/A. We N/A.
SOC PACK: Seasonal variations to Green Fee.
VIS RESTR'S: H'cap Cert required from Jun-Aug.
VIS GF - Round: Wd sk180. We sk210. Day: Wd N/A. We N/A.
FACILITIES: Restaurant, Pro-shop & Range.

KVARNBY GOLF CLUB MAP 13 B3

Klagerupsvagen Pl 135, 212 36 Malmö.
2km south-east of Malmö.

CONTACT: Secretary. Tel: +46 40 92339.
COURSE: 6,364m, PAR 72, SSS 73. Undulating parkland course.
SOC RESTR'S: Best time Wd. H'cap Cert required at the We.
SOC GF - Round: Wd sk150. We sk170. Day: Wd N/A. We N/A.
SOC PACK: On Application.
VIS RESTR'S: H'cap Cert required at the We.
VIS GF - Round: Wd sk150. We sk170. Day: Wd N/A. We N/A.
FACILITIES: Restaurant, Pro-shop & Range.

LJUNGHUSENS GOLF CLUB MAP 13 B3

Kanells vag, 236 42 Höllviken.
30km south of Malmö.

CONTACT: Secretary. Tel: +46 30 450384.
COURSE: 6,075m, PAR 72, SSS 73. Seaside/moorland course.
SOC RESTR'S: Max handicap 36 from May to end Sept.
SOC GF - Round: Wd sk210. We sk280. Day: Wd N/A. We N/A.
SOC PACK: Seasonal variations to Green Fee.
VIS RESTR'S: Max handicap 36 from May to end Sept.
VIS GF - Round: Wd sk210. We sk280. Day: Wd N/A. We N/A.
FACILITIES: 9-hole Course, Restaurant, Pro-shop & Range.

MALMÖ GOLF CLUB MAP 13 B3

Box 21068, 200 21 Malmö.
Situated north of Malmö.

CONTACT: Secretary. Tel: +46 40 292535.
COURSE: 6,078m, PAR 71, SSS 71. Parkland course.
SOC RESTR'S: Weekdays before 3.
SOC GF - Round: Wd sk150. We sk180. Day: Wd N/A. We N/A.
SOC PACK: On application.
VIS RESTR'S: Weekdays before 3.
VIS GF - Round: Wd sk150. We sk180. Day: Wd N/A. We N/A.
FACILITIES: Restaurant, Pro-shop & Range.

MÖLLE GOLF CLUB MAP 13 A3

Kullagarden, 260 42 Mölle.
3km north of Mölle.

CONTACT: Secretary. Tel: +46 42 347520.
COURSE: 5,843m, PAR 70, SSS 70. Undulating heathland course.
SOC RESTR'S: Max handicap 36.
SOC GF - Round: Wd sk180. We sk180. Day: Wd N/A. We N/A.
SOC PACK: On application.
VIS RESTR'S: Max handicap 36.
VIS GF - Round: Wd sk180. We sk180. Day: Wd N/A. We N/A.
FACILITIES: Restaurant, Pro-shop & Range.

RYA GOLF CLUB MAP 13 B3

Rya 5500, 255 92 Helsingborg.
10km south of Helsingborg.

CONTACT: P Lester, Professional. Tel: +46 42 220182.
COURSE: 5,599m, PAR 71, SSS 71. Parkland/Links.
SOC RESTR'S: Advisable to book.
SOC GF - Round: Wd sk180. We N/A. Day: Wd N/A. We N/A.
SOC PACK: On application.
VIS RESTR'S: Welcome.
VIS GF - Round: Wd sk180. We sk200. Day: Wd N/A. We N/A.
FACILITIES: Bar & Restaurant.

SVALÖVS GOLF CLUB MAP 13 B3

Mänstrot 1365, 268 00 Svalöv.
6km west of Eslov.

CONTACT: Secretary. Tel: +46 418 624 62.
COURSE: 6,542m, PAR 72, SSS 73. Undulating moorland course.
SOC RESTR'S: Weekdays only.
SOC GF - Round: Wd sk140. We N/A. Day: Wd N/A. We N/A.
SOC PACK: On application.
VIS RESTR'S: Phone for Weekend available.
VIS GF - Round: Wd sk140. We sk170. Day: Wd N/A. We N/A.
FACILITIES: 9-hole Par 31, Restaurant, Pro-shop & Range.

TOMELILLA GOLF CLUB MAP 13 B3

Box 129, 273 23 Tomelilla.
Located in the town of Tomelilla.

CONTACT: Secretary. Tel: +46 417 13420.
COURSE: 6,492m, PAR 73, SSS 73. Parkland course.
SOC RESTR'S: Please book with secretary.
SOC GF - Round: Wd sk160. We sk180. Day: Wd N/A. We N/A.
SOC PACK: On application.
VIS RESTR'S: None.
VIS GF - Round: Wd sk160. We sk180. Day: Wd N/A. We N/A.
FACILITIES: 9-hole Course (sk60), Restaurant, Pro-shop & Range.

STOCKHOLM

TRELLEBORGS GOLF CLUB   MAP 13 B3

Maglarp P1 401, 231 93 Trelleborg.
5km west of Trelleborg.

CONTACT: Secretary. Tel: +46 410 30644.
COURSE: 5,334m, PAR 68, SSS 68. Seaside/links course.
SOC RESTR'S: Max Handicap 36 Jun to Aug.
SOC GF - Round: Wd sk180. We sk190. Day: Wd N/A. We N/A.
SOC PACK: On application.
VIS RESTR'S: Max Handicap 36 Jun to Aug.
VIS GF - Round: Wd sk180. We sk190. Day: Wd N/A. We N/A.
FACILITIES: Restaurant, Pro-shop & Range.

YSTAD GOLF CLUB   MAP 13 B3

Box 162, 271 24 Ystad.
9km north-east of Ystad.

CONTACT: Secretary. Tel: +46 411 50350.
COURSE: 6,383m, PAR 72, SSS 72. Seaside/links course.
SOC RESTR'S: Best time - weekdays.
SOC GF - Round: Wd sk160. We sk160. Day: Wd N/A. We N/A.
SOC PACK: On application.
VIS RESTR'S: None.
VIS GF - Round: Wd sk160. We sk160. Day: Wd N/A. We N/A.
FACILITIES: Restaurant, Pro-shop & Range.

Stockholm

ÅGESTA GOLF CLUB   MAP 13 A1

123 52 Farsta.
Located in Farsta.

CONTACT: Secretary. Tel: +46 8 604541.
COURSE: 6,084m, PAR 72, SSS 72. Forest course.
SOC RESTR'S: Open Mar - Nov only. Best time - Weekdays.
SOC GF - Round: Wd N/A. We N/A. Day: Wd sk260. We sk260.
SOC PACK: On application.
VIS RESTR'S: None. Open Mar - Nov only.
VIS GF - Round: Wd N/A. We N/A. Day: Wd sk260. We sk260.
FACILITIES: 9-hole Course, Restaurant, Pro-shop & Range.

DJURSHOLM GOLF CLUB   MAP 13 A1

Hangbardsvägen 1, 182 63 Djursholm.
3km north of Djursholm.

CONTACT: Secretary. Tel: +46 8 7551477.
COURSE: 6,104m, PAR 71, SSS 73. Parkland course.
SOC RESTR'S: Open Mar-Oct only. Best time - Weekdays.
SOC GF - Round: Wd sk260. We sk310. Day: Wd N/A. We N/A.
SOC PACK: On application.
VIS RESTR'S: None. Open Mar-Oct only.
VIS GF - Round: Wd sk260. We sk310. Day: Wd N/A. We N/A.
FACILITIES: 9-hole Par 34 Course, Restaurant, Pro-shop & Range.

DROTTNINGHOLMS GOLF CLUB   MAP 13 A1

PO Box 183, 170 11 Drottningholm.
12km south of Stockholm.

CONTACT: Secretary. Tel: +46 8 759 0085.
COURSE: 6,294m, PAR 72, SSS 72. Parkland course.
SOC RESTR'S: Open Mar-Oct only. Best time - Tue - Fri.
SOC GF - Round: Wd sk260. We sk260. Day: Wd N/A. We N/A.
SOC PACK: Venue of the 1991 Scandinavian Masters.
VIS RESTR'S: Wd before 3pm, We after 3pm. Max H'cap 36.
VIS GF - Round: Wd sk260. We sk260. Day: Wd N/A. We N/A.
FACILITIES: Restaurant, Pro-shop & Range.

HANINGE GOLF CLUB   MAP 13 A1

Årstra Slott, 136 91 Haninge.
3.5km south-east of Handen.

CONTACT: Secretary. Tel: +46 8 500 32270.
COURSE: 6,362m, PAR 73, SSS 73. Forest/parkland course.
SOC RESTR'S: Open Mar-Oct only. Best time- Mon, Tue & Thur.
SOC GF - Round: Wd sk260. We N/A. Day: Wd N/A. We N/A.
SOC PACK: Seasonal alteration to Green Fee.
VIS RESTR'S: Wd before 1pm, We after 1pm.
VIS GF - Round: Wd sk260. We sk260. Day: Wd N/A. We N/A.
FACILITIES: 9-hole Par 37 Course, Restaurant, Pro-shop & Range.

INGARÖ GOLF CLUB   MAP 13 A1

Fogelvik, 130 35 Ingarö.
5km east of Saltsjobaden.

CONTACT: Secretary. Tel: +46 766 28655.
COURSE: 5,629m, PAR 71, SSS 71. Parkland course.
SOC RESTR'S: Open Mar-Oct only. Best time - Wd before 3.
SOC GF - Round: Wd sk210. We sk240. Day: Wd N/A. We N/A.
SOC PACK: On application.
VIS RESTR'S: None. Open Mar-Oct only.
VIS GF - Round: Wd sk210. We sk240. Day: Wd N/A. We N/A.
FACILITIES: Restaurant, Pro-shop & Range.

SWEDEN

LIDINGÖ GOLF CLUB MAP 13 A1

Box 1035, 181 21 Lidingö.
6km north-east of Stockholm

CONTACT: Secretary. Tel: +46 8 7657911.
COURSE: 5,451m, PAR 71, SSS 71. Parkland/forest course.
SOC RESTR'S: Open Apr-Oct only. Max H'cap 32.
SOC GF - Round: Wd sk250. We sk250. Day: Wd N/A. We N/A.
SOC PACK: On application.
VIS RESTR'S: Open Apr-Oct only. Max H'cap 32.
VIS GF - Round: Wd sk250. We sk250. Day: Wd N/A. We N/A.
FACILITIES: Restaurant, Pro-shop & Range.

ULLNA GOLF CLUB MAP 13 A1

Rosenkälla, 184 92 Åkersberga.
20km north of Stockholm via Route E18.

CONTACT: J Cockin, Professional. Tel: +46 8 510 26075.
COURSE: 5,775m, PAR 72, SSS 73. Forest with water.
SOC RESTR'S: Open Apr-Oct. H'cap Cert required.
SOC GF - Round: Wd sk300. We N/A. Day: Wd N/A. We N/A.
SOC PACK: On application.
VIS RESTR'S: Open Apr-Oct. H'cap Cert required.
VIS GF - Round: Wd sk300. We N/A. Day: Wd N/A. We N/A.
FACILITIES: Practice Area, Bar & Restaurant.

SKEPPTUNA GOLF CLUB MAP 13 A1

Skepptuna 195 93 Marsta.
20km north-east of Marsta.

CONTACT: Secretary. Tel: +46 762 93069.
COURSE: 5,983m, PAR 72, SSS 72. Meadowland/forest course.
SOC RESTR'S: Open Mar-Oct only. Best time - Weekday.
SOC GF - Round: Wd sk160. We sk160. Day: Wd N/A. We N/A.
SOC PACK: On application.
VIS RESTR'S: None. Open Mar - Oct only.
VIS GF - Round: Wd sk160. We sk160. Day: Wd N/A. We N/A.
FACILITIES: Restaurant, Pro-shop & Range.

VIKSJÖ GOLF CLUB MAP 13 A1

Fjällens Gärd, 175 45 Järfälla.
6km south of Järfälla.

CONTACT: Secretary. Tel: +46 8 580 31310.
COURSE: 6,369m, PAR 73, SSS 73. Parkland course.
SOC RESTR'S: Open Mar-15th Oct only. Best before 4 Mon-Thur.
SOC GF - Round: Wd sk230. We sk230. Day: Wd N/A. We N/A.
SOC PACK: On application.
VIS RESTR'S: None. Open Mar- 15th Oct only.
VIS GF - Round: Wd sk230. We sk230. Day: Wd N/A. We N/A.
FACILITIES: Restaurant, Pro-shop & Range.

STOCKHOLMS GOLF CLUB MAP 13 A1

Kevingestrand 20, 182 31 Danderyd.
8km north-west of Danderyd.

CONTACT: Secretary. Tel: +46 8 755 0031.
COURSE: 5,983m, PAR 71, SSS 71. Undulating parkland course.
SOC RESTR'S: Open Mar-Oct only. Best time - Weekday.
SOC GF - Round: Wd sk250. We sk285. Day: Wd N/A. We N/A.
SOC PACK: Start before 11 - Green Fee sk180.
VIS RESTR'S: None. Open Mar - Oct only.
VIS GF - Round: Wd sk250. We sk285. Day: Wd N/A. We N/A.
FACILITIES: Restaurant, Pro-shop & Range.

Western Region

TÄBY GOLF CLUB MAP 13 A1

Skälhamra Gärd, 183 43 Täby.
10km west of Täby.

CONTACT: Secretary. Tel: +46 8 510 23261.
COURSE: 6,273m, PAR 72, SSS 73. Undulating forest course.
SOC RESTR'S: Open Mar-Oct /Nov only.
SOC GF - Round: Wd sk225. We sk275. Day: Wd N/A. We N/A.
SOC PACK: On application.
VIS RESTR'S: Open Mar-Oct /Nov only. H'cap Cert required.
VIS GF - Round: Wd sk225. We sk275. Day: Wd N/A. We N/A.
FACILITIES: Restaurant, Pro-shop & Range.

BÄCKAVATTNETS GOLF CLUB MAP 13 A3

Box 288, 301 07 Halmstad.
10km east of Halmstad.

CONTACT: Secretary. Tel: +46 35 44271.
COURSE: 6,120m, PAR 72, SSS 72. Undulating forest course.
SOC RESTR'S: Open Apr-Oct only. Best time Weekdays.
SOC GF - Round: Wd sk180. We sk180. Day: Wd N/A. We N/A.
SOC PACK: On application.
VIS RESTR'S: Open Apr-Oct only. H'cap Cert required.
VIS GF - Round: Wd sk180. We sk180. Day: Wd N/A. We N/A.
FACILITIES: Restaurant, Pro-shop & Range.

WESTERN REGION

DELSJÖ GOLF CLUB MAP 13 A3

Kallebäck, 412 76 Göteborg.
4km south-east of Göteborg.

CONTACT: Secretary. Tel: +46 31 406959.
COURSE: 5,954m, PAR 71, SSS 71. Parkland course.
SOC RESTR'S: Open 15th Apr- 15th Oct only. Best time Weekdays.
SOC GF - Round: Wd sk210. **We** sk210. **Day: Wd** N/A. **We** N/A.
SOC PACK: On application.
VIS RESTR'S: None. Open 15th Apr- 15th Oct only.
VIS GF - Round: Wd sk210. **We** sk210. **Day: Wd** N/A. **We** N/A.
FACILITIES: Restaurant, Pro-shop & Range.

FORSGÅRDENS GOLF CLUB MAP 13 A3

Gamla Forsvagen 1, 434 47 Kungsbacka.
4km east of Kungsbacka.

CONTACT: Secretary. Tel: +46 300 13649.
COURSE: 6,096m, PAR 72, SSS 72. Open seaside course.
SOC RESTR'S: Best time Weekdays. Max H'cap 36.
SOC GF - Round: Wd sk210. **We** sk210. **Day: Wd** N/A. **We** N/A.
SOC PACK: On application.
VIS RESTR'S: None. Max H'cap 36.
VIS GF - Round: Wd sk210. **We** sk210. **Day: Wd** N/A. **We** N/A.
FACILITIES: Restaurant, Pro-shop & Range.

HALMSTAD GOLF CLUB (ONE) MAP 13 A3

302 73 Halmstad.
Tylosand, 9km west of Halmstad.

CONTACT: Starter. Tel: +46 35 30077/30280.
COURSE: 6,259m, PAR 72, SSS 74. Pine Forest.
SOC RESTR'S: H'cap Cert required. Open Apr-Oct.
SOC GF - Round: Wd N/A. **We** N/A. **Day: Wd** N/A. **We** N/A.
SOC PACK: On application.
VIS RESTR'S: Apr-Oct. H'cap Cert. With Member before 1 at We.
VIS GF - Round: Wd sk250. **We** sk300. **Day: Wd** N/A. **We** N/A.
FACILITIES: Practice Area, Bar & Restaurant.

HALMSTAD GOLF CLUB (TWO) MAP 13 A3

302 73 Halmstad.
Tylosand, 9km west of Halmstad.

CONTACT: Starter. Tel: +46 35 30077/30280.
COURSE: 5,787m, PAR 72, SSS 72. Sandy Forest.
SOC RESTR'S: H'cap Cert required. Open Apr-Oct.
SOC GF - Round: Wd N/A. **We** N/A. **Day: Wd** N/A. **We** N/A.
SOC PACK: On application.
VIS RESTR'S: Apr-Oct. H'cap Cert. With Member before 1 at We.
VIS GF - Round: Wd sk250. **We** sk300. **Day: Wd** N/A. **We** N/A.
FACILITIES: Practice Area, Bar & Restaurant.

KINDS GOLF CLUB MAP 13 A3

512 00 Svenljunga.
10km east of Kinna.

CONTACT: Secretary. Tel: +46 325 27298.
COURSE: 6,143m, PAR 72, SSS 72. Parkland course with water.
SOC RESTR'S: Best time Weekdays.
SOC GF - Round: Wd sk150. **We** sk210. **Day: Wd** N/A. **We** N/A.
SOC PACK: On application.
VIS RESTR'S: None.
VIS GF - Round: Wd sk150. **We** sk210. **Day: Wd** N/A. **We** N/A.
FACILITIES: Restaurant, Pro-shop & Range.

VARBERGS GOLF CLUB (EAST) MAP 13 A3

Torstorp, 430 16 Rolfstorp.
15km east of Varberg.

CONTACT: Secretary. Tel: +46 340 37470.
COURSE: 5,700m, PAR 72, SSS 73. Undulating parkland course.
SOC RESTR'S: Best time Weekdays.
SOC GF - Round: Wd sk160. **We** sk210. **Day: Wd** N/A. **We** N/A.
SOC PACK: Seasonal alterations to Green fee.
VIS RESTR'S: None.
VIS GF - Round: Wd sk160. **We** sk210. **Day: Wd** N/A. **We** N/A.
FACILITIES: Restaurant, Pro-shop & Range.

VARBERGS GOLF CLUB (WEST) MAP 13 A3

Torstorp, 430 16 Rolfstorp.
8km south of Varberg, near E6.

CONTACT: Secretary. Tel: +46 340 43445.
COURSE: 6,640m, PAR 72, SSS 76. Undulating parkland course.
SOC RESTR'S: Best time Weekdays.
SOC GF - Round: Wd sk160. **We** sk210. **Day: Wd** N/A. **We** N/A.
SOC PACK: Seasonal alterations to Green fee.
VIS RESTR'S: None.
VIS GF - Round: Wd sk160. **We** sk210. **Day: Wd** N/A. **We** N/A.
FACILITIES: Restaurant, Pro-shop & Range.

SWITZERLAND

IF a vote were to be taken among Europe's professionals as to which is the most scenic course regularly featured on the Tour, chances are that Crans-sur-Sierre would be among the favourites. The fact that for half the year the course is under several feet of snow, yet nothing short of perfect during the summer months, shows what can be achieved with first-rate greenkeeping and course management techniques and should act as a source of encouragement for other, similarly-affected countries.

Crans is on a plateau 5,000 feet up in the Bernese Alps and even in the height of summer, the mountains ringing the course remain snow-capped. At ground level, it's 6,800 yard-plus length would be challenging, but in the thin Alpine air, the ball seems to fly for ever. Low scores are commonplace, although none as yet lower that the 60 carded by Italy's Baldovino Dassu in the 1971 Swiss Open. A drive at Crans, soaring off towards the 300 yard mark, can do wonders for a short-hitter's confidence!

Founded in 1906, Crans is Switzerland's second-oldest course - Montreux is six years older. Of the newer layouts, Bonmont, just outside Nyon and some twenty miles north-east of Geneva, is said to be extremely good, as is its near and even newer neighbour, Domaine Imperial.

In common with other countries in Europe where golf courses are only open for play during the summer months, access at these times in Switzerland can be extremely tight and, in common with the cost of living throughout the country, a round can be expensive. However the magnificient scenery and the sheer exhilaration of hitting the ball prodigious distances does compensate a great deal! With the summer pressure on Swiss courses in mind, a pre-booked visit to Crans, or any other course, is perhaps best seen as an exciting accompaniment to a golf holiday in France, Germany or Italy - or combined with Austria, the ingredients would be there for a novel, and probably very good, Alpine golfing extravaganza.

BLUMISBERG G & C CLUB   MAP 12 A3

3184 Wünnewil.
15km south-west of Bern on the N12 in Blumisberg.
CONTACT: R Jenkinson, Club Manager. Tel: +41 37 363438.
COURSE: 6,048m, PAR 72, SSS 73. Hilly forest course.
SOC RESTR'S: Welcome Weekdays.
SOC GF - Round: Wd Sf 65. We N/A. **Day:** Wd Sf 65. We N/A.
SOC PACK: On application.
VIS RESTR'S: Weekdays only.
VIS GF - Round: Wd Sf 65. We N/A. **Day:** Wd Sf 65. We N/A.
FACILITIES: Swimming Pool, Range & Pro-shop.

BONMONT GOLF CLUB   MAP 12 A4

1261 Chéserex.
Lausanne - Geneva Motorway & take the Nyon exit. 3km on.
CONTACT: M Linde, Secretary. Tel: +41 22 692345.
COURSE: 6,120m, PAR 71, SSS 72. Undulating course.
SOC RESTR'S: Welcome Weekdays only.
SOC GF - Round: Wd N/A. We N/A. **Day:** Wd Sf 80. We N/A.
SOC PACK: On application.
VIS RESTR'S: Welcome Weekdays only.
VIS GF - Round: Wd N/A. We N/A. **Day:** Wd Sf 80. We N/A.
FACILITIES: Restaurant, Pro-shop & Rooms.

SWITZERLAND

BREITENLOO GOLF CLUB MAP 12 B3

Wassersdorf, 8309 Oberwil.
xkm from Zurich Airport.

CONTACT: T Villiger, Professional. Tel: +41 1 8364080.
COURSE: 6,144m, PAR 72, SSS 72. Parkland course.
SOC RESTR'S: Please book in advance.
SOC GF - Round: Wd Sf 70. **We** Sf 90. **Day:** Wd N/A. **We** N/A.
SOC PACK: No set package.
VIS RESTR'S: Welcome with Handicap Certificate.
VIS GF - Round: Wd Sf 70. **We** Sf 90. **Day:** Wd N/A. **We** N/A.
FACILITIES: Bar & Restaurant.

CRANS-SUR-SIERRE GOLF CLUB MAP 12 A4

3963 Crans-sur-Sierre-Montana.
30km east of Sion.

CONTACT: Secretary. Tel: + 41 27 412168.
COURSE: 6,260m, PAR 72, SSS 72. Undulating parkland course.
SOC RESTR'S: Best time Weekdays.
SOC GF - Round: Wd Sf 90. **We** N/A. **Day:** Wd N/A. **We** N/A.
SOC PACK: Seasonal alterations to Green Fee.
VIS RESTR'S: Welcome Weekdays. Weekends difficult.
VIS GF - Round: Wd Sf 90. **We** N/A. **Day:** Wd N/A. **We** N/A.
FACILITIES: 9-hole Course, Restaurant, Pro-shop & Range.

DOMAINE IMPÉRIAL GOLF CLUB MAP 12 A4

Villa Pragins, 1196, Gland.
Between Geneva & Lausanne, 20km north of Geneva.

CONTACT: E Henry, Director. Tel: +41 22 3644545.
COURSE: 6,297m, PAR 72, SSS 74. Set along lake Geneva.
SOC RESTR'S: Not allowed.
SOC GF - Round: Wd N/A. **We** N/A. **Day:** Wd N/A. **We** N/A.
SOC PACK: No groups allowed.
VIS RESTR'S: Welcome Weekday mornings only. Max H'cap 36.
VIS GF - Round: Wd Sf 90. **We** N/A. **Day:** Wd N/A. **We** N/A.
FACILITIES: Bar & Restaurant.

ENGADIN GOLF CLUB MAP 12 B4

7503, Samedan.
8km north-east of St. Moritz in Samedan.

CONTACT: Secretary. Tel: +41 82 65226.
COURSE: 6,080m, PAR 72, SSS 72. Hilly forest course.
SOC RESTR'S: Please book through Secretary.
SOC GF - Round: Wd N/A. **We** N/A. **Day:** Wd Sf 85. **We** Sf 85.
SOC PACK: On application.
VIS RESTR'S: Must reserve tee times.
VIS GF - Round: Wd N/A. **We** N/A. **Day:** Wd Sf 85. **We** Sf 85.
FACILITIES: Bar & Restaurant.

GENEVE GOLF CLUB MAP 12 A4

70 Route de la Capite, 1233 Cologny.
3km from City.

CONTACT: Secretary. Tel: +41 22 7357540.
COURSE: 6,250m, PAR 72, SSS 72. Forest course.
SOC RESTR'S: Welcome with prior agreement.
SOC GF - Round: Wd Sf 80. **We** N/A. **Day:** Wd N/A. **We** N/A.
SOC PACK: Available at time of booking.
VIS RESTR'S: Welcome Weekdays only.
VIS GF - Round: Wd Sf 80. **We** N/A. **Day:** Wd N/A. **We** N/A.
FACILITIES: Bar & Restaurant.

GOLF CLUB DE VERBIER MAP 12 A4

1936, Verbier, Valois.
In the town of Verbier.

CONTACT: N Marcel, President. Tel: +41 26 311566.
COURSE: 5,110m, PAR 70, SSS 70. Parkland course.
SOC RESTR'S: Welcome. Open June-Nov.
SOC GF - Round: Wd Sf 50. **We** Sf 70. **Day:** Wd Sf 50. **We** Sf 70.
SOC PACK: On application.
VIS RESTR'S: Welcome maximum Handicap limit 36.
VIS GF - Round: Wd Sf 50. **We** Sf 70. **Day:** Wd Sf 50. **We** Sf 70.
FACILITIES: 18-hole short Course, Swimming Pool & Pro-shop.

GOLF CLUB LENZERHEIDE MAP 12 B4

Postfach 7078, Lenzerheide.
Zurich-Chur-Lenzerheide, 1.5km towards Lantsch.

CONTACT: A Baselgia, Secretary. Tel: +41 81 341316.
COURSE: 5,274m, PAR 69, SSS 69. Parkland course with water.
SOC RESTR'S: Welcome 16th June - 31st October.
SOC GF - Round: Wd N/A. **We** N/A. **Day:** Wd Sf 60. **We** Sf 60.
SOC PACK: On application.
VIS RESTR'S: Please phone prior to play.
VIS GF - Round: Wd N/A. **We** N/A. **Day:** Wd Sf 60. **We** Sf 60.
FACILITIES: Bar, Restaurant & Pro-shop.

INTERLAKEN- UNTERSEEN MAP 12 A4

Postfach 110, 3800 Interlaken.
Located 2km west of Interlaken.

CONTACT: M Gadient, Secretary. Tel: +41 36 226022
COURSE: 5,970m, PAR 72, SSS 72. Parkland course.
SOC RESTR'S: Always welcome.
SOC GF - Round: Wd Sf 70. **We** Sf 90. **Day:** Wd Sf 70. **We** Sf 90.
SOC PACK: None.
VIS RESTR'S: Always welcome with Handicap Certificate.
VIS GF - Round: Wd Sf 70. **We** Sf 90. **Day:** Wd Sf 70. **We** Sf 90.
FACILITIES: Restaurant.

SWITZERLAND

LUGANO GOLF CLUB   MAP 12 B4

6983 Magliaso.
10km west of Lugano.

CONTACT: D Maina, Professional. Tel: +41 91 711557.
COURSE: 6,740m, PAR 72, SSS 71. Forest course.
SOC RESTR'S: Welcome with prior agreement
SOC GF - Round: Wd Sf 80. **We** Sf 110. **Day: Wd** N/A. **We** N/A.
SOC PACK: Available at time of booking.
VIS RESTR'S: Welcome. Handicap Certificate required.
VIS GF - Round: Wd Sf 80. **We** Sf 110. **Day: Wd** N/A. **We** N/A.
FACILITIES: Bar & Restaurant.

NEUCHÂTEL GOLF CLUB   MAP 12 A

2072 Saint-Blaise.
30km west of Bern on the A10. 5km north on Neuchâtel.

CONTACT: T Charpié, Professional. Tel: +41 22 692345.
COURSE: 5,840m, PAR 71, SSS 70. Parkland course.
SOC RESTR'S: Welcome by arrangement.
SOC GF - Round: Wd Sf 60. **We** Sf 80. **Day: Wd** N/A. **We** N/A.
SOC PACK: On application.
VIS RESTR'S: Welcome Weekdays only. H'cap Cert required.
VIS GF - Round: Wd Sf 60. **We** Sf 80. **Day: Wd** N/A. **We** N/A.
FACILITIES: Restaurant, Pro-shop & Rooms.

MONTREUX GOLF CLUB   MAP 12 A4

84 Rte. d'Evian, 1860 Aigle.
15km south of Montreux.

CONTACT: M. Jacques Nater, Manager. Tel: +41 25 264616.
COURSE: 6,143m, PAR 72, SSS 72. Undulating parkland course.
SOC RESTR'S: Please book through Manager.
SOC GF - Round: Wd Sf 70. **We** Sf 90. **Day: Wd** N/A. **We** N/A.
SOC PACK: On application.
VIS RESTR'S: Welcome except competition days.
VIS GF - Round: Wd Sf 70. **We** Sf 90. **Day: Wd** N/A. **We** N/A.
FACILITIES: Clubhouse & Pro-shop.

PATRIZIALE ASCONA GOLF CLUB MAP 12 B

Via al Lido 81, 6612 Ascona.
5km west of Locarno in Ascona.

CONTACT: F Codiga, Professional. Tel: +41 93 352132.
COURSE: 5,890m, PAR 72, SSS 71. Undulating parkland course.
SOC RESTR'S: Please book through Professional. Max H'cap 36.
SOC GF - Round: Wd Sf 70. **We** Sf 90. **Day: Wd** N/A. **We** N/A.
SOC PACK: On application.
VIS RESTR'S: Welcome except competition days. Max H'cap 36.
VIS GF - Round: Wd Sf 70. **We** Sf 90. **Day: Wd** N/A. **We** N/A.
FACILITIES: Clubhouse & Pro-shop.

KEY TO MAPS

AUSTRIA	11
BELGIUM	11
DENMARK	12
FINLAND	13
FRANCE	14 - 15
GERMANY	16
GREAT BRITAIN	1 - 10
ITALY	17
NETHERLANDS	18
NORWAY	13
PORTUGAL	18
SPAIN	19
SWEDEN	13
SWITZERLAND	12

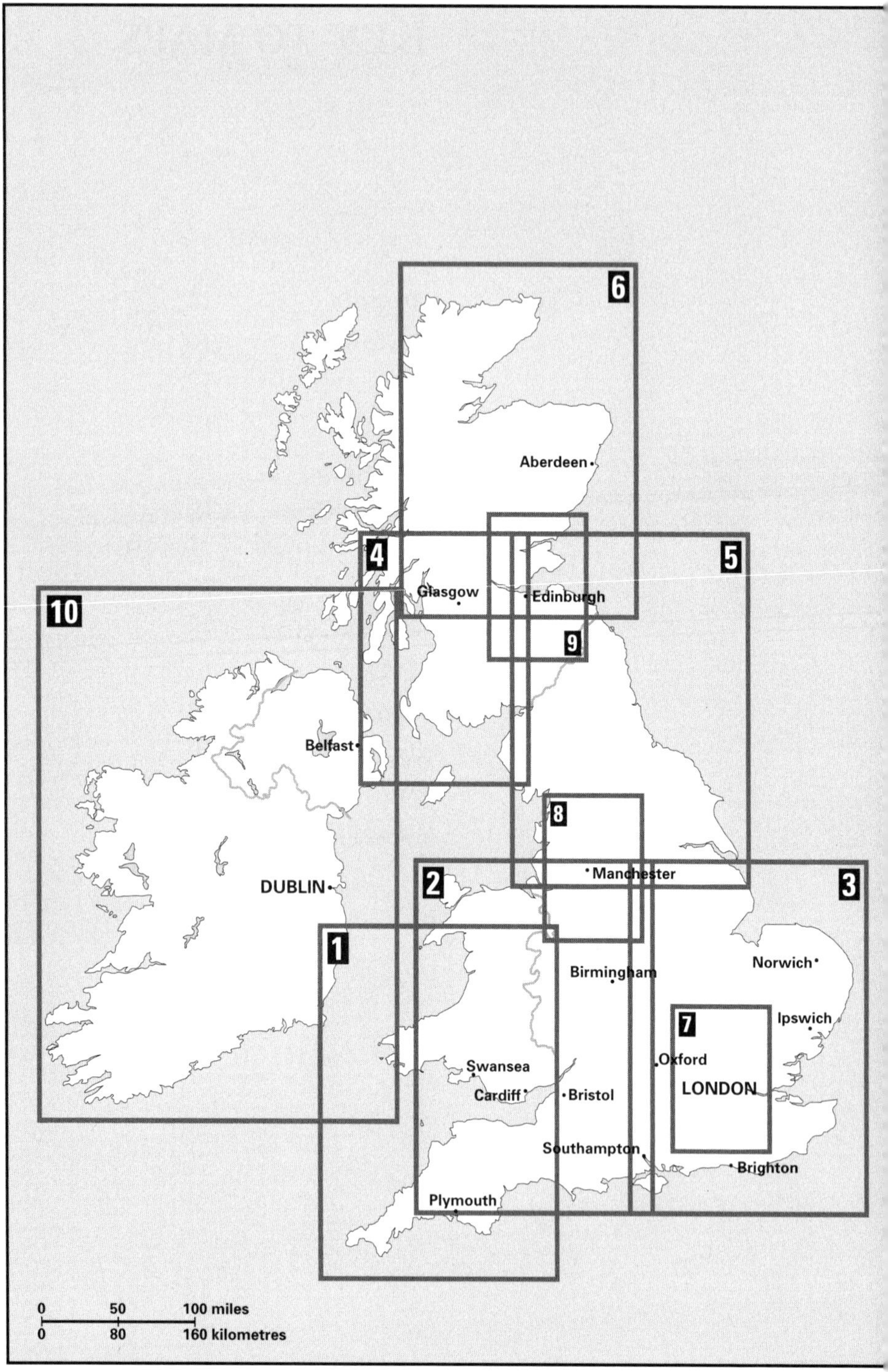
6
Aberdeen
4
5
10
Glasgow
Edinburgh
9
Belfast
8
DUBLIN
Manchester
2
3
1
Norwich
Birmingham
7
Ipswich
Oxford
Swansea
LONDON
Cardiff
Bristol
Southampton
Brighton
Plymouth
0
50
100 miles
0
80
160 kilometres

Nefyn & District
Criccieth
Porthmadog
Baia
Vale of Llangollen
Royal St David's
GWYNEDD
Oswestry
Llanymynech
Dolgellau
Welshpool
Welshpool
Church Stretton
Aberdovey
Borth & Ynyslas
Newtown
Aberystwyth
Aberystwyth
POWYS
Llandrindod Wells
Kington
Builth Wells
Builth Wells
Cardigan
DYFED
Fishguard
Cradoc
Brecon
Haverfordwest
Haverfordwest
Carmarthen
Glynhir
West Monmouthshire
Milford Haven
Monmouthshire
Pontardawe
Ashburnham
Morriston
Mountain Ash
Tenby
Neath
Aberdare
Bargoed
Swansea
GWENT
Fairwood Park
Rhonnda
Bryn Meadows
Pennard
Clyne
Maesteg
Newport
Mountain Lakes
Radyr
Pyle & Kenfig
Whitchurch
Creigiau
Cardiff
Royal Porthcawl
Southern Down
Dinas Powis
Brynhill Barry
Glamorganshire
Brean
Minehead & West Somerset
Illfracombe
Burnham & Berrow
Minehead
Saunton (East & West)
Enmore Park
Barnstaple
Bridgwater
Royal North Devon
Taunton
Taunton & Pickeridge
Bude
DEVON
Exeter
Axe Cliff
Manor House
Sidmouth
St Enodoc (Church)
St Mellion (Nicklaus & Old)
Trevose
CORNWALL
Bodmin
Plymouth
Torquay
Newquay
Newquay
Perranporth
Carlyon
West Cornwall
Penzance
Falmouth
Mullion
①
②
③
Ⓐ
Ⓑ

2

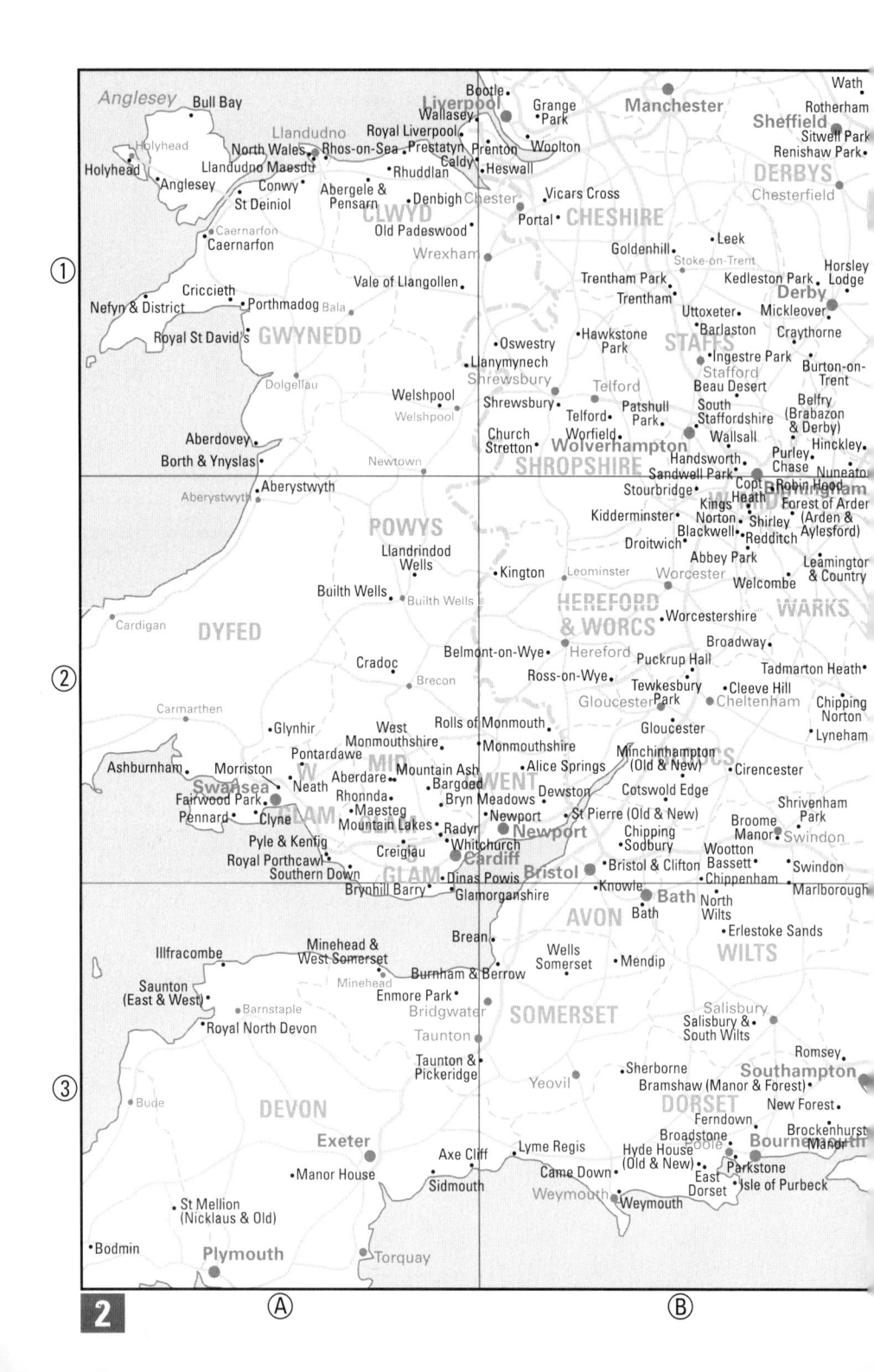

Regions and Locations

Anglesey / North Wales area (top left):
- Anglesey
- Bull Bay
- Holyhead
- Holyhead
- Llandudno
- Royal Liverpool
- North Wales
- Rhos-on-Sea
- Prestatyn
- Llandudno Maesdu
- Rhuddlan
- Caldy
- Anglesey
- Conwy
- Abergele & Pensarn
- St Deiniol
- Denbigh
- CLWYD

Liverpool / Manchester area:
- Bootle
- Liverpool
- Wallasey
- Grange Park
- Manchester
- Prenton
- Woolton
- Heswall
- Chester
- Vicars Cross
- Portal
- CHESHIRE
- Sheffield
- Rotherham
- Sitwell Park
- Renishaw Park
- DERBYS
- Chesterfield

Gwynedd / mid Wales:
- Caernarfon
- Caernarfon
- Old Padeswood
- Wrexham
- Leek
- Goldenhill
- Stoke-on-Trent
- Kedleston Park
- Horsley Lodge
- Derby
- Criccieth
- Vale of Llangollen
- Trentham Park
- Trentham
- Uttoxeter
- Mickleover
- Nefyn & District
- Porthmadog
- Bala
- Barlaston
- Craythorne
- Royal St David's
- GWYNEDD
- Oswestry
- Hawkstone Park
- STAFFS
- Llanymynech
- Ingestre Park
- Burton-on-Trent
- Dolgellau
- Shrewsbury
- Stafford
- Welshpool
- Telford
- Beau Desert
- Welshpool
- Shrewsbury
- Telford
- Patshull Park
- South Staffordshire
- Belfry (Brabazon & Derby)
- Aberdovey
- Church Stretton
- Worfield
- Wolverhampton
- Wallsall
- Purley Chase
- Hinckley
- Borth & Ynyslas
- Newtown
- Handsworth
- Sandwell Park
- Copt Heath
- Robin Hood
- Nuneaton
- SHROPSHIRE
- Aberystwyth
- Stourbridge
- Kings Norton
- Forest of Arden (Arden & Aylesford)
- Aberystwyth
- POWYS
- Kidderminster
- Blackwell
- Shirley
- Redditch
- Droitwich
- Abbey Park
- Leamington & Country
- Llandrindod Wells
- Kington
- Leominster
- Worcester
- Welcombe
- WARKS
- Builth Wells
- HEREFORD & WORCS
- Worcestershire
- Cardigan
- Builth Wells
- DYFED
- Broadway
- Cradoc
- Belmont-on-Wye
- Hereford
- Puckrup Hall
- Tadmarton Heath
- Brecon
- Ross-on-Wye
- Tewkesbury
- Cleeve Hill
- Gloucester Park
- Cheltenham
- Chipping Norton
- Carmarthen
- Glynhir
- West Monmouthshire
- Rolls of Monmouth
- Monmouthshire
- Gloucester
- Lyneham
- Pontardawe
- Minchinhampton (Old & New)
- Cirencester
- Ashburnham
- Morriston
- Aberdare
- Mountain Ash
- Alice Springs
- Swansea
- Neath
- Bargoed
- Dewston
- Cotswold Edge
- Fairwood Park
- Rhonnda
- Bryn Meadows
- Shrivenham Park
- Pennard
- Clyne
- Maesteg
- Mountain Lakes
- Radyr
- Newport
- St Pierre (Old & New)
- Broome Manor
- Swindon
- Pyle & Kenfig
- Creigiau
- Whitchurch
- Chipping Sodbury
- Wootton Bassett
- Royal Porthcawl
- Cardiff
- Bristol & Clifton
- Swindon
- Southern Down
- Dinas Powis
- Bristol
- Chippenham
- Marlborough
- Brynhill
- Barry
- Glamorganshire
- Knowle
- Bath
- North Wilts
- GLAM
- AVON
- Bath
- Erlestoke Sands
- WILTS
- Minehead & West Somerset
- Brean
- Wells
- Mendip
- Illfracombe
- Burnham & Berrow
- Somerset
- Saunton (East & West)
- Minehead
- Enmore Park
- Salisbury
- Barnstaple
- Bridgwater
- SOMERSET
- Salisbury & South Wilts
- Royal North Devon
- Taunton
- Romsey
- Taunton & Pickeridge
- Sherborne
- Southampton
- Yeovil
- Bramshaw (Manor & Forest)
- Bude
- DEVON
- DORSET
- New Forest
- Exeter
- Broadstone
- Ferndown
- Brockenhurst Manor
- Exeter
- Axe Cliff
- Lyme Regis
- Hyde House
- Poole
- Parkstone
- Bournemouth
- Manor House
- Sidmouth
- Came Down
- (Old & New)
- East Dorset
- Isle of Purbeck
- St Mellion (Nicklaus & Old)
- Weymouth
- Weymouth
- Bodmin
- Plymouth
- Torquay

① ② ③ Ⓐ Ⓑ

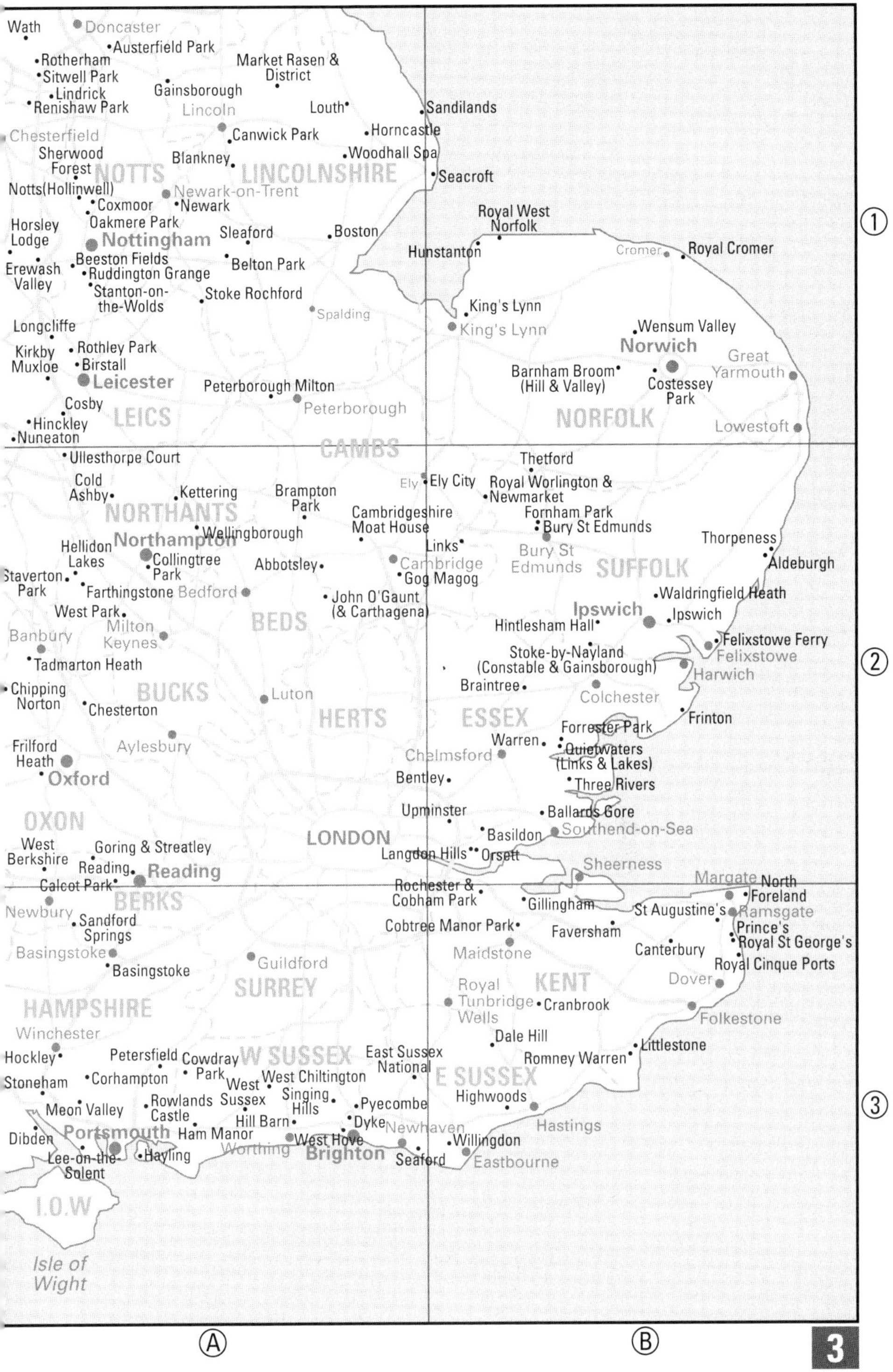
Wath
Doncaster
Austerfield Park
Rotherham
Sitwell Park
Lindrick
Renishaw Park
Market Rasen & District
Gainsborough
Lincoln
Louth
Sandilands
Chesterfield
Canwick Park
Horncastle
Sherwood Forest
NOTTS
Blankney
Woodhall Spa
LINCOLNSHIRE
Seacroft
Notts(Hollinwell)
Newark-on-Trent
Coxmoor
Newark
Royal West Norfolk
Horsley Lodge
Oakmere Park
Nottingham
Sleaford
Boston
Hunstanton
Cromer
Royal Cromer
Erewash Valley
Beeston Fields
Ruddington Grange
Belton Park
Stanton-on-the-Wolds
Stoke Rochford
Spalding
King's Lynn
King's Lynn
Longcliffe
Wensum Valley
Norwich
Kirkby Muxloe
Rothley Park
Birstall
Leicester
Barnham Broom (Hill & Valley)
Costessey Park
Great Yarmouth
Peterborough Milton
Peterborough
Cosby
LEICS
NORFOLK
Hinckley
Nuneaton
Lowestoft
CAMBS
Ullesthorpe Court
Thetford
Cold Ashby
Kettering
Brampton Park
Ely
Ely City
Royal Worlington & Newmarket
NORTHANTS
Cambridgeshire Moat House
Fornham Park
Bury St Edmunds
Wellingborough
Northampton
Thorpeness
Hellidon Lakes
Collingtree Park
Links
Bury St Edmunds
Aldeburgh
Abbotsley
Cambridge
SUFFOLK
Staverton Park
Gog Magog
Farthingstone
Bedford
John O'Gaunt (& Carthagena)
Waldringfield Heath
West Park
Ipswich
Ipswich
Milton Keynes
BEDS
Hintlesham Hall
Banbury
Felixstowe Ferry
Felixstowe
Stoke-by-Nayland (Constable & Gainsborough)
Tadmarton Heath
Harwich
Braintree
Chipping Norton
BUCKS
Luton
Colchester
Chesterton
HERTS
ESSEX
Frinton
Forrester Park
Aylesbury
Warren
Frilford Heath
Chelmsford
Quietwaters (Links & Lakes)
Oxford
Bentley
Three Rivers
OXON
Upminster
Ballards Gore
LONDON
Basildon
Southend-on-Sea
West Berkshire
Goring & Streatley
Langdon Hills
Orsett
Sheerness
Reading
Reading
Margate
North Foreland
Calcot Park
BERKS
Rochester & Cobham Park
Gillingham
St Augustine's
Ramsgate
Newbury
Sandford Springs
Cobtree Manor Park
Faversham
Prince's
Royal St George's
Basingstoke
Maidstone
Canterbury
Basingstoke
Guildford
Royal Cinque Ports
SURREY
Royal Tunbridge Wells
KENT
Dover
HAMPSHIRE
Cranbrook
Folkestone
Winchester
Dale Hill
Hockley
Petersfield
Cowdray Park
W SUSSEX
East Sussex National
Littlestone
Romney Warren
Stoneham
Corhampton
West Sussex
West Chiltington
E SUSSEX
Highwoods
Meon Valley
Rowlands Castle
Singing Hills
Pyecombe
Hill Barn
Dyke
Newhaven
Hastings
Dibden
Portsmouth
Ham Manor
West Hove
Willingdon
Worthing
Brighton
Lee-on-the-Solent
Hayling
Seaford
Eastbourne
I.O.W
Isle of Wight
①
②
③
Ⓐ
Ⓑ

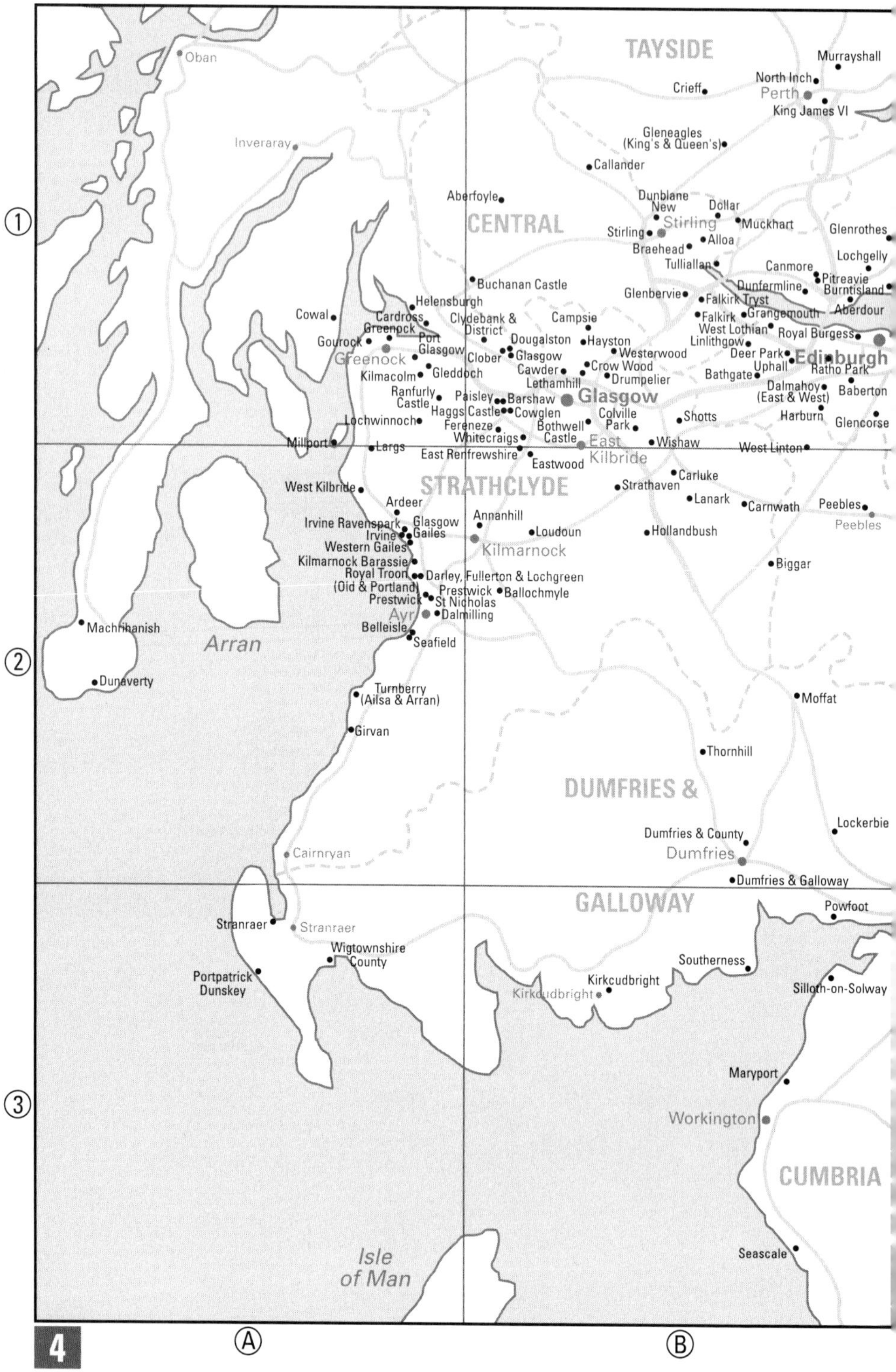
TAYSIDE
CENTRAL
STRATHCLYDE
DUMFRIES &
GALLOWAY
CUMBRIA
Arran
Isle of Man
Oban
Inveraray
Murrayshall
North Inch
Perth
King James VI
Crieff
Gleneagles (King's & Queen's)
Callander
Aberfoyle
Dunblane New
Dollar
Stirling
Muckhart
Glenrothes
Stirling
Alloa
Braehead
Lochgelly
Tulliallan
Canmore
Pitreavie
Dunfermline
Burntisland
Buchanan Castle
Glenbervie
Falkirk Tryst
Aberdour
Helensburgh
Cowal
Cardross
Clydebank & District
Campsie
Falkirk
Grangemouth
Greenock
West Lothian
Royal Burgess
Gourock
Port Glasgow
Dougalston
Hayston
Linlithgow
Greenock
Clober
Glasgow
Westerwood
Deer Park
Edinburgh
Cawder
Crow Wood
Uphall
Ratho Park
Kilmacolm
Gleddoch
Drumpelier
Bathgate
Lethamhill
Dalmahoy (East & West)
Baberton
Ranfurly Castle
Paisley
Barshaw
Glasgow
Haggs Castle
Cowglen
Colville Park
Shotts
Harburn
Glencorse
Lochwinnoch
Fereneze
Bothwell Castle
Whitecraigs
East Kilbride
Wishaw
West Linton
Millport
Largs
East Renfrewshire
Eastwood
Carluke
West Kilbride
Strathaven
Lanark
Carnwath
Peebles
Peebles
Ardeer
Annanhill
Irvine Ravenspark
Glasgow Gailes
Irvine
Loudoun
Hollandbush
Western Gailes
Kilmarnock
Kilmarnock Barassie
Biggar
Royal Troon (Old & Portland)
Darley, Fullerton & Lochgreen
Prestwick
Prestwick St Nicholas
Ballochmyle
Ayr
Dalmilling
Machrihanish
Belleisle
Seafield
Dunaverty
Turnberry (Ailsa & Arran)
Moffat
Girvan
Thornhill
Lockerbie
Dumfries & County
Dumfries
Cairnryan
Dumfries & Galloway
Powfoot
Stranraer
Stranraer
Wigtownshire County
Southerness
Portpatrick Dunskey
Kirkcudbright
Kirkcudbright
Silloth-on-Solway
Maryport
Workington
Seascale
①
②
③
Ⓐ
Ⓑ

Dundee
FIFE
Edinburgh
Magdalene Fields
Berwick-upon-Tweed
Berwick-upon-Tweed
Peebles
BORDERS
Selkirk
Dunstanburgh
Alnwick
NORTHUMBERLAND
Newcastle United
City of Newcastle
Newcastle-upon-Tyne
Whitburn
Hexham
Brampton
Slaley Hall
South Shields
TYNE & WEAR
Carlisle
Sunderland
Washington Moat House
Seaham
Mount Oswald
Brancepeth Castle
Durham City
Crook
Bishop Auckland
CLEVELAND
Penrith
DURHAM
Seaton Carew
(Old & Brabazon)
Woodham
Keswick
Appleby
Barnard
Castle
Middlesbrough
Darlington
Darlington
CUMBRIA
Whitby
Richmond
Scarborough North Cliff
Catterick
Garrison
Scarborough
Kendal
Kirkbymoorside
Scarborough South Cliff
NORTH YORKSHIRE
Ganton
Filey
Flamborough Head
Easingwold
Bridlington
Barrow-in-
Furness
Lancaster
Lancaster
York
Bridlington
Harrogate
York
Fulford
Pike Hills
Blackpool
North
Shore
Knott End
LANCASHIRE
HUMBERSIDE
Hornsea
Ashton &
Lea
Blackpool
Preston
Royal
Lytham
&
St Annes
Blackburn
Bradford
Leeds
Boothferry
Kingston-upon-Hull
Ganstead Park
Lytham
Green Drive
Penwortham
Shaw Hill
W.YORKSHIRE
Selby
Brough
Hillside
Chorley
Normanby Hall
Royal
Birkdale
Southport & Ainsdale
GRT.MAN.
Thorne
Immingham
Hickleton
Holme Hall
Grimsby
Grimsby
Formby
Ashton-in-
Makerfield
Haydock
Park
STH YORKS
Doncaster
Wath
Bootle
Manchester
Austerfield Park
Wallasey
Grange Park
Rotherham
Sitwell Park
Gainsborough
Market Rasen &
District
Liverpool
Sheffield
①
②
③
Ⓐ
Ⓑ

Scrabster
Thurso
Reay
Thurso
Wick
Wick
Brora
Golspie
Ullapool
Royal Dornoch
Tain
Moray (Old & New)
Hopeman
Spey Bay
Cullen
Strathlene
Buckpool
Fraserburgh
Inverallochy
Strathpeffer Spa
Dingwall
Banff
Royal Tarlair
Fortrose & Rosemarkie
Nairn
Nairn
Nairn Dunbar
Forres
Elgin
Garmouth & Kingston
Muir of Ord
Keith
Turriff
Peterhead
Peterhead
Inverness
Torvean
Inverness
Dufftown
MacDonald
Cruden Bay
HIGHLAND
Grantown-on-Spey
Oldmeldrum
Boat of Garten
GRAMPIAN
Kintore
Newmacher
Murcar
Aberdeen
Royal Aberdeen
Hazelhead(No1 & No2)
Bon Accord
Kingussie
Aboyne
Deeside
Balnagask
Newtonmore
Newtonmore
Braemar
Ballater
Banchory
Stonehaven
Fort William
Fort William
Edzell
Brechin
Montrose
Montrose Links
Pitlochry
Pitlochry
TAYSIDE
Taymouth Castle
Dundee
Perth
Inveraray
FIFE
CENTRAL
Stirling
Edinburgh
Greenock
Glasgow
①
②
③
Ⓐ
Ⓑ

Wavendon
Woburn (Duke's & Duchess)
Letchworth
Royston
Luton
Aylesbury
Bishop's Stortford
Redbourn
Mid-Herts
Welwyn Garden City
Whitehill
Whipsnade Park
Ashridge
Canons Brook
Potters Bar
Ellesborough
Porters Park
Cheshunt
West Herts
Hadley Wood
Trent Pk
W.Essex
Stapleford Abbotts (Abbotts & Priors)
Aldenham
Elstree
Arkley
Bushey Hall
Enfield
Sandy Lodge
South Herts
Bush Hill Park
Hartsbourne
Moor Park (High & West)
Chigwell
Hainault Forest
Finchley
North Middlesex
Muswell Hill
Pinner Hill
Harefield Place
Wexham Park
Winter Hill
Ealing
LONDON
West Middlesex
Royal Blackheath
Airlinks
Royal Mid-Surrey (Outer & Inner)
Stoke Poges
Wyke Green
Coombe Hill
Sundridge Park (East & West)
Fulwell
Wimbledon Park
Malden
London Scottish
Berkshire (Red & Blue)
Wentworth (East, West & Edinburgh)
Ruxley Park
Home Park
Cray Valley
Addington Court (Falconwood & Championship)
Langley Park
Sunningdale (Old & New)
Downshire
Mill Ride
Darenth Valley
Foxhills (Chertsey & Longcross)
St George's Hill
Banstead Downs
Selsdon Park
Cherry Lodge
Silvermere
Wildernesse Park (New & Old)
West Byfleet
Epsom
Walton Heath (Old & New)
Coulsdon Ct
Worplesdon
West Hill
Leatherhead
North Downs
North Hants
Southwood
Oaks Sports Centre
Kingswood
Knole Park
Tandridge
Guildford
Hankley Common
Bramley
Hindhead
Fernfell
Copthorne
Ifield
Blackmoor
Gatton Manor
Anderida
Cottesmore (Old & New)
Royal Ashdown Forest
Liphook
Old Thorns
Haywards Heath
Paxhill Park
①
②
③
Ⓐ
Ⓑ

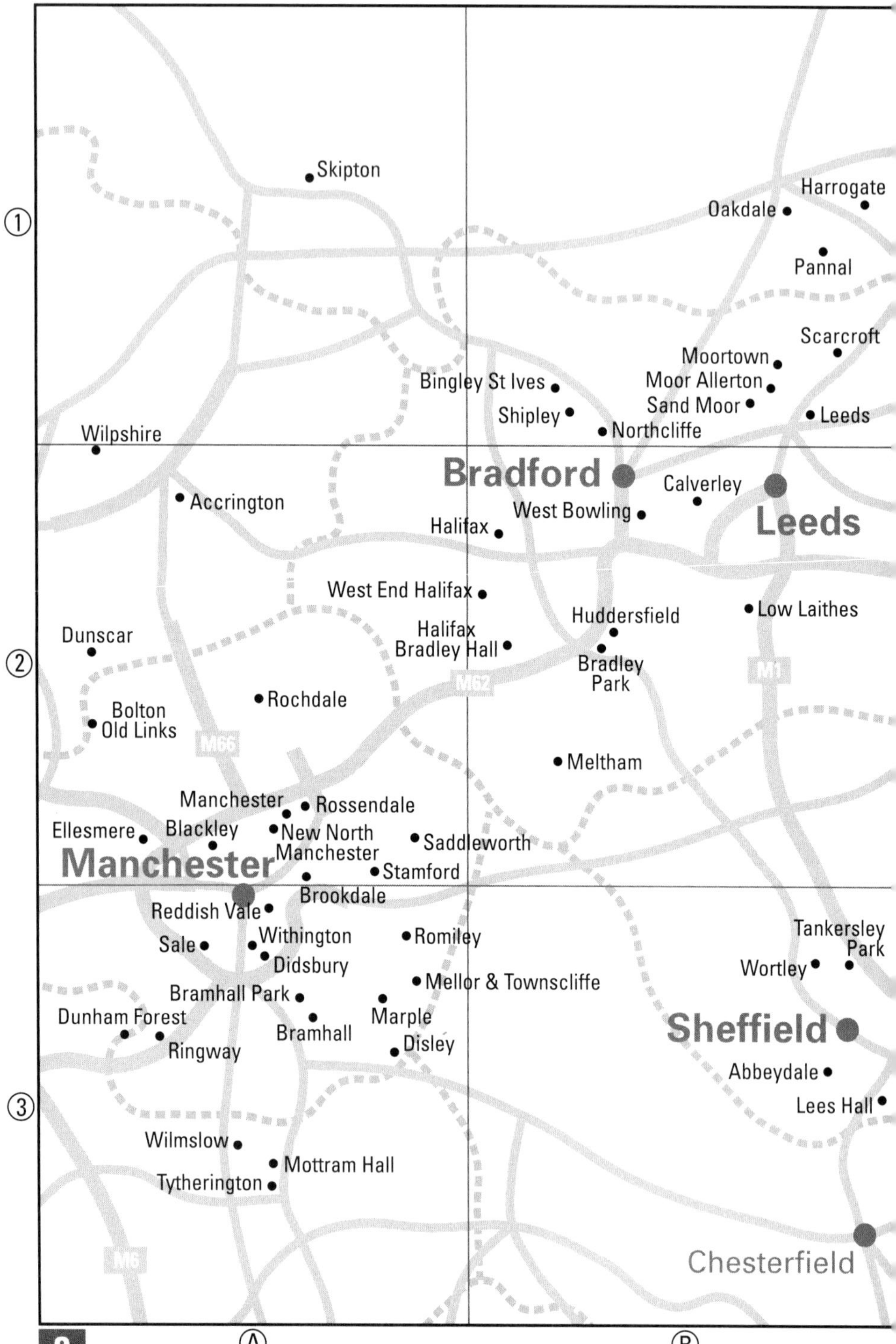

1
2
3
A
B
Skipton
Harrogate
Oakdale
Pannal
Scarcroft
Moortown
Moor Allerton
Sand Moor
Leeds
Bingley St Ives
Shipley
Northcliffe
Wilpshire
Bradford
Calverley
Leeds
West Bowling
Halifax
Accrington
West End Halifax
Huddersfield
Low Laithes
Dunscar
Halifax
Bradley Hall
Bradley
Park
M62
M1
Rochdale
Bolton
Old Links
M66
Meltham
Manchester
Rossendale
Ellesmere
Blackley
New North
Manchester
Saddleworth
Manchester
Stamford
Brookdale
Reddish Vale
Withington
Romiley
Tankersley
Park
Sale
Didsbury
Wortley
Mellor & Townscliffe
Bramhall Park
Dunham Forest
Marple
Sheffield
Bramhall
Ringway
Disley
Abbeydale
Lees Hall
Wilmslow
Mottram Hall
Tytherington
M6
Chesterfield

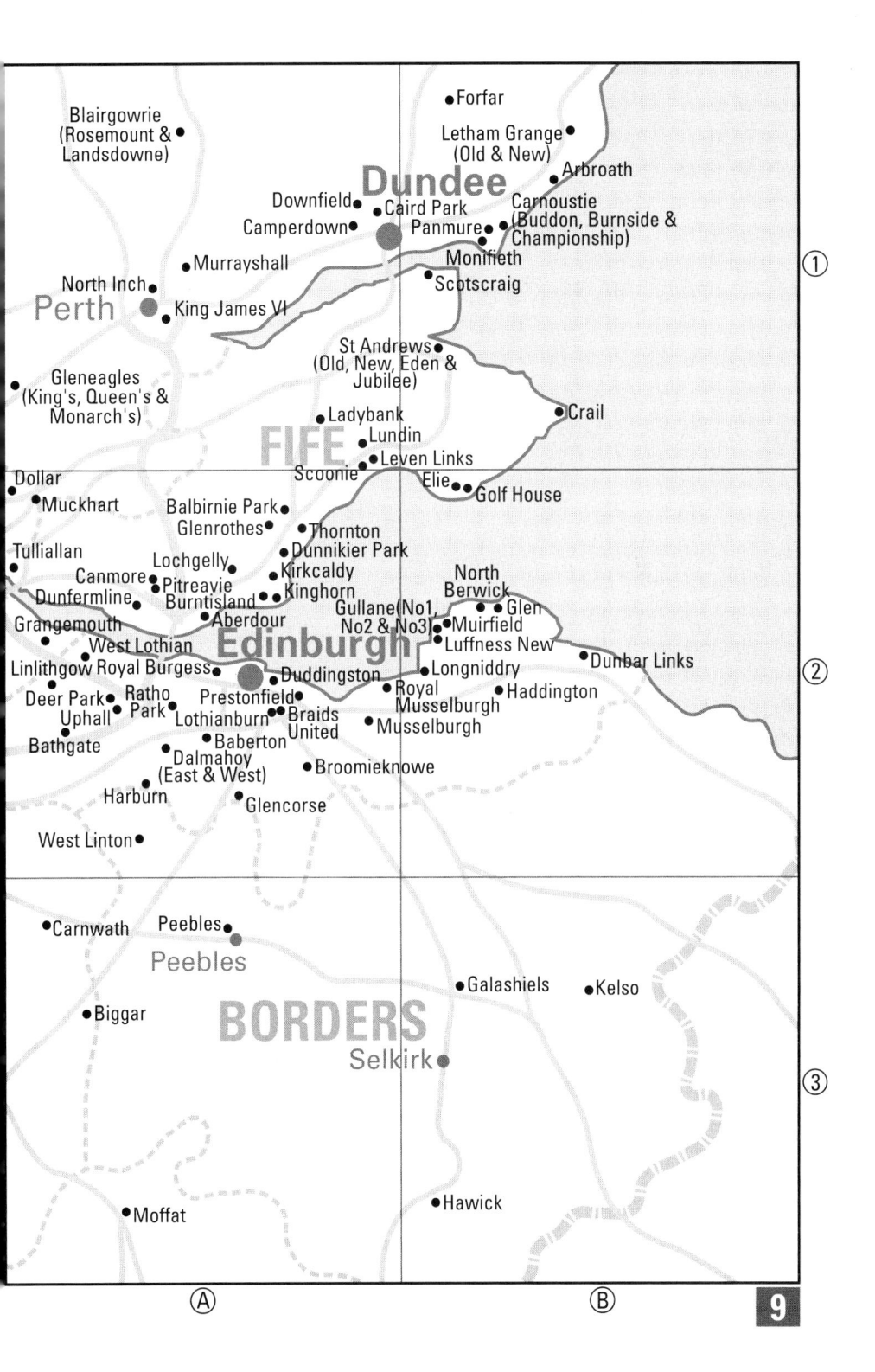

Map of golf courses in Scotland (Perth, Dundee, Fife, Edinburgh, and Borders regions)

- Forfar
- Blairgowrie (Rosemount & Landsdowne)
- Letham Grange (Old & New)
- Arbroath
- **Dundee**
- Downfield
- Caird Park
- Carnoustie (Buddon, Burnside & Championship)
- Camperdown
- Panmure
- Murrayshall
- Monifieth
- North Inch
- Scotscraig
- **Perth**
- King James VI
- St Andrews (Old, New, Eden & Jubilee)
- Gleneagles (King's, Queen's & Monarch's)
- Crail
- Ladybank
- Lundin
- **FIFE**
- Leven Links
- Dollar
- Scoonie
- Elie
- Muckhart
- Golf House
- Balbirnie Park
- Glenrothes
- Thornton
- Tulliallan
- Dunnikier Park
- Lochgelly
- Kirkcaldy
- North Berwick
- Canmore
- Pitreavie
- Kinghorn
- Glen
- Dunfermline
- Burntisland
- Gullane (No1, No2 & No3)
- Muirfield
- Grangemouth
- Aberdour
- Luffness New
- West Lothian
- **Edinburgh**
- Dunbar Links
- Linlithgow Royal Burgess
- Duddingston
- Longniddry
- Deer Park
- Ratho Park
- Prestonfield
- Royal Musselburgh
- Haddington
- Uphall
- Lothianburn
- Braids United
- Musselburgh
- Bathgate
- Baberton
- Dalmahoy (East & West)
- Broomieknowe
- Harburn
- Glencorse
- West Linton
- Carnwath
- Peebles
- Peebles
- Galashiels
- Kelso
- Biggar
- **BORDERS**
- Selkirk
- Hawick
- Moffat

Ⓐ Ⓑ ① ② ③

9

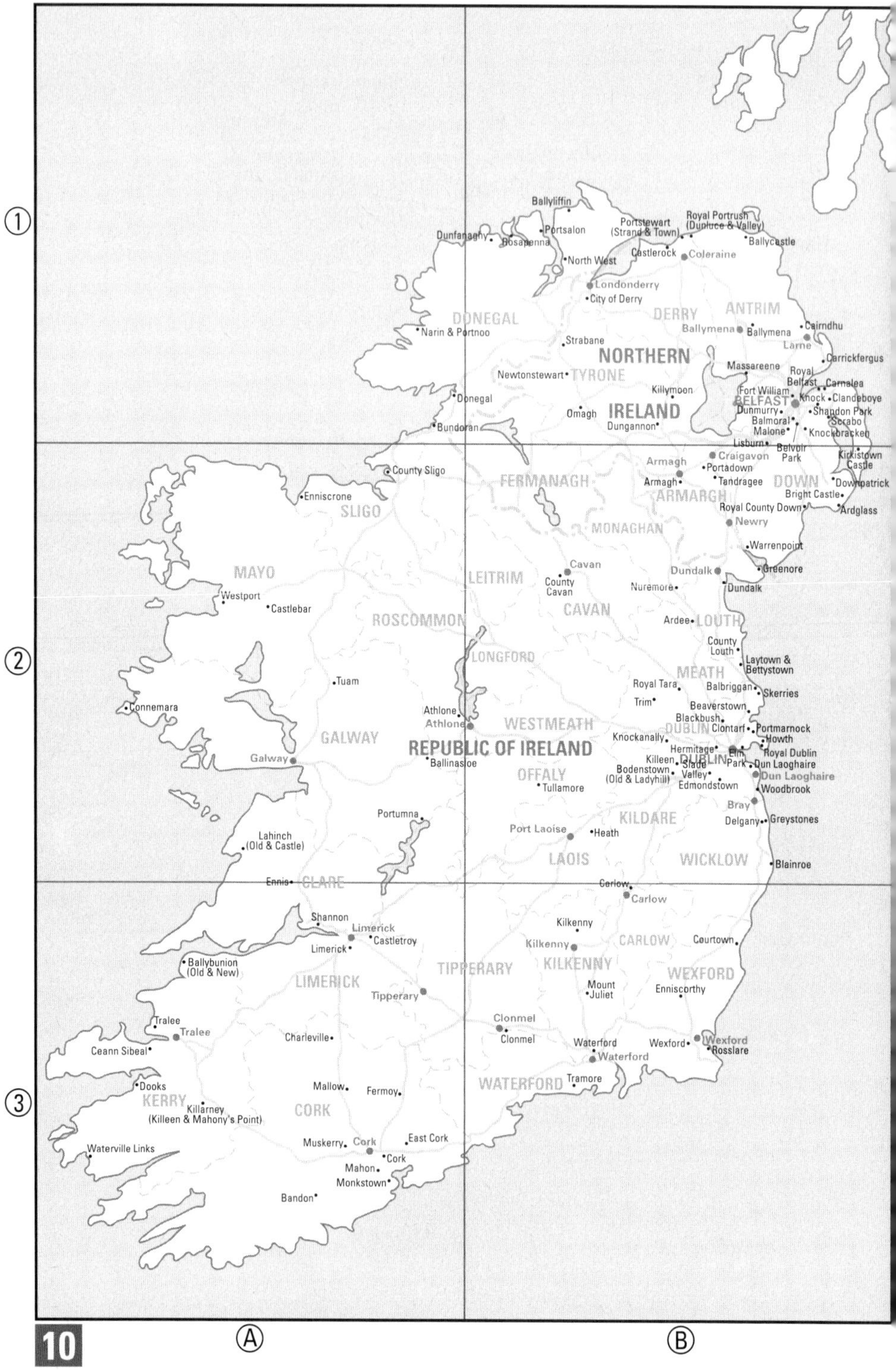

1
2
3
A
B
Ballyliffin
Portsalon
Dunfanaghy
Rosapenna
Portstewart (Strand & Town)
Royal Portrush (Dunluce & Valley)
Ballycastle
Castlerock
Coleraine
North West
Londonderry
City of Derry
DONEGAL
DERRY
ANTRIM
Narin & Portnoo
Ballymena
Ballymena
Cairndhu
Larne
Strabane
NORTHERN
Carrickfergus
Massareene
Newtonstewart
TYRONE
Royal Belfast
Carnalea
Killymoon
Fort William
BELFAST
Knock
Clandeboye
Donegal
Omagh
IRELAND
Dunmurry
Shandon Park
Scrabo
Balmoral
Dungannon
Malone
Knockbracken
Bundoran
Lisburn
Belvoir Park
Kirkistown Castle
Craigavon
Armagh
Portadown
County Sligo
FERMANAGH
Armagh
Tandragee
DOWN
Downpatrick
Bright Castle
Enniscrone
ARMAGH
Royal County Down
Ardglass
SLIGO
Newry
MONAGHAN
Warrenpoint
MAYO
Cavan
LEITRIM
County Cavan
Dundalk
Greenore
Nuremore
Dundalk
Westport
CAVAN
Castlebar
ROSCOMMON
Ardee
LOUTH
County Louth
LONGFORD
Laytown & Bettystown
MEATH
Tuam
Royal Tara
Balbriggan
Skerries
Trim
Beaverstown
Connemara
Athlone
Blackbush
Athlone
WESTMEATH
DUBLIN
Clontarf
Portmarnock
GALWAY
Knockanally
Howth
REPUBLIC OF IRELAND
Hermitage
Elm Park
Royal Dublin
Galway
Killeen
Slade Valley
DUBLIN
Dun Laoghaire
Ballinasloe
Bodenstown (Old & Ladyhill)
OFFALY
Edmondstown
Dun Laoghaire
Tullamore
Woodbrook
KILDARE
Bray
Portumna
Port Laoise
Delgany
Greystones
Heath
Lahinch (Old & Castle)
LAOIS
WICKLOW
Blainroe
Ennis
CLARE
Carlow
Carlow
Shannon
Kilkenny
Limerick
CARLOW
Courtown
Castletroy
Limerick
Kilkenny
Ballybunion (Old & New)
TIPPERARY
KILKENNY
WEXFORD
LIMERICK
Mount Juliet
Enniscorthy
Tipperary
Clonmel
Tralee
Clonmel
Tralee
Charleville
Waterford
Wexford
Wexford
Ceann Sibeal
Rosslare
Waterford
Tramore
WATERFORD
Dooks
Mallow
Fermoy
KERRY
Killarney (Killeen & Mahony's Point)
CORK
Waterville Links
East Cork
Muskerry
Cork
Cork
Mahon
Monkstown
Bandon

Map 11: Austria and Belgium

Scale (top map): 0 — 50 — 100 — 150 — 200 Kilometres

Austria (top panel)

- Waldviertel
- Linz
- Linz St Florian
- Colony Club Gutenhof (East & West)
- WIEN
- Brunn
- Wien
- Gut Altentann
- Schloss Ernegg
- Enzesfeld
- Donnerskirchen
- Bodensee
- Salzburg
- Salzkammergut
- Bregenz
- Gut Brandlhof
- Schloss Pichlarn
- Kitzbühel
- AUSTRIA
- Murhof
- Innsbruck
- Graz
- Fürstenfeld
- Gut Murstätten
- Austria-Wörther See
- Frauenthal
- Kärntner
- Klagenfurt

Belgium (bottom panel)

- North Sea
- Royal Zoute
- Royal Antwerp
- Royal Ostend
- Antwerp
- Ostend
- Damme
- Brugge
- Royal Bossenstein
- Latem
- Cleydael
- Gent
- Keerbergen
- Limburg
- Spiegelven
- BRUSSELS
- Winge
- Royal Waterloo (One & Two)
- Bercuit
- Hasselt
- BELGIUM
- Liège
- Rigenée
- Gomze
- Falnuée
- Mont Garni
- Namur
- Charleroi
- Arlon

Scale (bottom map): 0 — 25 — 50 — 75 — 100 Kilometres

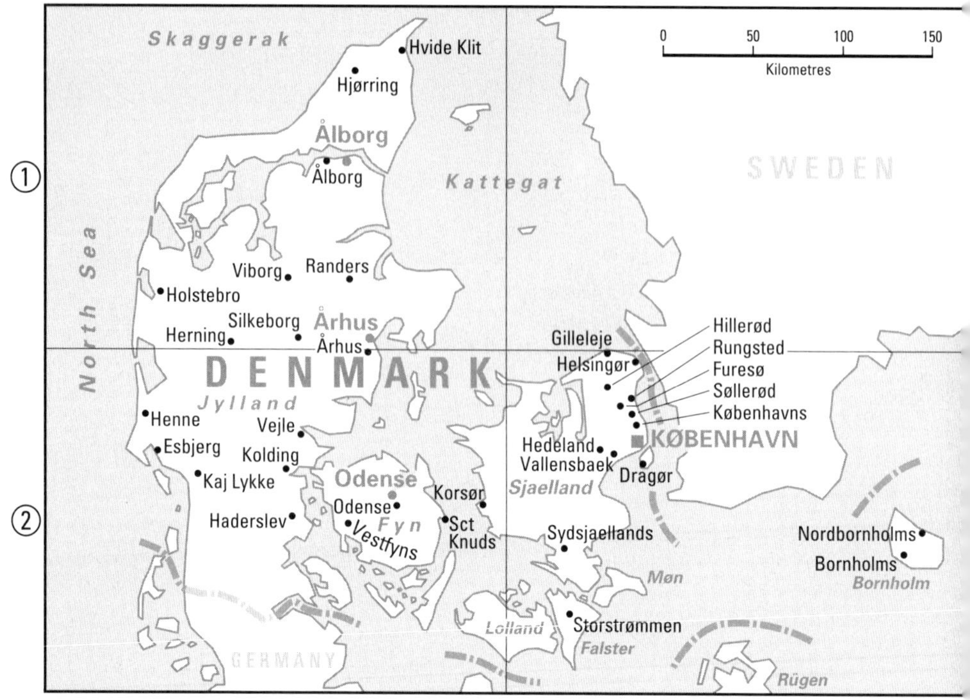
Skaggerak
Hvide Klit
Hjørring
Ålborg
Ålborg
Kattegat
SWEDEN
North Sea
Viborg
Randers
Holstebro
Silkeborg
Århus
Herning
Århus
Gilleleje
Hillerød
Rungsted
Furesø
Søllerød
Københavns
Helsingør
DENMARK
Jylland
Henne
Vejle
Esbjerg
Kolding
Hedeland
Vallensbaek
KØBENHAVN
Dragør
Kaj Lykke
Odense
Odense
Korsør
Sjaelland
Haderslev
Fyn
Vestfyns
Sct Knuds
Sydsjaellands
Nordbornholms
Bornholms
Bornholm
Møn
Lolland
Storstrømmen
Falster
GERMANY
Rügen
0 50 100 150
Kilometres

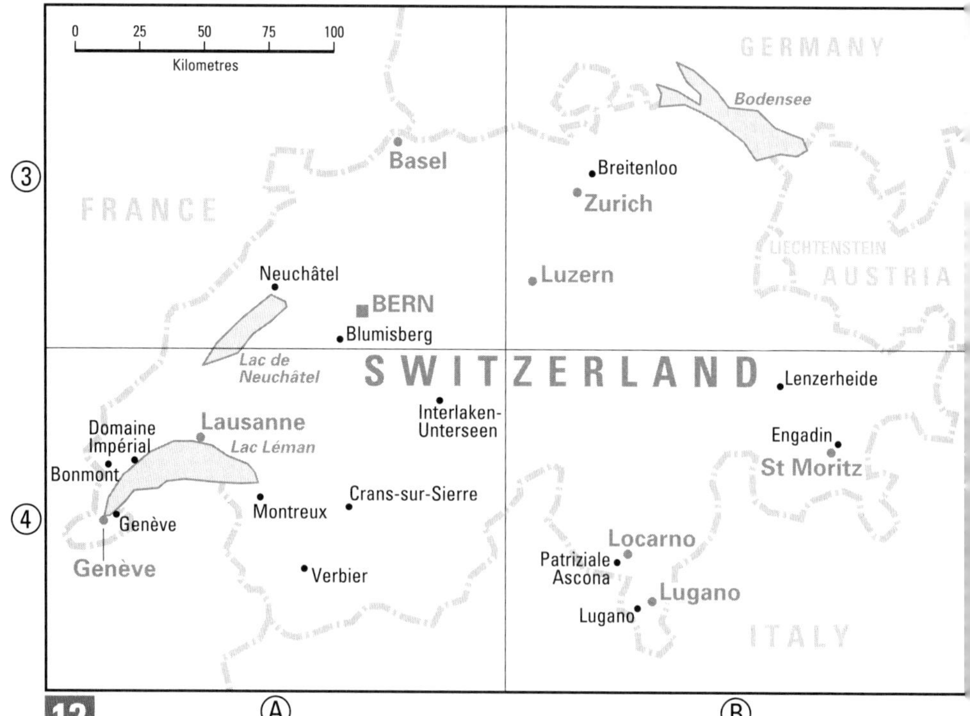
0 25 50 75 100
Kilometres
GERMANY
Bodensee
Basel
Breitenloo
Zurich
FRANCE
LIECHTENSTEIN
AUSTRIA
Neuchâtel
Luzern
BERN
Blumisberg
Lac de Neuchâtel
SWITZERLAND
Lenzerheide
Interlaken-Unterseen
Domaine Impérial
Lausanne
Lac Léman
Engadin
St Moritz
Bonmont
Montreux
Crans-sur-Sierre
Genève
Genève
Locarno
Patriziale Ascona
Lugano
Lugano
Verbier
ITALY

Ⓐ Ⓑ

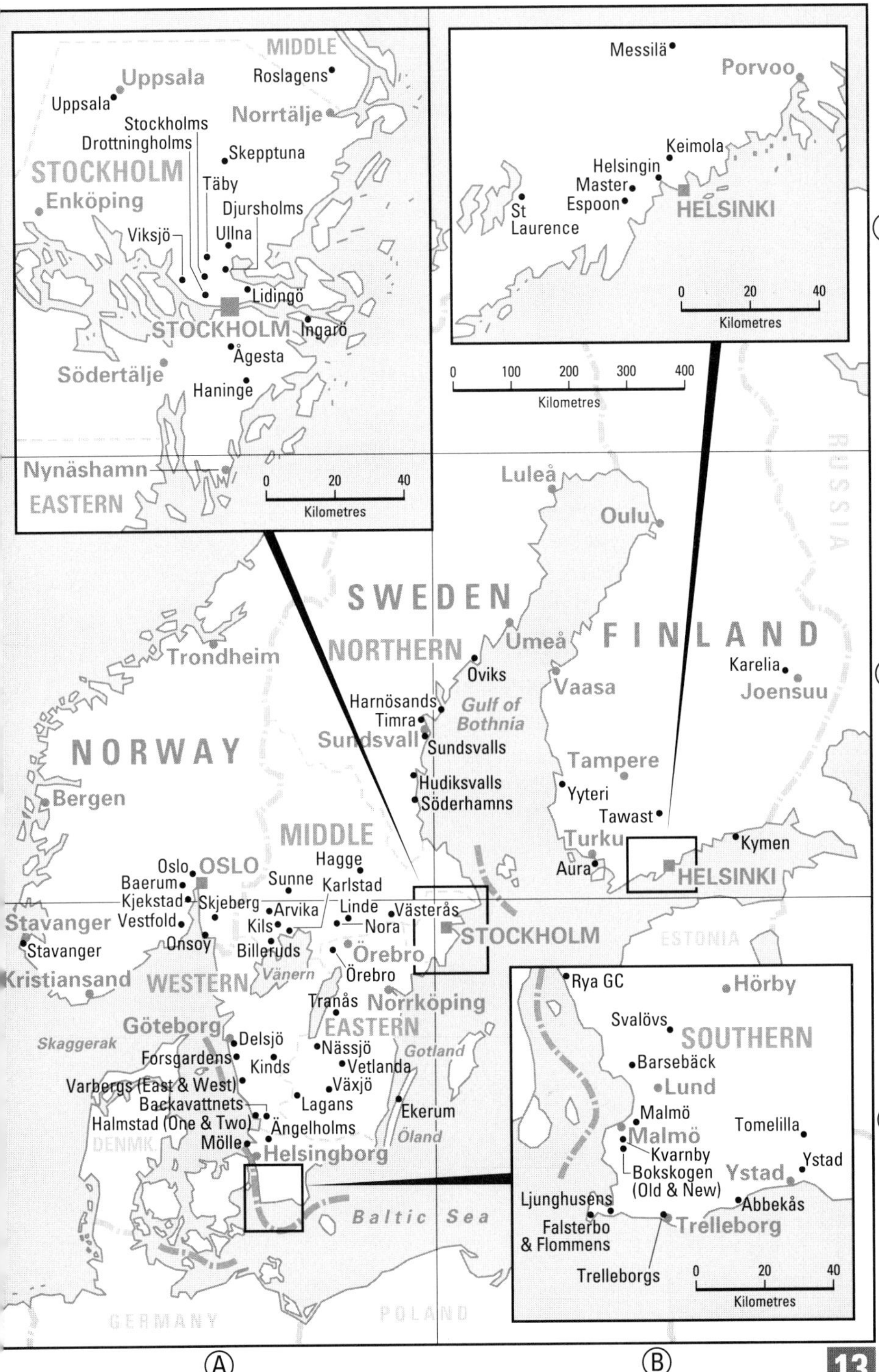
MIDDLE
Uppsala
Uppsala
Roslagens
Norrtälje
Stockholms
Drottningholms
Skepptuna
STOCKHOLM
Täby
Enköping
Djursholms
Viksjö
Ullna
Lidingö
STOCKHOLM
Ingarö
Ågesta
Södertälje
Haninge
Nynäshamn
EASTERN
0 20 40
Kilometres
Messilä
Porvoo
Keimola
Helsingin
Master
Espoon
St
Laurence
HELSINKI
0 20 40
Kilometres
0 100 200 300 400
Kilometres
RUSSIA
Luleå
Oulu
SWEDEN
NORTHERN
Umeå
FINLAND
Trondheim
Oviks
Karelia
Vaasa
Joensuu
Harnösands
Gulf of
Bothnia
Timra
Sundsvall
Sundsvalls
NORWAY
Tampere
Hudiksvalls
Yyteri
Bergen
Söderhamns
Tawast
MIDDLE
Turku
Kymen
Hagge
Aura
Oslo
OSLO
HELSINKI
Baerum
Sunne
Karlstad
Kjekstad
Skjeberg
Linde
Västerås
Arvika
Stavanger
Vestfold
Kils
Nora
STOCKHOLM
ESTONIA
Onsoy
Stavanger
Billeruds
Örebro
Kristiansand
WESTERN
Vänern
Örebro
Rya GC
Hörby
Tranås
Norrköping
Göteborg
Svalövs
EASTERN
SOUTHERN
Skaggerak
Delsjö
Nässjö
Gotland
Barsebäck
Forsgardens
Kinds
Vetlanda
Varbergs (East & West)
Växjö
Lund
Backavattnets
Lagans
Ekerum
Malmö
Halmstad (One & Two)
Ängelholms
Tomelilla
Öland
Malmö
DENMK.
Mölle
Kvarnby
Ystad
Helsingborg
Bokskogen
Ystad
(Old & New)
Ljunghusens
Abbekås
Baltic Sea
Trelleborg
Falsterbo
& Flommens
Trelleborgs
0 20 40
Kilometres
GERMANY
POLAND
①
②
③
Ⓐ
Ⓑ

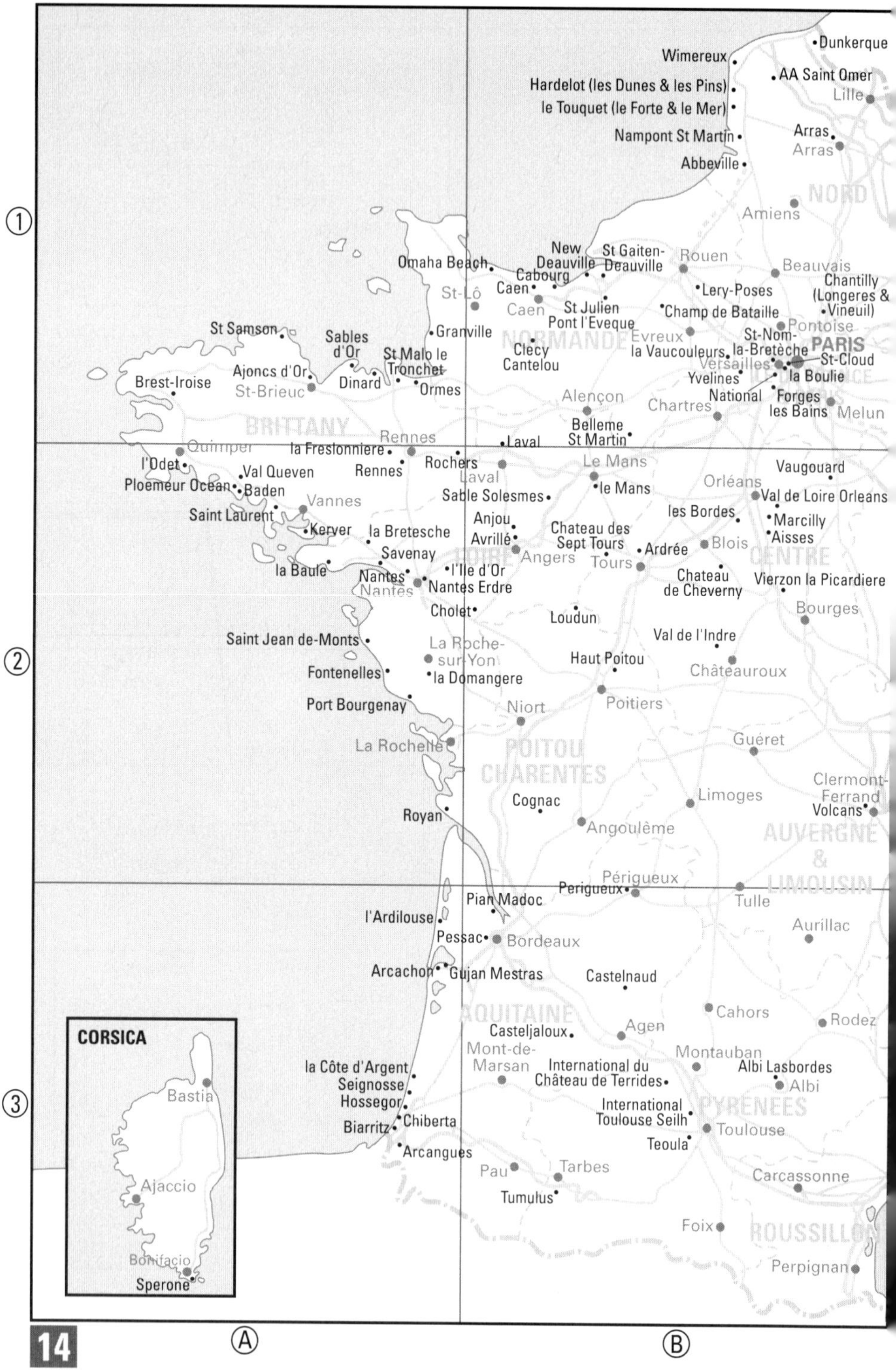

Dunkerque
Wimereux
AA Saint Omer
Hardelot (les Dunes & les Pins)
Lille
le Touquet (le Forte & le Mer)
Nampont St Martin
Arras
Arras
Abbeville
NORD
Amiens
Omaha Beach
New Deauville
St Gaiten-Deauville
Rouen
Beauvais
Cabourg
Chantilly (Longeres & Vineuil)
Caen
Lery-Poses
St-Lô
St Julien
Caen
Champ de Bataille
Pont l'Eveque
St Samson
Granville
NORMANDE
Evreux
Pontoise
Sables d'Or
Clecy
St-Nom-la-Bretèche
PARIS
St Malo le Tronchet
la Vaucouleurs
Ajoncs d'Or
Cantelou
Versailles
St-Cloud
Brest-Iroise
Dinard
Yvelines
la Boulie
St-Brieuc
Ormes
Alençon
National
Forges les Bains
Chartres
Melun
BRITTANY
Belleme St Martin
Rennes
Laval
Quimper
la Freslonniere
Rochers
Le Mans
l'Odet
Rennes
Laval
Vaugouard
Val Queven
le Mans
Orléans
Ploemeur Ocean
Baden
Sable Solesmes
Val de Loire Orleans
Vannes
les Bordes
Saint Laurent
Anjou
Chateau des Sept Tours
Marcilly
Kerver
la Bretesche
Avrillé
Aisses
Savenay
Angers
Ardrée
Blois
CENTRE
LOIRE
Tours
la Baule
Nantes
l'Ile d'Or
Chateau de Cheverny
Vierzon la Picardiere
Nantes
Nantes Erdre
Cholet
Bourges
Loudun
Saint Jean de-Monts
Val de l'Indre
La Roche-sur-Yon
Haut Poitou
Fontenelles
la Domangere
Châteauroux
Port Bourgenay
Poitiers
Niort
Guéret
La Rochelle
POITOU CHARENTES
Clermont-Ferrand
Cognac
Limoges
Royan
Volcans
Angoulême
AUVERGNE & LIMOUSIN
Périgueux
Perigueux
Tulle
Pian Madoc
l'Ardilouse
Aurillac
Pessac
Bordeaux
Arcachon
Gujan Mestras
Castelnaud
AQUITAINE
Cahors
Rodez
Agen
Casteljaloux
Mont-de-Marsan
Montauban
la Côte d'Argent
International du Château de Terrides
Albi Lasbordes
Seignosse
Albi
Hossegor
International Toulouse Seilh
PYRENEES
Biarritz
Chiberta
Toulouse
Teoula
Arcangues
Pau
Tarbes
Carcassonne
Tumulus
Foix
ROUSSILLON
Perpignan
CORSICA
Bastia
Ajaccio
Bonifacio
Sperone
1
2
3
A
B

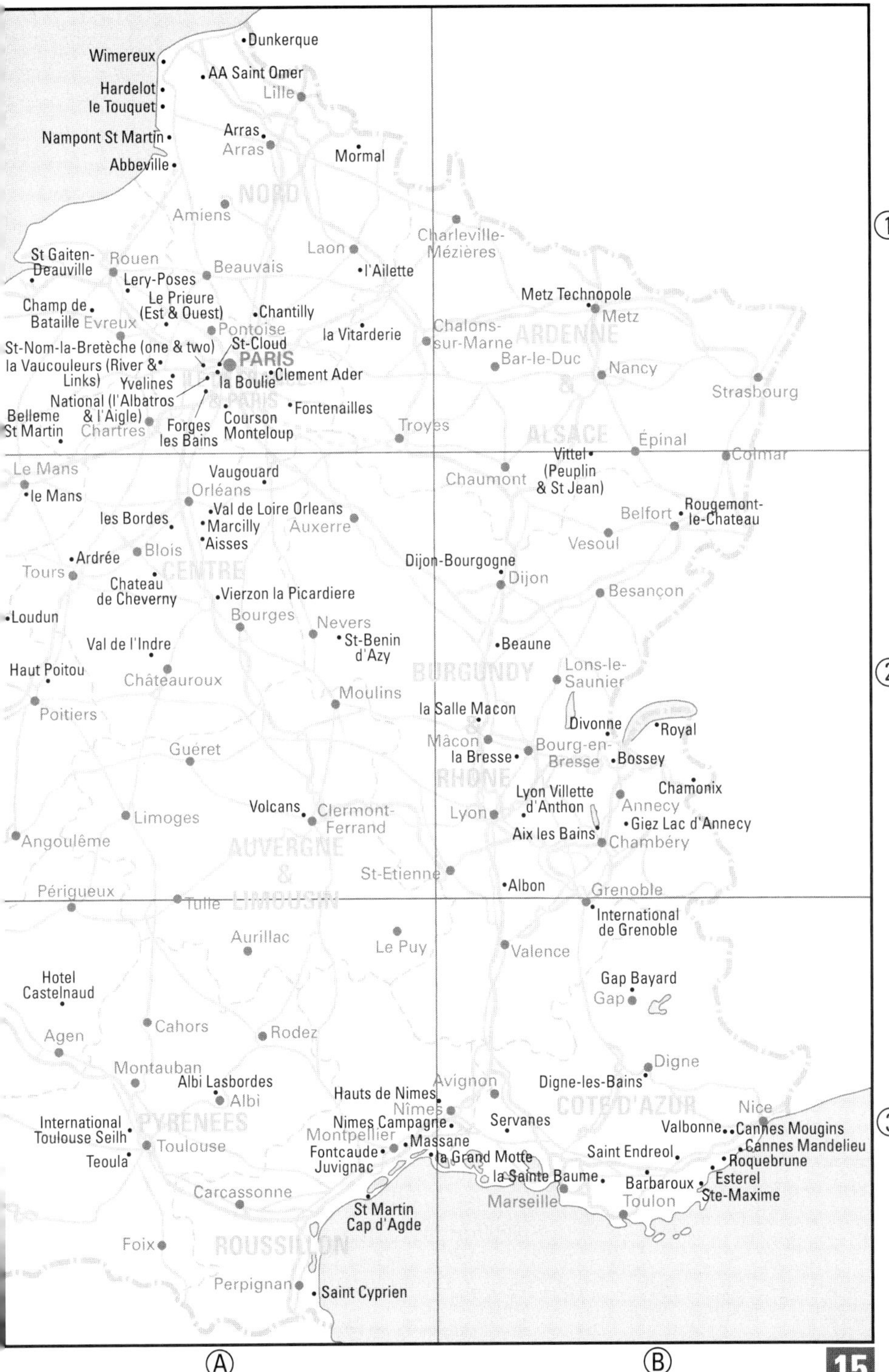
Dunkerque
Wimereux
AA Saint Omer
Hardelot
le Touquet
Lille
Nampont St Martin
Arras
Arras
Mormal
Abbeville
NORD
Amiens
Charleville-Mézières
Laon
St Gaiten-Deauville
Rouen
Beauvais
l'Ailette
Lery-Poses
Metz Technopole
Champ de Bataille
Le Prieure (Est & Ouest)
Chantilly
Metz
Evreux
Pontoise
la Vitarderie
Chalons-sur-Marne
ARDENNE
St-Nom-la-Bretèche (one & two)
St-Cloud
PARIS
Bar-le-Duc
la Vaucouleurs (River & Links)
Yvelines
la Boulie
Clement Ader
Nancy
&
Strasbourg
National (l'Albatros & l'Aigle)
Fontenailles
Belleme St Martin
Chartres
Forges les Bains
Courson Monteloup
Troyes
ALSACE
Épinal
Vittel (Peuplin & St Jean)
Colmar
Le Mans
le Mans
Vaugouard
Orléans
Chaumont
Val de Loire Orleans
Rougemont-le-Chateau
les Bordes
Marcilly
Auxerre
Belfort
Aisses
Vesoul
Ardrée
Blois
Dijon-Bourgogne
Tours
CENTRE
Dijon
Chateau de Cheverny
Vierzon la Picardiere
Besançon
Loudun
Bourges
Nevers
St-Benin d'Azy
Beaune
Val de l'Indre
Haut Poitou
BURGUNDY
Lons-le-Saunier
Châteauroux
Moulins
Poitiers
la Salle Macon
Divonne
Royal
Mâcon
Bourg-en-Bresse
la Bresse
Bossey
Gueret
RHONE
Chamonix
Lyon Villette d'Anthon
Volcans
Clermont-Ferrand
Annecy
Lyon
Limoges
Giez Lac d'Annecy
Aix les Bains
Chambéry
Angoulême
AUVERGNE
&
St-Etienne
Albon
Grenoble
Périgueux
Tulle
LIMOUSIN
International de Grenoble
Aurillac
Le Puy
Valence
Hotel Castelnaud
Gap Bayard
Gap
Cahors
Agen
Rodez
Digne
Montauban
Albi Lasbordes
Digne-les-Bains
Avignon
Hauts de Nimes
Albi
Nîmes
COTE D'AZUR
Nice
International Toulouse Seilh
PYRENEES
Nimes Campagne
Servanes
Valbonne
Cannes Mougins
Montpellier
Massane
Cannes Mandelieu
Toulouse
Fontcaude Juvignac
la Grand Motte
Saint Endreol
Roquebrune
Teoula
la Sainte Baume
Barbaroux
Esterel
Ste-Maxime
Carcassonne
Marseille
Toulon
St Martin Cap d'Agde
Foix
ROUSSILLON
Perpignan
Saint Cyprien
①
②
③
Ⓐ
Ⓑ

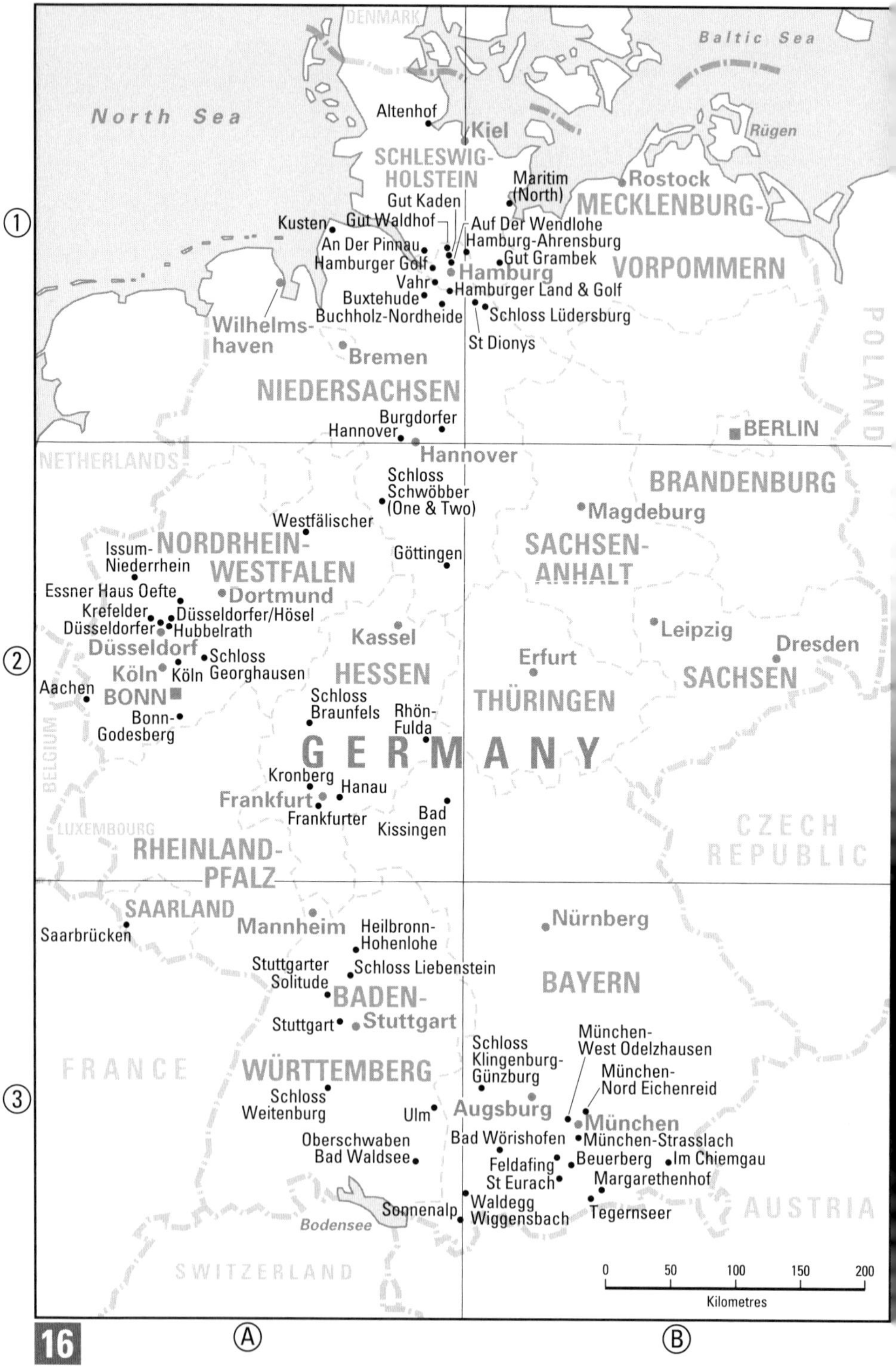
DENMARK
Baltic Sea
North Sea
Altenhof
Kiel
Rügen
SCHLESWIG-HOLSTEIN
Maritim (North)
Rostock
MECKLENBURG-VORPOMMERN
Gut Kaden
Kusten
Gut Waldhof
Auf Der Wendlohe
An Der Pinnau
Hamburg-Ahrensburg
Hamburger Golf
Gut Grambek
Hamburg
Vahr
Buxtehude
Hamburger Land & Golf
Buchholz-Nordheide
Schloss Lüdersburg
St Dionys
Wilhelmshaven
Bremen
POLAND
NIEDERSACHSEN
Burgdorfer
Hannover
BERLIN
Hannover
NETHERLANDS
BRANDENBURG
Schloss Schwöbber (One & Two)
Magdeburg
Westfälischer
NORDRHEIN-WESTFALEN
Issum-Niederrhein
Göttingen
SACHSEN-ANHALT
Essner Haus Oefte
Dortmund
Krefelder
Düsseldorfer/Hösel
Düsseldorfer
Hubbelrath
Kassel
Leipzig
Düsseldorf
Dresden
Schloss Georghausen
Erfurt
Köln
Köln
HESSEN
SACHSEN
Aachen
BONN
Schloss Braunfels
THÜRINGEN
Rhön-Fulda
Bonn-Godesberg
BELGIUM
GERMANY
Kronberg
Hanau
Frankfurt
Frankfurter
Bad Kissingen
LUXEMBOURG
CZECH REPUBLIC
RHEINLAND-PFALZ
SAARLAND
Nürnberg
Saarbrücken
Mannheim
Heilbronn-Hohenlohe
Stuttgarter Solitude
Schloss Liebenstein
BAYERN
BADEN-
Stuttgart
Stuttgart
München-West Odelzhausen
FRANCE
WÜRTTEMBERG
Schloss Klingenburg-Günzburg
München-Nord Eichenreid
Schloss Weitenburg
Ulm
Augsburg
München
Bad Wörishofen
München-Strasslach
Oberschwaben Bad Waldsee
Feldafing
Beuerberg
Im Chiemgau
St Eurach
Margarethenhof
Sonnenalp
Waldegg Wiggensbach
Tegernseer
Bodensee
AUSTRIA
SWITZERLAND
0
50
100
150
200
Kilometres
1
2
3
A
B

Italy Golf Course Map

SWITZERLAND / AUSTRIA / HUNGARY / SLOVENIA / CROATIA / BOSNIA-HERZEGOVINA

LOMBARDIA
- Monticello (One & Two)
- Carimate
- La Pinetina
- Barlassina
- Menaggio e Cadenabbia
- Alpino di Stresa
- Circolo Golf Villa d'Este
- Castelconturbia
- Bergamo
- Milano
- Zoate

VENETO
- Frassanelle
- Venézia
- Verona
- Pàdova
- Albarella
- Trieste

PIEMONTE
- I Roveri
- Le Fronde
- Biella "Le Betulle"
- Torino

EMILIA-ROMAGNA
- Modena
- Bologna
- Ravenna
- Croara
- Adriatic Cérvia

LIGURIA
- Gènova
- Rapallo
- Garlenda
- Degli Ulivi

TOSCANA
- Montecatini
- Firenze
- Firenze Ugolino
- Punta Ala
- Elba

Ancona

Ligurian Sea

ITALY

LAZIO
- Le Querce
- Olgiata
- ROMA
- Parco de Medici
- Castelgandolfo
- Roma
- Eucalyptus

Pescara

Adriatic Sea

PUGLIA
- Fòggia
- Bari
- Napoli
- Taranto
- Riva dei Tessali

SARDEGNA
- Pevero
- Sassari
- Cagliari
- Circolo Golf Is Molas

Tyrrhenian Sea

Cosenza

Mediterranean Sea

SICILIA
- Palermo
- Siracusa

Pantelleria

MALTA

ALGERIA / TUNISIA

0 — 100 — 200 — 300 Kilometres

Ⓐ Ⓑ **17**

18

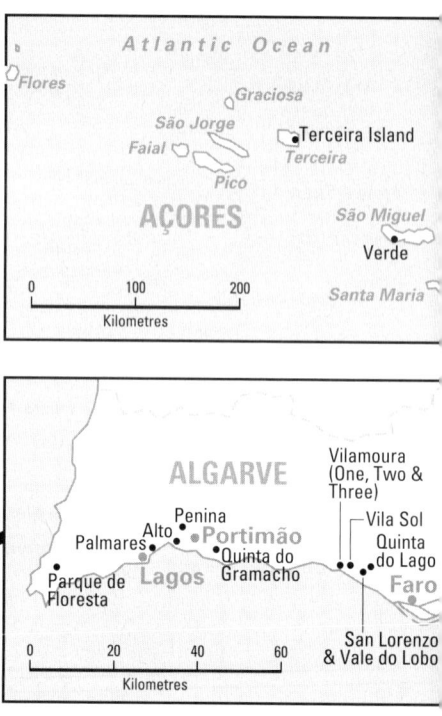

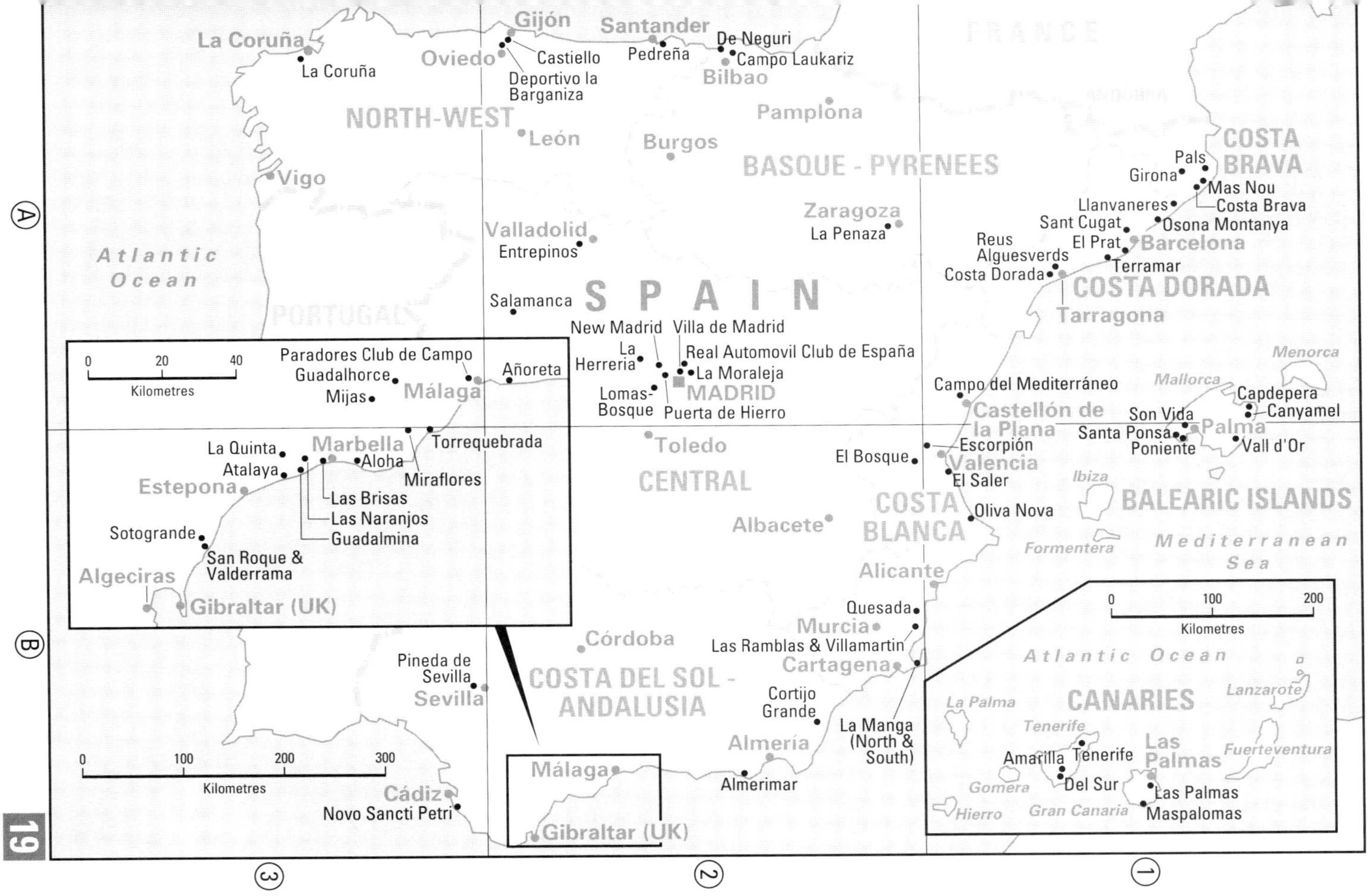

FRANCE
ANDORRA
La Coruña
Gijón
Santander
Oviedo
Castiello
Deportivo la Barganiza
Pedreña
De Neguri
Campo Laukariz
Bilbao
NORTH-WEST
León
Burgos
Pamplona
BASQUE - PYRENEES
Vigo
Valladolid
Entrepinos
Zaragoza
La Penaza
Atlantic Ocean
PORTUGAL
Salamanca
SPAIN
New Madrid
Villa de Madrid
La Herreria
Real Automovil Club de España
La Moraleja
Lomas-Bosque
MADRID
Puerta de Hierro
Toledo
CENTRAL
Albacete
COSTA BLANCA
Alicante
Córdoba
COSTA DEL SOL - ANDALUSIA
Pineda de Sevilla
Sevilla
Cádiz
Novo Sancti Petri
Málaga
Gibraltar (UK)
Murcia
Quesada
Las Ramblas & Villamartin
Cartagena
La Manga (North & South)
Cortijo Grande
Almería
Almerimar
0
100
200
300
Kilometres
COSTA BRAVA
Pals
Girona
Mas Nou
Costa Brava
Llanvaneres
Osona Montanya
Sant Cugat
El Prat
Barcelona
Reus
Alguesverds
Costa Dorada
Terramar
COSTA DORADA
Tarragona
Menorca
Mallorca
Capdepera
Canyamel
Campo del Mediterráneo
Castellón de la Plana
Son Vida
Santa Ponsa
Poniente
Palma
Vall d'Or
Escorpión
El Bosque
Valencia
El Saler
Ibiza
BALEARIC ISLANDS
Oliva Nova
Formentera
Mediterranean Sea
0
20
40
Kilometres
Paradores Club de Campo
Guadalhorce
Mijas
Málaga
Añoreta
Torrequebrada
La Quinta
Marbella
Atalaya
Aloha
Miraflores
Estepona
Las Brisas
Las Naranjos
Guadalmina
Sotogrande
San Roque & Valderrama
Algeciras
Gibraltar (UK)
0
100
200
Kilometres
Atlantic Ocean
CANARIES
La Palma
Tenerife
Lanzarote
Amarilla
Tenerife
Las Palmas
Fuerteventura
Gomera
Del Sur
Las Palmas
Hierro
Gran Canaria
Maspalomas
A
B
3
2
1

Index

AUSTRIA

AUSTRIA-WÖRTHER SEE GOLF CLUB	153
COLONY CLUB GUTENHOF (EAST)	153
COLONY CLUB GUTENHOF (WEST)	154
GOLF & COUNTRY CLUB BRUNN	154
GOLF CLUB DONNERSKIRCHEN	154
GOLF CLUB ENZESFELD	154
GOLF CLUB FRAUENTHAL	154
GOLF CLUB FURSTENFELD	154
GUT ALTENTANN GOLF CLUB	154
GUT BRANDLHOF GOLF CLUB	154
GUT MURSTÄTTEN GOLF CLUB	155
KÄRNTNER GOLF CLUB	155
KITZBÜHEL SCHWARZSEE	155
LINZ-SAINT FLORIAN GOLF CLUB	155
MURHOF GOLF CLUB	155
SALZKAMMERGUT GOLF CLUB	155
SCHLOSS ERNEGG GOLF CLUB	155
SCHLOSS PICHLARN GOLF CLUB	155
WALDVIERTEL GOLF CLUB	156
WIEN GOLF CLUB	156

BELGIUM

BERCUIT GOLF CLUB	157
BOSSENSTEIN GOLF CLUB	157
CLEYDAEL GOLF CLUB	158
DAMME GOLF CLUB	158
FALNUÉE GOLF CLUB	158
INTERNATIONAL GOMZE GOLF CLUB	158
KEERBERGEN GOLF CLUB	158
LIMBURG GOLF CLUB	158
MONT GARNI GOLF CLUB	158
RIGENÉE GOLF CLUB	158
ROYAL ANTWERP GOLF CLUB	159
ROYAL LATEM GOLF CLUB	159
ROYAL OSTEND GOLF CLUB	159
ROYAL WATERLOO CLUB (TWO)	159
ROYAL WATERLOO GOLF CLUB	159
ROYAL ZOUTE GOLF CLUB	159
SPIEGELVEN GOLF CLUB	159
WINGE GOLF CLUB	159

DENMARK

ÅLBORG GOLF CLUB	162
ÅRHUS GOLF CLUB	162
BORNHOLMS GOLF CLUB	161
DRAGØR GOLF CLUB	164
ESBJERG GOLF CLUB	162
FURESØ GOLF CLUB	164
GILLELEJE GOLF CLUB	164
GOLF CLUB HEDELAND	164
GOLF CLUB STORSTRØMMEN	164
GOLFKLUBBEN HVIDE KLIT	162
HADERSLEV GOLF CLUB	162
HELSINGØR GOLF CLUB	164
HENNE GOLF CLUB	162
HERNING GOLF CLUB	162
HILLERØD GOLF CLUB	164
HJØRRING GOLF CLUB	163
HOLSTEBRO GOLF CLUB	163
KAJ LYKKE GOLF CLUB	163
KØBENHAVNS GOLF CLUB	165
KOLDING GOLF CLUB	163
KORSØR GOLF CLUB	165
NORDBORNHOLMS GOLF CLUB	161
ODENSE GOLF CLUB	161
RANDERS GOLF CLUB	163
RUNGSTED GOLF CLUB	165
SCT KNUDS GOLF CLUB	161
SILKEBORG GOLF CLUB	163
SØLLERØD GOLF CLUB	165
SYDSJÆLLANDS GOLF CLUB	165
VALLENSBÆK GOLF CLUB	165
VEJLE GOLF CLUB	163
VESTFYNS GOLF CLUB	161
VIBORG GOLF CLUB	163

ENGLAND

ABBEYDALE GOLF CLUB	85
ABBEY PARK G & CC	82
ABBOTSLEY GOLF CLUB	20
ACCRINGTON GOLF CLUB	46
ADDINGTON COURT (CHAMPIONSHIP)	69
ADDINGTON COURT (FALCONWOOD)	69
AIRLINKS GOLF CLUB	57
ALDEBURGH GOLF CLUB	68
ALDENHAM G & CC	39
ANDERIDA GOLF CLUB	75
APPLEBY GOLF CLUB	25
ARKLEY GOLF CLUB	39
ASHRIDGE GOLF CLUB	39
ASHTON AND LEA GOLF CLUB	46
ASHTON-IN-MAKERFIELD G C	52
AUSTERFIELD PARK GOLF CLUB	85
AXE CLIFF GOLF CLUB	26
BALLARDS GORE GOLF CLUB	31
BANSTEAD DOWNS GOLF CLUB	69
BARLASTON GOLF CLUB	66
BARNARD CASTLE GOLF CLUB	30
BARNHAM BROOM (HILL)	59
BARNHAM BROOM (VALLEY)	59
BASILDON GOLF CLUB	31
BASINGSTOKE GOLF CLUB	35
BATH GOLF CLUB	17
BEAU DESERT GOLF CLUB	67
BEESTON FIELDS GOLF CLUB	62
BELFRY GOLF CLUB (BRABAZON)	79
BELFRY GOLF CLUB (DERBY)	79
BELMONT-ON-WYE GOLF CLUB	38
BELTON PARK GOLF CLUB	49
BENTLEY GOLF CLUB	31
BERKSHIRE GC (BLUE)	18
BERKSHIRE GC (RED)	18
BERWICK-UPON-TWEED	61
BINGLEY ST IVES GOLF CLUB	87
BIRSTALL GOLF CLUB	48
BISHOP AUCKLAND GOLF CLUB	30
BISHOP'S STORTFORD GC	39
BLACKBURN GOLF CLUB	46
BLACKLEY GOLF CLUB	53
BLACKMOOR GOLF CLUB	35
BLACKPOOL NORTH SHORE G C	47
BLACKWELL GOLF CLUB	38
BLANKNEY GOLF CLUB	50
BODMIN GOLF CLUB	22
BOLTON OLD LINKS	53
BOOTHFERRY GOLF CLUB	42
BOOTLE GOLF CLUB	55
BOSTON GOLF CLUB	50
BRADLEY PARK GOLF CLUB	87
BRAINTREE GOLF CLUB	31
BRAMHALL GOLF CLUB	53
BRAMHALL PARK GOLF CLUB	53
BRAMLEY GOLF CLUB	70
BRAMPTON GOLF CLUB	25
BRAMPTON PARK GOLF CLUB	20
BRAMSHAW (FOREST)	36
BRAMSHAW (MANOR)	35
BRANCEPETH CASTLE GOLF CLUB	30
BREAN GOLF CLUB	65
BRIDLINGTON GOLF CLUB	42
BRISTOL & CLIFTON GOLF CLUB	17
BROADSTONE GOLF CLUB	28
BROADWAY GOLF CLUB	82
BROCKENHURST MANOR G C	36
BROOKDALE GOLF CLUB	53
BROOME MANOR GOLF COMPLEX	80
BROUGH GOLF CLUB	42
BURNHAM & BERROW GOLF CLUB	65
BURTON-ON-TRENT GOLF CLUB	67
BURY ST EDMUNDS GOLF CLUB	68
BUSH HILL PARK GOLF CLUB	51
BUSHEY HALL GOLF CLUB	39
CALCOT PARK GOLF CLUB	18
CALDY GOLF CLUB	21
CALVERLEY GOLF CLUB	87
CAMBRIDGESHIRE MOAT HOUSE	20
CAME DOWN GOLF CLUB	28
CANONS BROOK GOLF CLUB	31
CANTERBURY GOLF CLUB	43
CANWICK PARK GOLF CLUB	50

Index

CARLYON BAY GOLF CLUB	22
CASTLETOWN GOLF CLUB	189
CATTERICK GARRISON GOLF CLUB	83
CHERRY LODGE GOLF CLUB	43
CHESHUNT GOLF CLUB	40
CHESTERTON GOLF CLUB	63
CHIGWELL GOLF CLUB	32
CHIPPENHAM GOLF CLUB	81
CHIPPING NORTON GOLF CLUB	63
CHIPPING SODBURY GOLF CLUB	17
CHORLEY GOLF CLUB	47
CHURCH STRETTON GOLF CLUB	64
CIRENCESTER GOLF CLUB	34
CITY OF NEWCASTLE GOLF CLUB	77
CLEEVE HILL GOLF CLUB	34
COBTREE MANOR PARK GC	43
COLD ASHBY GOLF CLUB	60
COLLINGTREE PARK GOLF CLUB	60
COOMBE HILL GOLF CLUB	70
COPT HEATH GLOF CLUB	79
COPTHORNE GOLF CLUB	75
CORHAMPTON GOLF CLUB	36
COSBY GOLF CLUB	49
COSTESSEY PARK GOLF CLUB	59
COTSWOLD EDGE GOLF CLUB	34
COTTESMORE COUNTRY CLUB (NEW)	76
COTTESMORE COUNTRY CLUB (OLD)	76
COULSDON COURT GOLF CLUB	70
COWDRAY PARK GOLF CLUB	76
COXMOOR GOLF CLUB	62
CRANBROOK GOLF CLUB	44
CRAY VALLEY GOLF CLUB	44
CRAYTHORNE GOLF CENTRE	67
CROOK GOLF CLUB	30
DALE HILL GOLF CLUB	74
DARENTH VALLEY GOLF COURSE	44
DARLINGTON GOLF CLUB	30
DIBDEN GOLF CENTRE	36
DIDSBURY GOLF CLUB	53
DISLEY GOLF CLUB	21
DOWNSHIRE GOLF COURSE	18
DROITWICH G & CC	82
DUNHAM FOREST G & CC	53
DUNSCAR GOLF CLUB	53
DUNSTANBURGH CASTLE	61
DURHAM CITY GOLF CLUB	30
DYKE GOLF CLUB	74
EALING GOLF CLUB	57
EASINGWOLD GOLF CLUB	83
EAST DORSET GOLF CLUB	28
EAST SUSSEX NATIONAL (EAST)	74
EAST SUSSEX NATIONAL (WEST)	74
ELLESBOROUGH GOLF CLUB	19
ELLESMERE GOLF CLUB	54
ELSTREE GOLF CLUB	40
ELY CITY GOLF CLUB	20
ENFIELD GOLF CLUB	58
ENMORE PARK GOLF CLUB	66
EPSOM GOLF CLUB	70
EREWASH VALLEY GOLF CLUB	26
ERLESTOKE SANDS GOLF CLUB	81
FARTHINGSTONE GOLF CENTRE	60
FAVERSHAM GOLF CLUB	44
FELIXSTOWE FERRY GOLF CLUB	68
FERNDOWN GOLF CLUB	28
FERNFELL GOLF CLUB	70
FILEY GOLF CLUB	83
FINCHLEY GOLF CLUB	51
FLAMBOROUGH HEAD GOLF CLUB	42
FOREST OF ARDEN (ARDEN)	79
FOREST OF ARDEN (AYLESFORD)	79
FORMBY GOLF CLUB	47
FORNHAM PARK G & CC	68
FORRESTER PARK GOLF CLUB	32
FOXHILLS (CHERTSEY)	70
FOXHILLS (LONGCROSS)	70
FRILFORD HEATH (RED)	64
FRINTON GOLF CLUB	32
FULFORD GOLF CLUB	83
FULWELL GOLF CLUB	58
GAINSBOROUGH GOLF CLUB	50
GANSTEAD PARK GOLF CLUB	42
GANTON GOLF CLUB	83
GATTON MANOR GOLF CLUB	70
GILLINGHAM GOLF CLUB	44
GLOUCESTER G & CC	34
GOG MAGOG	20
GOLDENHILL GOLF CLUB	67
GORING & STREATLEY GOLF CLUB	18
GRANGE PARK GOLF CLUB	55
GRIMSBY GOLF CLUB	42
HADLEY WOOD GOLF CLUB	40
HAINAULT FOREST GOLF CLUB	32
HALIFAX BRADLEY HALL GC	87
HALIFAX GOLF CLUB	87
HAM MANOR GOLF CLUB	76
HANDSWORTH GOLF CLUB	79
HANKLEY COMMON GOLF CLUB	71
HAREFIELD PLACE GOLF CLUB	58
HARROGATE GOLF CLUB	83
HARTSBOURNE G & CC	40
HAWKSTONE PARK (HAWKSTONE)	64
HAYDOCK PARK GOLF CLUB	55
HAYLING GOLF CLUB	36
HAYWARDS HEATH GOLF CLUB	76
HELLIDON LAKES G & CC	60
HESWALL GOLF CLUB	56
HEXHAM GOLF CLUB	61
HICKLETON GOLF CLUB	85
HIGHWOODS GOLF CLUB	74
HILL BARN GOLF CLUB	76
HILLSIDE GOLF CLUB	56
HINCKLEY GOLF CLUB	49
HINDHEAD GOLF CLUB	71
HINTLESHAM HALL GOLF CLUB	68
HOCKLEY GOLF CLUB	36
HOLME HALL GOLF CLUB	42
HOME PARK GOLF CLUB	71
HORNCASTLE GOLF CLUB	50
HORNSEA GOLF CLUB	43
HORSLEY LODGE GOLF CLUB	26
HUDDERSFIELD GOLF CLUB	87
HUNSTANTON GOLF CLUB	59
HYDE HOUSE GOLF CLUB (OLD)	28
HYDE HOUSE GOLF CLUB (NEW)	28
IFIELD GOLF & COUNTRY CLUB	76
ILFRACOMBE GOLF CLUB	27
IMMINGHAM GOLF CLUB	43
INGESTRE PARK GOLF CLUB	67
IPSWICH GOLF CLUB	68
ISLE OF PURBECK GOLF CLUB	29
JOHN O'GAUNT G C (CARTHAGENA)	17
JOHN O'GAUNT GOLF CLUB	17
KEDLESTON PARK GOLF CLUB	26
KESWICK GOLF CLUB	25
KETTERING GOLF CLUB	60
KIDDERMINSTER GOLF CLUB	82
KING'S LYNN GOLF CLUB	59
KING'S NORTON GOLF CLUB	38
KINGSWOOD G & CC	71
KINGTON GOLF CLUB	38
KIRBY MUXLOE GOLF CLUB	49
KIRKBYMOORSIDE GOLF CLUB	84
KNOLE PARK GOLF CLUB	44
KNOTT END GOLF CLUB	47
KNOWLE GOLF CLUB	17
LA MOYE GOLF CLUB	189
LANCASTER G & CC	47
LANGDON HILLS GOLF CLUB	32
LANGLEY PARK GOLF CLUB	44
LEAMINGTON & COUNTY GC	78
LEATHERHEAD GOLF CLUB	71
LEE-ON-THE-SOLENT GOLF CLUB	36
LEEDS GOLF CLUB	87
LEEK GOLF CLUB	67
LEES HALL GOLF CLUB	85
LETCHWORTH GOLF CLUB	40
LINDRICK GOLF CLUB	62
LINKS GOLF CLUB	69
LIPHOOK GOLF CLUB	36
LITTLESTONE GOLF CLUB	44
LLANYMYNECH GOLF CLUB	64
LONDON SCOTTISH GOLF CLUB	71
LONGCLIFFE GOLF CLUB	49
LOUTH GOLF CLUB	50
LOW LAITHES GOLF CLUB	88
LYME REGIS GOLF CLUB	29
LYNEHAM GOLF CLUB	64
LYTHAM GREEN DRIVE GOLF CLUB	47
MAGDALENE FIELDS GOLF CLUB	62
MALDEN GOLF CLUB	71
MANCHESTER GOLF CLUB	54
MANOR HOUSE GOLF CLUB	27
MARKET RASEN & DISTRICT G C	50
MARLBOROUGH GOLF CLUB	81
MARPLE GOLF CLUB	21
MARYPORT GOLF CLUB	25
MELLOR & TOWNSCLIFFE	54
MELTHAM GOLF CLUB	88
MENDIP GOLF COURSE	66
MEON VALLEY G & CC	37
MICKLEOVER GOLF CLUB	26
MID-HERTS GOLF CLUB	40
MILL RIDE GOLF CLUB	18
MINCHINHAMPTON (NEW)	34
MINCHINHAMPTON (OLD)	34
MINEHEAD & WEST SOMERSET	66
MOOR ALLERTON GOLF CLUB	88
MOOR PARK GOLF CLUB (HIGH)	40
MOOR PARK GOLF CLUB (WEST)	40
MOORTOWN GOLF CLUB	88
MOTTRAM HALL GOLF CLUB	21
MOUNT OSWALD GOLF CLUB	30
MULLION GOLF CLUB	23
MUSWELL HILL GOLF CLUB	51

263

Index

NEW FOREST GOLF CLUB	37
NEW NORTH MANCHESTER	54
NEWARK GOLF CLUB	62
NEWCASTLE UNITED GOLF CLUB	77
NEWQUAY GOLF CLUB	23
NORMANBY HALL GOLF CLUB	43
NORTH DOWNS GOLF CLUB	71
NORTH FORELAND GOLF CLUB	45
NORTH HANTS GOLF CLUB	37
NORTH MIDDLESEX GOLF CLUB	52
NORTH WILTS GOLF CLUB	81
NORTHCLIFFE GOLF CLUB	88
NOTTS GOLF CLUB	62
NUNEATON GOLF CLUB	78
OAKDALE GOLF CLUB	84
OAKMERE PARK GOLF CLUB	63
OAKS SPORTS CENTRE	72
OLD THORNS GOLF CLUB	37
ORSETT GOLF CLUB	32
OSWESTRY GOLF CLUB	65
PANNAL GOLF CLUB	84
PARKSTONE GOLF CLUB	29
PATSHULL PARK GOLF CLUB	65
PAXHILL PARK GOLF CLUB	76
PENWORTHAM GOLF CLUB	48
PERRANPORTH GOLF CLUB	24
PETERBOROUGH MILTON GC	20
PETERSFIELD GOLF CLUB	37
PIKE HILLS GOLF CLUB	84
PINNER HILL GOLF CLUB	58
PORTAL GOLF COMPLEX	21
PORTERS PARK GOLF CLUB	41
POTTERS BAR GOLF CLUB	41
PRENTON GOLF CLUB	56
PRINCE'S GOLF CLUB	45
PUCKRUP HALL GOLF CLUB	34
PURLEY CHASE G & CC	78
PYECOMBE GOLF CLUB	77
QUIETWATERS (LAKES)	33
QUIETWATERS (LINKS)	32
READING GOLF CLUB	18
REDBOURN GOLF CLUB	41
REDDISH VALE GOLF CLUB	54
REDDITCH GOLF CLUB	82
RENISHAW PARK GOLF CLUB	86
RINGWAY GOLF CLUB	54
ROBIN HOOD GOLF CLUB	80
ROCHDALE GOLF CLUB	54
ROCHESTER & COBHAM GC	45
ROMILEY GOLF CLUB	54
ROMNEY WARREN GOLF CLUB	45
ROMSEY GOLF CLUB	37
ROSS-ON-WYE GOLF CLUB	38
ROSSENDALE GOLF CLUB	48
ROTHERHAM GOLF CLUB	86
ROTHLEY PARK GOLF CLUB	49
ROWLANDS CASTLE GOLF CLUB	37
ROYAL ASHDOWN FOREST	75
ROYAL BIRKDALE GOLF CLUB	56
ROYAL BLACKHEATH GOLF CLUB	52
ROYAL CINQUE PORTS GOLF CLUB	45
ROYAL CROMER GOLF CLUB	59
ROYAL LIVERPOOL GOLF CLUB	57
ROYAL LYTHAM & ST. ANNES	48
ROYAL MID-SURREY (INNER)	72
ROYAL MID-SURREY (OUTER)	72
ROYAL NORTH DEVON GC	27
ROYAL ST. GEORGE'S GOLF CLUB	45
ROYAL WEST NORFOLK	59
ROYAL WORLINGTON & NEWMARKET	69
ROYSTON GOLF CLUB	41
RUDDINGTON GRANGE GOLF CLUB	63
RUXLEY PARK GOLF CENTRE	45
SADDLEWORTH GOLF CLUB	55
ST MELLION GC (NICKLAUS)	24
ST MELLION GOLF CLUB (OLD)	24
ST. AUGUSTINE'S GOLF CLUB	45
ST. GEORGE'S HILL GOLF CLUB	72
SALE GOLF CLUB	55
SALISBURY & SOUTH WILTS	81
SAND MOOR GOLF CLUB	88
SANDFORD SPRINGS GOLF CLUB	37
SANDILANDS GOLF CLUB	50
SANDWELL PARK GOLF CLUB	80
SANDY LODGE GOLF CLUB	58
SAUNTON GOLF CLUB (EAST)	27
SAUNTON GOLF CLUB (WEST)	27
SCARBOROUGH NORTH CLIFFE	84
SCARBOROUGH SOUTH CLIFFE	84
SCARCROFT GOLF CLUB	88
SEACROFT GOLF CLUB	51
SEAFORD GOLF CLUB	75
SEAHAM GOLF CLUB	31
SEASCALE GOLF CLUB	25
SEATON CAREW (BRABAZON)	22
SEATON CAREW (OLD)	22
SELBY GOLF CLUB	84
SELSDON PARK GOLF CLUB	72
SHAW HILL G & CC	48
SHERBORNE GOLF CLUB	29
SHERWOOD FOREST GOLF CLUB	63
SHIPLEY GOLF CLUB	88
SHIRLEY GOLF CLUB	80
SHREWSBURY GOLF CLUB	65
SHRIVENHAM PARK GOLF CLUB	81
SIDMOUTH GOLF CLUB	27
SILLOTH-ON-SOLWAY GOLF CLUB	26
SILVERMERE GOLF CLUB	72
SINGING HILLS GOLF CLUB	77
SITWELL PARK GOLF CLUB	86
SKIPTON GOLF CLUB	84
SLALEY HALL GOLF CLUB	62
SLEAFORD GOLF CLUB	51
SOUTH HERTS GOLF CLUB	52
SOUTH SHEILDS GOLF CLUB	78
SOUTH STAFFORDSHIRE	80
SOUTHPORT & AINSDALE	48
SOUTHWOOD GOLF CLUB	38
ST ENODOC G C (CHURCH)	24
STAMFORD GOLF CLUB	21
STANTON-ON-THE-WOLDS	63
STAPLEFORD ABBOTS (ABBOTS)	33
STAPLEFORD ABBOTS (PRIORS)	33
STAVERTON PARK GOLF COMPLEX	61
STOKE POGES GOLF CLUB	19
STOKE ROCHFORD GOLF CLUB	51
STOKE-BY-NAYLAND (CONSTABLE)	33
STOKE-BY-NAYLAND (GAINSBOROUGH)	33
STONEHAM GOLF CLUB	38
STOURBRIDGE GOLF CLUB	80
SUNDRIDGE PARK (EAST)	46
SUNDRIDGE PARK (WEST)	46
SUNNINGDALE GOLF CLUB (NEW)	72
SUNNINGDALE GOLF CLUB (OLD)	72
SWINDON GOLF CLUB	81
TADMARTON HEATH GOLF CLUB	64
TANDRIDGE GOLF CLUB	73
TANKERSLEY PARK GOLF CLUB	86
TAUNTON & PICKERIDGE	66
TELFORD G & CC	65
TEWKESBURY PARK GOLF CLUB	35
THETFORD GOLF CLUB	60
THORNE GOLF CLUB	86
THORPENESS GOLF CLUB	69
THREE RIVERS GOLF CLUB	33
TRENT PARK GOLF CLUB	52
TRENTHAM GOLF CLUB	67
TRENTHAM PARK GOLF CLUB	67
TREVOSE GOLF CLUB	25
TYTHERINGTON	21
ULLESTHORPE COURT GOLF CLUB	49
UPMINSTER GOLF CLUB	33
UTTOXETER GOLF CLUB	68
VICARS CROSS GOLF CLUB	22
WALDRINGFIELD HEATH	69
WALLASEY GOLF CLUB	57
WALSALL GOLF CLUB	80
WALTON HEATH (NEW)	73
WALTON HEATH (OLD)	73
WARREN GOLF CLUB	33
WASHINGTON MOAT HOUSE	78
WATH GOLF CLUB	86
WAVENDON GOLF CENTRE	19
WELCOMBE GOLF CLUB	79
WELLINGBOROUGH GOLF CLUB	61
WELLS (SOMERSET) GOLF CLUB	66
WELWYN GARDEN CITY	41
WENSUM VALLEY GOLF CLUB	60
WENTWORTH (EAST)	73
WENTWORTH (EDINBURGH)	73
WENTWORTH (WEST)	73
WEST BERKSHIRE GOLF CLUB	19
WEST BOWLING GOLF CLUB	89
WEST BYFLEET GOLF CLUB	73
WEST CHILTINGTON GOLF CLUB	77
WEST CORNWALL GOLF CLUB	25
WEST END GOLF CLUB (HALIFAX)	189
WEST ESSEX GOLF CLUB	52
WEST HERTS GOLF CLUB	41
WEST HILL GOLF CLUB	73
WEST HOVE GOLF CLUB	75
WEST MIDDLESEX GOLF CLUB	58
WEST PARK G & CC	61
WEST SUSSEX GOLF CLUB	77
WEXHAM PARK GOLF COURSE	19
WEYMOUTH GOLF CLUB	29
WHIPSNADE PARK GOLF CLUB	41
WHITBURN GOLF CLUB	78
WHITBY GOLF CLUB	85
WHITEHILL GOLF CLUB	41
WILDERNESSE PARK GOLF CLUB	46
WILLINGDON GOLF CLUB	75
WILMSLOW GOLF CLUB	22
WILPSHIRE GOLF CLUB	48
WIMBLEDON PARK GOLF CLUB	52

Index

WINTER HILL GOLF CLUB	19	GOLF NATIONAL (L'AIGLE)	180	GOLF DE LA GRANDE-MOTTE	188
WITHINGTON GOLF CLUB	55	GOLF NATIONAL (L'ALBATROS)	179	GOLF DE LA SAINTE-BAUME	178
WOBURN G & C C (DUCHESS)	20	GOLF SABLE SOLESMES	182	GOLF DE LA SALLE MACON	175
WOBURN G & C C (DUKE'S)	19	GOLF SAINT-BENIN D'AZY	175	GOLF DE LA VITARDERIE	171
WOODHALL SPA GOLF CLUB	51	GOLF D'ABBEVILLE	183	GOLF DES AISSES	176
WOODHAM GOLF CLUB	31	GOLF D'AIX-LES-BAINS	174	GOLF DES FONTENELLES	182
WOOLTON GOLF CLUB	57	GOLF D'ALBI LASBORDES	187	GOLF DES HAUTS DE NIMES	188
WOOTTON BASSETT GOLF CLUB	81	GOLF D'ARCACHON	169	GOLF DES ORMES	172
WORCESTERSHIRE GOLF CLUB	82	GOLF D'ARCANGUES	169	GOLF DES SABLES-D'OR-LES-PINS	173
WORFIELD GOLF CLUB	65	GOLF D'ARDREE	176	GOLF DES TUMULUS	187
WORPLESDON GOLF CLUB	74	GOLF D'ARRAS	183	GOLF DES VOLCANS	179
WORTLEY GOLF CLUB	86	GOLF D'AVRILLE	181	GOLF DES YVELINES	179
WYKE GREEN GOLF CLUB	58	GOLF D'HARDELOT 'LES DUNES'	183	GOLF DU CHATEAU DES SEPT TOURS	176
YORK GOLF CLUB	85	GOLF D'HARDELOT 'LES PINS'	184	GOLF DU COGNAC	186
		GOLF D'HOSSEGOR	169	GOLF DU PIAN MEDOC (NEW)	170
		GOLF DE BADEN	172	GOLF DU PIAN MEDOC (OLD)	170
		GOLF DE BEAUNE	174	GOLF DU VAL QUEVEN	173
		GOLF DE BELLEME-ST-MARTIN	185	GOLF DU VAL DE L'INDRE	176
		GOLF DE BOSSEY	174	GRANVILLE GOLF CLUB	185
FINLAND		GOLF DE BREST-IROISE	172	LA BAULE GOLF CLUB	182
		GOLF DE CAEN	185	LA BRESSE GOLF CLUB	175
		GOLF DE CASTELJALOUX	169	LA DOMANGERE GOLF CLUB	182
AURA GOLF CLUB	166	GOLF DE CHAMONIX	174	LA VAUCOULEURS (LINKS)	180
ESPOON GOLF CLUB	166	GOLF DE CHIBERTA	169	LA VAUCOULEURS (RIVER)	180
GREEN ZONE GOLF CLUB	166	GOLF DE CHOLET	181	LAVAL GOLF CLUB	182
HELSINGIN GOLF CLUB	166	GOLF DE CLECY CANTELOU	185	LE MANS GOLF CLUB	182
KARELIA GOLF CLUB	167	GOLF DE DIGNE-LES-BAINS	177	LE PRIEURE GOLF CLUB (EST)	180
KEIMOLA GOLF CLUB	167	GOLF DE DIJON-BOURGOGNE	174	LE PRIEURE GOLF CLUB (OUEST)	180
KYMEN GOLF CLUB	167	GOLF DE DINARD	172	LE TOUQUET 'LE FORTE'	184
MASTER GOLF CLUB	167	GOLF DE DIVONNE	174	LE TOUQUET 'LE MER'	184
MESSILÄ GOLF CLUB	167	GOLF DE DUNKERQUE	184	LERY POSES GOLF CLUB	186
ST LAURENCE GOLF CLUB	167	GOLF DE FONTENAILLES	179	LES BORDES GOLF INTERNATIONAL	176
TAWAST GOLF & COUNTRY CLUB	167	GOLF DE FORGES-LES-BAINS	179	LOUDUN GOLF CLUB	186
YYTERI GOLF CLUB	167	GOLF DE GIEZ LAC D'ANNECY	175	METZ TECHNOPOLE	171
		GOLF DE KERVER	172	NEW GOLF DEAUVILLE	186
		GOLF DE LYON VILLETTE-D'ANTHON	175	NIMES CAMPAGNE GOLF CLUB	188
		GOLF DE MARCILLY	176	OMAHA BEACH GOLF CLUB	186
		GOLF DE MASSANE	188	ROCHERS GOLF CLUB	173
FRANCE		GOLF DE MORMAL	184	ROUGEMONT-LE-CHATEAU	171
		GOLF DE NAMPONT-ST-MARTIN	184	ROYAL GOLF CLUB	175
AA SAINT-OMER GOLF CLUB	183	GOLF DE NANTES	181	ROYAN GOLF CLUB	187
AJONCS D'OR GOLF CLUB	171	GOLF DE NANTES ERDRE	181	SAINT ENDREOL	178
ALBON GOLF CLUB	174	GOLF DE PESSAC	170	SAINT JEAN DE-MONTS	183
ANJOU GOLF & COUNTRY CLUB	181	GOLF DE PLOEMEUR OCEAN	172	SAINT LAURENT	173
CABOURG GOLF CLUB	185	GOLF DE PORT BOURGENAY	182	SAINT MARTIN CAP D'AGDE	188
CHANTILLY (LONGERES)	183	GOLF DE RENNES	173	SAINT NOM-LA-BRETECHE (ONE)	180
CHANTILLY (VINEUIL)	183	GOLF DE ROQUEBRUNE	178	SAINT NOM-LA-BRETECHE (TWO)	180
CHATEAU DE CHEVERNY	175	GOLF DE SAINT CYPRIEN	188	SAINT-JULIEN PONT-L'EVEQUE	186
CHATEAU DE TERRIDES	187	GOLF DE SAINT SAMSON	173	SPERONE GOLF CLUB	178
COURSON MONTELOUP	179	GOLF DE SAINTE-MAXIME	178	VAL DE LOIRE ORLEANS	177
DE CANNES MOUGINS	177	GOLF DE SAVENAY	182	VITTEL GOLF CLUB (PEUPLIN)	171
DE CANNES MANDELIEU	177	GOLF DE SEIGNOSSE	170	VITTEL GOLF CLUB (ST JEAN)	171
GAP-BAYARD GOLF CLUB	177	GOLF DE ST GATIEN-DEAUVILLE	185		
GOLF CLEMENT ADER	179	GOLF DE ST MALO LE TRONCHET	173		
GOLF CLUB VIERZON LA PICARDIERE	176	GOLF DE TEOULA	187		
GOLF CLUB DE BARBAROUX	177	GOLF DE VALBONNE	178		
GOLF CLUB DE BIARRITZ	169	GOLF DE VAUGOUARD	176		
GOLF CLUB DE PERIGVEUX	169	GOLF DE WIMEREUX	184	**GERMANY**	
GOLF CLUB DE SERVANES	177	GOLF DE L'AILETTE	184		
GOLF CLUB DU CHAMP DE BATAILLE	185	GOLF DE L'ARDILOUSE	170	AACHEN GOLF CLUB	196
GOLF CLUB DU HAUT-POITOU	186	GOLF DE L'ILE D'OR	181	ALTENHOF GOLF CLUB	197
GOLF ESTEREL	178	GOLF DE L'ODET	172	AN DER PINNAU GOLF CLUB	197
GOLF GUJAN MESTRAS	170	GOLF DE LA BRETESCHE	182	AUF DER WENDLOHE GOLF CLUB	193
GOLF HOTEL CASTELNAUD	170	GOLF DE LA COTE D'ARGENT	170	BAD GODESBERG	196
GOLF INTERNATIONAL TOULOUSE-SEILH	187	GOLF DE LA FRESLONNIERE	172	BAD KISSINGEN	191

265

Index

BAD WÖRISHOFEN GOLF CLUB	191
BEUERBERG GOLF CLUB	191
BUCHHOLZ-NORDHEIDE	195
BURGDORF GOLF CLUB	195
BUXTEHUDE GOLF CLUB	195
CLUB ZUR VAHR	193
DÜSSELDORF HÖSEL CLUB	196
DÜSSELDORFER GOLF CLUB	196
ESSENER HAUS EFTE GOLF CLUB	196
FELDAFING GOLF CLUB	191
FRANKFURTER GOLF CLUB	194
GÖTTINGEN GOLF CLUB	195
GUT GRAMBEK GOLF CLUB	198
GUT KADEN GOLF CLUB	193
GUT WALDHOF GOLF CLUB	193
HAMBURG-AHRENSBURG	193
HAMBURGER GOLF CLUB	193
HAMBURGER LAND & GOLF CLUB	193
HANAU GOLF CLUB	194
HANNOVER GOLF CLUB	195
HEILBRONN-HOHENLOHE	190
HUBBELRATH GOLF CLUB (EAST)	196
IM CHIEMGAU GOLF CLUB	191
ISSUM-NIEDERRHEIN GOLF CLUB	197
KÖLN GOLF CLUB	197
KREFELDER GOLF CLUB	197
KRONBERG GOLF CLUB	194
KÜSTEN GOLF CLUB	194
MARGARETHENHOF AM CLUB	191
MARITIM GOLF CLUB (NORTH)	198
MÜNCHENER CLUB	192
MÜNCHEN-NORD EICHENRIED	192
MÜNCHEN-WEST ODELZHAUSEN	192
OBERSCHWABEN-BAD WALDSEE	190
RHÖN-FULDA GOLF CLUB	194
SAARBRÜCKEN GOLF CLUB	190
ST DIONYS GOLF CLUB	195
ST EURACH LAND & GOLF CLUB	192
SCHLOSS BRAUNFELS	194
SCHLOSS GEORGHAUSEN	197
SCHLOSS KLINGENBURG GÜNZBURG	192
SCHLOSS LIEBENSTEIN	190
SCHLOSS LÜDERSBURG	194
SCHLOSS SCHWÖBBER (ONE)	195
SCHLOSS SCHWÖBBER (TWO)	196
SCHLOSS WEITENBURG	190
SPORT & KURHOTEL SONNENALP	192
STUTTGART SOLITUDE CLUB	190
TEGERNSEER BAD WIESSEE	192
ULM GOLF CLUB	190
WALDEGG-WIGGENSBACH	192
WESTFÄLISCHER	197

IRELAND - NORTHERN

ARDGLASS GOLF CLUB	134
ARMAGH GOLF CLUB	134
BALLYCASTLE GOLF CLUB	132
BALLYMENA GOLF CLUB	132
BALMORAL GOLF CLUB	132
BELVOIR PARK GOLF COURSE	132
BRIGHT CASTLE GOLF CLUB	134
CAIRNDHU GOLF CLUB	132
CARNALEA GOLF CLUB	135
CARRICKFERGUS GOLF CLUB	132
CASTLEROCK GOLF CLUB	136
CITY OF DERRY GOLF CLUB	136
CLANDEBOYE GOLF CLUB	135
DOWNPATRICK GOLF CLUB	135
DUNGANNON GOLF CLUB	136
DUNMURRY GOLF CLUB	132
FORTWILLIAM GOLF CLUB	133
KILLYMOON GOLF CLUB	136
KIRKISTOWN CASTLE GOLF CLUB	135
KNOCK GOLF CLUB	133
KNOCKBRACKEN G & CC	133
LISBURN GOLF CLUB	133
MALONE GOLF CLUB	133
MASSEREENE GOLF CLUB	133
NEWTOWNSTEWART GOLF CLUB	136
OMAGH GOLF CLUB	137
PORTADOWN GOLF CLUB	134
PORTSTEWART (STRAND)	136
ROYAL BELFAST	135
ROYAL COUNTY DOWN	135
ROYAL PORTRUSH (DUNLUCE)	133
ROYAL PORTRUSH (VALLEY)	133
SCRABO GOLF CLUB	135
SHANDON PARK GOLF CLUB	134
STRABANE GOLF CLUB	137
TANDRAGEE GOLF CLUB	134
WARRENPOINT GOLF CLUB	135

IRELAND - REPUBLIC OF

ARDEE GOLF CLUB	148
ATHLONE GOLF CLUB	150
BALBRIGGAN GOLF CLUB	142
BALLINASLOE GOLF CLUB	144
BALLYBUNION (NEW COURSE)	145
BALLYBUNION (OLD COURSE)	145
BALLYLIFFIN GOLF CLUB	141
BANDON GOLF CLUB	140
BEAVERSTOWN GOLF CLUB	142
BLACKBUSH GOLF CLUB	149
BLAINROE GOLF CLUB	152
BODENSTOWN G C (LADYHILL)	146
BODENSTOWN GOLF CLUB (OLD)	146
BUNDORAN GOLF CLUB	141
CARLOW GOLF CLUB	139
CASTLEBAR GOLF CLUB	148
CASTLETROY GOLF CLUB	147
CHARLEVILLE GOLF CLUB	140
CLONMEL GOLF CLUB	151
CLONTARF GOLF CLUB	143
CONNEMARA GOLF CLUB	144
CORK GOLF CLUB	140
COUNTY CAVAN GOLF CLUB	139
COUNTY LOUTH GOLF CLUB	148
COUNTY SLIGO GOLF CLUB	150
COURTOWN GOLF CLUB	151
DELGANY GOLF CLUB	152
DONEGAL GOLF CLUB	141
DOOKS GOLF CLUB	145
DUN LAOGHAIRE GOLF CLUB	143
DUNDALK GOLF CLUB	148
DUNFANAGHY GOLF CLUB	142
EAST CORK GOLF CLUB	140
EDMONDSTOWN GOLF CLUB	143
ELM PARK GOLF CLUB	143
ENNIS GOLF CLUB	139
ENNISCORTHY GOLF CLUB	152
ENNISCRONE GOLF CLUB	150
FERMOY GOLF CLUB	140
GOLF CHUMANN CEANN SIBEAL	145
GREENORE GOLF CLUB	148
GREYSTONES GOLF CLUB	152
HEATH GOLF CLUB	147
HERMITAGE GOLF CLUB	143
HOWTH GOLF CLUB	143
KILKENNY GOLF CLUB	147
KILLARNEY (KILLEEN COURSE)	145
KILLARNEY (MAHONY'S POINT)	145
KILLEEN GOLF CLUB	146
KNOCKANALLY GOLF CLUB	146
LAHINCH (CASTLE COURSE)	139
LAHINCH (OLD COURSE)	139
LAYTOWN & BETTYSTOWN G C	149
LIMERICK GOLF CLUB	148
MAHON GOLF CLUB	140
MALLOW GOLF CLUB	141
MONKSTOWN GOLF CLUB	141
MOUNT JULIET G & C C	147
MUSKERRY GOLF CLUB	141
NARIN & PORTNOO GOLF CLUB	142
NORTH WEST GOLF CLUB	142
NUREMORE GOLF CLUB	149
PORTMARNOCK GOLF CLUB	143
PORTSALON GOLF CLUB	142
PORTUMNA GOLF CLUB	144
ROSAPENNA GOLF CLUB	142
ROSSLARE GOLF CLUB	152
ROYAL DUBLIN GOLF CLUB	143
ROYAL TARA GOLF CLUB	149
SHANNON GOLF CLUB	140
SKERRIES GOLF CLUB	144
SLADE VALLEY GOLF CLUB	144
TRALEE GOLF CLUB	146
TRAMORE GOLF CLUB	151
TRIM GOLF CLUB	149
TUAM GOLF CLUB	145
TULLAMORE GOLF CLUB	150
WATERFORD GOLF CLUB	151
WATERVILLE GOLF LINKS	146
WESTPORT GOLF CLUB	149
WEXFORD GOLF CLUB	152
WOODBROOK GOLF CLUB	144

ITALY

ADRIATIC CERVIA GOLF CLUB	200
ALBARELLA GOLF CLUB	204
ALPINO DI STRESA GOLF CLUB	203

Index

BARLASSINA COUNTRY CLUB	202	SPAARNWOUDE GOLF CLUB	208	BANCHORY GOLF CLUB	98
BERGAMO 'L'ALBENZA'	202	UTRECHTSE DE PAN	208	BARSHAW GOLF CLUB	109
BIELLA 'LE BETULLE'	203	ZEEGERSLOOT GOLF CLUB	210	BATHGATE GOLF CLUB	105
BOLOGNA GOLF CLUB	200			BELLEISLE GOLF CLUB	109
CARIMATE GOLF CLUB	202			BIGGAR GOLF CLUB	109
CASTELCONTURBIA GOLF CLUB	203			BLAIRGOWRIE (LANDSDOWNE)	117
CASTELGANDOLFO GOLF CLUB	200			BLAIRGOWRIE (ROSEMOUNT)	117
CIRCOLO GOLF IS MOLAS	205			BOAT OF GARTEN GOLF CLUB	102
CIRCOLO GOLF VILLA D'ESTE	202	**NORWAY**		BON ACCORD GOLF CLUB	98
CROARA GOLF CLUB	200			BOTHWELL CASTLE GOLF CLUB	109
DEGLI ULIVI GOLF CLUB	201	BAERUM GOLF CLUB	211	BRAEHEAD GOLF CLUB	92
EUCALYPTUS GOLF CLUB	200	KJEKSTAD GOLF CLUB	211	BRAIDS UNITED GOLF CLUB	105
FIRENZE UGOLINO GOLF CLUB	204	ONSOY GOLF CLUB	211	BRECHIN GOLF CLUB	117
FRASSANELLE GOLF CLUB	205	OSLO GOLF HOTEL	211	BROOMIEKNOWE GOLF CLUB	105
GARLENDA GOLF CLUB	201	SKJEBERG GOLF CLUB	212	BRORA GOLF CLUB	102
GOLF CLUB LE FRONDE	204	STAVANGER GOLF CLUB	212	BUCHANAN CASTLE GOLF CLUB	92
GOLF CLUB PARCO DE'MEDICI	200	VESTFOLD GOLF CLUB	212	BUCKPOOL GOLF CLUB	98
I ROVERI GOLF CLUB	204			BURNTISLAND GOLF HOUSE CLUB	95
LA PINETINA GOLF CLUB	202			CAIRD PARK GOLF CLUB	117
LA QUERCE GOLF CLUB	201			CALLANDER GOLF CLUB	92
MENAGGIO & CADENABBIA	202			CAMPERDOWN GOLF CLUB	117
MILANO GOLF CLUB	203			CAMPSIE GOLF CLUB	109
MODENA GOLF CLUB	205	**PORTUGAL**		CANMORE GOLF CLUB	95
MONTECATINI GOLF CLUB	204			CARDROSS GOLF CLUB	109
MONTOCELLO GOLF CLUB (ONE)	203	ALTO GOLF	214	CARLUKE GOLF CLUB	109
MONTOCELLO GOLF CLUB (TWO)	203	CLUB DE CAMPO DE AROEIRA	215	CARNOUSTIE (BUDDON)	118
OLGIATA GOLF CLUB	201	CLUB DE GOLF PALMARES	214	CARNOUSTIE (BURNSIDE)	118
PADOVA GOLF CLUB	205	DE GOLF DA QUINTA DO LAGO	214	CARNOUSTIE (CHAMPIONSHIP)	118
PEVERO GOLF CLUB	205	ESTELA GOLF CLUB	216	CARNWATH GOLF CLUB	110
PUNTA ALA GOLF CLUB	204	GOLF ESTORIL	215	CAWDER GOLF CLUB	110
RAPALLO GOLF CLUB	201	GOLF VILA SOL	214	CLOBER GOLF CLUB	110
RIVA DEI TESSALI GOLF CLUB	201	LISBON SPORTS CLUB	216	CLYDEBANK & DISTRICT GC	110
ROMA GOLF CLUB	201	OPORTO GOLF CLUB	216	COLVILLE PARK GOLF CLUB	110
VENEZIA GOLF CLUB	205	PARQUE DA FLORESTA	214	COWAL GOLF CLUB	110
ZOATE GOLF CLUB	203	PENHA LONGA GOLF CLUB	216	COWGLEN GOLF CLUB	110
		PENINA GOLF CLUB	214	CRAIL GOLFING SOCIETY	95
		QUINTA DA MARINHA GOLF	216	CRIEFF GC (FERNTOWER)	118
		QUINTA DO GRAMACHO	214	CROW WOOD GOLF CLUB	110
		SAN LORENZO GOLF CLUB	215	CRUDEN BAY GOLF CLUB	99
		TERCEIRA ISLAND GOLF CLUB	217	CULLEN GOLF CLUB	99
NETHERLANDS		TROIA GOLF	216	DALMAHOY G & CC (EAST)	105
		VALE DO LOBO GOLF CLUB	215	DALMAHOY G & CC (WEST)	105
ALMEERDERHOUT	207	VERDE GOLF & COUNTRY CLUB	217	DALMILLING GOLF CLUB	111
ANDERSTEIN GOLF CLUB	207	VILAMOURA ONE (OLD COURSE)	215	DARLEY GOLF CLUB	111
BEST GOLF & COUNTRY CLUB	209	VILAMOURA THREE	215	DEER PARK GOLF CLUB	105
BROEKPOLDER GOLF CLUB	210	VILAMOURA TWO (NEW COURSE)	215	DEESIDE GOLF CLUB	99
BRUNSSUM MERHEIDE	209			DOLLAR GOLF CLUB	92
CROMSTRIJEN GOLF CLUB	210			DOUGALSTON GOLF CLUB	111
CROSSMOOR GOLF CLUB	209			DOWNFIELD GOLF CLUB	118
DE PURMER GOLF CLUB	208			DRUMPELLIER GOLF CLUB	111
DE VERWAEYDE SANDBERGEN	207			DUDDINGSTON GOLF CLUB	106
DE ZUID LIMBURGSE GOLF & CC	209	**SCOTLAND**		DUFFTOWN GOLF CLUB	99
EINDHOVENSCHE GOLF CLUB	209			DUMFRIES & COUNTY GC	93
GREVELINGENHOUT GOLF CLUB	210	ABERDOUR GOLF CLUB	95	DUMFRIES & GALLOWAY GC	93
HET RIJK VAV NIJMEGEN	208	ABERFOYLE GOLF CLUB	91	DUNBAR LINKS GOLF CLUB	106
HILVERSUMSCHE GOLF CLUB	208	ABOYNE GOLF CLUB	98	DUNBLANE NEW GOLF CLUB	92
HOENSHUIS G & C CLUB	209	ALLOA GOLF CLUB	92	DUNFERMLINE GOLF CLUB	95
KENNEMER GOLF & CC	208	ANNANHILL GOLF CLUB	108	DUNNIKIER PARK GOLF CLUB	96
KLEIBURG GOLF CLUB	210	ARBROATH GOLF CLUB	117	EAST RENFREWSHIRE GC	111
NOORD BRABANTSE GOLF CLUB	209	ARDEER GOLF CLUB	108	EASTWOOD GOLF CLUB	111
NOORD NEDERLANDSE	207	BABERTON GOLF CLUB	105	EDZELL GOLF CLUB	118
NOORDWIJKSE GOLF CLUB	208	BALBIRNIE PARK GOLF CLUB	95	ELGIN GOLF CLUB	99
RIJSWIJKSE GOLF CLUB	210	BALLATER GOLF CLUB	98	ELIE GOLF CLUB	96
ROSENDAELSCHE GOLF CLUB	207	BALLOCHMYLE GOLF CLUB	109	FALKIRK GOLF CLUB	92
SALLANDSCHE DE HOEK	207	BALNAGASK GOLF CLUB	98	FALKIRK TRYST GOLF CLUB	92

267

Index

FERENEZE GOLF CLUB	111	LUFFNESS NEW GOLF CLUB	107	THORNTON GOLF CLUB	98
FORFAR GOLF CLUB	118	LUNDIN GOLF CLUB	97	THURSO GOLF CLUB	104
FORRES GOLF CLUB	99	MACDONALD GOLF CLUB	100	TORVEAN GOLF CLUB	104
FORT WILLIAM GOLF CLUB	102	MACHRIE GOLF CLUB	114	TULLIALLAN GOLF CLUB	93
FORTROSE & ROSEMARKIE GC	103	MACHRIHANISH GOLF CLUB	114	TURNBERRY GOLF CLUB (AILSA)	116
FRASERBURGH GOLF CLUB	99	MILLPORT GOLF CLUB	114	TURNBERRY GOLF CLUB (ARRAN)	116
GALASHIELS GOLF CLUB	91	MOFFAT GOLF CLUB	94	TURRIFF GOLF CLUB	102
GARMOUTH & KINGSTON GC	99	MONIFIETH GOLF LINKS (MEDAL)	119	UPHALL GOLF CLUB	108
GIRVAN GOLF CLUB	111	MONTROSE LINKS (MEDAL COURSE)	119	WEST KILBRIDE GOLF CLUB	116
GLASGOW GAILES GOLF CLUB	112	MORAY GOLF CLUB (NEW)	101	WEST LINTON GOLF CLUB	91
GLASGOW GOLF CLUB	112	MORAY GOLF CLUB (OLD)	101	WEST LOTHIAN GOLF CLUB	108
GLEDDOCH G & C CLUB	112	MUCKHART GOLF CLUB	93	WESTERN GAILES GOLF CLUB	116
GLEN GOLF CLUB	106	MUIR OF ORD GOLF CLUB	103	WESTERWOOD G & C CLUB	116
GLENBERVIE GOLF CLUB	93	MUIRFIELD GOLF CLUB	107	WHITECRAIGS GOLF CLUB	116
GLENCORSE GOLF CLUB	106	MURCAR GOLF CLUB	101	WICK GOLF CLUB	104
GLENEAGLES (KING'S COURSE)	118	MURRAYSHALL GOLF CLUB	119	WIGTOWNSHIRE COUNTY GC	95
GLENEAGLES (MONARCH'S)	119	MUSSELBURGH GOLF CLUB	107	WISHAW GOLF CLUB	117
GLENEAGLES (QUEEN'S COURSE)	119	NAIRN DUNBAR GOLF CLUB	103		
GLENROTHES GOLF CLUB	96	NAIRN GOLF CLUB	103		
GOLSPIE GOLF CLUB	103	NEWMACHER GOLF CLUB	101		
GOUROCK GOLF CLUB	112	NEWTONMORE GOLF CLUB	103		
GRANGEMOUTH GOLF CLUB	93	NORTH BERWICK GOLF CLUB	107		
GRANTOWN-ON-SPEY GOLF CLUB	100	NORTH INCH GOLF CLUB	120	# SPAIN	
GREENOCK GOLF CLUB	112	OLDMELDRUM GOLF CLUB	101		
GULLANE GOLF CLUB (NO. 1)	106	PAISLEY GOLF CLUB	115	ALOHA GOLF	223
GULLANE GOLF CLUB (NO. 2)	106	PANMURE GOLF CLUB	120	AMARILLA GOLF & CC	227
HADDINGTON GOLF CLUB	106	PEEBLES GOLF CLUB	91	AÑORETA GOLF CLUB	223
HAGGS CASTLE GOLF CLUB	112	PETERHEAD GOLF CLUB	101	ATALAYA PARK	223
HARBURN GOLF CLUB	106	PITLOCHRY GOLF CLUB	120	CAMPO DE GOLF MASPALOMAS	227
HAWICK GOLF CLUB	91	PITREAVIE GOLF CLUB	97	CAMPO DE GOLF DE SALAMANCA	219
HAYSTON GOLF CLUB	112	PORT GLASGOW GOLF CLUB	115	CANYAMEL GOLF CLUB	226
HAZELHEAD GOLF CLUB (NO. 1)	100	PORTPATRICK (DUNSKEY) GC	94	CAPDEPERA GOLF CLUB	226
HAZELHEAD GOLF CLUB (NO. 2)	100	POWFOOT GOLF CLUB	94	CASTIELLO GOLF CLUB	220
HELENSBURGH GOLF CLUB	112	PRESTONFIELD GOLF CLUB	107	CLUB GOLF DE PALS	222
HOLLANDBUSH GOLF CLUB	113	PRESTWICK GOLF CLUB	115	CLUB PINEDA DE SEVILLA	223
HOPEMAN GOLF CLUB	100	PRESTWICK ST NICHOLAS GC	115	CLUB TORREQUEBRADA	224
INVERALLOCHY GOLF CLUB	100	RANFURLY CASTLE GOLF CLUB	115	CLUB DE CAMPO LAUKARIZ	219
INVERNESS GOLF CLUB	103	RATHO PARK GOLF CLUB	108	CLUB DE CAMPO DEL MEDITERRANEO	221
IRVINE GOLF CLUB	113	REAY GOLF CLUB	104	CLUB DE GOLF COSTA BRAVA	222
IRVINE RAVENSPARK GOLF CLUB	113	ROYAL ABERDEEN GOLF CLUB	101	CLUB DE GOLF GIRONA	222
KEITH GOLF CLUB	100	ROYAL BURGESS GOLFING SOC	108	CLUB DE GOLF SANT CUGAT	225
KELSO GOLF CLUB	91	ROYAL DORNOCH GOLF CLUB	104	CLUB DE GOLF TERRAMAR	225
KILMACOLM GOLF CLUB	113	ROYAL MUSSELBURGH GC	108	CLUB DE GOLF VILLA MARTIN	221
KILMARNOCK (BARASSIE) GC	113	ROYAL TARLAIR GOLF CLUB	101	CLUB DE GOLF EL BOSQUE	221
KING JAMES VI GOLF CLUB	119	ROYAL TROON (OLD COURSE)	115	CORTIJO GRANDE	223
KINGHORN GOLF CLUB	96	ROYAL TROON (PORTLAND)	115	COSTA DORADA GOLF CLUB	225
KINGUSSIE GOLF CLUB	103	ST. ANDREWS (EDEN COURSE)	97	DE NEGURI GOLF CLUB	219
KINTORE GOLF CLUB	100	ST. ANDREWS (JUBILEE COURSE)	97	DE LA CORUNA GOLF CLUB	226
KIRKCALDY GOLF CLUB	96	ST. ANDREWS (NEW COURSE)	97	DEL SUR GOLF CLUB	227
KIRKCUDBRIGHT GOLF CLUB	94	ST. ANDREWS (OLD COURSE)	97	DEPORTIVO LA BARGANIZA	226
LADYBANK GOLF CLUB	96	SCOONIE GOLF CLUB	97	EL BOSQUE GOLF CLUB	221
LANARK GOLF CLUB	113	SCOTSCRAIG GOLF CLUB	97	EL SALER GOLF CLUB	221
LARGS GOLF CLUB	113	SEAFIELD GOLF CLUB	115	ENTREPINOS GOLF CLUB	219
LETHAM GRANGE (NEW COURSE)	119	SHOTTS GOLF CLUB	116	ESCORPION GOLF CLUB	221
LETHAM GRANGE (OLD COURSE)	119	SOUTHERNESS GOLF CLUB	94	GOLF ALMERIMAR	223
LETHAMHILL GOLF CLUB	113	SPEY BAY GOLF CLUB	102	GOLF OSONA MONTANYA	222
LEVEN LINKS GOLF CLUB	96	STIRLING GOLF CLUB	93	GUADALHORCE CLUB DE GOLF	224
LINLITHGOW GOLF CLUB	107	STONEHAVEN GOLF CLUB	102	GUADALMINA CLUB DE GOLF	224
LOCHGELLY GOLF CLUB	96	STRANRAER GOLF CLUB	94	LA HERRERIA GOLF CLUB	219
LOCHGREEN GOLF CLUB	114	STRATHAVEN GOLF CLUB	116	LA MANGA CLUB (NORTH)	221
LOCHWINNOCH GOLF CLUB	114	STRATHLENE GOLF CLUB	102	LA MANGA CLUB (SOUTH)	221
LOCKERBIE GOLF CLUB	94	STRATHPEFFER SPA GOLF CLUB	104	LA MORALEJA GOLF CLUB	220
LONGNIDDRY GOLF CLUB	107	TAIN GOLF CLUB	104	LA PENAZA GOLF CLUB	219
LOTHIANBURN GOLF CLUB	107	TAYMOUTH CASTLE GOLF CLUB	120	LA QUINTA GOLF & CC	224
LOUDON GOWF CLUB	114	THORNHILL GOLF CLUB	94	LAS BRISAS GOLF CLUB	224

Index

LAS PALMAS GOLF CLUB	228	MÖLLE GOLF CLUB	234	BRYNHILL (BARRY) GOLF CLUB	129
LAS RAMBLAS GOLF CLUB	221	NASSJO GOLF CLUB	230	BUILTH WELLS GOLF CLUB	128
LOMAS-BOSQUE GOLF CLUB	220	NORA GOLF CLUB	231	BULL BAY GOLF CLUB	121
LOS NARANJOS GOLF CLUB	224	ÖREBRO GOLF CLUB	231	CAERNARFON GOLF CLUB	125
MAS NOU GOLF CLUB	222	ÖVIKS GOLF CLUB	232	CLYNE GOLF CLUB	130
MIJAS GOLF CLUB (LOS LAGOS)	224	ROSLAGENS GOLF CLUB	231	CONWY GOLF CLUB	126
MIRAFLORES GOLF CLUB	224	RYA GOLF CLUB	234	CRADOC GOLF CLUB	128
NEW MADRID GOLF CLUB	220	SKEPPTUNA GOLF CLUB	236	CREIGIAU GOLF CLUB	129
NOVO SANCTI PETRI	225	SÖDERHAMNS GOLF CLUB	232	CRICCIETH GOLF CLUB	126
OLIVA NOVA GOLF CLUB	222	STOCKHOLMS GOLF CLUB	236	DENBIGH GOLF CLUB	122
PEDREÑA GOLF CLUB	226	SUNDSVALLS GOLF CLUB	232	DEWSTON GOLF CLUB	124
PONIENTE GOLF CLUB	227	SUNNE GOLF CLUB	231	DINAS POWIS GOLF CLUB	129
PUERTA DE HIERRO GOLF CLUB	220	SVALÖVS GOLF CLUB	234	FAIRWOOD PARK GOLF CLUB	130
QUESADA GOLF CLUB	222	TÄBY GOLF CLUB	236	GLAMORGANSHIRE GOLF CLUB	129
REAL AUTOMOVIL CLUB DE ESPANA	220	TIMRÅ GOLF CLUB	233	GLYNHIR GOLF CLUB	124
REAL CLUB DE GOLF EL PRAT	223	TOMELILLA GOLF CLUB	234	HAVERFORDWEST GOLF CLUB	124
REUS AIGUESVERDS CLUB	226	TRANÅS GOLF CLUB	230	HOLYHEAD GOLF CLUB	121
SAN ROQUE GOLF CLUB	225	TRELLEBORGS GOLF CLUB	235	LLANDRINDOD WELLS GC	128
SANTA PONSA GOLF CLUB	227	ULLNA GOLF CLUB	236	LLANDUDNO (MAESDU) GC	126
SON VIDA GOLF CLUB	227	UPPSALA GOLF CLUB	232	MAESTEG GOLF CLUB	127
SOTOGRANDE GOLF CLUB	225	VARBERGS GOLF CLUB (EAST)	237	MILFORD HAVEN GOLF CLUB	124
TENERIFE GOLF CLUB	228	VARBERGS GOLF CLUB (WEST)	237	MONMOUTHSHIRE GOLF CLUB	124
VALDERRAMA GOLF CLUB	225	VÄSTERÅS GOLF CLUB	232	MORRISTON GOLF CLUB	130
VALL D'OR GOLF CLUB	227	VÄXJÖ GOLF CLUB	230	MOUNTAIN ASH GOLF CLUB	127
VILLA DE MADRID	220	VETLANDA GOLF CLUB	230	MOUNTAIN LAKES GOLF CLUB	127
		VIKSJÖ GOLF CLUB	236	NEATH GOLF CLUB	130
		YSTAD GOLF CLUB	235	NEFYN & DISTRICT GOLF CLUB	126
				NEWPORT GOLF CLUB	125
				NORTH WALES GOLF CLUB	126
				OLD PADESWOOD GOLF CLUB	122
				PENNARD GOLF CLUB	130

SWEDEN

SWITZERLAND

				PONTARDAWE GOLF CLUB	130
				PORTMADOG GOLF CLUB	126
ABBEKAS GOLF CLUB	233			PRESTATYN GOLF COURSE	123
ÄNGELHOLMS GOLF CLUB	233	BLUMISBERG G & C CLUB	238	PYLE & KENFIG GOLF CLUB	128
ÅGESTA GOLF CLUB	235	BONMONT GOLF CLUB	238	RADYR GOLF CLUB	129
ARVIKA GOLF CLUB	230	BREITENLOO GOLF CLUB	239	RHONDDA GOLF CLUB	128
BÄCKAVATTNETS GOLF CLUB	236	CRANS-SUR-SIERRE GOLF CLUB	239	RHOS-ON-SEA GOLF CLUB	126
BARSEBÄCK GOLF & CC	233	DOMAINE IMPÉRIAL GOLF CLUB	239	RHUDDLAN GOLF CLUB	123
BILLERUDS GOLF CLUB	230	ENGADIN GOLF CLUB	239	ROLLS OF MONMOUTH	125
BOKSKOGEN GOLF CLUB (NEW)	233	GENEVE GOLF CLUB	239	ROYAL PORTHCAWL GOLF CLUB	128
BOKSKOGEN GOLF CLUB (OLD)	233	GOLF CLUB LENZERHEIDE	239	ROYAL ST. DAVID'S GOLF CLUB	126
DELSJÖ GOLF CLUB	237	GOLF CLUB DE VERBIER	239	ST. DEINIOL GOLF CLUB	127
DJURSHOLM GOLF CLUB	235	INTERLAKEN- UNTERSEEN	239	ST. PIERRE GOLF CLUB (NEW)	125
DROTTNINGHOLMS GOLF CLUB	235	LUGANO GOLF CLUB	240	ST. PIERRE GOLF CLUB (OLD)	125
EKERUM GOLF CLUB	229	MONTREUX GOLF CLUB	240	SOUTHERNDOWN GOLF CLUB	128
FALSTERBO GOLF CLUB	233	NEUCHATEL GOLF CLUB	240	TENBY GOLF CLUB	124
FLOMMENS GOLF CLUB	234	PATRIZIALE ASCONA GOLF CLUB	240	VALE OF LLANGOLLEN GOLF CLUB	123
FORSGÅRDENS GOLF CLUB	237			WELSHPOOL GOLF CLUB	129
HAGGE GOLF CLUB	231			WEST MONMOUTHSHIRE GC	125
HALMSTAD GOLF CLUB (ONE)	237			WHITCHURCH GOLF CLUB	129
HALMSTAD GOLF CLUB (TWO)	237				
HANINGE GOLF CLUB	235	## WALES			
HÄRNÖSANDS GOLF CLUB	232				
HUDIKSVALLS GOLF CLUB	232				
INGARÖ GOLF CLUB	235	ABERDARE GOLF CLUB	127		
KARLSTAD GOLF CLUB	231	ABERDOVEY GOLF CLUB	125		
KILS GOLF CLUB	231	ABERGELE & PENSARN GC	122		
KINDS GOLF CLUB	237	ABERYSTWYTH GOLF CLUB	123		
KVARNBY GOLF CLUB	234	ALICE SPRINGS GOLF CLUB	124		
LAGANS GOLF CLUB	230	ANGLESEY GOLF CLUB	121		
LIDINGÖ GOLF CLUB	236	ASHBURNHAM GOLF CLUB	123		
LINDE GOLF CLUB	231	BARGOED GOLF CLUB	127		
LJUNGHUSEN GOLF CLUB	234	BORTH & YNYSLAS GOLF CLUB	123		
MALMÖ GOLF CLUB	234	BRYN MEADOWS GOLF CLUB	127		

269

We'll find you lower cost car insurance. Here are the figures to prove it.

0800 678 000

Phone us now to find out how much we could save on your current motor insurance policy.

With the very latest in computer and communications technology we can instantly access the country's top insurers, such as Sun Alliance, Eagle Star and Royal Insurance to name but a few. We'll give you the best available motor insurance quote in a matter of minutes.

Take a look at what our streamline service offers you:

- The most competitive quote from Britain's best insurers.
- Special rates and offers not normally available to the general public thanks to our power of negotiation.
- An option to spread the co with monthly direct deb payments.

Why not let us give yo motor insurance some expe attention?

Call us now for a fre no-obligation motor insuran quote on **0800 678 000**. Or c tact your local branch, quotir reference RAC P5.

RAC INSURANCE *services*

One call does it all

RAC Insurance Brokers Ltd. are Lloyd's Brokers, Members of the British Insurance and Investment Brokers Association and regulated in the conduct of investment business by the Insurance Brokers' Registration Council. Registered office: 10-12 Hunting Gate, Hitchin, Herts SG4 0TT. Registered in England No. 4460

WIN A SET OF TOP QUALITY GOLF CLUBS IN THE

RAC
GOLF COURSES
in Great Britain & Ireland & Europe
COMPETITION

FILL IN THE ENTRY FORM OVER THE PAGE →

WIN A SET OF TOP QUALITY GOLF CLUBS!

GOLF COURSES
in Great Britain & Ireland & Europe
COMPETITION

Welcome to the first edition of RAC Golf Courses in Great Britain, Ireland and Europe.

To mark the launch of the guide we are offering the chance to win a set of top quality golf clubs in our launch competition, designed to test your knowledge of golf and golfing history.

To enter our competition all you have to do is answer the six questions on the entry form below. Once you've answered the questions send the completed form to

RAC Golf Courses Competition
PO Box 100
South Croydon
Surrey
CR2 6XW

RULES OF THIS COMPETITION
1 Entries must be on official forms only.
2 No correspondence can be entered into and there can be no cash alternative to the prize.
3 Not open to employees of the RAC.
4 Judges' decision is final.
5 Only open to entrants aged 18 and over.

The closing date for receipt of entries is 31/8/94.
All correct entries will be placed in a draw to take place on 2/9/94.
The winner will be chosen at random and will be notified by post no later than 9/9/94.

The questions are

1 In which year did Jack Nicklaus win his 6th US Masters title?......

2 Where was the 1990 US PGA Championship held?......

3 What was the final score in the 1993 Ryder Cup?......

4 Who was the last Englishman to win the Open?......

5 How many shots under par is an albatross?......

6 In men's golf, what is the shortest distance (in yards) for a par 5 in the UK?......

Name..........
Address ....
..........Postcode..........
Telephone number..........

RAC GOLF COURSES COMPETITION